Samuel Thomas Worcester

History of the Town of Hollis, New Hampshire

From its First Settlement to the Year 1879

Samuel Thomas Worcester

History of the Town of Hollis, New Hampshire
From its First Settlement to the Year 1879

ISBN/EAN: 9783337098483

Printed in Europe, USA, Canada, Australia, Japan

Cover: Foto ©ninafisch / pixelio.de

More available books at **www.hansebooks.com**

HISTORY

OF THE

TOWN OF HOLLIS,

NEW HAMPSHIRE.

From its First Settlement to the Year 1879.

WITH MANY BIOGRAPHICAL SKETCHES OF ITS EARLY SETTLERS

THEIR DESCENDANTS, AND OTHER RESIDENTS.

ILLUSTRATED WITH MAPS AND ENGRAVINGS,

BY SAMUEL T. WORCESTER.

IN MEMORIAM MAJORUM.

"Only the actions of the just
Smell sweet and blossom in the dust."

BOSTON:

A. WILLIAMS & CO.
283 WASHINGTON STREET.

1879.

Press of O. C. Moore, Nashua, N. H.

TO

THE INHABITANTS OF HOLLIS,

AND

THE DESCENDANTS OF ITS EARLY SETTLERS

WHEREVER SCATTERED,

AND TO ALL WHO HAVE RESIDED IN THE TOWN,

THIS HISTORY

IS RESPECTFULLY INSCRIBED,

BY THEIR FRIEND,

THE AUTHOR.

LIST AND PLACE OF ENGRAVINGS.

TO THE READER.

As this book will be found to contain very many short biographical *personal* sketches, it is hoped that it will not be looked upon as a matter of unpardonable egotism should it be introduced to the charitable reader with the like brief sketch of itself. Though a native of Hollis, the home of an honored ancestry for a hundred years and more, and my own, in childhood and youth, it has not been so for the last fifty years and more. It was my fortune to begin and spend a busy professional life of between thirty and forty years in a distant western State.

I am not aware that while living in Hollis I gained more knowledge of its early history and people than would ordinarily fall to the lot of other young persons in the like circumstances, and the many years of my absence from New England tended rather to lessen than add to the little I had before acquired.

But some years after my return to New Hampshire, having occasion when on a visit to Hollis to examine one or more volumes of its early town records, I chanced to find in the same depository with them many miscellaneous papers and documents, some scattered and loose, and the rest in ill-assorted packages—all relating to the early history of the town prior to or during the war of the Revolution. A cursory examination of these ancient documents, in connection with the older worn and mutilated volumes of the town records, interested me. Having at the time some leisure at command, I said to the Town Clerk who had these papers in charge, that if he would entrust them for a time to me, I would put them in a better condition for permanent preservation. With this understanding they were confided to me. Having procured for my purpose a large blank book, intended as a sort of supplement to the town records, I had it labelled "Hollis Historical Documents."

Into this book I caused to be inserted and bound all those ancient documents pertaining to the early history of the town. I also caused to be copied into the same volume a large number of original documents and records relating to its early history found in the offices of the Secretary of State and Adjutant General, both in Boston and Concord. There were also copied into the same book from the town records and methodically arranged, such other matters as were thought pertinent to its civil, ecclesiastical and educational history.

In the meantime, as I had leisure, I had written a number of articles relating to the early settlement and Revolutionary history of the town, some of which had been published in the New England Historical and Genealogical Register, and several, in other periodicals. All this however had been done without any purpose on my part of preparing for the press a connected history of the town, but yet with the hope that the materials so gathered might be preserved and some time used in the compilation of such history, by some one more competent to the task and less a novice in this kind of literary labor.

These fugitive historical scraps, as they had been published from time to time, had been read by some of the people of the town, and may have led to the insertion of an article in the warrant for the annual March meeting in 1878, " To see if the town would authorize the Selectmen to contract with some person to prepare and publish the early history of the town at its expense." By invitation I attended that meeting, and by request stated what had been done with the historical documents which had been entrusted to me. I also expressed my concurrence in the sentiment, strongly expressed by others, that a history of the town *ought* to be written, and also stated that though I had no purpose or wish myself to undertake the task, yet if some other person, satisfactory to the town, would undertake it, I would cheerfully and gratuitously place in his hands such materials for it as I had gathered, and also give such further aid, if desired, as convenient to me. After some further discussion of the question by others, the meeting unanimously " voted to refer the article relating to the publishing the early history of Hollis to the Selectmen, and that they be authorized to borrow money for the completion of the object, if in their judgment they should think it advisable, and that they be authorized to employ a committee to act with them."

The Selectmen chosen at that meeting were Messrs. Timothy E. Flagg, John A. Coburn and Charles W. Hardy, who shortly afterwards appointed as a committee to act with them, Messrs. John N. Worcester, Joseph E. Smith, John Farley and Charles S. Spalding. In the meanwhile, no one else having been found to prepare a history of the town as contemplated by the vote of the meeting, the wish was strongly expressed by the Selectmen and committee, that I would consent to undertake it. After one or more interviews with them, but without any specific proposals upon the subject on their part, or promises on my own, I set myself about gathering additional materials for the work, and putting in the shape and order in which they now appear, such as I had before collected.

It is needless for me here to speak of all the motives that led me to waive my objections to undertaking the task and going on with the compilation of this history, as I have now done. But among those motives, I may be permitted to say. was a sincere filial regard, not to say veneration, for the memory and character of the early settlers of the town as shown by the records of their doings, among whom, and its inhabitants afterwards, were three generations of both my paternal and maternal ancestors. I also participated in the sentiment felt and expressed by many others that it was but doing tardy justice to their memories, that their history should now be written, accompanied by the fear, also often expressed by those interested, that otherwise it might not be soon, if ever, done.

In my view it would also be needless, as well as tedious, here to enumerate the many books and public documents which have been consulted in the collecting of the facts presented in this history. The references to them, at least for the most part, will sufficiently appear to the patient reader in their proper connection. Suffice it to say that it has been my aim to gather these facts from all such pertinent original documents as were at my command, and from all other sources that seemed to me authentic and trustworthy, whether *books, letters* of correspondents or well-established *tradition.*

It has been said by a late author. " that one must write a book to know how courteous the world can be." It has been my fortune in the compilation of this history very fully and most cordially to appreciate that sentiment, and I take unfeigned pleasure in expressing my grateful acknowledgements to the very many correspondents who have aided me. and also to the librarians of the libraries I have had occasion to visit, and to the custodians of the public

records at Boston and Concord for their uniform courtesy and kindly
sympathy with my work.   My thanks are also due to the Selectmen of Hollis, and to the Publication Committee, for the active interest they have manifested in the undertaking, and likewise to the
people of the town for their unanimity and good wishes in respect
to it.   I further take leave to express my obligations to my brother
John N. Worcester, for the many matters furnished by him pertaining to the local history of the town, and also in respect to the personal history of many of its citizens, in regard to whom my own
information and memory were at fault.   The readers of this history, as well as myself personally, are also indebted to the town
for the engravings it has furnished, and to the individuals who
have gratuitously provided the portraits with which the book is
embellished.

For the last four years, the gathering of the materials for this
work, and its compilation, have busily, and for the most part pleas-
antly, employed very many of my leisure hours.   Conscious as any
one need be of its incompleteness and shortcomings, yet hoping to
some extent it may meet the reasonable expectations of the present
inhabitants of Hollis, and the widely scattered descendants of the
early settlers of the town, the work is respectfully dedicated to them
in the hope that the lessons of virtue, piety and patriotism taught in
the lives, doings and example of their worthy ancestors will not
soon fade from the memory of their posterity.

                                                         S. T. W.
NASHUA. N. H., April, 1879.

CONTENTS.

CHAPTER I.

OLD DUNSTABLE.

CHAPTER II.

WEST DUNSTABLE.

CHAPTER III.

THE PARISH OF WEST DUNSTABLE.

CHAPTER IV.

HOLLIS.

CHAPTER V.

BORDER TROUBLES WITH DUNSTABLE.

CHAPTER VI.

HISTORY OF MONSON.

CHAPTER VII.

MILITARY HISTORY.

CHAPTER VIII.

COLONIAL SCHOOL LAW AND SCHOOLS.

CHAPTER IX.

EARLY COLONIAL LAWS.

CHAPTER X.

THE NEW HAMPSHIRE GENERAL COURT.

CHAPTER XI.

BIOGRAPHICAL.

CHAPTER XII.

THE BEGINNING OF THE REVOLUTION.

CHAPTER XIII.

WAR OF THE REVOLUTION.

CHAPTER XIV.

WAR OF THE REVOLUTION CONTINUED.

CHAPTER XV.

THE THIRD YEAR OF THE WAR.

CHAPTER XVI.

THE FOURTH AND FIFTH YEARS OF THE WAR.

CHAPTER XVII.

THE SIXTH AND SEVENTH YEARS OF THE WAR.

CHAPTER XVIII.

THE LAST YEARS OF THE WAR.

CHAPTER XIX.

LIST OF THE HOLLIS SOLDIERS.

CHAPTER XX.

BIOGRAPHICAL.

CHAPTER XXI.

WAR OF 1812, AND WAR OF THE REBELLION.

CHAPTER XXII.

ECCLESIASTICAL HISTORY.

CHAPTER XXIII.

MUNICIPAL HISTORY.

CHAPTER XXIV.

POLITICAL HISTORY.

CHAPTER XXV.

STATISTICAL HISTORY.

CHAPTER XXVI.

EDUCATIONAL HISTORY.

CHAPTER XXVII.

BIOGRAPHY.

CHAPTER XXVIII.

BIOGRAPHY.

CHAPTER XXIX.

BIOGRAPHY.

CHAPTER XXX.

BIOGRAPHY.

CHAPTER XXXI.

LONGEVITY.

CHAPTER XXXII.

MARRIAGES.

CHAPTER XXXIII.

FAMILY REGISTERS.

HISTORY OF HOLLIS.

CHAPTER I.

CHARTERS OF THE PLYMOUTH AND MASSACHUSETTS COMPANIES.
GRANTS OF NEW HAMPSHIRE TO CAPT. JOHN MASON.—CHAR-
TER OF DUNSTABLE, AND HISTORY OF THAT TOWN FROM 1673
TO 1739.

When North America was first discovered by European navigators,
the fact of discovery, coupled with some act of possession, was regarded by the common consent of European governments as giving
a sufficient legal title to the sovereign or government in whose service the navigator was employed to all lands so discovered. By virtue of such discovery, prior to the settlement of any part of New
England, the largest part of the continent of North America had
become, as was claimed, the property of the sovereigns of Great
Britain, and rightfully subject to their disposal, with little or no regard to the possession and interests of the native inhabitants.

In the exercise of this supposed right, King James I. in the year
1620, by his letters patent granted to the Council of Plymouth, a
company instituted "for the planting, ordering and governing New
England," "all that part of North America lying between the 40th
and 48th degrees of north latitude, and of the same breadth throughout the main land from sea to sea."

In the following year, (1621,) the Plymouth company granted to
Capt. John Mason, a merchant of London, and a member of this
company, " all the land from the river Naumkeag round Cape Ann
to the river Merrimack ; and up each of those rivers to the farthest
head of them ; then to cross over from the head of the one to the
head of the other."*

---

*Holmes' Annals, Vol. I, pp. 164, 165.

In 1629 Capt. Mason procured a new patent from the Plymouth company. By this second patent that company conveyed to Mason " all the land from the middle of Merrimack river, near its mouth ; thence northward along the coast to the Piscataqua, thence up that river to its farthest head ; thence northwestward sixty miles from the first entrance of that river ; also up the Merrimack to its farthest head and so forward up into the land westward sixty miles ; thence to cross over to the end of the sixty miles from the mouth of the Piscataqua river, with all islands within five leagues of the coast."*

On the 19th of March, 1628, the Plymouth company, by their letters patent, granted and sold to Sir Henry Roswell and his associates " all that part of New England lying between three miles to the northward of Merrimack river and three miles to the southward of Charles river, and in length within the described breadth from the Atlantic Ocean to the South Sea." This grant to Sir Henry Roswell and his associates was afterwards in the year 1629 confirmed by King Charles 1. by letters patent, incorporating these grantees of the Plymouth Company by the name of the Governor and Company of Massachusetts Bay in New England," with perpetual succession, with the right to elect forever out of the freemen of the company, a Governor, deputy Governor and eighteen assistants, and to make laws not repugnant to the laws of England.†

It may be readily seen that these several grants to Mason and the Massachusetts company conflicted, a large tract of the same territory being embraced within the limits of each of them. As will appear in the sequel, this conflict of boundaries many years afterwards became the occasion of much trouble and tedious litigation between the heirs of Mason and New Hampshire on one side and Massachusetts on the other. Holding under this grant of the Plymouth Company, confirmed by the Royal Charter, the Massachusetts Company, afterwards acting through the General Court of the Province, from time to time made grants of land to individuals, corporations and companies, for Plantations and Townships. Such grants were made upon petition for them to the General Court, and were usually coupled with such conditions as it was believed would promote the common interest of the province and the welfare of the settlers. In this manner townships were originally granted, and became organized in Massachusetts without any more formal act of incorporation, and the

---

*Holmes' Annals, Vol. I, p. 199.
†Id, pp. 193, 195.

grantees named in the charter thus invested with the title to all the land within the boundaries of the township, subject to such conditions as might be imposed by the act making the grant.

For many years prior to 1679, the Provinces of New Hampshire and Massachusetts had been under the same government, but in that year, upon petition to the King, they were separated, and New Hampshire became a "royal province," the King being represented in its government by a Governor and Council of his own appointment. After this separation the like grants of townships and town charters were made in New Hampshire, as in Massachusetts, those in New Hampshire being granted by the Governor and Council of the province in the name of the King, subject to such conditions and limitations as were expressed in the charters, and supposed to be approved by the King.

CHARTER OF DUNSTABLE.

The old township of Dunstable, of which the present town of Hollis was a part, was chartered by the General Court of Massachusetts Oct. 16, 1673, O. S., corresponding to Oct. 27, 1673, N. S. More than one half of Dunstable, as chartered, was in the territory in dispute between the two provinces, but at the date of its charter, and for more than sixty years' afterwards, it was supposed to be wholly in Massachusetts, and formed a part of the county of Middlesex. It included within its chartered boundaries the present town of Tyngsborough, the east part of Dunstable, a narrow triangular gore on the north side of Pepperell, and a considerable tract in the northeast corner of Townsend — all still in Massachusetts. In the state of New Hampshire it embraced the towns of Litchfield and Hudson, the south-west part of Londonderry and the west part of Pelham, on the east side of Merrimack river: and on the west side of that river nearly all the present towns of Nashua and Hollis, all of Amherst and Merrimack south of the Souhegan river, and about two-thirds of each of the towns of Milford and Brookline.

The part of Dunstable west of the Merrimack was bounded north by the Souhegan river, south by Chelmsford and Groton, as previously chartered, and in part by "country land" (land not then in any chartered town), and west by a line running due north from its southwest corner to Dram Cup Hill, on the Souhegan, now in the town of Milford. The extreme length of the township from north to south, from the north line of Litchfield to Chelmsford, following

the course of the Merrimack was about seventeen miles; its least
length from the north line of Groton to the nearest point of Souhegan river not far from ten miles.   Its greatest breadth east and west
could not have been less than sixteen miles, the whole comprising an
area of near two hundred square miles or 128,000 acres.

It was still, at that time, a favorite home of the savage, covered
for the most part with the dense native forests, abounding in game,
and its rivers with fish, the Merrimack flowing from north to south
near its centre, the Souhegan on its northern border, and the Nashua
and Nissitissit in the south and southwest.   Besides all these beautiful rivers it was watered by hundreds of crystal brooks and springs,
and gemmed among its hills and valleys with scores of clear and
picturesque ponds.

From out this fair domain, between the years 1655 and 1673, many
grants had been made by the General Court of Massachusetts of
"Farms," so called, to individuals and corporations, mostly along
the Merrimack and Souhegan, varying in quantity from three hundred to fifteen hundred acres, and amounting in all to fourteen thousand acres or more.   The last of these grants, bearing date October
11, 1673, O. S., but a few days before the charter, was made to the
Boston Artillery Company, since known by the well-earned name
and title of the "Ancient and Honorable."   This last grant was of
one thousand acres, and was laid out on the north side of the Nashua
river, at its intersection with the Merrimack, extending north along
the Merrimack about one and a half miles, and on the Nashua to
Spectacle meadow and brook, about two miles, and including all the
compact part of the city of Nashua north of the river.   It appears
from the history of the Artillery Company that about seventy years
afterwards the company sold this tract to Col. Joseph Blanchard, a
gentleman of much note in the early history of Dunstable.   The remembrance of this grant has been affectionately perpetuated to our
times in the name of a small basin of water on the North Common
in Nashua, near the central part of the tract given to the Artillery
Company, and still known as "Artillery Pond."

PETITION FOR THE CHARTER.

The petition for this charter was dated Sept. 15, 1673, O. S., and
was signed by Thomas Brattle, Jonathan Tyng, and twenty-four
others, including a part of the owners of the "Farms" previously
granted.   The petitioners stated as reasons for granting the charter
that "the Land described in the Petition Was of little Capacity as it

then was to do the country service "—"that a considerable number
of persons of sober and orderly conversation, who stood in great
need of accommodations were ready to make improvement of this
vacant Land with whom the owners of the ' farms' previously granted
were ready to join and Encourage." The petition then concludes as
follows: " Yo^r Petitioners therefore Humbly request the favour of
this Honored Court that they will please to grant the said Tract of
Land to yor Petitioners and to such as will joyne with them in the
settlement of the Land aforementioned so that those who have already
improved their Farmes there and others also Who speedily intend to
doe the like may be in a way for the Enjoyment of the Publique ordinances of God; ffor without which the greatest part of the yeare
they will be deprived of; the farmes lying far remoat from any
towns ; and farther that this Honoured Court will please to grant the
like Immunities to this Plantation as they in their favors have for- ,
merly granted to other new Plantations. So shall your Petitioners
be ever engaged to pray &c.

THOS. EDWARDS,	THOMAS BRATTLE.
THO. WHEELER, Senior.	JONATHAN TYNG.
PETER BULKELEY.	JOSEPH WHEELER.
JOHN PARKER.	JAMES PARKER, Senior.
JOHN MORSS, Senior.	ROB'T GIBDS.
SAMUEL COMBS.	JOHN TURNER.
JAMES PARKER, Junior.	SAMPSON SHEAFE.
JOSIAH PARKER.	SAMUEL SCARLET.
JOSEPH PARKER.	WILLIAM LAKIN.
NATH. BLOOD.	ABRAHAM PARKER.
ROB'T PARRIS.	JAMES KNAPP.
JOHN JOLLIFFE.	ROBERT PROCTOR.
ZAFENEA LONG.	SIMON WILLARD."

The petition was granted, and the charter or act of incorporation,
as copied from the original manuscript record, is in the words following :

"The Magistrates Judge it Meet to grant the Petitioners Request herein; Provided that a
farme of Five Hundred Acres of Upland & Meadow be layed out for the Publick use, and that
they so proceed in settling ye Plantation as to finish it out within three years & procure & main-
tayne an able & Orthodox minister amongst them; the Magistrs have passed this, their brethren
the Deputies hereto consenting.

EDWARD RAWSON, SECRET.

16 October 1673.
The Deputyes consent hereto.

WILLIAM TORREY, CLERICUS."

Such, in those times, and for many years after, were the usual con
ditions upon which the General Court of Massachusetts granted
charters for towns. The procuring and maintenance of an " *able
and orthodox*" minister was an indispensable condition, and in case
a Town should be destitute of such *lawful* minister for six consecu-
tive months, it was made the duty of the Court of Sessions, at the

charge of the town, to procure and settle one that would answer the Law. By "finishing," or "finishing out the Plantation within three years," was undoubtedly meant, the procuring within that time of such number of settlers as would be competent to the support of such minister and the building of a meeting-house. That such was the meaning of the words "finish out the Plantation within three years" is more than implied in the action of the petitioners, and in the conditions upon which at the time, they made grants of "House Lotts," so called, to actual settlers : each settler being required by his contract to "clear, fence, break up, build a house, and Live upon his Lot within three years" from the date of the charter under the penalty of forfeiture. By the granting of this charter, the Twenty-Six Petitioners became the owners of all the ungranted Lands within the Boundaries of Old Dunstable, which, if equally shared, would have given to each of them not less than four thousand acres. About twelve years later, for the consideration of £20, as is said, the title of the Proprietors was confirmed by the Naticook & Wamesit Indians — the Naticooks then living about Thornton's Ferry, the Wamesits near Pawtucket Falls.

GRANTEES AND PROPRIETORS.

Many of the grantees of the "Farms" as well as of the petitioners for the charter were at the time men of note in the Province. Among the former were John Endicott, Governor of Massachusetts, and William Brenton, afterwards Governor of Rhode Island. Among the latter were William Brattle, whose name is perpetuated in Brattle Street, Brattle Street Church, and Brattle's End, Dunstable ; Peter Bulkeley, a fellow of Harvard College and Speaker of the Provincial Assembly ; Sampson Sheafe, a member of the Provincial Council of New Hampshire, and others of no less note.

PERAMBULATION AND SURVEY.

The Spring next after its incorporation, Dunstable was perambulated and the boundaries of the town established and marked by Jonathan Danforth of Billerica, who had laid off the grant to the Boston Artillery Company the fall previous, the towns of Chelmsford and Groton some years before, and who is spoken of in Mr. Farmer's biographical notice of him as one of the most eminent surveyors of his time. In an elegy written in memory of Mr. Danforth, it is said of him :

> " He rode the circuit ; chained great towns and farms
> To good behavior ; and by well marked stations
> He fixed their bounds for many generations."

NAME, ETC.

The name Dunstable is said to have been given to the new town in compliment to Madam Mary Tyng, wife of Hon. Edward Tyng, and mother of Jonathan Tyng, one of the grantees in the charter, Madam Tyng having come from a city of the same name in Bedfordshire, in the southerly part of England. This charter of Dunstable is older by near sixty years than that of any town in New Hampshire west of the Merrimack, that of Rumford, now Concord, incorporated in 1733, being among the next oldest.

COMPACT OF THE GRANTEES.

Before taking possession or making any division of their ample domains, the grantees, following the prudent example of the Pilgrims of the Mayflower, entered into a social written compact regulating their future polity in respect to the disposition and settlement of the town. In this compact, among other matters, it was agreed that each accepted settler, as a personal right should have a " house lott" of ten acres, one acre to be added to the ten for each £20 of estate, but no " house lott" to exceed thirty acres ; and all after-divisions of the common land to be apportioned according to house lots.

These lots were to be laid out in the same neighborhood and adjoining each other, for convenience of defence in case of hostile attack. " If any settler should fail to pay his dues or taxes, his lot to be seized by the town and held till payment." " To the end that they might live in peace and love with each other, every settler was to fence his garden, orchard and cornfield with a sufficient fence, four rails in height ; and all land not fenced was to be free and common to all the cattle of the proprietors."

HOUSE LOTS LAID OFF AND SETTLEMENT BEGUN.

These house lots, said to have been about eighty in all, were laid out not long afterwards, contiguous to each other, beginning at the " Neck," so called, near the mouth of Salmon Brook, and extending southerly along that brook, the Merrimack river and the main road in the direction towards the ancient burial ground near the present state line. Near by, and not far from the site of the old school-house in the present Harbor School District, the first fort or garrison house was built, to which the settlers could retire in case of danger.

It is very evident that settlements had been begun on these house

lots as early as the spring of 1674, as we find on the town records,
that on the 11th of May of that year, at a meeting of the "Farmers,"
"Proprietors" under the charter, and "township men" or new
settlers, it was "voted that the first meeting-house should be built
between Salmon Brook and the house of Lieutenant Wheeler as
convenient as may be for the accommodation of both."

Thus was begun, in the wilderness, two hundred years ago, the
infant settlement at Salmon Brook. For sixty years afterwards, it
stood there, solitary and alone, no town north of it this side of
Canada; none east of it, in New Hampshire to the west of Exeter—
fifty miles; none to the south-east, south or south-west, nearer than
Chelmsford, Groton and Lancaster, at the respective distances of
fourteen, fifteen and twenty-five miles.

KING PHILIP'S WAR.

The next year, in the summer of 1675, the bloody war begun
by the crafty and cruel King Philip for the extermination of the
English, broke upon the New England Colonies. The new towns
of Lancaster, Groton and Chelmsford were attacked and burnt, their
inhabitants murdered, carried into captivity or driven from their
homes. With the exception of the brave Jonathan Tyng, every
settler at Dunstable fled. Tyng alone refused to leave, and fortify-
ing his house he resolved to defend it to the last. He petitioned the
General Court of Massachusetts for a little "guard of three or four
men," saying in his petition "that he was living in the uppermost
house on the Merrimack, lying open to the enemy, but so seated as
to be, as it were, a watch-house for the neighboring towns." The
petition was granted, and with this little Spartan band, Tyng stoutly
defended his rude castle and held the town till the end of the war.

Jonathan Tyng thus nobly and gallantly earned the honor of being
the first permanent settler of Dunstable, and of all of that part of
New Hampshire west of the Merrimack, and of having his
name perpetuated by a grateful posterity in that of the town of
Tyngsborough.

In 1678, peace came again; the fugitive settlers at Salmon Brook,
or such of them as had survived the war, were at liberty to return,
and the same year it is said, the first meeting-house was built. At
one of their town meetings, about this time, it was "voted that the
number of settlers might be increased but not so as to exceed eighty
families in all." In 1679 the plantation was at last "*finished out*"
by the "procuring and maintaining" the Rev. Thomas Weld as

their first "learned and orthodox minister amongst them." Under the ministration of Mr. Weld, the settlement so increased and prospered that in 1685 it became necessary to build a larger meeting-house, "about the size of the one at Groton," as the town records have it.

BIRTHS, MARRIAGES AND DEATHS.

In the ancient records of births, marriages and deaths, we find that the first recorded birth was that of William, son of Jonathan and Mary Tyng, April 22, 1679. The first marriage that of John Sollendine, the Michael Angelo of the first meeting-house, and the architect of the first bridge across Salmon Brook, Aug. 2, 1680. The first recorded death that of the Hon. Edward Tyng, Dec. 22, 1681, aged 81.

KING WILLIAM'S WAR.

After an unquiet peace for about ten years, the beginning of the war, known in history as "King William's," was signalized in New England by the treacherous and horrible murder of Major Waldron and twenty-two other inhabitants of Dover by the Penacook and Eastern Indians, and the carrying off a still larger number as captives to Canada. The same party of savages had planned an attack at the same time upon Dunstable, but its execution was prevented by a timely discovery of the plot. Two companies of mounted scouts of twenty men each, afterwards reinforced by fifty, were promptly detailed to patrol the woods from Lancaster to Dunstable. But these precautions did not save the settlement at Salmon Brook from attack and massacre. The town records tell in graphic words, said to be in the handwriting of Mr. Weld, their first minister, the sad tale of two of these attacks.

Anno Domini 1691.

Benjamin Hassell Senior
Anna Hassell his wife
Benjamin Hassell, their son, } Were slain by our Indian Enemies
Mary Marks, Daughter of   Sept. 2 in the Evening.
Patrick Marks

Obadiah Perry and } Died by the hand of our Indian Enemies Sept. 28, 1691,
Christopher Perry   in the morning.

There were at this time in the settlement at Salmon Brook, four garrison houses, two of them having four soldiers each, one six and another seven. Such garrison houses, as described by Dr. Belknap, were surrounded with walls of timber built up to the eaves, with the gates as well as the house doors secured by iron bolts and bars. So much had the settlement been reduced by this war that in 1696 two-thirds of the inhabitants had fled, and in 1699 there were but twenty heads of families to contribute to the minister's wood rate. This war lasted ten years. Cotton Mather, who wrote its history, calls them " *Decennium Luctuosum* " — the decade of sorrows.

QUEEN ANNE'S WAR.

In the year 1703, after a short truce, the war known as Queen Anne's, broke upon the colonies, and also lasted ten years. The scholarly Penhallow, who, as a member of the New Hampshire Council, was an actor in it, and who wrote the history of the Indian wars, from 1703 to 1726, inscribes the title-page of his book with the sad, classic words : —

> " Nescio tu quibus es, Lector, lecturus ocellis
> Hoc scio, quod siccis, scribere non potui."
> (With what eyes, O reader, you will read this tale,
> I know not,
> This I do know, mine were not dry when writing it.)

The Eastern and Canadian Indians again took part with the French, and in the course of a few weeks more than two hundred settlers along our northern frontier were killed or captured and taken to Canada. " *Terror ubique tremor*,"says Penhallow — " fear and trembling everywhere."

In this war, the General Court, in retaliation of the example of the government of Canada, offered a bounty of £40 each for Indian scalps. Capt. John Tyng, of Dunstable, was the first to avail himself of this grim bounty, and went, in the depth of winter, says the historian, to the Indian headquarters and got five, for which he was paid £200. Early in the war the garrison house of Robert Parris, in the south part of the settlement, was attacked, and himself, wife and one daughter killed.

In 1706, the Weld Garrison, so called, then occupied by twenty troopers, was surprised by the savages, and one-half of the soldiers killed. The same party murdered six of the inhabitants of the town. The story of this last massacre is thus told in the town records : —

Nathan Blanchard Lydia Blanchard his wife Susannah Blanchard his daughter Mrs. Hannah Blanchard Goody Cumings wife of John Cumings.	Dyed July 3, 1706, at night.

Rachel Galusha, Dyed July 3, 1706.

At this time, including a block-house built by the government, there were seven garrison houses in the settlement, each having one or more soldiers, the town being still a " *Watch-house* " for the interior settlements.

LOVEWELL'S WAR.

In 1713 the Peace of Utrecht put an end to Queen Anne's War. A treacherous peace followed, till 1722, when the war was renewed. Dunstable, still on the extreme frontier, was attacked, two of her citizens captured and carried to Canada by a party of the enemy. The savages were pursued by soldiers from the town, who were ambushed, eight of them slaughtered, and all buried in the same grave.

The following epitaph in the ancient burial ground, " spelt by the unlettered Muse," tells the bloody tale.

" MEMENTO MORI.

" Here lies the body of Thomas Lund who departed
" this life Sept. 24, 1724, in the 42d year of his age.
" This man, with seven more that lies in this grave,
" Was all slew in a day by the Indians."

In the month of November after this slaughter, the " worthy Captain Lovewell " and his company of fearless and hardy men volunteered to "range the woods full wide " and fight the Indians for a year. I need not in this place repeat the story of the first, the second, or the last expedition of this band of daring backwoodsmen,

"What time the noble Lovewell came
With fifty men from Dunstable
The cruel Pequot tribe to tame
With arms and bloodshed terrible,

all familiar from our childhood as household words. From that day to our own, in our sober histories, in works of fiction, in oral tradition, in our most popular New England ballads, the names of " worthy Captain Lovewell " and Dunstable have been joined together, as it were, in holy wedlock, never to be put asunder. Of the seventy savages in the desperate conflict at Pequawkett, according to Penhallow forty were killed on the field and eighteen mortally wounded. Of the thirty-four men of Lovewell's company, in the battle fifteen were killed, including all the officers, besides many wounded. Well and worthily has a New Hampshire bard, upon visiting the battlefield one hundred years afterwards, sung of them,

" Ah! Where are the soldiers that fought here of yore!
The sod is upon them, they'll struggle no more,
The hatchet is fallen—the red man is low,
But near him reposes the arm of his foe.

The names of the fallen the traveller leaves
Cut out with his knife on the bark of the trees,
But little avail his affectionate arts,
For the names of the fallen are graved on our hearts.

Sleep, soldiers of merit! Sleep, gallants of yore,
The hatchet is fallen, the struggle is o'er,
While the fir tree is green or the wind rolls a wave,
The tear drop shall brighten the turf of the brave."

Though the combatants were so few, and this bloody conflict apparently a drawn battle (neither party being in a condition to pursue the other) yet so far as related to New England it had all the results of a decisive and complete victory. It was the last battle of the war; the power of the hostile savages was forever broken, and such of them as were left gradually withdrew from their ancient haunts and hunting-grounds in New England to the French settlements in Canada. Peace followed the ensuing winter, and from that time to the present the little settlement at Salmon Brook, so persistently and bravely defended for the preceding fifty years, has never been invaded by a hostile savage. From the breaking out of King William's War to the making of this peace was a period of thirty-seven years, twenty-three of this savage warfare, and but fourteen of treacherous, uncertain peace. During all these sad years the settlers in this ancient town, feeble and few in numbers, but always trusting in God, and literally keeping " their powder dry," were yet ever firm and defiant. Living for the most part in garrisons, felling the forests and planting their fields with their arms ready at hand — listening to the sermon on Sunday with their loaded muskets by their seats, or stacked at the meeting-house door — their bravest men waylaid and slaughtered — their wives and children massacred in their houses, or hurried off to a captivity often worse than death — they maintained this out-post of our modern Christian civilization with heroic courage to the end.

When we turn our eyes backward to the bloody scenes, to the terrors and sorrows of the past, and contrast those scenes and those sorrows with the peace and blessings of the present, and call to mind to what extent this quiet and these blessings are due to the sacrifices and sufferings of the early pioneers of Dunstable, what heart not palsied, can fail to throb with emotions of gratitude to our common Father for so worthy an ancestry.

It would be forgetfulness of a duty we owe alike to ourselves, to those who shall come after us when we are gone, to the institutions civil and religious they did so much to establish, and to our common humanity, should we neglect so far as in us lies to perpetuate the remembrance of their worthy and noble deeds.

POPULATION.

The population of Dunstable at this period, as stated by Mr. Fox, was as follows:

```
1680, 30 families, or about 120 inhabitants.
1701, 25    "      "   "   100      "
1711, 13    "      "   "    86      "
1730, 50    "      "   "   250      "
```

THE EFFECTS OF THE RETURN OF PEACE.

With the return of peace, both the town of Dunstable and all the country round, begun to experience a degree of prosperity never enjoyed before, and settlements were soon extended north and west of the Nashua, and east of the Merrimack. As we have already seen, no town before that time had been chartered north or west of Dunstable, in what is now New Hampshire, for the preceding fifty years. But such was the benign influence of peace, that within sixteen years after "Lovewell's Fight" twenty-eight towns, now in New Hampshire, had been chartered or granted by the General Court of Massachusetts, and more or less settled, extending north on the Merrimack, to Stevenstown (now Franklin and Salisbury) about sixty miles, and on the Connecticut to No 4, now Charlestown, near seventy miles.

FIRST DISMEMBERMENTS OF DUNSTABLE.

About this period, or a little before, began the legislative dismemberments and mutilations of the body politic of the town of Dunstable—afterwards continued with more or less frequency for near a century—a treatment little less unkind and cruel in its way than that suffered by the early settlers from the savages. The first of these excisions was in the year 1722 when its north-east extremity was cut off, to fill up a corner of the Town of Londonderry. The next, in 1731, when a small slice of it of about eighty acres, was taken from near its south-west corner to piece out a side of Townsend.

In the year 1732, all the remainder of the old town on the east side of the Merrimack, extending from the north line of Litchfield to Chelmsford, was incorporated into a new town then called Nottingham.

In the year 1734, the north part of the then new town of Nottingham, and a part of the present town of Merrimack, south of the Souhegan, at the junction of that river with the Merrimack, were incorporated into a town then and still called Litchfield.

Both of these towns being incorporated by the General Court of Massachusetts, were required within three years from the date of their respective charters to be "finished out" by procuring and "settling in each of them a learned and orthodox minister of good conversation, and making effectual provision for his comfortable and honorable support."

In 1739 that part of Dunstable lying west of the present east line of Hollis and the Nashua river was incorporated as a parish, known by the name of the West Parish of Dunstable. This charter of West Dunstable, as also that of Nottingham, authorized the assessment of a tax of two pence per acre upon all lands of non-resident owners, within their chartered limits for the space of five years for the building of a meeting house and the support of the ministry. The incorporation of West Dunstable was the last legislative act of the General Court of Massachusetts affecting that part of the old town now in New Hampshire.

CHAPTER II.

CHARTER OF THE PARISH OF WEST DUNSTABLE.— ITS SETTLEMENT
AND HISTORY FROM 1730 TO 1739.

Under the Laws of the Province of Massachusetts, in force at the time, the twenty-six petitioners for the charter of Dunstable, " with such as might joyn with them in the settlement," became owners in fee simple, as tenants in common, of all the ungranted land within the boundaries of the township. In the year 1682, shortly after the close of King Philip's war, a meeting of these proprietors was held, who formed themselves into an association for the purpose of settling their several rights — of making divisions of their lands from time to time among themselves in the modes and proportions mutually agreed upon — and also for the making of sales and setting off the lands disposed of to purchasers and actual settlers.

The meetings of these original proprietors, and of those who succeeded to their estates, afterwards continued to be held (sometimes at intervals of many years,) for more than a century, the last of them as late as 1816. The doings of this association, including the partitions and sales of land made by the proprietors were carefully recorded in books kept by them for the purpose, now worn and mutilated, but still to be found in the office of the city clerk of Nashua.

Before the year 1729, most of the land of these proprietors lying in the present towns of Nashua, Hudson and Litchfield, N. H., and Tyngsborough and Dunstable, Mass., had changed ownership, and much of it was then in the occupation of actual settlers. Previous to that year, no record of any sale or grant to any one of the early settlers of Hollis of land in that town is to be found in the books kept by these proprietors. But in the month of January, 1729-30, O. S., as is shown by these records, the modest quantity of 37 1-2 acres was set off by the proprietors to Peter Powers, in the right of John Usher. The survey of it was made by Col. Joseph Blanchard, an honored citizen of Dunstable, and a noted surveyor of the time, and was set off to Powers by Henry Farwell, Joseph French and William Lund as a committee acting for the association.   This tract is described in the record as lying in that part of Dunstable called "Nissitissit," which was the Indian name of Hollis.   It was laid out in an oblong 120 rods east and west, and 50 rods from north to south. Some years afterwards, as is shown by these records of the proprietors there were set off to Powers as purchaser and grantee, in a similar way several other tracts of land in Hollis, amounting in all to nearly 1400 acres, among which was one tract of 1000 acres lying between Long and Pennichuck ponds, but he is the only person among the early settlers of Hollis whose name is found as a grantee upon the books of that association.

Mr. Powers, afterward known as "Capt. Powers," and as a leading and prominent citizen of Hollis, was born at Littleton, Mass., in 1707.   In 1728 he was married to Anna Keyes of Chelmsford, and the same year removed with his wife to that part of Dunstable now known as Nashua.   During the summer and fall of 1730, he made the first clearing and built the first dwelling house in Hollis.   In the month of January, 1731, with his wife and two infant children he made his way through the then dense, unbroken forest to his new home and thus became the first permanent settler of the town.   The site of this humble dwelling, no doubt built of logs, was about one-half mile N. W. of the present Hollis meeting-house, but a short distance from the house formerly owned by Thomas Cumings, afterwards by his son-in-law, Mr. John S. Heywood, now deceased, where vestiges of the old cellar, as is said, may be still seen.   For nearly two years this family had no neighbor within about ten miles of them.   On the 9th of March, 1732, their eldest daughter, Anna Powers, was born, who was the first child of English descent born in the town.

In the summer of 1732, Eleazer Flagg from Concord, Mass., settled in the S. W. part of the town, on or near the place afterwards owned by his grandson, Capt. Reuben Flagg, and now by Timothy E. Flagg, Esq., about two miles from Mr. Powers.   The house of Mr. Flagg is said to have been fortified against the attacks of the Indians, and was used as a garrison house.   Mr. F. was the second settler.   The third family is said to have been that of Thomas Dinsmore from Bedford, Mass., who settled on the farm now owned by John Coburn, Esq., about one and a half miles south of the meeting-house, on the road from Hollis to Pepperell.   In the year 1736 the number of settlers is said to have increased to nine families.

The whole of the township of Dunstable, as we have already stated, from the date of the charter, till the new province line was settled in the spring of 1741, was believed to be in the county of Middlesex and a part of it.' The office of the Register of Deeds for that county was and still is at Cambridge, where, by the province law of the time, the deeds of all real estate within the county were to be recorded. But no records of deeds of land in Hollis, to persons known to have been early inhabitants of the town, are to be found in that office of a date prior to 1731.

Subsequent however to 1731 and before the spring of 1741 it is shown by these records that between those dates a very considerable number of deeds of land now in Hollis were made to the early settlers of the town. Many of these deeds, in addition to their date, a description of the land sold, and the name of the grantee, give also his occupation, and place of former residence. Among these deeds of land in Hollis, made before 1741, are to be found the following names of the early settlers of the town as grantees, viz., Thomas Dinsmore, weaver, David Nevins, carpenter, and widow Margaret Nevins, all of Bedford, Mass.; William Nevins, of Newton, Mass., husbandman; Jonathan Danforth and Joseph Farley, of Billerica; Eleazar Flagg and Jonathan Melvin, of Concord; Enoch Hunt and James McDonald, of Groton; Stephen Harris, of Littleton, and Samuel Cumings, of Groton.

Dunstable, as originally chartered, as we have seen, was bounded on the south, in part, by the north line of Groton. As chartered in 1655, Groton lay on each side of the Nashua River, its north-easterly corner being about two miles east of that river, at a place, then and still known as Buck Meadow, now in the town of Nashua, about one half mile from the south line of that town. The original north-west corner of Groton was in the line between the towns of Pepperell and Townsend, Mass., about one mile south of the present south line of New Hampshire. This corner is still marked by a stone monument now standing on the farm of Addison Wood. This old north line of Groton crossed the Nashua river, and the present state line at a point very near the Hollis Depot on the Worcester & Nashua Railroad.

In the summer and fall of 1738, a few of the settlers then living in the north part of Groton, and most of those residing in the west part of Dunstable, became desirous of being organized into a new township, and together with a considerable number of non-resident

(3)

proprietors, these settlers united in a petition to the Massachusetts
General Court for a township charter. The reasons for this application for a township charter are very clearly and pertinently set
forth in the following petitions, the originals of which, with the
doings of the General Court in respect to them, have been preserved
in the office of the Secretary of State at Boston.

PETITION OF THE INHABITANTS OF DUNSTABLE AND GROTON FOR A TOWN CHARTER.

"To his Excellency Jon[a] Belcher, Esq., Captain General and
Governor in chief, &c.; The Hon[ble] the Council and House of
Rep[tives] in General Court Assembled, at Boston, Nov. the 29th,
1738.

"The Petition of the subscribers, Inhabitants and Proprietors of
the Towns of Dunstable and Groton, Humbly Sheweth,

"That your Petitioners are situated in the westerly side of Dunstable Township, and the northerly side of Groton Township —
those in the Township of Dunstable, in general, their Houses are
nine or ten miles from Dunstable Meeting House, and those in the
Township of Groton, none but what lives at least on or near six
miles from Groton Meeting House — by which means your Petitioners are deprived of the benefit of preaching the greater part of the
year, nor is it possible at any season of the year for their families in
general to get to meeting; under which Disadvantages your Petitioners have this several years Labored, excepting the Winter Season for the two Winters past, in which they have at their own cost
and charges hired Preaching amongst themselves, which Disadvantages has very much prevented Peoples settling Land there.

" That there is a Tract of good Land well situated for a Township of the Contents of about six miles and a half square, bounded
thus, beginning at Dunstable Line by Nashaway River, so running
by the Westerly side of said River, Southerly one mile in Groton Land; then running Westerly, a parallel Line with Groton
North Line till it comes to Townsend Line; and then turning and
running North to Groton North-west Corner, and from Groton
North-west Corner by Townsend Line and by the Line of Groton
New Grant till it comes to be five miles and a half to the North
Ward of Groton North Line; from thence due East seven miles;
from thence South to Nashua River, and so by Nashua River,
South-westerly to Groton Line, the first mentioned bound. Which

described Lands can by no means be prejudicial to the Town of Dunstable or Groton, (it not coming within six miles or thereabouts of either of their Meeting Houses at the nearest place) to be taken off from them and erected into a seperate Township.

" That there is already settled in the bounds of the afore described Tract, near Forty Families, and many more ready to come on were it not for the difficulties and hardships aforesaid of getting to Meeting. These with many other Disadvantages we find very troublesome to us, our Living so remote from the Towns we respectively belong to.

" Wherefore your Petitioners most humbly pray that your Excellency and Honors would take the premises into your consideration and make an Act for the Erecting the aforesaid Lands into a seperate and distinct Township, with the Powers, Priviledges and Immunities of a distinct and seperate Township under such restrictions and Limitations, as you in your great Wisdom shall see meet.

"And whereas it will be a great benefit and advantage to the non-resident proprietors owning Lands there, by increasing the value of their Lands or rendering Easy settling the same, your Pet[rs] also pray that they may be at their proportionable part according to their respective interest in Lands there for the building a meeting house and settling a minister and so much towards Constant Preaching, as in your Wisdom shall be thought proper.

SETTLERS ON THE AFORESAID LANDS.

"OBADIAH PARKER	PETER POWERS	PHILIP WOOLERICH
JOSIAH BLOOD	ABRA'M TAYLOR. Jun	NATH'L BLOOD
JERAHMAEL CUMINGS	BENJ. FARLEY	WILLIAM ADAMS
EBEN'R PEARCE	HENRY BARTON	JOSEPH TAYLOR
WILLIAM COLBURN	PETER WHEELER	MOSES PROCTOR
STEPHEN HARRIS	ROBERT COLBURN	WILL'M SHATTUCK
THOMAS DINSMORE	DAVID NEVINS	THOS. NEVINS.

NON-RESIDENT PROPRIETORS.

SAMUEL BROWNE	JOSEPH EATON	JOHN MALVIN
W. BROWNE	JOSEPH LEMMON	JONA. MALVIN
JOSEPH BLANCHARD	JEREMIAH BALDWIN	JAMES CUMINGS
JOHN FOWLE Jun	SAM'L BALDWIN	ISAAC FARWELL
NATH'L SALTONSTALL	DANIEL REMANT	EBEN'R PROCTOR."

ORDER OF THE GENERAL COURT.

"In the House of Representatives Dec[r] 12, 1738.

Read and ordered that the Petitioners serve the Towns of Groton and Dunstable with Coppys of this Petition.

"In Council January 4th 1738-9.

Read and again ordered that the further consideration of this Petition be referred to the first Tuesday of the next May session, and that James Minot and John Hobson Esq^{rs}, with such as the Honorable Board shall joine be a Committee at the charge of the Petitioners to repair to the Lands petitioned to be Erected into a Township, first giving seasonable notice as well to the Petitioners as to the Inhabitants and non-resident Proprietors of Lands within the said Towns of Dunstable and Groton of the time of their going by causing the same to be published in the Boston Gazette : That they carefully view the s.d Lands, as well as the other parts of the s.d Towns so far as may be desired by the Partys or thought proper ; That the Petitioners, and all others concerned be fully heard in their Pleas and allegations for as well as against the Prayer of the Petition ; and that upon mature consideration on the whole the committee then report what in their opinion may be proper for the Court to do in answer thereto.   Sent up for concurrence.

J. QUINCY, Speaker.

In Council Jany 9th 1738-9.

            Read and concurred, and Thomas Berry Esqr is joined in the affair.

SIMON FROST Dep^{ty} Sec^{ry}.

Consented to.   J. BELCHER."

A very large majority of the settlers whose names appear on the above Petition lived in the west part of Dunstable. Many of the settlers residing at the time in the north part of Groton were not satisfied with this Petition, but wanted a much larger part of the new township to be taken from Groton than was contemplated by the signers of this first Petition.   With this purpose in view these settlers in Groton, with such of the residents of the west part of Dunstable as were willing to join with them, presented a second Petition to the General Court for a township to be formed from the two towns.   This second Petition bearing date Dec. 12, 1739, was as follows :

To his Excellency Jonathan Belcher, Esq., Captain General and Governor-in-Chief, &c, &c.

" The Petition of Richard Warner and others, Inhabitants of the Towns of Groton and Dunstable, most humbly sheweth :

" That your Petitioners dwell very far from the place of Public Worship in either of said Towns — many of them eight miles distant; and some more, and none less than four miles; whereof your Petitioners are put to great Difficulties in Travelling on the Lord's Day with ou

Families. Your Petitioners therefore pray your Excellency and Honors to take their circum stances into your wise and compassionate consideration, and that a part of the Town of Groton,—Beginning at the Line between Groton and Dunstable, where it crosses Lancaster (Nashua) River, and so up the said River until it comes to a place called and known by the name of Joseph Blood's Ford Way on said River—thence a West Point till it comes to Townsend Line, &c., with such a part and so much of the Town of Dunstable, as this Honorable Court in their great Wisdom shall think proper, with the Inhabitants thereon, may be Erected into a separate and distinct Township, that so they may attend the Public worship of God with more Ease than at present they can by reason of the great distance they live from the places thereof as aforesaid. And your Petitioners as in Duty bound Shall Ever Pray, &c.

INHABITANTS OF GROTON.

RICHARD WARNER, EBENEZER PIERCE, WILLIAM BLOOD,
BENJAMIN SWALLOW, SAMUEL FISK, JEREMIAH LAWRENCE,
WILLIAM ALLEN, JOHN GREENE, STEPHEN EAMES.
ISAAC WILLIAMS, JOSIAH TUCKER,
EBENEZER GILSON, ZECHARIAH LAWRENCE, JUN.,

INHABITANTS OF DUNSTABLE.

ENOCH HUNT, GIDEON HONEY, SAMUEL FARLEY,
ELEAZER FLAGG, JOSIAH BLOOD, WILLIAM ADAMS,
SAMUEL CUMINGS, SAMUEL PARKER, PHILIP WOOLERICH,
WILLIAM BLANCHARD,

Shortly after the presentation of this second Petition most of the settlers in Dunstable united in a Remonstrance against any part of Dunstable being set to Groton, and appointed Abraham Taylor, Jun., and Peter Powers to show forth their "earnest desire that a Township be made entirely of Dunstable Land."

This Remonstrance was dated at Dunstable, Dec. 21, 1739, and was as follows:

"We the Sub'rs Inhab'ts of ye Town of Dunstable, and resident in that part of it called Nissitisitt, Do hereby Authorize and fully Empower Abraham Taylor, Jun., and Peter Powers to represent to the General Court our unwillingness that any part of Dunstable should be sett to Groton to make a Township or Parish and to shew forth our Earnest Desire that a Township be made entirely out of Dunstable Land, Extending Six Miles North from Groton Line which will bring them on the Line on ye Brake of Land and just include the present settlement; or otherwise as ye Honorable Committee Reported, and Agreeable to the tenour thereof, as the Honorable Court shall see meet, and as in Duty bound, &c.

THOMAS DINSMORE, JAMES WHITING, PETER WHEELER,
JERAHMAEL CUMINGS, JAMES MCDANIELS, DAVID NEVINS,
JOSEPH WHITCOMB, RANDALL MCDANIELS, THOMAS NEVINS,
JONATHAN MELVIN, JOSEPH MCDANIELS, NATHANIEL BLOOD,
WILLIAM ADAMS, WILLIAM COLBURN, WILLIAM SHATTUCK,
WILLIAM WILSON, ROBERT COLBURN, JOSHUA WRIGHT,
MOSES PROCTOR, STEPHEN HARRIS, HENRY BARTON."

REPORT OF THE COMMITTEE APPOINTED BY THE GENERAL COURT.

"The committee appointed on the petition of the inhabitants and proprietors situated on the westerly side of Dunstable and northerly side of Groton, after notifying all parties, having repaired to the lands petitioned to be erected into a township and carefully viewed the same, find a very good tract of land in Dunstable, west of Nashaway river, between said river and Souhegan river, extending from Groton New Grant and Townsend line six miles east lying in a very commodious form for a township, and on said lands there is now about twenty families and many more settling. That none of the inhabitants live nearer to a meeting-house than seven miles, and if they go to their town have to pass over a ferry the greater part of the year.

We also find in Groton a sufficient quantity of land accommodable for settlement, and a considerable number of Inhabitants thereon, that in some short time, when they are well agreed, may be erected into a Precinct or Parish, and that it will be very inconvenient to erect a township in the form prayed for. * *

The committee are of opinion that the Petitioners in Dunstable are under such circumstances as necessitates them to ask relief which will be fully obtained by their being made a township. * *

The committee are further of the opinion that it will be greatly for the good and interest of the township that the non-resident proprietors have liberty of voting with the inhabitants as to the Building and Placing a meeting-house and that the lands be equally taxed, and that for the support of the Gospel ministry among them the lands of the non-resident Proprietors be taxed at two pence per acre for the space of five years.

All which is humbly submitted in behalf of the committee.

THOMAS BERRY."

ACTION OF THE GENERAL COURT UPON THE REPORT OF THE COMMITTEE.

"In Council Dec. 27, 1739.

Read and ordered that this report be so far accepted that the lands mentioned and described therein with the inhabitants there be erected into a separate and distinct Precinct and the said inhabitants are hereby vested with all such powers and privileges as any other Precinct in this Province have or by law ought to have or enjoy. And they are also empowered to assess and lay a tax of two pence per acre per annum for the space of five years on all the unimproved lands belonging to the non-resident proprietors to be applied to the support of the ministry according to the said Report.

Sent down for concurrence.

SIMON FROST, Dep'ty Sec'ty.

In the House of Representatives, Dec. 28, 1739

Read and concurred.   J QUINCY, Speaker.
Consented to.   J. BELCHER,   "

Such at that day was the mode of proceeding, and such the conditions under which townships and precincts or parishes were chartered by the General Court of Massachusetts. A parish was an ecclesiastical division of a township, vested with the power, (by the taxation of its inhabitants) and charged with the duty of building a meeting-house, and maintaining a " learned and orthodox minister." By the foregoing act of the General Court, that part of the old town of Dunstable, described in the report of the committee, became a parish, known for some years afterwards as *West Dunstable*. For all municipal purposes, other than ecclesiastical, it still remained a part of the old town. The new parish was bounded on the north by the Souhegan river, on the south by Groton, and west by the west line of the old town. On the east it was bounded in part by the Nashua river, and in part by a north and south line extending from that river to the Souhegan somewhat farther to the east than the present east line of Hollis, and in the records of the proceedings had some years afterwards, before the Governor and Council of New Hampshire for a change of the eastern boundary of Hollis, the parish of West Dunstable is said to have contained an area of 70.000 acres.

At the date of the charter the rude, primitive dwellings of the settlers who had petitioned for it with their stump-covered embryo farms were widely and sparsely scattered over a large part of the new parish. Robert and William Colburn, David, Thomas and William Nevins, Stephen Harris and Philip Woolerich had located on the south side of the extinct town of Monson, now the north part of Hollis; Samuel Farley, James, Joseph and Randall McDaniels, Melvin and Whitcomb, in the easterly part of Brookline, formerly the west part of Hollis. The house of Abraham Taylor was about 60 rods north of the present meeting-house in Hollis, on land now owned by Henry Blood; that of Samuel Cumings about 30 rods west of the meeting-house on the place now owned by Levi Abbot; that of Benjamin Farley, the inn-keeper, on the road leading to the south of the meeting-house, being a part of the same house now owned by Taylor G. Worcester; Jerahmael Cumings lived on the same road, with Farley, about 1-2 mile farther south; Josiah Blood, also on the same road, about 3-4 of a mile from Cumings, now known as the Fox place; Joshua Wright about 1-2 mile east of Blood on the farm now owned by the heirs of his grandson, Miles J. Wright; William Blanchard in the east part of the town, near Flint's hill; William Shattuck still farther east, near the old east school-house.

The farm of Peter Wheeler was in the north-west part of the town, about westerly from Long pond; Moses Proctor settled in the west part, on Proctor hill. Henry Barton in the westerly part, on land now owned by John C. Jewett. The house of William Adams is said to have been upon the site of the present south-west school-house, about 2 1-2 miles from the meeting-house. Samuel Parker lived in the same neighborhood on the farm now owned by Daniel M. Smith; James Whiting on the road to Brookline, near Whiting's hill; Nathaniel Blood in the same part of the town on the present farm of Franklin Colburn, and Enoch Hunt in the extreme south part, next to Pepperell, on the farm now owned by Luke Blood. Thus it may be seen that the settlers in the extreme north part of the settlement were from six to seven miles distant from those in the south part; and those living at the extreme east and west part were even more remote from each other.

CHAPTER III.

1739 TO 1746.—THE PARISH OF WEST DUNSTABLE AND DISTRICT OF
DUNSTABLE.—FIRST PARISH MEETING, AND FIRST MEETING
HOUSE. — THE NON–RESIDENT TAX.—SETTLEMENT OF THE
·FIRST MINISTER.

The report of the committee appointed to view the lands in the
north part of Groton and west part of Dunstable was carefully
preserved by the grantees of the charter of the parish of West
Dunstable, and is now to be found recorded at full length on the first
pages of the first volume of the Hollis town records.

These original records, in what I have to say of the early history
of Hollis, will be my principal guide. Where I can consistently do
so, I shall press them into my service and let them speak for me in
their own simple and homely dialect. We may occasionally observe
in the manuscript, wide, and sometimes grotesque departures from
the more modern orthography of Walker, Webster and Worcester,
and also from the grammar and syntax of Lowth and Murray. Yet
in these respects, they are less subject to unfavorable criticism than
many of our town records of a much more modern date. The style
of them is terse, plain, simple and direct, and the words well chosen
to express the ideas and matters to be recorded, and they contain the
municipal autobiography of our ancestors, commencing four generations ago, written down from year to year, and sometimes from
month to month, by persons appointed for the purpose, while what
they had done, or what they at the time proposed to do, was still
fresh in the minds of all.

BOUNDARIES AND AREA OF THE PARISH AND THE NON–RESIDENT
TAX.

The west parish of the old town of Dunstable, as we have seen,
extended north and south, from the Souhegan river to the south line
of the old town, a distance from 9 to 12 miles, and was not far from
10 miles in width, and was said to have contained an area of about

70,000 acres, being more than three times as large as Hollis now is. It included nearly all of the present town of Hollis, that part of Amherst south of the Souhegan, the most of Milford and Brookline, parts of the towns of Nashua and Merrimack, in the state of New Hampshire, and a small part of Pepperell in Massachusetts. The inhabitants of the parish, as we have seen by their charter, had authority to assess 2d. per acre on all the unimproved land of non-residents for the term of five years for the support of the ministry. At that time there were about 25 resident families. If each of these families owned, on an average, 800 acres (an estimate quite large enough), the resident settlers would have had 20,000 acres, leaving upon these estimates 50,000 to the non-residents. A tax of 2d. the acre on this last quantity would have yielded an annual fund of £416 13s., or about $1380 in the currency of the present time, calling the pound $3.33. We shall soon see what importance the first settlers of Hollis attached to this right to compel non-residents to pay for the preaching and meeting-houses of the resident settlers.

THE FIRST PARISH MEETING AND ITS DOINGS, AND THE FIRST
MEETING—HOUSE.

The first parish-meeting, under the parish-charter, was held at the inn of Lieut. Benjamin Farley, Jan. 22, 1739–40, O. S.   Mr. Farley's inn was the place where the parish-meetings were commonly held till the first meeting-house was built, and is said to have been upon the farm now owned by Taylor G. Worcester, a short distance south of the present meeting-house. The warrant for this meeting, like all similar warrants, was entitled, in its margin, "Middlesex SS.," meaning by these words, county of Middlesex, Massachusetts. It was under the hand and seal of Joseph Blanchard, Esq., of Dunstable, at that time one of "his majesty's" justices of the peace of that county, and was addressed to Abraham Taylor, as constable, to warn the meeting, who had been active in obtaining the charter, and who was annually elected parish-clerk till his death, about four years after.

At this first meeting Mr. Taylor was elected moderator and clerk; Mr. Taylor, Peter Powers and Benjamin Farley, assessors; Stephen Harris, treasurer; Thomas Dinsmore, collector of the non-resident money; and Peter Powers and Benjamin Farley a committee to procure preaching till the first of April following. Also it was "voted that Abraham Taylor, Peter Powers and Thomas Dinsmore be a committee to joyn with such Persons as the old Parish shall appoint for to raise Bounds between each Parish." At this meeting

also the following vote was passed in respect to a meeting-house ;
" Voted to build a House for the Public Worship of God : That
said House be Erected at or near Thomas Dinsmore's House Lot of
Land.   That the House be 22 feet one way and 20 the other — 9 foot
stud — well-boarded and shingled — One Floor — One Door — 3
windows and as many Seats as may be thought convenient — the
House to be Erected by the last of April next."

The house lot of Thomas Dinsmore, as was said, was upon the farm
now owned by John Coburn, Esq.   But no meeting-house was built
upon or near that site, the vote to that effect having been reconsid-
ered at a meeting in the following March.   After four or five other
sites had been proposed at various meetings and rejected, it was at
last, at a meeting held Nov. 5, 1740 : "Voted that the Meeting-
House should be Erected on Abraham Taylor's Land, about Sixty
Rods Southerly from said Taylor's Dwelling-House, on the highest
Knoll of Land thereabouts, and that the Burying Place for the Parish be ajoining the Place now appointed for ye Meeting-House."

This is the same pleasant and hallowed spot on which, a few
years later, the second meeting-house was built, the same where the
third, still standing, was erected more than sixty years after, the site
for it and the burial-ground having been given by Mr. Taylor, who
died in the spring of 1743, and was the first adult person buried in
it.   It appears that the new edifice was not wholly completed for a
year or more after its location was fixed, as we find that it was voted
at a parish-meeting, Oct. 23, 1741, " To have one Glace Winder in
the Meeting-House and to have it under-Pind as soon as possable."

THE FIRST PARISH TAX, WITH THE NAMES OF THE TAX-PAYERS.

In the month of November, 1740, by vote of a parish meeting, the
first tax was assessed upon the inhabitants " for defraying the necessary charges of the Parish," amounting to £16 2s. 2d.   This tax
list contains the names of 29 persons, viz. :

ZACHARIAH LAWRENCE, Jr.	JOSIAH BLOOD	NATHANIEL BLOOD
ENOCH HUNT	PETER POWERS	PHILIP WOOLERICH
ELEAZER FLAGG	BENJAMIN FARLEY	MOSES PROCTOR
SAMUEL CUMINGS	JERAHMAEL CUMINGS	JOHN BUTTERFIELD
WILLIAM BLANCHARD	SAMUEL FARLEY	ELNATHAN BLOOD
ABRAHAM TAYLOR	DAVID NEVINS	HENRY BARTON
STEPHEN HARRIS	WILLIAM NEVINS	THOMAS DINSMORE
WILLIAM COLBURN	Widow NEVINS	AMOS PHILIPS
ROBERT COLBURN	WILLIAM SHATTUCK	GIDEON BEHONEY,
PETER WHEELER	DANIEL KENDALL	

nearly all of them family names, familiar to the people of Hollis
from that time to this.

By a province law, then in force, all male persons of the age of eighteen years and over, with the exception of the governor, settled ministers, and a few others, were subject to a poll-tax. The above tax-list may be presumed to contain the names of all male persons above that age at that time inhabitants of the parish. Six of the list are charged with a poll-tax only ; the remaining twenty-three, including the widow Nevins, with both a poll and property-tax. Of the above tax of about £16, very near £13, or more than three-fourths of it, were assessed on twenty-eight persons as a poll-tax, and less than £3 upon real and personal estate. The sum assessed upon each poll was 9s. 2d., while the highest property-tax was only 6s. 7d. I may have occasion, in another connection, to advert again to this matter of taxation.

THE NON-RESIDENT'S MONEY, OR NON-RESIDENT TAX OF 2D. THE ACRE AND THE DISPOSAL OF IT.

As this tax was a matter of much interest and some trouble to the residents of the parish, it is entitled to further notice as illustrating the laws and usages of the good people of that time, and especially the ways and means which were supposed to be lawful and right for the raising of money for the support of "learned, able and orthodox" ministers.

The warrant for the third parish-meeting, held in March, 1740, with other articles to be voted on, contained the following :

1st. "To see what Encouragement the People will give to any Person or Persons for Killing Rattlesnakes in this parish.

2d. "To see if the Parish will agree to dispose of the Non-Resident money that shall be due and coming to this Parish for the space of five years from the first of January last to any Person or Persons who shall agree to Support the Gospel in this Parish. "

At the above meeting it was voted :

1st. "That if any Person shall make it appear to the Committee of the Parish that he has Killed one or more Rattlesnakes in this Precinct, in this present year, he shall have paid to him one shilling for every such snake so killed, out of the Parish Treasury. "

Also unanimously voted, "That Peter Powers & Abraham Taylor shall have the Total of all such sum or sums of money as is or shall be assessed on Land belonging to non-Resident Proprietors of this Parish for the space of five years from the 1st of January last, on condition that the said Powers and Taylor shall & do oblige them-

selves & Heirs with sufficient security to maintain and constantly
support Preaching in this Precinct for ye full term of ye said five
years —— and Erect a Meeting House for the Public Worship of God
agreeable to the tenor of the vote of said parish —— and likewise fully
acquit and discharge said Parish from the cost & charges that have
been expended in being set off from Dunstable & being erected into
a separate Precinct — and also from the cost and & charges that has
been expended in getting Timber for a Bridge across Nashaway
River, and also to pay Mr. Underwood for his Preaching with us in
this Parish."

The question was once asked, "Of whom do the Kings of the
Earth take custom or tribute, of their own children or of strangers?"
The answer was, "Of strangers." It would seem from the doings
of the above meeting that the early settlers of the west parish of Dunstable had taken lessons in finance from the "Kings of the Earth."

Within about a year from the time of this meeting, after a long
and angry controversy, the new province line between New-Hampshire and Massachusetts was surveyed and established where the
State line now is. Much to the chagrin and disappointment of the
inhabitants, that part of the old town of Dunstable now known as
Hollis, was found to be in New-Hampshire. In consequence of this
decision, the charter of the west parish in Dunstable, granted by the
general court of Massachusetts, was virtually annulled, that general
court having had at the time no power to grant it. With the charter
the legal right to assess this tax of two pence the acre on the land of
non-residents was also lost, and with the tax the very thrifty bargain
with Messrs. Powers and Taylor in respect to the disposal of it.

In this dilemma, the inhabitants promptly met (Feb. 19, 1741-2,)
and "voted to petition the Grate and General Court of N. Hampshire
that the Parish be made a Township, and also that the Parish may
have power to collect of delinquent persons, the several sums they
may have been assessed at agreeable to the Laws of the Massachusetts
Province."

But instead of granting this petition for a township-charter and to
legalize the non-resident tax, the general court, in March, 1742, organized all that part of old Dunstable north of the new province line
and west of Merrimack river, into a "District" for the collection of
province taxes, with authority for that purpose only, to elect district-
assessors or selectmen, and a district-clerk and collectors of taxes.

The first meeting for the election of District-officers, was held under
the direction of a committee of the general court, probably in the east

parish, April 23, 1742. At this meeting, Abraham Taylor was chosen clerk; Abraham Taylor, Thomas Harwood, Samuel Cumings and Jonathan Lovewell selectmen. The record for the year 1743 is lost. In 1744, John Boynton was district clerk; and John Boynton, Jonathan Lovewell and Jerahmael Cumings, selectmen or assessors. In 1745, John Boynton was district clerk; John Boynton, Jonathan Lovewell, and Jerahmael Cumings assessors or selectmen.

SETTLEMENT OF THE NEW PROVINCE LINE.

For a long time prior to the year 1739 the boundary line between the provinces of New Hampshire and Massachusetts had been the subject of protracted and acrimonious controversy. About seventy years before, Governor Endicott of Massachusetts had caused a monument to be fixed three miles northward of the junction of the two rivers forming the Merrimack in the present county of Belknap, and Massachusetts claimed all the territory in the present state of New Hampshire south of an east and west line passing through that point, and also all within three miles both east and north of the Merrimack.

On the other hand, New Hampshire claimed all the territory lying north of a line running due east and west through a point within three miles of the Merrimack, on its north side near its mouth. At last a royal commission was appointed to settle this controversy, which met for the purpose at Hampton Falls in this state in the year 1737, the General Court of each province attending the sittings of this commission. The Governor of Massachusetts in his coach, and the members of the General Court of that Province mounted on horseback, formed themselves into a procession at Boston, and marched in state to Hampton Falls to be present at the sessions of this tribunal. A description of this cavalcade has come down to us, as told by a wit of the time to a son of the Emerald Isle, in the following pasquinade, which I present as illustrating the customs of the colonial governments under the royal charters.

> "Dear Paddy you ne'er did behold such a sight,
>   As yesterday morning was seen before night;
> You in all your born days saw nor I didn't neither,
>   So many fine horses and men ride together;
> At the head, the lower house trotted two in a row,
>   Then all the higher house pranced after the low,
> Then the Governor's coach galloped on like the wind,
>   And the last that came foremost were the troopers behind;
> But I fear it means no good to your neck or mine,
>   For they say 'tis to fix the right place for the *Line*."

The Commission at Hampton Falls did not agree, and the question was reserved for the King in Council. A decision was finally made in the year 1740, fixing the Province line where the State line now is. This decision took from the Massachusetts claim, and gave to New Hampshire, not only all the disputed tract, but also a tract of territory south of that in controversy, fourteen miles in width and extending from the Merrimack River to the Connecticut, which New Hampshire had not before claimed, embracing all that part of old Dunstable north of the present State line.

This was for Dunstable " the most unkindest cut of all," being for the old town almost as troublesome, not to say as fatal, a " place for the line" as his neck could have been for the Paddy, cutting the body politic asunder from side to side through its most tender and vital parts, hard by the ancient meeting-house and burial ground. This new line was run in 1741, leaving in Massachusetts that part of the old town now in Tyngsborough and Dunstable in that State, and a narrow gore from the old parish of West Dunstable, now in Pepperell, and severing from Groton a small triangular tract now in the south part of Nashua along the State line.

EFFECTS OF THE DECISION.

This decision came upon the settlers in Dunstable, north of the new line, with mingled surprise and consternation. Dunstable was eminently and wholly a Massachusetts settlement. The settlers were nearly all from the neighboring towns in that Province, with whose people they were connected in sympathy, in business and by the ties of marriage and blood. Their town and parish charters and the titles to their lands and improvements were all Massachusetts grants, and their whole civil and ecclesiastical organizations under Massachusetts laws. This decision of the King in Council left them wholly out of the jurisdiction of that Province, and in legal effect made all their charters, the titles to their lands and improvements, and all statute laws regulating their civil and church polity wholly void. The decision of the King was final, and there was no appeal. Though disappointed, embarrassed and indignant, there was no alternative but submission.

Fortunately for them, in the course of a few years afterwards a compromise was effected with the adverse claimants of their lands and improvements, and their titles and possessions quieted. and they gradually became more reconciled to the change of their allegiance.

But this compromise and the quieting of their titles to their lands and improvements afforded these people no relief in respect to the support of the ministry and building meeting-houses.

Still, however, the inhabitants of West Dunstable continued to hold public meetings, elect officers and assess taxes much as before, and in the records of their doings their community was styled a "parish" or "precinct." Notwithstanding their disappointment in the loss of their charter, and at finding themselves citizens of New Hampshire against their wishes, they were not yet able to forget the "Non-resident Money," or to abandon the hope of obtaining it. With this hope in view, at a public meeting held in January, 1744, it was "Voted that Peter Powers should have all the non-residents' money that is not Collected for the four years past and the year to come, * * and for the said Powers to pay all the Parish Debt for Preaching and to any other Person for Sarvis Don the Parish before the ordination * * and to pay the Parish £40. O. T. at the end of the year." It is to be inferred from the doings of a parish meeting in the following December, that these non-resident land-owners had questioned the right of Mr. Powers to collect this tax, and that it was not paid so cheerfully as the purchaser had hoped. As a last remedy for this trouble, it was voted at this meeting, "that Capt. Powers represent the Parish at the General Court of New Hampshire to get ye Massachusetts Act for taxing ye land in said Parish confirmed if he will go at his own charges—*otherwise not to go.*"

The record does not show whether Capt. Powers accepted the honor of the office, with its condition, or not.

The charter of Hollis as a town bore date April 3, 1746, and embraced a territory much less than one half of that contained in the charter of West Dunstable. This town charter was wholly silent in respect to the right to tax non-residents for any purpose. To supply this omission, at a town-meeting held on the 22d of December of the same year it was "Voted to Raise two Pence per Acre Lawful Money on all the Land of Hollis for five years for ye Support of ye Gospel and ye arising charges of said Town, and to Petition the Grat and Generall Court for Streangth to Gather and Get the Money of Non-Residents." Samuel Cumings, Esq., was chosen a delegate to present this petition, which he did in the following April. In answer to this petition the general court of New Hampshire passed an act taxing all the land in Hollis for four years at two pence the acre for the support of the ministry and finishing the second meeting-house, the frame of which had then been raised. All the lands

in Hollis were taxed under this law for the next four years (as stated
in the town records), " for the Building and Repairing a Meeting-
House and the Supporting the Gospel Ministry." This tax was
assessed in the old-tenor currency, £4 of which at that date appear
to have been of the value of £1, lawful or silver money. In 1747
this tax amounted, in the old-tenor currency, to £394 17s. 8d. Of
that sum, £256 6s. 8d,, or more than two-thirds of it, were assessed
upon 33 non-resident land-owners, and the residue, £138 11s., on
48 residents. In 1748, £506 3s. were assessed for the like purpose,
of which £350 4s. 8d., again more than two-thirds of it, were
assessed on 31 non-residents, and the balance on 52 residents.
Whatever we may think of the justice of this law, it seems to have
had the good effect of lessening the number of non-residents, and also
the quantity of land in Hollis owned by them, and of adding to the
number of residents, and to their proportion of the land. In 1750,
the last year of the law, the resident land-owners had increased from
48, in 1747, to 70. And the non-residents had fallen off from 33 in
1747, to 24 in 1750, and the amount of the land-tax paid by the two
classes had become much more equal.

It seems, however, that all these non-residents did not acquiesce
in the justice of this law so cheerfully as they might have done. As
an instance of their dislike to it, we find that in 1748 Col. Prescott's
heirs were taxed under it the considerable sum of £48 13s. 4d. for
the support of preaching they could not hear, and that they had had
an article inserted in the warrant for the town-meeting asking for an
abatement of this tax. In response to this petition, as the record
states it, "It was put to vote to see if the Town would Ease Col.
Prescott's Heirs of any part of their Land Tax, and it was passed in
the negative."

To me, at least, as a native of the town, and one of the descendants
of these worthy people, their names and memories are sacred. "All
their failings leaned to virtue's side." Their ashes have slept for
near a century in peaceful and honored graves, and the foot of the
stranger who knows their worth would tread lightly upon them. I
have made these extracts from their annals with no irreverent or
unfilial feeling, but to illustrate some of the differences between the
laws, customs and sentiments that prevailed among good and Christian people in New-England one hundred and twenty years ago, and
those upon the like subjects under whose influence the last two gen-
reations have been educated.

PREACHING BEFORE THE SETTLEMENT OF THE FIRST MINISTER,
AND THE MANNER OF PROVIDING IT.

The new parish had no settled minister till the spring of 1743,—
more than three years after date of the charter.   In the mean time
the inhabitants had manifested a very commendable zeal in their
efforts to comply with the laws in respect to the support of the ministry.   At their first parish meeting, as we have seen, a committee
was chosen "to provide Preaching till the following April. "   In the
month of March previous, " Samuel Cumings and Eleazer Flagg"
were commissioned "to provide Preaching and Entertainment for the
minister for the next three months. "   In July, 1741, it was "voted
that Abraham Taylor and Peter Powers have the non-resident money
for the current year to pay Mr. Underwood and Mr. Towle * * *
and to procure Preaching till the first of January next, if the money
shall hold out. "   In September, 1741, the first article in the warrant
for a meeting then held, was " to see whether it be the minds of the
People to do any thing towards the Bringing forward the Settling of
a Larned and Orther Dox Minister in this Parish."   And in February, 1742, it was "Voted That any Person who shall hereafter
Entertain any Minister for this Parish shall have paid to him Eight
Shillings for one Sabbath day and 20ˢ a Week if he stay longer. "

DOINGS OF THE PARISH PREPARATORY TO THE SETTLEMENT OF
THE FIRST MINISTER.

At a parish meeting held in October, 1741, before it was publicly
known that any part of the town of Old Dunstable was on the wrong
side of the province line, it was voted,

1st. "That Stephen Harris, Abraham Taylor & Peter Powers be
joyned in Committee with Benjamin Farley and Samuel Cumings to
take some proper Measures to bring forward the settling of a Larned
and Orther Dox Minister in this Parish as soon as conveniency will
alow. "

2d. "That said Committee be directed to observe the following instructions, viz., That they wait upon the Rev. Mr. Trobridge, Mr.
Hemmingway, and the Rev. Mr. Bliss and Mr. Swan and desire
their assistance in keeping and solemnizing a Day of Fasting and
Prayer in this Parish and Seeking the Direction of Heaven in the
affair. "

3d. " That said Committee should make their Address to said
Ministers for their advice and Direction what Ministers to apply ourselves too to Preach with us on Probation. "

(4)

At a parish meeting Dec. 28, 1741, among the accounts presented and allowed were the following :

" Voted to alow Abraham Taylor —

" For Entertaining Ministers at the Fast   £3. 00ˢ. 0ᵈ.

" For Entertaining Ministers Five Sabbaths £2. 00ˢ. 0ᵈ."

The warrant for this meeting was the last in which the words " Middlesex ss." were written in the top margin. It soon became known to them that the parish of West Dunstable was not in the county of Middlesex, that their charter, as a legal instrument, was worthless, and that there was no law by which the minority of the inhabitants could be bound by the votes of a majority. Embarrassed by the decision in respect to the new line and the loss of their charter, our ancestors did not falter in their effort to bring forward and settle a " Larned and Orther Dox Minister."   With this end, and others in view, the inhabitants, as we have said before, met in February, 1742, and petitioned the General Court of New Hampshire for a township charter. No other public meeting of the inhabitants was held till the 17th of January, 1743, near a year after, when they came together by common consent, and by mutual agreement in their personal and individual capacity, invited the Rev. Daniel Emerson, the candidate of their choice, to become their minister. As I think the proceedings of this meeting and of that which next followed, cannot fail to interest others as well as myself, I have taken pains to transcribe the substance of them from the record.

THE CALL OF THE SOCIETY, ANSWER OF THE CANDIDATE, HIS SETTLEMENT AND SALARY, AND THE WAYS AND MEANS OF PROVIDING IT.

" Att a meeting of the Inhabitants of the West Parish in Dunstable regularly assembled January 17, 1742. 3. Abraham Taylor chosen moderator.

" Unanimously voted and chose Mr. Daniel Emerson for their Gospel Minister to take the Pastoral care of the Flock of Christ in said Place. Also,

" Unanimously voted and agreed to give said Mr. Emerson (on condition of his acceptance) for and toward his Settlement £400, common currency or £100 of the Massachusetts last Emition. Also

" Unanimously voted to give said Minister for his yearly Sallery, During his Ministry in said Place such a certain sum of Bills of Credit as will be equal to fifty Pounds of the Massachusetts last Emition . (new). Also,

" Voted to give Thirty Cords of Fire Wood, Cord Wood Length
att said Ministers Door yearly,   Also,

" Voted and chose Abraham Taylor, Samuel Brown, Enoch
Hunt, Eleazer Flagg, Samuel Cumings, Peter Powers, William
Colburn, Stephen Harris and Robert Blood to wait upon said Mr.
Emerson and communicate unto him the minds and Proposals of
said Parish and desire his answer therein in convenient time.

" In testimony whereof we have hereunto set our hands the Day
above said."

SAMUEL BROWN	BENJ. BLANCHARD	DAVID LOWELL
ABRAHAM TAYLOR	ZEDEKIAH DRURY	THOMAS NEVINS
ENOCH HUNT	PETER POWERS	THOMAS PATCH
WILLIAM SHATTUCK	JONATHAN DANFORTH	NATHANIEL BLODGETT
WILLIAM COLBURN	SAMUEL FARLEY	MOSES PROCTOR
STEPHEN HARRIS	WILLIAM ADAMS	JOHN BROWN
ELEAZER FLAGG	NICHOLAS FRENCH	DANIEL KENDALL
BENJAMIN FARLEY	ZERUBBABEL KEMP	JOSIAH BLOOD
JERAHMAEL CUMINGS	PETER WHEELER	WILLIAM NEVINS
SAMUEL CUMINGS	JOSIAH BROWN	SAMUEL DOUGLASS
DAVID NEVINS	WILLIAM BLANCHARD	JOSEPH MCDANIELS
JOSHUA WRIGHT	HENRY BARTON	JAMES MCDANIELS
JAMES STEWART	NATHANIEL BLOOD	JAMES WHITING
STEPHEN AMES	ELNATHAN BLOOD	JOSEPH FARLEY
ROBERT BLOOD		Making in all 43 names.

The parish committee were prompt in communicating the foregoing call to Mr. Emerson, and on the 4th of the following March
a meeting was called to consider his answer, which was entered upon
the record as follows:

" To the Inhabitants of the West Parish in Dunstable,"

" Whereas it has pleased the Great God (who has the Hearts of
all men in his Hands) — to dispose and incline your hearts to invite
me to take the oversight of you and to Labour among you in Word
and Doctrine as appears by a vote preferred to me by the Committee,
bearing date Jan. 17, 1742. 3, I have from that time taken that important matter into the most close consideration and have asked the
best advice and am (after many and great difficulties in the way)
come to this conclusion without Hesitation viz. :

" If you will fullfill your Promis as to the £400 Settlement in old
Tenor, only that the one part of it be in Forty Acres of Good Land,
near and convenient to the Meeting House, firmly and forever con-
vaied to me, and the other Part to be paid in Bills of Publique credit
within a year from the date of this Answer —— And that for my
yearly Sallary you give me such a certain Sum of Bills of Publique
credit yearly, as shall be equal to 150 ounces of coined Silver, which

is the sum you propose —— together with Thirty Cords of Wood
Cord Wood Length delivered at my Door —— And after your Parish
Town or District shall by the Providence of God be increased to the
number of 100 Families (and not desired or expected till then) you
make an addition to my yearly Sallary of five ounces of coined Silver per year till the same shall be equal to 200 Ounces of coined
Silver — there to abide till the number of your Families arise to 150
— and then to Raise Five Ounces of Coined Silver per year till it
arrives at 210 Ounces of Coined Silver — and there to abide and
be no more, which is equal to £70, of the Massachusetts last
Emition — Always expecting the Thirty Cords of Wood — And
that these Several Sums or Sum be continued to me, so long as I
continue a Ghospel Minister over you — Always and in an espetial
manner expecting that you will be Helpers with me by Prayer ——

"Now if these before mentioned conditions be freely and voluntarily acted on and secured to me — as you promist in the call —
then I as freely and willingly accept of the call and freely subscribe
myself yours to serve in the work of the Ghospel Ministry During
Life.

"Dunstable West Precinct March ye 4th 1743.

"DANIEL EMERSON."

The record continues. "It was thereupon Voted and agreed to
accept the Terms Mr. Emerson proposed in his answer bouth as to
settlement and sallary — Also Voted that Samuel Brown, Abraham
Taylor, Peter Powers, Eleazer Flagg and Samuel Cumings be a
committee to consult with Mr. Emerson in the choice of a council."

On the same day and at the same meeting, as it appears in the
record, a mutual additional agreement was entered into by the tax
payers, and signed by most of them, with a preamble setting forth
the reasons that made this new agreement necessary. the important
parts of which are as follows:

"Whereas his majesty by the late determination of the Northern
Boundary of the Massachusetts has left us the Subscribers, Inhabitants of the Westerly part of Dunstable out of the Province to
which we always supposed we belonged, and under whose
Laws we Exercised the Privileges of a Parish — but by the said determination it is supposed by some that said Inhabitants are Dis-
qualified to make any Act, Agreement or Determination by a majority of voters as they otherwise might have done that should be
Effectual to compel Persons to pay their honest Proportion of all

such Rates and necessary charges that shall arise in calling settling and maintaining a minister.

"Now therefore that we may Enjoy the Benefit of the Ghospel ordinances amongst us we have come into the following agreement and obligation viz."

The contract with Mr. Emerson is set forth in this new agreement, verbatim, and the record then continues as follows:

"Allso agreed that in the Payment of the Ministers Settlement & Sallary the assessors hereafter to be chosen Proportion such a certain part thereof to each Pole that when the Remainder thereof shall be levied upon Each Persons' Real and Personal Estate, agreeable to the Rules of the Massachusetts Province, that the highest Payer upon Estates shall be equal to a single Pole." * * * *

"To the Performance of the aforewritten agreement we hereby covenant and oblige ourselves in the Penal sum of £100, till such time as this society be incorporated a distinct Town or Parish."

Thirty-seven names were signed to this agreement, some of which were not upon the call. This agreement, as will be readily seen, was a voluntary compact, entered into by those who signed it as their best expedient for the lack of a town or parish charter.

Some other matters suggested by this *contract* between Mr. Emerson and his society are worthy of a few passing remarks, as illustrating the laws, customs and prevailing sentiments of the times as well in civil as in church affairs.

1st. It was agreed in this contract that the new minister for the present should receive for his yearly salary 150 ounces of coined silver, or their equal value in bills of public credit, the paper money of that day, and also 30 cords of wood. When the number of families in the society should reach 100, five ounces per year were to be added, till the salary should amount to 200 ounces, and it might afterwards be increased to 210 ounces.

The oz. Troy, used in weighing the precious metals, contains 480 grains. The American silver dollar contains 412 1-2 of those grains, making the value of the oz. of silver coin $1.14: 150 oz. = $171: 200 oz. = $228: and 210 oz. = $239.40, in standard federal coin.

Mr. Emerson was ordained April 20, 1743, and he continued a faithful, venerated and popular minister of that society till Nov. 27, 1793, a period of more than fifty years, without a change, "or wish to change his place." At the latter date the Rev. Eli Smith, who

had married his grand-daughter, was settled as his colleague, Mr.
Emerson retaining one-half of his salary till his decease, Sept. 30,
1801, at the age of 85 years.

During that long period the salary of the minister, in accordance
with the tenor of their contract, was assessed upon the inhabitants of
the town at the annual March meetings, and always voted, so far as
appears from the record, without dissent or opposition.   As we have
seen, in the acceptance of the proposals made to him by the society,
Mr. Emerson closed his answer with the words, " Yours to serve in
the work of the Ghospel ministry during life."   We have in the pastorate of Mr. Emerson, an apt illustration of what was understood
by our ancestors 130 years ago, by the settlement of a minister in a
country town in New England, " during life."

2d. We have seen that the society in their proposals to the candidate agreed to give him such a sum in bills of public credit as would
be equal to £50 of the " Massachusetts last Emition."   This Massachusetts last emission was, at that date, the latest issue of paper
money by that province, one pound of which, at that time, was
worth $3.33 in coin, but like all paper money was very liable to de-
preciate.   Not intending that the value of his pastoral services should
depreciate, as paper money might. Mr. Emersonin accepting the call,
with somewhat of worldly wisdom, not to say Yankee shrewdness,
took occasion to translate this £50 in paper money into its equivalent
at the time in hard cash.   By this thoughtful caution, he secured to
himself for the following fifty years and more, a fixed hard money
basis for the value of his parochial duties, a basis ever afterwards respected by the people of the town.

The variable and uncertain value of the paper money in use in
New Hampshire, as shown by the town records, from 1741 till
near the revolutionary war, and also during that war, is the best
commentary upon the caution and foresight of Mr. Emerson in making his contract as he did.   The General Court of Massachusetts
first issued bills of credit, as money, in 1690, of which a fac simile is
to be found in the Historical Collections of that state for the year
1863.   In the year 1748 that province had its bills of credit in circulation, issued at different times, to the nominal amount of £2,200,000.
These bills of credit at that time had so depreciated that £1 in silver
was equal in value to £11 in paper.   About that time this paper
money was redeemed at that rate(eleven for one) in Spanish dollars,
which had been received from England in payment of the services

of the Massachusetts troops, at the siege and capture of Louisburg,
in 1745. But in New Hampshire, from 1741 to 1765, there appears
to have been very little if any metallic money in use as a medium of
exchange. As shown by the town records, the taxes for all purposes, during that period, were assessed and collected in some sort of
paper money. Even the names by which the various kinds and
issues of this currency were known at the time, are to most of the
present generation an unsolved riddle.

Among these names we shall find on the records: "manufactory
bills." "Mass. old tenor." "N. H. old tenor," "Mass. new tenor,"
"N. H. new tenor," "Mass. new emission," "N. H. new
emission," "lawful money," &c., &c.; all apparently differing in
value as well as in name.

Prior to 1760 the number of families in Mr. Emerson's society had
not increased to one hundred, consequently he was not yet entitled to
an increase of his salary beyond the value of 150 oz. of silver, or of
that of the £50 of the Massachusetts last emission, as it was at the
time of his settlement.

For the payment of this salary (equal as we have seen to $171 in
federal money), we find that the inhabitants were assessed, in the
years named below, the following sums in the paper money then in
use. 1753. £777. 10ˢ. 6ᵈ. O. T. 1760. £404. 9ˢ. 8ᵈ. Mass. O. T
1761, £415. 6ˢ. N. H. N. Tenor. 1763. £447. 15ˢ. 6ᵈ. N. H. O. T.
1770, £67. 13ˢ. 8ᵈ. L. M. or silver money. In the year last named
paper money appears to have gone wholly out of use. The like
variation in the value of this currency is shown in the prices fixed for
the thirty cords of wood to be furnished yearly to the minister. This
wood was commonly assessed upon the tax payers from year to year
in kind, each of them being required to furnish at the minister's door
a certain number of feet. If not delivered at the time fixed by vote
of the town, the delinquent was to pay for it at a price voted at the
previous March meeting. The price of a cord of wood fixed in this
way for different years was: for 1748. £1.: 1750, £2. 10ˢ; 1760,
£6.; 1770, 3ˢ. 6ᵈ. lawful or silver money, equal to fifty-eight cents.

3d. We shall also find, by examination of these records, that the
mode of assessing taxes at that time, and the way in which they were
apportioned between polls and estates, were radically different from
our modern views and usages.

We have seen, in the agreement entered into among themselves
by the members of Mr. Emerson's society, that by mutual consent

they fixed upon a basis of taxation, as to polls and property, which, as stated in that instrument, " was agreeable to the rule of the Massachusetts province." This rule was to the effect, that the tax for the support of the minister should be so apportioned among such as had real and personal estate and those subject to a poll tax only, in such way that a single poll tax should be equal to the highest tax on property.   In other words, the whole amount of the property tax of the richest man in the town could be no more in amount than twice the poll tax of the poorest who was taxed at all.   Under the law of Massachusetts, as we have before seen, male persons were subject to a poll tax at eighteen, and the same law was at the time in force in New Hampshire.

In illustration of this rule of taxation, I will cite an example or two.   The first tax after the ordination of Mr. Emerson was for £35, assessed to pay for the entertainment of the ordaining council.   Of that sum, £27, 6s., or more than three-fourths of it, were assessed upon fifty-seven persons as a poll tax, and the balance, less than £8, upon property.

The next tax was for £635, 9s. 6d. for Mr. Emerson's settlement and salary for the first year.   Of that sum, £418, 9s. 6d. were assessed as a poll tax on sixty-two persons, or about two-thirds of the whole.

As in taxes assessed for other purposes, so in those for the support of the ministry, there was no law for the exemption of the person or property of any one except by vote of the town.   The law in this respect appears to have been in full accord with popular sentiment, and the majority of the people were sufficiently tenacious of their legal rights under it.   As an instance of public sentiment upon the question, we find that as late as 1785, Mr. Edward Spalding had an article inserted in the warrant for the annual March meeting: "To see if it were the minds of the people to exempt his estate from ministerial tax, for the reason that he belonged to the Baptist denomination."   This question being submitted to the meeting, "the minds of the people" found expression in the following clear and emphatic terms: "Voted, that the estate of Edward Spalding shall not be freed from minister's tax for the time past, present, or to come."

CHAPTER IV.

1746 TO 1750.—CHARTER OF HOLLIS, ETC. — ORIGIN OF THE NAME.
FIRST TOWN MEETING. — SECOND MEETING HOUSE. — PEW
GROUND AND PEWS. — CARE OF THE MEETING-HOUSE. — LAND
TAX. — SINGING, ETC.

The district organization of all that part of old Dunstable lying
north of the new Province line, and west of the Merrimack river, continued unchanged from 1742 till the spring of 1746. This district
organization, as we have seen, was for the single purpose of assessing and collecting Province taxes. Early in the year 1746, the
Governor and Council, with a view to the division of this district
into townships, appointed five Commissioners to examine the territory and to report in what way it could be best subdivided into
township corporations.

At the last public meeting of the inhabitants of West Dunstable,
held Feb. 18, 1746, John Boynton, Thomas Dinsmore, and Benjamin Parker were appointed a committee on the part of the people
to meet those Commissioners and to represent to them the wishes of
the settlers in West Dunstable in respect to the proposed incorporations. These Commissioners convened at the East parish. They
were waited upon there, as is said, by the Committee from West
Dunstable and requested to visit and view the west part of the District; but the Commissioners declined going any farther to the west.
In pursuance of the report of this commission, the district of Dunstable was very soon divided and incorporated into the four townships
of Dunstable, Holles, Merrimack and Monson. With the exception
of their boundaries, the charters of these townships were substantially alike, those of Dunstable and Monson, being dated April 1,
that of Merrimack, April 2, and that of Hollis, April 3, 1746.

CHARTER OF HOLLIS.

" Province of New Hampshire.   George the Second, by the
                                Grace of God of Great Brit-
    { Seal }   ain, France and Ireland, King,
                                Defender of the Faith. &c.

" To all to whom these Presents shall come.   Greeting.

" Whereas sundry of our loyal subjects. Inhabitants of a Tract
of Land within the Antient Boundary of a Town called Dunstable
in our Province of New Hampshire, on the Westerly Side of Merrimack river herein described, Have Humbly petitioned and requested of us that they may be erected and incorporated into a
Township and Enfranchised with the same Powers. Authorities and
Privileges which other Townships in our said Province have and
Enjoy.

" And it appearing to us to be conducive to the General Good of
our said Province as well as of said Inhabitants in particular, by maintaining Good order and Encouraging the Culture of the Land that
the same shall be Done.   Know ye therefore that Wee of our Special Grace, certain Knowledge and for the Encouragement and Pro-
moting the Good Purposes and Ends aforesaid ; — By and with the
advice of our trusty and beloved Benning Wentworth. Esq.. Governor and Commander in Chief. and of our Council for said Province. have erected. incorporated and ordained. and by these Presents for us and our Heirs and Successors Do will and ordain that
the Inhabitants of the Tract of Land aforesaid. bounded as follows
viz.. Beginning at Nashaway River where the Northerly Boundary
Line of the Province of Massachusetts Bay crosses that River :
Then running North Eighty Degrees West on said Line Six miles
and Ninety Six Rods : Then North by the needle on Dunstable Antient Head Line four Miles and one Hundred and Forty Rods :
Then South Eighty Degrees East by the Needle to Muddy Brook :
Then by Muddy Brook into Flint's Pond : Then by Flint's Brook to
Nashaway River : Then by Nashaway River to the Place Where it
first began ;   And (they who) shall inhabit the same be and by
these Presents are declared and ordained to be a Town Corporate and
are hereby Erected and Incorporated into a Body Corporate and Cor-
poration to have continuance forever by the name of *Holles* With
all the Powers and Authorities. Privileges, Immunities and Franchises Which other Towns within our said Province or any of them

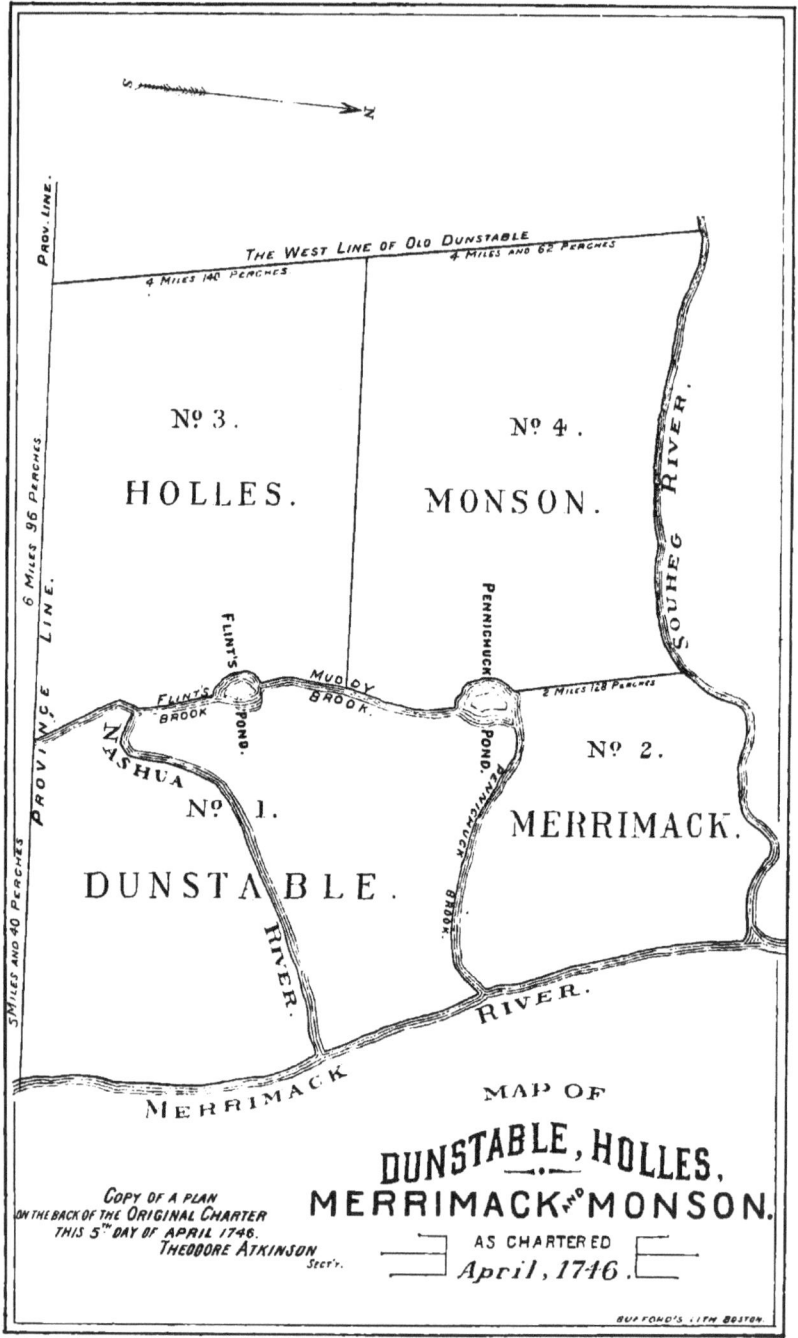

S —————→ N

PROV. LINE.

THE WEST LINE OF OLD DUNSTABLE

4 MILES 140 PERCHES   4 MILES AND 62 PERCHES

SOUHEG RIVER.

Nº 3.

HOLLES.

Nº 4.

MONSON.

6 MILES 96 PERCHES

PROVINCE LINE.

FLINT'S POND.

FLINT'S BROOK

MUDDY BROOK.

PENNICHUCK POND.

2 MILES 128 PERCHES

Nº 2.

MERRIMACK.

5 MILES AND 40 PERCHES

NASHUA Nº 1.

DUNSTABLE.

RIVER.

PENNICHUCK BROOK.

MERRIMACK   RIVER.

MERRIMACK

MAP OF

DUNSTABLE, HOLLES,
MERRIMACK AND MONSON.

AS CHARTERED
April, 1746.

COPY OF A PLAN
ON THE BACK OF THE ORIGINAL CHARTER
THIS 5TH DAY OF APRIL 1746.
THEODORE ATKINSON
Sec'y.

BUFFORD'S LITH BOSTON

by Law have and Enjoy. To have and to hold the said Powers
and Authorities, Immunities and Franchises to them the said Inhabitants and their Successors forever.

" *Always Reserving to us our Heirs and Successors, All White
Pine Trees growing and being, and which shall hereafter grow
on said Tract of Land fit for the use of our Royal Navy;* Also
the Power of Dividing the Said Town to us our Heirs and Successors
when it shall appear necessary or convenient for the benefit of the
Inhabitants thereof.

" And as the Several Towns Within our said Province are by the
Law thereof Enabled and Authorized to Assemble and by the Ma-
jority of Votes to chuse all such officers as are mentioned in Said
Law, We do by these Presents nominate Col. Joseph Blanchard to
call the first meeting of the Said Inhabitants to be held within the
Said Town at any time within thirty days from the date hereof.
Giving legal notice of the Time Place and Design of Holding Said
Meeting. In Testimony Whereof We have caused the Seal of our
Said Province to be hereunto affixed.

Witness, Benning Wentworth, Esq., our Governor, and Commander-in-Chief of our said Province the third day of April, in the
year of our Lord Christ, 1746, and in the 19th year of our Reign.

B. WENTWORTH.

By his Excellency's Command with the advice of Council,

THEODORE ATKINSON, Sect'y

BOUNDARIES OF DUNSTABLE, AS CHARTERED APRIL 1, 1746.

" Beginning at the River Merrimack at the Northern Boundary
Line of the Province of Massachusetts Bay and runs from the River
Merrimack, North, Eighty Degrees. West, five miles and forty rods
to Nashua River.   Then by said River to Flint's Brook ; thence by
Flint's Brook into Flint's pond : then by a run of water into Muddy
brook, and down Muddy brook into Pennichuck pond ; then by
Pennichuck brook into Merrimack river to the place where it first
begun."

BOUNDARIES OF MONSON.

" Beginning at the West Line of Dunstable, old Town, four miles
and one hundred and forty rods north, by the magnet, of the northern boundary line of the Province of Massachusetts Bay ; then south-

erly eighty degrees, east, to Muddy brook; then by that brook to Pennichuck pond and from the north end of said pond, north, by the magnet, to Souhegan river; then by the said river to the head line on the west side of old Dunstable; then south, by the magnet, on that line to the place where it begun."

ORIGINAL BOUNDARIES OF MERRIMACK.

" Beginning at the Merrimack river where Pennichuck brook comes into that river; then by Pennichuck brook to Pennichuck pond; then due north, by the magnet, to Souhegan river; then by that river to Merrimack river; then on the west side of Merrimack river to the place where it first begun."

On the 5th day of June, 1750, that part of the present town of Merrimack north of the Souhegan, was annexed to that town by an amendment of its original charter.

Nottingham West, now Hudson, on the east side of Merrimack river, being, as at first incorporated, wholly within ancient Dunstable, and *Pelham*, embracing its extreme eastern part were also incorporated as *towns* by the Governor and Council of New Hampshire, in 1746. *Litchfield*, as chartered by the General Court of Massachusetts, in 1734, as we have seen, lay upon both sides of the Merrimack, was also within old Dunstable. That part of Litchfield on the east side of the Merrimack was chartered as a town by the Governor and Council of New Hampshire, June 5, 1749.

All these New Hampshire town charters, unlike those granted by the General Court of Massachusetts, were wholly silent in respect to the " settlement and maintainance of able and orthodox ministers" and the building of meeting-houses. Benning Wentworth, at that time the royal Governor of New Hampshire, was an Episcopalian and a zealous adherent of the Church of England, and it may well be supposed that he had no special sympathy with the current orthodoxy of the times as taught in the Cambridge Platform and the Assembly's Catechism.

Instead of the like conditions as in the Massachusetts charters in respect to orthodox ministers and meeting-houses, Governor Wentworth in these New Hampshire charters expressly reserved, for the use of the royal navy, all suitable white pine trees then growing and being and which should afterwards grow in the towns so chartered, thus giving for the use of His Majesty's navy all such trees as were best adapted to the building of orthodox meeting-houses.

By a Province Law of New Hampshire, passed in 1714, it was enacted, "That it should be lawful for the free-holders of a town, convened in public Town Meeting to make choice of a minister for the supply of said town, and to agree what annual salary should be paid him," and it was made the duty of the selectmen "to make Rates upon the Inhabitants of the town for the payment of the Salary of the minister in the same manner as for other town charges." When a minister was chosen and settled under this law, all the tax-payers in the town were liable to be taxed for his support, it making no difference, as it would seem, as to this liability, whether the minister were a Calvinist, Episcopalian, Presbyterian, Baptist, or New Light.

> "Or Light that shines when few are nigh,
> For Spiritual trades to cozen by."

In Massachusetts, at that time, as has been shown, no minister satisfied the law unless "able, learned and orthodox."

THE NAME AND ITS ORIGIN.

Within my remembrance, there has been much controversy upon the question whether the name of Hollis should be spelt with the letter *i* or *e* in the last syllable, and also as to the person in whose honor the town was named. Mr. Farmer, in his Gazetteer of New Hampshire, spells it with an *i*, and tells us that the name was either derived from the Duke of Newcastle, whose family name was Hollis, or from Thomas Hollis, a distinguished benefactor of Harvard College; Mr. Farmer spelling both names "*Hollis.*" Hon. J. D. Hill, in his history of Mason, says the name was derived from that of the Duke of Newcastle, whose family name was *Holles*; Mr. Hill using the letter *e* in the last syllable. From the best evidence at my command upon the question, I have no doubt that Mr. Hill is correct, both in the orthography of the name and also in that of the person for whom the town was called. In the original record of the town charter, now at Concord, and in the copy of the charter on the Hollis record, the name is spelt *Holles.* In the town records for the twenty-five years and more before the war of the revolution the name occurs hundreds of times, and, so far as I have seen, is uniformly spelt Holles as in the charter, and is so spelt in the New Hampshire Laws published as late as 1815.

At the time Hollis was chartered, Benning Wentworth, as we have seen, was governor. Mr. Wentworth was appointed to that office in 1741, and held it till 1765. He was indebted to the Duke of Newcastle for this appointment, who was at the time, and for some years after, secretary of state for the colonies, this commission costing the friends of Gov. Wentworth £300 in fees and expenses of solicitation.

In a work entitled "Burke's Extinct Peerages of Great Britain," now in the library of the New England Historic, Genealogical Society in Boston, I find that the original name of this Duke of Newcastle was Thomas Pelham, (an English baron). This Thomas Pelham (whose mother was Grace Holles) was a nephew and the adopted son and heir of his uncle, the preceding Duke of Newcastle, who was childless, and whose family name was Holles. Upon the death of the old duke (his uncle), this nephew succeeded to his estates and titles, and assumed his family name and was afterward known as Thomas Pelham Holles.

It was very much a custom with Gov. Wentworth to name towns in New Hampshire, chartered by him, in honor of his friends and patrons connected with the home government. The towns of Monson, Hollis and Pelham were all chartered the same year, 1746, and while the Duke of Newcastle (Thomas Pelham Holles) was still secretary of state for the colonies. Monson was the family name of one of the board of the Lords of colonial trade, and that fact, I apprehend, accounts for the name of the extinct town of Monson. Pelham, the original family name of this Duke of Newcastle, was perpetuated in the name of the town of Pelham, in the same way and for the like reason that Holles, his name by adoption, was intended to be in that of the town of Hollis; the grateful governor, besides the £300, thus paying his patron the double compliment, — much in the same way as his successor, Gov. John Wentworth, commemorated the maiden name of his wife, Frances Deering, in the names of two of our neighboring towns, Francestown and Deering, as an expression of his gratitude for her acceptance of his hand at the end of two sad, lonely weeks of widowhood. Whatever may have been the special obligations of Benning Wentworth to the Duke of Newcastle, the people of New England had very little reason to think well of him. Mr. Bancroft, in his history, says of him, "that he was of so feeble a head and so treacherous a heart that Sir Robert Walpole called his name "Perfidy"; that Lord Halifax

used to revile him as a knave and fool, and that he was so igno-
rant of this continent, that it was said of him, that he addressed his
letters to the 'Island of New England.'"

Thomas Hollis, the generous benefactor of Harvard College, was
an eminent and wealthy merchant of London; of very exemplary
character, and liberal in his political principles. Mr. Hollis died in
1731,—ten years before Mr. Wentworth was appointed Governor,
and I know of no reason for supposing that the governor was personally acquainted with him. Hollis Hall at Cambridge, built and
dedicated just before the revolution, was named for this benefactor
of the college. The name of the London merchant, and also of
this hall, have been always spelt as the name of the town of Hollis
now is.

There can be no doubt that the people of Hollis, one hundred
years ago, well understood the character of the Duke of Newcastle,
and also that of the worthy London merchant, and it is not strange
that it should have been their choice that the name of the benefactor
of Harvard College should be commemorated in that of their town,
rather than any of the many names of the Duke of Newcastle,
whether original, adopted or bestowed by those who knew him as
well as did Sir Robert Walpole and Lord Halifax.

Accordingly, about the year 1775, when change and revolution
were the order of the day, in all their other important interests and
affairs, a slight orthographical revolution, as appears by their town
records, was for the first time initiated in the name of their town by
changing the e in the last syllable into i. During the revolutionary
war, and afterward to the end of the century, and in many instances
later, the name was spelt in the records and other public documents
in both ways, according to the opinion or caprice of the writer, and
it continued so to be spelt, as we have seen, as late as 1815. But
for the last fifty years, so far as I have known, it has with great uni-
formity been spelt as it now is, Hollis, like that of the benefactor of
Harvard College, and that orthography appears now to be permanently established both by common usage and the will of the people,
while Holles, the name of the Duke of Newcastle, has passed into
merited oblivion.

THE FIRST TOWN ELECTION.

The first Town Election in Hollis, (as provided in the charter), was called by Col. Joseph Blanchard, April 28, 1746, for the sole purpose of choosing officers for the new town. At this meeting the first town officers were chosen as follows:

SAMUEL CUMINGS, Moderator
SAMUEL CUMINGS, Town Clerk
SAMUEL CUMINGS,
BENJAMIN FARLEY,   } Selectmen
FRANCIS WORCESTER,
THOMAS DINSMORE,
FRANCIS PHELPS,
NICHOLAS FRENCH,   } Surveyors of Highwys
JAMES McDANIELS,
SAMUEL PARKER,

JAMES STEWART,
CHRISTOPHER LOVEJOY,   } Tithing Men
JONATHIIN DANFORTII,
BENJAMIN BLANCHARD,   } Fence Viewers
NICHOLAS FRENCH,
WILLIAM ADAMS,   } Hogreeves,
ELIAS SMITH, Pound Keeper,
ELIAS SMITH, Sealer of Weights and Measures
SAMUEL BROWN, Sealer of Leather

THE SECOND MEETING HOUSE.

In the month of March, 1745, as shown by the Tax List, the taxable inhabitants of West Dunstable had increased to the number of 77. They had had an acceptable and popular minister for near two years, and had begun to have a very painful sense of the small capacity of their first meeting house — " 22 feet one way —20 feet the other — 9 feet Studs — and one Glass Window." This feeling in respect to the dimensions of their meeting-house first found public expression in the doings of a parish meeting held at the first meeting-house Sept. 6, 1745, while the inhabitants were still without a town or parish charter. At this meeting, as shown by the record of it, it was " Voted unanimously to build a meeting-house 50 feet long — 44 feet wide — and 23 feet Posts in Hight." "Allso voted unanimously to sett the next meeting-house on yᵉ Lott of Land yᵉ present house stands on, which was given for yᵗ use." "Allso voted yᵗ John Boynton, Benjamin Farley, Elias Smith, Stephen Harris, Thomas Dinsmore and Zedekiah Drury be a committee to take the whole care in carrying on yᵉ work, and receiving yᵉ money yᵗ shall be subscribed for yᵗ use, and employ faithful men yᵗ shall appear to furnish Timber and other materials as shall be wanted for said House."

It will be observed that these doings of the inhabitants of West Dunstable, before its boundaries were changed by the town charter of the next year, were entirely unanimous.

The number of names on the first Tax List in the town of Hollis in 1746 was but 53, — 24 less than in West Dunstable the year before — a part of this last number living on the east side of West Dunstable having been set off by the acts of incorporation to the new town of Dunstable, and the rest of them on the north side to the town of Monson.

SEGOND MEETING HOUSE. BUILT 1746.

FIRST MEETING HOUSE.
BUILT 1744

At the second town meeting in Hollis, held May 20, 1746, " Voted unanimously to take on us the obligation to Mr. Emerson, as it now stands in the covenant for his yearly Salary so long as he remains our minister, and to raise £200, O. T., for his Salery the year ensuing." " Chose Jonathan Danforth and Benjamin Farley to run y⁰ Line between Holles and Monson." " Also voted to peti- tion y⁰ General Court of Massachusetts Bay for some Solders We being in Gratt Danger from y⁰ enemy." " Also voted that the Book we have used for the Parish Records, be used for a Town Book."

The third meeting of the town was called June 13, 1746, for the following purposes : " To see if the town will build a House for the Public worship of God." " To see if the town will Accept the Timber which is hewn and drawn together to build a House with, and chose a Committee to take charge of said Work." " To see if the Town will accept the acre of Land that was given the Parish to Sett the Meeting House on and for a Burying Place." " To see if the town will vote that the money due from Capt. Pow- ers shall be laid out in ammunition for a town Stock." " To see if the Town will provide a Pound and Stocks."

At this meeting the Town voted as follows :

1st, " To build a House for the Public Worship of God."

2d, " To accept the Timber that was prepared for said use to build said House with."

3d, " Chose Benjamin Farley, Benjamin Blanchard, and Capt. Powers a Committee to take care and see that said House is built."

4th, " To accept the Land that was given to the Parish to Sett the Meeting House on and for a Burying Ground."

5th, " That the Money due from Capt. Powers, shall be laid out to buy Powder, Bullets and Flints for a Town Stock."

6th, " To accept the old Pound for the present year and that the Selectmen provide Stocks."

It appears from the doings of a Town Meeting held the same year, a few months later, that Josiah Conant had been employed by the Selectmen to make the Stocks for the town, and that his account for making them was then accepted.

The *Pillory* for the confinement of the head and hands of the offender, *Stocks* for his feet, and the *Whipping Post* with the *cat o' nine tails* for his back, were in common use with our ancestors

(4)

of the last century, for the punishment of minor offences. A person, for instance, found guilty of profane swearing, for a first offence, was fined one Shilling — if not able to pay, he was set in the town stocks for two hours; for more than one profane oath at the same time, or for a second offence, he was set in the stocks for three hours.

The Hollis Whipping Post, standing on the west side of the Hollis Common, was in practical use after the beginning of the present century, and is still remembered by persons now living.

After the meeting of the 13th of June, such progress was made with the new meeting-house, that a special town meeting was called on the 28th of the following July, at which it was " voted that ye Meeting House be raised on the 13th of August next (1746). "Also Voted that ye Com^{ree} provide Victuals and Drink for ye People on Raising Day, and bring it to the Fraim at noon. If they Cant Get it among our Friends to Provide it Themselves."

To the doings of the last two meetings there was a very earnest and persistent opposition in respect to the location of the new meeting-house, and the building and raising it at that time, by a very considerable number of settlers then living in the west end of the town, most of them in that part of Hollis, some years afterwards set off to the present town of Brookline. Eight of these settlers had a written protest against the proceedings of these meetings entered upon the town records, setting forth their objections. After the meeting of the 28th of July, fixing the "Raising Day" for the 13th of August, thirteen of them united in a petition and complaint to the General Court of New Hampshire, dated August 5, 1746, stating their grievances, and praying for the "Appointment of a Committee to view the situation — and to fix upon a place for the Meeting-House, and that the Raising of it might be postponed till this Committee could report."

This petition conceded that the proposed " location for the Meeting-House was just and reasonable for the Parish of West Dunstable, as incorporated seven years before by the General Court of Massachusetts, but that it was unjust and unequal for the town of Holles as it then was. That by the late Act incorporating the town, above three miles off of the east end of the old parish were set to Dunstable bringing the east line of Holles within a mile and one half of the Meeting-House place. That the west line of Holles was near five miles from the Meeting-House place, and some inhabitants already settled at the outside. That the petitioners with others had applied to the Selectmen of Holles to call another meeting to consider the injustice of this location, but that their application had been refused. That if the Meeting-House should be built at the place proposed it would discourage settlements in the west end of the town, but that when further settlements should be made, the house would have to be pulled down, many changes made in the Highways — they loaded with great charges,— and room left for much contention and disturbance."

This Petition was signed by Stephen Ames, William Adams, Samuel Douglas, Isaac Farrar, James, Joseph and Randall McDaniels, John and Jonathan Melvin, Samuel Parker, Moses Proctor, James Whiting, and Jasher Wyman. It was presented to the General Court by Stephen Ames as agent of the Petitioners, read, considered and dismissed by the House of Representatives on the 11th of August, two days before "Raising Day," so that the "Raising" was not interrupted or postponed.

Afterwards, while the work on the new meeting-house was in progress, at a special town meeting held on the 22d of Dec., 1746, the town

" Voted to Raise two Pence per acre Lawful Money a year on all the Land in the Town of Holles for five years for ye support of the Gospel, and ye Arising charges of said town, and to Petition ye Generall Court for strength to Gather, and Get ye money of Non-Residents. And Allso Chose Samuel Cumings to prefer said Petition, and any other that may be thought proper and beneficiall for ye Town."

Early in the following spring, Mr. Cumings, as agent for the town, presented to the General Court the following petition for the passage of the proposed law. This petition may interest some of us at the present day, as clearly and forcibly setting forth the reasons that influenced the people of the town in asking for the law in question, and also as showing the popular sentiment of the times in respect to the justice and policy of taxing the property of non-resident landholders for the support of ministers and building meeting-houses.

"Province of New Hampshire ⎰ To his Excellency Benning Went-
worth, Esq., Gov., &c., The
Honble his Majesty's Council &
House of Representatives in Gen-
Assembly convened, March 31¹,
1747.

" The Petition of Saml Cumings in Behalf of the Town of Holles,
Humbly Sheweth, That the s^d Town has Lately settled A Minister and are now building a Meeting-House for the Publick Worship of God there.

" That the settlers of s^d Town have but lately entered thereon,
and altho a considerable progress in Agriculture has been made
(the only way we have for our support) yet find these charges very
burthensome.

" That a considerable part of the best Lands in s^d Town belong
to non-resident propri^{rs} who make no Improvement.

" That by the arduous begining the settlement & heavy charges
by us already paid has greatly advanced their Lands and they are
still rising in value Equal as the Resident propri^{rs} tho the charges
hitherto and for the future must Lye on y^r settlers only, unless we
obtain the assistance of this Honble court."

" Wherefore your Pet^r most humbly prays that y^r Excellency and
Hon^{rs} would take the Premises into consideration, and grant the
Whole of the Lands in s^d Township may be taxed annually for
five years next coming two pence new tenor p. acre to be applyed
for the support of the minister and finishing ye Meeting-House
and by Law Enabling us to collect the same & y^r Pet^r as in Duty
Bound shall pray &c.   SAMUEL CUMINGS."

This petition was favorably considered by the General Court, and
on the following 14th of May, 1747, an Act was passed taxing all
the lands in Hollis at two pence per acre for the support of the minister and finishing the meeting-house, but limiting the law to four
years.

In the meanwhile the work on the new edifice went on, and such
progress was afterwards made with the enterprise, that in about two
years after " Raising Day," a plan of the " Pew Ground," as it was
called, was made by a Committee appointed by the town and accepted by vote of a town meeting. The plan of this Pew Ground
embraced a space on the lower floor next the walls, wide enough

for a single range of pews on each of the four sides, and this space
was apportioned into sites or ground for about 20 pews.   At a town
meeting on the 12th of September. 1748. this Pew Ground was disposed of by vote of the town as follows :

" Voted that the highest in pay on Real Estate have the Pew
Ground on their paying £200. Old Tenor. to be applied towards finishing the Meeting-House and the Pew men are to take their Pews
for Themselves and Wives. the man and his wife to be seated according to their Pay."

That is, as I interpret this record, the men who at that time
paid the highest taxes on real estate were to have the luxury of owning and sitting in separate pews, the wife being indulged with the
privilege of sitting in the same pew with her husband upon the condition that the purchasers of the pew ground should build the walls
of their pews, and pay £200 Old Tenor towards the completion of the
building.

In December, 1748. this pew ground was disposed of by lot — those
entitled to do so drawing for choice.   Down to this day the records
of the town show the amount of the premium paid for each pew, by
whom it was paid, and the precise location of each pew in the
meeting-house, "with the man and his wife seated in it according to
pay on Real Estate." can be as readily understood from this record,
as from an ocular view.   " Mr. Enoch Hunt" drew the first choice,
paid for it £14. O. T.. and chose the second pew at the right hand of
the pulpit.   Mr. Elias Smith drew the second choice, paid £14, O.
T., and chose the second pew at the left hand of the pulpit.   "Capt.
Peter Powers." third choice. paid for it £13. O. T., and chose the
first pew on the left hand of the front door.   Lt. Benjamin Farley,
eighth choice. and took the third pew at the right hand of the east
door. and paid for it £11, O. T.   Dr. Samuel Cmings, thirteenth
choice ; paid for it £9. 10s., O. T., and took the first pew at the left
hand of the west door.   And so of the others.

The pulpit was not yet built ; but at the annual Town Meeting
in 1749 it was " Voted to Bould the Pulpit and the Ministerial Pew
and Stars as soon as the Bords wold do to work."   It was not told
how soon the " Bords wold do to work," yet it appears that when
that part of the joiner's work was first done. it was not thought so
good as it should have been. as I find at the annual meeting in 1754
the town " Voted that the Pew before the Pulpit be taken down. if
there may be a good Hansom Pew for the town built. and a

convenient Deacons' seat and good Hansom stairs to go to the
Pulpit." At the above annual meeting in 1749 it was put to vote
" To see if the Town would build two Porches to ye Meeting
House. and it passed in the Negative."

The question in respect to the building of porches to the meeting-
house was many times discussed in the town meetings for the next
twenty years. But none were built till about the year 1772, when a
small one was erected on the south side of the meeting house, for
passing into the main building. One on the east side high and large
enough for gallery stairs to the " Women's Gallery." and one on the
west side for stairs to the "Men's Gallery." with a belfry and
steeple.

This ancient second church edifice of Hollis, as originally completed, long ago was dust, and has passed away among the things
that once were but are not. All that was mortal of the worthy
people who built and worshipped in it is also dust. and for nearly a
century has reposed in the humble church-yard hard by. Yet from
the minutes and hints preserved by them in their town records it
would not require the genius of a Cuvier or Agassiz to reconstruct
this ancient edifice. both as to its interior and exterior. and to present in vivid perspective the old congregation of worshippers as it
would have appeared to the eye of a looker-on one hundred and
twenty years ago.

The stumps of the sturdy forest trees that had grown on the common before it. and in the burial ground behind. still stood firmly
rooted in their native soil. The roads that led to it. freshly cut. and
little better than bridle paths. unfenced. except here and there with
logs or brushwood through the scattered and stump-covered clear-
ings. wound their lonely way through the dense. primeval forest.

The building itself was a plain wooden structure. covered on its
outside with split clapboards. unpainted. except its doors. windows
and water " Troves." as yet without porches. with a single outside
door on each of its south. east and west sides : with a suitable number of horse blocks at convenient distances for the accommodation
of such of the congregation as rode to meeting upon the side saddle
or pillion. as well as of those who rode upon saddles with two
stirrups.

On the inside. upon the floor below. around next to the four
walls. was a single row of pews. in which. from Sabbath to Sabbath were seated the patriarchs and dignitaries of the town. the
" highest in pay on real estate." with their wives and families.

A broad aisle leading from the south door to the pulpit and deacons' seat divided the remainder of the lower floor into the east and west sides, the east being the "men's side." and the west the "women's side." This area was furnished with long seats for such as could not afford or were not permitted to enjoy the luxury and distinction of pews; yet in making and arranging these seats, the committee charged with their construction were directed by the town meeting to have them made and arranged "according to pay, having regard to age."

The galleries were also divided between the sexes in the same way with the lower floor — the west gallery belonging to the sterner, the east to the gentler sex, with separate flights of stairs in the southwest and southeast corners leading to each of them, with tithing men above as well as below to note all graceless irreverence and indecorum — especially in the youthful portion of the congregation.

The pulpit was at the end of the broad aisle, on the north side, next the wall, with a capacious sounding board raised over it so high that in after years it was ordered by the town to be placed lower, if "those who wished for the change would pay the expense of making it." By the side of the pulpit. and leading into it, was a flight of "Hansom stairs." such being the kind voted by the town. Immediately in front of the pulpit was the deacons' seat. where, in accordance with the usages and established proprieties of those times, Deacons Boynton. Cumings. Patch and Worcester. in their small clothes, long hose, knee and shoe buckles, took their seats as models of gravity and decorum to all the lay members of the congregation.

" *Cleanliness was said very long ago to be next to Godliness*," and *cleanliness* in respect to the care of their meeting-house was cultivated by our worthy forefathers as diligently as if it ranked among the Christian graces. At each annual town meeting a special officer was chosen to take care of the meeting-house for the coming year. The following extract from the town records of 1773 furnishes an example of these appointments. and of the duties expected to be performed by that officer: "Edward Carter. chosen to take care of ye meeting-house & he is to keep it well swept and clean: To open and shut the Doors in Good season. and shovell the snow from the Doors. and shovell Paths from the Doors to the Horse Blocks. and clean the Horse Blocks well. He is to have eighteen shillings if done to the acceptance of the Town,— if not, to have Nothing."

This picture of this ancient edifice cannot be truthfully embellished with stair or floor carpets, or with wood or coal stoves or
furnaces, or with any other modern invention for warming churches
in winter. The only implement or convenience for a like purpose,
then in use in country meeting-houses, was the little portable, tin foot
stove with its basin for coals and ashes, which the youthful members
of the congregation were educated to carry to meeting in their
hands for the use and comfort of their parents and seniors. Yet
this was an indulgence that popular sentiment did not seem to favor,
as is evident from a vote of the town, at the March meeting in
1776, of which a record was made in the following words : " Voted
that all Stoves that shall be left in the Meeting-House shall be forfeited to the *Saxton* Mr. John Atwell & he may sell them if the
owner shall refuse to pay 1-2 a Pistareen for the first offence & *Doble*
that sum for the second offence, and the said Atwell shall return the
overplus after he is paid for his trouble for the use of the Poor of the
Parish."

Nor are we able to garnish our picture with an organ, melodeon,
bass viol, or with duets, trios or quartettes, or with any choir of
trained vocal singers. All these helps and accompaniments of modern congregational worship were then unknown. Yet in the public
devotional exercises of that day the use of hymns and spiritual songs
was by no means omitted or neglected, and the singing was doubtless quite as solemn as other parts of the religious services either of
those times or the present. When a psalm was selected from Stern-
hold and Hopkins, or a hymn from Dr. Watts, it was slowly read by
the minister or senior deacon, one or at most two lines at a time,
and sung by the congregation as read from the pulpit or Deacons'
seat. When the reader had read from the book, " *Hark from
the tombs a doleful sound,*" or, " *My drowsy powers why sleep ye
so ?*" he was expected to take a rest till the congregation had sung
those lines before reading the next. The congregation in this way
would be quite sure to have some conception of the ideas intended
to be conveyed by the words of the hymn, a matter quite certain
not to be true in the ordinary opera performances of the modern
quartette.

The earliest reference to be found to a choir of singers in the
town records is in the doings of the annual town meeting in 1767.
The town then " Voted that those Persons that had taken pains to
instruct themselves in singing may have the two fore seats below on

the Men's Side."   The next notice we find of singing and singers is
in the record of the annual meeting in 1784.   It was then " Voted
That 12 Feet of the hind Body Seats below next the broad Aisle be
appropriated to the Use of Singers on condition that a certain number of them will give the Glass necessary to repair the windows."
Lastly, in the year 1788, it was " Voted That the Ground now occupied by singers shall not be appropriated to any other use, and that
the singers may be allowed to Sing once a Day Without Reading."

This was a final and decisive triumph on the part of the choir.
Thenceforth it not only secured toleration from the town meeting,
but approved recognition as a fitting adjunct and help to public worship. and also a place to sit and stand in the church without the
condition of paying for it by mending broken windows.   At length,
and before the end of the century, the choir was promoted to conspicuous seats in the front gallery where it might sing its pæans of
victory, and its songs of devotion and praise might be heard till
this venerable second meeting-house, having stood for nearly sixty
years, at last fell before the hand of time and modern innovation,
and the church edifice now standing was erected upon the same hallowed ground.

CHAPTER V.

1746 to 1773. — THE ONE PINE HILL CONTROVERSY. — ANNEXA-
TION OF ONE PINE HILL TO HOLLIS. — SECOND BORDER CON-
TROVERSY. — DISPUTE ABOUT BUILDING THE NASHUA RIVER
BRIDGE. — COMPROMISE.

The boundaries of the towns into which the parish of West Dunstable was divided do not appear to have been satisfactory to any
part of its early settlers. The boundary line between Hollis and
the new town of Dunstable, as established along Flint's brook and
pond and Muddy brook, soon became the occasion of a long, persistent and bitter controversy. The story of this controversy may
be best told by extracts from the original documents relating to
it still to be found in the office of the Secretary of State at Concord. Before, and at the time of these Acts of incorporation into
towns, there was a settlement of very worthy people, consisting of
about fifteen families, near the east side of West Dunstable, and east
of the new town line, known as "*One Pine Hill.*" This settlement had constituted an important part of the religious society
of West Dunstable. The settlers there had aided in the settlement
and support of Mr. Emerson, in the building of the new meeting-
house, in fixing the site of it and their burial ground, and in the
laying out and making the public roads. In this settlement, among
other worthy citizens, were William Cumings and Thomas Patch,
two of the deacons in the church of West Dunstable; also the
brothers David and Samuel Hobart, the first distinguished for his
gallantry as the colonel of a New Hampshire regiment at the battle of Bennington, and the latter as the first register of deeds of the
county of Hillsborough, and a member of the New Hampshire
Committee of Safety in the war of the Revolution. Much to their
vexation and disappointment, and also to the chagrin of the people in Hollis, these settlers on One Pine Hill, found themselves on

the wrong side of the town line and cut off from their former civil, social, and church relations with the settlers of West Dunstable. The only meeting-house in Dunstable, originally built for the accommodation of the settlers south of the new province line, as well as of those north of it, was from seven to eight miles distant from the settlers on One Pine Hill, while that in Hollis was less than half that distance. What was a matter to them of still more importance, the religious society in Hollis was well united in their popular and acceptable minister whose orthodoxy was without taint, while the society in Dunstable was distracted with bitter, chronic dissensions, mainly on account of the alleged heresy of their pastor, the Rev. William Bird, who was charged with being a *New Light* and follower of Rev. George Whitefield.

In these troubles of their neighbors, and late fellow parishioners, it was very natural that the kindly sympathies of the good people of Hollis should have been strongly with the settlers at One Pine Hill. The first reference we find in this matter in the Hollis records is in the proceedings of a town meeting, Oct. 26, 1747, at which the town " Voted to request of Dunstable the People of One Pine Hill with their Lands to be set off to Hollis, and chose Capt. Peter Powers, Thomas Dinsmore and Samuel Cumings to assist in that affair, and Rais Bounds between the Towns." It is very evident from the sequel of events that this very civil request of the people of Hollis was not hospitably entertained by their neighbors of Dunstable.

No further reference to this subject is to be found in the Hollis records till the annual town meeting in 1756, when the town " Voted to joyn with the One Pine Hill People so called to get them set off from Dunstable to be annexed to Holles." Again in 1759, the town " voted £50 O. T. for the assistance of the People on the westerly side of Dunstable in their Petition to be annexed to Holles;" and lastly, at the March Meeting in 1764, " Voted to give the People of One Pine Hill, so called, £200 O. T. towards expenses in Getting off from Dunstable." The foregoing votes sufficiently indicate the sentiments and wishes of the people of Hollis.

We again recur to the documents already referred to, pertaining to this controversy, to be found at Concord. It will be seen from these papers that the people of One Pine Hill, aided more or less by their helpful allies in Hollis, were in almost constant rebellion against the ecclesiastical and civil authorities of their own town, for

the seventeen years from 1746 to 1763. These original documents
will still be found interesting to many, not only as containing important and unique matter of local town history, but also as showing the
manner and spirit in which controversies of this sort were then conducted. They set forth very fully the questions in dispute, the arguments on each side, and somewhat of the evidence. To such as
are curious in such matters, these papers may also be further interesting as affording an insight into the temper that animated the
parties to this controversy and the sentiments which the good people
of Dunstable, Hollis and One Pine Hill mutually entertained of the
motives, conduct and Christian character of each other.

It appears from the town records of Dunstable, that the settlers
on One Pine Hill, very soon after they found themselves, against
their wishes, inhabitants of that town, petitioned the people of
Dunstable for their consent to be set off to Hollis. This petition
and all other amicable efforts on the part of the people of one Pine
Hill were refused by the Dunstable town meetings.

The oldest of the documents above referred to, as found in the
office of the Secretary of State at Concord, is a petition to the Governor and Council in the spring of 1756, signed by fifteen of the
settlers on the west side of Dunstable, and the Selectmen of Hollis.
In this Petition these signers from Dunstable say to the Governor
and Council,

"That your Petitioners live in, the west side of Dunstable and
so far from the Meeting-House, that it is almost empossable for
us to attend the Publick Worship of God there, for some of us live
7 1-2 miles and the nearest 5 1-2 miles from the Meeting-House so
that we Can't and Don't go to Meeting there * * * * for they
have set their Meeting-House to accommodate them Selves, and
seem not in the least to Regard us only to get our Money. Our
Difficulties are so exceeding great that make us Dispair of having
any comfortable reviving Gospel Priviledges unless we can obtain
the aid of your Excellency and Honnors."

"Wherefore your Petitioners pray that your Excellency and
Honnors would so far Compassionate our Circumstances as to Relieve us by setting us with our Land to Holles to which we once
belonged and helped settel our Minister and now go to attend the
Publick Worship of God. * * The furthest of us from Holles is
not more than 3 1-2 or 4 miles, and the bigest part about 2 1-2 or
3 miles to which we can go with some degree of comfort. We

therefore pray * * that you would be pleased to annex us to
Holles with about 2500 acres of Land which wee have described in
a Plan, which will greatly relieve us, * * and help us to a Comfortable Injoyment of Gospel Priviledges. * * And as in Duty
Bound, &c. Signed :

John Willoughby	Nicholas Youngman	David Hobart
Elnathan Blood	Gershom Hobart	Nehemiah Woods
John Phelps	Jonathan Hobart	William Cumings
John Mooar	Amos Phillips	Joseph Farley
Benjamin Parker,	Samuel Hobart	Anna Patch

Samuel Cumings ⎫
Samuel Goodhue ⎬ Selectmen of Holles."
Enoch Noyes ⎭

Upon being notified of this Petition, the people of Dunstable
promptly met in town meeting and " Voted not to set off the land
and inhabitants of One Pine Hill to Holles " and appointed Col.
Joseph Blanchard, with two others, a committee to oppose the petition. Col. Blanchard at the time was a member of the N. H.
Council, and made the answer to the Petition on the part of Dunstable. In this answer he stated that " About 1736, (9?) the old
town of Dunstable was divided into two parishes. That what was
then Holles & Monson with a part of Dunstable and Merrymac was
the West parish and contained about 70,000 acres." That they had
an annual tax of 2d. per acre for four years on the Land of non-
residents to build a meeting-house and support a minister, and an
after tax of about the same amount. More than was needed for it,
but they disposed of it all or divided it. That in 1741 the Province
Line was run leaving about 2-3 of the Inhabitants and Estates of
the East Parish in Massachusetts. * *

" On examination we find that Holles * * is about eight miles
in length East and West and about four and a half miles North and
South * * settled at each end. Some time after their Incorporation
Holles set up a Meeting-House with a part of the money we and
others paid for that use, and sett it about a mile and a half from their
East line Regardless of the complaints of the Inhabitants on the
Westerly part, so that many of them are eight miles from their
meeting, as they must travil, much further than any in Dunstable are
from our meeting-house.

" Wee are sencible that this vexatious Petition is stirred up and
encouraged by Holles purely to prevent Justice to their Western Inhabitants which they foresee will obtain unless they can Cloak it by
Ruining Dunstable.

" What Genius gave them *front* to mutter out this Motley Petition it is Difficult to guess.

" The Pretentions of Holles and the Pet^rs are totally Groundless Wherefore we pray that their Petition may be dismissed.

Signed   JOSEPH BLANCHARD, ⎫
              ZACCHEUS LOVEWELL, ⎬ Agts for Dunstable.
              JOSEPH FRENCH   ⎭

I do not find in the records at Concord how or when the above petition was disposed of. It is evident however that it was not granted. It was said in the answer of Dunstable to a like petition a few years later, that when it was found that Dunstable would answer it, the petitioners were afraid or ashamed to appear in its defence. In the fall of 1760 the settlers at One Pine Hill again petitioned Dunstable for permission to be set off to Hollis, at this time offering to pay to Dunstable £1500, O. T., for the privilege. A town meeting was called in Dunstable to consider this offer, which was promptly rejected, the town voting at the same time " not to change their Meeting-House Place."

After this last defeat open hostilities were suspended till the spring of 1763, when the contest was renewed and a second petition presented to the General Court by Col. Samuel Hobart as attorney for the settlers at One Pine Hill.

In this petition Col. Hobart says that " about the year 1747 (?), (1746), a Committee of five, two of them from Dunstable, was appointed by the Governor &c., to view the Lands about Merrymac River to see in what manner it was Best to Bound them in the Incorporations. * * that this Committee went no Farther Westward than the Old Town of Dunstable. That a Com^tee came down from Holles, and desired this Com^tee to go and view the Situation at Holles and One Pine Hill, and urged it hard. But the Com^tee could not be prevailed on to go any further that way, (the opposition we judge being made by Dunstable). * * Soon after Dunstable was Incorporated they got into Partys about Settling Mr. Bird. Each Party Courted Pine Hill's Assistance, promising to vote them off to Holles as soon as the matter was settled; and so Pine Hill was fed with *Sugar Plums* for a number of years, till at length Dunstable cast off the mask and now appears in their True Colours. * *

* * Under the Government of Massachusetts we belonged to Holles, and helpt Build a large Meeting-House and it was set to

accommodate us, and helpt settle a minister not in the least Doubting but we should always belong there." * *

"We have ever since attended the Public Worship of God at Holles and paid our Taxes to the Minister there, tho. in the mean time we have been called on to pay Ministerial Rates with Dunstable in full proportion, except some trifling abatement they made us to keep us quiet. We know of no other Real objection that Dunstable has to our going off, but reducing them to too small a number to maintain the Gospel. But if their Inclinations can be judged by their practice it can't be tho't that they have any inclination to settle a minister * * Dunstable as it lyes now consists of about 100 Families * * All we ask to be set off is but about twelve. * * So that their opposition must arise from some other quarter to keep us as whips to drive out every minister that comes among them, for they are always divided and which side we take must carry the Day."

The Selectmen of Dunstable, on being notified of this petition, at once called a town meeting which voted to continue their defence. and appointed a committee of three to answer the petition.

This answer begun with the assertion that this "Complaint of the People of One Pine Hill was groundless and *unreasonable*. * * As to Dunstable Meeting-House which Petitioners complain of as being at so great a distance from them. it was owing to themselves — for many of them voted to have it where it is — and none of them against it. * * That they so acted and voted for fear it might be moved to a place more just and equal and so they be prevented from being set off to Holles. * * As in Times past so they are now stired up by some Holles People to bring this petition in order to uphold the unjust Proceedings of Holles in setting their meeting-house where it is. * * And now Holles are endeavoring to have the south part of Monson anexed to them. and should that be don and also the Westerly half of Dunstable then their meeting-house where it now is will be aboute right. So could it now be obtained to breake up and ruin two Towns it may hereafter be something of a cover to hide the iniquity of Holles and help the private interests of some mercenary persons, but can't possably promote the Public Good nor help the Interest of these Towns."

The case was argued on both sides, and the evidence and arguments convinced the General Court that One Pine Hill with its Inhabitants ought no longer to remain a part of Dunstable. Accordingly. on the 13th of December. 1763. an act was passed.

entitled, " An Act Annexing One Pine Hill to Holles." This act
was prefaced by a preamble in which it was stated " That sundry
inhabitants of Dunstable had petitioned the General Assembly.
stating that they were more conveniently situated to belong to
Holles than to Dunstable — That Dunstable is large, rich and able
to spare them — which reasons and the arguments and objections
having been duly weighed, and it appearing reasonable to grant the
Petition.   *   *   Therefore be it enacted, &c."

Then follows a description of the part of Dunstable to be annexed
to Hollis, in accordance with a survey and plan made by Samuel
Cumings, the surveyor for Hollis and now at Concord. In running
this new east line of the town this survey begun at the *Pine tree*
standing on the hill called One Pine Hill, thence south 13 1-2°, west
372 rods to Nashua river. The line was then run northerly, beginning again at the same Pine tree, one mile and 225 rods — thence
westwardly one mile and 23 rods to the northeast corner of Hollis
as chartered in 1746 — thus taking from Dunstable all that part of
Hollis as it now is, east of Flint's brook and pond and Muddy
brook.

This once famous pine tree, thus made to mark the boundary of
the belligerent towns, and which gave its name to One Pine Hill, is
now no more.   It is said to have been a tall, straight pitch pine, near   •
a hundred feet high, with no other tree of its species near it, standing solitary and alone on the summit of the hill.   In early times, being conspicuous in all directions for a long distance, it served as a
beacon to mark a place of rendezvous for backwoodsmen and deer-
hunters, whose names in scores were cut in its bark, from its roots
many feet upward.

Thus at last ended by conquest the war between Dunstable and
One Pine Hill and its ever faithful allies of Hollis. a war which had
lasted, with varied fortune, nearly twice as long as the siege of Troy
— more than twice as long as our war of the Revolution, and, sad
to tell, no Homer has yet sung its heroes — no Marshall told its
history.

SECOND BORDER TROUBLE WITH DUNSTABLE, NASHUA RIVER
BRIDGE, COMPROMISE.

A second border trouble, in respect to the boundary between
Hollis and Dunstable, began soon after the conquest of One Pine
Hill.   This controversy grew out of a question in respect to the
support of an expensive bridge across the Nashua river, in the

south-east part of Hollis, near the place in the Hollis Records at
first called " Lawrehce's Mills," afterwards " Jaquith's," and in our
times known as " Runnell's Mills."   A bridge at this place was very
necessary to the people of Hollis, being on their main road to market; but much less needed by Dunstable. So indispensable was
this bridge to Hollis, that in 1740, as we have seen, provision was
made for building it out of the " non-resident tax of 2d. per acre "
granted by the parish charter for the support of the ministry. But
that tax being lost, with the parish charter, I do not find sufficient
evidence that any bridge was built at that place till many years after
the charter of Hollis and Dunstable as towns. These charters, as
has been seen, made the Nashua river from the Province line to
Flint's Brook the boundary of the two towns; the south line of Dunstable beginning at Merrimack river, and running on the Province
line " to " the Nashua, and the south line of Hollis, beginning " at "
the Nashua, and running westwardly on the Province line six miles
and ninety-six rods. A New Hampshire court in these times would
have probably held that this charter descriptive of this boundary
would have divided the river equally between the two towns, leaving
the town line in the middle or *thread* of the stream, instead of on its
banks, and each town under equal obligation to build the bridge.
But we shall see by and by that the town meetings in Hollis and
Dunstable did not take this view of the law.

In the early Hollis records there are many references to this
bridge, and to the troubles in respect to it. The first of these is
found in the record of the March meeting, in 1751 when the town
voted to help build a bridge " across Nashua river near Dea. Cumings." From this vote it is evident that the bridge had not been
then built, and that Dunstable was expected to help build it.

At the annual meeting in 1756, Hollis " chose Capt. Peter Powers, Samuel Cumings and Benjamin Abbott a Com^tee to see if Dunstable will joyn with Holles to bould a Bridge over Nashua river in
some convenant Place where the Road is laid out from Holles to
Dunstable." It seems that Dunstable did not accept this invitation
of the Hollis committee, for it is found that a special town meeting
in Hollis, in 1760, chose a " committee to Petition the Generall
Court for a Lottery to Bould a Bridge over Nashua river if they
think fit." But the " Generall" Court did not " think fit" to grant a
Lottery, as it appears that at the annual meeting in 1761, the town
without calling on Dunstable for help " Voted to have a Bridge
(6)

built over Nashua river near Lawrence's Mills," and chose a committee to obtain subscriptions for it.   The next year, 1762, the town
" Voted to raise Money to pay for the Building of the Bridge over
Nashua river the Money to be redukted out of the cost of the
Bridge that was subscribed out of town."   From this vote it is evident that as early as 1762 a bridge had been built across the Nashua
river mainly, if not wholly, by Hollis.   In May, 1765, at a special
town meeting, the town " Voted to Rebuild or Repair the Bridge
over Nashua river, and that the £800 voted at the March Meeting
for Making and Mending the Roads be laid out in Building and Repairing the Bridge."   From the above vote I infer that the bridge
built in 1762 was either washed away wholly in the spring of 1765,
or so much injured as to need costly repairs.   Though, in the language of the law, "often requested," the town of Dunstable, as it
seems, had given no aid in supporting this bridge, and the question
of the legal liability of that town to aid in it was allowed to sleep
till the annual meeting in Hollis in March, 1772.   At that meeting,
in pursuance of an article in the warrant, the town "Voted to appoint a committee to ask for and recover of Dunstable a share of
the Cost of Building and Repairing the Bridge across Nashua
River near Jaquith's Mills with power to prosecute if necessary."

This request of the people of Hollis, upon being submitted by the
committee to a town meeting in Dunstable, in the month of June
following, was curtly rejected, and it was " Voted that Dunstable
would not do anything towards building a bridge over Nashua
river."

But it fortunately so happened that not far from this time, the
Mills before known as "Lawrence's Mills," had become the property of Ebenezer Jaquith.   This Mr. Jaquith and Ensign Daniel
Merrill lived in the bend of Nashua river on the Dunstable side,
their two farms containing about 500 acres, and comprising all the
land in this bend.   These men were nearer to the meeting-house
in Hollis than to that in Dunstable, and like the saintly and sensible
settlers on One Pine Hill, wished to be annexed to Hollis and were
willing to pay something for the privilege.   With these new facts
in view, and the long and costly contest for the conquest of One
Pine Hill not yet forgotten, a special town meeting was called in
Hollis in December, 1772, at which it was "Voted that whereas,
there is a dispute with respect to the Bridge over Nashua river between Holles and Dunstable, and whereas Messrs. Merrill and Ja-

quith live more convenient to Holles than Dunstable, and are willing to pay something handsome towards the Building of said Bridge, and also considering the expense of Suits at Law in the Premises — now in order to an amicable settlement of the matter, and for the Preservation and Cultivation of Harmony between said Towns — Voted to accept said Families with their Lands, Provided Dunstable shall lay them off to us and assist in an amicable manner to get them incorporated with us. Also Voted that Samuel Hobart, Dea. Noyes and William Nevins be a Committee to treat with Dunstable on Bridge Affairs." The Hollis Committee soon communicated these amicable terms of peace to the Selectmen of Dunstable, who upon their receipt, summoned a town meeting of their constituents, by whom these neighborly overtures were disdainfully rejected and the meeting "Voted that the people of Dunstable would not pay anything towards the Building of the Bridge, nor would they consent to annex any more Land to Holles."

In the meanwhile the legal advisers of Hollis, "learned in the law," upon the examination of the charters of the two towns, had expressed the opinion that Nashua river, where it flowed between Hollis and Dunstable, was not in any part in either town, and that neither town was under any obligation to build a bridge across it. This opinion in respect to the law with the proposed remedy is set forth in the following preamble and resolution, adopted at a town meeting of Hollis, Jan. 20, 1773, called to consider the report of their Peace Ambassadors to Dunstable.

" Whereas it appears by the charters of Dunstable and Holles, that Nashua River is not in either town — That it is highly necessary that a Bridge be erected over said River, but that neither Town is obliged by Law to make or maintain the same — and Dunstable manifesting an unwillingness to do anything respecting the Building of a Bridge — therefore, voted that William Nevins be agent of the Town to Petition the Governor and Council and General Assembly that Dunstable and Holles may be connected so that a Bridge may be built over said River."

Again at the annual town meeting in Hollis, in 1773, Col. John Hale, William Nevins and Ensign Stephen Ames were chosen to represent the matter in respect to the bridge, to the Governor and Council.

This proposal to appeal to the General Court, or Governor and Council, very soon had the effect to render the people of Dunstable more placable, and more ready to accept the treaty of peace offered by Hollis the year before. The choice of evils now presented was another trial of their border troubles before the General Court or the acceptance of the proposed compromise, and it is manifest from the doings of a town meeting in Hollis on the ensuing 18th of March, that Dunstable had voted to submit to the least of the two evils. At this meeting Hollis voted

" To extend the easterly line of Holles so far east as to include Messrs. Merrill and Jaquith with their Improvements, provided it shall be done without expense to the Town, and that Dea. Boynton, Reuben Dow and Samuel Cumings be a committee to agree with Dunstable in respect to Boundaries."

At a town meeting on the following 12th of April this committee made report as follows :

" We have met the Dunstable committee and have mutually agreed that the Easterly Line of Holles shall be extended Eastwardly to the following Bounds : To Begin at a Stake and Stones fifteen Rods below Buck Meadow Falls, at the River. which is Mr. Jaquith's northerly corner ; Thence running southerly in a straight line to a Pine tree on the River Bank which is Mr. Jaquith's southwesterly corner. April 8, 1773."

This report was accepted by the town, and afterwards, in the month of May, 1773, at the joint request of Hollis and Dunstable, the General Court passed an act establishing the boundary line between the two towns as so agreed upon, where it has remained undisturbed from that day to this. These terms of settlement, though at first not willingly accepted by Dunstable, were exceedingly favorable to that town, and ought to have been ample satisfaction for the loss of One Pine Hill. It is true that Dunstable came out of the controversy short of 500 acres of territory, but in return for this loss, that town was relieved from the burden of aiding in maintaining this bridge in all future time ; a charge that has already cost Hollis much more than the value of all the land so annexed.

CHAPTER VI.

HISTORY OF MONSON.—TOWN OFFICERS.—EFFORTS TO MAINTAIN
PREACHING AND BUILD A MEETING–HOUSE, ETC.—REPEAL OF
CHARTER.—THE MILE SLIP.—CHARTERS OF RABY, WILTON,
MASON AND DUXBURY.—MILFORD.—1746 TO 1794.

The ancient, now extinct town of Monson, incorporated April 1,
1746, was bounded, as we have seen, on the north by the Souhegan
river, and south by Hollis. Its corporate existence lasted for twenty-four years, during which time it regularly held its annual town
meetings, elected its moderators, town clerks, selectmen, tithingmen,
hogreeves, deerkeepers and other town officers, but I am pained to
say that I find no evidence that it ever had a school, school house,
meeting-house or a "learned orthodox minister," or a minister not
orthodox. The only public structure ever owned by the town was
a pound, built for the confinement of disorderly cattle. Its first
town meeting was held May 1, 1746, under the direction of Col.
Joseph Blanchard, as provided in the charter, Col. Blanchard being
moderator. At this meeting town officers were chosen as follows:

ROBERT COLBURN, Town Clerk	SAMUEL LEEMAN, Surveyor of Highways	
BENJAMIN HOPKINS	ABRAHAM LEEMAN, Hogreeve	
ROBERT COLBURN } Selectmen	JOHN BURNS } Fence Viewers	
WILLIAM NEVINS	JAMES WHEELER	
THOMAS NEVINS, Constable		

At this meeting the town voted to build a pound, and also "to
buy a suteable Book to Record Votes in, and other things as the
town shall see meet."

During the twenty-four and one-half years of the corporate existence of Monson, I find from the record of votes kept in this "suteable Book," that the persons named in the following lists were chosen
at the annual town meetings to the respective offices of moderator,
town clerk and selectmen, the number of times set opposite their
names. *Moderator*,—William Nevins, twelve times; Benjamin

Hopkins, seven times: Robert Colburn and Benjamin Kenrick, twice each; Nathan Hutchinson, once. *Town Clerk*—Robert Colburn, thirteen times: Benjamin Kenrick. nine times; Archelaus Towne, three times. *Selectmen*—Robert Colburn, fifteen times; William Nevins, fourteen times; *Benjamin Hopkins and Benjamin Kenrick, ten times each; Nathan Hutchinson, six times; Josiah Crosby, four times; John Brown and Archelaus Towne, three times each; Daniel Kenrick and Samuel Leeman, twice each; Thomas Burns, Benjamin Farley, Joseph Gould. William Jones, Thomas Nevins and Jonathan Taylor, once each.

At the time Monson was chartered, the French and Indian War, (begun in 1744.) was still raging. A petition dated May 13, 1747, presented by the inhabitants of Monson to the New Hampshire General Court for soldiers for a guard, shows the extent and condition of the settlement at that time. This petition has fourteen names appended to it, probably those of all the householders then in the town. In this petition they say:

"That the town has just begun to settle, and but about fifteen families there—That they are one of the Frontier Towns West of the Merrimack River and the most northerly one already incorporated, lying between Holles and the new Plantation called Souhegan West. Could we be assisted by soldiers in such competent numbers as might enable us to Defend our Selves, we shall chearfully endeavor to stay there by which we shall serve as a Barrier in part to Holles, Merrimack and Dunstable. That last year we were Favored by Soldiers from the Massachusetts that prevented our Drawing off." * *

In answer to this petition, and one similar to it from Souhegan West, (now Amherst) the General Court gave orders for the raising of "fifteen good effective men to scout and guard Souhegan West and Monson till the 23d of the following October."

A petition of the selectmen of Monson to the General Court, six years later, dated April 25, 1753, asking that the inhabitants might be relieved from the payment of Province taxes, tells the story of the sad financial condition of the settlers at that time. In this petition the selectmen tell the General Court that there were then in Monson,

"But thirty-six Poles in the whole, severall of them transiently hired for a short space to Labor, * * without any Estate. But twenty-one Houses, chiefly small cottages only, for a present shelter, the charge of Building yet to come on. That they are all plain men Dwelling in these Tents; Husbandry their employment, their

Improvements very small, their Lands yet to Subdue. The Progress much retarded by the necessity to work out of town the prime
part of the year * * to procure Provisions. * * The few set-
lers are scattered all ab' the Town. Much Labour has & must be
spent in making and opening Roads and Bridges * * a burthen
too heavy for the small, weak number that is there. * * * They
therefore apprehend themselves utterly unable to Bear any Portion
of the Publick Taxes, as yet, * * but hope that their small Begining in Time may become usefull if they may be nurssed and
favoured now in their Infancy."

What, if anything, was done by the General Court in answer to
this pathetic petition, in respect to "nurssing" the infant suppliant,
does not appear in the Provincial records.

SCHOOLS, PREACHING, MEETING-HOUSE AND MEETING-HOUSE PLACE.

It is shown by the records of the doings of the annual town meetings in Monson that the attention of the inhabitants was many times
called to all of these topics, but always in vain.

Schools. An article first appeared in the warrant for the annual
town meeting in 1753. "To see if the town would raise a sum of
money for a school?" "Passed in the negative." The like articles
were inserted in the warrants for the annual town meetings in 1756
and 1760, and in each year, as before, "passed in the negative."
After 1760, I do not find that any effort was made for a tax either
for a school-house or school.

Preaching. In the year 1749, 1751, 1752, 1754 and 1757, the
question of raising a tax for the "support of Preaching amongst
them" was brought before the annual town meetings, and each year
either "passed in the negative," or was not acted on at all. But in
1763 the town "Voted a tax of £300, O. T., to support the Gospel, each person to pay where they *hear*." Yet it seems that this
tax was not collected, the town the next year having voted to
"*sink*" it. In 1764, at the annual meeting, a vote was passed "To
Raise £400, O. T., to make satisfaction to the Towns of Holles and
Amherst for the Privileges we Enjoy in attending Meeting with
them." But at a subsequent town meeting, in 1767, "Voted that
the money Raised in 1764, and assessed for the Towns of Holles
and Amherst shall not be collected," so that it does not appear that
any tax was ever collected in Monson, to pay for preaching either
in the town or out of it.

Building a Meeting-House.   Between the years 1752 and 1767, an article several times was inserted in the warrant for the annual town meeting to " see if the town will Vote to be taxed for the Building of a Meeting-House and Settling the Gospel amongst them."   And also " To see if the Town will Petition the General Court for a tax on the Land of Residents and non Residents to build a Meeting-House and setel the Gospel."   These various proposals all alike " passed in the negative ;" as also did a proposition, introduced in 1760 " to build a Meeting-house at the most convenient place near the Center of the Town or '*pick*' a new one."

In 1762, and again in 1765, Monson was coupled with Merrimack in sending a Representative to the New Hampshire General Court. In the former year these towns were represented by Major Joseph Blanchard, and in 1765, by Capt. John Chamberlain, both supposed to live in Merrimack.   At the census of New Hampshire taken in 1767, the population of Monson was 293.

PROPOSALS TO DIVIDE THE TOWN, AND FINAL REPEAL OF THE CHARTER.

The people of Monson, like their neighbors of Hollis, do not at any time seem to have been well content with their chartered boundaries. Several expedients in different years came before the annual town meetings proposing changes in the chartered limits of the town, some of them favoring additions to its territory, others, a division of it in various ways. Among the rest was a proposal adopted at the March meeting in 1760 " To annex the Land on the south side of Monson to Holles, and to Petition the Governor and Council for such part of Souhegan West to be added to the Remainder of Monson as will be sufficient to maintain the Gospel, and other incidental charges."   Again in 1761, the town " Voted to set off one mile and a half on the south side of Monson to Holles." This last vote it would seem was passed to favor a petition of Hollis to the General Court for the like purpose.   After this date all questions looking to a change in the boundaries of the town seem to have rested till the year 1770, when the people of Monson, having bandoned all hope of maintaining preaching, or of " settling the Gospel among them," or of building a meeting-house, or even of finding a suitable " Meeting-house Place," petitioned the General Court to put a final end to their unhappy and troubled corporate life by a repeal of their charter.   In their petition for this repeal,

they told the General Court as a reason for it, " That the Land in
and about the Center of Monson is so very poor, Broken, Baron and
uneaven, as cannot admit of many Settlers, so that those Families
that are in Town, are almost all planted in the Extreme parts of it."
* * *   " We have no prospect of ever Building a Meeting-House
in the Center or elsewhere, any ways to accommodate us, by which
Difficulties we think the Gospel will not be settled among us while
in the present situation. We therefore pray, &c."

The consent of Hollis to accept of two miles in width of the south
side of the suppliant town, and of Amherst all the residue, having
been first obtained, an Act was passed by the General Court, July
4, 1770, dividing Monson by an East and West line passing very
near its centre, annexing the south part to Hollis and the north to
Amherst. In this way, and in answer to its own humble entreaties,
this ancient town voluntarily surrendered its right to municipal life,
and for more than a century has been effaced from the map of New
Hampshire, and all memory or tradition of it is now nearly lost to
the present generation. Since the corporate death of Monson, its
remains have been subdivided into four fragments, the largest of
them being in the body politic of Milford, the smallest in Brookline,
the remainder about equally divided between Amherst and Hollis.

INCORPORATION OF RABY, WILTON AND MASON.—THE MILE SLIP.
DUXBURY.—MILFORD.

The west line of Hollis and Monson, as chartered in 1746, as already shown, was the original west line of old Dunstable, running
due south by the needle from Souhegan river to the new Province
line. The towns of Wilton and Mason, granted by the " Masonian"
proprietors in 1749, were afterwards chartered with the same boundaries as granted—Wilton in 1762 and Mason in 1768. The east
line of these towns also run due south from the Souhegan river to
the Province line, parallel with and about one mile distant from the
west line of Hollis and Monson, thus leaving, in the intermediate
space, a tract of unincorporated territory, about a mile wide, and
extending from the Souhegan river to the Province line. This tract
of land, at that time, and for some years later, was known as the
" Mile Slip," but often in the old records called the " Mile Strip,"
and sometimes " Strip town." A considerable number of families
had settled on the Mile Slip, who naturally felt the need of a town
charter. Their near neighbors at the west end of Hollis, as has

been seen, some years before had felt themselves much aggrieved at the location of the Hollis meeting-house, so far from themselves and so near to the east end of their town. Whether willing or not, these settlers in the west end of Hollis. as the Province laws then were, were taxable. both in person and estate, for the building of the meeting house and support of the ministry there, the same as the rest of the inhabitants. They had now, for many years, impatiently borne this injustice. So long as the boundaries of Hollis remained as fixed in the original charter of the town, these west end settlers doubtless cherished the hope that at some time in the future better justice would be done them, either by the erection of a new meeting-house, or the removal of the one already built nearer to the centre of the town. But all hope of this sort forever vanished in the year 1763, on the annexation of One Pine Hill to the east end of Hollis, thus bringing the centre of the town about two miles nearer to the west end, and the meeting-house so much nearer to the centre. The people in the other parts of Hollis were doubtless desirous of quieting the murmurs of their discontented and troublesome townsmen at the west end, provided it could be done consistently with the geographical symmetry and pecuniary interests of the old town. With this end in view, the expedient of forming a new town from this "Mile Slip," and the west end of Hollis, was first brought to the attention of the people of Hollis at their annual town meeting in the spring of 1764. less than three months after the conquest of One Pine Hill. At that meeting the town "Voted To measure *East* from the Meeting House to the Town Line—and then to Measure *West* from the Meeting House the same Length of Line—And all West by a North and South Line to be set off to the One *Mile Strip* so called."

The like vote was passed at the annual town meeting in 1768. In 1769. about a year after this last vote, the south part of the Mile Slip and a tract of territory about one mile and one-fourth wide, from off the west end of Hollis, were incorporated into a town by the name of Raby, so called from a town of that name, in the county of Durham, in the north part of England, from which some of its settlers first emigrated. It appears from the documents and records relating to Raby, that the petitioners for the charter asked for and expected a tract of land two miles in width from the west end of Hollis to be united with the Mile Slip. It is also evident that the people of Hollis were willing to spare the two miles,

provided it could be done and still leave their meeting-house equally
distant from the new east and west lines, otherwise they were not
willing. I infer from the language used in the charter of Raby,
that the Governor and Council tried to do their best to satisfy both
parties—that is, to give to Raby the two miles, and also to leave the
Hollis meeting-house no nearer the new west line than it then was
to the east line. Accordingly, with this end in view, they described
the south-east corner of the new town as being " at a stake and
stones about two miles from the South West corner of Hollis (as
Hollis then was) thence North by the needle to the North line of
Hollis, leaving the meeting house in the *middle* between this line
and the East line of said Hollis."

But unfortunately the west line of Hollis did not extend far enough
towards the setting sun, by three-fourths of a mile, to give to Raby
the coveted two miles, and at the same time to leave the Hollis
meeting-house at equal distances from the east and west lines of the
town. It not being possible to satisfy both conditions, the surveyor who run the town line appears to have come to the conclusion that it was of more importance that the Hollis meeting-house
should be equally distant from the east and west lines of the town,
than that the people of Raby should have all the land they expected.
Accordingly the line was so established as to take from Hollis a tract
of land about one mile and one-fourth in width. instead of two miles,
and leaving Hollis meeting-house the same distance from the east
line of Raby as it was from the west line of Dunstable. The people
of Raby were evidently disappointed with this result. and the
next year. at the annual town meeting in Hollis. an article was
inserted in the warrant, " To see if the town would set off to Raby
the Families and Lands they expected." This question being submitted to the meeting, it was " passed in the negative," and the
meeting-house in Hollis continued, for many years after, to divide
equally—a straight line passing through it—between the new west
and east lines of the town. The town of Raby, as at first chartered,
was but about two and one-half miles wide. and contained not more
than twelve square miles—an area not much more than one-third of
that of Hollis. The people of that town were not content with
these narrow limits. but the war and troubles of the Revolution
soon coming on, this discontent was allowed to sleep till the war
was well over. But in 1785. two years after the war was ended,
the people of Raby presented their grievances to the General Court

in a petition setting forth the small population and narrow limits of
their town, together with the alleged mistake in their boundaries
when chartered, occasioned as was charged by the "wrongs or
sharp practice of Hollis," and asking for the annexation from
Hollis of three-fourths of a mile more. Upon notice of this petition
a town meeting was soon called in Hollis and resolutions adopted
to oppose it, and Capt. Daniel Emerson, at that time their Representative in the General Court, was instructed to use his influence
against it. Notwithstanding the stout opposition of Hollis, the
General Court decided that Raby was in the right, and passed an
act setting off from the west end of Hollis to Raby another tract of
territory of the uniform width of three-fourths of a mile. This last
annexation to Raby left the length of the south line of Hollis four
miles and eighty-five rods instead of six miles and ninety-six rods as
in the original charter. In 1796 the name of Raby was changed to
Brookline by an act of the General Court upon a petition of the inhabitants of the town.

In the year 1776, upon application to the General Court of its inhabitants, the north part of the *Mile Slip*, including a tract of territory of about one thousand acres, known as the *Duxbury School
Farm*, was invested with limited town privileges. In a census of
New Hampshire taken in 1767, the Mile Slip had sixty-nine inhabitants ; in that taken in 1775, it had eighty-three. In the census of
1790 it was called *Duxbury*, and then had a population of one hundred and sixty-nine.

In 1794 the town of Milford was incorporated. The act charter-
ing Milford was entitled "an act to incorporate the south westerly
part of Amherst — the north-westerly part of Hollis — the Mile Slip
and Duxbury School Farm, into a town." Milford, as incorporated,
included a small part of Amherst north of the Souhegan river, much
the largest portion of that part of the old town of Monson, which
by the division of Monson in 1770 had been annexed to Amherst ;
all of the Mile Slip not included in Raby, with the Duxbury School
Farm, and an area of from 1000 to 1500 acres taken from the north-
west corner of Hollis. It does not appear that the people of Hollis
made any opposition to this contribution to the territory of their
new neighbor. The inhabitants living on the territory annexed
were nearer to the village in Milford than to the meeting-house in
Hollis, and probably, without objection, acquiesced in the transfer.
This tract annexed to Milford is the last loss or gain in territory
which has fallen to the lot of Hollis for the last three-quarters of

a century and more.   During that period the town has remained of
the same shape and dimensions, as left at the incorporation of Milford, without any encroachment from its neighbors since, or effort
on the part of its inhabitants to extend their borders.   According to
a survey and plan of the town, (now at Concord), made in the year
1806 by Nathan Colburn, a Hollis surveyor, still remembered, Hollis,
as it then was, and still is, contains an area of 19,620 acres, or
about 30 2-3 square miles, a territory not very much differing in extent from that of the town as first chartered.   In all these many
border troubles and controversies, which I have taken occasion to
notice, it cannot but be observed that the people of Hollis have uniformly had a wakeful eye to their own rights and interests, that they
at all times vigorously and vigilantly endeavored to hold their own,
and the present generation will find little reason to reproach the
memory of their ancestors for not guarding and striving to perpetuate the rights and interests of those who should come after them,

CHAPTER VII.

THE PROVINCIAL MILITIA LAW.— FIRST MILITIA COMPANY IN
HOLLIS.— HOLLIS IN THE FRENCH AND INDIAN WARS OF 1744
AND 1755.— PETITIONS FOR GUARDS.— NAMES OF OFFICERS
AND PRIVATE SOLDIERS.— 1744 TO 1763.

A law enacted by the New Hampshire General Court in the
year 1718. required all able bodied male persons between the ages of
sixteen and sixty, with the exceptions mentioned below, to do
military duty. These exceptions included members of the General
Court. ministers, deacons, schoolmasters, physicians, justices of
the peace, millers, ferrymen, and such persons as had before held a
military commission. Each private soldier was required to be furnished with a " *Fire Lock. Snap Sack, Cartouch Box, Worm
and Priming Wire, 1 Pound of Gun Powder. 20 Bullets. and
12 Flints*, " and to train four days in the year, and to muster once
in three years." It was also made the duty of each town in the Province to keep on hand a stock of ammunition for the town's use,
consisting of " one barrel of good Gun powder, 100 pounds of
bullets and 300 flints, for every sixty Soldiers," and also to provide
arms and ammunition for such poor soldiers as were not able to supply themselves. This law, with but little change, remained in force
till the war of the Revolution, and it explains the reasons for many
votes found in the records of Hollis for the assessment of " Rates "
for the " town stock of ammunition."*

In May 1744, the General Court passed an Act organizing the
6th Regiment of New Hampshire militia. This regiment, of which
Joseph Blanchard of Dunstable was Colonel, embraced the militia companies of a large part of the territory acquired by the settlement of the new Province line in 1741, being the towns and districts then known as Dunstable, the West Parish of Dunstable,
Rumford, (now Concord), Nottingham, (now Hudson), Souhegan

*Province Laws, pp. 92, 97.

East, (now Bedford,) Souhegan West. (now Amherst), and some others, making in all nine companies, of which that in West Dunstable was the ninth.   Of this last company, Peter Powers was appointed Captain by the Governor and Council.*   As we find in the Hollis records, shortly after the appointment of Captain Powers, the title of *Lieutenant* prefixed to the name of Benjamin Farley, of *Ensign* to that of Jerahmael Cumings, and of *Sergeant* to the name of James Stewart, there can be but little doubt that those persons held the offices indicated, in the first militia company of West Dunstable.   In those times of peril, when it was necessary for the defence of the hearth-stone and family from the midnight assault and scalping knife of the savage, that each citizen should be a soldier, military titles, as in after times, had not become an empty compliment.   Such titles as *Captain, Lieutenant* and *Ensign* indicated that the persons known by them were distinguished among their townsmen for such qualities as were most useful and most needed for the common safety, and for that reason most valued and honored.   When once duly bestowed, they virtually became a part of the name of such persons as were entitled to them, to be used alike in social intercourse and in the public records.

From the year 1745 to January 26, 1775, we find no roll of the Hollis militia company, nor have the names of its officers come down to us except as those names have been preserved in the Hollis tax lists, and other public documents, with their rank or title prefixed.   It appears from an original roll of the Hollis militia company of the last date, still existing, supposed to be in the handwriting of the town clerk of the time, that inclusive of officers Hollis then had 224 soldiers liable to do military duty, that being the number of names on this roll.   Of this company Joshua Wright was Captain, Reuben Dow Lieutenant, and Noah Worcester Ensign.

In addition to the military officers already mentioned, we find on the Hollis tax lists and other public documents prior to 1775, many names of Hollis men with military titles, most if not all of whom may be presumed to have held the commissions indicated by their several titles in the militia company of Hollis.   *Captains*—Benjamin Abbot, Zedekiah Drury and Leonard Whiting.   *Lieutenants,* —Robert Colburn, Amos Eastman, Samuel Farley, David Farnsworth, Amos Fisk, Samuel Gridley and James Taylor.   *Ensigns*— Stephen Ames, Josiah Brown, Jonas Flagg, Daniel Merrill and Benjamin Parker.

---

*'Prov. Papers' Vol. 5, p. 232.

THE FRENCH AND INDIAN WAR OF 1744.

In the month of March, 1744, the French and Indian war was begun, in which the Massachusetts and New Hampshire troops undertook the chivalrous expedition for the capture of Louisburg.* This war lasted till October, 1748. As in former wars, the Canada and Eastern Indians took sides with the French, who, coming in large numbers from Canada and Nova Scotia, prowled around our defenceless settlements, waylaying, murdering and scalping, or taking captive to Canada the settlers in the frontier towns, some of which no farther off than Peterborough, Lyndeborough and New Boston, were wholly deserted. The inhabitants of Hollis, Monson, Souhegan East, Souhegan West, and other places west of the Merrimack river, repeatedly petitioned the General Court for scouts and garrisons for their protection.

Among the earliest of these petitions was one from the old Parish of West Dunstable. On the 18th of June, 1744, about three months after war was declared, at a meeting of the inhabitants of West Dunstable, James Stewart was chosen their delegate to present this petition to the General Court. The Commission of Mr. Stewart for this purpose was in writing, signed by all, or very nearly all of the householders then in West Dunstable, forty-five in number, and was in substance as follows:

" DUNSTABLE, June 18, 1744.

" Wee, the Inhabitants of the West Parish in the District of Dunstable, do hereby authorise and depute Mr. James Stewart in our names and behalf, to make proper application to the Government of New Hampshire, Setting forth our being situated on the Frontier, and exposed to the Enemy, and the Necessity wee are in of a Guard, and Pray for a Sutable and Seasonable Relief there.

" Voted to Request Six Garasons and twenty-five soldiers."

Capt. PETER POWERS	WILLIAM COLBURN	JOSEPH McDANIELS
Lieut. BENJAMIN FARLEY	SAMUEL CUMINGS	RANDALL McDANIELS
Ensign JERAHMAEL CUMINGS	JONATHAN DANFORD	JONATHAN MELVIN
WILLIAM ADAMS	Rev. DANIEL EMERSON	DAVID NEVINS
STEPHEN AMES	SAMUEL FARLEY	THOMAS NEVINS
HENRY BARTON	JOSEPH FARLEY	BENJAMIN PARKER
BENJAMIN BLANCHARD	NICHOLAS FRENCH	SAMUEL PARKER
BENJAMIN BLANCHARD, Jr	STEPHEN HARRIS	THOMAS PATCH
WILLIAM BLANCHARD	WILLIAM HARTWELL	JOHN PHELPS
ELNATHAN BLOOD	STEPHEN HAZELTINE	AMOS PHILIPS
JOSIAH BLOOD	JOSIAH HOBART	MOSES PROCTOR
NATHANIEL BLOOD	ENOCH HUNT	JAMES WHEELER
JOHN BOYNTON, Jun	ZERUBBABEL KEMP	PETER WHEELER
JOHN BROWN	JONATHAN LOVEJOY	FRANCIS WORCESTER, Jr
JOSIAH BROWN	JAMES McDANIELS	JOSHUA WRIGHT."†

*Holmes Annals, Vol. 2, p. 23.   †Prov. Papers, Vol. 9, p. 195.

The following extracts from the petition soon after presented by Mr. Stewart set forth the reasons for it and the condition of the settlement at the time.

" The Memorial and Petition of James Stewart, in the name and behalf of the inhabitants of the West Parish of Dunstable, Humbly sheweth, That said Parish has been settled about 14 years, and a Gospell Minister ordained above a year. * *   That many Thousand Pounds has been spent in clearing and cultivating the Land there, and some Thousands more in Building Houses, Barns and Fences. * * *   The breaking up of which Settlements will not only ruin the Memorialists, but greatly diserve his Majesty's Interest."

" That it was by long and importunate Intercession of this Province (and not of the Memorialists seeking) that they are cast under the immediate care of this Government, which they conceive gives them so much the better right to its Protection. That as War is already declared against France, and a Rupture with the Indians hourly expected, your Memorialists, unless they have speedy help, will soon be oblidged to leave their Settlements. * *   Wherefore your Memorialists most humbly supplicate * *   such seasonable Relief as may enable them to subsist in the war, and (be) secure against the Ravages and Devastations of a blood thirsty and Merciless Enemy."

Near three years later, about one year after Hollis was chartered as a town, (the war still raging) at a town meeting held in April, 1747, Samuel Cumings was appointed a delegate to present to the General Court a second petition for " *scouts* " and " *guards*." The subjoined extracts from the petition of this delegate show the condition and needs of the town at that time. He says to the General Court in this petition, " That Holles is a Frontier town much exposed to Danger from the Indian Enemy, and the number of Effective men belonging to the same not exceeding fifty, who have all or most of them Families to take care of and being mostly new settlers, have much Labour on their hands to subdue and cultivate their Lands. That their situation is such that they dare not to venture to work without a guard * * which if they cannot have they must spend their time in *watching* and *warding*, in which case their families must suffer for want of the necessaries of life. * * * And they Humbly pray that they may be allowed a scout of ten or a dozen men for the ensuing season till the Danger of the Summer

(7)

and Fall of the year is over and the harvest past * * and as in duty bound &c."* In reply to these and other like petitions from the frontier settlements and towns west of and near the Merrimack in similar perils, the General Court at several different times detailed detachments of soldiers as patrols to scout through the woods west of that river, and at one time voted a force of ninety scouts to patrol the forests from the mouth of the Contoocook river to Hollos.

During this war the grim government bounty for Indian scalps for the encouragement of scouts and Indian hunters was increased by vote of the General Court from £100, paid for them in Lovewell's war, to £250, O. T., and at one time to £400, O. T., for each Indian scalp taken west of Nova Scotia, and produced to the Governor and Council. Probably owing to the efforts of the government, united with the vigilance of the settlers, it does not appear that any attack was made upon Hollis or any of the adjoining towns. I do not find that Hollis furnished any soldiers for the New Hampshire regiments raised in this war, and not more than two or three Hollis names appear in the printed lists of New Hampshire " scouts" published in the report of the Adjutant General for 1866. The protection of their own families and firesides was the first, and would seem the only military duty, in these years, asked or expected of the settlers in the towns on the extreme frontier.

THE WAR IN WHICH QUEBEC WAS TAKEN AND CANADA CONQUERED.

In 1754, about eight years after the peace of Aix La Chapelle, the last French and Indian War was begun, which ended in the capture of Quebec and the final conquest of Canada.† Hollis in this war was no longer on the extreme frontier, and was much less exposed to the attacks of the savages than in the preceding war. During the eight years of peace, the population of the town had very considerably increased, and its soldiers seem to have done their whole duty in filling up the ranks of the New Hampshire regiments called for by the Government. In the roll of a small detachment of New Hampshire troops posted on the Connecticut river in the fall of 1754, and to be found in the report of the Adjutant General for 1866, above referred to, I find the names of John Cumings, James French, Jonathan Hubbard, (Hobart) Samuel Parker and James Whiting, all names appearing on the Hollis records and believed to have been Hollis soldiers.

*Prov. Papers, Vol. 9, p. 399.
†Holmes' Annals, Vol. 2, p. 53.

In 1755, New Hampshire raised a regiment commanded by Col. Joseph Blanchard, to aid in the expedition against the French forts at Crown Point on the west shore of Lake Champlain. Of this regiment, Rev. Daniel Emerson was Chaplain, Dr. John Hale, Surgeon's Mate, and Jonathan Hubbard, (Hobart) Adjutant, all of Hollis.*

Nearly two-thirds of the Third Company of this regiment were also Hollis men. Of this company, Peter Powers was Captain, Benjamin Abbot, Lieutenant; William Cumings, Ensign; James Colburn, Clerk; David Hubbard, (Hobart) and Samuel Cumings. Sergeants; Jonathan Powers, Enoch Noyes, Stephen Hazeltine and James Brown, Corporals, and Samuel Brown, Drummer, all of Hollis. Among the private soldiers, or *sentinels*, we recognize the following Hollis names, viz. : Jacob Abbot, Ebenezer Ball, Samuel Barrett, Jabez Davis, John Flagg, Jonathan Fowler, Josiah French. John Goodhue, James Hill, George Lesley, Christopher Lovejoy. Levi Powers, Stephen Powers, Whitcomb Powers. Isaac Stearns. Nathaniel Townsend, Daniel Wheeler. James Wheeler, Peter Wheeler and John Willoughby. making in all thirty-four Hollis men in this regiment.

In August 1757, after the capture of Fort William Henry by the French and Indians, a battalion of two hundred and fifty New Hampshire troops was raised for the defence of Fort Edward. near Lake George, commanded by Major Thomas Tash. In the first company of this battalion there were eleven Hollis soldiers, viz. : Benjamin Abbot, Jacob Abbot, Stephen Ames, Ephraim Blood. Elnathan Blood, Robert Campbell, Timothy Emerson. John Hale, Samuel Hobart, (Sergt.) Jonathan Hobart and John Willoughby.

In 1758, a regiment of New Hampshire troops was raised, commanded by Col. John Hart of Portsmouth. a part of which was ordered to join a second expedition against Louisburg, and the remainder to serve on the western frontier. Of this regiment Rev. Daniel Emerson was Chaplain, and Dr. John Hale, Surgeon. Of its Sixth company, Ebenezer Jaquith was Second Lieutenant and Josiah Brown, Ensign. Besides the foregoing, there were also in the same company sixteen Hollis soldiers, making in all twenty Hollis men in this regiment, viz. : Nathaniel Blood, Joseph Easterbrook, Jonathan Fowler, James French, Samuel Hazeltine, James Hubbard, (Hobart), Thomas Nevins, Ebenezer Pierce, Whitcomb

---

*Vol. 2, Adjt. Gen. Rep. for 1866, pp. 97, 129, 131, 132.

Powers, Thomas Powers, Isaac Stearns, Samuel Stearns, James Taylor, Abel Webster, Peter Wheeler and John Willoughby.

In 1759, the year of the capture of Quebec, a New Hampshire regiment was raised and put under the command of Col. Zaccheus Lovewell, of Dunstable, with its rendezvous at that place. With the exception of two companies, the rolls of this regiment are lost, but as it was made up of drafts from the militia regiments of the whole province, and its headquarters being in an adjacent town, there can be no reasonable doubt that the Hollis soldiers were well represented in it.

In 1760, the year of the final conquest of Canada, New Hampshire furnished its last regiment of eight hundred men for this war, of which John Goffe was Colonel, having its headquarters at Litchfield. This regiment marched to its destination by the way of Monson, Keene, the Green Mountains, and thence to Crown Point. Its adjutant was Samuel Hobart, and on the roll of one of its companies I find the following names of Hollis soldiers : Joseph Taylor, Lieut., James Taylor, Sergeant, and among the privates, Jotham Cumings, Francis Powers, and Joshua Wright.*

In the foregoing lists there will be found sixty-one different names of men who as private soldiers or officers, in the several years of that war, went into the army from the territory now or at that time embraced in Hollis. How many other names of Hollis soldiers were on the lost rolls, cannot now be told. As no census had then been taken of which we have any knowledge, we have no means of learning the population of the town during that war with much approach to accuracy. The number of names on the Tax Lists, from 1754 to 1760, then varied from one hundred and eight to one hundred and seventeen, and the number of men furnished from the town in that war was equal to more than one half the number of tax payers, besides those that may have been on the lost rolls.

In February 1763, by the treaty concluded at Paris, peace was again proclaimed. For thirteen of the nineteen years beginning with 1744 and ending with 1763, our ancestors were engaged in this savage and bloody warfare for the defence of their lives and firesides, carried on by their enemies with the avowed purpose of driving the English from the country. We now look back upon the history of those years and the doings of our ancestors, with feelings of filial gratitude and admiration, knowing as we do that

---

*Adjt. Gen. Rep. for 1866, Vol. 2, pp. 191, 213, 214, 222, 241.

it was to their courage, constancy and sufferings that we owe the rich inheritance they have transmitted to us.   We would gladly know much more than it is now possible to learn of the personal history of these early pioneers of the town and State, but knowing as we do how soon the memorials of the dead fade from the recollections of the living, we may well be grateful that even the names of so many of these brave defenders of their country have come down to our times.

The militia company in Hollis, from the year 1768, formed a part of the 5th Regiment of the New Hampshire militia till the beginning of the war of the Revolution.   From 1768 to 1775, the field officers of that regiment were Edward G. Lutwyche of Merrimack, Colonel; its Lieut. Colonel was Dr. John Hale, and Samuel Hobart its Major.   Col. Lutwyche was a loyalist or tory, and is said to have left the country near the beginning of the war.   Major Hobart was appointed Colonel of the 2nd New Hampshire Regiment of minute men, by the New Hampshire Provincial Congress in September 1775, and in November of the same year, Lieut. Col. Hale was elected Colonel of the 5th Regiment of New Hampshire militia.

CHAPTER VIII.

COLONIAL SCHOOL LAW.—SCHOOLS IN HOLLIS BEFORE THE REV-
OLUTION.—SCHOOL DISTRICTS.—SCHOOL HOUSES.—THE GRAM-
MAR SCHOOL.—TEACHERS OF THE GRAMMAR SCHOOL.—COL-
LEGE GRADUATES, ETC., BEFORE 1800.—LETTER OF GOV. JOHN
WENTWORTH TO REV. MR. EMERSON.—1746 TO 1775.

By a Colonial law of New Hampshire passed in 1719, and remaining in force without any important change till after the Revolution, it was enacted " that each Town in the Province having the
number of fifty house holders shall be constantly provided of a
schoolmaster to teach children to read and write, and when any
town has one hundred families or house holders, there shall
also be a Grammar School set up and kept. * * And some discreet person of good conversation, well instructed in the *tongues*,
shall be procured to be master thereof. * * Every such school
master to be suitably encouraged and paid by the inhabitants. * *
And the Selectmen of Towns are hereby Empowered to agree with
such school masters for Salary, and to raise money by way of Rate
upon the Inhabitants to pay the same." The law also provided that
" If any such Town should neglect the due observance of the Law
for the space of six months, it should incur a Penalty of £20." In
1721 this law was so amended in respect to towns having one hundred families, as to subject the selectmen, instead of the town, to a
fine of £20, if their town for *one* month should be without a grammar school.

The above law was unlike the New Hampshire School Laws in
force during the present century in many important particulars.

1st. It provided for a single school only for teaching children to
read and write, in towns having fifty families and less than one hundred ; and for a grammar school in which the "tongues" or dead
languages were to be taught in towns having one hundred families
or more.

2nd. It was wholly silent as to school-houses, school districts and school committees.

3d. It contemplated the employment of *male* teachers only, "*School Masters.*"

4th. The hiring of "School Masters"—the whole management of the schools and the "raising of money by way of Rates" was entrusted wholly to the selectmen.

5th. It required, in its terms, both the school for teaching reading and writing, and also that for teaching the "Tongues" to be kept "constantly."

The foregoing suggestions in respect to the province school law tend to explain many matters relating to schools to be found in the early Hollis records, otherwise not so readily understood.

The first reference to public schools to be found in these records is in the doings of the annual town meeting of March, 1749. A few days previous to that meeting, the old first meeting-house had been offered for sale at public auction and bid off at £49. O. T., and it was then "Voted that the money the old meeting-house sold for be applied to the building of a school-house." But it afterwards appears from the records that this £49. O. T., was not paid, and that the old meeting-house still continued to belong to the town. In the year 1750 there were eighty-nine names on the tax list, and the number of families then in the town was doubtless fifty or more, a number making it the duty of the town "to provide a School Master to teach children to read and write." In that year the first tax was assessed for a public school amounting to £50, O. T. From that time till the war of the Revolution and after, with the exception of the years 1752, '53, '54, and 1756 the town at its annual meeting continued to vote a yearly tax for "a School" or "the School," varying in amount from £30. in silver or lawful money, to £800, O. T. In 1780, when the continental paper money had become so depreciated as to be nearly worthless, the nominal amount of the school tax in that currency was £4,000.

From 1750 to 1766, the school tax, like other taxes, was assessed in the Old Tenor paper currency, and varied from £50. O. T., the lowest amount in a year, to £800, the highest. During the war this tax as other taxes of the time, were assessed and payable in the Continental paper money, varying in amount from £50. in 1775, to £4,000, in 1780.

In 1753 the town "Voted to give Lieut. Samuel Cumings £52,

O. T., for his house which was Dea. Worcester's, for a school house, and he is to have the use of said house on Sabbath days." But in 1755 it was "Voted to give Samuel Cumings one half of the old meeting-house for the use of the house the Town bought of him for a School-house the three years they had it, and said Cumings is to have his house again." In 1760 an article was inserted in the warrant for the annual meeting, "To see if the Town would build a School-house." The question upon this article coming up in the meeting, it was "decided in the negative." From the doings of this meeting it is evident that the town owned no school-house in 1760.

Till the year 1771 it would be naturally inferred, from the language used in voting the yearly school tax, that but a *single* school was kept in the town at the same time—this tax being uniformly voted for "*a*" school, or "*the*" school, as if but one,—the school law in force at the time, apparently, contemplating but a single school in towns not having a sufficient number of families for a grammar school. Still it appears from other votes and doings of the town, that there may have been several schools kept at the same time in different parts of the town.

In 1752, it was "Voted that the school should be *moved* for the benefit of the town;" and in 1755, £100, O. T., were assessed as a school tax, and it was "Voted that the School should be kept in the four quarters of the town; Each quarter to draw £25, and to keep the school when and where they please." This was what was called the *movable* or "*perambulatory*" school.

The earliest approximation to any permanent local division of the town for school purposes is to be found in the records for 1757. The town that year voted £400, O. T. for "a school," "and that it be granted to every suitable number of persons that shall agree together in any part of the town (to have) their proportion for keeping a school among themselves, and those that dont joyn, their money is to be paid into the treasury for a school in the middle of the town." The like vote continued to be passed for many years after. These associations were wholly voluntary on the part of those who united in them, and are called in the records, "School Classes," "School Societies," and sometimes "School Squadrons," but in no instance, in the early records, "school districts." In 1760 a committee was chosen "to divide the town for schools, and to apportion the money between the summer and winter schools."

In 1761, Dea. Worcester, Benjamin Abbot, James Jewett, Stephen Ames and Samuel Cumings were chosen a committee to fix places for school-houses, and the next year, 1762, the town " voted that school houses should be built when there is a sufficient number that shall sign to any certain place to build the houses and each party is to build their own house." This is the last reference I find in the town records to school-houses, and I think there is no reasonable doubt that such houses were built in accordance with that vote, but if so, how many, when, in what parts of the town, and at what cost, these records do not tell us.

In 1771 the town " voted £36, in Lawful Money, (or silver) for schools to be laid out in the usual manner " and " that Mr. Emerson keep the Grammar School for the town as usual, viz,: to teach all those in the town that shall present themselves in the languages." The foregoing vote is the earliest notice of the Hollis Grammar School to be found in the records, but the words " *as usual*" imply that such a school had been kept for some years before.

According to the census of the town taken in 1767, Hollis then contained 809 inhabitants, and then had 150 names on its tax lists, and without doubt there were then in the town more than 100 families. If so it was the duty of the inhabitants, under the existing school laws, as early as that year, and probably earlier, to establish a grammar-school. In 1774 the town " Voted that the grammar-school should be kept the whole year in the four southern *squadrons*, the other *squadrons* to school out their money as usual." As that part of the town north of the meeting-house was somewhat larger in extent than the part south of it, we may fairly presume, that in 1771, there were as many as eight "*School Squadrons*" in the town, and not unlikely as many school-houses. In 1775 the town " Voted that Mr. William Cumings keep the grammar-school." The foregoing are all the minutes to be found upon the town records relative to the Hollis grammar-school, before the war of the Revolution, and we infer from them that such of the Hollis youth as wished for instruction in the " tongues," were taught by the Rev. Mr. Emerson, till the year 1775, when he was succeeded by Mr. Cumings. The name of this Mr. Cumings is found upon one of the Hollis military rolls in 1775 with the title of " School-Master." He was for many years a teacher in the Hollis schools, and long after his decease was gratefully and affectionately remembered, as " Master Cumings." In the two last years of the war, and several years after it, he held the office of Town Clerk, and the Hollis records of the time still exhibit abundant evidence of his neat and elegant penmanship, and of his ability not only to write his mother tongue correctly and in good taste, but also to garnish the productions of his pen with a somewhat pedantic display of his knowledge of Latin.

It is very evident from documents that yet exist, that the youth of Hollis, before the Revolution, were taught to " read and write," as required in the existing school law. I have seen and examined more than one hundred of the original signatures of the Hollis revolutionary soldiers, all, with but rare exceptions, written in a fair, legible hand, and but two " marksmen " among them all, and these supposed not to have been born in the town. Judging from the published histories of many towns, which I have read, it is very certain that the schools in Hollis were better cared for than in many towns both older and more populous. It was not uncommon, both in New Hampshire and Massachusetts, for towns or their selectmen to be indicted and fined for their neglect to comply with the school laws. Other towns sometimes voted to indemnify their selectmen for such neglects,—it costing less money to pay the fines than to support the schools. But no such vote is to be found in the doings of any Hollis town meeting, nor have I learned that any criminal complaint was ever made against the town or its selectmen for violation of the school laws.

This comparatively good condition of the public schools in Hollis is undoubtedly due, in great measure, to the efforts of their worthy minister, Mr. Emerson, and some of the prominent early settlers of the town, and the active interest they took in the cause of popular education. " The good which men do," as well as " the evil," lives after them, and there can be no doubt that the salutary influence of Mr. Emerson and his compeers, felt alike by parents and the youth of Hollis, continued long after their decease.

Some of the good fruits of this influence were to be seen in the unusually large number of the Hollis youth, born during the life of Mr. Emerson, who sought the advantages of a collegiate and professional education. In the short biographical notices that I have read of Mr. Emerson it was said of him that he was " a popular and successful minister," and that " his praise was in all the churches." The youth of Hollis who were born and grew up under his ministry, no doubt could say with equal truth, that his praise was in all the

schools.   Mr. Emerson, as we have seen, was settled in the ministry
over his society in 1743, and his connection with it as sole and associate pastor, continued till his death in 1801, a period of fifty-six years.
It will be seen from the lists of Hollis graduates of colleges, and of
ministers, physicians and lawyers, not graduates, that eleven of the
youth of Hollis, born before the war of the Revolution, were graduates of colleges, and an equal number, not graduates, also born before 1775, became ministers or physicians.   It may also be seen that
Hollis furnished twenty-eight graduates of colleges, born between
the years 1775, and 1800, during the pastorate of Mr. Emerson, a
number equal to more than one for each year during the last quarter
of the last century.

*The names of the Hollis Graduates of Colleges, and of Minis-
ters and Physicians, not Graduates, born before 1775, are presented in the following Lists:*

GRADUATES OF COLLEGES.

Rev. Peter Powers	born 1728	Rev. Samuel Worcester, D. D.	born 1770
" Josiah Goodhue	" 1735	" Daniel Emerson, Jun.	" 1771
" Henry Cumings, D. D.	" 1739	Jacob A. Cumings	" 1772
" Joseph Emerson	" 1759	" David Jewett	" 1773
Dr. Samuel Emerson	" 1764	Abel Farley	" 1773
Rev. Josiah Burge	" 1766		

MINISTERS AND PHYSICIANS NOT GRADUATES.

Dr. Abijah Wright,	born 1746	Rev. Leonard Worcester	born 1767
" Peter Emerson	" 1749	" Thomas Worcester	" 1768
Rev. Samuel Ambrose	" 1757	" David Smith	" 1769
" Noah Worcester, D. D.	" 1758	Dr. Joseph F. Eastman	" 1772
" Joseph Wheat	" 1759	Rev. David Brown	" 1773
Dr. William Hale	" 1762		

*The names of the Hollis Graduates of Colleges born between
the years 1775 and 1800 are presented below:*

Joseph Emerson, 2d	born 1777	Daniel Kendrick	born 1785
Mighill Blood	" 1777	William Tenney	" 1785
Manasseh Smith	" 1779	Eli Smith, Jr	" 1787
Stephen Farley Jun.	" 1779	Ralph Emerson	" 1787
Caleb J. Tenney	" 1780	Leonard Jewett	" 1787
Jonathan B. Eastman	" 1780	John Proctor	" 1787
Nehemiah Hardy	" 1781	Samuel E. Smith	" 1788
Benjamin Burge	" 1782	Luke Eastman	" 1790
Joseph E. Smith	" 1782	George F. Farley	" 1793
Benjamin M. Farley	" 1783	Wm. P. Kendrick	" 1794
Joseph E. Worcester	" 1784	David P. Smith	" 1795
Grant Powers	" 1784	Solomon Hardy	" 1796
Fifield Holt	" 1784	Eli N. Sawtelle	" 1799
Noah Hardy	" 1785	Taylor G. Worcester	" 1799

I am indebted to my kind friend the late Rev. Dr. Bouton, for the following very sensible and graceful letter written to Mr. Emerson, in 1770, by Gov. John Wentworth, upon committing to the tutorship of Mr. Emerson, a young orphan nephew. The letter is alike creditable to the head and heart of Gov. Wentworth, and is pleasant and pertinent evidence that the good reputation of Mr. Emerson as an instructor of youth and friend of education was well understood beyond the limits of Hollis.

"WENTWORTH HOUSE, WOLFEBOROUGH, }
28, July 1770. }

" *The Rev. Mr. Emerson at Hollis,*

"*Rev. Sir:*—In consequence of a letter I have just received from Major Hobart, who writes me that you are ready to receive my nephew, Mark Wentworth, and to take charge of his Education, I herewith send him and Earnestly beg your greatest care of his health and instruction. He is a fine boy, of great Spirit, which naturally leads him to playful negligence. He has also acquired idle habits which will be easily reformed under a strict discipline, equally removed from cruelty and levity. He must know that you in all things are to be obeyed and never suffer any sort of disobedience to your orders. This is more peculiarly necessary for him, as he has to be brought up in the Navy, where implicit obedience is necessary for the service and for him. As to his diet, I prefer simple, plain, and plentiful; his tender age admits no other instruction than reading and writing. But no age is too tender to receive inculcations of practical neatness, honor and virtue. With these, enriched by a just habitual piety, he cannot fail of being a good man, the first great object of Education. I hope hereafter to have opportunity to confer with you upon a future course of learning adapted to his genius and profession. In the mean time I beg leave to assure you, that I can never think any expense too great which he benefits by, and therefore gladly commit him to your care, not doubting but I shall rejoice in making you the most grateful acknowledgements for his improvement, which is the greatest and most earnest desire of Revd Sir,

Your most humble Servant,

JOHN WENTWORTH."

CHAPTER IX.

EARLY COLONIAL LAWS.—TOWN OFFICERS AND THEIR DUTIES.—MODERATORS.—SELECTMEN.—CONSTABLES.—FIELD DRIVERS.—TITHING MEN.—HOGREEVES.—DEER REEVES AND DEER.—WOLVES AND RATTLESNAKES.—QUALIFICATIONS OF VOTERS.—HOUSES OF CORRECTION.—THE POOR AND THEIR SUPPORT.—WARNING TO LEAVE TOWN.—SLAVERY IN NEW HAMPSHIRE.—1746 to 1775.

The town officers authorized to be elected at the annual town meeting in March, before the Revolution, were a Moderator for the town meetings, Town clerk, Treasurer, Selectmen or " *Townsmen*," Constables, Fence viewers, Field Drivers or "Haywards," Surveyors of highways, Surveyors of lumber, Sealers of weights and measures, Sealers of leather, Tithing-men, Deer-Reeves, Hogreeves, Pound-keepers, Overseers of the poor, and Overseers of houses of correction.

The Moderator then, as now, was the presiding officer of the town meeting. No person was allowed to speak in meeting without leave of that dignitary, nor "when any other person was speaking orderly," and all persons were to be silent at the request of the Moderator under the penalty of five shillings.*

The number of Selectmen might be three, five, seven or nine. Before the Revolution the number chosen in Hollis was either three or five, the last number having been chosen in fourteen out of twenty-nine years from 1746 to 1775. The selectmen were paid or not paid for their services, as decided by vote of the town at their election—the town sometimes voting to pay them for their time and expenses, sometimes their expenses only—and occasionally that they should have no pay for either. In respect to several matters of public concern the Selectmen, under the colony laws, had much

*Col. Laws, p. 72.

more power and a wider field of duty than at the present day. The law not providing for other assessors of taxes it was made the duty of the Selectmen to assess all the polls and estates of the inhabitants according to the known ability of each person for the support of the ministry, schools, the poor, and for all other town expenses.* They also had the whole charge of the public schools, including the providing of suitable buildings or rooms for teaching, and the employment and paying of teachers.†

Constables. One of the principal duties of Constables was to collect the taxes. Till the year 1765, but one Constable was elected in Hollis who was charged with the collection of the taxes for the whole town. After that year two were chosen, one of whom was for the west side or west half of the town, the other for the east half. Two corresponding tax lists were made, one for each constable, the one list containing the names of the taxpayers in the western division, the other those in the eastern.

Field Drivers. This office in this state has long since grown into disuse. In colonial times it was the duty of these officers to take up and impound neat cattle and other domestic animals found unlawfully running at large in the highways or upon the common land. For many years after the first settlement of Hollis, a very large part of the unimproved land was unfenced, the rights of the owners of such lands being in common. These common lands furnished much valuable pasturage, and by the Province law neat cattle and other domestic animals were not permitted to feed upon them without the consent of the land owners. If such animals were found at large upon such lands without the consent of the owners, it was the duty of the Field Driver to impound them, for which service he was allowed one shilling each for horses and neat cattle, and three pence each for sheep and swine, to be paid by the owner of the animals.

As early as 1747 the town meeting in Hollis "voted that the cattle belonging to the town be *booked* within a week and go at large upon the commons this year, and to proceed with cattle that dont belong to the town according to the law of the Province." The next year it was "voted that residents and non-residents turn out cattle according to their rights, and that all others be driven away." The like votes for the protection of the commons continued to be passed for many years after.

*Col. Laws, p, 138.
†Col, Laws. pp. 143, 163.

Tithing Men. The ancient office of Tithing-Man has also become obsolete, and the *name*, once a terror to rude and wayward youth, very nearly so. It was among the duties of these officers to inspect licensed houses, and to inform of all disorders in them. Also to inform of all idle and disorderly persons, profane swearers, and Sabbath breakers, and to aid in their arrest and punishment. They carried as a badge of their office a *black staff* two feet long, tipped at one end for about three inches with brass or pewter.* It was customary in Hollis to choose four of these officers, two of whom were known as Tithingmen " *below*," the other two as Tithingmen " *above*." All of them were expected to attend meeting on the Sabbath—the first two to have their seats on the lower floor, and to take note of all disorder and irreverence " below," the other two to be installed in the gallery, and to observe and report all disturbances and breaches of decorum " above."

Hogreeves. By a law of the Province passed in 1719, swine were not permitted to run at large, between the first day of April and the first day of October, without being yoked and rung in the way described in the law, and two persons were required to be chosen at the yearly town meeting to enforce the Act. The " regulation " hog yoke was to be of wood, to be in length equal to the depth of the swine's neck, above the neck, and half as long below. The ring was to be of strong flexible iron wire inserted in the top of the nose to prevent rooting, the ends of the wire being so twisted together as to project one inch above the nose.† By the custom of the town all the young men of Hollis, married within the year next preceding the annual elections, were entitled to the compliment of being chosen to this responsible office.

Deer Reeves. The forests in most parts of New Hampshire for many years after its first settlement abounded with deer. Both the flesh and skins of these animals being of great value to the settlers, laws were passed to punish the killing of them at such seasons as would diminish their increase. By a Province law of 1741 it was made a crime to kill deer between the last day of December and the first day of August. An offender against this law was liable to a fine of £10. If not able to pay he might be sentenced to work forty days for the Government, and fifty days if he should offend a second time. It was made the duty of the town at the annual election to choose two officers, known as *Deer Reeves*

*Col. Laws, p. 58.
†Col. Laws, p. 173.

or *Deer Keepers*, to see that this law was observed, with power to
enter and search all places where they had cause to suspect that the
skins or flesh of deer, unlawfully killed, was concealed. The first
Deer Reeves in Hollis were Samuel Farley, Josiah Brown and
William Adams, chosen in 1747—the last, John Cumings and
Elnathan Blood, in 1766.

Wolves and Rattlesnakes. Wolves, the natural and incorrigible
enemies both of deer and man, also abounded at the early settlement of the town, as also did Rattlesnakes, and were the objects of
wholly different laws and policy from those adopted in regard to
deer. By a province law passed in 1719, towns were empowered
to pay a bounty of 20s. per. head, (subsequently increased) for killing grown wolves, and one-half of the like bounty for "wolf
whelps." In pursuance of this law and its amendments, in the years
1760 and 1761, the town voted to pay any Hollis man, who should
kill a wolf within the town a bounty of 40s. and in 1766 this bounty
was increased to $10.00.

The policy of extermination in respect to *Rattlesnakes*, with
which parts of the town were then infested, was adopted earlier than
that in regard to wolves. At the third parish meeting, held in
West Dunstable, in March, 1740, it was "Voted that if any person
should make it appear to the Parish Committee that during the year
he had killed one or more rattlesnakes within the parish, he shall
be paid from the parish treasury one Shilling for each snake so
killed."

Voters and their qualifications. Prior to the Revolution, the
qualifications for voting in town meetings varied with the objects
of the meetings. To be qualified to vote for town officers, the person offering his vote was required to be a free holder in the town or
to have other taxable estate of the value of £20.*

In the choice and settlement of a minister for a town or parish,
and fixing his salary, the right to vote was limited to the owners of
real estate.† Nothwithstanding this restriction of the right to vote,
the taxes for the support of the minister were assessed by the Selectmen on land, *personal estate and polls* in the same manner as
taxes for other town charges. To be competent to vote for a delegate to the General Court, the elector was required to be the
owner of real estate in the town of the value of £50, and the candidate, in order to be eligible to that office, to be possessed of real
estate of the value of £300.

---

*Col. Laws, p. 137.   †Ib. p. 55.

Houses of Correction. A province law passed in 1719 provided
for the erection and regulation of *Houses of Correction* "for the
keeping, correcting and setting to work of *rogues, vagabonds,
common beggars* and *lewd* and *idle persons.*" Such persons on conviction before the Court of Sessions or a Justice of the Peace were
to be sent to the House of Correction and set to work under the master or overseer of that institution. Upon his admission, the unlucky
culprit was to be put in shackles or to be whipped, not to exceed
ten stripes, unless the warrant for his commitment directed otherwise. By an act of the General Assembly adopted in 1766, the law
for the maintenance of Houses of Correction was extended to towns
with the like powers and duties in respect to them.* It appears
from the following vote of a special town meeting, on the 18th of
March, 1773, that the people of Hollis had availed themselves of the
right to establish such an institution for the town. It was then
" Voted that Capt. Joshua Wright be overseer of the House of Correction, and take all who may be sent there according to law."
The foregoing vote is the only notice I find in the records of such an
asylum for rogues and vagabonds. Both the records and traditions
are alike silent in respect to the place of its location and the time it
was continued, and also as to the names and numbers of its inmates,
sent to the overseer to be welcomed on their introduction with
shackles and *stripes.*

The Stocks and Whipping Post. The punishment of malefac-
tors, " by making their feet of the offender fast in the stocks," is as
ancient as the days of Job,† and it is very evident from the recorded
experiences of the Apostles Paul and Silas that neither the stocks nor
whipping posts were unknown in their times. Sustained alike by
abundant Biblical precedent as well as by the laws of the province,
our order-loving ancestors were not slow in providing their town
with both of these terrors of evil-doers. At a special town meeting
in June, 1746, about two months after the town was incorporated,
" Voted that the Selectmen provide stocks ;" and at a town meeting
in the month of January next after, " Voted to Accept the Account
of Josiah Conant for making the Stocks." The town whipping-
post, the fitting companion of the stocks, held its place near the
front of the meeting-house, not far from the west line of the common,
till after the commencement of the present century, and was in use

*Col. Laws, pp. 74, 139, 202.
†Job, Chap. 13, v. 27.

(8)

within the memory of persons still living, with its inseparable associate, the " cat o' nine tails."   The varied practical uses to which
the stocks and whipping-post were applied may be readily inferred
by reference to a few of the cotemporary criminal laws for the punishment of minor offences, most of which were within the jurisdiction of justices of the peace.   Some of these punishments were as
follows ;

Profane Cursing and Swearing.   " For the first offence—a
fine of one shilling.   " If not paid the culprit to be set in the stocks
two hours—For more than one profane Oath at the same time—a
fine of two shillings and to be set in the stocks not more than three
hours."

Drunkenness.   " For first offence, a fine of 5 shillings—if not
able to pay, the convict to be set in the stocks not more than three
hours."

Defamation.   If found guilty the offender to be fined 20 shillings.
If not paid to be set in the stocks not more than three hours.*

Robbing Gardens and Orchards.   If the prisoner was not able
to pay his fine to be set in the stocks or whipped at the discretion of
the Justice.†

Insolence or Violence to Women on the Highway.   For first
offence, whipping not exceeding ten stripes.   For second offence, to
be burnt in the hand.†

Petit Larceny.   The offender to forfeit treble the value of the
property stolen, and to be fined not exceeding £5, or whipped not
more than twenty stripes.   If not paid, the culprit to be sold for a
term of time to be fixed at the discretion of the court.

The following sentence of one *Charles Newton,* convicted of steal-
ing property of the value of three shillings, is copied from the early
court records of Grafton County.   It is here presented as illustrating the state of the law in like cases in the times of King George.
The person from whom the property was stolen, and who was
charged with the duty of selling the culprit into servitude, was *Dea.
John Willoughby,* one of the many worthy emigrants from Hollis,
to Plymouth just before the war of the Revolution.

" *Grafton, ss. Superior Court, June Term, 1774.*

" Dominus Rex. v. Charles Newton. It is considered by the
Court that the said Charles Newton pay a fine to his Majesty of

---

*Col. Laws. p. 31.
†Col. Laws, p. 189.

Ten Shillings, or be whipped ten stripes on the naked back by the
hands of the common whipper, between the hours of 11 o'clock
A. M., and 2 o'clock, P. M., to-morrow, being the 16th day of
June, A. D., 1774.—Also that he pay to John Willoughby nine
shillings, being treble the value of the goods stolen and costs of
prosecution. That in want of the payment of the said nine shillings and cost, he be sold into servitude by the said Willoughby to
any of his Majesty's liege subjects for the Term of Six months
to commence on the 15th day of June, A. D. 1775, and that he
stand committed till sentence be performed."

" Attest,   GEORGE KING, Clk."

The Poor and their Support.   By a law of the province of
1719, continued in force till long after the Revolution, all persons
having dwelt in a town for three months, without being legally
warned to depart, became inhabitants, and in case of inability to
support themselves from sickness or other cause, were required to
be relieved by the town. By the same law the town could protect
itself from the risk of the liability for the support of all new
comers by warning them to leave town within the three months
after their first coming. By an Act passed in 1771, the time for
this warning to leave was extended to one year. The warrant for
this " Warning out," as it was called, was issued by the selectmen
to a constable, commanding the new comer to depart from the
town within a time fixed in the warrant, and in case of his neglect
to leave, the law authorized the issuing of a second warrant for his
removal to his former residence. If a person so removed afterwards returned, he could be dealt with as a " vagabond," and sent
to the house of correction.

The province laws of the times provided for the election by
towns of Overseers of the Poor, and in 1749, Capt. Peter Powers,
Zedekiah Drury, and Nathaniel Townsend were chosen to that
office. This is the only instance I find in the early records of an
election to that office, and the instances were very rare in which
any special tax was levied for the support of the poor. The care
of the poor as well as the protection of the town from the increase
of paupers by the " Warning out" of new settlers appear to have
been left wholly to the selectmen. It is very evident from the many
entries upon the records of the issuing and return of these notices
that this harsh and invidious duty of warning new settlers to leave

the town was very diligently performed by the Hollis selectmen and constables from its first settlement, till near the commencement of the present century.

The first of these notices found in the records was in June, 1746, the year of the charter, and was directed to Wid. Mary Blanchard. The next in time, now to be found, was dated July 6, 1749, and served upon James Ferguson and John Thompson, requiring them " to depart from the town in 14 days." Between 1746 and 1797 there are records of nearly two hundred of the like warrants and notices, a part of them to single individuals, but much the largest portion embracing whole families, giving the names of the husband, wife and children. All new comers, indiscriminately, appear to have been exposed to these inhospitable notices, whether likely to become paupers or not. As evidence of this lack of discrimination, I find in these warrants between 1767 and 1774, the names of no less than seven persons who were afterwards Hollis soldiers in the Revolution, and the like number who had been in the army, and were warned to leave after the war was ended. It is very evident, however, that the persons so warned did not ordinarily obey this summons to leave, nor does it appear that they were expected to do so, as we find in these warrants not only the names of so many Hollis soldiers, who did not go away, but also the names of many others, who were served with the like notices, and afterwards remained, and became substantial freeholders and valuable and respected citizens. It is but just to say that this odious and barbarous custom had the sanction of a general law of the province, and I find no reason to believe that it was executed more offensively in Hollis than in other New Hampshire towns.

Slavery. African slavery existed in New Hampshire under the sanction of the province laws till near the close of the war of the Revolution. According to a census taken in 1767, the whole population of the province was 52,700, of which number 384 were slaves, of whom there were two in Hollis. In 1775 the whole population of New Hampshire had increased to 82,200, and the slaves to 656, of whom four were in Hollis.

I am indebted to a granddaughter of Col. David Webster for the original deed of sale made to him of two negro slaves. A copy of this deed is presented below, showing the mode of transferring the supposed legal title to this kind of property in human flesh in accordance with the laws then in force in New England. ' Col.

Webster was a distinguished New Hampshire officer in the war of the Revolution, who for some years before the war resided in Hollis. and removed from Hollis to Plymouth about the year 1765.

" Know all Men by these Presents that I Jacob Whittier of Methuen in the County of Essex in the Province of Massachusetts Bay. Yeoman. in consideration of the Sum Sixty pounds lawful money paid me by David Webster of Plymouth in the Province of N. Hampshire. Gent. have sold and by these Presents do sell unto the said David Webster, one negro man named Cicero. and also one Negro Woman. named Dinah. both being servants for life. and now in my possession. To have and to hold the said Negroes during the natural life of each of them Respectively to the said David Webster, his heirs and assigns. according to the common usage and Laws of said Provinces. In Witness Whereof I have hereunto set my hand and seal the 13th day of December Anno Domini 1769, in the 10th year of his Majesty's reign.
Signed Sealed and delivered in presence of us.

JACOB WHITTIER.   [Seal.] "

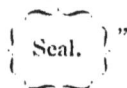

EBEN V. BARKER.
ABIGAIL BARKER.

CHAPTER X.

THE NEW HAMPSHIRE GENERAL COURT.—MEMBERS FROM HOLLIS
AND THE OLD DUNSTABLE TOWNS BEFORE THE REVOLUTION.
CONTESTED ELECTION IN 1762.—DIVISION OF THE PROVINCE
INTO COUNTIES.—ORGANIZATION OF HILLSBOROUGH COUNTY.
COUNTY OFFICERS FROM HOLLIS.—THE PINE TREE LAW.—ITS
UNPOPULARITY AND TROUBLE IN ENFORCING IT.—RIOT AT
WEARE.—GOV. JOHN WENTWORTH.—HIS PERSONAL POPU-
LARITY.—ADDRESS FROM THE PEOPLE OF HOLLIS.—JURORS
TO HOLLIS.—THE FIRST TRIAL FOR MURDER IN HILLSBOROUGH
COUNTY.—POPULATION BEFORE 1775.—1741 TO 1775.

THE NEW HAMPSHIRE GENERAL COURT.

From 1741. (the year when the new province line was settled).
till 1775. the New Hampshire General Court consisted of a Governor and twelve Councillors appointed by the King. and a House of
Representatives varying in number from thirteen to thirty-one.
elected by the towns. The only member of the Governor's Council.
from the towns formed out of the territory of Old Dunstable, was
Col. Joseph Blanchard. a resident of the new town of the same
name. who was appointed in 1741. and held his office till his death
in 1758.

MEMBERS OF THE HOUSE FROM HOLLIS AND THE OLD DUNSTABLE TOWNS.

There was no member of the House of Representatives from
either of the old Dunstable towns till 1752. when Jonathan
Lovewell was chosen for Dunstable and Merrimack. From 1762 to
1768 these towns were coupled together and represented as follows:

1762. Dunstable and Hollis—Dr. John Hale.
Merrimack and Monson—Joseph Blanchard. Esq.
Nottingham West and Litchfield—Capt. Samuel Greeley.
1768. Dunstable and Hollis—Dr. John Hale.
Merrimack and Monson—Capt. John Chamberlain.
Nottingham West and Litchfield—James Underwood. Esq.

I find the following scrap of characteristic political history in respect to the election for Hollis and Dunstable in 1762, in the New Hampshire Historical Collections (v. 1, p. 57) which is here presented as follows:

" What is now Hollis was formerly the West Parish of Dunstable. For a number of years after Hollis was incorporated, the two towns were classed together to send a man to represent them to the General Court. Dunstable being the older town, required the Elections to be uniformly held there, until Hollis became the most populous, when it was requested by Hollis that they should be held in those towns alternately, that Each might have an Equal chance. But Dunstable did not consent to this proposal. Hollis feeling some resentment, mustered all its forces, leaving at home scarcely man or horse. Previously to this time the person chosen had been uniformly selected from Dunstable. But on this occasion the people of Dunstable, finding they were outnumbered, their town clerk mounted a pile of shingles and called on the inhabitants to bring in their votes for Moderator for *Dunstable*. The town clerk of Hollis mounted another pile and called on the inhabitants of *Dunstable* and *Hollis* to bring in their votes for Moderator for *Dunstable* and *Hollis*. The result was that —— Lovewell, Esq., was declared Moderator for Dunstable and Dea. Francis Worcester, Moderator for Dunstable and Hollis. Each Moderator proceeded in the same manner to call the votes for Representative. Jonathan Lovewell, Esq., was declared chosen to represent Dunstable and Dr. John Hale was declared chosen to represent Dunstable and Hollis. Accordingly both repaired to Portsmouth to attend the General Court. Lovewell was allowed to take his seat, and Hale rejected. Hale, however, instead of returning home, took measures to acquaint the Governor with what had transpired and waited the issue. It was not long before Secretary Theodore Atkinson came into the House and proclaimed aloud, ' I have special orders from his Excellency to dissolve this House : Accordingly you are dissolved.' · *God save the King.*'"

It appears from the Journal of the House that the election of both Lovewell and Hale was set aside, and the House immediately dissolved by the Governor. A very few days after, a second election was held, and Hale was returned by the sheriff, and at once obtained his seat without further objection.*

*Prov. Papers, Vol. 6, p. 806.

Dr. Hale was afterwards re-elected and continued to represent Hollis and Dunstable till 1768, when he was succeeded by Col. Samuel Hobart, who, as appears from the Journal, represented Hollis only for the next six years till the Revolution. In 1767 Dr. Hale was Lieut. Colonel of the Regiment of Militia to which Hollis was attached, and Col. Hobart, Major of the same regiment. In 1775, Hale was appointed Colonel of that regiment, and Hobart Colonel of the Second New Hampshire Regiment of Minute Men, ordered to be raised by the New Hampshire Provincial Congress in September, 1775.*

Before the Revolution, Justices of the Peace as well as the Governor and Council held their commissions, as Magistrates, from the King. The only persons in Hollis known or supposed to have been so commissioned were Samuel Cumings, Sen., the first Town clerk, his son Samuel Cumings, Jun., John Hale, Samuel Hobart and Benjamin Whiting, the first sheriff of Hillsborough County. Samuel Cumings, Jun., and Whiting were Loyalists or Tories, and are supposed to have left the State early in 1777 and never afterwards returned, and together with Thomas Cumings, a brother of the former, were proscribed by an act of the New Hampshire General Court passed in 1778, forbidden to return and their estates confiscated.†

ORGANIZATION OF HILLSBOROUGH COUNTY.

. Previously to 1771 there had been no division of New Hampshire into counties. Till that year the province, in law, was but a single county, and the courts of law, as well as the sessions of the General Court, were ordinarily held at Portsmouth, near the S. E. corner of the province. That part of New Hampshire between the Merrimack and Connecticut rivers had for many years been largely settled, and the settlers west of the Merrimack had for a long time been greatly dissatisfied with the inconvenience, delays and expense incident to their being so remote from the courts of justice and seat of government. As early as 1754 the people of Hollis, with a very large portion of the settlers west of the Merrimack, united in petitions to the General Court setting forth their grievances,

and praying for a division of the province into counties. But
no such division was made till 1771. On the 19th of March of that
year the General Court passed an act dividing the province into the
five original counties of Rockingham. Strafford. Hillsborough,
Grafton and Cheshire. These counties were so named by Governor Wentworth in honor of some of his friends in England connected with the English government.*

The county of Hillsborough was organized the same year, with
the county seat at Amherst. The town meeting in Hollis, held in
August of that year, "Voted to raise £100. for a prison at Amherst,
provided it should be built on the South side of the Souhegan
river."

Two of the first Judges of the Court of Sessions for the county
were Matthew Thornton, of Merrimack, and Samuel Hobart, of
Hollis. Benjamin Whiting, also of Hollis, was the first high
Sheriff, and Hobart the first county Treasurer and Register of
Deeds, his office being kept in Hollis.

THE PINE TREE LAW. ITS UNPOPULARITY AND TROUBLE IN ENFORCING IT.

It will be remembered by the careful reader of the town charter of Hollis that all *White Pine Trees* growing within the town
and fit "for the royal navy" were reserved to the King for that
use. The same reservations of white pine trees for the like purpose were made in other New Hampshire town charters granted
by the royal governors. As early as 1722, the New Hampshire
General Court passed an act making it a penal offence for any
person to cut White Pine Trees of twelve inches in diameter and
over, a law that was continued in force till the Revolution. By this
law the fine for cutting such trees of 12 inches in diameter was £5,
—12 to 18 inches in diameter, £10,—from 18 to 24 inches, £20,—
exceeding 24 inches, £50,—and all lumber made from trees unlawfully cut was forfeited to the King.†

It may well be supposed that this law was not popular with the
New Hampshire owners of saw mills, and farmers whose lands
abounded with those trees, which were quite as useful and needful
for the dwelling-houses and meeting-houses of the inhabitants as
for the King's navy. At the time Hillsborough County was

*Belknap, p. 341.
†Col. Laws, pp. 226, 229.

organized. Gov. John Wentworth held the office of " *Surveyor of
the King's Woods*," coupled with the authority and duty of enforcing this hated law, and he had in different parts of the province his
deputies to aid in its execution.   It was among the duties of these
deputies, at the expense of the land owner, to mark all of the
King's Pine Trees, on land proposed to be cleared, before the
owner should begin his clearing.   If lumber made from the
King's trees, marked or unmarked, was found at saw-mills or elsewhere, it was made the duty of the deputies to seize and sell it for
the benefit of his Majesty's treasury.

PINE TREE RIOT IN WEARE.

In the spring of 1772 an incident occurred in the town of Weare,
in the northerly part of Hillsborough county, that well illustrates
the bitter and settled hostility of public sentiment to this odious
law.   A citizen of that town of the name of *Mudgett*, with others,
had been charged by a deputy surveyor with unlawfully cutting the
king's trees, the lumber made from which was then at one of the
saw-mills in Weare.   A complaint was made against the offender
and a warrant issued for his arrest, and put into the hands of Sheriff
Whiting for execution.   The sheriff, taking with him an assistant,
repaired forthwith to Weare and made prisoner of the accused.
The arrest being late in the afternoon, the prisoner suggested that if
the officer would wait till the next morning he would furnish the
necessary bail for his appearance to the next court.   The sheriff
acquiesced in this suggestion, and he, with his assistants, went to a
tavern near by to pass the night.   The coming of the sheriff, with
the nature of his mission, to Weare, was very soon made known to
the townsmen of the accused, who, to the number of twenty or
more, met together, and during the night made their plans for bail
of a different sort from that understood by the sheriff the evening
before. , Very early in the morning, while the sheriff was yet in
bed, he was roused from his slumbers by his prisoner who told him
that his bail was waiting at his door.   Whiting complained at being
so early disturbed in his slumbers.   The proposed bail, however,
without waiting to listen to any complaints of this kind, promptly
entered his sleeping-room, each furnished with a tough, flexible
switch, an implement better adapted for making his mark upon the
back of the sheriff than for writing the name of the bail at the
foot of a bail bond.   Without allowing their victim time to dress

himself. one of the company, as is said, held him by his hands, and
another by his feet. while the rest in turn proceeded to make their
marks upon the naked back of the sheriff more to their own satisfaction than for his comfort or delight.   Having in this way, as they
said. squared and crossed out their pine tree accounts with the
principal. they afterwards settled substantially in like manner with
his assistant.   Having in this manner satisfied their accounts with
these officials their horses were led to the door of the tavern. ready
saddled and bridled. with their manes, tails and ears closely
cropped, and their owners invited to mount and leave.   Being slow
to do so, they were assisted upon their horses by some of the company and in that plight rode away from Weare. followed by the
shouts and jeers of the rioters.

The sheriff was not of a temper to overlook or forgive such gross
abuse and insults.   He at once appealed to the colonels of the two
nearest regiments of militia. and with their aid called out the *posse
comitatus*, who, armed with muskets, marched to Weare to arrest
the offenders.   The rioters for the time disappeared, but afterwards
surrendered themselves, or were arrested. and eight of them were
indicted for assault and riot. at the September Term of the Superior
Court, 1772.   At that term they were arraigned and all pleaded
that they "would not farther contend with our Lord the King but
would submit to his Grace."   Upon this plea the court fined them
the very moderate sum of twenty shillings each with cost.   This
very slight punishment for such an outrage upon the high sheriff.
when executing the legal process of the court. would seem to indicate that the sympathies of the bench were quite as much with the
prisoners at the bar and popular sentiment as with the sheriff and
the Pine tree law.   This law as it was enforced was more oppres-
sive and offensive to the people of those times than the Stamp tax
and Tea tax. and there is little doubt that the attempted execution
of it contributed quite as much as either or both of those laws to
the remarkable unanimity of the New Hampshire yeomanry in
their hostility to the British Government in the civil war that soon
followed.

CHARACTER OF GOVERNOR WENTWORTH.

Notwithstanding Governor Wentworth continued to hold this
odious office of "Surveyor of the King's Woods." he was personally
very popular with the people of New Hampshire till the out-break

of the war, when, still adhering to the cause of the King, he left
the country. Mr. Sabine, in his Biographies of the Tories of the
Revolution, says of him :

"That his talents were of a high order, his judgment sound, and
his views liberal. That he was a friend of learning, gave to
Dartmouth College its Charter, did much to encourage Agriculture
and to promote the settlement of the province : Zealously labored
to increase its importance, and at the last retired from his official
trusts with a character unimpeached, and with the respect of his
political opponents.*"

Still, in the face of this great popularity, Peter Livius, one of his
council, having been disappointed in his ambition for office, became
his bitter enemy, and in the summer of 1772, made complaint
against the governor to the home government, charging him, among
other things, with oppression in office and corrupt interference with
the courts of justice.

COMPLIMENTARY ADDRESS TO GOVERNOR WENTWORTH.

In reference to this attack upon Governor Wentworth, the people
of Hollis, at their annual town meeting in 1773, unanimously voted
a highly complimentary address to him, the most of which is copied
in the following extracts from the record of the meeting :

"*May it please your Excellency:*

"We, the inhabitants of Holles, being assembled at our annual
town meeting, having been informed that Peter Livius, Esq., has
presented a memorial to the Lords of Trade, * * wherein it is
signified that your Excellency, together with the Honorable Council,
have obstructed the channels of Justice in this Province, &c., &c.
* * We, the Inhabitants of Holles, being sensible of the many
obligations this county and Province are under to your Excellency,
for the repeated and continued instances of your goodness to them
* * in all respects but more especially in your unwearied endeav-
ors that Justice might be duly and impartially administered : * *
We beg leave to assure your Excellency that we shall hold ourselves
in the greatest readiness to bear testimony against all such false
aspersions of your Excellency's administration, and think ourselves
in duty bound to give our voice publickly—and we do it cheerfully
and sincerely in favor of your Excellency's Administration * * *

*Sabine, Vol. 2, p. 411.

and we have no doubt that it has been to the satisfaction of the
people of this county and province * * We beg leave to add that
it is our earnest desire that the Divine Blessing may attend your
Excellency, and that you may be continued in the important place
you now fill for many years to come.

" Voted that Hon. Samuel Hobart and Col. John Hale, Esq.,
wait on his Excellency with this address."

FIRST JURORS FROM HOLLIS.

The names of the first and only jurors from Hollis, to the courts
held at Portsmouth, to be found in the records are under the date of
July 24, 1769, when Ensign Stephen Ames was "*chosen*" Grand
Juror and Noah Worcester, Petit Juror. The first Superior Court
for Hillsborough County was held at Amherst in September, 1771.
The Grand Jurors from Hollis for this court were Lt. Reuben Dow
and William Nevins—Petit Jurors, Capt. Joshua Wright and Dea.
Stephen Jewett.

FIRST TRIAL FOR MURDER AT AMHERST.

The first trial for a capital crime in Hillsborough County was that
of Israel Wilkins, Jun., of Hollis, who was tried upon an indictment
found against him by the Grand Jury in September, 1773, charging
him with the murder of his father, Israel Wilkins, Sen., at Hollis,
Nov 2, 1772. It appears from the proceedings and indictment that
this homicide was the result of a sudden quarrel, in which the deceased was mortally wounded, "by a blow upon the head with a
certain billet of wood in the hand of the defendant of the value 3d,
thereby giving the said deceased upon his left temple, a mortal wound,
of the length of three inches and the depth of one inch, of which
mortal wound the said deceased, after languishing for the space of
three days, then and there died." So says the indictment.

The jury upon the evidence found the defendant guilty of *man-
slaughter* only, that crime being at that time punishable with death,
the same as premeditated murder. The record of the trial, after
reciting the arraignment and plea of the prisoner, the doings of the
court, and the verdict of the jury, concludes as follows : "It being
demanded of the said Israel Wilkins, Jun., Why sentence of Death
should not be passed upon him, the said Wilkins prayed the *benefit
of clergy*, which was granted. Whereupon the prisoner, the said
Wilkins, was burned with a hot iron in the form of the letter T, on

the brawny part of the thumb of his left hand, and it is further considered that the said Wilkins forfeit all his Goods and Chattels to the King."

Not having space in this connection to speak of the origin and history of the ancient popish plea of the "Benefit of Clergy," I take leave to refer the reader, who is curious in such inquiries, to Blackstone's Commentaries on the Laws of England (vol. 4, p. 364.) He would most likely search in vain the New Hampshire court records, as also those of any other American State, for any case in which such a plea has been allowed for the last hundred years. Without further comment I leave the matter as I find it to the curiosity of the bar, and for the "benefit of the clergy" of our times.

POPULATION BEFORE THE REVOLUTION.

I do not find that any census was taken of Hollis prior to 1767. Before that year the best approximation to the number of its inhabitants is to be found in the annual tax-lists. The number of names in those lists in the years mentioned below was as follows :

1746, 75.   1750, 93.   1755, 107.   1760, 117.   1765, 131.   1767, 161.

By the Provincial census, taken in 1767, the population of the old Dunstable towns was as below :

Dunstable, 520.   Merrimack, 400.   Nottingham West, 583.
Holles,   809.   Litchfield, 234.   Monson,   298.

At that time Dunstable had four slaves, Hollis and Nottingham West two each, Litchfield twelve, Merrimack three, Monson none.

In 1775, in September of that year, a second census was taken by the New Hampshire convention. The following statistics relating to the old Dunstable towns are taken from that census :

	whole pop.,		Men in the army,	Slaves,
Dunstable,	705.		40.	7.
Hollis,	" " 1,255.		" " " " 60.	" 4.
Litchfield,	" " 284.		" " " " 13.	" 10.
Merrimack,	" " 606.		" " " " 19.	" 13.
Nottingham West,	" " 649.		" " " " 22.	" 4.
Total,	3499.		154.	38.

Before the taking of that census, Hollis had lost eleven of her soldiers, of whom nine had been killed, and two died of disease.

THE SETTLEMENT OF PLYMOUTH, NEW HAMPSHIRE.—A HOLLIS COLONY.

The war for the conquest of Canada ended in 1761. Many of the soldiers from Hollis who had been in that war, in their toilsome marches through the northern wilderness, had become acquainted

with the fine country on the upper branches of the Connecticut and
Merrimack. They returned to their homes with so favorable im-
pressions of that part of New Hampshire, that in the fall of 1762,
a party of eight men from Hollis went to what is now Plymouth,
to explore the country with a view to settlement there. This ex-
ploration, with their report of it, resulted the next year in obtaining a charter of the town of Plymouth from Benning Wentworth,
then Governor, dated July 16, 1763. Of about sixty grantees
named in this charter, near two-thirds were Hollis men. Emigra-
tion from Hollis at once commenced, and within the next three
years a large number of the former residents of Hollis became settlers in Plymouth, of whom many were afterwards known as in-
fluential and respected citizens of that town. Among them were
Col. David Hobart, afterwards distinguished for his bravery and
good conduct as the Colonel of a New Hampshire Regiment under
Gen. Stark at the battle of Bennington, and Col. David Webster,
who commanded a Regiment of New Hampshire troops at the
taking of Burgoyne at Saratoga, and was afterwards sheriff of
Grafton County. Besides the foregoing, there were Dea. Francis
Worcester, for many years a deacon of the Hollis church and town
treasurer, and afterwards a representative to the General Court from
Plymouth in the war of the Revolution : also three Captains of
companies in the army, viz. : Jotham Cumings, John Willoughby
and Amos Webster, the last of whom was killed at the battle at
Saratoga in the command of a company of infantry attached to Col.
Morgan's famous rifle corps.*

_____

*New Hampshire Hist. Coll., Vol. 3, p. 274.

CHAPTER XI.

BIOGRAPHICAL SKETCHES OF A PORTION OF THE EARLY SETTLERS OF HOLLIS PRIOR TO THE CLOSE OF THE FRENCH WAR OF 1754.

ABBOT, CAPT. BENJAMIN

was from Andover, Mass. His name was on the Hollis Tax Lists in 1750. In 1755 he was Lieutenant in Capt. Power's company, Col. Blanchard's regiment, in the expedition to Crown Point, and was again in the army in 1757. He was selectman in 1752, '53 and '54. His son Benjamin was a soldier in the Revolution. Died January 5, 1776, æt. 46.

ADAMS, WILLIAM

was in West Dunstable in 1738, and signed the petition for the charter of West Dunstable. Married Mary Spears, May 29, 1744. Was a town officer in 1746. His son William was a soldier at Bunker Hill and Bennington. Died August 3, 1757, æt. 39.

AMES, ENSIGN STEPHEN

came from Groton, Mass. Married Jane Robbins in Groton, in 1731. Was in West Dunstable in 1739, selectman in 1747 and 1748, and was a soldier in the French war in 1757. Representative to the New Hampshire General Court, in 1775, '76 and '77. His sons Jonathan and David were soldiers in the Revolution.

BALL, EBENEZER

came from Concord, Mass. His name was on the Hollis Tax List in 1749, and he was a soldier in the French war in 1755, in the company of Capt. Powers. His sons Ebenezer, Nathaniel, William and John were soldiers in the Revolution.

BAILEY, DANIEL

was from Marlborough, Mass. Settled in the part of Hollis known as Monson, about the year 1754. Himself and three of his sons, viz. Joel, Andrew and Daniel, Jun., were Revolutionary soldiers. Died January 15, 1798, æt. 69.

BARTON, HENRY

was in West Dunstable in 1738 and signed the petition for the charter. Was Parish Assessor in 1741 and Collector in 1743. Died
April 20, 1760. æt. 54.

BLANCHARD, BENJAMIN

is supposed to have come from Dunstable, N. H. He was in West
Dunstable, in 1743, and signed the call to Rev. Mr. Emerson.
Married Kezia Hastings Dec. 31, 1744. Was tithing-man in 1747,
and selectman in 1750 and 1754.

BLOOD, ELNATHAN

supposed from Groton, Mass. His name is on the first tax list
for West Dunstable, in 1740. Married Elizabeth Boynton in
Groton, in 1741. He was a soldier in the French war in 1757, and
selectman in 1773.

BLOOD, JOSIAH

was from Dracut, Mass. Was in West Dunstable in 1738 and
signed the petition for the charter : was a soldier in the Revolution,
as was also his son Josiah. Jr., and is supposed to have died at Ticonderoga in September. 1776.

BLOOD, NATHANIEL

supposed from Groton, Mass. He was in West Dunstable in 1738
and signed the petition for the charter, and was a soldier in the
French war in 1758. Five of his sons. viz., Nathaniel, Francis,
Daniel, Timothy and Nathan. were soldiers in the Revolution, the
last named of whom was killed at Bunker Hill.

BOYNTON, DEA. JOHN

supposed from Newbury. Mass. Was in West Dunstable in 1743 :
parish clerk in 1744. Married Ruth Jewett of Rowley in 1745.
Chosen deacon in 1755, and selectman in 1758, 1761, and 1762, etc.
His sons John and Jacob were soldiers in the Revolution, the last
of whom was killed at Bunker Hill. Died Oct. 29. 1787. æt. 67.

BOYNTON, JR., JOHN

supposed also from Newbury. He was in West Dunstable in
1745. Married Lydia Jewett of Rowley, in May. 1745. His sons.
Isaac and Joel, were Revolutionary soldiers.

(9)

BOYNTON, JOSHUA

was in West Dunstable in 1745, and a town officer in 1747. Three of his sons, viz., Joshua. Jun., Benjamin and Elias, were soldiers in the Revolution.

BROWN, ENSIGN, JOSIAH

came from Salem, Mass., and was in West Dunstable in 1743, and a town officer in 1747 and 1748. He was an ensign in the French war in 1758. Removed to Plymouth. N. H., in 1764.

BROWN, JOHN

was also from Salem, and was in West Dunstable in 1743 and signed the call to Rev. Mr. Emerson. Married Kezia Wheeler October 9, 1744. Died May 6, 1776.

BURGE, EPHRAIM

was from Chelmsford, Mass. Settled in Hollis about 1760. Was a soldier in Capt. Emerson's company in 1777. His oldest son Ephraim B., Jun., was for many years a deacon of the Hollis church, and his sons, Rev. Josiah B. and Dr. Benjamin B., were graduates of Harvard College. (q. v.) Died July 21, 1784, æt. 46.

CONANT, JOSIAH

was from Salem, Mass. Came to West Dunstable in 1744. Married Catharine Emerson, February, 1745. His two sons, Josiah, Jun., and Abel, were soldiers in the Revolution, and both deacons of the Hollis church. Died December 14, 1756, æt. 44.

COLBURN, LIEUT. ROBERT

came from Billerica, Mass., was in West Dunstable in 1738, and signed the petition for the charter. Married Elizabeth Smith in 1747. Settled in the part of Hollis known as Monson. His sons, Robert, Benjamin and Nathan, were Revolutionary soldiers. Died July 9, 1783, æt. 66.

CUMINGS, ESQ., SAMUEL

was born in Groton, Mass., March 6, 1709; married Prudence Lawrence of Groton, July 18, 1732. Was in West Dunstable in 1739 and signed the second petition for the charter. He was the first justice of the peace in Hollis and was chosen town clerk in twenty-two different years, between 1746 and 1770. He was

sergeant in Capt. Powers's company in the French war in 1755.
Two of his sons, Samuel and Thomas, were loyalists in the Revo-
lution. and Benjamin, his youngest son, was a Continental soldier.
Died January 18, 1772, æt. 62.

CUMINGS, JERAHMAEL.

was a brother of Samuel Cumings, and born in Groton, October 10.
1711. Married Hannah Farwell in 1736; was in West Dunstable
in 1738, and signed the first petition for the charter. He was the
father of R ev. Henry Cumings, D. D., the first minister of Billerica, and of Capt. Jotham Cumings, a soldier in the French war
of 1755, and an officer in the war of the Revolution. Died October
25, 1747, æt. 36.

CUMINGS, DEA. WILLIAM

is supposed to have come from Groton, and was in West Dunstable
in 1744, and chosen Deacon of the Hollis church in 1745. He was
ensign in the French war in 1755, in the company of Capt. Powers,
and all his three sons, Ebenezer, William and Philip, were soldiers
in the Revolution. Died September 9, 1758, æt. 46.

DANFORTH, JONATHAN

came from Billerica, and was in West Dunstable in 1743, and signed
the call to Rev. Mr. Emerson. He was a grandson of the noted
Massachusetts surveyor of the same name, and was a town officer in
1746. Died March 3, 1747, æt. 33.

DINSMORE, THOMAS

came from Bedford, Mass., was in West Dunstable previous to 1736,
and was the third settler, and lived on the farm in Hollis now owned
by John Coburn on the road to Pepperell. Died December 10, 1748.

DRURY, ZEDEKIAH

was also from Bedford, and by trade a blacksmith; was in West
Dunstable in 1743, and signed the call to Mr. Emerson. About the
year 1765 he removed to Temple, N. H.

FARLEY, LIEUT. SAMUEL.

came from Bedford, Mass., was in West Dunstable in 1739, and was
a petitioner for the charter. Married Hannah Brown October 7,
1744. His son Benjamin was a soldier in the Revolution. Died
November 23, 1797, æt. 79.

FARLEY, LIEUT. BENJAMIN

was also from Bedford. Was in West Dunstable in 1738 and a petitioner for the charter and was the first inn keeper in West Dunstable. He lived first on the farm now owned by T. G. Worcester, about one-fourth of a mile south of the meeting-house. He was parish assessor in 1740 and 1741, and selectman in 1746. Three of his sons, Ebenezer, Christopher and Stephen, were Revolutionary soldiers. Died November 23, 1797, in his 80th year.

FARLEY, JOSEPH

came from Billerica, and was in West Dunstable in 1743. Killed by the fall of a tree, November 24, 1762, æt. 49.

FLAGG, ELEAZER

came from Concord, Mass., and was the second settler in West Dunstable. He lived in the south-west part of the town, and during the French war of 1744 his house was fortified as a guard house. He was parish assessor in 1742. His son John was a soldier in the French war, 1755, and his son Jonas in that of the Revolution. Died August 14, 1757, æt. 53.

HARDY, PHINEAS

came to Hollis from Bradford, Mass. His name is first on the Hollis tax lists in 1752. He was a soldier in the garrison at Portsmouth, N. H., in 1776, and his sons, Phineas, Thomas, Noah and Jesse, were all soldiers in the army. Died March 7, 1813, æt. 86.

HARRIS, STEPHEN

was from Littleton, Mass., and settled in what is now the north part of Hollis about 1735. He was a petitioner for the charter of West Dunstable in 1738, and first treasurer of West Dunstable in 1740. Died September 20, 1775, æt. 75.

JEWETT, DEA. STEPHEN

is supposed to have come to Hollis from Rowley, Mass., in 1751, and married Hannah (Farwell) Cumings, widow of Ensign Jerahmael Cumings, in 1752. He was chosen selectman in 1766, deacon of the Hollis church in 1770, and a delegate to the County Congress at Amherst in 1774 and 1775. All of his three sons, Stephen, Jun., Noah and Jonathan, were soldiers in the Revolution. Died May 23, 1803, æt. 75.

KEMP, ZERUBBABEL

was born in Groton, Mass., October 12, 1705. Married Abigail Lawrence, in Groton, November 23, 1737. Was in West Dunstable in 1743, and a town officer in 1748.

McDONALD, JAMES

also came from Groton and was in West Dunstable in 1739, and a signer of the second petition for the charter. He was a town officer in 1748 and a soldier in 1777 in the company of Capt. Goss. Died April 11, 1801, æt. 83.

NEVINS, WILLIAM

came from Newton, Mass., and his name appears in the first tax list in West Dunstable in 1740. He was selectman in 1771 and 1772, and moderator in 1773 and 1774. Five of his sons, viz., William, Joseph, Benjamin, John and Phineas, were Revolutionary soldiers. Died February 15, 1785, æt. 67.

NEVINS, DAVID

was from Bedford, Mass., and was in West Dunstable in 1738 and signed the first petition for the charter. He was parish collector in 1741. Removed from Hollis to Plymouth among the first settlers of Plymouth.

NOYES, DEA. ENOCH

came from Newbury, Mass. His name first appears on the Hollis tax lists in 1747. He was selectman in 1751, and chosen deacon in 1755. His two sons, Enoch and Elijah, were soldiers in the Revolution. Died September 1796, æt. 80.

PATCH, DEA. THOMAS

was from Groton. Married Anna Gilson in 1741, in Groton. He was in West Dunstable in 1743, and was chosen deacon in 1745. His sons, Thomas and David, were soldiers in the Revolution. Died May 1, 1754, æt. 40.

POOL, WILLIAM

was from Reading, Mass. Married Hannah Nichols, at Reading, June 19, 1751, and came to Hollis during the French war of 1754, his name being first found on the Hollis tax lists in 1758. He was selectman in 1771. Died in Hollis, October 27, 1795, æt. 70. His oldest son, William W., was a soldier in the Revolution in 1775, and

again in 1778. James, the second son, settled in Maine, and became a successful merchant. His youngest son, Hon. Benjamin
Pool, born January 17, 1771, settled in Hollis, and was many times
chosen to important town offices. He was justice of the peace from
1810 to 1822, and justice of the peace and quorum from 1822 till his
decease. He was also representative to the New Hampshire
General Court from 1804 to 1809, and State senator in the years
1818, '19, '20 and '21. Beside these three sons, Mr. Pool had
eleven daughters, ten of whom lived to adult age, and were all
married, and most of them became the mothers of large families.
He died April 20, 1836, æt. 65.

POWERS, CAPT. PETER

was the first settler in Hollis. Was born in Littleton, Mass., and
married Anna Keyes of Chelmsford in 1728. Settled in West Dunstable in 1730. He was parish committee in 1740 and held many
other important parish and town offices. He was the first Captain
of the West Dunstable militia, the commander of an expedition to
explore the Coos country in 1754, and captain of the Hollis company in the expedition to Crown Point in 1755. Stephen, Whitcomb and Levi, three of his sons, were soldiers in the French war
in the same company : and four of them, viz., Stephen, Francis,
Nahum and Samson were soldiers in the Revolution. Died August
22, 1757, æt. 50.

PROCTOR, MOSES

came from Chelmsford, Mass. Was in West Dunstable in 1738,
and signed the first petition for the charter. He settled in the west
part of the town on Proctor hill, which was named for him. His
name is found on the first West Dunstable tax list in 1740, and he
was selectman in 1740. The life of Mr. Proctor is said to have
been shortened by the bite of a rattlesnake, and he afterwards waged
so successful a war of extermination against those reptiles that no
rattlesnakes have been known in Hollis since his death. Died
May 21, 1780, æt. 73.

TAYLOR, ABRAHAM

was born in Concord, Mass., and came to West Dunstable previously to 1738, and was agent of the inhabitants with Capt. Powers in
obtaining the charter. In 1740 he gave the land for the Hollis
meeting-house, burial ground and common. He was parish assessor in 1740, '41, '42 and '43. Died June 3, 1743, æt. 36.

TENNY, WILLIAM

came to Hollis from Rowley. Mass. His name appears first on the
Hollis tax lists in 1747. He was selectman in 1769 and 1770.
His son. Capt. William Tenny, was a soldier in the Revolution.
Died March 22. 1783. æt. 61.

WHEELER, PETER

is said to have come from Salem. Mass., and settled in the part of
Hollis known as Monson. He was a petitioner for the charter of
West Dunstable in 1738. and his name was on the first West Dunstable tax list in 1740. He is said to have been noted in his day for
his exploits and success in hunting. especially of bears. He was a
soldier in the French war in 1755. and his sons, Ebenezer and
Lebbeus. were soldiers in the Revolution. Died March 28. 1772,
æt. 67.

WILLOUGHBY, JOHN

came from Billerica. He was in West Dunstable in 1745 and was a
soldier in the French war. in the years 1755. 1757. and 1758. His
son. John W.. Jun.. was a captain in the war of the Revolution in
the regiment of Col. Webster. Died February 2. 1793. æt. 85.

WORCESTER, REV. FRANCIS

was born in Bradford. Mass.. June 7. 1698. Married Abigail
Carleton. of Rowley. in 1720. Was settled as a Congregational
minister in Sandwich. Mass.. for ten years before coming to Hollis.
Removed to Hollis in 1750. Afterwards preached as an evangelist
in New Hampshire. but was not again settled in the ministry. He
was the author of a small volume of "Meditations" in verse. written
in his sixtieth year. Also of several moral and religious essays
reprinted in 1760. entitled "A Bridle for Sinners and a Spur for
Saints." His oldest son was Dea. Francis Worcester. His second
son. Jesse. was a soldier in the French war. was taken prisoner,
and died at Montreal. in 1757. His youngest son was Capt. Noah
Worcester. Died October 14. 1783. æt. 85.

WORCESTER, DEA. FRANCIS

was the oldest son of Rev. Francis Worcester. Born at Bradford,
March 30. 1721. Married Hannah Boynton. of Newbury. Mass.,
October 28. 1741. Came to West Dunstable in 1744. Was chosen
deacon of the Hollis church in 1746. He was selectman in Hollis

six years, moderator of the annual town meeting eleven years, and
town treasurer twenty years, between 1746 and 1768. In 1768 he
removed to Plymouth, N. H., and was deacon of the church at Plymouth ; representative to New Hampshire General Court in 1777
and 1778, and State councillor in 1780, 1781 and 1783. Died October 19, 1800, æt. 79.

WRIGHT, CAPT. JOSHUA

came from Woburn, Mass., was in West Dunstable in 1739, and
signed the second petition for the charter. He was selectman in
1749 and 1769. A soldier in the French war in 1760, and Captain
of the Hollis militia company, in 1775, and previously. His sons,
Lemuel and Uriah, were soldiers in the Revolution. Died August
5, 1776, æt. 60.

HOLLIS TAX LISTS.

NAMES ON THE HOLLIS "EAST SIDE" AND "WEST SIDE" TAX
LISTS IN JANUARY 1, 1775.

The following lists, copied from the records, present all the
names of the tax payers, January 1, 1775, then on the Hollis tax
lists, with the amount of the province tax for 1774, assessed to each
in pounds, shillings and pence. This was the last tax collected in
Hollis under the authority of the King. The names marked thus*
will be found in the lists of the Hollis soldiers in the Revolution.

ON THE EAST SIDE.

	£	s.	d.		£	s.	d.
Wd. Elizabeth Abbot,		1	5	John Boynton, Jun.,		3	6
Jeremiah Ames,		6	3	*William Brooks,		5	7
Ens. Stephen Ames,		5	9	*John Brooks,		2	10
*Jonathan Ames,		2	6	*Ephraim Burge,		8	8
Nathaniel Ball,		8	6	*John Campbell,		2	8
*Nathaniel Ball, Jun.,		2	8	*Sam'l Chamberlain,		7	6
Wd. Abigail Barron,		1	5	*James Colburn,		7	2
Phineas Bennett,		2	10	*Josiah Conant,		7	6
Joshua Blanchard,		2	3	Sam'l Cumings, Esq.,		6	10
*Josiah Blood,		5	2	*John Cumings,		5	6
*Josiah Blood, Jun.,		3	9	*Lt. Reuben Dow,		10	11
*Nathaniel Blood,		7	8	Peter Eads,		2	3
*Francis Blood,		6	6	Lt. Amos Eastman,		6	5
Ebenezer Blood,		4	9	*Amos Eastman, Jun.,		3	5
*Nathan Blood,		3	11	*Jonathan Eastman,		4	9
Caleb Blood,		2	3	*Christopher Farley,		4	8
Dea. John Boynton,		9	4	Lt. Sam'l Farley,		10	9
*Joshua Boynton,		7	3	Benjamin Farmer,		2	8
*Benjamin Boynton,		3	3	*Minott Farmer,		5	3

	£	s.	d.		£	s.	d.
*David Farnsworth,		8	3	James Nutting,		3	3
*Ens. Jonas Flagg,		7	5	Benjamin Parker,		4	2
James French,		3	2	Elea'r Parker,		2	3
John French,		4	8	Sam'l Parker,		0	2
Josiah French,		5	2	Sam'l Parker, Jun.,		2	3
*Timothy French,		3	0	*Ephraim Pierce,		3	3
*John Goss,		7	6	*Solomon Pierce,		2	6
*Col. John Hale,		14	2	Barzillai Pierce,		2	3
*Lemuel Hardy,		4	9	Richard Pierce,		4	8
*Samuel Hill,		2	3	Simon Pierce,		5	9
*Hon. Samuel Hobart,	1	3	8	Jona. Philbrick,		8	9
Shubael Hobart,		8	8	Wd. Anna Powers,		2	2
*Parmeter Honey,		2	3	*Samson Powers,		3	2
Richard Hopkins,		2	8	*Stephen Powers,		0	11
*Ephraim How,		2	3	William Pool,		9	2
*Joseph How,		4	2	Cyrus Proctor,		3	6
Wd. Hannah Hunt.		1	2	Moses Proctor,		5	8
Josiah Hunt,		4	8	*Moses Proctor, Jun.,		5	2
*Ebenezer Jaquith,		0	5	Philip Proctor,		2	3
*Thomas Jaquith,		0	3	Nehemiah Ranger,		2	9
*Jacob Jewett,		7	5	William Read,		6	8
Dea. Stephen Jewett,		8	5	*James Rideout,		3	9
Dea. Nath'l Jewett.		10	0	William Searl,		4	8
*Ebenezer Jewett.		4	0	Ebenezer Shed,		5	6
Edward John,		2	6	Abel Shipley,		8	11
*Samuel Jewett,		7	11	Joshua Simonds,		1	6
Zach'h Kemp,		5	2	Jacob Smith,		2	3
*Israel Kinney,		2	5	*Joshua Smith,		6	2
Oliver Lawrence,		14	3	*Isaac Stearns,		4	8
Zach'h Lawrence,		7	11	*Caleb Stiles,		2	3
Zach'h Lawrence, Jun.,		3	6	Edward Taylor,		4	9
Joseph Lesley,		5	3	Benjamin Tenney		2	11
*Jonas Lesley,		2	6	William Tenney,		7	0
Chris'r Lovejoy,		2	5	*William Tenney, Jun.,		2	8
Daniel Lovejoy,		6	3	Daniel Wheeler,		2	6
Daniel Lovejoy, Jun.,		2	3	*Ens. Noah Worcester,		12	4
Wid. Patience Martin,		1	6	Capt. Joshua Wright.		15	0
Ens. Daniel Merrill,		8	0	*Lemuel Wright,		5	0
*James McConnor,		2	3	Timothy Wyman,		3	6
Dea. Enoch Noyes,		7	8				

ON THE WEST SIDE.

	£	s.	d.		£	s.	d.
Samuel Abbot,		2	3	*Daniel Blood, Jun.,		3	8
*John Atwell,		7	3	Elnathan Blood,		5	11
Benjamin Austin,		3	4	*Jonas Blood,		2	3
*Daniel Bailey,		5	9	*Abel Brown,		2	3
*Joel Bailey,		2	3	Joseph Brown,		2	8
*Joseph Bailey,		2	10	William Brown,		8	8
*Richard Bailey,		2	6	Edward Carter,		4	8
Timothy Bailey,		2	3	*Edward Carter, Jun.,		2	3
*Ebenezer Ball,		6	6	Lt. Robert Colburn,		8	6
*Eleazer Ball,		5	3	*Robert Colburn, Jun..		4	0
*Joshua Blanchard, Jun..		2	3	William Colburn,		1	6
*Ebenezer Ball, Jr.,		2	11	*John Conroy,		1	0
*Daniel Blood,		2	9	*John Conroy, Jun..		2	11

	£	s.	d.		£	s.	d.
*Samuel Conroy,		2	3	Benj'n Nurse,		2	6
Timothy Cook, ,		2	0	Josiah Parker,		6	8
*Philip Cumings,		2	8	*Thomas Patch,		4	11
Jonathan Danforth,		3	3	John Phelps,		7	2
*Jacob Danforth,		2	8	*Nathan Phelps,		2	3
*Thomas Emerson,		3	11	*John Philbrick,		3	9
*Dan'l Emerson, Jun.,		5	0	Thomas Powers,		4	0
Joseph Estabrooks,		2	3	*Thomas Pratt,		2	3
*Caleb Farley,		7	6	*Ezekiel Proctor,		2	8
Ebenezer Farley,		2	0	Benj'n Reed,		2	3
*Ebenezer Farley, Jun.,		4	3	*Jacob Reed,		3	6
*James Fisk,		2	5	*Jonathan Russ,		3	8
Oliver Fletcher,		3	5	*Benj'n Saunderson,		4	2
Ephraim French,		2	3	*Robert Seaver,		0	3
*Isaac French,		2	3	*Jerem'h Shattuck,		2	3
*Nehemiah French,		2	9	*Wm. Shattuck,		3	6
Nicholas French,		3	3	Zach'h Shattuck,		5	11
*William French,		0	11	*Zach'h Shattuck, Jun.		3	3
John Goodhue,		4	2	Benj'n Simpson,		3	5
*Samuel Goodhue,		6	2	Thomas Smith,		3	6
Samuel Gridley,		2	11	Wd. Mary Smith,		9	8
Moses Hadley,		3	2	*Joseph Stearns,		2	6
*Aaron Hardy,		4	9	Sam'l Stearns, Jr.,		4	3
*Nehemiah Hardy,		2	6	Isaac Stevens,		2	8
*Phineas Hardy,		4	3	*Isaac Stevens, Jun.,		2	8
*Phineas Hardy, Jun.,		2	3	*Jonathan Taylor,		7	3
Stephen Harris,		4	8	*David Wallingford,		6	6
Samuel Hayden,		5	0	Solomon Wheat,		2	11
*John Hobart,		4	3	*Thomas Wheat,		9	6
Jonathan Hobart,		0	3	*Thomas Wheat, Jun.,		3	6
*Jona. Hobart, Jun.,		2	3	*Ebenezer Wheeler,		4	6
Jacob Jewett, Jr.,		5	8	*Lebbeus Wheeler,		2	3
*James Jewett,		5	11	*Thaddeus Wheeler,		5	2
*Edward Johnson,		2	8	Benj'n Whiting, Esq.,		6	2
*Samuel Johnson,		2	6	Capt. Leonard Whiting,		10	6
*Daniel Kendrick,		7	11	*Bray Wilkins,		7	2
*Abner Keyes,		3	0	*Jonas Willoughby,		3	6
Abra'm Leeman,,		3	6	John Willoughby,		3	8
Sam'l Leeman,		3	2	Sam'l Willoughby,		5	0
*Sam'l Leeman, Jun.,		2	3	*Israel Wilkins,		7	2
Israel Mead,		1	5	*Nehemiah Woods,		4	2
*James McDaniels,		5	6	*Benj'n Wright,		3	6
*Daniel Mooar,		2	9	Sam'l Wright,		0	3
*Joseph Minott,		2	0	*Sam'l Wright, jun.,		2	8
William Nevins,		0	2	*Jesse Wyman,		3	9
*Wm. Nevins, Jun.,		4	11	Timo. Wyman, Jun.,		2	6
*Benj'n Nevins,		2	3	*Ebenezer Youngman,		2	3
*Joseph Nevins,		2	0	*Nicholas Youngman,		3	0

Whole number of names on the above tax-lists, 239. Number marked thus *, as having been in the army, 130.

CHAPTER XII.

Written history as well as tradition, and the provincial and early
State records, alike with the records of many of the older towns in
New Hampshire, bear ample testimony to the unanimity, courage,
constancy and sacrifices of the people of the then province in the
cause of our national independence. The town meeting of those
times, the family gathering of a sturdy, grave and thoughtful yeomanry, was near of kin and the next door neighbor to the family altar
and hearth-stone. It was an original New England invention—the
rude, it may be, but fitting cradle of American Independence—alike
the admiration and despair of the friends of constitutional liberty
the world over.

> "Stern rugged nurse, thy rigid lore
> With patience many a year she bore,
> What sorrow was thou hadst her know "

One could hardly find or hope for a better or more perfect working model of this novel political machinery than was to be met with
in the town meetings of Hollis from the year 1775 to 1783. There
is abundant evidence that the like spirit and patriotism animated
many of the other New Hampshire towns as were manifested in the
town meetings and doings of the people of Hollis, though it is believed that in but few of them were their revolutionary records and
documents, at the time, so carefully kept, and since then so well
preserved. In what I have to say of the doings of Hollis, in the
Revolution, it is not my wish or purpose to make any invidious comparison between those doings and what was done in the same cause
in the same years by other New Hampshire towns, but rather to

present this sketch of Hollis as an illustration of the predominance of the public sentiment of the province. *Ab uno disce omnes.*

Hollis (spelled Holles in the town charter as well as in all the early town records) was on the south line of the province, adjoining Pepperell, about forty-five miles northwest of Boston and twenty-three from Concord, Mass. By the census taken in September, 1775, the whole number of its inhabitants was 1255, of whom 174 were males between the ages of 16 and 50, 71 males over 50, 60 of its men then in the army, besides the eleven who had before been killed in the service or died of sickness.* There were also in the town one hundred and thirty-one fire-arms, and one hundred and eleven pounds of powder, the property of private persons, but none at that date in the town store, the ammunition of the town having been all exhausted the spring previous.

In respect to what was done by the town in the war that followed, the "*coming events cast their shadows before*" in the resolutions and doings of several town meetings held long before the first blood was shed at Lexington. The records of these first gatherings, and of all other meetings of the town, for the like purpose held till the war was ended, tell their own story in plain, blunt, terse Anglo Saxon, and need no comment of mine to add force or point to their meaning, or to make them more intelligible. Where my limits will permit, it is my purpose to let them speak in their own language.

In the record of a special town meeting held November 7, 1774, more than five months before the battle at Lexington, I find the first recorded allusion to the existing political troubles and forthcoming conflict. This meeting was called to choose delegates for the town to a County Congress (so-called) for Hillsborough County, to be held the next day, (November 8,) at Amherst, this being the first of three special Hollis town meetings called for the like purpose. After having made choice of "Dea. Stephen Jewett, Ensign Stephen Ames and Lieut. Reuben Dow" to represent the town at that Congress, the following preamble and resolution, with three other resolutions of the like tenor, were adopted by the meeting:

"PREAMBLE.—We, the inhabitants of the town of Holles, having taken into our most serious consideration the precarious and most alarming affairs of our land at the present day, do firmly enter into the following resolutions:

---

* N. H. Hist. Coll., v. 1, p. 233.

1st. " That we will at all times endeavor to maintain our liberty and privileges. both civil and sacred, even at the risque of our lives and fortunes, and will not only disapprove, but wholly despise all such persons as we have just and solid reasons to think even wish us in any measure to be deprived of them."

This year, (1774) it appears from the tax list, that the sum of £27. 16s. 3d. was assessed upon the inhabitants for ammunition for the town. as a part of the annual tax.

The next special town meeting was held December 30,1774 to choose delegates to a Provincial Congress at Exeter, called to advise in respect to a Continental Congress. At this meeting, as shown by the record, the following votes were passed:

" 1st. Voted to send a delegate to Exeter to meet the delegates of this province to consult on a Continental Congress, and John Hale, Esq., was chosen said delegate.

" 2d. Voted that we do cordially accede to the just statement of the rights and grievances of the British colonies and the measures adopted and recommended by the Continental Congress for the restoration and establishment of the former, and for the redress of the latter.

"3d. Voted that Col. John Hale, Dea. Stephen Jewett, Dea. John Boynton, Ensign Stephen Ames, Dea. Enoch Noyes, Ensign Noah Worcester, Daniel Kendrick, Jeremiah Ames, William Brown and William Nevins or the major part of them, be a committee in behalf of the town to observe the conduct of all persons touching the association agreement.

" 4th. Voted to raise £16. 13s. 8d. as a donation to the poor of Boston."

There are still to be found among the revolutionary documents of Hollis, three original rolls of military companies, all made in the year 1775. The two oldest of these rolls bear date January 26, 1775, and the third of them June 7, of the same year, ten days before the battle of Bunker Hill. The heading of one of the two oldest rolls is "*A List of the Company of Militia in Holles under the command of Capt. Joshua Wright, made January 26, 1775.* Of this company, Reuben Dow was Lieutenant and Noah Worcester, Ensign. There were also four Sergeants, viz., John Atwell, Jacob Jewett, Jun., John Cumings and William Brooks. Besides these officers, this roll contains the names of one Corporal, one Drummer, one Fifer, and 214, rank and file—224 in

all—supposed to have been the names of all the able bodied men
in the town liable under the law to do military service.

The caption of the second roll is the "Alarm List" made January 26th, 1775. On this list are 100 names, and it is supposed to
include the names of all such able bodied men of the town as by
the province law were exempt from military duty, either on account of age or other cause specified in the law. The list contains
the names of two millers, viz., Thomas Jaquith and Enoch Noyes,
—millers then being excused from doing military duty. It also
contained the names of twenty-seven persons who were designated
with the title *senior*, indicating that each of the twenty-seven had a
son of the same name. For the purpose of exhibiting the character
of this roll as a curiosity of the times the first twenty-four names,
copied from it in the order in which they stood upon the list, are
presented below with the several titles prefixed or appended to each
of them. Whether or not this order is intended to indicate the relative social rank and standing of these dignitaries is left to con-
jecture.

Capt. Leonard Whiting,	Ensign Daniel Merrill,
Benjamin Whiting, Esq.,	Ensign Jonas Flagg,
Richard Cutts Shannon, Esq.,	Ensign Benjamin Parker,
Samuel Cumings, Esq.,	Rev. Daniel Emerson,
Daniel Emerson, Jun., Esq.,	Dea. Samuel Goodhue,
Lieut. Benjamin Farley,	Dea. Nathaniel Jewett,
Lt. Samuel Farley,	Dea. Enoch Noyes,
Lt. David Farnsworth,	Dea. John Boynton,
Lt. Amos Eastman,	Dea. Stephen Jewett,
Lt. Robert Colburn,	William Cumings, Sch. Master,
Lt. Samuel Gridley,	John Hale, Physician,
Ensign Stephen Ames,	Samuel Hosley, do.

The title of the third of those rolls is as follows : " *The List of
the present Militia Company of Holles. Exclusive of the Minute Men and all that have gone into the army June ye 7th, 1775.*"
Of this Company Noah Worcester was Captain, Daniel Kendrick,
Lieutenant, and Jacob Jewett, Ensign, and inclusive of these
officers this roll contains 122 names, 102 less than the militia company roll made on the previous 26th of January.

In the record of the annual town meeting of March 6, 1775, no
reference in any way was made to the impending troubles, but on
the 3d of April following, a special town meeting was summoned
to choose delegates to a second County Congress to be held at Amherst on the 5th of that month, " and to see what method should be
taken to raise money for the Continental Congress at Philadelphia."

Having made choice of "Dea. Stephen Jewett" and "Dea. Enoch Noyes" as delegates to that Congress, and voted such instructions to them as the meeting thought prudent. it also " Voted that all persons who shall pay money by subscription to send *now* to the Continental Congress, shall have the same deducted out of their Province Rates."

The next special town meeting was held April 23, 1775, upon the receipt of the following letter from Col. John Wentworth, written the day after the battle of Lexington, to the selectmen of Hollis. in behalf of the New Hampshire Committee of Safety, and which forms a part of the record of the meeting :

" *Gentlemen :* This moment melancholy intelligence has been received of hostilities being commenced between the troops under the command of General Gage and our brethren of the Massachusetts Bay.   The importance of our exerting ourselves at this critical moment has caused the provincial committee to meet at Exeter, and you are requested instantly to choose and hasten forward a delegate or delegates to join the committee and aid them in consulting measures necessary for our safety.

J. WENTWORTH.
In behalf of the Committee of Safety."

" Province of New Hampshire.   } Special town meeting. April
  Hillsborough County, SS.   }   23, 1775.

" Pursuant to the above notice and request. the inhabitants of the town of Holles being met. unanimously voted. that Samuel Hobart. Esq.. be and hereby is appointed to represent this town at Exeter. with other delegates. that are or shall be appointed by the several towns of this Province for the purpose above mentioned.

NOAH WORCESTER, Town Clerk."

The following is a copy of the full record of a town meeting. April 28. 1775, called to raise soldiers for the army. nine days after the battle of Lexington :

" Province of New Hampshire.   } Special meeting April 28. 1775.
  Hillsborough County. SS.   }   Col. John Hale, Moderator.

" At a meeting of the town of Holles called on a sudden emergency in the day of our public distress.

" 1st.   Voted, that we will pay two commissioned officers. four non-commissioned officers. and thirty-four rank and file, making in the whole forty good and able men to join the army in Cambridge.

paying said officers and men the same wages the Massachusetts men receive, and will also victual the same till such time as the resolution of the General Court or the Congress of the Province of New Hampshire shall be known respecting the raising of a standing army the ensuing summer.

" 2nd.   Voted, that the selectmen provide necessaries for sundry poor families where the men are gone into the army till further orders, and the amount be deducted out of their wages.

" 3d.   Voted, that what grain was raised for the poor of Boston shall be one half sent to the army, and the other half to be distributed to the above families."

The sequel of the doings of the town, both in the first and following years of the war, furnishes abundant evidence that this vote of the 28th of April was not an empty boast, and that the patriotic pledges then made were amply and faithfully redeemed.

The extract presented below is copied from the proceedings of a town meeting, May 11, 1775, called to choose delegates to the Provincial Congress at Exeter, to be holden May 17th.

" Voted and chose Col. John Hale and Deacon Enoch Noyes Delegates to the Provincial Congress to meet at Exeter on the 17th of May inst.   Also, Voted and instructed our delegates to join the other Governments in raising and paying their proportions in men and money in the defence of the Liberties of these Colonies."

Next below is presented a copy in full of the record of the third town meeting, May 18, 1775, to appoint and instruct delegates to the third and last County Congress to be held at Amherst, on the following 24th of May.

"Province of New Hampshire, } Speci'l town meeting May 18. 1775.
    Hillsborough County, SS. } Ensign Noah Worcester, moderator.

" At a meeting of the inhabitants of the town of Holles, May the 18th, in the day of our public distress, occasioned by a letter from Mr. Daniel Campbell and Mr. Jonathan Martin, a committee for calling a Congress for this county, which Congress was called for the following purpose :

" 1. To go into some measures for the better security of the internal policy of the county to prevent declining into a state of nature.

" 2. To see if the Congress will appoint a committee of correspondence to wait on or join the Congress of Massachusetts Bay.

" 3. To enforce a strict adherence to the Association Agreement of the Continentel Congress.

"Mr. William Nevins, Mr. Jeremiah Ames and Lieut. Samuel
Farley, chosen delegates for the Congress which is to be holden at
Amherst on the 24th of May next. As to the article in the letter of
Messrs. Campbell and Martin respecting the sending a committee
to the Massachusetts Congress.

"Voted unanimously that as we have a Provincial Congress now
sitting, which will doubtless send to them—therefore it appears to us
not best for this county to take it upon them to send such a committee."

It is very evident from the foregoing proceedings and vote that the
people of Hollis were in no degree in sympathy with a part, at least,
of the supposed purposes of this County Congress. On the contrary
they regarded some of the objects and doings of that Congress as
usurpations, and as tending to disunion. This view of the people of
the town will more fully appear in an able and thoughtful memorial of their Committee of Safety (still preserved) and addressed to
the County Congress in July of that year. A copy of this memorial
may be found in the "New Hampshire Provincial Papers, vol.
VII. page 450."

It is shown by the town records that the style "*Province of New
Hampshire,*" was used in the margin of all warrants for town meetings till after the battle of Bunker Hill, June 17, 1775. After that
date, till July 4. 1776, the word "*Colony*" was used in those warrants, in the place of Province. After the Declaration of Independence the word "*State*" took the place of colony and province.

The following is a copy of the record of the last Hollis town
meeting in 1775, and shows among other things how the right to
vote of soldiers absent in the army was settled by our ancestors one
hundred years ago.

"Colony of New Hampshire.) Special meeting, Dec. 12, 1775.
Hillsborough County, SS.) Col. John Hale, Moderator.

"Voted and chose Ensign Stephen Ames a delegate to the Congress or Assembly at Exeter for a year.

"SOLDIERS' VOTES.—A dispute arose respecting some votes
which were brought in writing of persons gone into the army,
which being put to vote they were allowed as if the men were
present themselves."

(10)

THE COMPANY OF HOLLIS MINUTE MEN FOR LEXINGTON AND CAMBRIDGE.

Late at night on the 18th of April the detachment of British troops under command of Lt. Col. Smith crossed over from Boston common to East Cambridge on their march to Lexington and Concord. The distance from Hollis to Cambridge, by the roads then travelled, was forty-two miles. The alarm of this expedition was at once spread through the country by mounted express. According to well established tradition the news of it was brought to Hollis about noon of the 19th, by Dea. John Boynton, who lived in the south part of the town, near the province line, and was one of the committee of observation. Dea. Boynton came riding through the town at the top of his horse's speed, calling out to his townsmen, as he passed, "*the Regulars are coming and killing our men.*" Dea. Boynton (as the tradition tells the story). riding at full speed, and out of breath, announced his message at the door of Capt. Worcester. another member of the same committee, living a little south of the Hollis common, who had just risen from his dinner, and was then standing at his looking glass with his face well lathered, and in the act of shaving. Capt. Worcester, without stopping to finish his work, with his face still whitened for the razor, at once dropped that instrument, hurried to his stable. mounted his horse, and in that plight assisted in spreading the alarm. Other mounted messengers were soon despatched to the several parts of the town to carry the news, and in the afternoon of the same day ninety-two minute men were rallied and met on the Hollis common. with their muskets,—each with his powder horn, and one pound of powder from the town's stock and twenty bullets.

A story is told in the same connection of five brothers of the name of Nevins, then living in the north part of the town, all of whom were afterwards in the army, which illustrates the spirit and promptness with which these minute men met this alarm. Early in the afternoon of the 19th of April three of these brothers were at work with their crowbars in digging stone for a farm wall at a short distance from their home. At the coming in sight of the messenger, they had partially raised from its place a large flat stone embedded in a farm roadway. Seeing the messenger spurring towards them at full speed, one of the brothers put a small boulder under the large stone to keep it in the position to which it had been raised, and all stopped and listened to the message of the horseman.

Upon hearing it, leaving the stone as it was in the roadway, with the little boulder under it, they hastened to the house, and all three of them, with their guns and equipments, hurried to the Hollis common to join their company. One of those brothers was afterwards killed at Bunker Hill; another, the spring following, lost his life in the service in New York. As a family memento of this incident, this large stone, with the small one supporting it, was permitted to remain for more than seventy years afterward, in the same position in which the brothers had left it on the 19th of April.

Having made choice, the same afternoon, of Reuben Dow as Captain, John Goss, first Lieutenant, and John Cumings, 2d Lieutenant, this company on the evening of the 19th, or before daylight the next morning, was on its march from Hollis to Cambridge. The names of all the officers of the company, and also of the private soldiers, are presented in the list below, copied from an original company roll, preserved by Capt. Dow, and now with the Hollis documents, showing the date of enlistment, time of service, daily wages of officers and privates, pay for travel from Hollis to Cambridge, and back, and the amount of money paid to each of them by the town. This document is entitled, "A Muster Roll of Capt. Reuben Dow's Company of Minute Men who marched from Holles the 19th of April, 1775," and may be found in full, in the October number of the New England Historical and Genealogical Register. pp. 282, 283.

Reuben Dow, Capt.,	Richard Bailey, Private.	Ebenezer Gilson, Private
John Goss, 1st Lieut.,	Daniel Blood, "	Manuel Grace, "
John Cumings, 2d. Lieut.,	Francis Flood, "	Aaron Hardy, "
Nathan Blood, Sergt,	Jonas Blood, "	Samuel Hill, "
Joshua Boynton, "	Benj'n Boynton, "	Samuel Hosley "
William Nevins, "	Elias Boynton.	Ephraim How, "
Minot Farmer, "	Abel Brown, "	Ebenezer Jaquith, "
Samson Powers, Corp'l.	John Campbell, "	Samuel Jewett, "
James McIntosh, "	James Colburn, "	Edward Johnson, "
James McConnor, "	Nathan Colburn, "	Sam'l Johnson, "
Ephraim Blood, "	Thomas Colburn, "	Thomas Kemp. "
David Farnsworth, drummer,	Samuel Conroy, "	Abner Keyes, "
Noah Worcester, Jr., Fifer,	Benj'n Cumings "	Israel Kinney, "
Benjamin Abbot. Private,	Jacob Danforth, "	Samuel Leeman, "
David Ames, "	James Dickey. "	Randall McDaniels. "
Jonathan Ames, "	Amos Eastman, "	Joseph Minot, "
John Atwell, "	Jonathan Eastman, "	Benjamin Nevins, "
Ebenezer Ball, "	Benj'n Farley, "	Joseph Nevins, "
Nathaniel Ball. "	Ebenezer Farley, "	Thomas Patch, "
Job Bailey, "	James Fisk, "	Nathan Phelps, "
Joel Bailey, "	Josiah Fisk, "	John Philbrick, "
Joseph Bailey. "	William French, "	Ephraim Pierce,. "

Nahum Powers, Private.	Amos Taylor, Private	Bray Wilkins, Private,
Thomas Pratt, "	Daniel Taylor, "	Israel Wilkins, "
Ezekiel Proctor, "	William Tenney, "	William Wood, "
Jacob Reed, "	David Wallingford, "	Benjamin Wright, "
Jonathan Russ, "	Nathaniel Wheat, "	Benj. Wright, Jun., "
Benjamin Sanders, "	Thomas Wheat, "	Uriah Wright, "
Robert Seaver, "	Ebenezer Wheeler, "	Jesse Wyman, "
Jacob Spalding, "	Thaddeus Wheeler, "	Ebenezer Youngman, private.
Isaac Stearns, "	Lebbeus Wheeler, "	

Thirty-nine of the privates of the company, after an absence of from five to twelve days, returned to Hollis. The remaining fifty-three, with but few if any exceptions, stayed at Cambridge and volunteered in other companies to serve for eight months. Much the largest part of those who remained at Cambridge re-enlisted for eight months in a new company under Capt. Dow, of which John Goss was also 1st Lieutenant, and John Cumings, 2d Lieutenant. This company was afterwards mustered into the Massachusetts regiment commanded by Col. William Prescott, the hero of Bunker Hill, who at the time lived near the north line of the adjoining town of Pepperell, a large part of his farm being in Hollis. Thomas Colburn and Ebenezer Youngman, two of these minute men, enlisted in the company of Capt. Moor, of Groton, Mass., in the same regiment, and were both killed in the fight at Bunker Hill. Job Bailey, Ephraim How, and Samuel Leeman, three others of them, joined the company of Capt. Levi Spalding of Nottingham West, (now Hudson) in the New Hampshire regiment, that fought at Bunker Hill under Col. Reed, and were all present in the battle. Six others of them, viz., Joel Bailey, Richard Bailey, Nathan Colburn, Abner Keyes, David Wallingford, and Bray Wilkins, volunteered in the company of Capt. Archelaus Town, of Amherst, New Hampshire, afterwards mustered into the 27th Massachusetts regiment, commanded by Col. Hutchinson. Of this company, Wallingford was 2d Lieutenant, and Wilkins, one of the Sergeants.

It is shown by the original company roll of the Hollis minute men, that the wages paid to the private soldiers of the company were one shilling and five pence per day, equal to about 24 cents in federal money. They were also paid one penny a mile each way for travel, making in all 84d. or 7s., the distance from Hollis to Cambridge being 42 miles. The wages of the Captain were 4s. 6d., or about 75 cents per day; those of the 1st Lieutenant, 2s. 10d.; of the 2d Lieutenant, 2s. 6d.; of the Sergeants, 1s. 8 3-4, or some less than 30 cents per day. The full amount paid by the town for the services of this company, as shown by this same roll, was £65. 12s. 7d.

CHAPTER XIII.

1775 CONTINUED.—HOLLIS COMPANY AT BUNKER HILL.—ROLL,
AND DESCRIPTIVE LIST.—CAPT. DOW'S COMMISSION.—BATTLE
OF BUNKER HILL.—HOLLIS MEN KILLED AND WOUNDED.— LOSS
OF EQUIPMENTS.—THE NEW HAMPSHIRE REINFORCEMENTS.—
CAPT. WORCESTER'S COMPANY.—NUMBER OF HOLLIS SOLDIERS
IN 1775 AND THEIR WAGES.— MILITARY COATS.—STORY OF A
PATRIOTIC HOLLIS WOMAN.

The new company of Capt. Dow, enlisted at Cambridge, for
eight months, including its officers, consisted of fifty-nine men, that
number making a full company under the law of Massachusetts
for organizing the troops of that province.   It is shown by an original return roll of this company, dated October 6, 1775, presenting
the names of the dead and wounded as well as of those then living,
now in the office of the Secretary of State, at Boston, that all the
men were from Hollis.   This roll is preserved with the other company rolls of the regiment of Col. Prescott, and it may be seen on
inspection of them that Capt. Dow's was the only company of the
regiment, in which all the officers and privates were from one and
the same town.

The names of the officers and privates of the company, as first
organized, are here presented, copied from an original roll pre-
served in the family of Capt. Dow.   *Captain*, Reuben Dow; 1st
Lieutenant, John Goss; 2d *Lieutenant*, John Cumings.   *Ser-
geants*, 1st, Nathan Blood; 2d, Joshua Boynton; 3d, William
Nevins; 4th, Minot Farmer.   *Corporals*, 1st, Samson Powers; 2d,
James McIntosh; 3d, James McConnor; 4th, Ephraim Pierce.
Drummer, David Farnsworth.   *Fifer*, Noah Worcester, Jun.

PRIVATES.

William Adams,	Jacob Boynton,	Benjamin Cumings,
David Ames,	Abel Brown,	Philip Cumings,
Ebenezer Ball,	John Campbell,	Peter Cumings,
Francis Blood,	Wilder Chamberlain,	Evan Dow,
Elias Boynton,	Abel Conant,	Caleb Eastman,

William Elliot,
James Fisk,
Josiah Fisk,
Samuel Hill,
Isaac Hobart,
Samuel Hosley,
Samuel Jewett,
Thomas Kemp,
Israel Kinney,
Phineas Nevins,
Nathaniel Patten,

Nehemiah Pierce,
John Platts,
Peter Poor,
Nahum Powers,
Francis Powers,
Jonathan Powers,
Thomas Pratt,
Ezekiel Proctor,
Jacob Read,
Jeremiah Shattuck,

Jacob Spalding,
Isaac Stearns,
Amos Taylor,
Daniel Taylor,
Moses Thurston,
Ebenezer Townsend
Thomas Wheat,
Lebbeus Wheeler,
William Wood,
Uriah Wright.

Five members of the company, viz., the 2d. Lieut., John Cumings ; Ebenezer Ball, Ephraim Blood, Jonathan Powers and Isaac Stearns, were soldiers in the last French and Indian war, begun in the year 1754, and which resulted in the final conquest of Canada.

An original descriptive roll of fifty of the non-commissioned officers and private soldiers of the company still exists, showing their height, age and complexion. From this roll it appears that Jonathan Powers, who was of the age of sixty years, was the oldest, and that Peter Cumings, a son of the 2d Lieutenant, and but thirteen. was the youngest. The next youngest, was Noah Worcester, Jun., the fifer, who was sixteen the November previous. The four tallest of the men were each six feet in height—the shortest was the boy, Peter Cumings, who was but five feet. Fourteen of the men were of " dark " complexion, the remaining thirty-six, " light."

COPY OF THE DESCRIPTIVE ROLL.

	Age.	Complexion.	Height.		Age.	Complexion.	Height.
William Adams	20	Light,	5 ft. 5 in.	James McConner	31	Light,	5 ft. 7 in.
Ebenezer Ball	45	Dark,	5 ft. 6 in.	James McIntosh	30	"	5 ft. 6 in.
Nathan Blood	28	Light,	6 ft.	Phineas Nevins	17	"	5 ft. 6 in.
Francis Blood	27	"	6 ft.	Nathaniel Patten	41	Dark,	5 ft. 6 in.
Ephraim Blood	37	"	5 ft. 11 in.	Nehemiah Pierce	20	Light,	5 ft. 7 in.
Jacob Boynton	19	Dark,	5 ft. 9 in.	John Platts	27	"	5 ft. 9 in.
Elias Boynton	20	"	5 ft. 10 in.	Peter Poor	21	"	5 ft. 5 in.
Joshua Boynton	30	Light,	5 ft. 6 in.	Nahum Powers	35	Dark,	5 ft. 9 in.
John Campbell	20	"	5 ft. 9 in.	Francis Powers	33	Light,	5 ft. 6 in.
Abel Conant	19	"	5 ft. 6 in.	Jonathan Powers	60	"	5 ft. 9 in.
Philip Cumings	27	"	5 ft. 6 in.	Samson Powers	26	"	5 ft. 10 in.
Benjamin Cumings	19	"	5 ft. 11 in.	Thomas Pratt	35	"	5 ft. 10 in.
Peter Cumings	13	"	5 ft.	Ezekiel Proctor	40	Dark,	5 ft. 6 in.
Evan Dow	21	"	5 ft. 6 in.	Jacob Read	48	"	5 ft. 10 in.
Caleb Eastman	22	Dark,	5 ft. 8 in.	Jeremiah Shattuck	20	"	5 ft. 10 in.
William Elliot	20	Light,	5 ft. 7 in.	Jacob Spalding	20	Light,	5 ft. 4 in.
Minot Farmer	25	"	5 ft. 8 in.	Isaac Stearns	38	"	5 ft. 5 in.
David Farnsworth	21	"	6 ft.	Amos Taylor	27	"	5 ft. 8 in.
James Fisk	37	Dark,	5 ft. 9 in.	Moses Thurston	48	"	5 ft. 6 in.
Josiah Fisk	20	Light,	5 ft. 5 in.	Ebenezer Townsend	22	"	5 ft. 10 in.
Samuel Hill	21	"	6 ft.	Thomas Wheat	24	Dark,	5 ft. 8 in.
Isaac Hobart	19	"	5 ft. 6 in.	Lebbeus Wheeler	23	Light,	5 ft. 6 in.
Samuel Hosley	23	"	5 ft. 7 in.	William Wood	23	"	5 ft. 6 in.
Samuel Jewett	19	Dark,	5 ft. 6 in.	Noah Worcester, Jr.	16	"	5 ft. 10 in.
Thomas Kemp	27	"	5 ft. 7 in.	Uriah Wright	21	Dark,	5 ft. 6 in.

Besides the fifty-nine eight months' men in the company of Capt.
Dow, Thomas Colburn, Samuel Conroy, Samuel Wright, and
Ebenezer Youngman, enlisted in the company of Capt. Moor, of
Groton, in the same regiment, and eight other Hollis soldiers, viz.,
Andrew Bailey, Job Bailey, Phineas Hardy, Thomas Hardy,
Ephraim How, Samuel Leeman, Jun., Ephraim Rolfe, and Ephraim
Smith, enlisted in the company of Capt. Spalding, in the New
Hampshire regiment under Col. Reed, and all of them were present
at the battle of Bunker Hill.   Joel Bailey, Richard Bailey, Josiah
Bruce, Nathan Colburn, Joseph French, Nehemiah French, Abner
Keyes, David Wallingford and Bray Wilkins, nine other Hollis
men, enlisted for the like time in the company of Capt Towne of
Amherst, which, as appears from the company roll, still preserved,
afterwards joined the 27th Massachusetts regiment, which served at
the siege of Boston under Col. Hutchinson.   These several numbers, added to the fifty-nine names in the company roll of Capt.
Dow, make in all, eighty eight months' soldiers who went from
Hollis in the spring or early in the summer of 1775.

The original commission of Capt. Dow, dated May 19, 1775,
with the autograph signature of Gen. Joseph Warren, president
pro tem. of the Massachusetts Congress, who was killed at Bunker
Hill about four weeks after, is now among the Hollis documents.
A copy of this commission is here presented.

" THE CONGRESS OF THE COLONY OF MASSACHUSETTS BAY.

" To REUBEN Dow, gentleman.

" Greeting.

" We reposing especial trust and confidence in your courage and
good conduct, do by these presents constitute and appoint you, the
said Reuben Dow, to be Captain in the —— company in the Regiment of foot commanded by William Prescott, Esq., Colonel,
raised by the Congress aforesaid for the defence of said colony.

" You are, therefore, carefully and diligently to discharge the
duty of a Captain in leading, ordering and exercising the said com
p any in arms, both inferior officers and soldiers, and to keep them
in good order and discipline; and they are hereby commanded to
obey you as their Captain; and you are, yourself, to observe and
follow such orders and instructions as you shall from time to time
receive from the General and commander in chief of the forces

raised in the colony aforesaid, for the defence of the same, or any
other your superior officers according to military rules and discipline in war, in pursuance of the trust reposed in you.

"By order of the Congress,

"Jos. WARREN, President P. T.

"Watertown, the 19th of May, A. D., 1775.
    "Sam¹. Freeman, Secretary P. T."

The regiment of Col. Prescott, with other Massachusetts regiments, was stationed at Cambridge till the battle of Bunker Hill.
About nine o'clock on the night of the 16th of June the companies
of Captains Dow and Moor, with the regiment of Col. Prescott,
and detachments from two or three other regiments, by orders of
the Massachusetts Committee of Safety, with their arms, spades
and other intrenching tools, marched from Cambridge common to
Charlestown, and took possession of the heights upon which, the
next day, was fought the battle of Bunker Hill. Col. Prescott was
at the head of the detachment, in a simple appropriate uniform,
with a blue coat and three cornered hat. Two Sergeants carrying
dark lanterns were in front of him, and the intrenching tools in
carts in the rear. The men had been ordered to take with them
in their knapsacks, one day's rations, but many of them neglected
to obey this order. After one or more halts, for consultation
of the officers, the detachment reached the hill to be fortified about
midnight. Working with their spades and pickaxes the whole of
the rest of the night and the next forenoon in the intense heat of a
June sun, without sleep and many of them suffering for the want
of food and drink, they threw up the redoubt, which their heroism
soon made forever memorable. To inspire his men with courage
and confidence while busy with their intrenching tools, the gallant
Prescott, on the forenoon of the 17th, mounted the parapet of the
redoubt, and continued to walk leisurely around on the top of it in
full view of the British ships and troops, inspecting the works,
giving directions to his officers and men, encouraging them by his
example and approval, or amusing them by his humor. Gen.
Gage, seeing through his spy glass, the tall, commanding form of
Prescott, asked of Willard, one of the Council, "who he was?"
Willard replied, "He is my brother-in-law." "Will he fight?"
again asked Gage. "Yes, Sir;" said Willard, "he is an old
soldier, and will fight to the last drop of blood in him."

The men, hungry and weary, having worked through the night
and till noon of the next day, without sleep, and many of them without food or drink, some of their officers, in view of the impending
conflict, urged Col. Prescott to send a request to Gen. Ward, commanding at Cambridge, that the men who had built the fort might
be relieved and fresh troops might be sent over for its defence. Col.
Prescott fully understood the spirit and temper of his men—many
of them were his neighbors, and he promptly said to the officers
making that request, that he would not consent to their relief.
"The men," said he, "who have raised these works will best
defend them ; they have had the merit of the labor and should have
the honor of victory, if attacked."

Very many histories of the battle of Bunker Hill have already
been written. It is not my purpose to add another, but simply to
tell, in few words, the share the town of Hollis and Hollis soldiers
had in it.

HOLLIS, AND OTHER NEW HAMPSHIRE SOLDIERS IN COL. PRESCOTT'S REGIMENT.

Besides the company of Capt. Dow, and the four Hollis soldiers
in the company of Capt. Moor, it is shown by the original return
rolls of Col. Prescott's regiment, now at Boston, that there were
fifty or more other New Hampshire soldiers in the same regiment,
mostly from towns in the vicinity of Hollis. Of these, eleven were
from Merrimack, eleven from Londonderry, seven from Raby (now
Brookline), others from Amherst, Mason, New Ipswich, and other
towns, making in all between one hundred and ten and one hundred
and twenty New Hampshire men in that regiment. Yet, so far as
I am aware, no New Hampshire history of the battle of Bunker Hill
makes any reference to the New Hampshire soldiers in the regiment
of Col. Prescott. It is said in "Frothingham's Siege of Boston,"
page 401, that not more than three hundred of Col. Prescott's
regiment marched with him to Charlestown on the night of the 16th
of June. If such was the fact, it is not improbable that one-fourth
of the three hundred were New Hampshire soldiers, and at least
one-sixth of them from Hollis.

CASUALTIES.

James Fisk and Jeremiah Shattuck, two of Capt. Dow's company,
died of sickness, at Cambridge, on the 29th of May. Caleb
Eastman was killed at Cambridge, two days after the battle, by the

accidental bursting of his gun. Nathan Blood, the 1st Sergeant, Jacob Boynton, Isaac Hobart, Phineas Nevins, Peter Poor and Thomas Wheat, of Capt. Dow's company, and also Thomas Colburn and Ebenezer Youngman, two of the Hollis soldiers in Capt. Moor's company, were killed in the battle, making eight in all lost on the field, and a total loss of eleven. There were also six of the Hollis company wounded in the battle, viz., Reuben Dow, the Captain, Ephraim Blood, Francis Blood, Francis Powers, Thomas Pratt and William Wood; Dow and Wood, so severely that they were afterwards pensioners for life. The number of killed in Col. Prescott's regiment, (according to Frothingham, page 193,) was forty-two; wounded, twenty-eight. Of the killed in that regiment, the loss of Hollis was nearly one-fifth, and more than that proportion of the wounded.

From a letter written by Col. Stark, to Matthew Thornton, two days after the battle, it appears that the loss of his own regiment in killed and missing was fifteen, that of the regiment of Col. Reed, but four, making nineteen in all.* From the above statements, it appears that the loss of Hollis, in killed, was fully equal to two-fifths of the killed and missing in the two New Hampshire regiments, and greater, as is believed, than that of any other town in New Hampshire or Massachusetts. It is shown by the return rolls at Boston, that the town of Pepperell lost six in killed, which is believed to be the next largest loss of a single town. Of the Hollis men, above named, who had died of disease or been killed, Fisk, Shattuck, Blood and Wheat were married and heads of families. Boynton, Eastman, Hobart, Youngman, Nevins and Poor, were young, unmarried men, the oldest supposed to be 22, and the youngest but 17.

LOSS OF EQUIPMENTS, ETC., IN THE BATTLE.

It is shown by the rolls of Capt. Dow's company, that his men furnished all their own equipments, and also their clothes, as did the soldiers generally, the first year of the war. The following statement, to which are appended the names of twenty-eight members of the company, present at the battle, not including the commissioned officers, or the killed, exhibits the articles lost by each of them, with their estimated value.

---

*New Hampshire Hist. Coll., Vol. 2, p. 145.

"CAMBRIDGE, Dec. 22, 1775."

"This may certify that we the subscribers in Capt. Reuben Dow's company, in Col. William Prescott's regiment, in the Continental army, that we lost the following articles, in the late engagement on Bunker Hill on the 17th of June last."

	value £0 1s. d.
William Adams 1 knapsack, 1s.,	" 2 6
David Ames, 1 knapsack 1s. 4d. 1 tumpline 1s. 2d.,	" 2 6
Ephraim Blood, 1 knapsack 1s. 8d. 1 tumpline 1s. 4d. 1 gun £2, 14s.,	" 2 17
Francis Blood, 1 knapsack 1s. 4d. 1 tumpline 1s. 2d.,	" 2 6
Elias Boynton, 1 gun £2, 2s.,	" 2 2
Abel Brown, 1 tumpline 1s. 2., 1 gun 18s., 1 cartridge box 4s.,	" 2 3 2
Wilder Chamberlain, 1 knapsack 1s 4d.,	" 1 4
Abel Conant, 1 knapsack 1s. 8d., 1 tumpline 1s. 4d.,	" 3
Benjamin Cumings, 1 knapsack 1s. 8d., 1 tumpline 1s. 4d.,	" 3
Minot Farmer, 1 knapsack 1s. 4d., 1 tumpline 1s 4d., 1 sword 10s.,	" 12 8
David Farnsworth, 1 knapsack 1s. 8d., 1 tumpline 1s. 2d.,	" 2 10
Josiah Fisk, 1 knapsack 1s. 8d., 1 tumpline 1s. 2d., 1 cartridge box 4s. 8d.	" 7 8
Samuel Hill, 1 knapsack 1s. 4d., 1 tumpline 1s. 8d.,	" 3
Samuel Jewett, 1 knapsack 1s. 8d., 1 tumpline 1s. 2 d.,	" 2 10
Israel Kinney, 1 knapsack 1s. 4d., 1 tumpline 1s. 2d.,	" 2 6
James McConnor, 1 knapsack, 1s. 4d., 1 tumpline, 1s. 2d. 1 gun £2, 2s. 1 hat 12s	" 2 16 6
James McIntosh, 1 knapsack 1 s. 8d., 1 tumpline 1s. 4d., 1 jacket 8s,	" 13
William Nevins, 1 knapsack 1s. 8d., 1 tumpline 1s. 4d., 1 jacket £1, 4s.,	" 1 7
Nathaniel Patten, 1 knapsack 1s 4d., 1 tumpline 1s 2d., 1 jacket 16s.,	" 18 6
Nehemiah Pierce, 1 knapsack 1s. 8d., 1 tumpline 1s. 4d., 1 hat 18s.,	" 1 1
Francis Powers, 1 gun £2, 14s., 1 bayonet 6s.,	" 3
Nahum Powers, 1 knaps'k 1s. 4d., 1 tump'e 1s, 2d., hat 3s., jacket 8s., bayonet 6s	" 19 6
Thomas Pratt, 1 knapsack 1s. 4d., 1 tumpline 1s. 2d., 1 gun £1, 16s.,	" 1 18 6
Isaac Stearns, 1 knapsack 1s. 4d., 1 gun £2, 14s.,	" 2 15 4
Lebbeus Wheeler, 1 knapsack 1s. 8d., 1 tumpline 1s. 2d., 1 hat 6s.,	" 8 10
Noah Worcester, Jun., 1 knapsack 1s. 8d., 1 tumpline 1s. 2d.,	" 2 10
William Wood, 1 knapsack 1s. 8d., 1 tumpline 1s. 2d., 1 gun £2, 8s.,	" 2 10 10
Uriah Wright. 1 knapsack 1s. 8d., 1 tumpline 1s. 3d.,	" 2 11

It appears from the above certificate, that twenty-five of these men lost their knapsacks, twenty-three their tumplines,* eight their guns, three their cartridge boxes, two their bayonets, and one his sword; five of them their short coats or "Jackets," and three their hats.

How many of Capt. Dow's company, besides the killed and commissioned officers, were present in the battle and lost no part of their equipments, cannot now be known—doubtless some, and it may be most of them.

The following copy of an original certificate in the hand writing of Capt. Dow, and preserved by him, with other papers relating to his company, shows the loss of equipments of the six men belonging to it, killed in the battle.

---

*A Tump-line was a strap to be placed across the forehead, to assist a man in carrying a pack on his back.—WORCESTER'S QUARTO DICTIONARY.

CAMBRIDGE, Dec. 22, 1775."

"Nathan Blood,   Isaac Hobart,   Jacob Boynton,
Thomas Wheat,   Peter Poor,   Phineas Nevins."

"The men whose names are above written belonged to Capt. Dow's company, and Col. William Prescott's regiment and were all killed in the battle of Bunker Hill, on the 17th of June last, and were furnished each of them with a good gun, judged to be worth Eight Dollars apiece—also were furnished with other materials, viz. Cartridge Boxes, Knapsacks and Tump-lines—and were well clothed for soldiers—Also had each of them a good blanket. Nathan Blood had a good Hanger."

It appears that the eight Hollis men in Capt. Spalding's company, in the New Hampshire regiment of Col. Reed, were all present in the battle, and that each of them lost portions of his clothing or equipments, as is shown from the returns of losses made after the battle, now to be found in the "New Hampshire Provincial Papers," Volume 6, page 592." These losses with their appraised value were as follows:

	value,	£2.	os.	8d.
Andrew Bailey, 1 coat, 1 shirt, trousers, stockings,				
Job Bailey, 1 cartridge box, knapsack, and shirt,	"		15	
Phineas Hardy, 1 blanket, coat, shirt, breeches,	"	1	12	
Thomas Hardy, 1 blanket, coat, jacket, stockings,	"	2	6	8
Ephraim How, 1 gun, breeches and shirt,	"	1	5	1
Samuel Leeman, 2 coats and 1 blanket,	"	2	13	4
Ephraim Rolfe, 1 gun, blanket, shirt, stockings,	"	3	9	4
Ephraim Smith, 1 knapsack, shirt, stockings,	"		11	4

At this late day it is difficult to ascertain all the reasons that may have induced the company of Capt. Dow to join the Massachusetts regiment of Col. Prescott. But the following well established facts undoubtedly had much influence. Col. Prescott at the time lived upon his farm on the north side of Pepperell, adjoining Hollis, (still the country seat of his descendants) a large part of the farm then being in Hollis. Capt. Dow and Lieut. Goss lived in the south part of Hollis, and were the neighbors and friends of Col. Prescott. A very large part of the early settlers of Hollis were from Billerica, Chelmsford, Groton and Pepperell and other towns in Middlesex county in which most of the companies in Col. Prescott's regiment were enlisted. It may be added to these reasons, that Col. John Hale, one of the leading friends of the Revolution, in Hollis, was a brother-in-law of Col. Prescott, he having married Abigail Hale, a sister of Col. Hale.

THE NEW HAMPSHIRE REINFORCEMENTS IN DECEMBER, 1775.

The time of service of the men enlisted for eight months expired in December. On the 30th of November an express was sent by Gen. Sullivan, then in command of the Continental troops at Winter Hill, near Boston, to the New Hampshire Committee of Safety, informing them that the Connecticut regiments had refused to remain longer in the service, and urging for reinforcements from New Hampshire to supply their places.

LETTER OF GEN. SULLIVAN TO THE NEW HAMPSHIRE COMMITTEE OF SAFETY.

"WINTER HILL. Nov. 30, 1775.

" *Sirs :* Gen. Washington has sent to New Hampshire for thirty-one companies to take possession of and defend our lines in room of the Connecticut forces who most scandalously refuse to tarry till the 1st of January. I must therefore intreat your utmost exertions to forward the raising those companies, lest the enemy should take advantage of their absence and force our lines. As the Connecticut forces will at all events leave us at or before the 10th of next month, pray call upon every true friend of his country to assist with heart and hand in sending forward these companies as soon as possible. Sirs. I am in extreme haste your Obt. Serv't,

"JOHN SULLIVAN."

" To the Committee of Safety at Exeter."*

In answer to this call, New Hampshire, with patriotic and characteristic promptness, sent to Cambridge 31 companies of 63 each, of the New Hampshire " Minute Men," numbering in all 2000, or more. These troops continued in the service, till the middle of March, 1776, when the British army evacuated Boston.

Two-thirds or more of the 26th company of this force volunteered from Hollis. Of this company Noah Worcester was Captain, and Robert Seaver. 2d Lieutenant, both of Hollis. and Obadiah Parker of Mason, 1st Lieutenant.

No roll of this company containing the names of all the men in it is known now to exist. But there are now among the Hollis Revolutionary papers two documents presenting the names of most of the Hollis men who were in the service in the several years of the war, with the amount of the wages and bounties paid to each of

*N. H. Prov. Papers, Vol. 7, p. 677.

them by the town. One of these documents entitled the " *Great
Return* " was made out by the selectmen of the town about eight
years after the war was ended, in obedience to a resolution of the
New Hampshire General Court. The other was prepared by Capt.
John Goss, who was chosen by the town in the year 1777, as a
member of a committee appointed for that purpose, and who was
Captain of the Hollis company at the battle of Bennington. These
documents together contain the names of forty-four Hollis soldiers.
The name of the 2nd Lieutenant, Robert Seaver, is not found on
either of them, though he was one of the company that marched
from Hollis to Lexington and Cambridge on the 19th of April, and
also his name at the time and for many years after was on the Hollis
tax lists as a resident tax payer.

It appears from the " Great Return " that thirty-seven men of this
company were paid by the town £3 each, and two others £2, 5s.
each. The names of five others of the company, with the wages
supposed to have been paid them, are found in the " Return " of
Capt. Goss, but not in the other document. The names of these
soldiers, forty-five in all, are here presented :

Noah Worcester, Capt.	Stephen Farley,	Ephraim Lund,
Robert Seaver, 2d Lieut.	Isaac French,	Elijah Noyes,
Samuel Ambrose,	Ebenezer Gilson,	Daniel Patch,
Eleazer Ball,	Nehemiah Hardy,	Nathan Phelps,
Daniel Bailey,	Jonathan Hobart,	Solomon Pierce,
Joshua Blanchard,	Joshua Hobart,	Wm. W. Pool,
Daniel Blood,	Parmeter Honey,	John Read,
Joel Boynton,	Joseph How,	Jonathan Russ,
Eliphalet Brown,	Ebenezer Jaquith,	William Shattuck,
James Colburn,	Thomas Jaquith,	Zachariah Shattuck,
Robert Colburn,	Jacob Jewett, Jun.,	Jacob Taylor,
Josiah Conant,	Stephen Jewett,	Jonathan Taylor,
John Conroy,	Oliver Lawrence,	William Tenney,
Benjamin Farley,	Asa Lovejoy,	Nathaniel Wheat,
Joseph Farley,	Jonathan Lovejoy,	James Wheeler.

NUMBER OF HOLLIS SOLDIERS THE FIRST YEAR OF THE WAR.

Minute men who went to Cambridge in April,	92
Eight months' men : In Capt. Dow's Company, 59 : Capt.	
Moor's, 4 ; Spalding's, 8 ; Towns, 9 : in all,	80
In Capt. Worcester's Company,	45
Making in all,	217

The names of 61 of the 92 minute men who went to Cambridge
in April will be found in the foregoing lists of men enlisted for
eight months, or in that of the Hollis men in Capt. Worcester's

company. Deducting the 61 from 217, there will remain a total of 156 different names of Hollis soldiers who were in the military service of the country during a part of the first year of the war, a number very nearly equal to one in eight of the whole population.

It is shown by the "Great Return" made by the selectmen above referred to, that the town paid in the year 1775, for the wages or bounties for these soldiers. the following sums;

	s.	d.
To the eight months' men at £12. per man, (£1 10s. per month),	£792. 00. 00.	
To the men in Capt. Worcester's company,	115. 10. 00.	
For the 92 Minute men to Cambridge in April,	93. 07. 07.	
Making an aggregate of	£1000. 17. 07.	

WAGES OF SOLDIERS IN 1775.

In the common histories of the war of the Revolution, but very little information is to be gleaned in regard to the wages paid to the brave men by whose valor and privations our national independence was won. Several of the original Hollis documents, still existing. throw much light upon this subject in respect to the pay of the soldiers who went from the town in 1775, and in the other years of the war. The pay roll of the first company of ninety-two minute men has already been adverted to, showing the daily wages paid to both the officers and privates of that company. It appears from a pay roll of the company of Capt. Dow, made in August, 1775, after the men had been at Cambridge near four months. that the monthly wages of the private soldiers were £2, or $6.67, or about 24 cents a day, reckoning twenty-eight days to the month. In addition to these wages the men were credited with 1d. a mile for travel. The wages of the drummer. fifer and corporals appear to have been £2, 5s. per month—those of the Sergeants £2, 10s.. the Second Lieut.. £3, the First Lieut.. £4, and of the Captain. £6. or about $20.00 per month.

THE MILITARY COAT VOTED AS A BOUNTY TO EIGHT MONTHS' MEN.

From the following copy of an original certificate and receipt now in the office of the Secretary of State. at Boston, it is shown that the soldiers in Capt. Dow's company received a military coat. voted by the Massachusetts Congress in the spring of 1775. as a bounty to men enlisted for eight months.

"CAMBRIDGE, Nov. 20, 1775.

"*To the Honorable Committee of Supplies:*

"This may certify that we who have hereunto subscribed our names do declare that we being under officers and soldiers enlisted under Captain Reuben Dow of Holles, in Col. William Prescott's regiment, have received each of us a coat according to a vote of the late Congress held at Watertown, and provided by the committee of supplies, we say received of Lieutenant John Goss of said company."

The above certificate was signed by forty-seven members of the company, being all the non-commissioned officers and privates, except the nine of them who had been previously killed or died of sickness. There was endorsed upon this certificate the receipt of Lieut. Goss, as follows :

"Rec'd of the committee on cloathing forty-seven coats for the within mentioned soldiers as per Receipt on back, of this date.

"Nov. 20, 1775"   "JOHN Goss, Lieut."

It also appears from the three following certificates and vouchers to be found in the same depository at Boston, that the heirs or widows of the nine deceased men received pay for these military bounty coats.

1st Voucher.   "To the Honorable the Committee of Supplies of Massachusetts Bay. Be pleased to pay or deliver to Capt. Reuben Dow the money due to the following men for their military coats, viz., Sergt. Nathan Blood, Thomas Wheat, Isaac Hobart, Jacob Boynton, Phineas Nevins, James Fisk and Caleb Eastman, in Capt. Reuben Dow's company, in Col. William Prescott's regiment, deceased. and this shall be your Receipt for the same, per us"

"WILLIAM NEVINS	ENOCH NOYES
JOHN BOYNTON	ABIGAIL WHEAT
AMOS EASTMAN	her
SHUBAEL HOBART	SARAH X FISK."
	mark

William Nevins, John Boynton, Amos Eastman and Shubael Hobart were respectively the fathers of Phineas Nevins, Jacob Boynton, Caleb Eastman and Isaac Hobart; Abigail Wheat and Sarah Fisk, the widows of Thomas Wheat and James Fisk, and Enoch Noyes was the father-in-law of Sergt. Nathan Blood.

2d Voucher. "We hereby certify that the widow Experience Shattuck is the proper person to receive the clothing belonging to

Jeremiah Shattuck who belonged to Capt. Reuben Dow's Company in Col. Wm. Prescott's regiment and is dead.

> "NOAH WORCESTER,
> JACOB JEWETT,   } Selectmen."
> OLIVER LAWRENCE,

" Holles. y° 16th of March, 1776.

" To the Honorable Committee of Supplies of Massachusetts Bay. Gentlemen, Be pleased to pay to Capt. Reuben Dow, the money due to Jeremiah Shattuck. deceased, who belonged to Capt. Reuben Dow's Company in Col. Wm. Prescott's regiment, and this order shall be your discharge for the same, per me.

> her
> EXPERIENCE X SHATTUCK."
> mark.

Holles. March 14, 1776.

3d Voucher. " We hereby certify that Capt. Reuben Dow is the only proper person to receive the clothing that is due to Peter Poor, a transient person who enlisted in his Company, and last resided in this Town and went away in debt. Said Poor was killed in Bunker Hill fight.

> "NOAH WORCESTER, OLIVER LAWRENCE,
> STEPHEN AMES, JACOB JEWETT,   } Selectmen of
> DANIEL KENDRICK.   Holles."

" Holles. Feb. 10, 1776.

STORY OF A HOLLIS WOMAN.—CAPTURE AND SURRENDER OF A HOLLIS TORY.

Among the citizens of Hollis in 1775, were four known as tories, whose sympathies were strongly with the royal government. These four were Benjamin Whiting, the first sheriff of Hillsborough county; his brother, Capt. Leonard Whiting; and Samuel and Thomas Cumings. two of the sons of Samuel Cumings, Sen., the first town-clerk of Hollis. We copy the following notices of the two Whitings from Sabine's "Loyalists of the American Revolution," Vol. 2. p. 422.

" Whiting, Benjamin, Sheriff of Hillsborough County, N. H. He was proscribed and banished and his property confiscated."

" Whiting, Leonard, of Hollis, N. H. A noted Tory. In 1775, Whiting was the bearer of despatches from Canada to the British in Boston, and was arrested in Groton, Mass., under the following circumstances. After the departure of Col. Prescott's Regiment of ' Minute Men,' Mrs. David Wright, of Pepperell, Mrs. Job Shattuck,

(11)

of Groton, and the neighboring women, collected at what is now Jewett's bridge, over the Nashua river, between Pepperell and Groton, clothed in their absent husbands' apparel, and armed with muskets, pitchforks, and such other weapons as they could find, and having elected Mrs. Wright their commander, resolutely determined that no foe to freedom, foreign or domestic, should pass that bridge. Rumors were then rife that the Regulars were approaching, and frightful stories of slaughter flew rapidly from place to place and from house to house. Soon there appeared Mr. Leonard Whiting (the subject of this notice), on horseback, supposed to be treasonably engaged in carrying intelligence to the enemy. Whiting, by direction of Mrs. Wright in her assumed character of Sergeant of the Bridge Guard, was seized, taken from his horse, searched, and detained a prisoner. Despatches were found in his boots, which were sent to the Committee of Safety, and Whiting himself was committed to the custody of the Committee of Observation of Groton."

The maiden name of Mrs. David Wright was Prudence Cumings, a sister of Samuel and Thomas Cumings, two of the Hollis tories before mentioned, and also of Benjamin Cumings, a younger brother, who was in the company of Capt. Dow at Bunker Hill, and was afterwards a soldier in the Continental army. It appears from the Hollis Records of Births and Marriages, that Prudence Cumings was born at the parish of West Dunstable, now Hollis, Nov. 26, 1740, and that she was married to David Wright, of Pepperell, Dec. 28, 1761.

CHAPTER XIV.

1776.—HOLLIS SOLDIERS THE SECOND YEAR OF THE WAR.—THE
HOLLIS LOYALISTS OR TORIES.

COMMITTEE OF SAFETY.

At the annual March election of 1776 "Capt. Reuben Dow,
Capt. Noah Worcester, Ensign Stephen Ames, Capt. Daniel Kendrick, Jacob Jewett, Oliver Lawrence, and Samuel Chamberlain,"
were chosen a *Committee of Safety ;* Noah Worcester, Stephen
Ames, Daniel Kendrick, Jacob Jewett, and Oliver Lawrence, Selectmen ; and on the 26th of November, at a special election, Stephen
Ames was chosen Representative to the General Court for one year.

HOLLIS SOLDIERS THE SECOND YEAR OF THE WAR.

In the year 1776 the seat of the war was removed from the vicinity of Boston to Canada, and the States of New York and New
Jersey.   But a few of the company or regimental rolls of the troops
furnished from New Hampshire the second year of the war are now
known to exist, or if in existence, some of the most interesting and
important of them, supposed to be in the office of the Secretary of
State at Washington, under the inhospitable rules of that office, are
not accessible to the historical enquirer.   I have examined the very
few of them at Concord, but in these researches I have been
obliged to rely mainly upon the town records and documents for
the names, numbers, time of service and wages of the Hollis soldiers for this year.

It appears from these documents that four Hollis soldiers, viz.,
David Ames, Minot Farmer, David Patch and Eli Stiles, enlisted
in the detachment of troops, under Gen. Arnold, who with so
much privation and suffering, made their way, in the depth of
winter, through the forests of Maine in 1775–6, by the way of Ken-
nebec river, to Canada and Quebec.   Minot Farmer, who had been

a Sergeant in Capt. Dow's company at Bunker Hill, was taken
prisoner at the assault on Quebec, and died in captivity in the month
of May of this year.

In 1776, and afterwards till near the end of the war, New Hampshire furnished three regiments or battalions of regular troops,
known as the 1st, 2d and 3d New Hampshire Continental regiments, commanded severally by Colonels Cilley, Hale and Scammel. Dr. John Hale and his son-in-law, Dr. Jonathan Pool, both
of Hollis, were respectively Surgeon and Assistant Surgeon of the
1st New Hampshire regiment, from 1776 to 1780. Dr. Hale had
previously been Colonel of the New Hampshire regiment of militia,
to which Hollis was attached, which office he resigned in the month
of June of the former year.

The private soldiers in these Continental regiments were at first
enlisted for a single year. Besides the Surgeon and Assistant Surgeon for the 1st regiment, Hollis furnished for those regiments
twenty-one men, a part of whom are said to have enlisted in the
sixth company of the 1st regiment, commanded by Capt. John
House of Hanover, and a part in the first company of the 3d regiment under Capt. Isaac Frye of Wilton. Of this last company
Samuel Leeman, Jun., of Hollis, was Ensign. The history and
doings of these gallant regiments are too well known to require or
permit special comment here. They were in the hard-fought battles of this year near New York city, and their bravery and good
conduct were conspicuous in the victories won at Trenton and
Princeton in New Jersey. The wages of the men paid by the town
were £24 for the year, or £2 each per month. Their names were

Elias Boynton,	Thomas Hardy,	Ezra Proctor,
Abel Brown,	Israel Kinney,	John Read,
Abel Conant,	Sam'l Leeman, Jun.,	Stephen Richardson,
Benjamin Cumings,	William Nevins,	Ephraim Rolfe,
Stephen Conroy,	Jonathan Parker,	Ephraim Smith,
Jacob Danforth,	Thomas Pratt,	Jacob Taylor,
William Elliot,	Ezekiel Proctor,	Thomas Youngman.

William Nevins is said to have been taken captive near New
York city, and to have died while a prisoner, probably in a British
prison ship. Ezra Proctor, as shown by the Hollis records, was
drowned at New York on the 15th of May of this year.

HOLLIS MEN IN COL. WINGATE'S REGIMENT.

About the middle of July of this year a regiment of New Hampshire Volunteers was enlisted to re-enforce the army then in Canada and placed under the command of Col. Joshua Wingate of

Dover. In the third company of this regiment, of which Daniel Emerson, Jun., of Hollis was Captain, were twenty-five Hollis soldiers, supposed to have been in service about six months.

The wages paid them by the town were £12 each. In consequence of the retreat of the Continental troops from Canada, this regiment went no farther north than Ticonderoga. The names of these men were,

David Ames,	Samuel Hill,	Solomon Pierce,
John Ball,	John How,	Joseph Stearns,
Daniel Blood, Jun.,	Oliver Lawrence, Jun.,	Isaac Stevens, Jun.,
Josiah Blood,	Elijah Noyes,	Ebenezer Townsend,
Daniel Emerson, Jun., Capt.	Enoch Noyes, Jun.,	Jesse Worcester,
Thomas Emerson,	Thomas Patch,	Lemuel Wright,
Ralph Emerson,	Nathaniel Patten,	John Youngman,
Benjamin Farley, Jun.,	Samuel Phelps,	Nicholas Youngman.
Josiah Fisk,		

It appears from an inventory of the equipments and clothing of Josiah Blood, one of these soldiers, now among the Hollis Documents, dated at Mt. Independence, September 16. 1776, that he died in the army about that time.

MEN IN COL. LONG'S REGIMENT.

Early in August of this year, a small regiment of seven companies was organized by order of the New Hampshire Committee of Safety, afterwards commanded by Col. Pierce Long, and stationed at Newcastle, near Portsmouth. About the last of November, 1776, this regiment was ordered to the State of New York for the defence of Ticonderoga. In the third company of this regiment, of which Timothy Clements, of Hopkinton, was Captain, were twelve Hollis soldiers, supposed to have served about a year, and were paid by the town £12 each. and whose names were

Ebenezer Ball,	David French,	Isaac Shattuck,
Larnard Cunings.	Richard Hopkins,	Enoch Spaulding,
Caleb Farley,	Abner Keyes,	Thomas Wheat,
Christopher Farley,	Stephen Powers,	Samuel Worcester.

Isaac Shattuck, one of these soldiers, a son of Zachariah Shattuck. and a young, unmarried man, died in this service.

MEN IN COL. BALDWIN'S REGIMENT.

In the month of September, of this year. a regiment of New Hampshire troops was raised, commanded by Col. Nahum Baldwin, of Amherst, to reinforce the Continental army, then at White Plains, near New York city. In the second company of this

regiment of which William Reed was Captain, were twenty-one
Hollis soldiers, who, with one exception, were paid by the town
£5 7s. each, and supposed to have been in the service about three
months. It is shown by a roll of this company, now at Concord,
that the men on enlisting were paid a bounty of £6 each, and
allowed a penny a mile for travel, and the same in lieu of a baggage
wagon. The names of these men were

Daniel Bailey, Jun.,	Stephen Dow,	Asa Lovejoy,
Daniel Blood,	Isaac French,	Ephraim Pierce,
Timothy Blood,	Stephen Goodhue,	John Platts,
Benjamin Boynton,	Noah Jewett,	Benjamin Sanderson,
Joel Boynton,	Stephen Jewett, Jun.,	Joshua Smith,
Edward Carter,	Thomas Kemp,	William Tenney,
Nathan Colburn,	Jonas Lesley,	Ebenezer Wheeler.

MEN IN COL. GILMAN'S REGIMENT.

In the month of December of this year, another New Hampshire
regiment was enlisted to reinforce the army in New York, commanded by Col. David Gilman. In the second company of this regiment, of which William Walker, of Dunstable, (now Nashua) was
Captain, there were thirteen Hollis soldiers, as appears by the rolls
at Concord and Hollis documents, eight of whom were paid by the
town £4 each, and are supposed to have been in the service for two
months. The names of these men are presented in the following
list :

Samuel Chamberlain,	Jonathan Hobart,	David Sanderson,
William Cumings,	Samuel Johnson,	William Shattuck,
Amos Eastman,	Randall McDaniels,	Benjamin Wright,
Ebenezer Farley,	James Rolfe,	Jesse Wyman.
John Hale, Jun.,		

It is shown by the company roll at Concord, that the men were
allowed £3, each, being advanced pay for one month and £2 2s.
each for "_billeting_" or expenses to New York.

It is also shown by the "Great Return" above referred to made
by the selectmen, that in 1776 four Hollis soldiers served in the
garrison at Portsmouth, for about three months, (as is supposed),
they having been paid by the town £4 10s. each. The names of
these men were John Atwell, Andrew Bailey, Phineas Hardy, and
Phineas Hardy, Jun.

OTHER HOLLIS SOLDIERS IN 1776 IN CAPT. GOSS'S "RETURN."

In addition to the soldiers for 1776, whose names appear in the
foregoing lists, I find in the "Return" made by Captain Goss, the

names of twenty-five others who in his "Return" are credited
with wages varying from £2 to £12, each, for services, as would
appear in another expedition to Ticonderoga under Capt. Emerson.
The names of these men, with the amount credited to each of them,
appear in the list below.

Nathaniel Ball,	£6.	Thomas Jaquith,		Daniel Mooar,	£3.
Elnathan Blood,	3.	Nathaniel Jewett,	£2.	John Phelps,	12.
William Brown,	4.	Jacob Jewett,	6.	Richard Pierce,	6.
Ephraim Burge,	4.	James Jewett,	6.	William Pool,	4.
Deacon Goodhue,	4.	Stephen Jewett,	4.	Edward Taylor,	3.
John Goodhue,	4.	Edward Johnson,	4.	Solomon Wheat,	3.
Lemuel Hardy,	6.	Daniel Lovejoy,	12.	Ensign Willoughby,	6.
John Hobart,	3.	Daniel Merrill,	3.	Nehemiah Woods,	4.
Ebenezer Jaquith,	2.		4.		

From the foregoing lists it appears that 125 Hollis men were in
the army the whole or a part of the year 1776, a number nearly
equal to one in ten of the whole population. The amount paid by
the town in 1776, as wages and bounties, according to the Great
Return, was £1018, 7s.

THE HOLLIS TORIES OR LOYALISTS.

As has been, in another connection, already stated, there were in
Hollis, at the commencement of the war, four of its citizens, viz.,
Benjamin and Leonard Whiting, and Samuel and Thomas Cumings,
who were understood by their fellow townsmen to be loyalists or
tories and opposed to the independence of the colonies. To these
four should probably be added Richard Cutts Shannon, a lawyer
from Portsmouth who had settled in Hollis just before the
Revolution.

About the first of March, 1776, or it may be somewhat earlier,
the four men first named were summoned for trial, upon a charge of
the character referred to, before the Committees of Safety of the towns
of Hollis, Dunstable, Merrimack and Litchfield. Upon the petition
of the accused, shortly after the first of March, the case was transferred for hearing to the New Hampshire General Court then sitting
at Exeter. Capt. Reuben Dow, of Hollis, as chairman of the
Committees of Safety, appeared before the General Court and filed
his complaint in their behalf with the evidence charging all the
accused as "persons suspected of being inimical to the Rights and
Liberties of the United Colonies." The accused appeared at the
trial by their counsel and made their defence, and at the final hearing on the 20th of June, following, it was decided that the testimony
was not sufficient to sustain the complaint and all of them were

discharged.* But events very soon proved that the suspicions and charges of the Committees of Safety were well grounded.

In the same month of June, as shown by the court records, Thomas Cumings was indicted before the Superior Court, and gave bail for his appearance to the following September term of the Court to answer to the charge. In the meanwhile he left his family, the town and country, failed to appear, forfeited his bond and never returned. Some months later, Samuel Cumings and Benjamin Whiting left the town and State, both leaving their families, and remained " absentees," and all the three died in exile. The names of all of them, with those of seventy-three other New Hampshire tories, were embraced in the "Act of Banishment," passed by the New Hampshire General Court, in November, 1778—the estates of Samuel Cumings and Benjamin Whiting were confiscated, all of them forbidden to return under the penalty of transportation, and in case of a second return, they were to suffer death. It is to be inferred that Thomas Cumings and Whiting both died within a very few years after leaving the country, Grace Whiting, the deserted wife of Sheriff Whiting, (as appears from the Hollis records) having been married to Burpee Ames, of Hollis, May 28, 1782, and upon her decease, which occurred shortly after this marriage, Mr. Ames married for his second wife, Hannah Cumings, the deserted wife of Thomas Cumings.

Capt. Leonard Whiting did not leave the country, but continued to reside in Hollis for many years after the war. But for a large portion of the years 1777 and 1778 he was imprisoned in the jail at Amherst, with several other accused persons, all under the charge of being "*inimical to the Rights and Liberties of the United Colonies.*"† It appears also that Richard Cutts Shannon, the Hollis lawyer, at the time, for a part of the year 1777 was imprisoned in the jail at Amherst, with Whiting and others under the like charge.‡ Yet it seems that the offence of Mr. Shannon, whatever it may have been, was afterwards so far forgotten or forgiven by the people of Hollis, that in the year 1782 he was chosen Representative of the town to the General Court.

*Prov. Papers, Vol. S, pp. 82, 106, 156.
†N. H. Prov. Papers, Vol. S, p. 636.
‡N. H. Prov. Papers, Vol. S, pp. 601, 636.

CHAPTER XV.

1777.—WAR OF THE REVOLUTION CONTINUED.—COMMITTEE OF SAFETY FOR 1777.— HOLLIS SOLDIERS THE THIRD YEAR OF THE WAR.— PATRIOTIC AGREEMENT OF FORTY-EIGHT HOLLIS MINUTE MEN.—THE TICONDEROGA ALARM.—COMPANY TO BENNINGTON.—DEPRECIATION OF CONTINENTAL PAPER MONEY.

HOLLIS COMMITTEE OF SAFETY IN 1777.

From the Town Records. An. T. M. March 3, 1777.— " Voted and chose for a Committee of Safety, this year, Capt. Noah Worcester, Ensign Stephen Ames, Capt. Daniel Kendrick, Oliver Lawrence and Jacob Jewett, and also voted that we will stand by the Committee of Safety and defend them and do all we can to assist them in the cause of liberty. Chose Capt. Daniel Emerson Powder keeper, and Capt. Reuben Dow, Capt. John Goss, Capt. Daniel Emerson, Capt. William Read and Dea. John Boynton a committee to make out a list of the men who have been in the army, in defence of American liberty, and set a valuation on their services."

At a town meeting held on the 25th of the following November, this committee, in respect to these services, made the following report which was then accepted by the town, including in the report the Hollis soldiers who afterwards, the same year, went to Bennington and Portsmouth.

		£	s.
" 1775.	To Cambridge, £1, 10s. per month, 8 months,	£12,	s.
1776.	To New York and Canada for the year,	24	
1776.	To Ticonderoga, each time,	12	
1776.	To New York with Capt. Reed,	5	7
1776.	To New York with Capt. Walker,	4	
1777.	To Bennington with Capt. Goss,	7	
1777.	To Portsmouth 1 month,	1	10 "

THE TOWN'S QUOTA FOR THE CONTINENTAL ARMY.

Special Town Meeting April 2, 1777. "Voted to give each
man that shall enlist for three years, or during the War to make out
our Quota of thirty men £46, including the Continental and State's
Bounty and to raise the money by Tax, and also that the Selectmen
shall give Security to each man that enlists for the sum that is to be
given to the thirty men by the town."

THE TOWN'S QUOTA FOR THE CONTINENTAL ARMY.

*Adjourned Special Town Meeting, May 4.—From the
records.* "The officers having received new orders to raise our
men, (if they could not be got for three years, or during the war,)
for eight or twelve months, if the town would supply their places
with other men at the end of said time. Voted that the Committee
appointed at this meeting should agree with the men for eight
months. The Committee having reported that they had agreed
with the men for eight months for £20, that sum was voted to them
accordingly, and also that the Selectmen give security to the men
to their satisfaction."

HOLLIS SOLDIERS IN 1777, IN THE CONTINENTAL ARMY.

In 1777, as in the year preceding, the State of New Hampshire,
under the laws and resolutions of Congress, was required to furnish
three regiments for the regular Continental army, commanded severally this year, as in 1776 by Colonels Cilley, Hale and Scammel.
The men to be raised for these regiments were assigned by the New
Hampshire State authorities to the respective regiments of the State
militia in proportion to their numbers and to the several towns, in
accordance with the number of the militia in each town. The
number so set to the town, was known as the town's "*Quota*," and
the law made it the duty of the town to keep its "Quota" constantly
filled. The number set to Hollis, in this apportionment, was *thirty*,
and that number continued to be the Hollis quota for the regular
army, till near the end of the war. It is shown by the returns of
Col. Nichols, the commander of the regiment in 1777, to which the
Hollis company of militia belonged, that the thirty men whose
names are in the lists below composed the Hollis quota for that
year, and were enlisted in the winter or spring of 1777. It appears
from the same "return" that twenty of these men enlisted for three
years and the rest for eight months.

For three years.	For three years.	For eight months.
David Ames,	Samuel Hill,	John Ball,
Daniel Blood,	Asa Lovejoy,	Andrew Bailey,
Isaac Boynton,	Nathaniel Patten,	Joel Bailey,
Ebenezer Cunings,	Thomas Pratt,	John Brooks,
Edward Carter,	Stephen Richardson,	John Boynton, 3d,
William Connick,	David Sanderson,	James Colburn,
Jacob Danforth,	Ebenezer Townsend,	Jonathan Parker,
Ralph Emerson,	Lebbeus Wheeler,	Nehemiah Pierce,
John Godfrey,	John Youngman,	Eli Stiles,
William Hale,	Thomas Youngman,	Jacob Taylor.

Twenty of the men in the above lists enlisted in the sixth company
of the 1st New Hampshire regiment, commanded by Capt. John
House, of Hanover, the rest of them, with but one or two exceptions, in the first company of the 3d regiment of which Isaac Frye
of Wilton was Captain. Of this last named company Samuel
Leeman, Jun., of Hollis, was the Ensign, and was killed at one of
the battles at the taking of Gen. Burgoyne and his army at Saratoga in October, 1777. All three of the New Hampshire Continental regiments fought in these battles and acquitted themselves
with their accustomed fidelity and heroism. After the capture of
Burgoyne and his army, the theatre of war was removed further
south to New Jersey and the vicinity of Philadelphia. The New
Hampshire troops being formed into a distinct brigade, shared in all
the services and hardships of the campaign in New Jersey and
Pennsylvania. At the battle of Monmouth, a part of them, including the 1st New Hampshire regiment, under Col. Cilley, be-
haved with such gallantry, as to merit and receive the particular approbation of Gen. Washington.

Poorly shod, clad and fed, in the hard winter of 1777–8, they
patiently shared with their companions in arms the privations and
sufferings at the ill-provided winter quarters in the huts at Valley
Forge. The people of Hollis, at home, in the mean time, were
not forgetful of the wants and sufferings of their townsmen in the
army. I find from the Hollis documents still preserved, that about
the first of January, 1778, there were collected by contribution, and
sent to them in the camp at Valley Forge, "*20 Pairs of Good
Merchantable Shoes, 20 Pairs of Good Woolen Stockings, 15
Shirts made of Good Merchantable Cloth,*" besides many other
articles for the use and comfort of these soldiers.

PATRIOTIC AGREEMENT OF THE HOLLIS MINUTE MEN.,

Early in May 1777, Gen. Burgoyne assumed command of the large British army in Canada, composed of British Regulars, Hessians, Tories and Indians, collected and organized for the invasion of the Northern States, in the hope and expectation of putting a speedy end to the so-called rebellion. At the same time a formidable British fleet was cruising along the coast of New England ready for an attack upon the sea-board. The whole north was in constant and fearful alarm, uncertain upon what points the gathering storm would first break.

The patriotic agreement below presented, drawn up at this crisis, and in view of the impending perils, is in the hand writing of its first signer, Capt. Reuben Dow, and is still preserved. It has appended to it the original autograph signatures of forty-eight Hollis minute men, and tersely tells the manner and spirit with which they were ready to meet and to aid in welcoming the invaders. As the names of the signers merit honorable mention and grateful remembrance, they are also presented.

"HOLLIS, May 15, 1777."

"Whereas it appears that the enemies of the United States of America are laying every Plan in their power to ruin and destroy us—and it being hourly expected that a Fleet and Army will arrive on some part of our coast in order to prosecute their wicked purpose—we apprehend it to be the Duty of all the Inhabitants of these States to be in the greatest Readiness and Preparation to exert themselves in defence of their country in this hour of danger."

"Wherefore we whose names are hereunto subscribed do promise and engage to equip ourselves immediately, with Arms, Ammunition, &c., and to be ready at a minute's warning by night or by day, to go and assist our Brethren wherever they may be attacked—that upon an *alarm*.* we will immediately appear upon the Parade at the Meeting House in Holles, and be under the command of such officer and officers as we shall choose ourselves or the major part of us, and that each of us will be provided with a good Horse in order that we the sooner may get to the place attacked."

---

*An alarm was three guns fired in quick succession.

" Reuben Dow,
Daniel Emerson, Jun.,
Benjamin Abbot,
Jonathan Ames,
Benjamin Austin,
Daniel Bailey, Jun.,
Eleazer Ball,
William Ball,
Daniel Blood, Jun.,
Francis Blood,
Josiah Blood,
Joshua Boynton,
Eliphalet Brown,
Ephraim Burge,
Benjamin Colburn,
Robert Colburn,

Robert Colburn, Jun.,
Josiah Conant,
John Cumings,
Evan Dow,
Stephen Dow,
Amos Eastman, Jun.,
Benjamin Farley, Jun.,
Christopher Farley,
Ebenezer Farley,
Stephen Farley,
Josiah French,
Jacob Jewett, Jun.,
Thomas Kemp,
Oliver Lawrence,
Oliver Lawrence, Jun.,
Nathaniel Leeman,

Enoch Noyes, Jun.,
Solomon Pierce,
Nathan Phelps,
John Platts,
Francis Powers,
Abel Shipley,
Isaac Stearns,
James Taylor,
William Tenney, Jun.,
Moses Thurston, Jun.,
Joseph Wheat,
William Wood,
Noah Worcester, Jun.,
Benjamin Wright,
Lemuel Wright,
Uriah Wright."

THE TICONDEROGA ALARM.

About the 20th of June of this year, Gen. Burgoyne with his fleet and army advanced up Lake Champlain, towards the important fortress at Ticonderoga, and soon after arrived with his forces at Crown Point, within a few miles of it, where he halted for a short time. Upon the news of this advance, known as the " *Ticonderoga Alarm*," a company was at once enlisted and organized at Hollis to aid in the defence of Ticonderoga. This company consisted of fifty-eight men, inclusive of officers, fifty of whom were from Hollis. The commissioned officers of this company were Daniel Emerson, Jun., Captain, Robert Seaver 1st Lieutenant, and David Wallingford 2d Lieutenant, all of Hollis. The company started from Hollis on the 30th of June, (the same day the British troops took possession of Ticonderoga) made a rapid march of sixty-five miles to Walpole, there had orders to return and reached Hollis again on the 4th of July. The next day the company received orders to march a second time for Ticonderoga, started on the 5th of July, proceeded as far as Cavendish, Vermont, (one hundred miles) and there met a New Hampshire regiment, under Col. Bellows, on their retreat, Ticonderoga having been abandoned by its garrison. At Cavendish the company had orders a second time to return home, reached Hollis on the 15th of July and was disbanded. The wages of the private soldiers on these expeditions were three shillings a day, and three pence a mile for travel.

NAMES OF THE HOLLIS MEN IN THIS COMPANY.

Daniel Emerson, Jun., Capt.
Robert Seaver, 1st Lieut.,
David Wallingford, 2d Lieut.,
Joshua Boynton, Ser'gt,
Ephraim Burge, "
Isaac Stearns, Corp.,
Noah Worcester, Jun., Fifer.

PRIVATES.

Benjamin Abbot,
Jonathan Ames,
Eleazer Ball,
William Ball,
Daniel Bailey,
Francis Blood,
Josiah Blood,
Reuben Blood,
Oliver Bowers,

Eliphalet Brown,
Benjamin Colburn,
Stephen Conroy,
William Cumings,
Stephen Dow,
Joseph Farley,
Josiah Fisk,
Nehemiah French,
Lemuel Hardy,
Noah Hardy,
John Hobart,
Joshua Hobart,
Solomon Hobart,
Ebenezer Jaquith,
Ebenezer Jewett,
Jonathan Jewett,
Samuel Jewett,

Nathaniel Leeman,
Ephraim Lund,
Samuel Merrill,
Joseph Nevins,
Elijah Noyes,
Ephraim Pierce,
Moses Proctor,
Jacob Spalding,
Moses Thurston, Jun.,
Ebenezer Townsend,
Joseph Wheat,
Abner Wheeler,
Jonas Woods,
Nehemiah Woods,
Jesse Worcester,
Lemuel Wright,
Uriah Wright.

HOLLIS SOLDIERS AT BENNINGTON.

Upon the news of the fall of Ticonderoga, the New Hampshire General Court promptly met on the 17th of July, and, in a session of three days, adopted the most decisive and vigorous measures for the defence of the country and to stop the advance of Gen. Burgoyne. An appeal was made to the New Hampshire militia and minute men which was at once responded to with the like spirit and patriotic devotion as in the years before. In the course of a very few days a brigade composed of three regiments of New Hampshire volunteers was enlisted and organized, and placed under the command of the brave and popular Gen. Stark, two of these regiments consisting of ten companies each, and one of them of but five. These regiments were commanded severally by Colonels Nichols of Amherst, Stickney of Concord, and David Hobart of Plymouth, to which place he had removed from Hollis, a few years before. Of the 6th company of Col. Nichols' regiment, John Goss was Captain and David Wallingford, 2d Lieutenant, both of Hollis. This company left Hollis on the 20th of July, and was present and shared in the honors of the brilliant and ever memorable battle and victory fought and won at Bennington, mainly by the New Hampshire volunteers, on the following 16th of August. The company afterwards marched as far west as Stillwater, N. Y., and was discharged on the 28th of September, having been in service two months and nine days. It is shown by the Hollis documents and the return of Capt. Goss now at Concord, that in his company there were forty-two men from Hollis, inclusive of officers, and that the wages paid the private soldiers were £4 10s, per month, and 3d. per mile for travel. The names of these men were

John Goss, Capt.,	Thomas Kemp,	Jonathan Russ,
David Wallingford, Second Lt.	Archibald McIntosh,	Ephraim Rolfe,
William Adams,	James McDonald,	Jonas Shed,
Simeon Blood,	Samuel Merrill,	Isaac Stearns,
Henry Bowers,	Daniel Mooar, Jun.,	Joseph Stearns,
Eliphalet Brown,	Jacob Mooar,	Ebenezer Townsend,
John Campbell,	Benjamin Messer,	Abner Wheeler,
John Connick,	Benjamin Nevins,	William Wood,
Jonathan French,	John Nevins,	Jonas Woods,
Timothy French,	Ephraim Pierce,	Nehemiah Woods,
Stephen Hazeltine,	Francis Powers,	Noah Worcester, Jun.,
Joshua Hobart,	Samson Powers,	Benjamin Wright,
Ephraim How,	James Rideout,	Samuel Wright,
Joseph How,	Stephen Runnells,	Jesse Wyman.

Two other Hollis soldiers, viz., Samuel Goodhue and Jesse Worcester, served a part of this year in the garrison at Portsmouth, and were paid by the town £1, 10s. each.

I do not find that any Hollis soldier, this year, died of disease in the service or was killed in battle, with the exception of Ensign Samuel Leeman, Jun., killed at Saratoga, at the taking of Gen. Burgoyne and his army. He was the son of Samuel Leeman, Sen., and born in Hollis, Aug. 7, 1749, æt. 28 years at the time of his death.

In the foregoing lists of the Hollis soldiers fourteen of the names occur twice, the men having enlisted more than once. Making the proper deduction, it will appear that there are in these lists one hundred and ten different names—a number equal very nearly to one in eleven of the population.

THE AMOUNT PAID BY THE TOWN IN 1777 FOR BOUNTIES AND WAGES WAS AS FOLLOWS:

	£	s.
To thirty Continental Soldiers, £20 each,	£600,	
To men in Capt. Emerson's Company, "Ticonderoga alarm,"	38,	4,
To men in Capt. Goss' Company to Bennington, &c.,	234,	
To two men to Portsmouth,	3,	
Making for this year	£875,	4,

DEPRECIATION OF THE PAPER CURRENCY, AND THE LAW REGULATING PRICES.

During most years of the war there was no money in circulation as a medium of exchange, except the Continental paper money issued by Congress or the bills of credit of the States. This currency was issued in such quantities, both by the State and Congress, that both from its excess and also from the fact of its being extensively counterfeited, it begun to depreciate rapidly, and to an alarming extent, as early as the second year of the war.   This depreciation is very plainly indicated in comparing the wages paid to soldiers in 1775 with those paid in 1777.   In the former year the wages paid to the Hollis soldiers who were at Cambridge and Bunker Hill were £2, or about $6.67, per month, and 1d. a mile for travel.   In 1777 the wages paid to the Hollis soldiers who went to Bennington and New York in July of that year, were £4 10s. per month, and 3d. per mile for travel, nominally more than twice as much for wages and travel as in 1775.   Both the General Court and the people became greatly and justly alarmed at this condition of the only currency then in use, and in the hope of lessening or wholly arresting the evil, the New Hampshire legislature, early in the spring of 1777, passed a law limiting and regulating the prices at which the common necessaries of life might be sold.   A portion of the articles named in this law with the prices fixed for them are presented below.

	s. d.		s. d.		s. d.
Wheat per bushel,	7, 6,	Cheese per lb.	0, 6,	Beef per lb.	0, 3,
Rye " "	4, 6,	Butter " "	0, 10,	Tow Cloth per yard,	2, 3,
Indian Corn, "	3, 6,	Coffee, " "	1, 4,	Flannel " "	3, 6,
Oats, "	2, 0,	Cotton, " "	3, 0,	Linen Cloth " "	4, 0,
Peas, "	8, 0,	Wool, " "	2, 2,	N. E. Rum, per gal.,	3, 10,
Beans. "	6, 0,	Flax, " "	1, 0,	W. I. " " "	7, 8,
Salt, "	10, 0,	Pork " "	0, 4.1-2,	Molasses, " "	4, 0.

DEPRECIATION OF THE PAPER CURRENCY.

On the second of June, 1777, a special town meeting in Hollis was summoned to consider what should be done by the town in reference to this law, from the record of which meeting we make the following extracts : " Voted to choose a Committee agreeably to the late Act of the General Court, called *An Act in addition to an Act regulating Prices of Sundry articles therein enumerated*, and that Capt. Reuben Dow, Dea. Enoch Noyes, Capt. Noah Worcester, Capt. Daniel Kendrick, and Capt. Daniel Emerson, be said committee."

At a subsequent special town meeting, on the 28th of September of the same year, called to consider the same subject, the town passed the following vote : " Voted that we highly disapprove of the conduct of any persons in endeavoring to forestall or unreasonably raise the prices of the necessaries of Life ; and that we will

hold every such person inimical to our present cause; and that
we will treat all such Persons with neglect and will have no Dealings with them. and that the Committee of Safety of the Town
shall judge and determine when any Person shall transgress the
true intent and meaning of this Vote, and shall post every such Person's name in the Public Houses in town and in the Public Prints."

But all these vigorous. well meant and patriotic efforts of the
General Court. town meetings, and Committees of Safety, to
check this growing evil. were wholly fruitless, and this paper currency, from month to month. continued to lessen in value, so that
before the end of the war it became utterly worthless.   The people of Hollis, however. seem at last to have gained a sensible idea
of the only practicable remedy for this excessive issue of irredeem-
able promises to pay, as is shown by the doings and votes of a
special town meeting on the 27th of November of this year.   At
this meeting, as appears from the record, the town " Voted, 1st,
To give our Representative, the following Instructions, viz., to use
his Influence to *sink* our State money by way of Taxes, and 2d,
also Voted that it is our mind to pay a Tax of *twelve double* of
what it was last year."

(12)

CHAPTER XVI.

RESOLUTIONS AND VOTES OF THE TOWN MEETINGS IN 1778.

Articles of Confederation and Union. On the 15th of November, 1777, the Continental Congress adopted articles of confederation and perpetual union of the States, to be submitted to the States severally for their approval. On the 19th of January, 1778, a town meeting in Hollis was called to consider, among other things, these articles of confederation, at which the town's approval of them was expressed as follows: "Voted unanimously our approbation of the articles of confederation and perpetual union recommended by the Continental Congress to all the States."

The Town's Quota for the Army. Also at the same meeting, "Voted that the Militia Officers, Selectmen and Committee of Safety of the town agree with the men to supply the places of our eight months' men as cheap as they can, and give the security of the Town for their services in the Continental Army."

Committee of Safety for 1778. Annual Town Meeting, March 2, 1778. "Chose for Committee of Safety this year, Noah Worcester, Esq., Mr. Oliver Lawrence, Mr. Edward Taylor, Dea. Enoch Noyes and Mr. Nehemiah Woods. Also Voted that the Selectmen take care of the Continental Soldiers families if they stand in need."

War Tax. Special Town Meeting April 6, 1778. "Voted to raise £830, to be levied by a Tax on the Town to defray the charges of our ten Continental men."

Soldiers' Families. "Voted that Capt. Daniel Emerson, James Jewett and Jonathan Taylor, be a Committee to provide for the Continental Soldiers' Families, and that they have the Necessaries of life at the price stated in 1777, and that the overplus be paid *out of the Town Treasury.*"

Representatives to Concord. "Chose Noah Worcester, Esq., and Dea. Enoch Noyes to represent this Town in the General Convention of the State to be held at Concord on the 10th of June next."

This convention was called in pursuance of a resolution of the General Court, to agree upon and present to the people for their acceptance a system or "Plan for a State Government."* It appears that the plan of government agreed upon and proposed by this convention, on being submitted to the people, was rejected.†

Soldiers for Rhode Island. Special Town Meeting, June 15. 1778. From the Town Records. "At a meeting of the Inhabitants of the town of Hollis, called on account of orders from Col. Nichols for four men to be raised from this town to go to Providence to join Col. Peabody's regiment. Voted to give to each man that will enlist £3 3s. 6d. per month from the time they shall enlist till discharged, and that if enough do not enlist, that the men who are drafted and go and serve shall receive the same sum ; and also voted that the Selectmen join with the commissioned officers to draft men at all times when there is occasion."

Soldiers' Families. Special Town Meeting, Oct. 5, 1778. "Voted that the Committee appointed to take care of the Continental Soldiers' families adhere strictly to the law of the State, in respect to them, and that they take care of the families of the Widows' Cumings and Wheeler as if their husbands were alive." The deceased soldiers referred to in this vote were Ebenezer Cumings and Lebbeus Wheeler, both of whom enlisted for three years in the Continental army in the spring of 1777. Cumings had died in the army of small pox, leaving (as appears from the Hollis records of births) a widow and eight children, among whom was Jacob Abbot Cumings, born Nov. 2, 1772, afterwards a graduate of Harvard College, and the author of Cummings' School Geography and other literary works. Wheeler was a son of Peter Wheeler, born in Hollis, October 15, 1750, and died in the army of "disease or wounds," July 10, 1778, leaving a widow and one child.

*Prov. Papers, Vol. 8, pp. 774—5.
†Belknap, p. 383.

Representative to General Court.   Special Town Meeting,
Dec. 1, 1778. "Chose Capt. Reuben Dow to represent the town
in the General Assembly to be held at Exeter on the 3d Wednesday
of December next."

RECRUITS FOR THE CONTINENTAL ARMY.

In the month of January, 1778, ten men were wanted to fill the
Hollis Continental quota to supply the places of the men who had
enlisted for eight months only. On the 19th of that month, as we
have seen, a special town meeting was promptly called to supply
this deficiency, and the Selectmen, Committee of Safety with the
militia officers, were instructed to engage the men and to pledge the
security of the town for their services. It is shown by the returns
of Col. Nichols, (now at Concord) that these ten recruits were very
soon engaged and that most of them were mustered into the company of Capt. John House, in the 1st New Hampshire Continental
regiment. It appears from the "Great Return" of the Selectmen
of Hollis, that nine of them were paid from £40 6s. 8d. to £50
each. Their names were

John Auld,	John Conroy, Jun.,	Jacob Danforth.
Reuben Blood.	Stephen Conroy.	Nathaniel Patten,
Simeon Blood,	William Cowen,	Joel Proctor.
Samuel Boyd,		

It is stated in the return of Col. Nichols that Auld and Cowen
belonged to Merrimack, and Boyd to Goffstown, but that they were
all enlisted for and paid by Hollis. It appears from the rolls at
Concord, that John Conroy, Jun., died in hospital at Danbury, Conn.,
in September of this year. He was the oldest son of John Conroy,
Sen., and born in Hollis, December 28, 1761. Daniel Blood,
another Hollis soldier, who enlisted for three years, in the spring of
1777, died in the army of "wounds or disease," November 28,
1778, making a loss by death this year of four of the Hollis
Continental quota.*

Men in Col. Peabody's Regiment. About the middle of June
of this year, a brigade of New Hampshire troops was raised for
service in Rhode Island, commanded by Brig. Gen. Whipple.
One of the regiments of this brigade was commanded by Col.
Stephen Peabody, of Amherst. In the Second company of this
regiment, of which Ezekiel Worthen of Kensington, was Captain,
were three Hollis soldiers, viz., Jonathan Jewett, Oliver Lawrence

*Kidder's History of First N. H. Regiment, p. 134.

and Enoch Spalding. The regiment was discharged June 3, 1779, having been in the service six months and twenty-five days. The wages of the men were £4 10s. per month, and they were allowed for travel in going to Rhode Island 3d. per mile, and 8d. per mile on their return home. The town paid the three Hollis men a bounty of £6 each.

Hollis Volunteers to Rhode Island in August, 1778. The brigade of Gen. Whipple was raised in the summer of 1778 to reinforce the Continental army in Rhode Island in a proposed attack upon the British troops then in possession of the island of Rhode Island. In this attack it was expected that a powerful French fleet, then on the coast, under the command of Admiral Count D'Estaing, would co-operate with the army. But the fleet having been disabled and dispersed by a violent storm just before the time fixed for the intended attack, the expedition failed.

About the 6th of August of this year, a company of volunteers to aid in this expedition was raised in Hollis. The company, including its officers, consisted of forty-three men. It was commanded by Capt. Daniel Emerson, and was the 1st company of a regiment commanded by Col. Moses Nichols of Amherst. The men were in the service from the 6th to the 28th of August, and were then discharged, in consequence of the misfortune to the French fleet. The wages of the private soldiers in this expedition were at the rate of £5 per month, and 8d. per mile for travel, one hundred miles each way, in going and returning. They were also paid by the town £1 3s. each. It is to be inferred also that the men were all mounted and furnished their own horses, as it is shown by the return of Col. Nichols that the company had forty-three horses, for which they were allowed £10 each, making £430. The roll below presents a list of this company with its officers, all from Hollis.

Daniel Emerson, Capt.,	Nathaniel Blood, Jun.,	Jacob Jewett, 3d.,
Caleb Farley, Lieut.,	Timothy Blood,	Daniel Kendrick,
William Brooks, Ensign,	Thomas Carter,	Asa Lawrence,
Daniel Bailey, Sergeant,	Benjamin Colburn,	Daniel Merrill, Jun.,
Josiah Conant, "	Reuben Dow,	Samuel Merrill,
Stephen Runnells, "	Josiah Fisk,	Elijah Noyes,
Abel Conant, Corporal,	Jonas Flagg,	Jonathan Parker,
Elias Boynton, "	Jonathan French,	William W. Pool,
Evan Dow, "	Stephen Goodhue,	Ephraim Rolfe,
Andrew Bailey, Fifer.	David Hale,	Jacob Spalding,
PRIVATES.	John Hale, Jun.,	Joseph Wheat,
Benjamin Abbot,	Noah Hardy,	Jonas Woods,
David Ames,	Joshua Hobart,	Noah Worcester, Sen.,
John Atwell,	Solomon Hobart,	Jesse Worcester.
Nathaniel Blood,	John How,	

It may be seen from the foregoing data, that including the town's quota of thirty Continental soldiers, Hollis in 1778 had seventy-six men in the service, for the whole or a part of that year.

VOTES AND RESOLUTIONS OF THE TOWN MEETINGS IN 1779.

Committee of Safety. Annual Town Meeting, March 1, 1779.
" Voted and chose Noah Worcester, Esq., Mr. Oliver Lawrence, Mr. Jacob Jewett, Ensign Stephen Ames and Mr. Edward Taylor, Committee of Safety, Correspondence, and Inspection."

Soldiers' Families. "Voted that the Overseers of the Poor take care of the Continental Soldiers' Families, and have particular regard to the families of those that have died in the army."

Capt. Leonard Whiting's War Rate. "Mr. Samuel Chamberlain, one of the constables of Hollis, having informed the town that Capt. Leonard Whiting refused to pay his War Tax, Voted to defend said Chamberlain and that he be indemnified in recovering the same, so far as he has acted according to law."

QUOTA OF CONTINENTAL SOLDIERS.

Special Town Meeting, March 31, 1779. "Chose Noah Worcester, Esq., Capt. Reuben Dow, and Capt. Daniel Emerson, to take the method they shall think best and proper to get our Quota of Continental men."

Special Town Meeting, July 5, 1779. "Voted that the Committee chosen at the last meeting be joined with the Selectmen, and Militia officers to assist in getting our Continental Men, either by draft or otherwise as they shall think best for the town."

Special Town Meeting, July 19, 1779. "Voted 1st, to raise the men called for to fill up the New Hampshire Battalions, being our proportion of the Continental Army, as a town for one year, and chose Ensign Jeremiah Ames, Dr. Jonathan Fox, and Jacob Jewett, Jun., a Committee to hire for one year our nine Continental Men."

" 2d. Voted that said Committee be empowered to give the Town's Security to each of said nine men for any sum of money that they may agree with them for, and the Town to be responsible to said Committee for said Sums, and the Committee's trouble in raising said men, and that the Selectmen be empowered to assess the Polls and Estates of this town the sum of money that it shall cost to raise said men."

On the 2d of August, about two weeks after this last meeting, this committee made their report in writing to the town showing that they had engaged eight of the nine men wanted, with their names and the bounties agreed to be paid to each of them for the year's service.

A copy of this report is presented below as follows :

"The Inhabitants of the Town of Holles to Jeremiah Ames, Jonathan Fox and Jacob Jewett, Jun.. a Committee chosen by said Town to agree with and hire nine men to go into the Continental Army for one year for said town.   Dr.

"*Aug. 2, 1779. To cash and our security given to Eight men as a Bounty from said Town to go into said service.*

To Caleb Stiles,	Cash, £300	10 Bushels of Rye.	10 Do. of Ind. Corn.
" Caleb Stiles, Jun.,	" £300	10 Bushels of Rye.	10 Do. of Ind. Corn.
" Ephraim Pearce,	" £300	10 Bushels of Rye.	10 Do. of Ind. Corn.
" Francis G. Powers,	" £300	10 Bushels of Rye.	10 Do. of Ind. Corn.
" Jerathmael Bowers,	" £300	10 Bushels of Rye.	10 Do. of Ind. Corn.
" Jacob Hobart,	" £300	10 Bushels of Rye.	10 Do. of Ind. Corn.
" Joseph Stearns,	" £177	17 Bushels of Rye.	20 Do. of Ind. Corn.
" Simeon Foster,	" £210	10 Bushels of Rye,	10 Do. of Ind. Corn.
Lawful Money,	£2,187.	87 Bushels of Rye.	90 Bushs. Ind. Corn.

JEREMIAH AMES.
JONATHAN FOX.
JACOB JEWETT, Jun."

"Holles, Aug. 3, 1779."

The "Return" of Col. Nichols for the regiment shows that the ninth man enlisted for the town under this call was Joseph Wheat, but it does not appear what bounty was paid him.

VOLUNTEERS FOR RHODE ISLAND AND PORTSMOUTH.

In the spring or summer of this year a regiment of New Hampshire troops was raised for service in Rhode Island, commanded by Col. Hercules Mooney, of Lee. In this regiment were six Hollis men. viz., Daniel Emerson, Jun.. who was captain of the 5th company, Dr. Peter Emerson, a brother of Captain Emerson, (the surgeon of the regiment,) Daniel Bailey. Daniel Kendrick, John Hobart. and Samuel Emerson. another brother of Capt. Emerson, then in his fifteenth year, afterwards a graduate of Harvard college. and an eminent physician. The men were discharged on the first of January, 1780, having been in the service near six months. The wages of the private soldiers were £12 per month. Bounty paid by the town, £9. All owed for travel to Providence 2s. per mile—from Providence, home, 3s. per mile.

The original commission of Capt. Emerson, as a Captain in this regiment, signed by Meshech Weare, President of the New Hampshire Council, has been preserved in the family of a grandson, and a copy of it is presented below.

The Government and people of the State of New Hampshire to Daniel Emerson, Esq., Greeting.

{ Seal. }

" We reposing especial trust and confidence in your courage and good conduct, do by these *Presents* constitute and appoint you the said DANIEL EMERSON, *Captain* of a company in a regiment raised within said State, for the defence of the State of Rhode Island, of which regiment *Hercules Mooney*, Esq., is Colonel. You are therefore carefully and diligently to discharge the duty of a Captain in leading, ordering and exercising the said company in arms, both inferior officers and soldiers, and to keep them in good order and discipline, and they are hereby required and commanded to obey you as their *Captain*, and you are yourself to observe and follow such orders and instructions as you shall from time to time receive from the General and Commander-in-Chief of the *Continental Forces*, or any other your superior officers according to Military Rules and Discipline in war in pursuance of the trust reposed in you.

In Testimony whereof we have caused the Seal of said State to be hereunto affixed.

Witness, MESHECH WEARE, Esq., the President of our Council, at Exeter this 30th day of June, A. D., 1779.

M. WEARE.

E. THOMPSON, Secretary.

It also appears from the Revolutionary rolls, preserved in Concord, that in the year 1779, John Goodhue, Joseph Hardy and Silas Hardy, all of Hollis, enlisted in the company of Capt. Hezekiah Lovejoy, to serve for six months in the garrison at Portsmouth.

At a special town meeting Aug. 25th of this year, " Voted to allow Dea. Enoch Noyes £21 2s., and Noah Worcester, Esq., £46 9s. for services in attending the Convention to agree upon and settle a Plan of State Government," also at the same meeting, " chose Col. John Hale to represent this town in the Convention to be held at Concord on the 23d of September next."

This was a general convention of delegates from the State, called together in the vain hope of being able to devise some farther expedients to arrest the rapid depreciation of the paper currency by limiting and regulating the prices of the necessaries of life. The extent at this time of this alarming depreciation may be readily inferred by comparing the wages and bounties paid to soldiers at the beginning of the war, with those paid, as may be seen above, in the month of August, 1779. In 1775, the wages paid by the town to the eight months' men who went to Cambridge were £1 10s. per month, or at the rate of £18 per year. In 1776, the men who enlisted for the year were paid in all £24 by the town, or at the rate of £2 per month. In 1779 there were paid by the town to the Hollis soldiers for a years' service, £300 and 10 bushels of rye, and 10 bushels of corn.

The Concord convention, as appears, met as proposed, and agreed upon a schedule of prices of certain commodities and necessaries, leaving it for the towns to state and limit the prices of others. The convention having finished its work, a town meeting was called on the following 21st of October to consider the report and proceedings of that body and to determine what further should be done by the town. From the record of this meeting we quote as follows:

PLAN OF FIXING PRICES BY THE CONCORD CONVENTION.

Special Town Meeting, Oct. 21, 1779. "Voted unanimously our entire approbation of the Proceedings of the Convention held at Concord, in September last Stating Prices, &c." "Voted to pursue the Plan laid down by the Convention for Stating Prices, and to State the Prices for articles for this town, not stated by the Convention—to see the Plan carried into effect—and to correspond with other towns,—and chose Col. John Hale, Capt. Daniel Kendrick, Dea. John Boynton, Capt. John Goss, Ephraim Burge, Ebenezer Runnells, Jacob Jewett, Christopher Farley, Josiah Fisk and Lt. Ebenezer Jewett, said Committee. Adjourned to Nov. 16.

Adjourned Town Meeting, Nov. 16, 1779. "Voted to accept the Report of the Committee."

In the mean time, previous to the 16th of November, the foregoing committee prepared their report and submitted it to the meeting held on that day. The report was then accepted by the town as shown by the record of the meeting as follows:

Adjourned Town Meeting, Nov. 16, 1779. " Voted to accept the Report of the Committee appointed on the 21st of October, and that each person in town govern himself accordingly *under the penalty of being treated as an enemy of his Country*, and that copies of the same be posted up in the public houses in town attested by the town clerk.

" At this meeting a paper that had been set up at Runnell's (Mills) by order of the town, attested by the town clerk, being brought in and exhibited to the meeting much defaced, upon view of which, the Town voted unanimously their resentment of the matter, and that the Committee should enquire into the affair and report at the next meeting."

Zachariah Lawrence Jun., and his offence. It appearing from the report of the committee to the next town meeting, held on the 9th of December, that Zachariah Lawrence, Jun., was guilty of defacing the paper containing the list of prices set up by the town clerk at Runnells, " Voted that the Committee of Safety be empowered to settle the affair with Zachariah Lawrence, Jun., for his offence in defacing a certain paper as they shall think proper, and that if said Lawrence refuses to settle to their satisfaction to pursue him in the law and make report to the town as soon as may be."

SCALE OF DEPRECIATION OF PAPER MONEY.

In the year 1781, the New Hampshire General Court prepared and adopted what was called an " Authorized Scale of Depreciation of Continental Paper Money," in accordance with which, contracts made at different dates during the war might be equitably settled with silver money. The following table copied from that scale indicates the value of £100 in silver as compared with its equivalent in Continental paper money in different years as fixed by the General Court.

June, 1777,	£100 in silver equal to	£120 Continental paper.
" 1778,	£100 "	" £425 " "
" 1779,	£100 "	" £1342 " "
" 1780,	£100 "	" £5700 " "
" 1781,	£100 "	" £12000 " "

After the last date Continental paper money became worthless.

SMALL POX IN HOLLIS.

It is stated by Rev. Grant Powers, in his Centennial address, delivered in 1830, " That in the year 1779 the small pox broke out in the town, supposed to have been communicated by the Enemy of our Country, and two houses were improved as Hospitals. One of these houses was afterwards owned and occupied by Lemuel Wright, and the other by James Rideout. In the last named of these houses there were at one time more than one hundred patients. About one hundred and fifty persons were inoculated, of whom three died, and five others who took the disease from exposure to the infection, also died."

It appears from the town records that Col. John Hale was put in charge of these hospitals, with a supervisory committee, consisting of " Noah Worcester, Stephen Ames, Oliver Lawrence, Capt. Daniel Emerson, Solomon Rogers, Dea. Stephen Jewett and Edward Taylor, who were to take security of Col. Hale and place him under proper restrictions."

CHAPTER XVII.

1780 AND 1781.—VOTES AND RESOLUTIONS.—HOLLIS CONTINENTAL
QUOTA.—WAGES OF SOLDIERS.—MILITIA FOR WEST POINT AND
NORTHERN FRONTIER.—THEIR WAGES AND BOUNTIES.—TAXES
ASSESSED TO PAY THEM.—BEEF FOR THE ARMY IN 1780, 1781.
—REDUCTION OF NEW HAMPSHIRE TROOPS.—REDUCTION OF
THE HOLLIS QUOTA.—TWELVE CONTINENTAL SOLDIERS CALLED
FOR AND ENGAGED.—THEIR NAMES.—BEEF FOR THE ARMY IN
1781 AND HOW OBTAINED.—THE TOWN DIVIDED INTO CLASSES.
NEW CALL FOR TWELVE SOLDIERS.—RUM FOR THE ARMY.—
REPRESENTATIVE IN 1781.

VOTES AND RESOLUTIONS OF THE TOWN MEETINGS IN 1780.

Annual Town Meeting, March 6, 1780. "Chose Ephraim Burge,
Lt. Ebenezer Jewett and Ebenezer Runnells a committee to take
care of Soldiers' Families, and voted that the Selectmen and commissioned officers settle with the Rhode Island men for 1779 and
the men who went to Portsmouth last Fall, as to what they shall
receive on account of the fall of Money, agreeably to our agreement with them, and also voted that Ebenezer Runnells, Noah
Worcester and Jacob Jewett be a committee to procure the Grain
for the last Continental men and settle with them and that the Selectmen assess the amount on the Polls and Estates of the town."

No new Committee of Safety was chosen this year or after 1779.

RECRUITS FOR THE CONTINENTAL ARMY

Special Town Meeting, June 28, 1780. It is shown by the
record of a special town meeting held June 28th of this year, that
there was then a deficiency of nine men in the Hollis Continental
quota. At this meeting the town "voted to hire nine able-bodied
men to serve in the Continental Army till the last day of December
next, and that Jonathan Fox, Jacob Jewett, Jun., and Ephraim

Burge be a committee to hire said men, and to give security in behalf of the Town in any way they think proper." On the 4th of July, within a week after this meeting. this committee made the following report of its doings :

"The Inhabitants of the Town of Hollis to Jonathan Fox. Jacob Jewett, Jun., and Ephraim Burge as a committee chosen by said Town to agree with and hire nine men to go into the Continental Army for six months for said Town.   Dr.

July 4. 1780.   To cash and our security given to nine men. Viz.

To Jacob Danforth.	Cash, £210.	90 Bushels of Rye.	& 10 Bushels of Ind Corn.		
" Stephen Conroy,	" £210 & 90	"	"		
" Nathaniel Patten.	" £510 & 79	"	"		
" Asa Lovejoy, .	" £210 90	"	"	and one Blanket.	
" Abel Lovejoy.	" £210 90	"	"	and one Blanket.	
" Jesse Worcester.	" £210 90	"	"	and one Blanket.	
" Lemuel Blood,	" £210 90	"	"	and one Pair of Shoes.	
" Reuben Blood,	" £210 90	"	"	and one Pair of Shoes.	
" Nathaniel Blood.	" £210 90	"	"	and one Pair of Shoes.	

Lawful Money,   £2,190   799 Bushels of Rye, 3 Blankets, 3 Pair of Shoes.

N. B. The wages of the nine six months' men belong to the Town."

It appears from the above note that the full amount of the wages of these men was paid in advance by the town. the men being unwilling. probably on account of the state of the currency. to give credit to the State or Congress.

MILITIA TO WEST POINT.

It is shown also by the "Great Return" of the Selectmen of Hollis before often referred to, that Abel Blood. another Hollis soldier, enlisted at the same time with these nine. in the Continental army. and was paid the like amount of wages.

MILITIA FOR WEST POINT AND THE NORTHERN FRONTIER.

Early in July of this year a further call was made upon the town for fifteen men for three months to aid in the defence of West Point, and for three others to serve for six months on the northern frontier. On the 3d of July a town meeting was called to act upon this subject, and also to raise money to pay the "nine" men who. had enlisted in the Continental army.

Special Town Meeting. July 3d. 1780.   Extracts from the Record. "Voted that the Selectmen procure the money for the nine men the committee have engaged the best way they can, and that Dr. Jonathan Fox, Jacob Jewett. Jun.. and Ephraim Burge be a committee to assist in raising the eighteen men now called for."

Within about two weeks after this meeting, this committee made report to the town that they had procured fourteen of the men for three months to go to West Point and two of those to serve on the northern frontier. The bounties agreed upon for the men to go to West Point were to be paid wholly in either rye or corn, as follows : to one of them thirty-five bushels of rye ; to two others, thirty bushels of corn each ; to another, forty-five bushels of corn ; to each of ten others, fifty bushels of corn. These fourteen men were all to retain their government wages. To Simeon Blood and Thomas Youngman, the two men engaged to serve for six months on the northern frontier, the committee agreed to pay ninety bushels of rye and £210 each in money.—"*the government wages of these two to belong to the town.*" It appears from the "Great Return," that two others, paid the like bounties with the fourteen, were engaged for West Point, making sixteen for that place, and the whole eighteen called for from the town.

NAMES OF THE MEN FOR WEST POINT.

Andrew Bailey,	Jesse Hardy,	Silas Lawrence,
Richard Bailey,	Lemuel Hardy,	Nathaniel Leeman,
Josiah Blood,	Lieut. Ebenezer Jewett,	Daniel Merrill, Jun.,
John Conroy,	Jacob Jewett, 3d.,	Stephen Parker,
Stephen Dow,	Nicholas Lawrence,	Francis Grant Powers.
Jonas Flagg,		

These sixteen men were enlisted in the company of Capt. William Barron, in a regiment commanded by Col. Nichols. It is shown by the regimental returns now with the army rolls at Concord, that these men were enlisted July 6, 1780, and were discharged on the 22d of the following October, having been in the service three months and sixteen days. The wages paid by the government were £134 per month and 6s. per mile for travel. It is stated in the Hollis Centennial address, that Francis Grant Powers, one of these sixteen soldiers, was killed at Crown Point. He was a son of Francis Powers, and a grandson of Capt. Peter Powers, the first settler of Hollis, and was born January 8, 1764.

PAY FOR THE HOLLIS SOLDIERS.

" *Special Town Meeting,* November 23, 1780. Chose Dr. Jonathan Fox, Jacob Jewett, Jun., and Mr. Ephraim Burge a committee to settle with the soldiers they have hired and report to the town what sum of money to raise. Adjourned to December 5." *Adjourned Special Town Meeting,* December 5, 1780,

The committee above appointed having reported in respect to the soldiers, " Voted to raise £32,000 to pay the money borrowed for said soldiers, and to procure the grain engaged to the three and six months men, and that Capt. Daniel Emerson, Mr. Ephraim Burge and Lieut. Ebenezer Jewett be a committee to purchase said grain."

BEEF FOR THE ARMY.

The town in August of this year was called upon to furnish 16,000 pounds of beef for the army, and at a town meeting held on the 31st of August the town voted a tax of £25,000 for the purchase of this 16,000 lbs. of beef, being at the rate of £1 11s. 6d., or somewhat more than $5 per pound. On the 23d of November, 1780, Col. John Hale was chosen to represent the town in the General Court to be holden at Exeter on the 3d of the following December.

REDUCTION OF NEW HAMPSHIRE TROOPS IN 1781..

By an act of the General Court, passed January 12, 1781, the number of New Hampshire troops for the regular army was reduced to one thousand three hundred and fifty-four, to be organized into two regiments, and to serve for three years or during the war.

The number of men to be furnished for this force by Hollis was reduced from thirty, the old quota, to a new quota of but twenty. At that date, as appears from the army rolls, there were nine Continental soldiers in the army, who had been previously enlisted to serve during the war. The names of these soldiers were

Samuel Boyd,	Stephen Richardson,	Eli Stiles,
Thomas Pratt,	Lemuel Rogers,	Joseph Wheat,
Joel Proctor,	David Sanderson,	Jabez Youngman.

Boyd, Pratt, Proctor, Richardson, Sanderson and Youngman enlisted in the 1st New Hampshire regiment, and were in that regiment December 31, 1782, and afterwards, as supposed, till the regiment was discharged in 1783.*

The time of the service of a large part of the Hollis quota having expired about this time, a town meeting was summoned on the 19th of February, 1781, to supply such deficiencies as might exist in the new quota. At this meeting Capt. Daniel Emerson, Dr. Jonathan Fox and Mr. Ephraim Burge were appointed a committee to enquire into the subject, to engage the soldiers wanted, and to make report to the next town meeting. This committee afterwards, at the

*Kidder's History of 1st N. H. Regiment, p. 162.

adjourned annual town meeting held on the 12th of March, made report, that twelve men were then wanted to complete the new quota. Upon this report being made, the town, at that meeting, instructed this committee to engage the men, and to give security in behalf of the town for such wages or bounties as they should agree with them for, and also voted a war tax of £800 for the war charges of the year, and appointed "Noah Worcester, Esq., Jonathan Taylor and John Atwell, a committee to hire the money till this tax could be collected."

BEEF FOR THE ARMY IN 1781.

The town also at the same meeting voted a tax of £800, " new emission," to purchase the town's quota of beef for this year, and appointed Capt. Daniel Emerson, Ephraim Burge and Jeremiah Ames a committee to procure it. The report of the committee for hiring these twelve men is not found, and is probably lost. But the returns and army rolls at Concord show that they all enlisted for three years, and the returns of the Hollis Selectmen also show that the town paid each of them a bounty of £60, or $200. As the old Continental paper money had now become worthless these bounties were doubtless paid in specie or its equivalent, amounting in all to £720, or $2,400. Instead of entailing this amount as a debt upon the town to be paid by posterity, as has been too often done in more modern times in like cases, our ancestors at their annual town meeting assessed a war tax of £800 or $2,666.67, to meet it, to be collected and paid the same year. The names of these twelve men were

John Bonner,	Benjamin W. Grace,	Stephen Parker,
Elijah Clark,	Isaac Hobart,	Ezekiel Proctor,
Edward Deane,	Jacob Hobart,	James Rolfe,
John Godfrey,	John McHendley.	Asahel Twiss.

At a special town meeting held on the 14th of May of this year a resolution was adopted, that for the purpose of engaging soldiers in answer to future calls, the town should be divided into *Classes*, and the Selectmen and Mr. Ephraim Burge were chosen as a committee to " class the town." It appears that in pursuance of this resolution the town was divided into eight " classes."

THE TOWN'S QUOTA OF BEEF FOR 1781.

Special Town Meeting, June 25, 1781. At this meeting the town " Voted that as the town is now divided into eight classes, the quantity of beef we have to get be divided to each class according to valuation, (except as to non-residents) and that the Selectmen set down each man's portion of beef to his name and that if any class or person refuse to pay their or his proportion of beef the same shall be committed to the Constable to collect, and that the Selectmen shall set such sum in specie to such delinquent as will be sufficient to pay for his proportion of beef."

NEW CALL FOR SOLDIERS.

In the month of July of this year a requisition was made by the State upon the town for twelve men to serve in the army for three months. In consequence of this call a town meeting was held on the 19th of July, at which it was " voted that the eight classes into which the town was divided should be so coupled that each two classes should procure three good effective men." The Great Return shows that nine of these three months' men were enlisted and paid by the town. No record or other evidence is found in respect to the other three. A bounty of £15, or $50 each, was paid to the nine men engaged. They enlisted in the company of Capt. John Mills, in a small, incomplete regiment commanded by Col. Daniel Reynolds of Londonderry. It is not known where this regiment was employed, or that in fact it ever left the State. The war at this time was substantially at an end, and the regiment soon disbanded, and most probably for these reasons, the three remaining Hollis men were not engaged. The names of the nine men in Capt. Mills' company were,

Capt. William Brooks,	Abner Keyes,	B. Woods Parker,
Asa Chamberlain,	Daniel Merrill,	Thomas Powell,
Robert Connick,	Jacob Mooar,	Samuel Read.

Including the nine three months' men and the twenty "Continentals," Hollis had this year in the service, in all, but twenty-nine soldiers, a number much less than that of any preceding year.

RUM FOR THE ARMY.

On the 1st of October of this year a town meeting was called to see what method should be taken to procure *the Rum* required of the town for the army, and Robert McGaw was chosen agent of the town to provide it. The town's quota in gallons is not stated in the record but at a subsequent town meeting, in December of this year a tax of £100, or $333 was voted to pay for it, and the necessary charges of the town.

(13)

CHAPTER XVIII.

1782–83. — THE LAST YEAR OF THE WAR. — NEW PLAN OF GOV-
ERNMENT. — THE NEW HAMPSHIRE RANGERS IN 1782. — LAST
SOLDIER OF THE HOLLIS QUOTA. — NUMBER AND NAMES OF
HOLLIS SOLDIERS. — SENTIMENTS IN RESPECT TO THE RETURN
OF THE TORIES. — LAST WAR TAX. — HOLLIS RECORDS AND
DOCUMENTS. — NAMES OF THE COMMITTEES OF SAFETY AND
COMMISSIONED OFFICERS. — SOLDIERS LOST IN THE WAR.

NEW PLAN OF GOVERNMENT.

In the month of June, 1781, a State Convention was held at Concord to agree upon and propose a new "Plan" or system of State
Government. Hollis had no delegate in this convention, the town,
in the month of May previous, having voted not to elect. In the
month of September next afterwards the convention reported its
"plan" to be submitted to the people of the State at their town
meetings. Early in January, 1782, a town meeting was called in
Hollis to consider this plan, at which a committee of sixteen was
chosen to examine it and make report of their sentiments in respec
to it at an adjourned meeting on the 16th of January. Upon the
coming in of the report of this committee, the town voted as follows :
" 1st, to accept the Bill of Rights with an amendment reported by
the Committee." " 2d, To have a Governor under certain restrictions, but that the power of the Governor set forth in the "Plan
is too large." " 3d, That the present mode of representation be
adopted and that each town pay its own representative."

This first plan reported by the convention was not accepted by
a majority of the people of the State and the convention again me
and made a second report in September, 1782. A town meeting
was called on the 16th of December of this year to consider and
act upon this new report. The extracts from the record of the
meeting presented below exhibit the sentiments and doings of this

meeting. " Voted to reject said Plan of Government as it stands, yeas, 10, nays, 36." " It then being submitted to the town what amendment they would have instead of a Supreme Head to be styled a ' Governor,' Voted that we would choose to be governed similar to what we now are by a council and assembly—the President of the Council to be the Supreme Head of the State and in the recess, the General Court to have a Committee of Safety to assist the President."

It is said that this new plan was generally approved in the State but was not fully completed at the time news of peace arrived. The old form of government, having expired with the war, it was revived by the votes of the people and kept in force for one year longer. In the year following the new form was finished, and the name of " Governor " being changed to " President " it was printed a third time, and declared to be the civil Constitution of the State, and continued in force till the adoption of the present Constitution in September 1792.

NEW HAMPSHIRE RANGERS IN 1782.

Although the danger was not supposed to be great, yet as a matter of precaution, companies of New Hampshire Rangers were kept in service on the northern frontier, known as the " Coos Country," in the summer and fall of 1782, to protect the inhabitants from threatened raids of the Indians in Canada. On the 4th of July of this year, Andrew Henderson of Hollis enlisted in a company of these Rangers, (in which he was a Sergeant) commanded by Capt. Jonathan Smith of Surry. Also on the 6th of July Jonas Willoughby of Hollis volunteered in a company employed in the same service commanded by Capt. Ebenezer Webster of Salisbury, the father of Hon. Daniel Webster. These companies were discharged about the middle of November, having been in the service about four and one-half months.

THE LAST SOLDIER OF THE HOLLIS CONTINENTAL QUOTA.

Previously to the beginning of 1782, active hostilities between the contending armies had virtually ended, yet the Continental Congress regarded it prudent that the ranks of the regular army should be kept filled. About the middle of July of this year, upon investigation being made by a committee of the town, one man was found to be wanting in the Hollis quota. At a town meeting then held

the town " voted unanimously that one man more be raised by the
town to serve in the Continental army and that the committee for
that purpose procure him at discretion, immediately." It appears
from the regimental returns of Col. Nichols, that on the 15th of
July 1782, Jabez Youngman had enlisted as a soldier for Hollis for
three years, thus making the Continental quota of the town complete. Youngman was the last soldier who volunteered for Hollis,
and the only one called for this year for the regular army. His name
is found on the roll of the 1st New Hampshire Continental regiment, in December, 1782, and he is supposed to have been in the
service till the regiment was discharged, the next year, at the conclusion of peace. The town paid him a bounty of £60 or $200,
the same as paid to the Continental soldiers enlisted for three years,
in 1781.

NUMBER AND NAMES OF THE HOLLIS SOLDIERS.

It will be found on examination of the various lists and rolls,
still existing, of the Hollis soldiers in the Revolution, that most of
them enlisted more than once, and many of them on three or more
different occasions ; but counting each name but once, it will appear
that Hollis, at different times during the war, as nearly as can now
be ascertained, furnished, with but few exceptions, from its own
citizens, more than three hundred soldiers who for a longer or shorter time were in the military service—a number but little less than
one-fourth of its whole population.

Of these soldiers, there was one each of the names of Abbot,
Adams, Ambrose, Atwell, Auld, Blanchard, Bonner, Boyd, Bruce,
Burge, Campbell, Clark, Cowen, Danforth, Davis, Deane, Dickey,
Elliot, Farmer, Farnsworth, Flagg, Foster, Gilson, Godfrey, Goss,
Hazeltine, Henderson, Hill, Honey, Hopkins, Hosley, Kemp,
Kendrick, Keyes, Kinney, Lesley, Lund, McConnor, McHendley,
Messer, Minot, Patten, Philbrick, Platts, Poor, Powell, Pratt,
Richardson, Rideout, Rogers, Runnells, Russ, Seaver, Shed,
Stevens, Tenney, Thurston, Townsend, Twiss, Wallingford, Wood
and Wyman.

Two each of the names of Ames, Brooks, Carter, Conant,
Connick, Fisk, Grace, Jaquith, Johnson, Leeman, McDaniels,
McIntosh, Mooar, Noyes, Pool, Rolfe, Sanderson, Smith, Spalding,
Stearns, Wilkins, Willoughby and Woods.

Of the names of Bowers, Chamberlain, Dow, Eastman,

Goodhue, How, Merrill, Parker, Patch, Phelps, Read and Stiles, three each.

Four each of the names of Brown, Conroy, Hale, Lawrence, Lovejoy, Pierce, Proctor, Shattuck and Worcester. Of the names of Ball, Colburn, Emerson. Nevins, Taylor, Wheat, Wheeler, Wright and Youngman, five each. Six of the name of Powers. Of the names of Bailey, Boynton. Cumings, Farley and French, seven each. Eight of the name of Hobart, nine of Jewett, ten of that of Hardy, and sixteen of the name of Blood.

Representative to the General Court. At a special town meeting held on the 28th of October of this year Richard Cutts Shannon was elected to represent the town in the General Court to be holden at Portsmouth in December 1782.

1783. Annual Town Meeting. Increase of the State Tax. At the annual March meeting of this year the town ·· Voted to *enlarge* the State tax £200 to defray the necessary charges of the war. and chose Dea. Daniel Emerson, Noah Worcester. Esq., Capt. Daniel Kendrick and Ephraim Burge a committee to assist the Selectmen in settling with the Continental soldiers."

THE SENTIMENTS OF THE PEOPLE OF HOLLIS IN RESPECT TO THE TORIES.

As stated in the early part of this narrative, four of the citizens of Hollis were known as loyalists or tories, one of whom for a time was imprisoned for disloyalty. The remaining three left the country early in the war. and their names were included in the act of confiscation. passed in 1778. by the New Hampshire General Court. and they, with many others, were forbidden to return to the country under the penalty of death.

After the end of the war. the British Commissioners, in their negotiations for peace. were persistent in their efforts to provide for the return of the banished adherents of the crown. and the restoration of their confiscated estates : and this subject was widely and warmly discussed by the American press of the time, and in the primary assemblies of the people. A special town meeting in Hollis was called to consider this subject in the spring of 1783, "and to see if the Town would give their Representative any Instructions in respect to the Absentees from this State and their returning." As will appear from the following extract, which we copy from the record of that meeting. the sentiments of the people

of the town upon this question found expression in language more
vigorous and emphatic than forgetful or forgiving, as follows:

"The minds of the people being tried in respect to the Returning
of those Miserable Wretches under the name of Tories, Absentees
or Conspirators,"

"Voted unanimously that they shall not be allowed to return or
regain their forfeited Possessions."

"Voted that a Committee be chosen to give the Representative
of this Town particular Instructions which may convey to him the
unanimous sentiments of the people in respect to the Absentees
above mentioned."

"Voted that Col. John Hale, Noah Worcester, Esq., Master
Cumings, Dea. Boynton, Captains Dow, Goss and Kendrick be a
Committee to give the Instructions above mentioned."

Representative to the General Court.   On the 26th of December of this year Dea. Daniel Emerson was chosen Representative to
the General Court to be held at Concord in June.

Annual Town Meeting March 1, 1784.   At the annual town meeting of this year Dea. Daniel Emerson was again chosen Representative to the General Court to meet at Concord in June.   At the same
meeting the town "Voted to raise £210 to defray the charges of
four Continental soldiers, viz., Elijah Clark, John Godfrey, Jacob
Hobart and Jabez Youngman, and also that the selectmen should
assist the Continental soldiers in preferring a petition to the General
Court for a redress of Grievances in respect to their wages."

THE LAST TOWN MEETING IN RESPECT TO THE CONTINENTAL
SOLDIERS, MAY 2, 1785.

"Voted that Noah Worcester and Daniel Emerson, Esqrs., and
Mr. William Cumings be a Committee to look into matters
relating to the Continental soldiers and see how matters stand in
relation to making them or any of them a consideration for their
services, and report at a future meeting."

At a special town meeting held afterwards on the 15th of September this committee reported as follows: "That the Town in
Justice ought to give *free gratis* to Thomas Pratt, David Sanderson,
Joel Proctor, John Youngman and Thomas Wheat £18 to each of
them, for their voluntary service in the Continental Army."   This
report was accepted by the town and a tax for the amount assessed
at the same meeting.   Such was the honorable and characteristic
close of the Hollis war meetings.

THE HOLLIS RECORDS AND REVOLUTIONARY DOCUMENTS.

In the foregoing narrative it has been my aim to gather as far as practicable, from authentic sources, and to present in as little space as was consistent with perspicuity and historical accuracy, the annual doings of the people of Hollis in the seven years' war of the Revolution, and also somewhat of the sentiments and spirit which animated their efforts in the struggle for National Independence. Notwithstanding all the care I have used in my researches, it may be that some errors have escaped me.

In view of the lapse of one hundred years since our Revolution, and the long time since the last of the actors in its story have passed away, it would be passing strange if some mistakes have not unwittingly found their way into this narrative, which, if detected, I hope may be pardoned and corrected. But in the hope of avoiding important errors, I have in the main adhered closely to the Revolutionary documents and records of the State and town.

These records and documents of Hollis which I have so freely used and copied, and which so fully tell of the doings and purposes of the men who made them, I cannot but look upon as a precious and sacred legacy to their posterity, and to the present and future inhabitants of the town. We find in them all no sentiment of our ancestors which we would forget, no recorded act which does not do honor to their memories. The story as here told to some who may read it may seem needlessly prolix, and in some of its details tedious, still I am conscious that very many matters have been omitted, highly creditable to the actors in them, which interested me to know, and which if told would doubtless interest others as well. ' Yet I trust that in this imperfect narrative enough has been said, to satisfy all who have curiosity in such inquiries, that upon all occasions, from the beginning of the war to its end, our ancestors of Hollis did what at the time they believed to be their duty to their country, their own generation, and to their posterity, intelligently, promptly, and patriotically, with unfaltering courage, and the hopeful assurance of final success.

In 1774, when that dark and portentous war cloud was still in the horizon, undismayed by its threatenings, they proclaimed in the face of it and inscribed upon their public records. " *We will endeavor at all times to maintain our liberties and privileges, both civil and sacred, at the risk of our lives and fortunes.*" When a few months later that cloud first burst at Lexington, the Hollis minute men with full ranks hastened to the scene of conflict.

On the night of the 16th of June the Hollis company, under the eye of the gallant Prescott, without sleep or food, were busy with their spades and pickaxes upon the earthworks at Bunker Hill. They were a part of that force, worn and weary with the work of the night, of whom it was curtly said by their brave Colonel, on the morning of the battle, in answer to a proposal to relieve them, and call fresh troops to the defence of the works they had built— " *The men who built this fort will best defend it.*"

In the fall after that battle, when the ranks of the army at Cambridge were thinned and weakened by the base desertion of the Connecticut regiments, another company, mainly of Hollis volunteers, with the New Hampshire reinforcements, promptly marched to the seat of war to supply the places of the mutineers.

In 1776 we find Hollis soldiers with the army in Canada, at Ticonderoga, in the garrisons at Portsmouth, at White Plains, and sharing in the bloody campaigns in New Jersey.

The next year, when Gen. Burgoyne was on his march from Canada to Ticonderoga, a company of fifty or more Hollis minute men is seen hastening to its defence. The same summer, after the fall of that fortress, we find a company, chiefly of Hollis soldiers, under the gallant Stark at the decisive battle and brilliant victory at Bennington. In the hard winter of 1777–8, when their Continental soldiers were in the ill-supplied camp at Valley Forge, some of them barefoot and in rags, the nimble fingers of their mothers and sisters at home are seen busy for their relief.

In the summer of 1778, when Rhode Island was threatened with invasion, a company of forty-three mounted Hollis soldiers marched to aid in the defence. When in 1780 West Point was endangered by the base treason of Gen. Arnold, we have seen how readily our ancestors responded to the call for volunteers. And in 1782, after the last battle of the war had been fought, when the Continental Congress thought it prudent to keep the ranks of the regular army filled, this last call was at once cheerfully and promptly met.

If we follow the campaigns of the regular army we shall find the Hollis Continental quota in the New Hampshire regiments with Washington at the battles of Trenton, Princeton, Monmouth and Germantown; with Gen. Gates at Stillwater and Saratoga; with Gen. Sullivan in the war against the Six Nations, and again with Washington at the final battles and surrender at Yorktown. The New Hampshire Continental regiments known as the " Hampshire Boys" from the beginning to end of the war, were noted for their fidelity to duty, their good conduct and intrepidity, and their commanders, the gallant Cilley, Poor and Scammell, could at all times rightfully say with the Trojan Hector, in face of the dangers of battle,

> " Where heroes war the foremost place we claim,
> The first in danger as the first in fame."

HOLLIS COMMITTEE OF SAFETY IN 1776.

Capt. Reuben Dow,	Capt. Daniel Kendrick,	Oliver Lawrence,
Capt. Noah Worcester,	Jacob Jewett,	Samuel Chamberlain.
Ensign Stephen Ames,		

1777.	1778.	1779.
Noah Worcester,	Noah Worcester,	Noah Worcester,
Stephen Ames,	Dea. Enoch Noyes.	Stephen Ames,
Daniel Kendrick,	Oliver Lawrence,	Oliver Lawrence,
Oliver Lawrence,	Nehemiah Woods,	Edward Taylor,
Jacob Jewett,	Edward Taylor,	Jacob Jewett.

HOLLIS COMMISSIONED OFFICERS.

Samuel Hobart, Colonel of 3nd N. H. regiment of minute men, and paymaster of N. H. troops in 1775.

Regimental Surgeons,	John Hale,	Peter Emerson.
Assistant Surgeon,	Jonathan Pool.	

Captains.	First Lieutenants.	Second Lieutenants.
Reuben Dow,	Caleb Farley,	William Brooks,
Daniel Emerson, Jun.,	Ebenezer Jewett,	John Cumings,
John Goss,	Robert Seaver,	Samuel Leeman, Jun.
Noah Worcester.	David Wallingford.	

HOLLIS SOLDIERS KILLED OR DIED IN THE ARMY OF DISEASE OR WOUNDS.

James Fisk,	died at Cambridge,	May 29,	1775.
Jeremiah Shattuck,	" "	May 29,	1775.
Nathan Blood,	killed at Bunker Hill,	June 17,	1775.
Jacob Boynton,	" " "	" " "	
Thomas Colburn,	" " "	" " "	
Isaac Hobart,	" " "	" " "	
Phineas Nevins,	" " "	" " "	
Peter Poor,	" " "	" " "	
Thomas Wheat,	" " "	" " "	
Ebenezer Youngman,	" " * "	" " "	
Caleb Eastman,	"	" 19	"
Josiah Blood,	died	Sept.	1776
Minot Farmer,	"	May	"
William Nevins,	"		"
Ezra Proctor,	"	May 15	"
Isaac Shattuck,	"		"
Samuel Leeman, Jun.,	killed	Oct.	1777.
Ebenezer Cumings,	died		1778.
Lebbeus Wheeler,	"	July 19	"
John Conroy,	"	Sept.	"
Daniel Blood,	"	Nov. 28	"
Francis G. Powers,	killed		1780

The number of names in the list of deaths, is twenty-two. The Rev. Grant Powers, in his Centennial Address, states the loss of Hollis in the war, in killed or by disease, at thirty. He probably included in that number eight persons who in 1779 died in Hollis of the small pox, which he tells us was supposed to have been communicated by the enemy. The eight who died of that disease, added to the twenty-two, would make the Hollis loss of thirty as Mr. Powers states it.

The Hollis soldiers who received pensions from the Government, on account of permanent disabilities suffered in the service, either from wounds or disease, were Capt. Reuben Dow, Ensign William Wood, Thomas Pratt, (all wounded at Bunker Hill) Samuel Boyd and Stephen Richardson.

CHAPTER XIX.

ALPHABETICAL LIST OF HOLLIS SOLDIERS, SHOWING IN WHAT YEARS THEY ENLISTED WHEN AND HOW LONG THEY WERE IN THE SERVICE.

(*" 1775 L."* *denotes enlisted, April 19, 1775, for Lexington and Cambridge;* " *Cam.,*" *Cambridge;* " *B. H.,*" *at the Battle of Bunker Hill;* " *C. A.,*" *Continental Army;* " *Port.,*" *in Garrison at Portsmouth, N. H.;* " *Wh. P.,*" *at White Plains;* " *Ti.,*" *Ticonderoga;* "*1777 Al. T.,*" *Ticonderoga Alarm, June, 1777;* " *Ben,*" *in the company of Capt. Goss, at Bennington, July 1777;* " *W. Pt.,*" *West Point;* " *R. I.,*" *Rhode Island;* " *G. R.,*" *names in the Return of Capt. Goss, p. 167.*)

Abbot, Benjamin, '75, L., '78, R. I., 22 d.

Adams, William, '75, Cam., B. H., 8 m.

Ambrose, Samuel, '75, Cam., 3 mon.

Ames, David, '75, Cam., B. H., 8 m., '76, C. A. 1 y, '77 C. A., 3 y.

Ames, Jonathan, '75, L., '77 Al. T.

Atwell, John, '75, L., '76, Port., 3 m., '78, R. I., 22 d.

Auld, John, '78, C. A., 3 y.

Bailey, Andrew, 75, 'Cam., B. H., 8 m., '76, Port. 3 m., '77, C. A., 8 m. '78, R. I., 22 d.

Bailey, Daniel, '75, Cam. 3 m., '77, Al. T., '78, R. I., 22 d., '79, R. I., 5 m.

Bailey, Daniel, Jun., '76, Wh. P. 5 m.

Bailey, Job, '75, Cam. B. H., 8 m.

Bailey, Joseph, '75, L.

Bailey, Joel., '75, Cam., 8 m., '80, W. Pt., 3 m.

Ball, Ebenezer, '75, Cam., B. H., 8 m., '76, Port. and N. Y., 12 m.

Ball, Eleazer, '75, Cam. 3 m., '77, Al. T.

Ball, John, '76, Ti., 6 m., '77 C. A., 8 m.

Ball, Nathaniel, Jun., '75, L.

Ball, William, '77, Al. T.

Blanchard, Joshua, '75, Cam. 3 m.

Blood, Abel, '80, C. A., 6 m.

Blood, Daniel, '75, Cam. 3 m., '77, C. A., 3 y.

Blood, Daniel, 2 d, '75, L., '76, Ti., 6 m.

Blood, Elnathan, '76, Ti., G. R.

Blood, Ephraim, '75, Cam. B. H., 8 mo.

Blood, Francis, '75, Cam. B. H., 8 m.

Blood, Josiah, '76, Ti., 6 m.

Blood, Josiah, Jun., '77, Al. T., '80 W. Pt., 3 m.

Blood, Lemuel, '80, C. A., 6 m.

Blood, Nathan, '75, L., '75, Cam. B. H., 8 m.

Blood, Nathaniel, '78, R. I., 22d., '80, C. A. 6 m.

Blood, Nathaniel, Jun., '78, R. I., 22 d.

Blood, Jonas, '75, L.

Blood, Reuben, '77, Al. T., '78, C. A., 2 y., '80, C. A., 6 m.

Blood, Simeon, '77, Ben., '78, C. A., 2 y., '80, N. Frontier, 6 m.

Blood, Timothy, '76, Wh. P., 5 mo., '78, R. I. 22 d.

Bonner, John, '81, C. A., 3 y.

Bowers, Henry, '77, Ben.

Bowers, Jerathmael, '79, C. A., 1 y.

Bowers, Oliver, '77, Al. T.

Boyd, Samuel, '78, C. A., 2 y., '80, C. A. 3 y.

Boynton, Benjamin, '75, L., '76, Wh. P., 5 m.

Boynton, Elias, '75, Cam. B. H., 8 m., '76, C. A., 1 y., '78, R. I., 22 d.

Boynton, Isaac, '77, C. A. 3 y.

Boynton, Jacob, '75, Cam. B. H., 8 m.
Boynton, Joel, '75, Cam. 3 m., '76, Wh. P., 5 m
Boynton, John, 3 d., '77, C. A., 8 m.
Boynton, Joshua, '75, Cam. B. II., 8 m., '77, Al. T.
Brooks, John, '77, C. A., 8 m.
Brooks, Lt. William, '78, R. I., 22 d., '81, 3 m.
Brown, Abel, '75, Cam. B. II., 8 m.
Brown, William, '76, Ti., G. R.
Brown, Eliphalet, '75, Cam. 3 m., '77, Al. Ti., '77, Ben.
Brown, Joseph, '76, N. Y., 2 m.
Bruce, Josiah, '75, Cam. 8 m.
Burge, Ephraim, '77, Al. T.
Campbell, John, '75, Cam. B. II., 8 m., '77, Ben.
Carter, Edward, '76, Wh. P. 5 m., '77, C. A. 3 y.
Carter, Thomas, '78, R. I., 22 d.
Chamberlain, Asa, '81, 3 m.
Chamberlain, Samuel, '76, N. Y., 2 m.
Chamberlain, Wilder, '75, Cam. B. II., 8 m.
Clark, Elijah, '81, C. A., 3 y.
Colburn, Benj., '77, Al. T., '78, R. I., 22 d.
Colburn, James, '75, Cam., 3 m., '77, C. A. 8 m.
Colburn, Nathan, '75, L., '75, Cam. 8 m., '76, Wh. P., 5 m.
Colburn, Robt., '75, Cam. 3 m.
Colburn, Thomas, '75, L., '75, Cam. B. II., 8 m.
Conant, Abel, '75, Cam. B. II., 8 m., '76, C. A., 1 y., '78. R. I., 22 d.
Conant Josiah, '75, Cam. 3 m., '78, R. I., 22 d.
Connick, Robt., '81, 3 m.
Connick William, '76, Wh. P., 5 m., '77, C. A., 3 y., '80, C. A., 6 m.
Cowen, William, '78, C. A., 2 y.
Cumings, Benj., '75, L., '75, Cam. B. II. 8 m., '76, C. A., 1 y.
Conroy, John, '75, Cam. 3 m., '80, W. Pt., 3 m.
Conroy, John, Jun., '78, C. A. 2 y.
Conroy, Samuel, '75, L., '75, Cam. B. II., 8 m.
Conroy, Stephen, '76, C. A., 1 y., '78, C. A., 2 y., '80, C. A., 6 m.
Cumings, Ebenezer, '77, C. A., 3 y.
Cumings, En. John, '75, L., '75, Cam., B. II. 8 m.
Cumings, Larnard, '76, Port. and N. Y., 12 m.
Cumings, Peter, '75, Cam. B. II., 8 m.
Cumings, Philip, '75, Cam. B. II., 8 m.
Cumings, Wm., '76, N. Y., 2 m., '77, Al. T.
Danforth, Jacob, '76, C. A., 1 y., '77, C. A., 3 y., '80, C. A., 6 m.
Davis, Joshua, '76, Ti. 6 m.
Deane, Edward, '81, C. A. 3 y.
Dickey, James, '75, L., '77, Al. T.
Dow, Capt. Reuben, '75, L., '75, Cam. B. II., 8 mo., '78, R. I., 22 d.

Dow, Evan, '75, Cam. B. H., 8 m,. '78, R. I., 22 d.
Dow, Stephen, '77, Al. T., '80, W. Pt., 3 m.
Eastman, Amos, '75, L., '76, N. Y., 2 m.
Eastman, Caleb, '75, Cam. B. H., 8 m.
Eastman, Jonathan, '75, L.
Elliot, William, '75, Cam. B. II., 8 m., '76, C. A., 1 y.
Emerson, Capt. Daniel, '76, Ti. 6 m., '77, Al. T., '78, R. I., 22 d., '79, R. I., 5 m.
Emerson, Dr. Peter, '79, R. I., 5 m., Reg. Surg.
Emerson, Ralph, '76, Ti., 6 m., '77, C. A., 3 y.
Emerson, Samuel, '79, R. I., 5 m.
Emerson, Thomas, '76, Ti., 6 m.
Farley, Benj., '75, L., '75, Cam. 3 m.
Farley, Benj., Jun., '76, Ti., 6 m.
Farley, Lt. Caleb, '76, Port. and N. Y., 12 m., '78 R. I., 22 d.
Farley, Christopher, '76, Port. and N. Y., 12 m.
Farley, Ebenezer, '75, L., '76, N. Y., 2 m.
Farley, Joseph, '75, Cam., 3 m.
Farley, Stephen, '75, Cam., 3 m.
Farmer, Minot, '75, L., '75, Cam., B. H. 8 m. '76, C. A., 1 y.
Farnsworth, David, '75, L., '75, Cam. B. II., 8 m.
Fisk, James, '75, L., '75, Cam. 8 m.
Fisk, Josiah, '75, Cam. B. H., 8 m.
Flagg, Jonas, '78, R. I., 22 d., '80, W. Pt., 3 m.
Foster, Simeon, '79, C. A., 1 y.
French, David, '76, Port. and N. Y., 12 m.
French, Isaac, '75, Cam. 3 m., '76, Wh. P. 3 m.
French, Jonathan, '77, Ben., '78, R. I., 22 d.
French, Joseph, '75, Cam., 8 m.
French, Nehemiah, '75, Cam., 8 m., '77, Al. T.
French, Timothy, '76, N. Y., 2 m.
French, William, '75, L.
Gilson, Ebenezer, '75, L., '75, Cam., 3 m.
Godfrey, John, '77, C. A., 3 y., '81, C. A. 3 y.
Goodhue, Samuel, '77, Port. 1 m.
Goodhue, John, '79, Port. 6 m.
Goodhue, Stephen, '70, Wh. P., 5 m. '78 R. I., 22 d.
Goss, Capt. John, '75 L., '75, Cam., B. H., 8 m., '77, Ben.
Grace, Benjamin W., '81, C. A., 3 y.
Grace, Manuel, '75, L.
Hale, Dr. John, Reg. Surgeon from '76 to '80.
Hale, John, Jun., '76, N. Y., 2 m., '78, R. I., 22 d.
Hale, David, '78, R. I., 22 d.
Hale, William, '77, C. A., 3 y.
Hardy, Aaron, '75, L.
Hardy, Jesse, '80, W. Pt., 3 m.
Hardy, Lemuel, '77, Al. T., '80, W. Pt., 3 m.
Hardy, Joseph, '79, Port., 6 m.
Hardy, Nehemiah, '75, Cam. 3 m.

Hardy, Noah, '77, Al. T., '78, R. I., 22 d.

Hardy, Phineas, '76, Port. 3 m.

Hardy, Phineas, Jun., '75, Cam., B. II., 8 m., '76, Port., 3 m.

Hardy, Silas, '79, Port., 6 m.

Hardy, Thomas, '75, Cam., B. II., 8 m., '76, C. A., 1 y.

Henderson, Andrew, '82, N. Frontier, 6 m.

Hill, Samuel, '75, Cam., B. II., 8 m. '76, Ti., 6, m. '77, C. A., 3 y.

Hobart, Isaac, '75, Cam. B. II., 8 m.

Hobart, Isaac, 2d., '81, C. A., 3 y.

Hobart, Jacob, '81, C. A., 3 y.

Hobart, John, '77, Al. T., '79, R. I., 6 m.

Hobart, Jonathan, '75, Cam., 3 m., '76, N. Y., 2 m.

Hobart, Joshua, '75, Cam., 3 m., '77, Ben., '78, R. I., 22 d.

Hobart, Col. Samuel, '75, Paymaster.

Hobart, Solomon, '77, Al. T., '78, R. I., 22 d.

Honey, Parmeter, '75, Cam., 3 m.

Hopkins, Richard, '76, Port., and N. Y., 12 m.

Hosley, Samuel, '75, Cam., B. II., 8 m.

How, Ephraim, '75, Cam. B.H., 8 m., '77 Ben.

How, John, '76, Ti., 6 m., '78, R. I., 22 d.

How, Joseph, '75, Cam., 3 m.

Jaquith, Ebenezer, '75, Cam., 3 m.

Jaquith, Thomas, '75, Cam., 3 m.

Jewett, Lieut. Ebenezer, '77, Al. T., '80, W. Pt., 3 m.

Jewett, Jacob, '75, Cam., 3 m.

Jewett, Jacob, 3d., '78, R. I., 22 d., '80, W. Pt., 3 m.

Jewett, James, '76, Ti., G. R.

Jewett, Jonathan, '78, R. I., 6 m.

Jewett, Dea. Nathaniel, '76, Ti., G. R.

Jewett, Noah, '76, Wh. P., 5 m.

Jewett, Samuel, '75, Cam., B. H., 8 m.

Jewett, Stephen, Jun., '75, Cam., 3 m., '76, Wh. P., 5 m.

Johnson, Edward, '75, L.

Johnson, Samuel, '76, N. Y., 2 m.

Kemp, Thomas, '75, Cam., B. II., 8 m., '76, Wh. P., 5 m., '77 Ben.

Kendrick, Capt. Daniel, '78, R. I., 22 d.

Keyes, Abner, '75, Cam., 8 m., '76, Port. and N. Y., 12 m. '81, 3 m.

Kinney, Israel, '75, Cam., B. II., 8 m., '76, C. A., 1 y.

Lawrence, Asa, '78, R. I., 22 d.

Lawrence, Nicholas, '80, W. Pt., 3 m.

Lawrence, Oliver, '75, Cam., 3 m., '78, R. I., 6 m.

Lawrence, Silas, '80, W. Pt., 3 m.

Leeman, Nathaniel, '77, Al. T., '80, W. Pt., 3 m.

Leeman, Ensign Samuel, '75, Cam., B. II., 8 m., '76, C. A., 1 y., '77, C. A., 3 y.

Lesley, Jonas, '76, Wh. P., 5 m.

Lovejoy, Abel, '80, C. A. 6 m.

Lovejoy, Asa, '75, Cam., 3 m., '76, Wh., P. 5 m., '77, C. A., 3 y.

Lovejoy, Daniel, '76, Ti., G. R.

Lovejoy, Jonathan, Jun., '75, Cam., 3 m.

Lund, Ephraim, '75, Cam., 3 m.

McConnor, James, '75, Cam., B. H., 8 m.

McDaniels, James, '77, Ben.

McDaniels, Randall, '75, L.

McHendley, John, '81, C. A., 3y.

McIntosh, Archibald, '77, Ben.

McIntosh, James, '77, Cam., B. H., 8 m.

Merrill, Daniel, '76, Ti., G. R.

Merrill, Daniel, Jun., '78, R. I., 22 d. '80, W. Pt., 3 m., '81, 3 m.

Merrill, Samuel, '77, Al. T., '77, Ben., '78, R. I. 22 d.

Messer, Benjamin, '77, Ben.

Minot, Joseph, '75, L.

Mooar, Daniel, '77 Ben.

Mooar, Jacob, '77, Ben., '81, 3 m.

Nevins, Benjamin, '75, L., '77, Ben.

Nevins, John, '77, Ben.

Nevins, Joseph, '75, L., '77, Al. T.

Nevins, Phineas, '75, Cam., B. H., 8 m.

Nevins, William, '75, L., '75, Cam., B. II., 8 m. '76, C. A., 1 y.

Noyes, Elijah, '75, Cam., 3 m., '76, Ti., 6m., '77 Al. T., '78, R. I., 22 d.

Noyes, Enoch, Jun., '76, Ti., 6 m.

Parker, Benjamin W., '81, 3 m.

Parker, Jonathan, '76, C. A., 1 y., '77, C. A., 8 m., '78, R. I., 22 d.

Parker, Stephen, '80, W. Pt., 3 m., '81, C. A., 3 y.

Patch, David, '76, C. A., 1 y.

Patch, Daniel, '75, Cam., 3 m.

Patch, Thomas, '75, L., '76 Ti., 6 m.

Patten, Nathaniel, '75, Cam., B. H., 8 m., '76, Ti., 6 m., '77, C. A., 3 y., '80, C. A., 6 m.

Phelps, John, '76, Ti., G. R.

Phelps, Nathan, '75, L., '75, Cam., 3 m.

Phelps, Samuel, '76, Ti., 6 m.

Philbrick, John, '75, L.

Pierce, Ephraim, '75, L., '76, Wh. P., 5 m., '77 Al. T., '77, Ben., '79, C. A., 1 y.

Pierce, Nehemiah, '75, Cam., B. II., 8 m., '77, C. A., 8 m.

Pierce, Solomon, '75, Cam., 3 m., '76, Ti., 6 m.

Pierce, Richard, '76 Ti., G. R.

Platts, John, '75, Cam., B. II., 8 m., '76 Wh. P. 5 m.

Pool, Dr. Jonathan, Assist. Surgeon, '76 to '80

Pool, William, '76, Ti., G. R.

Pool, William W., '75, Cam., 3 m., '78, R. I. 22 d.

Poor, Peter, '75, Cam., B. H., 8 m.

Powell, Thomas, '81, 3 m.

Powers, Francis, '75, Cam., B. II., Sm., '77, Ben.

Powers, Francis G., '79, C. A., 1 y., '80, W. Pt., 3 m.

Powers, Jonathan, '75, Cam., B. II. S m.

Powers, Nahum, '75, L., '75, Cam., B. II. S m.

Powers, Samson, '75, L., '75, Cam., B. II. S m. '77, Ben.

Powers, Stephen, '76, Port. and N. Y., 12 m.

Pratt, Thomas, '75, L., '75 Cam., B. II. S m. '76, C. A. 1 y., '77, C. A., 3 y., '81, for the war.

Proctor, Ezekiel, '75, L., '75, Cam., B. II., S m. '76, C. A., 1 y. '81, C. A., 3 y.

Proctor, Ezra, '76, C. A., 1 y.

Proctor, Joel, '78, C. A., 2 y., '81, for the war.

Proctor, Moses, '77, Al. T.

Read, Jacob, '75, L., '75, Cam., B. II., S m.

Read, John, '75, Cam., 3 m., '76, C. A. 1 y.

Read, Samuel, '81, 3 m.

Richardson, Stephen, '76, C. A., 1 y., '77, C. A., 3 y., '81, C. A. for the war.

Rideout, James, '77, Ben.

Rogers, Lemuel, '81, C. A., for the war.

Rolfe, Ephraim, '75, Cam., B. II., S m., '77, Ben. '78, R. I. 22 d.

Rolfe, James, '81, C. A. 3 y.

Runnells, Stephen, '77, Ben., '78, R. I., 22 d.

Russ, Jonathan, '75, L., '75, Cam., 3 m., '77, Ben.

Saunderson, Benjamin, '75, L., '76, Wh. P., 5 m.

Saunderson, David, '76, N. Y., 2 m., '77, C. A. 3 y., '80, for the war.

Seaver, Robert, '75, L., '75, Cam., 3 m., '77, Al. T.

Shattuck, Isaac, '76, Port. and N. Y., 12 m.

Shattuck, Jeremiah, '75, Cam. S m.

Shattuck, William, '75, Cam. 3 m., '76, N. Y. 2 m.

Shattuck, Zachariah, '75, Cam. 3 m.

Shed, Jonas, 77, Ben.

Smith, Ephraim, '75, Cam., B. II. S m., '76, C. A., 1 y.

Smith, Joshua, '76, Wh. P., 5 m.

Spaulding, Enoch, '76, Port. and N. Y., 12 m. '78, R. I., 6 m.

Spaulding, Jacob, '75, L., '75, Cam. B. II. S m. '77, Al. T., '78, R. I., 22 d.

Stearns, Isaac, '75, L., '75, Cam., B. II., S m. '77, Al. T., '77. Ben.

Stearns, Joseph, '76, Ti., 6 m., '77, Ben., '79, C. A. 1 y.

Stevens, Isaac, Jun., '76, Ti., 6 m.

Stiles, Caleb, '79, C. A., 1 y.

Stiles, Caleb, Jun., '79, C. A., 1 y.

Stiles, Eli, '76, C. A., 1 y., '77, C. A., S m., '80, C. A., for the war.

Taylor, Amos, '75, L., '75, Cam. B. II., S m.

Taylor, Daniel. '75, L., '75, C. B. II., S m.

Taylor Edward, '76, Ti., G. R.

Taylor, Jacob, '75, Cam. 3 m., '76, C. A., 1 y., '77, C. A., S m.

Taylor, Jonathan, '75, Cam. 3 m.

Tenney, Wm., Jun., '75, L., '75, Cam., 3 m., '76, Wh. P., 5 m.

Thurston, Moses, '75, Cam., B. II., S m.

Townsend, Ebenezer, '75, Cam., B. II., S m., '76, Ti., 6 m., '77, C. A., 3 y.

Twiss, Asahel, '81, C. A., 3 y.

Wallingford, Lt. David, '75, Cam., S m., '77, Al. T., '77, Ben.

Wheat, Joseph, '77, Al. Ti., '78, R. I., 22 d., '79, C. A., 1 y., '80, for the war.

Wheat, Nathaniel, '75, L., '75, Cam., 3 m.

Wheat, Solomon, '76, Ti., G. R.

Wheat, Thomas, '76, Port. and N. Y., 12 m.

Wheat, Thomas, Jun., '75, L., '75, Cam., B. II., S m.

Wheeler, Abner, '77, Al. T., '77, Ben.

Wheeler, Ebenezer, '75, L., '76, Wh. P. 5 m.

Wheeler, James, Jun., '75, Cam., 3 m.

Wheeler, Lebbeus, '75, L., '75, Cam., B. II., S m., '77, C. A., 3 y.

Wheeler, Thaddeus, '75, L.

Wilkins, Bray, '75, L., '75, Cam., S m.

Wilkins, Israel, '75, L.

Willoughby, Jonas, '82, N. Frontier, 6 m.

Willoughby, Samuel, '76, Ti., G. R.

Wood, William, '75, L., '75, Cam. B. II., S m., '77, Ben.

Woods, Jonas, '77, Al. T., '77, Ben., 78, R. I., 22 d.

Woods, Nehemiah, '77, Al. T.

Worcester, Capt. Noah, '75, Cam. 3 m., '78, R. I., 22 d.

Worcester, Noah, Jun., '75, L., '75, Cam., B. II., S m., '77, Ben.

Worcester, Jesse, '76, Ti., 6 m., '77, Al. T., '77, Port. 1 m., '78, R. I., 22 d., '80, C. A. 6 m.

Worcester, Samuel, '76, Port. and N. Y., 12 m.

Wright, Benj., '75, L., '76, N. Y., 2 m.

Wright, Benj., Jun., '75, L.

Wright, Lemuel, '76, Ti., 6 m., '77, Al. T.

Wright, Samuel, '75, Cam., B. II., S m., '77, Ben.

Wright, Uriah, '75, L., '75, Cam., B. II., S m., '77, Al. T.

Wyman, Jesse, '75, L., '76, N. Y., 2 m., '77, Ben.

Youngman, Ebenezer, '75, L., '75, Cam. B. II. S m.

Youngman, Jabez, '82, during war.

Youngman, John, '76, Ti., 6 m., '77, C. A., 3 y., '80, C. A., for the war.

Youngman, Nicholas, '76, Ti. 6 m.

Youngman, Thomas, '76, C. A., 1 y., '77, C. A., 3 y., '80, N. Frontier, 6 m.

CHAPTER XX.

BIOGRAPHICAL SKETCHES OF SOME OF THE HOLLIS REVOLUTIONARY OFFICERS AND SOLDIERS.

BLOOD, NATHAN

son of Nathaniel Blood, was born in Hollis April 4, 1747. Married Elizabeth Noyes, daughter of Dea. Enoch Noyes, April 16, 1772. Enlisted April 19, 1775, and was First Sergeant in the company of Capt. Dow at Bunker Hill, where he was killed June 17, 1775.

BROOKS, LIEUT. WILLIAM

came to Hollis about 1757. Married Abigail Kemp, in Hollis, March 29, 1759. Enlisted in 1778 in Captain Emerson's company to Rhode Island, in which he was Second Lieutenant. Enlisted again in 1781, in the company of Capt. Mills, regiment of Col. Reynolds. Removed from Hollis after the Revolution.

CONANT, DEA. JOSIAH

son of Josiah Conant. Born in Hollis, October 17, 1746. Enlisted December, 1775, in the company of Capt. Worcester for Cambridge. Enlisted again in 1778 in the company of Capt. Emerson for Rhode Island, in which he was Sergeant. Deacon of the Hollis church in 1787, till his death in Hollis, August 21, 1807, æt. 60.

CONANT, DEA. ABEL

son of Josiah Conant, born in Hollis October 3, 1755. Enlisted April 19, 1775, and was in the company of Capt. Dow at the battle of Bunker Hill. Enlisted in 1776 in the Continental army for one year. and in 1778 in Capt. Emerson's company for Rhode Island. Married Pegga Jewett in Hollis, November 20, 1781. Chosen a deacon of the Hollis church in 1787. Removed to Hardwick, Vt., in 1813, where he died May 2, 1844, æt. 88.

CUMINGS, ENSIGN JOHN

born in Groton, Mass., March 16, 1737. His name was on the Hollis tax lists in 1758. Enlisted April 19, 1775, and was Ensign

or Second Lieutenant in the company of Capt. Dow at Bunker Hill.
Removed after the war to Hancock, as is supposed.

CUMINGS, CAPT. JOTHAM

son of Jerahmael Cumings, and a younger brother of Henry
Cumings, D. D., of Billerica, Mass. Born December 19, 1741.
He was a soldier in the French war in 1758. Married Anna
Brown, of Hollis, April 27, 1763. Removed from Hollis to
Plymouth, N. H., in 1764. Was Lieutenant in a company of New
Hampshire Rangers in 1775 and was for many years a deacon of the
Plymouth church. Died at Plymouth, April 1, 1808, æt. 66.

CUMINGS, WILLIAM

was born in Groton, Mass., October 2, 1741. Came to Hollis about
the year 1760. Married Mehitabel Eastman of Hollis, June 28,
1768. Was Master of the Hollis Grammar School in 1775, and for
many years after. Was Town Clerk and First Selectman in Hollis
in 1771 and 1772—and again from 1782 to 1788 inclusive. Enlisted
in the army in 1776 and again in 1777. About the year 1790 he
removed to Hebron, N. H., where he died October 2, 1831, æt. 90.

DOW, CAPT. REUBEN

came from Salem, N. H., and was in Hollis in 1761, and Selectman
in 1769 and 1770. Lieutenant of the Hollis Militia company in
January, 1775. Chosen captain of the Hollis company of Minute
men to Cambridge, April 19, 1775. Commissioned as captain of
the Hollis company in Col. William Prescott's regiment, May 19,
1775. Wounded at the battle of Bunker Hill and was afterwards a
United States' pensioner for life. He was chairman of the Hollis
Committee of Safety in 1776, and Representative to the New
Hampshire General Court in 1778. His two sons, Evan and
Stephen, were Revolutionary soldiers. Died February 11, 1811,
æt. 81.

EASTMAN, LIEUT. AMOS

was a son of Amos Eastman, Senior, born in Penacook, now
Concord, N. H., April 28, 1751, and came to Hollis with his
father about the year 1759. Married Ruth Flagg, of Hollis,
January 6, 1774. Enlisted April 19, 1775, and again in 1776 in the
regiment of Col. Gilman. He was for many years a Justice of the
Peace, and Town clerk and First Selectman in 1806. Died August
. 2, 1832, æt. 81.

In the year 1752, his father, Amos Eastman, Senior, then living at Penacook, being on a hunting expedition, in the northerly part of New Hampshire, with Gen. John Stark and others, was, with Stark, taken prisoner by the Indians, and both of them taken to an Indian village in Canada. On their arrival at the village, both the captives were compelled to run the gauntlet between two files of savages, each armed with a switch or club with which to strike them as they passed between the lines. Stark, as is said, escaped with but slight injury, but Eastman was cruelly beaten, and was afterwards sold to a French master, kindly treated by him and soon after redeemed and went home.*

EMERSON, CAPT. DANIEL

son of Rev. Daniel Emerson, born in Hollis, December 15, 1746. Married Ama Fletcher November 17, 1768. Chosen deacon of the Hollis church in 1775. Appointed Coroner and High Sheriff of Hillsborough county in 1776. He was Captain of the Hollis company that went to Ticonderoga in July of that year, and was also Captain of the company enlisted in Hollis in June 1777, upon the *Ticonderoga Alarm*. He was also in 1778 Captain of a mounted Hollis company that went to Rhode Island in the summer of that year, and also of a company in Col. Mooney's regiment raised for the defence of Rhode Island in 1779. Capt. Emerson was Town Clerk and First Selectman in 1780 and 1781. A member of the New Hampshire Council in 1787—of the New Hampshire Constitutional Convention in 1791,—and a Representative to the New Hampshire General Court in nineteen different years, between 1780 and 1812. His two oldest sons, Rev. Daniel Emerson, Jun., and Rev. Joseph Emerson, were graduates of Harvard, his third son, Rev. Ralph Emerson, D. D., of Yale (*q. v.*) His youngest son, William, was Colonel of the regiment to which Hollis was attached and was for many years a deacon of the Hollis church.

The following epitaph is inscribed on the tomb stone of Capt Emerson in the Hollis central burial ground.

" In Memory of Daniel Emerson, Esq.
Having faithfully and industriously served his generation
As an officer of the Church
As a Defender of Freedom
As a Magistrate and Legislator
As a friend of the Poor
And as a Zealous Promoter of the Redeemer's Kingdom.
He rested from his labors
October 4, 1820, æt. 74."

---

*See Bouton's History of Concord, p. 192.

EMERSON, DR. PETER

second son of Rev. Daniel Emerson, born in Hollis, November 30,
1749. Appointed Surgeon of the regiment of Col. Mooney, in 1779.
Settled as a physician in Hillsborough, N. H., and died at
Hillsborough in 1827, æt. 78.

EMERSON, LIEUT. RALPH

son of Rev. Daniel Emerson, born March 4, 1761. Enlisted July
1776 at the age of fifteen in his brother's company for the defence of
Ticonderoga. In April, 1777, he enlisted in the Continental army
for three years. Married Alice Ames, May 13, 1784. On his
tombstone in the Hollis burial ground is the following inscription :

> " Erected to the Memory of Lieut. Ralph Emerson
> Who was instantly killed by the accidental discharge
> Of a cannon while exercising the matross,
> October 4, 1790, in the 30th year of his age.
> We drop apace,
> By nature some decay
> And some the gusts of fortune sweep away."

FARLEY, CAPT. CALEB

was born in Billerica, Mass., October 19, 1730. Married Elizabeth
Farley, October 11, 1754. He was a soldier from Billerica in the
French war of 1755, and came to Hollis in November, 1765, and
was Selectman in 1767. He enlisted in 1776 in the regiment of
Col. Pierce Long for New York and Canada, and in 1778 he was
Lieutenant in Capt. Emerson's mounted company, enlisted in Hollis
for the defence of Rhode Island. Died in Hollis, April 5, 1833,
æt. 102 years, 5 months.

FARMER, MINOT

son of Benjamin Farmer, born 1750. Enlisted April 19, 1775, in
the Hollis company of minute men in which he was a Sergeant, and
he was also a Sergeant in the company of Capt. Dow, at the battle
of Bunker Hill. Married Abigail Barron, September 15, 1775.
In the fall or winter of 1775, he enlisted in Gen. Arnold's expedition
to Canada. Was taken prisoner in the attack on Quebec, and died
in captivity, May 9, 1776, æt. 26. He is supposed to have held the
rank of Ensign.

GOSS, CAPT. JOHN

was born at Salisbury, Mass., February 13, 1739. His name first
appears on the Hollis tax lists in 1770. Married Catharine Conant,
of Hollis, February 10, 1774, and was Selectman in Hollis the same

year. He was Lieutenant in the Hollis company of minute men, that went to Cambridge April 19, 1775, and also in the Hollis company at the battle of Bunker Hill. In the year 1777 he was the Captain of the Hollis company that went to Bennington. About the year 1805 he removed with his family to Hardwick, Vt., where he died September 26, 1821, æt. 82.

HALE, COL. JOHN

was born in Sutton, Mass., October 24, 1731. Settled, as a physician in Hollis, at the age of about 24. He was Assistant Surgeon in 1755 in the regiment of Col. Joseph Blanchard, in the French war, and Surgeon in Col. Hart's regiment, in 1758 in the same war. He was Representative to the New Hampshire General Court from Hollis and Dunstable from 1762 to 1768. In 1767 he was Lieutenant-Colonel of the Fifth regiment of the New Hampshire Militia, and Colonel of the same regiment in 1775, and the same year he was Representative from Hollis to the New Hampshire General Court, and also to the New Hampshire Provincial Congress. He was Surgeon of the First New Hampshire Continental regiment, from 1776 to 1780, and a member of the New Hampshire Council in the year last named. After the war was ended he continued in the practice of his profession in Hollis, in which he was distinguished, till his death in 1791. His three sons, John, Jun., David and William were all soldiers in the war. The following epitaph is inscribed on his tombstone in the central burying ground.

> " Erected to the Memory of
> **Dr. John Hale,**
> Who was born October 14, 1731.
> Died October 22, 1791.
> How soon our new born light attains to full age'd noon
> And that how soon to gray haired night,
> We spring, we bud, we blossom, and we blast
> Ere we can count our days they fly so fast."

HALE, DR. WILLIAM

son of Col. John Hale, born in Hollis, July 27, 1762. Enlisted for three years in the Continental Army, April, 1777, when in his fifteenth year. After his discharge from the army studied medicine with his father and succeeded him in his practice. He was a man of great energy, and had a large practice in his profession. Died October 10, 1854, æt. 92, and he is said to have been the last survivor of the 1200 men whose names are found on the rolls of the First New Hampshire Continental regiment.

HOBART, COL. DAVID

son of Peter Hobart and grandson of Gershom Hobart, the third
minister of Groton, Mass., born in Groton, August 21, 1722.
Settled in that part of Hollis known as "One Pine Hill," about
1748, and was a Sergeant in the company of Capt. Powers in the
French war in 1755. He was one of the grantees of Plymouth, N.
H., and one of the first settlers of that town. His name last
appears on the Hollis tax lists in 1765. In 1777 he was Colonel of
the Twelfth New Hampshire regiment of militia and had command
of a New Hampshire regiment under Gen. Stark at the battle of
Bennington, where he greatly distinguished himself for his gallantry
and good conduct, for which he received due commendation from
Gen. Stark in his report of the battle. In that battle Col. Hobart
with Col. Stickney led the attack against the Tory breast-work on
the right where the contest was most desperate—the Tories it is said
" fighting like tigers," and neither asking nor giving quarter. Col.
Hobart having lost his wife, after the war removed to Haverhill,
Mass., married a second wife and died soon after at Haverhill. The
name of this heroic officer is erroneously spelt "Hubbard" in
" Belknap's History of New Hampshire," as it also was said to have
been in Gen. Stark's report of the battle.

HOBART, COL. SAMUEL

a younger brother of Col. David Hobart, born in Groton, August
11, 1734. Settled in Hollis during the French war of 1755. Was
a Sergeant in that war in 1758. Adjutant of Col. Goffe's regiment in 1760, and an Ensign in 1761. In 1767 he was Major of the
Fifth New Hampshire regiment of militia. Representative to the
General Court from Hollis for six years, from 1768 to 1774. In the
year last named was appointed Colonel of the Second New
Hampshire regiment of minute men, and was a delegate from
Hollis to the New Hampshire Provincial Congress. Upon the
organization of Hillsborough county in 1771, he was appointed
Register of Deeds, County Treasurer and one of the Justices of the
county court. In 1775 he was appointed Muster Master, and also
Paymaster of the New Hampshire regiments at Cambridge. In 1777
he contracted with the State government to manufacture gunpowder
for the State, and removed from Hollis to Exeter. Was representative to the General Court from Exeter in 1777 and 1778, and a
member of the State Committee of Safety in 1779 and 1780. Anna
Hobart, the first wife of Col. Hobart, died in Hollis, May 20, 1773.

After he removed from Hollis he continued to reside in Exeter for several years after the war, married a second time, and finally removed to Kingston, N. H., where he died June 4, 1798, æt. 63.

JEWETT, LT. EBENEZER

son of Dea. Nathaniel Jewett, born 1743, enlisted in June, 1777, in the company of Capt. Emerson, on the "Ticonderoga Alarm," and in 1780 in the company of Capt. Barron, regiment of Col. Nichols, for the defence of West Point, in which company he was Lieutenant. Was Selectman in 1782. He married Mary Rideout in 1793. Died Oct. 6, 1826, æt 83.

JEWETT, JUN., DEACON STEPHEN

son of Dea. Stephen Jewett, born in Hollis, October 4, 1753. Enlisted in 1775 in the company of Capt. Worcester for Cambridge, and in 1776 in the company of Capt. Reed for White Plains. Married Elizabeth Pool, November 16, 1778. Chosen deacon of the Hollis church, 1805. Died February 22, 1829, æt. 75.

KENDRICK, CAPT. DANIEL

born 1736, son of Daniel Kendrick. Selectman in 1775, '76, and '77. Member of the Hollis Committee of Safety in 1776 and 1777. Enlisted in Capt. Emerson's mounted company for Rhode Island in 1778. Married Mary Pool, February 13, 1782. His oldest son, Daniel, was a graduate of Brown University. His youngest, William P., of Harvard. (q. v.) Died May 20, 1789, æt. 53.

LEEMAN, JUN., ENSIGN SAMUEL

son of Samuel Leeman, born in Hollis August 7, 1749. Enlisted April 19, 1775. Was at the battle of Bunker Hill in the company of Capt. Spalding, regiment of Col. Reed. Enlisted in 1776 in the Continental army, and again in the Continental army in 1777 in the company of Capt. Frye, 1st New Hampshire regiment, in which he was Ensign. Killed at the battle near Saratoga, October 10, 1777, æt. 28.

NEVINS, JUN. ENSIGN WILLIAM

son of William Nevins, born in Hollis, July 26, 1746, married Rebecca Chamberlain, March 24, 1768. Enlisted April 19, 1775, and was Sergeant, and also a Sergeant in the company of Capt. Dow at Bunker Hill. Enlisted in 1776 for one year in the Continental army. Died in New York, 1776. æt. 30.

POOL, DR. JONATHAN

son of Eleazer Pool, born at Woburn, September 5, 1758. Studied medicine with Col. John Hale in Hollis, was Assistant Surgeon in the 1st New Hampshire regiment from 1776 to 1780. Married Elizabeth Hale, daughter of Col. John Hale, December 7, 1780, and settled as a physician in Hollis, where he died July 25, 1797, æt. 38.

SEAVER, CAPT. ROBERT

born 1743, name first on the Hollis tax lists in 1767. Enlisted April 19, 1775, was Lieutenant in Capt. Worcester's company for Cambridge in 1775, and also in Capt. Emerson's company in June 1777. Died November 3, 1828, æt. 85.

TENNEY, CAPT. WILLIAM

was the son of William and Anna Tenney and was born in Hollis, March 17, 1755. April 19, 1775, he enlisted in the company of the Hollis minute men ; and in December 1775 in the company of Capt. Worcester, for Cambridge, and again in 1776 in that of Capt. Reed, for White Plains. Married Phebe Jewett in 1776 by whom he had ten children, five sons and five daughters. His sons, Caleb Jewett, and William, were graduates of Dartmouth. (*q. v.*) Died June 16, 1806, æt. 51.

His youngest son, Hon. Ralph E. Tenney, born October 5, 1790, settled as a farmer in Hollis, upon his paternal homestead. He was for many years a Justice of the Peace and Quorum, and was frequently elected by his townsmen to offices of honor and trust. For his first wife he married Olive Brown, of Hollis, November 12, 1812, by whom he had one daughter. After her decease, he married, August 14, 1818, for his second wife, Miss Phebe C. Smith, born in Dracut, Mass., June 2, 1790. At an early age Miss Smith went to Merrimack, N. H., to reside with her step father, Simeon Cumings, Esq., upon whose decease she came to Hollis with her mother to care for her, in her declining years. She was afterwards, in her earlier years, widely known in Hollis as an excellent and popular school teacher, and as an assistant of Mr. Ambrose Gould, in his store.

She had by Mr. Tenney a family of nine children, and upon her marriage became an honored wife and a devoted, faithful and beloved mother. She was also a kind neighbor and an efficient and cheerful helper in works of benevolence and charity, and a

THE TENNEY HOMESTEAD FOR FIVE GENERATIONS.

Home of WILLIAM TENNEY   1747 to 1785.   Home of RALPH E. TENNEY 2d.   1874 to 1879.   Home of RALPH E. TENNEY   1806 to 1854
"   " CAPT W.N. TENNEY   1777 " 1806.   "   " WILLIAM N. TENNEY   1854 " 1874

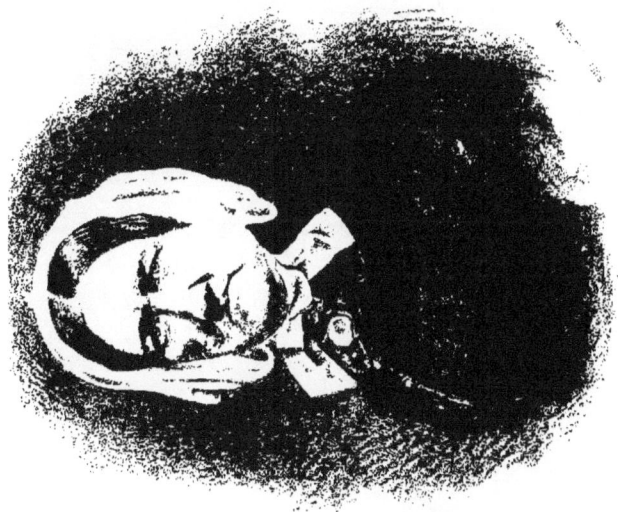

consistent and exemplary member of the church for more than half a century. Died February 17, 1864, æt. 73.

In addition to his other offices, Mr. Tenney was Representative from Hollis to the New Hampshire General Court, in 1832, '33, '34, and in 1845, and a member of the New Hampshire Senate in 1847 and 1848. Died October 19, 1854, æt. 64.

WALLINGFORD, LIEUT. DAVID

son of Jonathan Wallingford, born in Bradford, Mass., September 25, 1744. Married Elizabeth Leeman, of Hollis, March 25, 1767. His name was first on the Hollis tax lists in 1770. He enlisted April 19, 1775. in the company of Hollis minute men, commanded by Capt. Dow. In 1775, he was afterwards Lieutenant in the company of Capt. Town, in the Massachusetts regiment, under Col. Hutchinson. In June, 1777, he was also Lieutenant in the company of Capt. Emerson, and again Lieutenant, in July, 1777, in the company of Capt. Goss, that went from Hollis to Bennington. Died in Hollis, March 12, 1791, æt. 46.

WEBSTER, COL. DAVID

son of Stephen Webster, was born in Chester, N. H., December 10, 1738. Removed from Hollis to Plymouth, N. H., among the first settlers of that town in 1764, and is said to have driven the first ox team to Plymouth. He was a soldier in the French war, in 1757, and again in 1760. He was Ensign in the militia company of Plymouth; enlisted in the army, and rose to be Colonel of a New Hampshire volunteer regiment which he commanded at the taking of Gen. Burgoyne, in 1777. He was, after the war, High Sheriff of Grafton county for thirty years. Died at Holderness, N. H., May 8, 1824. æt. 85.

WEBSTER, CAPT. AMOS

was a brother of Col. David Webster, and also born in Chester. N. H. He also removed from Hollis to Plymouth among its earliest settlers. He was Lieutenant in the Third New Hampshire Continental regiment in 1776, and a Captain in the same regiment in 1777. and was killed at the battle at Saratoga, in October of that year. Just before he expired, he asked: " *Which side gave way?*" Being told, " *The British.*" he replied: " *It is enough, I die in peace.*"

WOOD, ENSIGN, WILLIAM

enlisted April 19, 1775, and was afterwards in the company of
Capt. Dow at the battle of Bunker Hill, at which he was so severely
wounded, that he became a United States pensioner for life. In
1777, he again enlisted, and was in the company of Capt. Goss at
the battle of Bennington, August 18, 1777. He married Susannah
Wright, daughter of Capt. Joshua Wright, by whom he had five
sons and nine daughters, all of whom, with the exception of one
son, lived to adult age and were married and had families. Died
1826, æt. 73.

WILLOUGHBY, CAPT. JOHN

son of John Willoughby, born in Billerica, Mass., in 1736. Capt.
Willoughby removed from Hollis to Plymouth, among the first settlers of that town, and was a Captain in Col. David Webster's regiment at the battles of Stillwater and Saratoga. He afterwards was
deacon of the Plymouth church for 67 years, and died at Plymouth,
June 22, 1834, æt. 98.

WORCESTER, CAPT. NOAH

youngest son of Rev. Francis Worcester, born at Sandwich, Mass.,
October 4, 1735, married Lydia Taylor, daughter of Abraham
Taylor, February 22, 1757. He was Captain of the Hollis militia
company in 1775, and of the Hollis company to Cambridge in December of that year. He enlisted in the Hollis company to Rhode
Island in 1778. Was Town clerk and first Selectman in 1775, '76,
'77, '78, and '79; chairman of the Hollis Committee of Safety in
1777, '78 and '79; appointed Justice of the Peace in 1777, and held
that office forty years; chosen a member of the Constitutional Convention of 1778; was moderator of the Hollis annual Town meetings in fifteen different years, between 1782, and 1801, and was an
active member of the Hollis church for sixty years. His two oldest sons, Noah and Jesse, were soldiers in the Revolution; and four
of them, viz., Noah, Leonard, Thomas and Samuel, became clergymen. (q. v.) Died at Hollis, August 13, 1817, in his 82d year.

WORCESTER, JESSE

2d son of Capt. Noah Worcester, born in Hollis, April 30, 1761.
Enlisted July, 1776, in the company of Capt. Emerson, for Ticonderoga; in 1777 in the garrison at Portsmouth; in 1773, in Capt.

THE WORCESTER HOMESTEAD FOR FIVE GENERATIONS.

Home of REV. FRANCIS WORCESTER 1759 to 1783.
" " CAPT. NOAH WORCESTER 1757 :: 1817.
" " JESSE WORCESTER 1794 :: 1834.
Home of JOHN N. WORCESTER 1826 to 1834
" " TAYLOR G. WORCESTER 1834 :: 1879
" " WILLIAM WORCESTER 1870 :: 1879.

Sarah Worcester

Jno. Worcester

Emerson's company to Rhode Island, and in 1780 in the Continental Army. In June, 1782, he married Sarah Parker of Hollis, by whom he had nine sons and six daughters, who all lived to adult age, and fourteen of whom became teachers in the public schools or academies. In 1782, he removed to Bedford, New Hampshire, and returned again to Hollis in 1794, and settled upon his ancestral homestead, where he resided till his decease, Jan. 20, 1834, in his 73d year. Mr. Worcester was for many years a teacher in the public schools in Bedford and Hollis, an occasional contributor to the public journals of the day, and was the author of an unpublished work called the " *Chronicles of Nissitissit.*" Seven of his nine sons aspired to a collegiate education. The eldest, Jesse Worcester, Jun., died after being prepared to enter the Junior class at Dartmouth. The youngest, David, after spending two years at Harvard, left college and became a teacher. Joseph E. and Henry A., were graduates of Yale; Taylor G., Samuel T., and Frederick A. of Harvard. The third son, Leonard, was a machinist; John N., the fifth son, settled in Hollis as a farmer, at first upon the paternal homestead, and was chosen State Councillor in the years 1858 and 1859.

CHAPTER XXI.

HOLLIS IN THE WAR OF 1812.—AND IN THE WAR OF THE RE-
BELLION.—HOLLIS SOLDIERS IN THE WAR OF 1812.—SOLDIERS
FURNISHED FROM THE TOWN FOR THE SUPPRESSION OF THE
REBELLION.—REGIMENTS IN WHICH THEY ENLISTED.—DATE
OF ENLISTMENT, AND TIME OF SERVICE.—CASUALTIES, ETC.—
SOLDIER'S AID SOCIETY AND SOLDIER'S MONUMENT.—CAPT.
AMES.—LIEUT. WORCESTER.—LIEUT. FARLEY.

The Declaration of War by the United States against Great
Britain in 1812 was not generally approved in New England, nor
in this part of it was this war afterwards popular. Party feeling in
respect to it was highly excited and violent, and but little was done
in the first years of the war to favor voluntary enlistments. A decided
majority of the voters in Hollis shared strongly in this common
sentiment of disapproval. No special call is known to have been
made upon the town for the regular army, either for drafted men or
volunteers, and but few Hollis men are known to have enlisted in
the regular service, and of those few it is now difficult to learn the
names or number.

Capt. Jonathan B. Eastman, of Hollis, was at the time a Captain
in the regular army and afterwards promoted to United States'
Paymaster, and Capt. Levi Powers. a son of Samson Powers, was
employed as a recruiting officer, and is said to have held a commission as captain in the army. In the report of the Adjutant-General
for 1868, I find the names of Jacob Hobart and Benjamin Ranger,
two Hollis soldiers, who enlisted in the regular army in 1812.
Besides Hobart and Ranger, Abel Brown. William N. Lovejoy and
Isaac Hardy are known to have been in the regular service. Lovejoy
died of disease in the service, and Hardy, who was in the navy, was
killed in the naval batttle on Lake Erie, fought under Com. Perry,
September 10, 1813.

In the summer and early in the fall of 1814, a powerful British fleet was cruising along the north coast of New England, and an attack was apprehended upon Portsmouth. In consequence of this apprehension, Gov. Gilman issued a proclamation, calling for New Hampshire troops for the defence of that city, and a number of regiments of "Detached Militia," so called, was raised for this purpose—some for sixty and the rest for ninety days, and ordered to Portsmouth. The whole number of men assigned to Hollis not having been obtained by voluntary enlistment, a draft was ordered from the two Hollis militia companies to supply the deficiency. In view of this draft at a special town meeting held October 17, 1814, the town voted to "each of the soldiers who had been drafted $15 per month, including their Continental pay."

In the report of the Adjutant General for 1868, above referred to, I find the following names of Hollis men who went to Portsmouth, viz., William Emerson, who was an Ensign in the regiment of Lieut. Col. Foot, and Daniel Lawrence, Jun., and Phineas Cumings who served in a regiment of artillery. Besides the men above named I find in that report credited to Hollis, the names of Leonard Blood, Isaac Butterfield, John Butterfield, John Drew, Hezekiah Kendall and David Powers. It is also known that Ephraim Burge, Jun., and Nathaniel Hobart, names not found in that report, were also soldiers from Hollis for the defence of Portsmouth. Some of the men above named are known to have been volunteers, the rest of them were drafted, or were substitutes for drafted men.

LISTS OF THE NAMES OF THE SOLDIERS FURNISHED BY HOLLIS IN THE WAR FOR THE SUPPRESSION OF THE SOUTHERN REBELLION.

There is not in this history space, nor is it pertinent here to speak at length of what was done by the people of New Hampshire in aid of the National Government in the war for the suppression of the late Southern Rebellion. Nor is it needful here to tell. The story of the doings of the State in this war has been well, if not fully told in histories already written and now before the public. In addition to these histories the names of the officers and private soldiers in the twenty or more regiments raised in the State, telling also of their campaigns and the parts of the country where they served and of the many battles in which they fought, have been published by authority of the State in an official State record of the war. Suffice it here to say, that in this war to save the nation and to perpetuate the union of the States, which the people of New Hampshire, one hundred years ago so freely and nobly shed their blood and lavished their treasure to establish, the good name and fair fame of the State suffered no dishonor. In the war of the Rebellion as in that of the Revolution, each call upon the State for enlistments and re-enforcements was promptly and cheerfully met, and in the war to save the nation, as in that in which its independence was won, the New Hampshire regiments were distinguished for their intrepidity, good conduct and devotion to duty. In most of the great and hard fought battles of the war, the blood of New Hampshire men flowed freely and mingled in full proportion with that of the brave soldiers from all the other loyal States, and their graves are marked and numbered by thousands in the cemeteries about the battle-fields where they fell and near the hospitals in which they pined and died.

The people of Hollis in this fearful struggle for the nation's life were at no time forgetful of their duty to their country, or of the memory and example of their worthy and patriotic ancestors. As in the war of the Revolution so in that of the Rebellion, the quota of soldiers allotted by the State to the town, on the many calls for troops, was not only as then promptly filled, but it appears from the official returns, that the number actually furnished, as in many other New Hampshire towns, was in excess of the number required.

The names of the Hollis soldiers, with the date of their enlistment or mustering, time of service, and the regiments and companies in which they served, are presented in the following lists.

HOLLIS SOLDIERS ENLISTED IN 1861, 1ST NEW HAMPSHIRE REGIMENT.

This regiment was raised in answer to the call of President Lincoln of April 15, 1861, for 75,000 men for three months. This regiment was commanded by Col. Mason W. Tappan of Bradford, —had its rendezvous at Concord—was mustered in that place on the 4th of May—left for Washington and the seat of war on the 25th—and upon the expiration of its term of service, returned to and was mustered out at Concord on the following 9th of August. This first regiment, for most of its term of service was on duty along the Potomac river, between Washington and Harper's Ferry. It was engaged in some skirmishes with the enemy, but in no memorable battle. All the other regiments raised in New Hampshire in 1861, were enlisted under the call of the President, for three years. The Hollis men in this regiment were,

French, William F. Enlisted, company F, May 3, 1861. Mustered out August 9, 1861.
Jaquith, Asa W. Enlisted, company F, May 3, 1861. Mustered out, August 9, 1861.

SECOND NEW HAMPSHIRE REGIMENT ENLISTED FOR THREE YEARS.

This regiment had its rendezvous at Portsmouth, and was commanded by Col. Gilman Marston of Exeter. The men were enlisted in the months of May and June, and the regiment was mustered in on the 4th of June and left Portsmouth for Washington and Virginia on the 20th of that month. This regiment was present at the first battle at Bull Run, at Gettysburg, and most of the great battles of the war fought in Virginia.

HOLLIS SOLDIERS IN THE SECOND REGIMENT.

Beard, Samuel J. Enlisted June 5, 1861, company G. Wounded at Fair Oaks, Virginia, June 25, 1862. Discharged for disability, December 9, 1862.

Worcester, George. Enlisted, company C, June 1, 1861. Mustered out June 21, 1864.

Greeley, George P. Appointed Assistant Surgeon, May 3, 1861. Resigned June 3, 1861. Appointed Assistant Surgeon Fourth New Hampshire Regiment, August 1, 1861. Promoted to Surgeon October 8, 1862. Honorably discharged, October 23, 1864.

THIRD NEW HAMPSHIRE REGIMENT ENLISTED FOR THREE YEARS, AUGUST, 1861.

This regiment was organized at Concord. Its first Colonel was Enoch Q. Fellows of Sandwich, who resigned June 26, 1862, and was succeeded by Col. John H. Jackson of Portsmouth, who upon being honorably discharged, February 24, 1864, was succeeded by Col. John Bedel of Bath. The regiment was enlisted under the Act of Congress of July 22, 1861, authorizing the enlistment of 500,000 volunteers for three years, and was mustered into the United States service about the last of August. It left Concord September 3, for Long Island, thence on the 14th to Washington, and from Washington, on the following 19th of October, it was ordered to the seat of war in South Carolina. It was on duty in South Carolina and Florida till the spring of 1864, and in the meanwhile was present at nearly all the battles in those States, including the bloody assault upon Fort Wagner. The regiment was ordered to Virginia near the last of April, 1864, and was in most of the battles afterwards fought in that State till the end of the war.

The Hollis soldiers, whose names appear below, enlisted in company F., of this regiment, Aug. 23, 1861.

Blood, Stillman. Re-enlisted February 13, 1864. Mustered out, May 15, 1865.

Chase, Charles F. Promoted to 2nd Lieutenant, 3d South Carolina Volunteers.

Chase, James L. Wounded June 15, 1862. Re-enlisted February 13, 1864.

Conroy, Leonard. Mustered out, August 23, 1864.

Davis, Caleb. Wounded August 16, 1864. Mustered out, August 23, 1864.

Doherty, John O. Discharged for disability, September 15, 1862.

FOURTH NEW HAMPSHIRE REGIMENT.

This regiment was enlisted and organized at Manchester, was mustered in at Manchester, September, 1861, and left that city for South Carolina, by way of Washington and Fortress Monroe, September 27, under command of Col. Thomas J. Whipple of Laconia. It was on duty in South Carolina and Florida till April, 1864, when it was ordered to Virginia, and was in service in that State and North Carolina till the close of the war. Among the many battles in which it fought was the assault on Fort Wagner, July, 1863, the battle of Bermuda Hundred, Va., May, 1864, and in that at Fort Fisher, N. C., January, 1865. In company B, of this regiment, were two Hollis soldiers who enlisted September 18, 1861, and whose names were

Jewett, Perley J., who died of disease at Morris Island, S. C., December 3, 1863.
Mansfield, William. Mustered out September 27, 1864.

SEVENTH NEW HAMPSHIRE REGIMENT, ENLISTED FOR THREE YEARS.

This regiment was also enlisted and had its rendezvous at Manchester and was mustered into the United States service December 14, 1861, under Col. Haldimand S. Putnam, of Cornish. Col. Putnam was killed July 18, 1863, in the assault on Fort Wagner, and was succeeded in the command by Col. Joseph C. Abbott, of Manchester. The regiment left Manchester, for Florida, by the way of New York, January 14, 1862, and was in the service in Florida and South Carolina till April 1864, when it was ordered to Virginia.

While in the two former States, among other battles in which this regiment was engaged, it was present and lost heavily in the assault on Fort Wagner, July 18, 1863, and also at the bloody and disastrous battle at Olustee, Fla., February 20, 1864. After coming north it was present and engaged in many of the battles near Richmond, Va., and also in the capture of Fort Fisher, N. C. In company H of this regiment were forty-one Hollis soldiers, mustered in for three years, December 14, 1861, the survivors of whom not before discharged or re-enlisted, were mustered out at the expiration of their term, at Manchester, December 22, 1864. The names of these men are presented in the following list:

Ames, Nathan M. Commissioned Captain of Company H, December 14, 1861. Mustered out December 22, 1864.
Austin, Mark J. Promoted to Fifth Sergeant December 14, 1861. Mustered out December 22, 1864.

Ball, Henry. Accidentally killed himself at Beaufort, S. C., June 26, 1862.

Bartemus, George H. Mustered out December 22, 1864.

Bills, John P. Killed at Fort Wagner, July 18, 1863.

Boynton, John F. Wounded at Olustee, Fla., February 20, 1864. Re-enlisted February 28, 1864. Promoted to Corporal January 26, 1865. Promoted to Sergeant June 13, 1865. Mustered out July 20, 1865.

Burge, Charles H. Discharged for disability at St. Augustine, Fla., January 4, 1863.

Burge, George A. Promoted to Corporal May 25, 1862. Promoted to Sergeant December 9, 1863. Mustered out December 22, 1864.

Coburn, John A. Promoted to Fourth Sergeant December 14, 1861. First Sergeant December, 28, 1863. Re-enlisted Veteran, February 28, 1864. Promoted to Captain Company E, December 12, 1864. Mustered out July 20, 1865.

Colburn, Edward S. Transferred to Invalid Corps, March 29, 1864.

Colburn, Josiah. Wounded at Bermuda Hundred, Va., May 20, 1864. Mustered out December 22, 1864.

Colburn, Daniel W. Promoted to Corporal December 14, 1861. Died of disease, at Hollis, February 28, 1862.

Day, Henry M. H. Promoted to Corporal December 14, 1861. Wounded at Olustee, Fla. February 20, 1864. Mustered out December 22, 1864.

Duncklee, Ebenezer P. Discharged for disability, February, 1862.

Farley, Benjamin L. Discharged for disability at Fort Jefferson, Fla., June 26, 1862.

Farley, Charles H. Promoted to First Sergeant, December 14, 1861. Second Lieutenant June 30, 1862. First Lieutenant August 6, 1863. Wounded, mortally, at Olustee, Fla., February 20, 1864.

Fletcher Charles H. Died of disease at Beaufort, S. C., August 10, 1862.

Hayden, Daniel W. Promoted to Corporal December 5, 1862. Wounded at Fort Wagner, July 18, 1863. Promoted to Sergeant February 3, 1864. Wounded at Olustee, February 20, 1864. Discharged for disability April 29, 1864.

Hayden, John W. Promoted to Corporal December 14, 1861. Died of disease at New York City, February 8, 1862.

Hayden, J. Newton. Wounded May 14, 1864. Mustered out December 22, 1864.

Hills, Albert F. Wounded at Olustee, Fla., February 20, 1864. Mustered out December 22, 1864.

Hills, Alfred F., Mustered out December 22, 1864.

Hobart, Jonathan B. Died of disease at Morris Island, S. C., August 23, 1863.

Hood, Frank P. Wounded at Fort Wagner, July 18, 1863. Discharged on account of wounds, Nov. 25, 1863.

Howard, James C. Wounded at Fort Wagner July 18, 1863. Mustered out December 22, 1864.

Howe, Norman R. Promoted to Corporal, December 14, 1861. Died of disease at Beaufort, S. C., Aug. 15, 1862.

Jaquith, George D. Mustered out December 22, 1864

Lovejoy, Francis. Promoted to 3d Sergeant December 14, 1861. To 2d Lieutenant, August 6, 1863. Honorably discharged April 28, 1864.

Lund, John. Discharged for disability at Fort Jefferson, Florida, June 26, 1862.

Lund, William. Transferred to Veteran Reserve Corps, March 29, 1864. Mustered out December 22, 1864.

Price, Stephen H. Promoted to Corporal, Dec. 14, 1861. Re-enlisted Veteran, February 28, 1864. Mustered out July 20, 1865.

Rideout, Charles C. Mustered out December 22, 1864.

Smith, Freeman H. Discharged for disability at Fort Jefferson, July 20, 1862.

Spalding, Wm. F. Promoted to 1st Sergeant, December 14, 1861. To 1st Lieutenant, July 18, 1863, Company C. Mustered out December 22, 1864.

Spalding, Winslow J. Promoted to Corporal October 10, 1862. Promoted to Sergeant. Captured at Fort Wagner July 18, 1863. Exchanged, January 21, 1864. Mustered out December 22, 1864.

Truell, Nathaniel L. Promoted to Corporal December 14, 1861. Mustered out December 22, 1864.

Worcester, Charles H. Promoted to Corporal December 14, 1861. To Sergeant, October 9, 1863. Wounded near Richmond, Virginia, October 1, 1864. Mustered out December 22, 1864.

Worcester, John H. Promoted to 2d Lieutenant, December 14, 1861. To 1st Lieutenant, June 30, 1862. Mortally wounded, July 18, 1863, at Fort Wagner. Died of wounds July 26, 1863.

Worcester, William. Mustered out December 22, 1864.

Wright, Ezra S. Mustered out December 22, 1864.

Wright, Nathaniel H. Died of disease at St. Augustine, Florida, November 27, 1862.

EIGHTH NEW HAMPSHIRE REGIMENT.

This regiment was also enlisted at Manchester in the fall and early in the winter of 1861, and was mustered in at Manchester December 23, 1861, commanded by Col. Hawkes Fearing, Jun., of that city. It left Manchester Jan. 24, 1862, for Ship Island, Mississippi, by the way of Boston, and was afterwards in the service in Louisiana and other States bordering on the Mississippi river till the expiration of its term of enlistment. The Hollis soldiers named below enlisted for three years in this regiment in the fall or winter of 1861.

Austin, Albert S. Company E, enlisted December 20. Transferred to Veteran Reserve Corps, April, 1864.

Conant, Andrew H. Company E, enlisted December 20. Promoted to Corporal, February 14, 1863. Re-enlisted, January 4, 1864. Died at Natches, Miss., October 10, 1865.

Elkins, Freeman. Company E, enlisted December 20. Discharged for disability, at Ship Island, Miss., April 10, 1862.

Jones, James, W. D. Company A, enlisted October 25. Died at camp Kearney, La., October 26, 1862.

Patch, Joseph T. Company A, enlisted October 25. Discharged for disability. Died at Nashua, July 18, 1863.

Prior to the month of August, 1862, no bounties to volunteers, to fill the quota of Hollis in the war, had been offered or paid by the town. Till that date all the several calls upon the town for enlistments had been cheerfully and fully met by its patriotic young men. But owing in part to the large number of Hollis men then in the army, and in part also to a depreciation of the paper currency then in use, the calls for enlistments after the first of August, 1862, were not so promptly filled. In view of this state of facts, and to stimulate enlistments, the town, at a meeting held on the 12th of August of that year, " voted to pay a bounty of $200 to any inhabitant of Hollis who would enlist for three years, or during the war, or should volunteer or be drafted for nine months, and be mustered into the United States service." In pursuance of this vote the town paid as bounties to thirty men, between the first of September, 1862, and July first, 1863, $200 each, amounting to $6,000. Most of these men enlisted for nine months in the 15th New Hampshire regiment; the rest in other regiments for three years.

FIFTEENTH NEW HAMPSHIRE REGIMENT.

This regiment was raised for nine months, under the call of President Lincoln for 300,000 men for that time. It had its rendezvous at Concord, and was mustered into service at that place November 12, 1862, under the command of Col. John W. Kingman of Durham. It left Concord the next day for New Orleans, and afterwards served its time with the union army in Louisiana. The regiment reached New Orleans on Christmas day, and was engaged in garrison and guard duty near that city till about the 20th of May, 1863, many of the men in the meantime having suffered much from the diseases of the climate. About the last of May, it was ordered, with other regiments, to Port Hudson, and shared in the sanguinary but finally successful siege of that place, which ended in its unconditional surrender on the 9th of July following. At the expiration of its term of service the regiment returned to Concord, and was mustered out on the 13th of August. In company E of this regiment, commanded by Capt. William E. Stearns of Manchester, and of which Francis A. Wood of Hollis was 2d Lieutenant, were twenty-two Hollis soldiers, enlisted between October 9 and November 2, 1862, all of whom, with the exception of John C. Smith, returned and were mustered out with the regiment. The names of these men are presented in the following list:

Adams, Charles F.	Hayden, Samuel F.	Smith, John C. Died of disease
Annis, George H.	Hull, George S.	at Hollis, August, 10, 1863.
Chamberlain, Caleb W.	Patch, Granville P.	Tenney, George F.
Colburn, Ai	Pond, Aaron	Vandyke, Isaac
Humblet, Charles S.	Pond, Frank E.	Willoby, Harvey M.
Hanscom, Alfred A.	Portwine, Rufus	Willoby, Oliver H.
Hardy, Isaac	Rideout, David J.	Wood, Francis A., 2d Lieu-
Hardy, John H.	Smith, Freeman H.	tenant.

OTHER HOLLIS SOLDIERS ENLISTED IN 1862.

Cameron, Henry G. Enlisted company I, 13th regiment, September 20, 1862. Promoted to Sergeant. Discharged for disability at Falmouth, Virginia, January 14, 1863.

Chickering, Frank N. Enlisted company B, 2d regiment Aug 21, 1862. Promoted to Sergeant. Wounded June 3, 1864. Mustered out June 9, 1865.

Jaquith, John G. Enlisted company H, 7th regiment, March 14, 1862. Mustered out, April 21, 1865.

Roby, David T. Enlisted company I, 13th regiment, September 20, 1862. Wounded September 30, 1864. Mustered out June 21, 1865.

Smithwick, Peter. Enlisted company E, 13th regiment, September 26, 1862. Transferred to Veteran Reserve Corps, March 31, 1864.

Sullivan, Joseph. Enlisted company B, 10th regiment, August 25, 1862. Mustered out May 16, 1865.

Woods, John L. Enlisted August 21, 1862, company B, 2d regiment. Discharged for disability June 23, 1863.

(15)

HOLLIS SOLDIERS ENLISTED AND DRAFTED IN 1863.

Baker, Patrick. Enlisted December 7, 1863, company H, 7th regiment. Mustered out July 20, 1865.

Buss, Joseph. Enlisted December 7, 1863, company A, 14th regiment. Died of disease at Fort Munroe, Virginia, October 13, 1864.

Bills, Jason W. Enlisted August 14, 1863, company A, heavy Artillery. Mustered out September 11, 1865.

Hale, Charles A. Enlisted May 18, 1863, company H, 7th regiment. Wounded July 18, 1863 at Fort Wagner. May 10, 1864, at Drury's Bluff, Virginia. June 16, 1864, at Bermuda Hundred, Virginia. Mustered out July 20, 1865.

Hall, Harvey M. Enlisted November 4, 1863, company C, 9th regiment. Died of disease at Washington, D. C., September 1, 1864.

Kendall, Hiram R. Drafted September 1, 1863, company G, 8th regiment. Died of disease at Natchez, Miss., November 3, 1864.

In the month of July 1863, ten soldiers were lacking to fill the Hollis quota, and for want of voluntary enlistments, ten of the Hollis enrolled men were drafted, all of whom, with the exception of Hiram R. Kendall, above named, furnished non-resident substitutes at an average cost of about $500, of which the town paid $300 as a bounty; the town at a meeting September 3, 1863, having voted to pay that sum as a bounty to every drafted man of the town or his substitute, after having been for ten days mustered into the United States service.

In October of this year a further call was made upon the town for fourteen men to fill its quota, twelve of whom, (all non-residents) were engaged by the Selectmen, and who were paid bounties by the town averaging about $235 each, in addition to a State bounty of $300. Patrick Baker and Joseph Buss, two resident volunteer citizens, made up the number then called for, each of whom was paid a bounty by the town of $300 in addition to that paid by the State.

HOLLIS SOLDIERS FURNISHED IN 1864.

Three veteran Hollis soldiers, whose terms of service were about to expire, re-enlisted under a call made by the President in February of this year, viz., John F. Boynton, John A. Coburn and Stephen H. Price, all of whom were mustered out in July 1865. The town's quota being still deficient, about the first of March 1864, six other Hollis enrolled men were drafted, each of whom, at the cost to himself of about $315, furnished a non-resident substitute— these substitutes being also paid a bounty by the town of $300 each.

At a town meeting held June 11, of this year, Enoch Farley, Esq., one of the Selectmen for 1864, was appointed sole agent in

behalf of the town to engage men to fill all future calls. Afterwards, about the middle of July, a further requisition was made upon
the town for twenty-eight additional men who were enlisted for
three years. Only three residents of Hollis enlisted under this call,
viz., Charles S. Hamblet, September 6, 1864, in the heavy artillery, and Aaron Pond, September 26, and Charles F. Chase, Dec.
28, 1864, in the Veteran Reserve Corps. These were the last residents of Hollis who enlisted in this war. The remaining twenty-
five of the twenty-eight, all non-residents and most of them aliens,
were engaged by the agent of the town, the whole twenty-eight
being paid bounties averaging to each about $680, including the
bounty paid by the State and that of $300 paid by the town.

SOLDIERS FURNISHED IN 1865.

At a meeting held on the 5th of January of this year, the town
" voted to pay a bounty of $300 to any enrolled man of the town,
or citizen of the town who would himself enlist or furnish a substitute to fill the quota of the town in anticipation of future calls
to the amount of the town's quota for 500,000 men in addition to
the present call for 300,000."

In pursuance of this vote, sixteen enrolled citizens of the town
engaged substitutes at the average cost of about $816 each, of which
sum the town paid as a bounty, $300, and the State also $300. In
the foregoing recitals I have purposely omitted the names of all the
non-resident substitutes who were engaged during the last years of
this war. I am glad to be able to say that none of them were citizens or residents of Hollis. With but few exceptions they were all
aliens, belonging mainly to that class of worthless vagabonds,
known at the time as "Bounty Jumpers," of no service in the army,
a curse to the country, and a reproach to human nature.

THE HOLLIS SOLDIERS' AID SOCIETY.

The history of Hollis in the war of the Rebellion would be un-
pardonably incomplete should it fail to tell of the patient, faithful
and fruitful labors of the Hollis ladies. Like their grandmothers
in the war of the Revolution, they were at all times mindful of their
fathers, sons and brothers in the field, camp and hospital, and not
forgetful of those of them in the rebel prisons. In the year 1861,
near the beginning of the war, a Ladies' Soldiers' Aid Society was
organized, and continued in active and successful operation till its
close.

The president of this society was Mrs. Taylor G. Worcester—
its Treasurer, Mrs. Pliny B. Day—and its Directors in different
years, Mrs. James Ball, Mrs. Cyrus Burge, Mrs. Levi Abbot, Mrs.
William P. Saunderson, Mrs John S. Heywood, and Misses
Roxana Read, Elizabeth Fletcher, and Martha Worcester.

It had a numerous membership, but unfortunately for the historical chronicler, it preserved no written record of its members nor of
its very liberal contributions in various ways to the needs and comforts of the men in the army. A better and more fitting record of
their good works than that kept in day books and ledgers still
exists in the hearts and memories of the grateful recipients of their
bounty.

Besides the work done for the soldiers, by these ladies at their
own homes, they continued to meet during the war on the afternoon
of the first Tuesday of each month (and at times much oftener) to
fashion, make and provide articles of necessity and comfort, such
as lint, bandages, comfortable clothing and bedding, canned fruits,
wines, etc., for the sick and wounded in the hospitals, and necessaries for the use, convenience and health of the men in the field
and camp, and also for the relief of such of them as were doomed
to pine and suffer in the infamous rebel prisons. The value of these
good deeds and kind offices is not to be estimated in " greenbacks "
or gold. Still, Rev. Dr. Day in his anniversary New Years' sermons during the war, as well as before and after it, was accustomed
to present a statement of the amount of the contributions of the
people of his society to the various benevolent enterprises of the
time, including with the rest during the war the estimated appraised value in money of the yearly contributions of the Ladies'
Soldiers' Aid Society to the comforts and wants of the men in the
army.

Unfortunately these annual sermons of Dr. Day during the war,
with but one or two exceptions, cannot now be found. But the true
estimated money value of these contributions for the four years of
the war may be proximately gathered from his annual sermon, still
preserved, delivered in January 1864, from which it appears that
these benefactions for the soldiers and freedmen for the year 1863
were appraised in cash, at somewhat more than $1,500, and it may
be added, that it is believed, by the late officers and members of
the society most conversant with its doings, that the entire cash
value of its contributions during the war, including the money
donated by its members, was not less than $4,000.

SOLDIERS' MONUMENT.
"THOSE THAT FELL".

1st LIEUT. JOHN H. WORCESTER.
1st LIEUT. CHAS. H. FARLEY.
CORP. WEBSTER D. COLBURN.
CORP. NORMAN R. HOWE.
CORP. JOHN W. HAYDEN.
HENRY BALL.
JOHN P. BILLS.
JOSEPH E. BUSS.
CHARLES H. FLETCHER.

HARVEY M. HALL.
JONATHAN B. HOBART
PERLEY J. JEWETT.
JAMES W. D. JONES.
HIRAM R. KENDALL.
JOSEPH T. PATCH.
JOHN C. SMITH.
SYLVESTER T. WHEELER
NATHANIEL H. WRIGHT.

THE HOLLIS POST OF THE GRAND ARMY.

The JOHN H. WORCESTER Post of the Grand Army, having twenty-six members, was organized April 1, 1875. The officers of the Post then chosen were Capt. John A. Coburn, Commander, Francis Lovejoy, Senior vice Commander, Charles H. Worcester, Junior vice Commander, and Daniel W. Hayden, Adjutant.

THE SOLDIERS' MONUMENT.

Not very long after the end of the war of the Rebellion, the question was brought before the people of the town of providing some suitable monument in honor of the Hollis soldiers whose lives had been sacrificed in the service of the country in the war to save the nation, and also in that in which its independence was won. The interest felt in this subject shortly afterwards led to a voluntary subscription for this purpose on the part of the citizens of near $800, and finally resulted in a vote of the town at its annual meeting in March 1872, to raise by tax a sum not exceeding $2,500, for the erection of a monument in memory of the Hollis soldiers, who perished "in the war of the Revolution, in that of 1812, and in the war of the Rebellion." At the same meeting a committee, consisting of Dea. Noah Farley. Capt. John A.Coburn, George H. Bartemus, Henry G. Cameron, Isaac Vandyke, Levi Abbot, Charles F. Chase, William E. Howe, and Nathaniel L. Truell, was appointed to locate and contract for the monument.

The action of this committee, in July following, resulted in the selection of the site for the monument where it now stands, on the Hollis common, about five rods south of the meeting-house, and afterwards in making a contract for its erection, with Moses Davis of Nashua as architect and builder, in accordance with a plan made by him and approved by the committee.

This monument as it now stands is of the best Concord granite, of four equal sides, all smoothly cut or polished, and its several parts all artistically and symmetrically proportioned to each other. Including its base, die and shaft, it is 22 1-2 feet in height, six feet square at its foundation. its diameter gradually growing less from its base to the vertex. On the east side of the die are inscribed the names of eighteen Hollis soldiers lost in the Rebellion. Upon its west side are the words, " In honor of the Hollis soldiers who fell in the wars of 1775 and in 1812." The names of those lost in the Revolution were not inscribed upon the monument at the time it

was erected, for the reason that the committee had not then succeeded in obtaining a complete list of them. But from careful investigation since made, it is believed that this list is now full, as
presented on page 201 of this history, and there seems no longer
sufficient reason for further delay in the inscription of their names
on the monument, as originally designed.

The entire cost of this monument, including the foundation and
curbing, was $2120.77, of which sum $790.37 were paid by private
subscription of the citizens, and the balance $1330.40, by the town.

The dedication took place at the Hollis meeting-house, on the
afternoon of Decoration day, (May 30) 1873, the graves of the fallen
soldiers having been first strewed with flowers, by the comrades now
belonging to the (Hollis) John H. Worcester Post of the Grand
Army, and the pulpit and windows of the church beautifully gar-
landed with bouquets. The exercises consisted, first of music by
the Hollis Brass Band, next of singing by choirs of children, then
prayer by Rev. Mr. Laird, followed by patriotic songs and hymns
by the Hollis church choir. The dedicatory address was delivered
by Rev. Charles Wetherby of Nashua, in which he paid an eloquent and just tribute to the early settlers of Hollis, especially to
the virtues, courage and patriotism of the Revolutionary fathers of
the town, and to the Hollis soldiers in the war of the Rebellion,
whose bravery and good conduct had proved them worthy descendants of their Revolutionary ancestors—not forgetting to commend
the liberal and grateful spirit of the people of the town as manifested in the erection of so chaste, appropriate and durable a monument to perpetuate to future generations the memory and names of
their fellow townsmen who had thus given their lives for their
country.

AMES, CAPT. NATHAN M.
(By J. H. H.)

was the only son of William Ames, Esq., and Lydia (Merrill)
Ames, and was born in Hollis June 4, 1827. Capt. Ames settled
in Hollis as a farmer and continued in that business till the breaking
out of the civil war in 1861. Naturally vigorous and active, he
manifested great energy in all enterprises he undertook, and was
earnestly engaged in the promotion of the agricultural interests of
the town.

At the age of eighteen, he held a position in the staff of the
brigade with which he was connected in the militia of the State,

J. H. Worcester

and in 1860 he organized a temporary militia company in Hollis, called the *Hollis Phalanx*, of which he was first Lieutenant. This company attended the Muster of that year at Nashua, and won great praise for its soldierly appearance and discipline. Many of the members of this company formed the nucleus of the organizations that enlisted from Hollis in the civil war that soon followed. ·

When the war broke out Capt. Ames at once begun the labor of recruiting a company for the service. His original purpose was to have his company mustered into the Fifth New Hampshire Regiment of infantry. But the ranks of that regiment having been filled, before his company was complete, he concluded to have it united with the Seventh New Hampshire infantry.

He was with his regiment during most of its period of service till its discharge. In 1863, for a short time, he was Provost Marshal at Fernandina, Florida, and in the summer of 1864 he was appointed Chief of Ambulance in the Tenth Army Corps, at Bermuda Hundred, Va. While in this position he was assigned to a place on the staff of Gen. Birney.

At the expiration of the time for which his company had enlisted, he returned with it to New Hampshire, and resumed his former occupation on his farm in Hollis. In 1870 he removed from Hollis to Vineland, N. J., where he bought a farm and engaged in the cultivation of fruits for the Philadelphia market. Although he made this change for the reason that from his experience of army life at the South, he believed that the climate of New Jersey would be better adapted to his health than that of New Hampshire, yet early in 1872, he was attacked with bronchial consumption of which he died September 5, 1872, æt. 45. Captain Ames was married June 20, 1848, to Miss Asenath Hardy, of Hollis, who now survives, and by whom he had three children, who survived him at his decease. He was a kind and affectionate husband and father, and at all times, in whatever position in life he was placed, he was ever ready to do his duty conscientiously, faithfully and promptly.

WORCESTER, LIEUT. JOHN H.

son of John N. and Sarah (Holden) Worcester, was born in Hollis, January 18, 1839. In his boyhood he attended the public schools in Hollis, and afterwards had the benefit of a good academic education. Before the Southern Rebellion he had been a student at the law school at Cambridge, and at the commencement of the civil war he was nearly ready to engage in the practice of his intended profession with flattering prospects of success.   But when the nation summoned its young men to its defence, his love of country and stern sense of duty found from him a prompt response.

In the summer of 1861, he enlisted as a private soldier in Company H, of the Seventh New Hampshire regiment, and upon its organization was chosen Second Lieutenant of his company.   In June, 1862, upon the resignation of the First Lieutenant, (Potter,) Lieutenant Worcester was promoted to his place, and was afterwards constantly in the service with his regiment, in Florida and South Carolina, till his decease at Hilton Head, S. C., July 26, 1863, æt. 24 years and 6 months.

The Seventh regiment was present and took part in the fearful and bloody assault upon Fort Wagner, S. C., on the evening of July 18, 1863.   Lieutenant Worcester having succeeded, at the head of his men, in gaining the top of the parapet of the Fort, while cheering them on, was severely wounded in his left leg, so that when the order to retreat was given, he was unable to leave the field.   Having remained all night on the battle ground, he was taken prisoner, the next morning, carried into Charleston, his leg amputated, and on the 25th he was returned under a flag of truce, sent to Hilton Head and put on board a vessel to be sent north with other wounded men.   But the following night the gangrene struck his limb, and before morning he breathed his last.   When he found he could not live, he calmly resigned himself to his fate, and said to a wounded comrade lying at his side, " *Give my love to my men, and say to them that I shall be with them no more, and tell my friends at home all you know of me.*"   His remains were buried at Hilton Head, under a military escort, and afterwards disinterred, taken to Hollis and buried in the family cemetery.

In a tribute to his memory on the occasion of his funeral at Hollis, Rev. Dr. Day said of him, " Lieutenant Worcester was just the man the country wanted.   Firm in his convictions, active and forcible, he was a right arm of strength in her service.   Nature had fitted him for a popular and successful officer.   His form was large and commanding.   He had a happy faculty of mingling with his men freely and socially, and yet maintaining a complete command of them. It was a command, not common in the army—that of respect and love.   He endeavored to make the most of his men by increasing their virtues.   His counsel and example were always against the

Chas. H. Farley

use of intoxicating drinks, tobacco, profanity and gambling, and he knew how to urge his views upon others without giving offence."

Dr. Boynton, the regimental Surgeon, wrote of him, "No officer in the regiment was before Lieutenant Worcester in promise. He was a general favorite with officers and men, and no one whose lot it was to fall on that fatal night was more universally lamented." Lieutenant Potter, to whose place Lieutenant Worcester was promoted, in a short obituary notice says of him: "Lieutenant Worcester in the discharge of every duty was faithful and persevering. No effort was too great for him if he could benefit the condition of a private soldier or serve a friend. Such honesty—such fidelity—such energy and such kindness won for him the highest esteem of all who knew him. His character was unexceptionable —his habits strictly temperate—his principles unwavering. His service short, faithful and earnest, is ended. But his example still lives. and will be felt so long as a remnant of his company shall survive."

The JOHN H. WORCESTER Post of the Grand Army, composed of his surviving comrades in the war, in and about Hollis, was so named, on its organization, from an affectionate and respectful regard for his memory.

FARLEY, LIEUT. CHARLES H.

son of Dea. Leonard W. and Clarissa (Butterfield) Farley, was born in Hollis July 31, 1835, and died at Lake City, Florida, February 24, 1864, æt. 28 years and six months. Calmly weighing the consequences, and acting from a deep sense of duty, he was among the first of the young men of Hollis to enlist in the service of his country. Early in the fall of 1861 he volunteered as a private soldier in the 7th New Hampshire regiment, and on the organization of Company H he was appointed Orderly Sergeant. June 30, 1862, he was promoted to 2nd Lieutenant, and to 1st Lieutenant August 6, 1863. He faithfully served with his regiment in Florida and South Carolina through the years 1862 and 1863, and till mortally wounded at the battle of Olustee, Florida, February 20, 1864.

Lieut. Farley was one of the gallant band who fought their way into Fort Wagner on the night of July 18, 1863. Wading the ditch and scaling the parapet under a raking fire of the enemy, he stood by the side of the brave and lamented Col. Putnam, when he fell. fighting the enemy hand to hand with his revolver. He was twice struck with balls, one passing through his clothes, without serious injury, the other warded off by the testament in his pocket which probably saved his life. He remained till the fall of Col. Putnam and the retreat ordered.

The battle of Olustee commenced on the afternoon of February 20, and Lieutenant Farley was mortally wounded in the first part of it. The Union troops were soon driven from the part of the field where he fell, and he was taken prisoner, and carried by the enemy to Lake City, about twenty miles distant. He was found the next day in a confederate hospital by two ladies formerly from New Hampshire, taken to their own home and kindly cared for by them, and also by the rebel Surgeon. But all efforts to save his life were unavailing, and he expired four days after the battle. His funeral was attended by the Mayor of Lake City, his remains kindly interred in the public burial ground, and afterwards removed for burial at Hollis in the family burial lot. Rev. Dr. Day in a tribute to his memory, delivered at his funeral at Hollis, says of Lieutenant Farley, "That at the early age of sixteen he made a public profession of religion and united with the Baptist church in Hollis, and ever after till his death lived a consistent Christian life. He never fell into any of the vices so common in the camp, never resorted to the gaming table, to the intoxicating cup nor to the fumes of the poisonous weed. As an officer he was a universal favorite. The soldiers knew him so well, that for him to indicate his wishes, was authority. He never threatened, censured harshly nor spoke defiantly. His courage was never doubted, and no one ever saw him agitated, hurried or disconcerted on the eve of battle. He was calm, self-possessed and trustful in that Providence in which he had been taught to believe, and which was a cardinal point in his religious faith."

CHAPTER XXII.

THE CONGREGATIONAL CHURCH AND SOCIETY.— MEMBERSHIP.—
MINISTERS.— MR. EMERSON. MR. SMITH, MR. PERRY, MR. AIKEN,
MR. GORDON, DR. DAY, MR. LAIRD, MR. KELSEY, MR. SCOTT.—
DEACONS.— YOUNG MEN'S ASSOCIATION.— THIRD MEETING-
HOUSE.— PHILANTHROPIC SOCIETY.— BENEVOLENT ASSOCIA-
TION.— FEMALE CHARITABLE SOCIETY.— BAPTIST SOCIETY.

In a former chapter I have spoken of the efforts of the first settlers of Hollis, while yet a parish, in providing for the support of
the ministry—of the building of their first and second meeting-
houses—of the call and settlement of Rev. Daniel Emerson, the
first and only minister of the church for some more than fifty years
—of his character, public spirit, the high esteem in which he was
held, and his favorable influence in the town through all its early
history.

There is now to be found no existing record of the original formation of his church, and the well authenticated facts in respect to its
history for the first fifty years of its existence are but few.   As Mr.
Emerson was ordained April 20, 1743, it is supposed that the
church was organized either at that time, or but a short time before.
It is stated in a short historical manual of the church published in
1871, that its first sacrament or communion service, was celebrated
June 5, 1743. It appears from the church records, that on the 31st
of July, 1745, a church covenant then " *renewed* " and adopted,
was signed by ten persons, besides the pastor, that number probably including all its male members at that date, viz.

Daniel Emerson,	Jerahmael Cumings,	Nathaniel Blood,
John Boynton,	Benjamin Blanchard,	Joseph Fletcher
Henry Barton,	Elias Smith,	Jonathan Danforth.
Samuel Brown,	Enoch Hunt,	

It is shown by the same original records that on the 25th of December, 1745, William Cumings and Thomas Patch were chosen

its first deacons, and that February 17, 1747. Francis Worcester, Jun., was chosen the third deacon.

As no confession of faith is mentioned or referred to in the records previously to 1794, it is supposed that none was formally adopted before that time. A *Creed or Confession of Faith* adopted in that year, and the covenant in previous use, were revised in 1831, and continued without change, (as is stated in the church manual), till 1871, when they were revised and adopted as they now are.

It is said also in the same manual, that for the first fifty years, no records were kept of the members admitted to the church, but that incidental statements show "that from the beginning, it enjoyed the labors of a faithful and successful ministry." In 1755, during the last French and Indian war, Mr. Emerson asked permission of his church to be absent for a time, as chaplain to the regiment of Col. Joseph Blanchard in the expedition of the army to Crown Point. In a meeting of the church to consider the request, it appears that forty-seven members voted, a number nearly equal to one-half of the tax payers at that time, the latter numbering that year but one hundred and seven.

The following names of members of the church, copied from this manual, are found on the Hollis tax lists, as resident tax payers before the war of the Revolution, viz.,

Benjamin Abbot,	Thomas Dinsmore,	Abraham Leeman,
John Atwell,	Zedekiah Drury,	Samuel Leeman,
Henry Barton,	Amos Eastman,	Jonathan Lovejoy,
Benjamin Blanchard,	Daniel Emerson, Jun.,	William Nevins,
Nathaniel Blood,	Benjamin Farley,	Enoch Noyes,
John Boynton,	Samuel Farley,	Thomas Patch,
Josiah Brown,	Amos Fisk,	Peter Powers,
Samuel Brown,	Eleazer Flagg,	Moses Proctor,
Ephraim Burge,	Samuel Goodhue,	William Shattuck,
Robert Colburn,	John Goss,	Zachariah Shattuck,
William Colburn,	John Hale,	Elias Smith,
Josiah Conant,	Phineas Hardy,	Jonathan Taylor,
Jerahmael Cumings,	David Hobart,	Nathaniel Townsend,
John Cumings,	Samuel Hobart,	John Willoughby,
Samuel Cumings,	Enoch Hunt,	Francis Worcester,
William Cumings,	Stephen Jewett,	Noah Worcester,
Jonathan Danforth,	Ebenezer Jewett,	Benjamin Wright.

At the close of Mr. Emerson's active ministry, in 1793, the resident members of the church numbered about two hundred.

Rev. Dr. Davis, in his Centennial address before the Hollis association of ministers in September, 1862, after short biographical sketches of some other of the early members of that association, in speaking of Mr. Emerson, says of him, "Of the Rev. Daniel Emerson of Hollis we have more distinct notions derived from sketches furnished by his distinguished grandsons.   He was a man of large and active intellect, a convert of Whitefield, and partaking largely of his spirit. he was uniformly evangelical, and often a very eloquent preacher.   His chief excellencies in preaching were sound doctrine, deep feeling and zeal at times almost overwhelming.   His labors were by no means confined to the pulpit.   He was interested in public affairs, serving as chaplain in the army and accompanying it to Crown Point.*   An able counsellor, he was often called from home to aid feeble churches.   Interested in the cause of ministerial education, and much blessed with revivals of religion, among his own people, he animated a large number of young men to become preachers of the gospel.   Very assiduous in his attendance on the meetings of this association, he manifested an energy like that of Baxter, whom in person he was said to resemble.   From his talents and position the Hollis minister was for many years a leading mind in the association."

In another connection I have spoken of the interest Mr. Emerson manifested in the cause of popular education and of the indebtedness of the youth of Hollis to him on that account.

Upon the monument erected over his grave in the Hollis central burial ground is inscribed the following epitaph:

"Beneath this Monument lies the Mortal part of
Rev. Daniel Emerson.
He was born at Reading, Mass., May 20, 1716.
Graduated at Harvard University, 1739
And was ordained April 20, 1743 to the Pastoral care
Of the Church and Congregation in Hollis
Which then consisted of only 30 Families.
He was an honest man, given to Hospitality:
An affectionate Husband and tender Parent:
A faithful Friend and Patriotic Citizen:
An Evangelical, zealous and unusually successful Preacher
Of the Gospel of Jesus Christ.
Highly Esteemed by his people, his praise was in all the Churches.
A. D. 1793, he voluntarily relinquished one-half his Salary
To promote the settlement of a Colleague,
From which time his pious walk and occasional labors
Evinced an unabating love for the cause of Christ,
Until nature failed and he fell asleep in Jesus,
September 30, 1801, aged 85 years.

---

*When at Crown Point it is said of him that when the men of his regiment were ordered to present their *arms* for inspection, Mr. Emerson presented his *Bible* to the inspecting officer as his *weapon*.

Upon the same monument is also inscribed the following epitaph in memory of his beloved and venerated consort.

"Here are also deposited the remains of
Hannah Emerson, wife of the above and
Daughter of Rev. Joseph Emerson of Malden.
She lived a pattern of filial obedience, respect and affection,
And an example of conjugal love and duty;
A most tender, indulgent and faithful Parent,
The delight of her Friends and ornament of the Church;
She lived the life of a true Disciple of Christ,
In the constant exercise of active faith in His promises,
And died in triumphant hope of everlasting life in those
Regions where Charity never faileth,
February 28, 1812, aged 90."

Mr. Emerson and Mrs. Emerson were the parents of thirteen children—seven sons and six daughters. Two of the sons, Joseph and Samuel, were graduates of Harvard College. (*q. v.*) Hannah Emerson, the oldest daughter, married Manasseh Smith of Hollis, three of whose sons were also graduates of Harvard College. (*q. v.*)

SMITH, REV. ELI

second minister. On the 27th of November, 1793, Rev. Eli Smith was settled as colleague pastor of the Hollis church with Rev. Mr. Emerson. Mr. Smith was born at Belchertown, Mass., September 17, 1759, and was a graduate of Brown University in 1792.

Rev. Dr. Day in a biographical sketch of Mr. Smith, written for the "History of the New Hampshire Churches," says of him: "That he was a man of strong natural talents, a firm and energetic defender of the truth and a successful pastor. During his pastorate of a little more than thirty-seven years, between four and five hundred persons were admitted to the church. * * * The great revival of his ministry was in the years 1801 and 1802. At that time one hundred and forty-two new members were united to the church. In 1811 there was another revival when thirty or forty persons were added to the church. In 1817 there was still another, of which about fifty more were made subjects. Mr. Smith was dismissed, (at his own request,) in February, 1831, and died in Hollis, May 11, 1847."

Mr. Smith, like his predecessor, Mr. Emerson, was an active and zealous friend of the public schools, and such was the interest he took in them, that some years after his settlement, the town manifested its appreciation of his services by a cordial vote of thanks. From 1806 to 1830, inclusive, he was annually elected chairman of the school committee, a position he continued to fill with much

Eli Smith.

fidelity and advantage to the schools. He was settled upon an annual salary of £90 and twenty cords of wood, which is not known to have been materially changed during his pastorate.

The following epitaph is inscribed upon his monument in the central burial ground.

" Rev. Eli Smith.
Born September 17, 1759. Graduated, 1792. Ordained, 1793.
Was Pastor of the Church in Hollis 37 years.
Died May 11, 1847.
Mr. Smith was distinguished for energy and decision of character,
for piety, faithfulness and success in his ministry."

Mr. Smith was twice married. His only son by Catharine Sheldon, his first wife, was Rev. Eli Smith, Jun., a graduate of Dartmouth college. (q. v.). By his second wife, Ama Emerson, daughter of Dea. Daniel Emerson, he had six children—four sons and two daughters. The oldest of these died in childhood. Luther, the third son, was a graduate of Brown University, (q. v.). Joseph E., the fourth, settled in Hollis, as a farmer, upon the paternal homestead, who, beside being elected many times to important town offices, was chosen representative to the New Hampshire General Court in 1838 and 1839. John R., the youngest son, studied medicine, and settled in his profession in Missouri. Ama, the oldest daughter, married Rev. Noah Emerson, of Baldwin, Me. ; the youngest, Catharine H., Rev. Darwin Adams of Camden, Me.

PERRY, REV. DAVID

the third minister of this society, was born at Worcester, Mass., July 26, 1798, graduated at Dartmouth College in 1824, at the Theological Seminary at Andover in 1827, and was ordained at Cambridgeport, Mass., May, 1828. He was dismissed at Cambridgeport, afterwards installed as pastor of the church in Hollis, February 23, 1831, and dismissed, at his own request, June 13, 1842, after a pastorate of some more than ten years. During his ministry not far from one hundred and fifty persons were admitted to the church by profession or letter.* Mr. Perry died at Wareham, Mass., Aug. 27, 1876, æt. 78, and was buried in Hollis, where he had resided for several years near the close of his life.

AIKEN, REV. JAMES

the fourth minister, was born at Goffstown, New Hampshire, Nov. 14, 1810, graduated at Dartmouth College in 1839, and at Union Theological Seminary in 1842. Mr. Aiken was ordained as pastor

*New Hampshire Churches, p. 186.

of the church and society in Hollis, August 30, 1843, and retained his office as pastor near five years, in which time about sixty members were added to the church.   Dismissed July 3, 1848.*

GORDON, REV. MATTHEW D.

fifth minister, was born at Blantyre, Scotland, Dec. 10, 1812.   He came to this country with his parents in 1817, graduated at Middlebury College in 1840, and at Union Theological Seminary in 1846. March 21, 1849, he was ordained as pastor of the church at Hollis, as successor of Rev. Mr. Aiken, and dismissed in consequence of ill health June 7, 1852.   Died at Hoosic Falls, N. Y., August 21, 1853, æt. 40.

DAY, D. D., REV. PLINY BUTTS

sixth minister was born at Huntington, Mass., April 21, 1806, graduated at Amherst college in 1834, and at the Theological Seminary at Andover in 1837.   Dr. Day was ordained as pastor of the church at Derry, N. H., Oct. 4, 1837, dismissed at Derry in 1851, and installed as pastor of the church and society in Hollis, July 7, 1852.   He received the honorary degree of D. D. from Dartmouth college in 1864, of which institution he was a trustee for several years previous to his death.   Died at Hollis July 6, 1869, æt. 63.   The annual salary of the three ministers next preceding Dr. Day was $600. That of Dr. Day was at first $700, but afterwards increased to $1000.

The esteem in which Dr. Day was held by his brethren in the ministry, and also by the people of Hollis, is well expressed in the following resolution of the Hollis Association of ministers, adopted August 2, 1869, at its first meeting after his decease.

" Resolved that while we humbly submit to the Divine Providence that has thus removed our greatly esteemed and beloved brother, we feel deeply pained and bereft at his departure.   Rev. Dr. Day we received as a true, Christian gentleman: courteous, amiable, possessed of superior mental endowments, judicious, wise ; his mind well trained and furnished with extensive, varied and useful knowledge ; a sound theologian, an able sermonizer ; an earnest, impressive preacher ; a faithful teacher, pastor and spiritual Christian ; and an eminently discreet and useful minister of Jesus Christ.

---

*New Hamp 'hire Churches, p. 186.

P. B. Day

We record our deep conviction of the loss sustained in his death by this Association—by the church and people of which he was so long pastor and teacher—by the Congregational churches throughout the State ;—by our State college of which he was an esteemed trustee ; —by the interests of education generally—of patriotism—of Christian benevolence—of sound morals—and of philanthropy."

The published writings of Dr. Day are *Letters from Europe,* 1851 ; *Two Sermons,* the Sabbath after his installation, 1852 ; *New Year's Address,* 1854 ; *Sermons:* at the funeral of Benjamin F. Nichols, 1854 ; at the funeral of John H. Cutter, 1860 ; *Fare- well to Soldiers,* 1861 ; in memory of John H. Worcester, 1864 ; *Victory and its Dangers.* 1865 ; in memory of Abraham Lin- coln, 1865 ; at the funeral of Benjamin M. Farley, 1865. Dr. Day was also a valued contributor to the *Congregationalist* and *Con- gregational Journal.*

LAIRD, REV. JAMES

seventh minister, was born at Huntingdon, Canada East, Septem- ber 4, 1833. Fitted for college at Monson, Mass. Entered Amherst College in 1857, passed the first two years of his college course at Amherst, the last two at Oberlin College, Ohio, at which he gradu- ated in 1861. He afterwards entered the Theological Seminary at Andover. Graduated at Andover in 1864. Was ordained as pastor of the Congregational church at Guildhall, Vt., March 15, 1866 ; dismissed at Guildhall and afterwards installed as pastor of the church at Hollis, May 25, 1870. Died at Hollis after a long and lingering sickness, May 25, 1870. æt. 36. The annual salary of Mr. Laird was $1,250.

KELSEY, REV. HIRAM L.

eighth minister, was born at Wheelock, Vt., August 31, 1835. Graduated at the Wesleyan University, Middletown, Conn., 1861. Was ordained as a minister of the Methodist Episcopal church, April 16, 1865. Mr. Kelsey was installed as pastor of the church and society at Hollis, June 1, 1875, and dismissed, (at his own re- quest,) March 1, 1878. About two months after his dismissal at Hollis he was installed as pastor of a Congregational church at Brockton, Mass., where he now resides.

Annual salary of Mr. Kelsey at Hollis, $1,500 and use of the parsonage.

(16)

SCOTT, REV. D. B.

from Milton, N. H., in the fall of 1878, was engaged as minister of the society for one year and is now the acting pastor of the church.

DEACONS OF THE HOLLIS CONGREGATIONAL CHURCH.

William Cumings,	chosen	1745,	died September 9, 1858,	aged 46 years.
Thomas Patch,	"	1745,	" May 1, 1754,	" 40 "
Francis Worcester,	"	1747,	" October 19, 1800,	" 79 "
Enoch Noyes,	"	1750,	" September, 1796,	" 80 "
John Boynton,	"	1755,	" October 29, 1787,	" 67 "
Stephen Jewett,	"	1770,	" May 23, 1803,	" 75 "
Daniel Emerson, Jun.,	"	1775,	" October 4, 1820,	" 74 "
Josiah Conant,	"	1787,	" August 21, 1807,	" 61 "
Abel Conant,	"	1787,	" May 2, 1844,	" 88 "
Ephraim Burge,	"	1803,	" March 3, 1843,	" 78 "
Thomas Farley,	"	1803,	" March 17, 1832,	" 63 "
Stephen Jewett, Jun.,	"	1808,	" February 22, 1829,	" 75 "
Benoni Cutter,	"	1814,	" January 17, 1816,	" 44 "
Enos Hardy,	"	1816,	" May 18, 1857,	" 85 "
Phillips Wood,	"	1820,	" January 14, 1858,	" 76 "
William Emerson,	"	1832,	" December 3, 1873,	" 82 "
Isaac Farley,	"	1832,	" February 25, 1874,	" 90 "
John B. Hardy,	"	1838,		
Rev. Leonard Jewett,	"	1846,	" February 16, 1862,	" 74 "
Rev. James D. Hills,	"	1857,		
Noah Farley,	"	1860,	" April 4, 1876,	" 76 "
Enoch J. Colburn,	"	1863,		
Perry M. Farley,	"	1875,		
George M. Bradley,	"	1875,		

THE HOLLIS YOUNG MEN'S CHRISTIAN ASSOCIATION OF THE LAST CENTURY.

I think it pertinent to the History of the society and church, and as some evidence of the moral and religious training and culture of the youth of Hollis one hundred years and more ago, to present in this connection the following articles of association signed by nearly one hundred of them. The document was preserved among the papers of Miss Mary S. Farley, the generous benefactor of the Hollis High School, and whose grandfather, Christopher Farley, was a member of the association. There is no date upon the paper, but the fact that two members of the association, whose names were signed to it, were killed at Bunker Hill, June 17, 1775, and one of them at Cambridge two days after, is conclusive evidence that the association was organized before that time.

It may interest some persons who belong to the *Young Men's Christian Associations* of the present day to know that the like associations existed in New Hampshire three generations ago, and also to learn in what manner they were organized and conducted. They may also have some curiosity to know somewhat of the *qualifications* for membership in this ancient association—of the *duties* of its members to each other. as well as to the community at large—of its *rules* for the *admission* or *expulsion* of disorderly or unworthy members—and of the trust and confidence reposed by these young men in the pastor and deacons of the church. in making them the final arbiters in all matters that might disturb their harmony.

"THE ARTICLES OF ASSOCIATION."

"Hoping that we are disposed by the influence of the spirit of God to seek those things which are above and made in some measure sensible of the danger of bad company by which many have fallen into temptation and the snare of the devil. and calling to mind that we are given up to God in holy baptism, as well as desiring to remember our Creator in the days of our youth and become the unfeigned servants of the Lord Christ. we determine to associate in the following manner, viz. :

1st. We will endeavor to spend about two hours every Sabbath evening in praying, reading and singing in the ensuing order. first asking God's presence and blessing, then reading a portion of sacred Scripture, then each one praying in his turn beginning with the oldest, then sing part of a psalm or hymn, then read a sermon or a part of some profitable book. then another prayer, then sing, then ask a question in the Assembly's Catechism to every member by the person who prayed last.

2nd. By Christ strengthening us we will watch over each other with a spirit of love and concern—not divulging one another's infirmities but lovingly inform them of what we shall know or hear to be a fault—nor will we manifest ourselves offended when we are charitably reproved, although the reproof be not administered in such manner as we should wish, but endeavor immediate reformation.

3d. If any of our members shall fall into scandalous sin we will admonish and suspend him for a longer or shorter time, according to the nature of the offence, nor will we receive him again without visible tokens of repentance and reformation.

4th. We will spend the evening of the fourth Lord's day in every other month in prayer for the increase of the kingdom of our

blessed Lord and Saviour through the world, especially for the con-
version of the young people where we live, and invite one or two
brethren of the church to join with and lead us on said evenings
when these articles shall be audibly read.

5th. If any member shall absent himself for more than two evenings successively without known reason we will send one or two
to enquire, and if no answer be given, but such as discovers apos-
tacy—without reformation, in one month his name shall be exposed
before the society.

6th. Any one who is desirous of joining with us shall be pro-
pounded by one of the members, one evening beforehand, and if
allowed shall present himself the next, when, hearing our articles, if
he pleases to sign them, it shall be his admission into our number.

7th. We will cheerfully contribute each of our parts towards the
necessary expenses of the society.

8th. If there arises any difficulty between any of us which we
cannot heal among ourselves we will submit the whole affair to our
Rev. Pastor and deacons of the church for the time being, and their
judgment shall be the final issue of the difficulty."

There were appended to the foregoing articles the names of
ninety-four youths and young men, all supposed to have been residents of Hollis, and most of them sons of the early settlers of the
town. So far as can now be learned, the two youngest of the members were Ralph Emerson, a son of the minister, and Jesse
Worcester, a son of Noah Worcester, each of whom in June, 1775,
was in his fifteenth year. Among the oldest, were Daniel Emerson,
Jun., who was a Captain in the war, and Nathan Blood, who was a
Sergeant in the Hollis company at Bunker Hill, each of whom was
then in his twenty-ninth year. Forty-eight, or more than one-half
of the members of this fraternity were soldiers in that war, the most
of them having been in the service the first year of it. The names
of these soldiers are presented in the following list, thirteen of
whom marked thus, (*) were in the Hollis company at Bunker
Hill. Two of the thirteen, viz., Nathan Blood, aged twenty-eight,
and Jacob Boynton, aged nineteen, were killed in the battle.

Samuel Ambrose,	*Evan Dow,	*James Mc Conner,
John Atwell, Jun.,	*Caleb Eastman	*William Nevins, Jun.,
Andrew Bailey,	Jonathan Eastman,	Elijah Noyes,
John Ball,	*William Elliot,	Enoch Noyes, Jun.,
Nathaniel Ball,	Daniel Emerson, Jun.,	Thomas Patch,
Daniel Blood,	Christopher Farley,	William W. Pool,
*Nathan Blood,	*Josiah Fisk,	John Philbrick,

THIRD CONGREGATIONAL MEETING-HOUSE
BUILT 1804   RECONSTRUCTED 1849.

Benjamin Boynton,	Joseph French,	*Nahum Powers,
John Boynton,	Jacob Jewett, Jun.,	*Thomas Pratt.
*Joshua Boynton,	Jonathan Jewett,	Edward Taylor,
*Jacob Boynton,	Noah Jewett,	Jacob Taylor,
James Colburn,	Stephen Jewett, Jun.,	William Tenney,
Jotham Cumings,	Abner Keyes,	Amos Webster,
*Philip Cumings,	Asa Lovejoy,	*Noah Worcester, Jun.,
William Cumings,	Jonathan Lovejoy.	Jesse Worcester,
Joshua Davis,	Ephraim Lund,	Samuel Worcester.

THE THIRD HOLLIS MEETING HOUSE.

At the annual town meeting in 1799, an article was inserted in the warrant " *To see if the town would build a new Meeting House or repair the old one.*" At that meeting the town " voted to build a new Meeting House in three years," and chose the following committee to decide where it should be placed, viz., David Danforth of Amherst, Jeremiah Pritchard of New Ipswich, Jacob Blodgett of Townsend, James Brazier of Pepperell and Frederick French of Dunstable. The report of this committee was soon after made and formally accepted. At the same meeting Emerson Smith, David Smith and Benjamin Wright were appointed a committee to report a " Plan " for the new house, which they did the same season—this plan, as appears, having been copied from that of the meeting-house at Billerica, which with some modifications was accepted and adopted.

The foregoing proceedings seem to have contemplated that the new meeting-house should be built at the expense of the town ; but at a town meeting in May, 1801, the town " voted to proceed with the building provided it could be erected without a Town tax " and then chose a committee to devise the means to effect it, and at the same time to pay the owners of pews in the old meeting-house the appraised value of their pews. This committee of " *ways and means*" consisted of Daniel Emerson, Esq., Noah Worcester, Jeremiah Ames, Daniel Emerson, 3d, William Brown, Solomon Wheat, Ephraim Burge, Amos Eastman and David Smith.

In the following September, this committee made a report (which was adopted) to the effect " that the town should choose a committee to sell the pews, as described in the ' plan,' reserving a ministerial pew, and every seventh pew below, and each fifth pew in the gallery, till the rest should be sold. If the sales should fall short of the cost of the house—the purchasers of the pews to make good the deficiency—if they should exceed the cost, the purchasers to have the excess in proportion to the amounts severally paid by them." The committee afterwards chosen to make these sales consisted of Dea. Daniel Emerson, Benjamin Wright, William Tenney, Amos Eastman, and William Brown.

After the new plan was adopted, the town voted that the new house should be finished on or before November 1st, 1803, but afterwards voted to extend the time one year longer. At the annual town meeting in March, 1804, the town instructed the building committee to take down the old house at the expense of the purchasers of the pews in the new house, and also voted that the " new house might be finished with a tower and steeple if it could be done without expense to the town." The foregoing was the last town meeting held in respect to the building of the third meeting-house.

This new meeting-house (built as is supposed) substantially after the model of that at Billerica, was finished in the fall of 1804. It continued to be occupied, as originally constructed, without material change outside or inside, till the year 1849, when its west end was turned around to the south—its south side to the east, and the whole building remodelled, renovated, and altered substantially to the condition in which it now is.

Hundreds of people still living have a vivid remembrance of it as originally constructed and finished. It stood upon the same spot with the first meeting-house built in Hollis more than sixty years before, the main building being sixty-eight feet long, east and west, and fifty-four feet wide north and south. It was two stories in height, well clapboarded and painted white, with windows of twenty-four panes each of glass, nine inches by twelve, on its sides and ends, and porches on its two ends and south side, with a wide door in each porch opening into the main building or audience room. The east porch was of two stories with entrance doors on the east and south sides, with a stairway ascending to the east or *women's* gallery. The south porch was of but one story with outside doors on its east, south and west sides. The west porch was also of two stories, with stairs to the west or *men's* gallery, and surmounted with a belfry, cupola and steeple. All of the outside doors of the porches had well finished steps or stairways of hammered stone for ascent to them, and those at the east and west porches were each furnished at one end with a neatly finished and convenient horse-block of the like hammered stone.

The pulpit stood at the middle of the north wall of the audience room, facing south, with stairs on each side of it, and the seats for

the four deacons, and the communion table hung on hinges directly
below, in front, the central broad aisle leading to it from the inside
door of the south porch. There was in front of the deacons' seat an
aisle extending east and west across the audience room, separating
the north wall pews, from two ranges of long free seats for the
aged and *deaf*, one-half of these free seats being east of the broad
aisle, for *women*—the other half west of that aisle, for *men*.

The pews were six feet long, east and west, and five feet wide,
neatly panelled and painted, the partitions between them being finished at the top with a miniature balustrade. There were in all
ninety-five of them, of which sixty-eight were below and twenty-
seven in the gallery. There was a single row of them next to the
wall on the lower floor, with a step or stair in front of each pew,
all raised a foot or more above the outside aisles leading to them,
which with the wall pews, extended around on the two sides and
both ends of the audience room. Of these wall pews there were
ten, (including those in the corners,) on each of the north and south
sides of the lower floor, and six at each end. Of those on the sides
five were on the east and five on the west side of the south door, and
five on the right side, and five on the left of the pulpit. Of those
at the ends, three were on each side of the east and west doors.

The intermediate space between the four outside aisles, (including the long seats for the aged,) was occupied with six rows of six
pews each, all parallel with the broad or central aisle—there being
three rows on each side of it—the east and west rows of the six being separated from the others by a narrow alley leading from the
south aisle to the long seats for the aged.

The gallery, supported by round, wooden, well painted Ionic
columns was finished in front with panel work, and a heavy cornice,
and extended around on the south side and east and west ends of the
audience room, with a range of pews next to the walls, eleven of
them being on the south side and eight at each end, with aisles leading to them. The front part of the south gallery was appropriated
to the singers. The front part of the east gallery, not occupied by
pews, was furnished with long, unpainted free seats for women, and
was known as the " women's gallery." The corresponding portion
of that on the west end was provided with the like kind of free seats
for men and known as the " men's gallery."

The pews were all provided with panelled and painted doors
hung on hinges, and with wide, hard uncushioned seats on the side

facing the pulpit, each about two feet long, and also with like seats in the corners, all also hung on hinges. In those times, the worshippers, as was the custom, stood during prayers. When they rose their seats were all lifted up and turned back against the sides of the pews. At the close of each prayer the " amen " of the minister was the signal for carelessly dropping the seats again to their places with a noise and rattle not unlike a musketry salute of a raw, poorly drilled militia company. Some of these pews were supplied with flag-bottomed arm chairs for the grand-parents, and most of them with long, narrow " leaning boards," so called, to be placed lengthwise of the pews in front of the occupants as they sat, upon which they might rest their listless heads, when their " drowsy powers " got the better of their interest in the services. The top ceiling of the audience room was slightly arched and painted of a light sky blue, with a dark, angry, portentous thunder-cloud in its north west corner. With but few if any exceptions, there were no blinds to the windows on the outside to protect the patient audience from the heat and sun in summer, nor curtains nor shades on the inside— nor stoves nor furnaces to soften the cold of winter. The principal substitutes in winter for these last modern luxuries, were warm fur muffs and tippets for the hands, arms and necks of such of the gentler sex as could afford them, and thick socks of fur or wool for the feet, but more than all the small tin hand stove with its little basin of bright coals and ashes carried in the hand to the pews by the younger members of the family and kindly and quietly slipped around from one pair of cold feet to another.

No sound of a church-going bell was ever heard from the belfry of this meeting-house till 1821. In that year a subscription was raised by the people of the town of near $740 for the purchase of one, and a bell weighing 1263 lbs. bought and hung the same year. This bell proved to be of a very fine tone, but about twenty years afterwards it was unfortunately cracked, and taken down and sold, and the one now in use procured by a like subscription and hung in its place.

THE HOLLIS PHILANTHROPIC SOCIETY.

On the 15th January, 1801, thirty or more of the citizens of Hollis, interested in the maintenance of the ministry in the Congregational society, met for the purpose of devising a " plan" for its permanent support without taxation. At that meeting, a preamb was reported, adopted and signed by them, expressive of their wishes and purposes, a substantial copy of which with the names of the signers, is here presented, as follows:

" Considering the gospel of Jesus Christ the sole foundation and source of happiness to man, * *—and that this gospel should be respectably maintained and publicly taught in such way as will most harmoniously tend to promote public tranquility and individual piety, * *—we the subscribers, inhabitants of the town of Hollis, do hereby associate ourselves together under the name of the " *Hollis Philanthropic Society* " for the purpose of devising, according to the best of our ability, some plan for the perpetual support of the gospel in the town in which we live, and although we dare not promise ourselves a speedy accomplishment of our purposes, yet we view it of such consequence to the well being of society that we deem it an object highly worthy of our attention, and that we cannot transmit to posterity a more valuable legacy." Signed,

Noah Worcester,	John Ball,	William Tenney,
Daniel Emerson, Jun.,	Benoni Cutter,	Benjamin Wright,
Stephen Jewett,	Wilder Chamberlain,	David Holden,
Ephraim Burge,	Jesse Hardy,	Amos Eastman, Jun.,
Nathan Colburn,	Jesse Worcester,	Reuben Flagg,
Thomas Farley,	Daniel Lawrence,	Eli Smith,
Nathan Holt,	James Bradbury,	William Ferguson,
Daniel Emerson, 3d,	William Merrill,	Aaron Bailey,
Solomon Wheat,	Josiah Conant, Jun.,	Samuel Smith,
David Smith,	William Brown,	Enos Hardy,
David Burge,	David Hale,	Timothy Lawrence.

At that meeting a committee, consisting of Daniel Emerson, 3d, Noah Worcester, Jesse Worcester, Stephen Jewett, and Ephraim Burge, was appointed to prepare and report a plan and rules for carrying into effect the objects of the association. These proceedings, with the report of this committee finally resulted in procuring from the General Court an Act of Incorporation, authorizing the association to raise funds by donation and contribution, the income of which (as contemplated) might permanently support the ministry in this church and society. The association began its operations for the objects proposed the same year, and has continued in existence, under its original and amended charters, from that time to the present.

The original charter provided that when the funds of this association should reach the sum of $7,000, five-sixths of its income should be paid to the Selectmen of Hollis for the time being for the support of the gospel in this church and society. In 1831, the

original charter was altered, authorizing the association, when its
funds should amount to $3,500, to pay to the standing committee of
that society twelve-thirteenths of its yearly income. In the year
1832 the invested funds of the association, having increased to
$3,536, the association that year paid $200 of its income for the
support of the ministry in that society, and continued to pay the
like sum yearly till 1849,—from 1849 to 1854, $250 per year.
Since 1854, the average annual amount so paid has been near $267.
It appears from the annual report of the association, made in January 1878, that its permanent fund, including interest, had increased
to $5,703.95.

THE HOLLIS BENEVOLENT ASSOCIATION.

If the amount of the contributions in money of the Congregational society in Hollis in aid of the various charitable and religious enterprises of the day does not equal that of some other
larger and more wealthy societies in the county, still it is believed
that in this respect its good name will not suffer in comparison with
most of them. In January, 1836, a charitable organization was
formed, composed of its leading members, which then adopted the
name, and has since been known, as the " *Hollis Benevolent Association.*" It appears from the written Constitution of this association, that it was one of its main purposes, by means of a *single*
organization, in place of *several*, to furnish material aid to each of
the charitable religious enterprises of the day, in which the members
of this association felt interested. These enterprises included the
Bible Society, Foreign and Domestic Missions, the Tract, Education, and Sabbath School Societies. It is shown by the accounts of
its doings, kept in the records of this association, that the amount
in money contributed to its objects for the first six years of its existence, was $3,644, being at the rate of $607 per year. It also appears that the amount raised by it from 1853, to 1869, (being sixteen years of the pastorate of Rev. Dr. Day) was very nearly equal
to an annual average of $500, and making an aggregate of $7,794.

THE HOLLIS FEMALE READING AND CHARITABLE SOCIETY.

This association composed of ladies belonging to the Congregational church and society was formed in the year 1829, and has been
in active operation from that year to the present. It appears from
its Constitution, then adopted, that its leading objects were the pro-

promotion of social intercourse, mental culture and improvement, and active and worthy charities. Its regular meetings were to be held during the entire year on the first Thursday afternoon of each month, and while listening to some useful and instructive reading by one of its members, the time of the rest was to be occupied in working for some object of beneficence to be approved by a majority of them.

The records of the doings of this society have been, from year to year, neatly written out and kept for near half a century. One of the primary objects of its charities seems to have been to aid the unfortunate, deserving poor at home, but the amount of its benefactions bestowed in this way does not appear in its records, nor in the early years of its existence was the annual report of its treasurer recorded at all. Still, though the record of its good works is thus incomplete, yet it is shown by the report for 1878 of its present secretary, Mrs. Jefferson Farley, that it appears from these records that more than $1,000 have been received by the society, mainly from self-imposed taxes and fees for membership. Aside from its home charities and work, the objects of the bounty of the association have been many and various, including in them, Home and Foreign Missions and Missionaries, the Seaman's Friends' Society, the Home of the Friendless in New York city, and the New Hampshire Orphan's Asylum, at Franklin. As the fruits of the labors and beneficence of these busy and faithful workers, boxes filled with clothing, bedding, and other valuable articles for household use have been made by them and from year to year forwarded to their destination in aid of the charitable enterprises above named, of the aggregate appraised value of $3,305.

THE HOLLIS BAPTIST SOCIETY.

It appears from the published minutes of the Boston and New Hampshire Baptist Association, that a Baptist church existed in Hollis as early as 1791, and that in the years 1810 and 1811 it numbered forty-nine members, but I do not find that the society then had either minister or meeting-house. As those "minutes" contain no report of any Baptist church in Hollis between 1811 and 1836 it is to be presumed that the church first formed, was dissolved soon after 1811. But it is within the recollection of many persons now living, that between the years 1816 and 1823, Rev. Benjamin Paul, a very worthy colored Baptist minister, had charge of a small Baptist

society composed of members living in part in the east part of
Hollis and partly in Dunstable. No record of this society is known
to exist and it is supposed also to have been dissolved.

After 1823 no Baptist society is known to have been formed in
Hollis till March 31, 1836, when a new society of that denomina-
tion was organized, and the following officers then chosen, viz.,
William N. Bradstreet and Amos Hagget, Directors; William F.
Burrows, Clerk; William N. Bradstreet, Treasurer, and Asa
Jaquith, Collector. The church was formed June 6, 1837, then
consisting of twenty-eight members, and took the name of the
"First Baptist Church in Hollis." The Deacons of the church
at that time chosen were Abraham Temple Hardy and Amos
Hagget. In April 1841, on the removal of Dea. Hardy from the
town, Dea. Leonard W. Farley was elected in his place. The
church from the time of its formation continued to increase, from
year to year, till September 1843, when it consisted of one hundred
members, with a Sabbath school of one hundred and twenty pupils.
After 1843, its numbers gradually diminished. The clergymen who
have acted as pastors of the church have officiated in the following
order: Rev. Phineas Richardson, Rev. Daniel P. Deming, Rev.
H. W. Dalton, Rev. Bartlett Pease and Rev. George B. Bills. In
the year 1838 this society built a convenient and substantial meeting-house, on the east side of the Hollis common, with fifty pews,
and at a cost of $2,000.

Rev. Mr. Richardson is said to have begun to preach in Hollis
the year before this society was formed, and was a popular, faithful
and successful pastor of the church for about twelve years. He was
born in Methuen, Mass., February 2, 1787, and was self educated,
with the exception of studying for a few months with Rev. Dr.
Chaplin of Danvers. He was ordained to the work of the ministry
at Methuen, in 1817, and was for some years afterwards employed
as an evangelist, but for eighteen years next previous to his coming
to Hollis he was pastor of the Baptist church in Gilmanton, N. H.
Mr. Richardson resigned his pastorate in Hollis on account of feeble
health and removed to Lawrence, Mass. His last pastorate of four
years was at New Hampton, N. H. Died at Lawrence, January
25, 1860, in his 83d year.

Mr. Richardson was succeeded in the pastorate at Hollis by Rev.
Mr. Deming who supplied the pulpit for about six years, till the
year 1854, when he removed to Goffstown, and was pastor of the

Baptist church at Goffstown for the next four years. Upon his removal from Goffstown he became the pastor of the Baptist church at Cornish, N. H. for the next seven years. Mr. Deming (1879) now resides in Plainfield, N. H. He was succeeded in Hollis by Rev. Mr. Dalton, who officiated as pastor for about two years, and upon his removal the church was supplied for a short time by Rev. Mr. Pease, who was succeeded by the Rev. Mr. Bills, the last minister of the society, for about a year. For the last sixteen years, the church has had no minister or stated preaching, and in the year 1869, in pursuance of a vote of the society, the meeting-house, built in 1838, was sold, taken down and removed to Nashua.

CHAPTER XXIII.

PARISH OFFICERS OF WEST DUNSTABLE FROM 1739, TO 1746.—
OFFICERS OF THE DISTRICT OF DUNSTABLE FROM 1742 TO
1746.—FULL LISTS OF THE TOWN OFFICERS OF HOLLIS FOR
THE FIRST AND THIRD YEARS.—MODERATORS OF THE ANNUAL
TOWN MEETINGS.—TOWN CLERKS.—TREASURERS AND SELECT-
MEN FROM 1746 TO 1878.

PARISH OFFICERS OF WEST DUNSTABLE.

First Election January 2, 1739-40. O. S.

Abraham Taylor, Moderator.
Abraham Taylor, Assessor.
Peter Powers,   "
Benjamin Farley,   "
Moses Proctor, Collector.
Thomas Dinsmore, Collector non-resident
    Taxes.

Stephen Harris, Treasurer.
Benjamin Farley, Auditor.
Moses Proctor,   "
Abraham Taylor, Com. to run Parish lines.
Peter Powers,   "   "   "
Thomas Dinsmore,   "   "   "

Second Election, March, 1740-1, O. S.

Peter Powers, Moderator.
Abraham Taylor, Clerk.
Benjamin Farley, Assessor.
Willam Colburn,   "
Jerahmael Cumings,   "

Thomas Dinsmore, Treasurer.
Stephen Harris, Parish Committee.
Thomas Dinsmore,   "   "
Peter Powers,   "   "
David Nevins, Collector.

Third Election, March 4, 1742-3, O. S.

Abraham Taylor, Moderator.
Abraham Taylor, Clerk.
Peter Powers, Collector.
Abraham Taylor, Assessor.

Eleazer Flagg, Assessor.
Enoch Hunt,   "
Jonathan Danforth   "
Thomas Patch,   "

Fourth Election, March, 1743-4, O. S.

Samuel Cumings, Moderator.
John Boynton, Clerk.
John Boynton, Assessor.
Samuel Cumings,   "

Jonathan Danforth, Assessor.
Jerahmael Cumings, Treasurer.
Sephen Harris, Collector.
Henry Barton,   "

Fifth Election, March 12, 1744-5, O. S.

Samuel Brown, Moderator.
John Boynton, Assessor.
Thomas Patch,   "
Jerahmael Cumings, "

John Boynton, Clerk.
Elias Smith, Treasurer.
Josiah Blood, Collector.
Stephen Ames,   "

OFFICERS OF THE DISTRICT OF DUNSTABLE, FROM 1742 TO 1746.

The district of Dunstable, as we have stated, (pp. 44, 45, ante.) was organized by the New Hampshire General Court in March, 1742, for the purpose of assessing and collecting province taxes, and comprised all the territory afterwards embraced in the towns of Dunstable, Hollis, Merrimack and Monson, as chartered in April, 1746. The meetings for the choice of district officers appear to have been held, alternately, in the East Parish of Dunstable, and at the old or first meeting-house in West Dunstable. The district officers chosen at these meetings were, a Moderator, Clerk, Assessors and Collectors, and were about equally divided in respect to residence, between the East and West Parishes. Of the officers named in the lists below, Blanchard, Harwood, Lovewell, Lund and Parker lived in the East Parish, and Boynton, the two Cumings, Hunt, Proctor, Smith and Taylor in West Dunstable, now Hollis.

First District Election, April 23, 1742.

Joseph Blanchard, Moderator.
Abraham Taylor, Clerk.
Enoch Hunt, Collector.
Henry Parker,   "

Abraham Taylor, Assessor.
Thomas Harwood,   "
Samuel Cumings,   "
Jonathan Lovewell, "

Second Election, September 18, 1744.

Joseph Blanchard, Moderator.
John Boynton, Clerk.

John Boynton, Assessor.
Jonathan Lovewell, "
Jerahmael Cumings, "

Third Election, September 19, 1745.

Elias Smith, Moderator.
John Boynton, Clerk.
Moses Proctor, Collector.
Jonathan Lund,   "

John Boynton, Assessor.
Jonathan Lovewell, "
Jerahmael Cumings, "

The charter of Hollis as a town, as we have seen, was dated April 3, 1746, and the town officers chosen at the first and second town elections, are presented in the lists below.

First Town Election, April 28, 1746.

Samuel Cumings, Moderator.
Samuel Cumings, Clerk.
Samuel Cumings, Selectman.
Benjamin Farley,   "

Thomas Dinsmore, Surveyor of Highways.
Francis Phelps,   "   "
Nicholas French,   "   "
James Mc Daniels, "   "

Francis Worcester, Selectman.
Elias Smith, Constable.
James Stewart, Tithing man.
Christopher Lovejoy,   "
Jonathan Danforth, Fence Viewer.
Benjamin Blanchard,   "

Samuel Parker, Surveyor of Highways.
Nicholas French, Hog Reeve.
William Adams,   "
Elias Smith, Pound Keeper.
Elias Smith, Sealer of Weights and Measures.
Samuel Brown, Sealer of Leather.

Third Town Election, March 7, 1748.

Samuel Cumings, Moderator and Clerk.
Francis Worcester, Treasurer.
Samuel Cumings, Selectman,
Benjamin Farley,   "
Samuel Brown,   "
Stephen Ames,   "
Elias Smith,   "
Benjamin Blanchard, Constable.
Josiah Conant, Tithing Man.
Nathaniel Blood,   "   "
Nicholas French, Hog Reeve.
David Nevins,   "   "
Zerubbabel Keinp, "   "
Elias Smith, Pound Keeper.

Josiah Blood, Fence Viewer.
Josiah Brown,   "   "
Samuel Farley, Field Driver.
Wm. Blanchard,   "   "
Wm. Shattuck,   "   "
Zedekiah Drury, Surveyor of Highways.
Francis Phelps,   "   "   "
Benj. Blanchard, Jr., "   "   "
James McDonald,   "   "   "
Nathaniel Blood,   "   "   "
Sam'l Brown, Sealer of Weights and Measures
William Tenney, Sealer of Leather,
Zedekiah Drury, Deer Reeve,
Samuel Farley,   "   "

Such as shown in the preceding lists were the town officers, chosen at the annual March meetings in Hollis, in most years, from 1746 till the war of the Revolution and for some years afterwards. Under the Province laws in force before the Revolution, the number of Selectmen, as has been before said, might vary in different years, a town being at liberty at its annual meeting to choose either three, five, seven or nine of these officers as might be decided at the time, by vote of the town. Before the Revolution the number of Selectmen annually chosen in Hollis was either three or five, each of these numbers having been elected about an equal number of times.

The following lists present the names of the persons who have held the several offices of Moderator of the annual town meetings, Town Clerk, Treasurer and Selectmen from the year 1746 to 1878, with the years in which they were respectively chosen.

MODERATORS OF THE ANNUAL TOWN MEETINGS.

Samuel Cumings, 1746, '47, '48, '49 and '55.
Francis Worcester, 1750, '51, '52, '53, '54, '58, '60, '62, '63, '64 and '68.
Samuel Goodhue, 1756 and '57.
John Hale, 1761, '65, '66, '67, '69, '70, '71, '72 and '82.
William Nevins, 1773 and 1774.
Benjamin Abbot, 1759.
Stephen Jewett, 1776.
Enoch Noyes, 1777, '78, and '79.
John Boynton, 1780 and '81.
Noah Worcester, 1783, '84, '85, '86, '87, '88, '90, '92, '93, '94, '95, '96, '97, '99 and 1800.

Jonathan Danforth, 1789.
Reuben Dow, 1791.
Daniel Emerson, 1798, 1801, '02, '03, '04, and '09.
Amos Eastman, 1805 and 1806.
Samson Powers, 1807.
Benjamin W. Parker, 1808.
Stephen Jewett, Jun., 1810 and 1811.
Joseph F. Eastman, 1812, '13, '14, '15, '17, '18, '19 '22, '23, '25, '26, '29, '30, '31 and 1834.
Ambrose Gould, 1816.
Benjamin M. Farley, 1820, '24, '38 and 1839.
Jonathan B. Eastman, 1821.

William Emerson, 1827 and 1828.
Benjamin Pool, 1832, '33.
Ralph E. Tenney, 1835 to 1837, 1840 to 1844, '46, '51, '52.
Stillman Spaulding, 1845, 1847 to 1853, '56, 1861, to 1864, '69, '71, '72, '74, '75, '77, '78.

Reuben Baldwin, 1854.
Ambrose H. Wood, 1855.
Luther Proctor, 1857 to 1860, '67, '70, '73.
Timothy E. Flagg, 1865, '66, '76.
Nathan M. Ames, 1868.

TOWN CLERKS FROM 1746 TO 1878.

Samuel Cumings, 1746 to 1770, except 1753, '54, and '66.
Samuel Goodhue, 1753, '54.
John Hale, 1766.
William Cumings, 1771, '72, and 1782 to 1788.
Samuel Cumings, Jun., 1773, '74.
Noah Worcester, 1775 to 1779.
Daniel Emerson, 1780, 1781.
Solomon Wheat, 1789 to 1793, 1800, 1801, and 1809 to 1816, except 1812 and 1813.
Jesse Worcester, 1799.
Daniel Emerson, Jun., 1802 to 1805.
Amos Eastman, 1806.
Benjamin Pool, 1807, 1808.
Ambrose Gould, 1812, 1813.
Christopher P. Farley, 1817 to 1819.
Benjamin M. Farley, 1820 to 1823.

William Ames, 1823, '24.
Jonathan T. Wright, 1825 to '29.
Noah Hardy, 1830, 1831.
Joseph E. Smith, 1832, '33, '42, '46, '47, and 1854 to '59.
Moses Proctor, 1834, '35.
William P. Hale, 1836, '37, '39, '40, '41, '50, '51.
Edward Emerson, 1838 and 1852.
Reuben Baldwin, 1843 to '45, '61, '62.
John Coburn, 1848.
William P. Saunderson, 1849.
Luther Proctor, 1853 and '60.
William A. Trow, 1863 to '65.
Ebenezer T. Wheeler, 1866 to '70.
Isaac Hardy, 1871 to '74.
George A. Burge, 1875 to '78.

TOWN TREASURERS FROM 1746 TO 1878.

John Boynton, 1746, '47.
Francis Worcester, 1748 to 1767.
Samuel Cumings, 1768 to 1770.
Noah Worcester, 1771 to 1773.
Daniel Emerson, 1774 to 1779, '98, 99.
Josiah Conant, 1780.
Solomon Rogers, 1781 to 1785.
Christopher Farley, 1786 to 1788.
Benjamin Wright, 1789 to 1797 and 1800 to 1806.
Peleg Lawrence, 1806 to 1808.
Joseph F. Eastman, 1809 to 1817.

Josiah Conant, 1818 to 1830.
Benjamin Farley, 1831 to 1849, except 1833.
Moses Proctor, 1833.
Ebenezer Baldwin, 1850, '51, '52, '53.
Joseph Gates, 1854.
Christopher F. Smith, 1855.
David W. Sawtell, 1856 to 1860.
Edward Hardy, 1861 to 1864.
Charles B. Richardson, 1865 to 1874.
Henry N. Smith, 1875.
George A. Burge, 1876.
Silas M. Spaulding, 1877, '78.

SELECTMEN FROM 1746 TO 1878.

Samuel Cumings, 1746 to 1770, except 1753, 1754 and 1766.
Benjamin Farley, 1746, '47, and 1748.
Francis Worcester, 1746, '47, '48, '62, '63 and 1765.
Stephen Ames, 1747, '48, '62, '67, '73, '75, '76, '77, and 1779.
Nathaniel Townsend, 1747 and '52.
Samuel Brown, 1748.
Elias Smith, 1748.
Enoch Hunt, 1749.
Joshua Wright, 1749 and 1767.
Moses Proctor, 1749.
Enoch Noyes, 1749, 1751 to 1754, 1756 to 1760, 1778.

Samuel Goodhue, 1750, '51, '53, '54, and 1756.
Benjamin Blanchard, 1750 and 1754.
Zachariah Lawrence, 1754 and 1757.
John Cumings, 1751.
Josiah Conant, 1751 and 1755.
Benjamin Abbot, 1752, '53, '54, '59, '60, and 1761.
John Boynton, 1758, '61, '62, '66, '68, '80, and 1781.
John Hale, 1761, '64, and 1766.
Abel Webster, 1761.
Stephen Webster, 1762, '63 and 1765.
Samuel Hobart, 1764 and 1766.
Stephen Jewett, 1766.
Jonas Flagg, 1766.

(17)

Caleb Farley, 1767.

Jonathan Philbrick, 1767 and 1768.

Noah Worcester, 1769, '75, '76, '77, '78 and '79.

Reuben Dow, 1769, '70, '78 and 1788.

William Tenney, 1769.

James Jewett, 1769.

William Brown, 1771, '72, '95, and 1796.

William Pool, 1771.

Ebenezer Kendall, 1771, '72.

William Cumings, 1771, '72, and 1782 to 1788.

William Nevins, 1771 and 1772.

Samuel Cumings, Jun., 1773 and 1774.

Jacob Jewett, Jun., 1773, '75, '76.

Nathaniel Ball, 1773.

Elnathan Blood, 1773.

Amos Eastman, 1772.

Leonard Whiting, 1774.

John Goss, 1774, '80, '85, '86, '87, '88.

Daniel Kendrick, 1775, '76 and 1777.

Oliver Lawrence, 1775, '76 and 1779.

Daniel Emerson, 1780, '81.

Jonathan Fox, 1780 and 1781.

William Read, 1780.

Solomon Wardwell, 1782 '83.

Ebenezer Jewett, 1782, '83, '84.

Jeremiah Pritchard, 1784.

Jeremiah Ames, 1785, '86.

Thaddeus Wheeler, 1787, '89, '90, 1806, '07 and 1808.

Nathan Colburn, 1789, '90, '91, '92, '94, and '97.

Jonas Willoughby, 1789.

Solomon Wheat, 1789 to 1798, 1800, '01, '09, '10, '11, '14, '15 and '16.

Jonathan Danforth, 1789.

William Tenney, Jun., 1791, '92, '93, '94, '98, '99 and 1800.

Ephraim Burge, 1795 and 1796.

Jesse Worcester, 1797, '99 and 1800.

Benjamin Wright, 1798, '99.

Benjamin Pool, 1801 to 1808, 1833, '34.

Stephen Dow, 1801.

Daniel Bailey, 1802, '03, '04, '05, '09, '10, '11, '12, and 1813.

Amos Eastman, Jun., 1806.

Samson Powers, 1807 and 1808.

Enos Hardy, 1809, '10, '12 and 1819.

David Hale, 1811.

Ambrose Gould, 1812 and 1813.

Jonathan Saunderson, 1813, '14, '15, '16 and '17.

Benjamin M. Farley, 1815, '16, '17, '18, '20, '21, '22, '25, '26, '27, '28, and '29.

Christopher P. Farley, 1814, '17, '18, and '19.

Nathaniel Jewett, 1818.

Jonathan T. Wheeler, 1819, '20 and '21.

William Ames, 1820, '21, '22, '23 and '24.

Ralph W. Jewett, 1822.

Thomas Cumings, 1823 and 1824.

Jonathan T. Wright, 1823 to 1829 and 1835.

William Emerson. 1825.

Ralph E. Tenney, 1826, '27, '28, '30, '31, 32.

Benjamin Farley, 1829.

Noah Hardy, 1830 and '31.

William Hale, 1830, '31, '32.

Joseph E. Smith, 1832, '33, '42, '46, '47, and 1854 to 1859.

William Merrill, 1833 and '34.

Moses Proctor, 1834 and '35.

Leonard Farley, 1835, '36, '39.

William P. Hale, 1836, '37, '39, '40, '41, '50, '51.

Almon D. Marshall, 1836, '37.

Phillips Wood, 1837, '38.

John N. Worcester, 1838.

Edward Emerson, 1838 and '52.

Ezekiel M. Bradley, 1839, '40.

James Wheeler, 1840, '41.

Samuel Little, 1841, '42.

John Farley, 1842, '43.

Reuben Baldwin, 1843, '44, '45, '61, '62.

John L. Pool, 1843 to '46.

Wm. P. Saunderson, 1847, '49.

Amos Hardy, 1844, '45, '46.

Thomas Brown, 1847.

John Coburn, 1848.

David J. Wright, 1848, '49.

Wm. N. Tenney, 1848, '49.

Luther Proctor, 1850, '51, '52, '53, '60, '70, '71.

Nehemiah Boutwell, 1850.

Noah Johnson, 1851.

Nathan M. Ames, 1852, '53, '54, '65.

Stillman Spaulding, 1853.

James W. Wheeler, 1854, '56, '57.

Dexter Greenwood, 1855.

Daniel Bailey, 1855.

Warner Read, 1856, '57.

Edward Hardy, 1858, '59.

Ebenezer T. Wheeler, 1858.

Joseph D. Parker, 1859, '60.

David M. Farley, 1860.

John Mooar, 1861.

Jefferson Farley, 1861, '62.

Enoch Farley, 1862, '63, '64.

Wm. A. Trow, 1863, '64.

Oliver P. Eastman, 1863, '64.

Charles A. Read, 1865, '66, '67.

Francis A. Wood, 1865.

Enoch J. Colburn, 1866.

John Woods, 1866 to '69.

Frederick A. Wood, 1867 to '69.

Charles H. Worcester, 1868.

George Moore, 1869, '70.

Daniel M. Smith, 1870, '71.

George A. Burge, 1871 to '73.

Silas M. Spaulding, 1872 to '75.

James E. Hills, 1872 to 1875.

Adkins J. Turner, 1874, '75.

Timothy E. Flagg, 1876 to '78.

John A. Coburn, 1876 to '78.

Charles W. Hardy, 1876 to '78.

CHAPTER XXIV.

REPRESENTATIVES AND DELEGATES TO THE GENERAL COURT, ETC., FROM 1739 TO 1878.— VOTES FOR STATE PRESIDENT FROM 1784 TO 1792.— VOTES FOR GOVERNOR FROM 1792 TO 1878.

DELEGATES.

1739. Abraham Taylor and Peter Powers, delegates of the settlers in West Dunstable to the Massachusetts General Court upon their petition for a *Charter*.

1744. James Stewart, delegate of the inhabitants of West Dunstable to the New Hampshire General Court, to present their petition for *Garrisons* and *Soldiers* for protection against the Indians.

1746. Stephen Ames, delegate of the settlers in the west part of Hollis to the New Hampshire General Court, upon their petition for a committee to locate the new *Meeting House*.

1747. Samuel Cumings, delegate of the town to the New Hampshire General Court, upon its petition for an act for *taxing the land* of non-residents for the support of the ministry, and also upon the petition of the town for *scouts* for *protection against the Indians*.

REPRESENTATIVES TO THE GENERAL COURT BEFORE THE REVOLUTION.

1762 to 1768, Dr. John Hale, Representative to the New Hampshire General Court, six years, from 1762 to 1768.

1768 to 1774. Col. Samuel Hobart, Representative to the New Hampshire General Court, six years, from 1768 to 1774.

REPRESENTATIVES AND DELEGATES TO THE GENERAL COURT, CONVENTIONS, ETC., DURING THE WAR OF THE REVOLUTION.

1774. Stephen Ames, Reuben Dow and Stephen Jewett, delegates to the First County Congress, at Amherst, Nov. 8, 1774.

1775, Stephen Jewett and Enoch Noyes, delegates to the Second County Congress, held April 5, 1775.

William Nevins, Jeremiah Ames and Samuel Farley, delegates to the Third County Congress at Amherst, held May 24, 1775.

Col. John Hale, delegate to the Provincial Convention at Exeter, January 25, 1775. to consult in respect to a Continental Congress.

Col. John Hale, Representative to the General Court at Portsmouth, February 23, 1775.

Col. Samuel Hobart, delegate to the Provincial Congress at Exeter, April, 1775.

Col. John Hale and Deacon Enoch Noyes, chosen delegates to the Provincial Congress to meet at Exeter, May 13, 1775. Col. Hale not being able to attend, Col. Hobart was elected in his place May 21.

1775. November 12, Stephen Ames chosen Representative to the General Court for one year.

1776, November 26, Stephen Ames again chosen Representative to the General Court for one year.

1777, November 25. Stephen Ames chosen Representative a third time to the General Court, for one year.

1778, December 12, Capt. Reuben Dow chosen Representative to the General Court.

April 6, Capt. Noah Worcester and Dea. Enoch Noyes chosen delegates to the convention at Concord to form a " new plan " of government.

1779, Col. John Hale, August 12. chosen delegate to the convention held at Concord, September 23, 1779, to "state prices."

December 2, Col. John Hale chosen Representative to the General Court.

1780, November 23. Col. Hale again chosen Representative to the General Court.

1781, November 21, Capt. Daniel Emerson chosen Representative to the General Court.

1782, October 28, Richard Cutts Shannon chosen Representative to the General Court.

1791, August 28, Capt. Daniel Emerson chosen delegate to the New Hampshire Constitutional Convention.

REPRESENTATIVES TO THE GENERAL COURT, FROM 1783 TO 1778.

Capt. Daniel Emerson, 1783 to 1791, '98, '99, 1801, '02, '03, '09, '10 and 11.
Jeremiah Ames, 1792 to '97 and 1800.
Benjamin Pool, 1804 to 1808.
Nathan Thayer, 1812, '19, '20 and '21.
Daniel Bailey, 1813.
Benjamin M. Farley, 1814 to 1818 and 1824 to 1829.
Ralph W. Jewett, 1822 and '23.
Jonathan T. Wright, 1830 and '31.
Ralph E. Tenney, 1832, '33, '34 and '45.
Moses Proctor, 1835, '36 and '37.
Joseph E. Smith, 1838 and '39.
Leonard Farley, 1840, '41 '42.
William Merrill, 1843 and '44.
William P. Hale, 1846, '47 and 48.

John L. Pool, 1849 and '50.
Almon D. Marshall, 1851 and 1852.
John Farley, 1853 and '54.
John S. Haywood, 1855.
Maj. James Wheeler, 1856 and '57.
John H. Cutter, 1858 and '59.
Minot Farley, 1860 and 1861,
Luther Proctor, 1862.
Reuben Baldwin, 1863 and '64.
John Coburn, 1865 and '66.
Timothy E. Flagg, 1867 and '68.
Charles B. Richardson, 1869 and '70.
Charles H. Worcester, 1871 and '72.
John Woods, 1873 and '74.
Charles A. Reed, 1875 and '76.
Franklin Worcester, 1877 and 1878.

Under the Constitution or "Plan" of Government in force in New Hampshire from 1784 to the adoption of the present Constitution, September 5, 1792, the chief magistrate of the State had the title of "*President*" instead of *Governor*, and was elected in the like manner as the Governor now is under the present Constitution.

VOTES FOR STATE PRESIDENT FROM 1784 TO 1792 INCLUSIVE.

1784, Meshech Weare,	87	1789, John Pickering,	35
John Langdon,	1	Josiah Bartlett,	18
1785, John Langdon,	153 all cast.	John Sullivan,	17
1786, John Langdon,	103 " "	Woodbury Langdon,	15
1787, John Langdon,	106	1790, John Pickering,	85 all cast.
John Sullivan,	14	1791, Josiah Bartlett,	105 " "
1788, John Langdon,	110	1792, Josiah Bartlett,	103 " "
John Sullivan,	8		

VOTES FOR GOVERNOR (EXCEPT SCATTERING) FROM 1793 TO 1878, INCLUSIVE.

1793, John Taylor Gilman,	75	1803, John Taylor Gilman,	116
Josiah Bartlett,	23	John Langdon,	42
1794, John Taylor Gilman,	78 all cast.	1804, John Langdon,	92
1795, John Taylor Gilman,	83 "	John Taylor Gilman,	79
1796, John Taylor Gilman,	105 "	1805, John Langdon,	127
1797, John Taylor Gilman,	113 "	John Taylor Gilman,	105
1798, John Taylor Gilman,	115 "	1806, John Langdon,	129
1799, John Taylor Gilman,	123 "	Timothy Farrar,	99
1800, John Taylor Gilman,	97	1807, John Langdon,	116
Timothy Walker,	15	Timothy Farrar,	44
1801, John Taylor Gilman,	87	1808, John Langdon,	122
John Langdon,	27	Timothy Farrar,	1
1802, John Taylor Gilman,	95	1809, Jeremiah Smith,	139
John Langdon,	53	John Langdon,	118

1810, Jeremiah Smith,	133	
John Langdon,	108	
1811, Jeremiah Smith,	138	
John Langdon,	108	
1812, John Taylor Gilman,	141	
William Plumer,	107	
1813, John Taylor Gilman,	157	
William Plumer,	105	
1814, John Taylor Gilman,	169	
William Plumer,	105	
1815, John Taylor Gilman,	167	
William Plumer,	111	
1816, James Sheafe,	134	
William Plumer,	107	
1817, James Sheafe,	146	
William Plumer,	102	
1818, William Hale,	142	
William Plumer,	97	
1819, William Hale,	127	
Samuel Bell,	67	
1820, Samuel Bell,	96	
1821, Samuel Bell,	84	
David L. Morrill,	17	
1822, Samuel Bell,	94	
1823, Levi Woodbury,	130	
Samuel Dinsmore,	65	
1824, Jeremiah Smith,	100	
David L. Morrill,	79	
Levi Woodbury,	50	
1825, David L. Morrill,	194	
1826, David L. Morrill,	176	
Benjamin Pierce,	34	
1827, Benjamin Pierce,	76	
David L. Morrill,	23	
1828, John Bell,	198	
Benjamin Pierce,	81	
1829, John Bell,	159	
Benjamin Pierce,	116	
1830 Timothy Upham,	155	
Matthew Harvey,	136	
1831, Samuel Dinsmore,	150	
Ichabod Bartlett,	146	
1832, Samuel Dinsmore,	141	
Ichabod Bartlett,	123	
1833, Samuel Dinsmore,	175	
Charles H. Atherton,	18	
1834, William Badger,	133	
1835, William Badger,	134	
Joseph Healey,	95	
1836, Isaac Hill,	114	
1837, Isaac Hill,	99	
1838, James Wilson, Jun.,	168	
Isaac Hill,	135	
1839, James Wilson, Jun.,	152	
John Page,	131	
1840, John Page,	152	
Enos Stevens.	135	
1841, John Page,	163	
Enos Stevens.	137	
1842, Henry Hubbard.	159	
Enos Stevens,	108	
1843, Henry Hubbard.	157	
Anthony Colby.	83	
1844, John H. Steele.	151	
Anthony Colby,	81	
Daniel Hoyt,	33	
1845, John H. Steele.	138	
Anthony Colby.	66	
Daniel Hoyt,	28	
1846, Jared W. Williams.	131	
Anthony Colby.	92	
Nathaniel S. Berry.	37	
1847, Jared W. Williams.	156	
Anthony Colby,	107	
Nathaniel S. Berry.	33	
1848, Jared W. Williams.	168	
Nathaniel S. Berry,	150	
1849, Samuel Dinsmore.	151	
Levi Chamberlain,	118	
Nathaniel S. Berry.	20	
1850, Samuel Dinsmore.	156	
Levi Chamberlain.	130	
1851, Samuel Dinsmore.	152	
Thomas E. Sawyer.	107	
John Atwood,	43	
1852, Noah Martin,	157	
Thomas E. Sawyer.	126	
John Atwood,	29	
1853, Noah Martin,	157	
James Bell,	90	
John H. White,	23	
1854, Nathaniel B. Baker.	135	
James Bell,	96	
Jared Perkins,	37	
1855, Ralph Metcalf,	155	
Nathaniel B. Baker.	142	
James Bell,	11	
1856, Ralph Metcalf,	141	
John S. Wells,	162	
Ichabod Goodwin.	10	
1857, William Haile.	157	
John S. Wells,	165	
1858, William Haile.	171	
Asa P. Cate,	168	
1859, Asa P. Cate,	197	
Ichabod Goodwin,	171	
1860, Ichabod Goodwin.	148	
Asa P. Cate,	184	
1861, Nathaniel S. Berry.	141	
George Stark,	179	
1862, Nathaniel S. Berry.	138	
George Stark,	150	
1863, Ira A. Eastman,	164	
Joseph A. Gilmore.	131	

1864, Joseph A. Gilmore,	149		1872, Ezekiel A. Straw,	167
Edward W. Harrington,	156		James A. Weston,	161
1865, Frederick Smyth,	174		1873, Ezekiel A. Straw,	155
Edward W. Harrington.	156		James A. Weston,	140
1866, Frederick Smyth,	175		1874, Luther McCutchins,	151
John G. Sinclair,	147		James A. Weston,	132
1867, Walter Harriman.	189		1875, Person C. Cheney,	160
John G. Sinclair,	144		Hiram R. Roberts,	143
1868, Walter Harriman.	179		1876, Person C. Cheney,	172
John G. Sinclair,	158		Daniel Marcy,	145
1869, Onslow Stearns.	168		1877, Benjamin F. Prescott,	168
John Bedell,	144		Daniel Marcy,	136
1870, Onslow Stearns,	154		1878, Benjamin F. Prescott,	162
John Bedell,	136		Frank A. McKean,	148
1871, James A. Weston.	152		1878, (Nov,) Natt Head,	157
James Pike,	153		Frank A. Mc Kean,	139 .

CHAPTER XXV.

AREA. — SOIL. — PRODUCTIONS. — STREAMS AND PONDS. — FOREST
TREES. — COOPERING. — POPULATION. — BIRTHS AND DEATHS. —
POSTMASTERS. — TAVERN-KEEPERS. — JUSTICES OF THE PEACE.
BURIAL GROUNDS. — PUBLIC ROADS. — MUTUAL INSURANCE COM-
PANY.

AREA, SOIL AND PRODUCTIONS.

Hollis is in latitude 42 degrees, 44 minutes north, lying on the
south line of the State, and bounded north by Amherst and Milford,
east by Nashua, south by Pepperell, Mass., and west by Brookline.
It is forty-two miles northwest of Boston, and thirty-six south of
Concord, and has an area of 19,620 acres or about 30 2-3 square
miles. Its surface is much diversified with hills and valleys, but
generally more level than that of most towns in the county, there
being no mountains, and Flint's and Birch hills, its highest eleva-
tions, not exceeding about three hundred feet in height above the
surrounding plains. The soil in different parts varies; a small
portion of it being light and sandy, some of it in the north and
west hard and stony, but an unusual proportion of it in other sec-
tions, consisting of a rich, somewhat pebbly or slaty loam, well
adapted to pasturage, and the raising of hay, corn, small grains,
fruits, potatoes and other vegetables. It has, for many years,
been noted for its abundance of good fruit, especially apples, the
produce of its orchards, according to the returns of the census, being
more in value than that of any other town in the county. That
very excellent and popular apple, known as the "Nod head," sometimes called in fruit books, "Jewett's fine red," originated in Hollis,
about one hundred years ago, in the orchard of Dea. Stephen Jewett,
hence the last name. The town in all parts of it is well watered,
scarcely any of its farms being without perennial brooks or springs.

The householders of the town, from its first settlement, have been

mostly farmers, with such numbers of traders, inn-keepers, black-
smiths, carpenters, shoemakers and other mechanics as were needed
for the wants of the other inhabitants.   In the past, as now, the
farms have been of moderate size, ordinarily varying from fifty
acres to one hundred and fifty.   The New Hampshire Gazetteer of
1874 says of it, "That Hollis is one of the wealthiest towns in the
county, and that everything pertaining to the farms and farmhouses
betokens an air of wealth and thrift."   A compliment well deserved
as to many of them, but subject to exceptions.

   In 1783, as shown by the census then taken, there were in the
town 1,392 inhabitants, 174 dwelling-houses and 144 barns.   Numbers of those dwelling-houses are still standing, many and it may
be most of them of two stories, and of generous size.   In 1800 the
population had increased to 1,557, about 500 more than at present ;
and there can be no doubt that the number of farms and farm-houses
in the town, and of acres tilled, was quite as large then as now,
and also that the quantities of grain, and the numbers of oxen and
sheep were larger.   Sixty years ago the hay raised in the town was
fed out on the farms where it grew.   Now a large portion of it,
with the other surplus agricultural and horticultural produce of the
farms. finds its way to the neighboring markets.   *Then* substantial
and thrifty farmers had each his flock of sheep and patch of flax,
and the farmer's wife and daughters were skilled in the use of the
distaff, spinning-wheel and hand-loom, for making the family clothing from the wool and flax furnished from the farm.   Now such
implements of female thrift and industry are known only as historical curiosities.   Large quantities of excellent butter and also of
cheese, of a much superior quality to that which the markets now
furnish from our modern cheese factories, were made in the family,
first for the family's use, but with a generous surplus for sale.
Now this industry to a very great extent has been abandoned, and
in place of it, the milk produced in the town, to the amount, as
reported, of 350,000 quarts yearly, is sent to market.   Formerly
large quantities of corn, rye and other grains raised in the town
were also annually sent to market abroad ; now, to a considerable
extent, Hollis itself has become a market for the purchase of the
like products.

   Still it may be that the aggregate wealth of the town, with its
diminished population and lessened productions in some articles, is
greater now than sixty years ago.   In 1872 its assessed value for

taxation was $803,435, true value estimated at $1,205,152,— money at interest and stocks, $41,692,—money in Savings Banks, $168,710 —these items being larger, with but one or two exceptions, than the like items in any other town in the county, mainly agricultural.

It is shown by the United States census of 1870 that there were then in the town 10,805 acres of improved land, 203 horses, 1,171 neat cattle, 123 sheep and 237 swine, of the aggregate value of $72,425. Also that there were raised that year in the town 1,090 bushels of rye, 7,769 of corn, 6,844 of oats and barley, 26 of wheat, 320 of peas and beans, 11,368 of potatoes, and 511 pounds of wool. That there were also made 25,510 pounds of butter, 4,505 of cheese, and 2,370 of sugar. The value of the products of the orchard the same year was $10,436; of animals sold or slaughtered $16,183; gallons of milk sold, 88,310; tons of hay raised, 2,575; the aggregate value of farm products (including betterments) being $133,321.

According to the same census there were then in the town seven saw-mills, with a capital of $13,000, employing thirteen hands, with a pay-roll of $3,000, and sawing 1,400,000 feet of lumber, of the value of $21,000; also one grain mill. The whole amount of capital then invested in manufactures of different kinds was $28,000, employing thirty-four men, with a pay-roll of $12,000, and with a product for the year of the value of $43,000. In 1820, as stated in Farmer's New Hampshire Gazetteer, there were in Hollis five grain mills, six saw mills, one clothing mill, one carding machine, one tannery, two taverns and four stores. In 1878 (as appears) but one grain mill, no clothing mill, carding machine, tannery or tavern, and but one store.

RIVERS, PONDS AND BROOKS.

As has been said already, the town, in all parts of it, is well watered. Its south-east part is crossed by the Nashua river, and its south-west by the Nissitissit. Besides several smaller ponds, there are in the town four large ones, viz., Flint's pond in the east, Rocky in the north-west, Pennichuck in the north-east, and Long pond north of the centre, varying in area from fifty to one hundred acres. Brooks of considerable size form the outlet of each of these ponds, viz., Flint's brook, flowing into the Nashua, of Flint's pond; Pennichuck, emptying into the Merrimack, of the pond of the same name, and also of Long pond, and Rocky Pond brook, flowing into the Nissitissit, of Rocky pond. Many other smaller brooks flow into these ponds and rivers, some of which, as well as the rivers and the other brooks, furnish eligible sites for saw and other mills.

FOREST TREES, LUMBER AND COOPERING.

Since its first settlement, the forests of Hollis have abounded in a large variety of the most valuable forest trees, including white and other species of Oak, Pine, Chestnut, Walnut, White and Sugar Maple and many other kinds. The great abundance and good quality of its oak and chestnut timber, early in the present century, led many of the citizens of the town to engage in the manufacture of barrels and other casks for the Boston market, very many of the farmers having a *cooper's shop* near the farm house. This business for many years was carried on to such extent that it was sometimes said by their neighbors of other towns, "that all the Hollis folks were coopers, except their minister, and that he hooped his own cider barrels!" The manufacture of casks of different kinds is still carried on to considerable extent, but by a less number of persons than formerly, pine lumber being now mainly used for this purpose. in place of oak and chestnut.

POPULATION.

No official provincial census of Hollis, taken prior to 1767, has come down to us. The best means now available for approximating to the number of its inhabitants before that year, are furnished by the names of the tax payers, on the annual tax lists. The number of names on the tax lists in West Dunstable, in 1740, was twenty-nine.—in 1745, seventy-seven ; on the Hollis tax list in 1746, the year of its incorporation, fifty-three. The number of names found on these lists from 1746 to 1783, was as below.

1746, 53.	1755, 107.	1765, 131.	1775, (at the beginning of the war,) 279.
1750, 77.	1760, 117.	1771, 231.	1783, (at the end of the war,) 293.

One Pine Hill was annexed in 1763. and the south part of Monson in 1770. which accounts in part for the increase of names on the tax lists in 1765 and 1771. The whole population in 1767 was 809, including one male and one female slave. In 1775, whole population 1,255, of which four were slaves. According to the several censuses taken in different years since, the population was as presented below.

1783, 1392.	1800, 1557.	1820, 1543.	1840, 1333.	1860, 1317.
1790, 1441.	1810, 1529.	1830, 1501.	1850, 1293.	1870, 1079.

The whole population of New Hampshire in 1767 was 52,880 ; in 1775, 82,200.

BIRTHS AND DEATHS FROM 1794 TO 1818.

It appears from the Hollis church records, as kept by Rev. Eli Smith from 1794 to 1818, that it was his custom to enter in those records, the yearly number of births in the town, with the name of the father of the several children born. It is shown by this record, that for the twenty-five years from 1794 to 1818, the number of births in the town annually was as follows:

1794, 41.	1799, 30.	1804, 45.	1809, 32.	1814, 27.
1795, 46.	1800, 29.	1805, 40.	1810, 33.	1815, 25.
1796, 50.	1801, 55.	1806, 37.	1811, 32.	1816, 23.
1797, 57.	1802, 55.	1807, 40.	1812, 27.	1817, 18.
1798, 41.	1803, 51.	1808, 37.	1813, 25.	1818, 11.

Making in all 907 *births* in the twenty-five years. It is shown in Farmer's New Hampshire Gazetteer, published in 1823, that the number of *deaths* in Hollis for the same twenty-five years was 557, being an excess of births over deaths of 340.

POSTOFFICE AND POSTMASTERS.

The first postmaster appointed in Hollis was Major Ambrose Gould in the year 1818. Prior to that year, there had been no postoffice in Hollis, and letters and other matters sent by mail, addressed to Hollis people, were sent to the postoffice at Amherst. The following list, copied mainly from the New Hampshire Annual Registers, exhibits the names of the Hollis postmasters from 1818 to 1879, with the years in which they severally held the office.

Ambrose Gould,	from 1818 to 1830.	William N. Tenney,	" 1856 " 1858.
Benoni G. Cutter,	" 1830 " 1835.	David W. Sawtell,	" 1858 " 1862.
Moses Proctor,	" 1835 " 1836.	Ebenezer T. Wheeler,	" 1862 " 1867.
William Butterfield,	" 1836 " 1840.	William A. Trow,	" 1867 " 1875.
Franklin Wright,	" 1840 " 1845.	Henry N. Smith,	" 1875 " 1877.
Edward Emerson,	" 1845 " 1854.	George A. Burge,	" 1877 " 1879.
Reuben Baldwin,	" 1854 " 1856.		

In the year 1794, with a population in the State of 141,885, the number of postoffices in the State was but five. In 1802—population of the State, 183,858. Number of postoffices, twenty-eight. In 1818—population, 214,460. Number of postoffices, sixty-eight. In 1860 — population 326,073. Number of postoffices three hundred and seventy-two. Since 1860 the number of postoffices in the State is supposed to have considerably increased.

TAVERN KEEPERS FROM 1792 TO 1821.

With but one or two exceptions, I have been unable to learn the names of the *Tavern Keepers* in Hollis previously to 1792. In that year the New Hampshire General Court passed an Act authorizing the Selectmen of towns to grant licenses to keep tavern to "suitable persons," having "accommodations" who might make application, with the right to sell by retail *rum, brandy, wine, gin* and other spirituous liquors—such license, unless renewed, to continue but one year. It appears from a record of their doings kept by the Selectmen, that between the years 1792 and 1821, licenses to keep tavern in Hollis were granted to the several persons named below, and to most of them in several different years. In 1793, to William W. Pool and to widow Sarah Eastman; 1794 to Capt. Leonard Whiting; 1795 to Leonard Whiting. Jun. ; 1796 to Capt. B. Woods Parker, and John Smith ; 1806 to Daniel Emerson, Esq., Benjamin Pool, Daniel Merrill and Ambrose Gould ; 1812 to Benjamin Farley, Peleg Lawrence and Nehemiah Woods; 1818 to Charles Farley, Luther Parker and Joseph Patch : 1821 to Miss Mary Woods, Dr. Noah Hardy. and Samuel G. Jewett.

JUSTICES OF THE PEACE.

The Justices of the Peace in Hollis, prior to the war of the Revolution, have been spoken of in a former chapter. During the war, (in the year 1777) Noah Worcester was appointed to this office and continued to hold it afterwards till his death in 1817. Also during the war, or soon after it, Dea. Daniel Emerson was commissioned a Justice of the Peace and Quorum, which office he continued to hold till his decease in 1820. From the close of the war till 1808, a period of near thirty years, with a population in Hollis averaging near 1500, Messrs. Emerson and Worcester were the only Justices of the Peace in the town. For the next twenty-two years, from 1808 to 1830. but seven other citizens of Hollis were appointed to that office, viz.. in 1808, Benjamin Pool. Amos Eastman and William Ames : in 1813, Benjamin Farley : in 1816, Benjamin M. Farley ; in 1822. Nathan Thayer. and in 1830. Christopher P. Farley.

In the early civil history of our State. this office of Justice of the Peace involved responsible and very important public duties and also implied capacity on the part of such magistrates to discharge those duties intelligently and acceptably. But in view of the numbers and frequency of such appointments for the last thirty years or more. with the supposed reasons for many of them, one may be permitted to doubt whether the office, in all cases, is now looked upon as involving such duties to the public, or competency for their performance. In many, not to say in a majority of instances, the commission of Justice with the title conferred by it, seem to be looked upon as a matter of cheap fashionable ornament, intended for personal gratification and distinction, rather than as of any important practical use to the public. Such commissions, as is understood, add *one dollar* each to the revenues of the State, and the New Hampshire Governors and Council have become exceedingly obliging and liberal in the issue of official compliments of this sort to their fellow citizens in all parts of the State—especially to such of them as were known to be of like politics with themselves. There is no evidence that the good people of Hollis have been more bountifully favored with these complimentary commissions than the citizens of most towns in other parts of the State, yet it appears from the statistics to be found in the New Hampshire Annual Registers, that since the year 1830, no less than *fifty* of the worthy citizens of Hollis have been so favored, (an average of more than one a year), and that no less than twelve of them held such commissions in 1878. Of this last number, *four*, as appears, were Justices of the Peace for the State at large, having jurisdiction in all parts of it—and *one*, of the quorum, all *ex-officio*, having the right to be addressed by the title of "Esquire,"—also to issue writs both in civil and criminal cases—hold courts—and try causes—and in all proper cases to join in wedlock, and read the riot act—the number of these officials in the town, each with all these powers and duties, being equal to one for each ninety of the whole of the present population.

BURIAL GROUNDS.

There are now in the town, in all, five of those sacred reposito_ ries of the remains of the dead, the most ancient of them near the meeting-house, older in fact than the town charter ; the next oldest on the road to Amherst, in the north part of the town, within the limits of the extinct town of Monson ; one at Pine Hill in the east part ; a fourth about a mile south of the meeting-house, on the road to Pepperell, laid out about fifty years ago ; the fifth near a mile east of the meeting-house, which has been in use about sixteen years. All of these grounds are of moderate extent, no one of them containing more than two or three acres. It may be that all of these sacred repositories are kept in as good condition, and the graves, monuments and gravestones in them as well preserved and cared for as in most like public burial grounds in this part of the State, which is saying but very little in their favor. Still no one of these cemeteries in Hollis is now fenced, cared for and ornamented in a way to do justice to the feelings and sentiments which the descendants of its early inhabitants entertain of the moral worth of the many excellent and patriotic men, and exemplary and virtuous women, whose mortal dust reposes in them. If the attention of the people of Hollis is once properly called to this subject, no doubt should be indulged that in this matter, better justice would soon be done alike to themselves and to the memories of an ancestry of which they feel justly proud.

THE PUBLIC ROADS.

The public roads in Hollis, now leading to Amherst, Pepperell, Nashua, Merrimack and Brookline, were originally laid out three rods wide, most of them substantially on the lines where they still run. Previous to or at the time the town was incorporated in 1746, it was divided into five road districts, and that number of Surveyors of Highways was chosen at the first town election. Between that date and the end of the war of the Revolution, the number of road districts was increased to twelve, with the like number of Surveyors of Highways. At that time it was the custom to determine by vote at the annual meeting, the amount of the yearly tax "for making and mending the highways" (all to be paid in labor on the roads) and also to fix by the like vote, the sum to be allowed for a day's work both of men and oxen. The amount of the road tax, as also the wages allowed for labor, varied in different years, according to the state of the currency. From 1746 to 1765, the money in circulation was mainly what was afterwards known, as the "Old Tenor" paper money. This currency fluctuated in value from year to year, and the amount of the road tax, and wages, varied with the value of the currency. For example, in 1752 the road tax was £400 O. T.—allowed for a day's work for a man 30 shillings—for a pair of oxen 10 shillings. In 1760, the road tax was £1000—allowed for a day's work for a man £5, do. for oxen, 30 shillings. In 1768, after the Old Tenor paper had gone out of use, and "lawful" or silver money had taken its place, the annual tax for "making and mending the highways," was £35—allowed for a man's days work, 2 shillings and 5 pence. or about 40 cents, in Federal money—for a pair of oxen 12 1-2 pence, or about 18 cents.

During the war of the Revolution, when the taxes were assessed and paid in the old Continental paper money, the amount of the road tax, and the wages for a day's work, fluctuated from year to year in like manner as from 1746 to 1765. The public roads in Hollis, as is evident from the town records, were an object of much attention, and appear to have been uniformly well cared for from its first settlement, and during the present century, at least, they have been kept well graded, smooth and safe, and now afford pleasant drives, whether for business or pleasure, in all parts of the town.

THE HOLLIS MUTUAL FIRE INSURANCE COMPANY.

Some more than thirty years since, many of the citizens of Hollis believing that they might secure themselves from losses by fire at less expense than through the joint stock, or other fire insurance companies then existing, resolved to try the experiment of a town organization for their mutual protection from such losses. With this purpose in view, a public meeting was held April 7, 1846, at the hall of Truman Hardy, of which Dr. Oliver Scripture was chairman, and resolutions (then reported upon the subject), adopted and signed by fifty-three of their number. At the same meeting, a committee of six of them, consisting of William P. Saunderson, Joseph E. Smith, Leonard Farley, David J. Wright, Joel Hardy and Edward Emerson, was appointed to draft a constitution and by-laws, and also to take the proper steps to obtain a charter for the association. These proceedings resulted in the procuring for the association an act of incorporation at the June session of the General Court of the same year. by the name of the " Hollis Mutual Fire Insurance Company."

The company was organized August 3, 1846, with the following officers then chosen, viz.: President, Ebenezer Fox; Secretary and Treasurer, Edward Emerson; Directors, Leonard Farley, David J. Wright, David W. Sawtell, William P. Saunderson, Joel Hardy and Ambrose H. Wood.

The losses of this company for the thirty-two years of its existence to December 1, 1878, have been $3,081.74; amount of property insured $216,202; amount of premium notes now held by the company, $13,174.95. The officers of the company the present year (1879) are, President, Edward Hardy; Secretary and Treasurer, Ebenezer T. Wheeler; Directors, Edward Hardy, Jefferson Farley, Silas M. Spaulding, Ira H. Proctor, Timothy E. Flagg, Joseph Gates and Isaac Vandyke.

CHAPTER XXVI.

THE PUBLIC SCHOOLS.—SCHOOL LAWS AND TAXES.—SCHOOL
DISTRICTS.—STATE LITERARY FUND.—SCHOOL COMMITTEES.—
TEACHERS, THEIR QUALIFICATIONS TO TEACH, AND EXAMINA-
TION.—THE HIGH SCHOOL.—MISS MARY S. FARLEY.—HOLLIS
LIBRARY.—LYCEUMS AND PUBLIC LECTURES.—GRADUATES OF
COLLEGES.

In a former chapter I have spoken of the school law in force in
New Hampshire prior to, and for some years after the Revolution,
and somewhat of the public schools in Hollis under that law.
It was shown by that law, that each New Hampshire town having
fifty families was required to support a public school for teaching
children in the town to " read and write," and towns having one
hundred families or more, to maintain a Grammar school in which
the " tongues" or dead languages should be taught. These schools,
as has been seen, were sustained by an annual tax, voted at the yearly
March meeting, and were wholly under the charge and control of
the Selectmen. This school law remained in force without material
change till 1789.

The following exhibit presents the yearly amount of the school
tax voted at the annual town meetings in Hollis, from 1750 for the
following thirty-nine years. From 1750 to 1767, this tax was assessed
in the " Old Tenor" paper currency ; from 1767 inclusive, to 1776
in " Lawful Money" or silver ; during the war, in Continental paper
money or New Hampshire bills of credit : after the war, again in
lawful money or silver.

SCHOOL TAXES FROM 1750 TO 1789.

In 1751, £50, O. T. In 1752, 1753 and 1754, no school tax ;
1755, £100, O. T. In 1756, no school tax. In 1757, £200, O. T. :
1758, £300. In 1759, 1760, 1761, 1762 and 1763, £400, yearly. In
(18)

1764 and 1765, £800, each year; 1766, £600. In 1767, £35, lawful money or silver. In 1768, 1769 and 1770, £30, lawful money each year. In 1771, 1772 and 1773, £30 lawful money, yearly. In 1774 and 1775, £50 lawful money, each year. In 1776 and 1777, £50 ; 1778, £80 ; 1779, £200 ; 1780, £4000, all in Continental paper money. In 1781 and 1782, £50 each year, lawful money, and in 1783, £65 ; 1784, £50, all in lawful money. In 1785, 1786, 1787, 1788 and 1789, £75, lawful money, yearly.

THE SCHOOL LAW OF 1789.

An Act of the General Court passed in 1789, for the maintaining and regulating the New Hampshire public schools, repealed the school laws till that time in force, and made it the duty of the Selectmen, yearly to assess upon the inhabitants of each town £45 upon each 20 shillings of the town's proportion of the public taxes, for the teaching the children and youth of the town " reading, writing and arithmetic." It may be seen that by the law of 1789 that " arithmetic " was required to be taught in the public schools, in addition to " reading and writing." " Shire towns and half shire towns," by the same law, were required to maintain a Grammar school, for teaching " Latin and Greek." This Act of 1789 is supposed to have continued in force till 1805.

SCHOOL TAXES ASSESSED UNDER THE SCHOOL LAW OF 1789.

In 1790, £90. In 1791, £85. In 1792, 1793, 1794 and 1795, £90 yearly. In 1796, $400. From 1797 to 1803, inclusive, $450 yearly. In 1804 and 1805, $500 each year. In 1806, 1807 and 1808, $700 yearly.

SCHOOL DISTRICTS.

I find no statute school law, in New Hampshire passed, previous to the year 1805, requiring or seeming in its terms to contemplate the division of towns, for school purposes into school districts. In that year an Act was passed by the General Court, conferring *authority* upon towns, at a legal meeting called for the purpose, to organize school districts (should the inhabitants so choose), and define their boundaries. This Act, a few years later, was so amended as to make this subdivision of the towns into school districts *imperative* upon the town authorities.

Still, as has been before stated, it appears from the town records that some years before the Revolution Hollis was, in fact, divided into local subdistricts for the support of its public schools. These divisions appear to have been wholly voluntary on the part of such of the inhabitants as were affected by them, and as we have seen were called in the records, school "classes," school "societies," or "squadrons," but I have not been able to find any record in respect to their location or the manner in which they were organized. How many of these school "classes" or "squadrons" there may have been at the time the law was passed requiring towns to be divided into school districts, with fixed boundaries, cannot now be ascertained with certainty, but probably there were not less than eight or ten of them. It is shown by the town records that as early as the year 1774 the town voted, "that the Grammar school should be kept the whole year in the four *southern squadrons*, the other squadrons to school out their money as usual, except their proportion of the Grammar school." As the part of the town north of the meeting-house was quite as large in extent as that south of it, and probably quite as populous, there can be but little doubt that before the Revolution there were as many as eight or nine of these school ' squadrons."

After the passage of the law requiring towns to be divided into school districts, with fixed boundaries, we find that as early as the year 1818 there were in Hollis as many as twelve of these districts, and this number, by subdivision, was afterwards increased to fourteen. These districts were designated numerically, from No. 1 to No. 14. and were also familiarly known and called by the following names : No. 1, *Middle*, or *Centre*; No. 2, *Pool*; No. 3, *Pine Hill*; No. 4. *Corner*; No. 5. *White*; No. 6, *Southwest* : No. 7, *Red*; No. 8. *North*; No. 9. *Beaver Brook*; No. 10. *Northwest*, or *Bailey*; No. 11. *Willoughby*; No. 12, *East*; No. 13, *Brick*; No. 14, *Hardy*.

This number of districts continued till 1874, when Nos. 1, 5, 9, 13 and 14. known as the "Middle." "White,"" Beaver Brook," "Brick" and "Hardy," were united and consolidated into a single district, since known as the *Union School District*. thus reducing the whole number of districts in the town to ten. Upon the union of these districts being consummated, the old school buildings in all of those five districts were abandoned for school purposes and sold, and the new Union district at once proceeded to purchase a beautiful and sightly school-house lot on Main street, near the centre of the town, and to erect upon it for the use of its schools, a spacious, commodious, well-finished and furnished two-story school-house, with convenient and suitable out-buildings and fixtures at the cost of about $10,000, in which its schools have since been kept. In the year 1876, the "Pine Hill" and "East" districts were united into one, thus reducing the whole number of school districts in the town to *nine*, the present number.

With perhaps the exception of the school in the first or middle district, I am aware of no special facts of general interest, which in any marked degree would distinguish the public schools in Hollis from the like country schools in most other New Hampshire country towns. For the first twenty-five years of the present century, all these schools, generally, if not uniformly, were kept by *male* teachers in winter, and by school mistresses in summer, and from well ascertained facts which have come to my knowledge, I am led to the belief that the average attendance of pupils upon them fifty years ago was more than double of what it has been for the last twenty-five years. During the period last named, many and it may be most of these schools have been taught by female teachers both winter and summer.

The following somewhat curious and unique facts pertaining to the "middle" school district in Hollis are below presented, substantially as published in the Nashua Weekly Telegraph about two years since. I am indebted for them to my brother, John N. Worcester, who has spent his life in Hollis, and has kept himself well posted in its local history, and who, with myself, in our boyhood, was a member of the school in that district. With but slight changes the article, as it appeared in the Telegraph, was as follows:

"HOLLIS SIXTY YEARS AGO."

"In the year 1812, there were in the First or Middle school district in Hollis forty-two dwelling-houses, at that time occupied by forty-eight families, including widowed mothers whose husbands, then deceased, had been residents of the district. Three of these forty-eight families had no children; the remaining forty-five of them had had, in all, three hundred and eighty-four, averaging eight and eight-fifteenths to each family. Nine of the forty-five families had six children each; seven of them, seven each; four of them eight each; eight of them nine each; four, ten each; two, eleven each; three, twelve each; two, thirteen each; one fourteen, one fifteen, and one sixteen.

"Of these three hundred and eighty-four children, three hundred and twenty-nine lived to adult age ; sixteen of the fathers of them were soldiers in the war of the Revolution : and twenty-two of the sons born in twelve of these families had the benefit of a collegiate education.

"Both the father and mother of one of these families of twelve children are still living, (March 1, 1879), the father in his 92d year, the mother in her 88th, they having been married November 21, 1811, sixty-seven years ago. The several mothers of the rest of the three hundred and eighty-four children are all deceased. The respective ages of forty-two of these forty-five mothers, at the time of their decease, are known.

"The sum of the ages of twelve of the forty-two was six hundred and twenty-three years, making the average age of each of the twelve, fifty-one and eleven-twelfths years. The aggregate ages of twelve others of the forty-two were nine hundred and twenty-two years, making their average age seventy-six and ten-twelfths years. The sum of the ages of the remaining eighteen of the forty-two was fifteen hundred and ninety years, making the average of the eighteen, eighty-eight and one-third years. The foregoing data have been gathered from sources believed to be correct and reliable, and they may interest others as well as myself who take pleasure in recalling memories of

"OLDEN TIMES."

SCHOOL TAXES FROM 1808 TO 1828.

In 1808 the law relating to the amount of taxes to be raised for the public schools was so amended as to require each town to raise for its schools a sum equal to $70 for every one dollar of the town's portion of the public taxes. In 1827 this per centage was increased to $90 for each one dollar of the town's share of other public taxes. The amount of school taxes, annually assessed in Hollis under these laws from 1808 to 1828, was as follows : In 1809, $500. In 1810, 1811 and 1812, $700 each year. In 1813, $500. From 1814 to 1828 inclusive, $700 each year.

THE STATE'S LITERARY SCHOOL FUND.

In the year 1828 a law was passed by the General Court in pursuance of which all the banks in the State were taxed at the rate of one-half of one per cent. on their capital stock for the support of the public schools. The tax so raised was known as the *State's Literary Fund*, and was required to be divided among the towns in the proportion of each town's share of the public State tax. The share of Hollis in this fund has greatly varied in the several years from 1828 to 1878, amounting in some years to about $250, and in others to less than $100.

Since the year 1828 the law in respect to the amount of taxes to be assessed for the public schools has been several times changed. Previously to 1842, the percentage to be assessed on the town's proportion of the State tax was increased from $90 to $100 upon each dollar of the town's proportion of that tax : and again in 1852 this percentage was increased to $135, and at last in 1867 to $250 upon each dollar of the town's share of other public taxes.

SCHOOL TAXES FROM 1828 TO 1878.

In addition to the Literary Fund, there were assessed for the public schools in Hollis in each of the years named below, the following sums annually, viz., 1829 and 1830, $700 ; 1831, $660 ; 1832 and 1833, $700 ; 1834, 1835 and 1836, $800 ; 1837, $600 ; 1838, 1839, 1840, $700 ; 1841, '42, '43. '44, '45, '46, '47, '48 and 1849, $800 ; 1850, $1000 ; 1851 and 1852, $800 ; 1853 and 1854, $1000 ; 1855, '56, '57, '58, '59, '60, '61, '62.'63. '64 and 1865, " the amount only 'required by law." 1866, $300, in addition to the amount required by law ; 1867. '68, '69, '70, '71 and 1872, the amount only required by law ; 1873, $1500 ; 1874, '75 and 1876, the amount required by law ; 1877, $400 in addition : 1878, $500 in addition.

COMMITTEES TO VISIT AND EXAMINE SCHOOLS.

By the law in force in New Hampshire for about twenty years prior to 1827, each town in the State, at its annual meeting, was required to appoint three or more suitable persons to visit and examine all the public schools in the town, at such times as might be convenient. The first appointment of committees for this purpose, to be found in the Hollis records, was in the year 1806. This first committee consisted of Rev. Eli Smith, Dea. Daniel Emerson, Ensign Samuel Willoughby, Capt. Leonard Whiting and Mr. Amos Eastman. The powers and duties of these committees appear to have been limited to the visiting and examination of the schools without any authority to examine teachers.

EXAMINATION AND QUALIFICATIONS OF TEACHERS.

It was enacted by the school law passed in 1808, that no person should be deemed qualified to teach a public school in this State "unless he or she should produce to the Selectmen or School Committee a certificate from some able and reputable Grammar School Master, Minister of the Gospel, or President, Professor, or Tutor in some college, that he or she is well qualified to teach such school ; and also a certificate of good moral character, from the Selectmen, or Minister of the Parish to which the candidate belonged. Provided, (however) that the qualifications of School Mistresses be required to extend no further than that they should be able to teach the *various sounds and powers of the letters of the English language, Reading, writing and English Grammar.*" It may be observed that this law did not require female teachers to be examined at all in respect to their qualifications to teach Arithmetic.

In the year 1827 this school law was so amended as to require female teachers as well as male to be qualified to teach the rudiments of Arithmetic and Geography ; and, again, some years afterwards, it was so changed as to require *all* teachers in the public schools to be qualified to teach the elements of History and such other suitable studies as the School Committee should judge proper for the school.

EXAMINING SCHOOL COMMITTEES FROM 1806 TO 1827.

Rev. Eli Smith, 1806, '08, '09, '10, '12, and from 1812 to 1827.
Dea. Daniel Emerson, 1806 and 1811.
Ensign Samuel Willoughby, 1806 and 1810.
Capt. Leonard Whiting, 1806.
Amos Eastman, 1806 and 1807.
Noah Worcester, 1807.
William Brown, 1807, '08, '09, '12, '13, and 1816.
Dea. Stephen Jewett, 1808.
Dea. Ephraim Burge, 1809.
Benjamin M. Farley, 1809, '12, '13, '14, '15, '16, and from 1819 to 1826.
Jesse Worcester, 1811, '16, '20, and 1826.

Ambrose Gould, 1811, '15, and 1820.
John French, 1812, '13, '14, and 1815.
Abijah Gould, 1815, '17, '18, '19 and 1821.
Dr. Noah Hardy, from 1816 to 1827.
Nathan Thayer, 1817, '18, '21, '22, '25 and 1827.
Dr. Peter Manning, 1817
Capt. Jonathan B. Eastman, 1817, '18, '19, '21, '22, and 1824.
Dr. Joseph F. Eastman, 1823 and 1824.
William Emerson, 1823 and 1825.
Capt. Jonathan T. Wright, 1825 and 1827.
William Ames, 1826 and 1827
Ralph E. Tenney, 1827.

SUPERINTENDING SCHOOL COMMITTEES.

In the year 1827, this school law was amended in respect to school committees, making it the duty of towns at their annual meetings to elect or appoint a Superintending School Committee of not less than three in number, whose duty it should be to examine all candidates for teaching in the public schools of the town, and also to visit and inspect each of the schools at least twice in each year. Under this law, the Superintending Committee in Hollis varied in number in different years, from three to seven.

Some years afterwards the law was so altered as to permit the town to elect by ballot for this committee so many persons only as the voters at the annual meeting might think fit. In pursuance of this law, so amended, the town at several of its annual meetings elected but one person as Superintending Committee, the person so elected being charged with the whole duty of examining candidates for teaching, and visiting and inspecting the schools.

MEMBERS OF THE SUPERINTENDING SCHOOL COMMITTEES FROM 1827 TO 1878.

Rev. Eli Smith, 1828, '29 and 1830.

Dr. Noah Hardy, 1828, '29, '31, '32, '37, '38, '39, '40, '43 and 1849.

William Ames, 1828, '33, '34, '35, '36, '37, and 1840.

Nathan Thayer, 1828, '29 and 1830.

Joseph Greeley, 1829.

Rev. Leonard Jewett, 1829, '45 and 1846.

Benjamin M. Farley, 1830, '31, '32, '33, '35, '37, '38, '39, '41, '42 and 1843.

Edward Emerson, 1830, '31, '32, '36, '43, '47, and 1854.

John N. Worcester, 1830, '31, '32 and 1847.

Rev. David Perry, from 1831 to 1842, and 1871.

Dr. Oliver Scripture, 1833.

Moses Proctor, 1833 and 1838.

Joseph E. Smith, 1834, '35, '36, '43, '44, '51, and 1852.

Taylor G. Worcester, 1834, '35, '36, '38, '44, '48, '60 and 1871.

Rev. Phineas Richardson, from 1839 to 1844.

Benjamin F. Farley, 1845 and 1846.

Joseph F. Eastman, Jun., 1841 and 1842.

William P. Hale, 1843 and 1844.

Rev. James Aiken, 1844.

William P. Saunderson, 1845 and 1846.

Nathan Willoughby, 1847 and 1848.

Dr. John L. Colby, 1848.

Cyrus Burge, 1849.

James Blood, 1849 and 1850.

Rev. Daniel P. Deming, 1850.

Dr. Lockhart B. Farrar, 1850.

Timothy E. Flagg, 1851 and 1852.

Andrew Willoby, 1852, '53, and 1854.

Nathan M. Ames, 1852 and 1858.

Dr. Henry Boynton, 1855, '56 and 1857.

Rev. Pliny B. Day, from 1854 to 1866.

Dr. Henry W. Willoughby, 1855, '56, '57, '58, '59, '62, '67, '68, '69 and 1870.

Dr. George P. Greeley, 1860.

Dea. James D. Hills, 1861.

David Worcester, 1867.

Rev. James Laird, 1871 and 1872.

Levi Abbot, 1873, '74, '75 and 1878.

Rev. Hiram L. Kelsey, 1876 and 1877.

STATISTICS OF THE HOLLIS SCHOOLS IN 1873.

According to the report of the State Superintendent of the New Hampshire Public Schools for 1873, the year previous to the formation of the Union School District in Hollis, there were then in the town fourteen school districts, two hundred and sixty-two children and youth of school age, with an average attendance of two hundred and four—value of school-houses, $3,000, or about $215 average value—amount of money for the year raised for schools, $2,245.36, being $8.56 per scholar, for those of school age.

HOLLIS HIGH SCHOOL.
ESTABLISHED 1877

THE HOLLIS HIGH SCHOOL.

In several different years prior to 1876, earnest efforts had been made by many of the friends of popular education in Hollis to establish a *High School*, as authorized by the law of the State, of which the youth in all parts of the town might enjoy the benefit, and a number of town meetings had been held specially to consider the question. But previously to the year above named all such efforts had wholly failed.

This worthy and beneficent object has however been at last happily accomplished by means of the generous bequest of Miss Mary S. Farley, the only daughter and heir-at-law of Capt. Christopher P. Farley, a grandson of Lieut. Benjamin Farley, one of the first settlers of the town. Miss Farley deceased July 27, 1875, leaving by her will a legacy to the town of near $10,000, the annual interest of which was to be used for the support of a High School for the benefit of the whole town, on condition that the town would accept it by providing within two years from her decease a suitable site and buildings for such a school near the centre of the town, and also for the future would take proper care of her family burial lot in the south burial ground. If the town should not accept the legacy with the conditions annexed to it, then it was to be paid to the Trustees of the New Hampshire Orphans' Home at Franklin.

On the 14th of May, 1876, a special town meeting was held to consider this bequest, at which the town voted to accept it, and at the same meeting voted to provide a school-house in compliance with the conditions of the will. At a subsequent town meeting, on the second day of September following, it was voted to organize the town into a High School District in accordance with the State law.

Afterwards, at a meeting of the *Union School District* in the November following, that district voted for a nominal consideration, to convey to the *High School District* one equal undivided half of its school lot, and the whole of the second story of its school building for the use and accommodation of the High School, with all such appertaining rights and privileges as would be proper and needful for its occupation for school purposes. This vote on the 7th of January, 1877, was consummated and made effectual by a deed of the premises made by the Union District to the High School District, to the acceptance of the latter. A high school for the benefit of the youth of the whole town has thus been fortunately provided and made permanent, and now for near two years has been in successful operation.

MISS MARY SHERWIN FARLEY,

(By Gen. T. S., her cousin.)

daughter of Capt. Christopher P. and Mary (Sherwin) Farley, was born in Hollis, Nov. 2, 1813.   Her father was a grandson of Lt. Benjamin Farley, one of the earliest settlers in Hollis, and followed the business of tanning, by which he acquired an ample estate, and was justly esteemed for his uprightness and sound judgment. January 18, 1813, he married Mary Sherwin, daughter of David Sherwin, of New Ipswich, who died about two weeks after the birth of her daughter.   Left so soon a widower, the affections and hopes of the father, perhaps, turned the more strongly to his child, whose life in her infancy seemed to hang upon the most slender thread.   In her early years she was most tenderly cared for by a sister of her father.   Her health, exceedingly frail and delicate from her birth, was never vigorous.   In her girlhood, she could rarely join in the pastimes of those of her own age, nor was she ever able to attend regularly upon the school terms, though for one year, when of the age of fifteen, she was placed in a boarding school.

While her father lived, the two were almost constant companions. She accompanied him in his walks and rides, became familiar with his interests and business—in this way gaining practical knowledge and habits of thought, which helped to form her character, and were of great value to her.   After the death of her father, July 22, 1848, (a loss to her that few can realize), she continued to live at the paternal homestead till her death, July 27, 1875.

Occupied with the care of her pleasant farm, busying herself in the culture of flowers, making occasional journeys to visit friends, and oftener in the hope of gaining health and strength, she passed a life, though not eventful, yet marked through its whole course by acts of kindness and charity.   In matters of business she was methodical and exact, manifesting more than usual insight and good judgment in the management of her affairs.   But above all it was her aim to be just to others.   She was in the highest degree conscientious, and would at any time sacrifice her own interest rather than that another should suffer wrong.

Her memory of persons and events was uncommonly quick and retentive.   Matters of history gained from her reading were rarely forgotten.   Her recollection of dates and places was somewhat phenomenal, and she often surprised her friends by recounting events in their own lives, which had quite escaped the memory of all but herself.

Mary S. Farley

Firm and sincere in her friendships, she attracted to herself all those of her acquaintance who knew her sufficiently well to appreciate the kindliness, generosity and purity of her character. Nowhere could a more cordial hospitality be found than in her pleasant old fashioned homestead, standing amidst fertile, well cultivated acres, and shaded by the huge buttonwood in the door yard.

She had a strong affection for children and young people—enjoyed having them about her—entered into their sports and plans—encouraged their efforts for improvement and often gave them substantial aid. She was at all times deeply interested in the prosperity and welfare of her native town, and especially in its public schools, and besides her other benefactions for them, during life, bequeathing by her last will, as we have seen, a fund of near $10,000 for the endowment and permanent support of a High school. In addition to other charitable benefactions bequeathed by her will, was a legacy of $5,000 to the funds of the New Hampshire Orphan Asylum at Franklin.

THE HOLLIS SOCIAL LIBRARY.

The Hollis Social Library, so called, was incorporated by an act of the General Court, June 11, 1799, and is believed to be one of the oldest associations of the kind in the State. The corporators named in the charter were Rev. Daniel Emerson, then in his 84th year, Rev. Eli Smith, Noah Worcester and Daniel Emerson, Jun., who, with their associates, were made a body corporate, with perpetual succession, with power to establish and maintain a library, and to make all needful rules and by-laws in respect to it. The original capital was $1,000—since increased by an amendment of the charter to $50,000. The two last-named corporators were authorized to call the first meeting, and under this charter a small library of from one hundred to three hundred well chosen books was soon collected, which number has since been increased to between nineteen hundred and two thousand bound volumes, besides pamphlets.

The officers of the Association consist of a President, three Directors, Secretary, Treasurer and Librarian, chosen annually. Any inhabitant of the town could become a member of the Association, and entitled to the privileges of the library, upon paying an initiation fee of fifty cents, being afterwards chargeable with an annual tax of twenty-five cents, afterwards increased to fifty cents. The

number of names now on the list of membership is one hundred and
sixty-seven. This library for many years after its establishment was
kept at the house of the librarian, elected from time to time, but
since the year 1851 it has been kept in a room, provided and furnished for it by its directors, in the Congregational meeting-house.
The books furnished to the people of Hollis from this library have
been of great use to them, from the time of its foundation, in the
promotion of useful knowledge and in cultivating and supplying a
taste for reading among the inhabitants generally, the extent of
which may in some measure be seen from the fact stated in one of
the last annual reports, that in the preceding year there had been
given out to be read between twenty-four hundred and twenty-five
hundred volumes, the same book, however, in many instances,
having been given out more than once.

THE HOLLIS LYCEUM AND PUBLIC LECTURES.

During most of the winters since 1851, either lyceums or courses
of public lectures have been maintained in Hollis for the intellectual entertainment and improvement of its citizens. The constitution of the lyceum has commonly provided for a monthly election
of its officers, and also for its exercises, including select readings
and recitations, vocal and instrumental music, a discussion of some
topic or question of general interest to its members, and a paper,
known as the "Lyceum Reporter," edited by some of its lady members, appointed for that purpose. The exercises of this association
have usually been public. Separate committees have ordinarily
provided for the selection of the subjects for these exercises, and the
assignment and acceptance of their various parts, and when these
duties of the committees have been faithfully performed, the public
interest in them has been so general as to insure a large attendance
at the meetings.

The public lectures have commonly been provided for by voluntary subscriptions of the citizens, and have been free to all who
wished to attend them. They have embraced a great variety of
subjects of interest, and some of the lecturers engaged have been
persons of distinction in this and other States. Also a club for the
rehearsal and acting of dramas has occasionally existed, and public
entertainments given by it, highly creditable to the performers, and
very acceptable to the audiences. This club at present numbers
about fifty members.

GRADUATES OF COLLEGE FROM HOLLIS, WITH THE YEARS OF
THEIR GRADUATION.

Graduates of Harvard College.

Peter Powers,	1754	Joseph E. Smith,	1804
Josiah Goodhue,	1755	Benjamin Burge,	1805
Henry Cumings,	1760	Samuel E. Smith,	1808
Joseph Emerson,	1774	John Proctor,	1813
Samuel Emerson,	1785	George F. Farley,	1816
Josiah Burge,	1787	William P. Kendrick,	1816
Daniel Emerson, Jun.,	1794	Taylor G. Worcester,	1823
Joseph Emerson, 2d,	1798	Jonathan Saunderson,	1828
Manasseh Smith,	1806	Samuel T. Worcester,	1830
Jacob A. Cumings,	1801	Frederick A. Worcester,	1831
Benjamin M. Farley.	1804	Francis J. Worcester,	1870

Graduates of Yale College.

Ralph Emerson,	1811	Joseph Emerson,	1830
Joseph E. Worcester,	1811	Benjamin F. Farley.	1832
Henry A. Worcester.	1828	Ralph H. Cutter,	1858

Graduates of Dartmouth College.

Samuel Worcester,	1795	Noah Hardy,	1812
Abel Farley,	1798	Luke Eastman,	1812
Mighill Blood,	1800	David P. Smith,	1823
Caleb J. Tenney,	1801	William P. Eastman.	1842
David Jewett,	1801	Charles Cummings.	1842
Jonathan B. Eastman,	1803	Charles H. Mooar,	1848
Nehemiah Hardy, Jun.,	1803	Edward F. Johnson,	1864
Stephen Farley, Jun.,	1804	Joseph B. Parker,	1869
William Tenney, Jun.,	1808	John H. Hardy,	1870
Eli Smith, Jun.,	1809	Franklin Worcester,	1870
Leonard Jewett.	1810	Charles L. Day,	1877
Grant Powers.	1810	George W. Saunderson,	1877

Graduates of Middlebury College.

Fifield Holt,	1810	Solomon Hardy,	1824

Graduates of Amherst College.

Thomas A. Farley,	1838	Amos F. Shattuck,	1859

Graduates of Brown University.

Daniel Kendrick.	1810	Luther Smith,	1824

Graduates of Maryville College, Tenn.

Phillips Wood,	1831	Leonard Wood,	1832

Greenville, Tenn.   Union. N. Y.

Eli N. Sawtell,	1823	Benjamin F. Emerson,	1830

Of the sixty-two college graduates named above thirty-three
studied Theology, four Medicine, twenty-three became Lawyers or
are now studying law, one an Author, one an Author and Bookseller, and one an army officer.

CHAPTER XXVII.

BIOGRAPHICAL SKETCHES OF HOLLIS GRADUATES OF COLLEGES.—
GRADUATES OF HARVARD AND YALE.

REV. PETER POWERS,

the first Hollis college graduate, was the son of Capt. Peter Powers, the first settler of Hollis, and Anna (Keyes) Powers, was born in old Dunstable, November 29, 1728, and came with his father to that part of Dunstable. afterwards known as Hollis, in 1730. He graduated at Harvard College in 1754. Rev. Grant Powers, his nephew, in his " History of the Coos Country," says of his uncle, " that in his early youth, he had a very strong desire for a college education, a wish in respect to which he had often spoken to his parents. But his parents had other plans for their son. and, regarding his project for such an education as a vision of youth that would soon pass away, gave him no encouragement. Young Peter, afterwards, for a considerable time remained silent in respect to the matter, till at length. one evening, he was found to be missing at the customary nine o'clock family prayers, and remained absent the whole night. Early the next morning, the father upon going out of the door saw his son just coming out of the woods. He, however, put off calling upon Peter for an explanation of his absence till the close of his family morning prayers, when in presence of the whole family the Captain asked his son, " *Where he had passed the night.*" " *In the woods,*" answered the youth. " *And what were you doing in the woods?*" asked the father. " *I was praying,*" said the son. " *And for what were you praying?*" continued the Captain. " *That I might go to college,*" replied Peter. " *And for what do you wish to go to college?*" added the father. " *That I may prepare myself to preach the Gospel,*" rejoined the youth.

Capt. Powers was so moved by these answers, that for the time he was unable to say more, but upon Peter's leaving the room he said to his wife, " Anna, I don't see but that we must give up the point, and let Peter go to college." The result was a collegiate education, and a life of eminent usefulness.

Mr. Powers graduated at the age of twenty-two, and in June 1755, the year after he left college, he received his first call to settle in the ministry at New Ipswich. After some negotiation this call was finally declined, and the next year he was settled as pastor of the church in the parish of Newent, Connecticut, then a part of the town of Norwich. He remained at Newent till 1764, when he was dismissed, and early the next year was settled as pastor of a church and society in the towns of Haverhill, New Hampshire, and Newbury, Vermont. His connection with this society continued till 1784, when he was dismissed, and the year after was settled as pastor of the church in Deer Isle, Maine, where he died, May 13, 1800, æt. 71. In a biographical sketch of Mr. Powers, in Volume II. of the New Hampshire Collections, it is said of him, "that he was a faithful and discriminating preacher, and possessed of superior talents."

Publications of Mr. Powers.—An *Installation* sermon preached by himself with the following title, " A sermon preached at Holles, February 27, 1765, at the Installation of Rev. Peter Powers, A. M., for the towns of Newbury and Haverhill, at a place called *Coos*, in the Province of New Hampshire, by *myself*, published at the desire of many that heard it, to whom it is Humbly dedicated." Also a sermon preached at the funeral of D. Bailey, 1772.*

REV. JOSIAH GOODHUE,

the second Hollis college graduate, was the son of Dea. Samuel and Abigail (Bartlett) Goodhue, born 1735. His father was among the early settlers of Hollis, but his family register is not found in the town records. Allen in his "American Biographies" and Farmer in his " New Hampshire Gazetteer" speak of the son as having been born in Hollis. He graduated in 1755, at the age of 20, and was first settled as pastor of the Congregational church in Dunstable, Mass., June 8, 1757, at the age of twenty-two. Dismissed by a mutual council, September 28, 1774, and recommended by it " as a person of conspicuous seriousness and piety."† He afterwards settled as pastor of a church in Poultney, Vt., where he died November, 1797, æt. 62.

---

*See Allen's Am. Biographies, p. 625, and History of the Coos Country, by Rev. G. Powers.
†Allen's Am. Biographies, p. 386.

REV. HENRY CUMMINGS,* D. D.,

was the son of Ensign Jerahmael and Hannah (Farwell) Cummings, and was born in Hollis, September 16, 1739. His father, Ensign Cumings, was from Groton, (*q. v.* p. 131.) and died October 25, 1747, leaving his widow with five young children, of whom the oldest was ten years of age, and the youngest, an infant. He prepared for college in Hollis, with Rev. Mr. Emerson, and graduated in 1760 at the age of twenty-one.

In Rev. Dr. Sprague's "Biographies of the American Pulpit" it is said that " the mother of Dr. Cummings was a woman of distinguished piety—of great strength of character and greatly devoted to her children. That some years after the death of her husband she received proposals for a second marriage which she accepted. But shortly before the contemplated wedding, the prospective bridegroom intimated to her, that he did not expect her children would come with her to the new home, and asked her how she expected to dispose of them? To this question the mother promptly replied: ' If you do not take my children you cannot take me. I have a mother's duty to perform for them and by God's help I shall perform it,' and immediately gave her suitor leave to retire."

Young Cummings early gave such indications of so vigorous a mind as to attract the attention of his pastor, Rev. Mr. Emerson, and to justify unusual efforts to give him a collegiate education, and so as to induce Mr. Emerson personally to take charge of his preparatory studies. He entered college in 1756 and maintained a high rank both for scholarship and good conduct. As pleasant evidence of the esteem in which he was held at home, it is shown by the Hollis church records that in the last year of his course, the Hollis church contributed £70 O. T. towards his college expenses.

He left college at the age of twenty-one, and but a few months after was invited to preach in Boston, and elsewhere, and soon became one of the most popular preachers of the time. In the fall of 1762, at the age of twenty-two, he had a call to settle as pastor of the church in Billerica, Mass., which he accepted, and was ordained at Billerica, January 26, 1763. The sermon at his ordination was preached by his old friend and pastor, Rev. Mr. Emerson, from

---

*This name which very often occurs in the old Hollis records is in them uniformly spelt with but a single " M," " Cumings." The same name, for the last fifty years or more, has been more commonly spelt " Cummings," doubling the " M."

Heb. xiii : 17. He was the only minister of Billerica from 1762 to 1814, fifty-two years, when Rev. Nathaniel Whitman was settled as his colleague.

After his ordination, Dr. Cummings devoted himself to his studies with great assiduity, became an excellent classical scholar, and so well versed in the Hebrew, as not only to read, but also to write it with ease. During the Revolution, he was an earnest friend of Independence, and *in*, as well as *out* of the pulpit, labored to diffuse the spirit of patriotism and to give strength to the new government.

He is described as having been a fine specimen of physical, moral and mental nobility. His countenance evinced a high order of intelligence and dignity. His excellent social qualities rendered him a most agreeable companion, and he did not withhold his sympathy and kindness even from the unworthy. His public discourses were characterized with great boldness of style and delivered with a voice of much power. Among his published writings are the following : " Thanksgiving Sermons", 1766, 1775, 1785 and 1799. "Public Fast," 1801. Sermon at the "Anniversary of the Battle of Lexington," and also "General Election" sermon, 1783. Sermons on "Natural Religion," 1795, also in 1796. At the ordination of Rev. Caleb Bradley, 1800. " Eulogy on Washington," 1801. "Charity" sermon at Roxbury, 1802. "Half Century" sermon at Billerica, 1813. Received the honorary degree of D. D. from Harvard College, 1800. Died at Baltimore, Maryland, September 5, 1823, æt. 84 nearly.*

REV. JOSEPH EMERSON,

son of Rev. Daniel and Hannah Emerson, born in Hollis, September 28, 1759, and graduated at Harvard college in 1776, at the age of seventeen. He studied for the ministry with his father in Hollis, and died in Hollis, July 27, 1781, in his twenty-second year. For sometime previous to his death, he had preached as a candidate and had accepted a call to settle in the ministry as pastor of the Congregational church and society in Temple, New Hampshire, but was taken sick and died but a short time before his expected ordination. It is said that the church at Temple, in manifestation of their esteem and affection for him, attended his funeral at Hollis in a

---

*Sprague's American Unitarian Pulpit, pp. 55, 56. Allen's American Biography, p. 274.
(19)

body. The following tribute to his memory, expressive of his character, is inscribed on his gravestone in Hollis.

"JOSEPH EMERSON,
Son of Rev. Daniel and Mrs. Hannah Emerson,
Born September 28, 1759.
Rec'd the degree of A. B. in 1776, and the degree of A. M.
at Harvard University in 1779.
Possessed of good mental powers and disposition,
Sedate, Contemplative and Studious,
A dutiful son, an affectionate brother, a respectable scholar,
An agreeable companion, a faithful and benevolent man,
An Exemplary Christian, a solid and devotional preacher,
Died July 27, 1781, in the 22d year of his age,
Much lamented, not only by the family but by a numerous
Circle of friends and acquaintances, particularly the
Church and Congregation at Temple, who had given
him an invitation to settle with them in the work of
the Gospel Ministry. His mortal part here deposited
Rests until it rises in glory and immortality."

DR. SAMUEL EMERSON

was the 6th son of Dea. Daniel and Hannah Emerson, born in Hollis, September 6, 1764. In 1779, when in his fifteenth year, he enlisted as a fifer in a company commanded by his brother, Capt. Daniel Emerson, in the regiment of Col. Hercules Mooney. After the war he fitted for college with his father, and graduated at Harvard college in 1785. He subsequently studied medicine, and settled as a physician in Kennebunkport, Maine. Dr. Emerson was highly educated, an excellent English and classical scholar, and is said to have retained his taste and interest in classical literature till his death. He was also very fond of music, and played well on the violin, flute, clarionet and organ. He had a laborious and extensive practice, and was much distinguished and very popular in his profession, but it is said of him that he could never be persuaded to send a bill for his services to a poor man. Died at Kennebunkport, August 7, 1851, in his eighty-seventh year. George B. Emerson, A. A. S., a graduate of Harvard college in 1817, an eminent Boston teacher, naturalist, and author, and for several years President of the Boston Society of Natural History, was a son of Dr. Emerson.

REV. JOSIAH BURGE,

son of Ephraim and Anna (Abbot) Burge, born in Hollis, April 15, 1766. Graduated at Harvard college, 1787, at the age of twenty-one. Studied for the ministry with the Rev. Seth Payson, D. D., at

Rindge, N. H., and was licensed to preach; but after having preached about nine months, his health failed, and he died at Hollis, March 24, 1790, in his 24th year.

REV. DANIEL EMERSON, JUN.,

son of Dea. Daniel and Ama (Fletcher) Emerson, born in Hollis, July 15, 1771. Graduated at Harvard college, 1794. For several years after leaving college, he engaged in business as a merchant, first in Charlestown, Mass., and afterwards in Hollis, and was Town Clerk and First Selectman in Hollis in the years 1802, 1803, 1804 and 1805. He afterwards studied for the ministry with his brother, Rev. Joseph Emerson, at Beverly, Mass., and began to preach in 1806. He was ordained as pastor of the Congregational church at Dartmouth, Mass., October 14, 1807, and died at Dartmouth, November 16, 1808, æt. 36. Two of his sons, Benjamin F. and Joseph, were college graduates. (q. v.)

REV. JOSEPH. EMERSON, 2D.,

son of Dea. Daniel and Ama (Fletcher) Emerson, born in Hollis, October 13, 1777, and graduated at Harvard college, 1798. After graduating, he was for a time college tutor at Harvard. He studied Theology with Rev. Nathaniel Emmons, D. D., of Franklin, Mass. Was ordained as pastor of the Congregational church at Beverly, Mass., September 21, 1803; resigned his pastorate at Beverly, September 21, 1816; removed to Byfield, Mass., in 1818, and the same year established there a seminary for the higher education of young ladies. In 1821 he removed to Saugus, Mass., and established his seminary at that place, and remained in Saugus till 1824, preaching in the meantime on the Sabbath. In the latter part of the year last named, in compliance with an invitation of the people of Wethersfield, Conn., through his townsman and friend, Rev. C. J. Tenney, D. D., his seminary was removed to Wethersfield, which he continued to conduct with great acceptance at that place, till about a year before his death. He was reputed an excellent and accomplished scholar, and a faithful and popular teacher. His seminary had a wide reputation, and is believed to have been the first institution of the kind in New England. Mr. Emerson died at Wethersfield, May 13, 1833, æt. 55. An interesting biography of him by his brother, Prof. Ralph Emerson, was published in 1834.

Mr. Emerson was the author of several publications, among

which was the "Evangelical Primer," 1810: "Writings of Miss
Fanny Woodbury, with Notes," 1814 ; "Lectures on the Millen-
ium," 1819 ; "The Union Catechism," 1821 ; "Poetic Reader," 1831.

MANASSEH SMITH, JUN., ATTORNEY AT LAW,

the oldest son of Manasseh and Hannah (Emerson) Smith, was
born in Hollis, August 16, 1779. Graduated at Harvard college in
1800. Afterwards read law and settled in his profession in
Wiscasset, Maine, where he died in 1822, æt. 43.

JACOB ABBOT CUMMINGS, AUTHOR AND BOOKSELLER,

son of Ebenezer and Elizabeth (Abbot) Cummings, was born in
Hollis, November 2, 1772. His father enlisted in the Continental
Army in April, 1777, and died in the service the next year. Mr.
Cummings graduated at Harvard college in 1801. After leaving
college he became a teacher for several years, and afterwards a
bookseller and publisher, and a member of the well-known Boston
publishing house of Cummings and Hilliard. He was also the
author of several elementary educational works, among which were
"New Testament Question," published in 1817, and a "Spelling
Book" and "School Geography Ancient and Modern," with an
atlas." His publications for schools were highly esteemed, and his
industry, useful labors, and amiable qualities procured him much
respect.*

BENJAMIN M. FARLEY, ATTORNEY AT LAW,

son of Benjamin and Lucy (Fletcher) Farley, and grandson of Lt.
Samuel Farley, one of the first settlers of Hollis, was born April
8, 1783, in that part of Hollis afterwards set off to Brookline. Mr.
Farley prepared for college at the academy in New Ipswich ; graduated at Harvard college in 1804 ; read law with Hon. Abijah Bige-
low in Leominster, Mass. ; admitted to the bar and settled in his
profession in Hollis in 1808, and continued to reside in Hollis till
1855, when he removed to Boston. Upon being established in his
profession, he soon rose to a high rank in it, and for many years he
had no superior at the Hillsborough bar, of which he was for several years president.

Distinguished for his legal ability, as well as for his fidelity to his
clients, he spared no pains in the preparation of their cases for the
court, and it is said of him that he made the cases of his clients so

---

*Allen's American Biographies, p. 274.

Benjamin M. Farley

much his own, that he examined witnesses, and addresssed the jury as if himself personally were on trial. In the popular acceptation of the term, Mr. Farley was not noted for eloquence. He relied more for his eminent success upon a carefully arranged and lucid statement of the evidence to the jury, and a clear presentation of his points of law to the court, than upon figures of rhetoric, or appeals to sympathy, and his presentation, both of the evidence and law, were made so clear and distinct that neither the jury nor court could misunderstand him.

Mr. Farley was not only industrious, faithful and prompt, but what he undertook to do he did with his might. His temperament was not impulsive, but having once settled upon his course, he was not easily diverted from it. If it required loss of sleep or exposure to heat or cold, he was ready to meet them, and he knew no such thing as failure if by his personal efforts success were attainable. He had so trained himself to these habits from early life that he seemed hardly conscious that advancing years had lessened his strength, and as he approached the age of fourscore it could hardly be perceived that "his eye had become dim, or his natural force abated." He was naturally conservative, and this trait of his character grew upon him with his years. He had acquired an ample competence by his profession, yet in his pecuniary investments he made no ventures, nor did he readily become a convert to new teachings in education, morals, or social changes. He does not in any part of his life seem to have been an eager aspirant for political office or distinction. Though decided and outspoken in his political preferences and opinions he had but little taste for party politics, yet his standing and personal popularity with his fellow townsmen are shown by the fact that between the years 1809 and 1844 he was twenty-five times chosen a member of the School Committee, and from 1814 to 1829 he was elected in fifteen different years to represent the town in the General Court. As a member of the legislature Mr. Farley was highly respected, and, though in his political relations often in the minority, he never failed to exert an important influence upon its deliberations. His ability as a lawyer was well known and felt, and being often on the judiciary committee of the House, it is said that some of our important statute laws originated with him. Knowing himself but too well the evils and uncertainties of litigation, as well as its expense, Mr. Farley was in the habit of dissuading his own townsmen from engaging in it. Owing in great part to this cause, it is said that the people of Hollis were but seldom represented in the courts. His wise counsel in this direction rarely failed of success, he not wishing to add to his own fortune at the cost of the peace of his neighbors. Died at Lunenburg, Mass., September 16, 1865, æt. 82.

JOSEPH E. SMITH, ATTORNEY AT LAW,

son of Manasseh and Hannah (Emerson) Smith, born in Hollis, March 6, 1782. Graduated at Harvard college 1804. Read law and settled in his profession in Boston. Mr. Smith is reputed to have been well read in his profession, an able and successful advocate, and highly esteemed for his integrity and moral worth. Died 1837, æt. 55.

BENJAMIN BURGE, M. D.,

son of Ephraim and Anna (Abbot) Burge, born in Hollis, August 5, 1782. Graduated at Harvard college in 1805. Was for a time a tutor at Bowdoin college, and received the honorary degree of A. M., at Bowdoin in 1815. He studied medicine and settled in his profession in Vassalborough. Maine. Died in Hollis, June 11, 1816, æt. 33.

SAMUEL E. SMITH, ATTORNEY AT LAW,

son of Manasseh and Hannah (Emerson) Smith, and grandson of Rev. Daniel Emerson, born in Hollis. March 12, 1788. Graduated at Harvard college in 1808. He held a high rank in his class, and graduated with distinguished honors. He read law with the Hon. Samuel Dana, of Groton, Mass., and with his brother, Joseph E. Smith, in Boston. He was admitted to the bar in Boston in 1812, and afterwards settled in his profession in Wiscasset, Maine. Mr. Smith was a member of the General Court of Massachusetts in 1819, and of that in Maine in 1820, and was a Judge of the Court of Common Pleas of Maine from 1822 to 1830. He was elected Governor of Maine in the years 1831, 1832 and 1833; and was reappointed Judge of the Court of Common Pleas in 1835, resigned in 1837, and the same year was appointed one of the Commissioners to revise the Statutes of Maine.

In an obituary notice in the Harvard Necrology it is said of him, " that he was unostentatious in his intercourse with his fellow citizens—honest in all his dealings—exemplary in his habits and respected by all who knew him." Died at Wiscasset, March 3. 1860. æt. 71.

JOHN PROCTOR, ATTORNEY AT LAW,

son of Cyrus and Sybil (Farnsworth) Proctor, was born January 28, 1787. Graduated at Harvard college in 1813. Read law and settled as an attorney at law in Rockport, Indiana. Died at Rockport in 1844, æt. 57.

GEORGE F. FARLEY, ATTORNEY AT LAW,

son of Benjamin and Lucy (Fletcher) Farley, was born April 5, 1793, and graduated at Harvard college in 1816. He read law in the office of his brother, Hon. B. M. Farley, of Hollis, and Hon. Luther Lawrence, of Groton, Mass., and was admitted to the bar, and commenced the practice of his profession at New Ipswich in 1821. In the year 1831, he was a member of the New Hampshire General Court from New Ipswich, and the same year removed to Groton, Mass., and practised his profession, with distinguished ability and success till his death at that place, November 8, 1855, æt. 62. Several years before his death, Mr. Farley established a law office in Boston, and was regarded as one of the most eloquent and able lawyers at the Massachusetts bar.

REV. WILLIAM P. KENDRICK,

son of Capt. Daniel and Mary (Pool) Kendrick, born June 20, 1794, graduated at Harvard college in 1816, and at the Theological seminary at Andover, Massachusetts, in 1819. He was ordained as a home missionary in 1823, and for many years afterwards was employed as a home missionary or "stated supply" in western New York, and at length removed to the State of Illinois, and became pastor of a church at Bristol in that State, where he died November 5, 1854, æt. 50.

TAYLOR G. WORCESTER,

son of Jesse and Sarah (Parker) Worcester, born April 6, 1799. Graduated at Harvard college in 1823, at Andover Theological seminary in 1827, and was licensed to preach the same year. He afterwards preached in several places in New Hampshire and Massachusetts, but was never settled in the ministry. He still (1879) resides in Hollis on the old ancestral homestead. While in college and at Andover he became interested in the doctrines of the New Jerusalem church as taught in the writings of Emanuel Swedenborg, and was the editor of a revised translation of the work of that author, entitled the "True Christian Religion," and also aided in the revision of the translation of some of the smaller works of the same author.

JONATHAN SAUNDERSON, ATTORNEY AT LAW,

son of Jonathan and Lucy (Pool) Saunderson, born December 30. 1802, prepared for college at the academy at Westford, Mass., and graduated at Harvard college in 1828. Read law in Hollis with Hon. B. M. Farley and at the law school in Cambridge, and settled in the practice of his profession in Philadelphia.

SAMUEL T. WORCESTER, ATTORNEY AT LAW,

son of Jesse and Sarah (Parker) Worcester, born August 30, 1804, prepared for college at the academies in Pembroke, N. H., and Andover, Mass., and graduated at Harvard college in 1830. After leaving college, taught an academy for one year at Weymouth. Mass., and also for one year at Cambridge. Read law in the office of Hon. B. M. Farley in Hollis, and also at the law school in Cambridge, settled in his profession in Norwalk, Ohio, in 1835, and continued in the practice of the law in that place till the summer of 1867, when he removed to Nashua, N. H., where he still resides (1879). May 13, 1835, married Mary F. C. Wales, daughter of Samuel Wales, Esq., of Stoughton, Mass., who deceased at Nashua. April 29, 1874. Was a member of the Ohio Senate in the years 1849 and 1850; elected district judge of the 10th Ohio judicial district in October, 1859, and while holding that office was elected a member of the United States Congress in the spring of 1861. Publications: 1831, "Sequel to the Spelling Book;" 1833, "American Primary Spelling Book;" 1871, Revised Editions of "Worcester's Comprehensive and Primary Dictionaries;" 1871, "Old and New, or the School Systems of Ohio and New Hampshire compared."

FREDERICK A. WORCESTER, ATTORNEY AT LAW,

son of Jesse and Sarah (Parker) Worcester, born January 28, 1807; prepared for college in part at the Pinkerton Academy, in Derry, New Hampshire, and in part at the Phillips Academy, in Andover; graduated at Harvard college in 1831. Read law with Hon. B. M. Farley in Hollis and at the law school in Cambridge, admitted to the bar and commenced the practice of law in Bangor, Maine,

Saml T. Worcester

in 1834. Soon afterwards removed to Townsend, Massachusetts, where he still resides and yet continues (1879) in the successful practice of his profession.

FRANCIS J. WORCESTER, ATTORNEY AT LAW,

son of Taylor G. and Lucy (Bell) Worcester, born in Hollis, November 1, 1848, graduated at Harvard college in 1870. Read law in New York city, and was there admitted to the bar, and commenced the practice of his profession in 1877, and still resides in New York.

GRADUATES OF YALE COLLEGE.

JOSEPH E. WORCESTER, L. L. D.,

son of Jesse and Sarah (Parker) Worcester, was born in Bedford, N. H., August 24, 1784, and in 1794, when in his tenth year, came to Hollis with his parents. His youth, till the age of majority, was passed in agricultural labor on his father's farm in Hollis, but he early manifested an ardent love of knowledge and availed himself of every attainable means for mental improvement. After reaching his majority he prepared himself for college, partly at the academy in Salisbury, N. H., and in part at Phillips Academy in Andover, and entered the sophomore class at Yale in 1809, and graduated at Yale in 1811. After leaving college he was for several years employed as a teacher of a private school at Salem, Mass., he afterwards passed two years at Andover, Mass., and in 1819 removed to Cambridge, where he devoted himself to literary pursuits, and to the preparation for the press of his numerous and valuable publications, till his decease, October 27, 1865, æt. 81. He was married June 29, 1841, to Amy Elizabeth McKean, (who still survives), daughter of Rev. Joseph McKean, D. D., formerly Professor of Rhetoric and Oratory at Harvard college.

The first literary work of Dr. Worcester was his "Universal Gazetteer, Ancient and Modern," in two volumes octavo, of near 1000 pages each, published at Andover in 1817 ; the next a "Gazetteer of the United States," one volume octavo, of 372 pages, published in 1818. This was followed in 1819 by his "Elements of Geography, Ancient and Modern, with an Atlas," a work that was received with such favor that it passed through several stereotype editions. In 1823 this Geography was succeeded by an illustrated work in two volumes duodecimo, entitled "Sketches of the Earth and its

Inhabitants." In 1825 upon being elected a member of the American Academy, he communicated to that association an elaborate essay, entitled, "Remarks upon Longevity," which was published with the memoirs of the academy. His "Elements of Ancient and Modern History," with an "Historical Atlas," appeared in 1826, a work from that time to the present very extensively used as a standard text book in our public high schools and academies.

His first work in lexicography was an edition of "Johnson's Dictionary, combined with Walkers's Pronunciation," an octavo volume of 1156 pages, first published in 1828. In 1829, against his own inclination, he was induced, through the persistent urgency of the publisher of Webster's Quarto Dictionary (who was his personal friend) to prepare an abridgement of that work, a task to which he was strongly averse, and at first refused, a refusal to which he afterwards regretted that he did not adhere. This work appeared in 1830, in an octavo volume of 1071 pages, into which he incorporated much valuable matter which he had prepared for his own dictionaries. The same year he published the first edition of his "Comprehensive Dictionary," a duodecimo volume of 420 pages. This work was the first of his own dictionaries, and at once had an extensive sale and soon passed through many editions.

In 1831 he made a voyage to Europe where he spent many months in visiting places of interest, and in the collection of works in the departments of philology and lexicography, for use in his future publications.

Upon his return from Europe, he became the editor of the "American Almanac," a statistical, closely printed, duodecimo Annual, each number containing about 350 pages, which he continued to edit for eleven years, with his accustomed care and fidelity. In 1846, his "Universal and Critical Dictionary" was first published—a large, closely printed royal octavo volume of 1031 pages, and also the same year, his "Elementary School Dictionary."

In 1847, Dr. Worcester was threatened with total loss of sight. His eyes had yielded to his long, unbroken intellectual labor, and for two years he was nearly blind. In the meanwhile, three operations were performed on his right eye (which became wholly blind), and two on the left eye, which was happily saved. After the partial recovery of his sight, Dr. Worcester published the following works:

1850, "Primary Dictionary for Public Schools," 16mo, 384 pages. Revised edition, 1860.

1855, "Academic Dictionary", for High Schools and Academies, duodecimo, 565 pp.

1857, " Pronouncing Spelling Book," duodecimo, 180 pp.

1859, " Quarto Dictionary of the English Language," with 1000 illustrations, 1284 pp.

1860, " Elementary Dictionary," Revised edition, duodecimo, 400 pp.

1860, "Comprehensive Dictionary," Revised edition, duodecimo, 612 pp.

1864, " Comprehensive Spelling Book," duodecimo, 156 pp.

From a memoir of Dr. Worcester read before the American Academy, by Ezra Abbot, LL. D., Librarian of Harvard college, a few lines are here transcribed, presenting an estimate of his literary labors by one who was familiar with them. " All the works of Dr. Worcester, (says the author of this memoir,) give evidence of sound judgment and good taste, combined with indefatigable industry, and a conscientious solicitude for accuracy in the statement of facts. The tendency of his mind was practical, rather than speculative.

" As a lexicographer, he did not undertake to reform the anomalies of the English language. His aim was rather to preserve it from corruption. In regard to both *Orthography and Pronunciation*, he took great pains to ascertain the best usage, and perhaps there is no lexicographer whose judgment respecting these matters in doubtful cases deserves higher consideration."

Dr. Worcester was a member of the Massachusetts Historical Society—of the American Academy—of the American Oriental Society, and an Honorary member of the Royal Geographical Society of London. He received the honorary degree of LL. D., from Brown University in 1847, and from Dartmouth college in 1856.

In a biographical sketch of Dr. Worcester, by Hon. George S. Hillard, it is said of him. " His long and busy life was passed in unbroken literary toil. Though his manners were reserved, and his habits retiring, his affections were strong : and benevolence was an ever active principle in his nature. * * He was a stranger to the impulses of passion and the sting of ambition. His life was tranquil, happy and useful. A love of truth and a strong sense of duty

were leading traits in his character. Little known, except by name,
to the general public, he was greatly honored and loved by that
small circle of relatives and friends who had constant opportunities
of learning the warmth of his affections and the strength of his
virtues."*

REV. RALPH EMERSON, D. D.,

was a son of Dea Daniel and Ama (Fletcher) Emerson, born in
Hollis, August 18, 1787. Graduated at Yale in 1811, and at the
Theological seminary at Andover in 1814. He was tutor at Yale
college from ·814 to 1816; ordained as pastor of the Congregational
church at Norfolk, Conn., 1816, where he remained till 1829, when
he was appointed Professor of Ecclesiastical History and Pastoral
Theology in the Theological seminary at Andover. He continued
to discharge the duties of that professorship with eminent ability
for twenty-five years, till 1854, when he resigned. He afterwards
resided in Newburyport, Mass., for about five years, and then
removed to Rockport, Ill., where he died May 20th, 1863, æt. 75.
Publications: Prof. Emerson was the author of an interesting and
appreciative "Biography" of his brother, Rev. Joseph Emerson, published in 1834, and also of a translation of Wiggin's "Augustinism"
and "Pelagianism," with copious notes, published in 1840. He was
also a frequent and able contributor to the " Bibliotheca Sacra"
the ·" Christian Spectator," and to other theological publications.†

REV. HENRY A. WORCESTER,

son of Jesse and Sarah (Parker) Worcester, born in Hollis, September 22, 1812 ; graduated at Yale college in 1828 ; studied for the
ministry at the theological seminary at New Haven, and was
licensed to preach in 1833. Mr. Worcester embraced the doctrines
of the New Jerusalem church as taught in the writings of Emanuel
Swedenborg, and commenced preaching to the New Jerusalem
society at Abington, Mass., in 1833. After remaining at Abington
for some months, he removed to Portland, Me., and was the acting
minister of the New Jerusalem societies in Portland, Bath and Gar-
diner, till his decease at Portland, May 24, 1841, æt. 38. A small
volume containing twelve of his sermons, on various doctrinal subjects, was published in 1837, and he was also the author of a small
work on the " Sabbath," which has been reprinted since his death.

---

*See also Allibone's Dictionary of Authors, Vol. 3, pp. 2838-39.
†See Allen's American Biographical Dictionary, p. 305.

Ralph Emerson

In an obituary notice of Mr. Worcester, published soon after his decease, it was said of him "that his amiable, frank and social qualities gained him many warm friends, and his character and acquirements were such as to ensure to him universal esteem."

REV. JOSEPH EMERSON,

son of Rev. Daniel and Esther (Frothingham) Emerson, was born September 4, 1808, graduated at Yale college in 1830, and at the Theological seminary at Andover in 1835. Ordained October 12, 1836. Mr. Emerson was agent of the American Education Society from 1836 to 1839, and agent of the Western College Society from 1849 to 1853. Settled as pastor of the Congregational church at Rockford, Ill., from 1854 to 1859; District Secretary of the American Foreign Christian Union from 1859 to 1871, and District Secretary of the A. B. C. F. M. from 1871 to ——. He now resides (1879) in Andover, Mass.*

BENJAMIN F. FARLEY, ATTORNEY AT LAW,

son of Benjamin M., and Lucretia (Gardner) Farley, born November 20, 1808, graduated at Yale college in 1832, read law in the office of his father in Hollis, and for a time practised his profession with him. Afterwards he engaged in mercantile business, and also in farming; now (1879) resides in Worcester, Mass.

RALPH H. CUTTER, ATTORNEY AT LAW,

son of John H. and Susan (Poole) Cutter, born in Louisville, Ky., November 4, 1835, came to Hollis with his parents in 1849, graduated at Yale college in 1858, read law in Nashua, N. H., and for some years practised his profession in that place,—afterwards removed to the State of Georgia. His father, John H. Cutter, son of Dr. Benoni Cutter, was born in Hollis, August 16, 1807, was settled for many years in business at Louisville, and afterwards returned with his family and settled in Hollis.

---

*Andover Triennial Catalogue.

CHAPTER XXVIII.

GRADUATES OF DARTMOUTH, MIDDLEBURY, AMHERST AND
OTHER COLLEGES.

REV. SAMUEL WORCESTER, D. D.,

son of Noah and Lydia (Taylor) Worcester, was born in Hollis,
November 1, 1770. He labored on the farm of his father in Hollis,
till 1791, and after attaining to his twenty-first year, prepared for
college, partly at the academy at New Ipswich, and in part with
Rev. Dr. Wood in Boscawen; entered Dartmouth college in
1792, and graduated in 1795. He was preceptor of New Ipswich
academy in 1796; afterwards studied for the ministry with the
Rev. Dr. Austin in Worcester, Mass., and was ordained as pastor
of the Congregational church and society at Fitchburg, Mass.,
September 27, 1797. He was dismissed at Fitchburg, by mutual
council, September 8, 1802; afterwards installed as pastor of the
Tabernacle church in Salem Mass., April 20, 1803, and chosen
Professor of Theology at Dartmouth college June 1804, which appointment he declined. "In 1810, at the first meeting of A. B.
C. F. M., he was chosen Corresponding Secretary of the Board, and
peformed the duties of that office with eminent ability and success,
in connection with the pastorate of the Tabernacle church, till July,
1819, when he was relieved of a part of his duties as pastor by the
settlement of a colleague." These relations with the American
Board and the Tabernacle church continued till his decease, at
Brainerd, East Tennessee, June 7, 1821, in his fifty-first year. He
was buried at Brainerd and a monument erected there by the Board
to his memory, with the following inscription from the pen of Hon.
Jeremiah Evarts, his successor, as Corresponding Secretary :

"As a minister of the Gospel, Dr. Worcester labored for more than
twenty years with zeal, fidelity and success. As a distinguished
agent in exciting and directing the missionary enterprise of the
American churches, he displayed eminent talents, and was impelled

S. Worcester

by an ardent desire for the salvation of the heathen. To the promotion of this divine work he applied all his faculties till exhausted by his arduous labors he fell asleep in Jesus while on a visit of kindness to the Cherokee people." His remains were afterwards disinterred and removed to Salem in 1844, and deposited in the Harmony Grove cemetery.

He received the honorary degree of D. D. from Princeton college in 1811. Very many of the sermons, public addresses and other writings of Dr. Worcester have been published, and among them the following : "Orations," at Dartmouth college, July 4, 1795 ; at New Ipswich, July 4, 1796; "On the Death of Washington," at Fitchburg, 1800. "Sermons." Six sermons on "Eternal Judgment," 1800 ; "Farewell," at Fitchburg, 1802 ; "Dedication" sermon at Beverly, 1803 ; "Righteousness as conducive to Happiness." 1804 : "The Messiah of the Scriptures," 1808 ; "Funeral of Mrs. Eleanor Emerson," 1809 ; "Ordination of Rev. E. L. Parker,' 1810; "State Fast." and at the "Ordination" of Rev. Henry Griffin, 1811 ; "National Fast," 1812 ; "Before the Foreign Missionary Society of Salem, 1813 ; "Funeral of Rev. Rufus Anderson," 1814 ; "Paul on Mars Hill," 1815 ; "At the First Anniversary of the American Education Society," 1816 ; "Before the Massachusetts Society for the Suppression of Intemperance," 1817 ; "Posthumous Sermons," one volume duodecimo, pp. 500, 1823 : "Letters to the Rev. Thomas Baldwin, on Baptism, 1807 ; three letters to Rev. Dr. Channing, on "American Unitarianism," 1815 ; "Christian Psalmody," and "Watt's Entire and Select Hymns," 1818.

"His letters to Dr. Channing, in connection with the Unitarian Controversy, have been considered as almost unrivalled specimens of polemic theological discussion, and his published sermons are rich in evangelical thought, logically and luminously presented."*

REV. ABEL FARLEY,

son of Capt. Caleb and Elizabeth Farley, was born in Hollis, July 17. 1773, graduated at Dartmouth college, 1798, and studied for the ministry in Hollis, with Rev. Eli Smith. Ordained as pastor of the Congregational church at Manchester, Vermont, February 6. 1805. Resigned at Manchester in 1812 ; afterwards removed to Goshen, Massachusetts, and was the acting pastor of the Congregational church at Goshen, till his death at that place, March 22, 1817, æt. 43.

---

* See Allibone's Dic. of Authors, Vol. 3, p. 2839, and Sprague's Am. Pulpit, Vol. 2, p. 398.

REV. MIGHILL BLOOD,

son of Daniel and Mary (Putnam) Blood, born in Hollis, December 13, 1777. Graduated at Dartmouth college, 1800; ordained as pastor of the Congregational church at Buckstown, now Bucksport, Maine, May 12, 1803; dismissed in 1840. He afterwards resided in Ellsworth, Maine, but subsequently returned to Bucksport, "and there terminated an humble and valuable life," April 6, 1852, æt. 74.*

REV. CALEB J. TENNEY, D. D.

The ancestors of Dr. Tenney were from Rowley, county of Yorkshire, in the northerly part of England, and came to New England, and settled in Rowley, Massachusetts, about the year 1638. His grandfather, William Tenney, came from Rowley, Massachusetts, and settled in Hollis about the year 1746. Dr. Tenney was the son of Capt. William and Phebe (Jewett) Tenney, and was born in Hollis, May 3, 1780. He graduated at Dartmouth college, in 1801, with the first rank and honors of his class, of which Hon. Daniel Webster was a member. He studied for the ministry, with Rev. Dr. Burton, Thetford, Vt., and Rev. Dr. Spring of Newburyport, Mass., and was ordained as pastor of the Congregational church at Newport, R. I., September 12, 1804. Married Ruth Channing of Newport, 1810. Resigned his charge at Newport, on account of ill health in May, 1814. He was afterwards installed as pastor of the Congregational church at Wethersfield, Ct., March 27, 1816. He received the honorary degree of D. D., from Yale, in 1829. Resigned his pastorate at Wethersfield, in consequence of impaired health and failure of his voice, January 1841. In 1842, he removed to Northampton, Mass., and in 1843 was appointed agent of the American Colonization Society, and for the remainder of his life, gave himself wholly to that work in which he had eminent success. His last address in behalf of this society was delivered at North Amherst, September 19, 1847, but nine days before his death, which took place at Northampton, September 28, 1847, at the age of 67. In Dr. Sprague's "Annals of the American Pulpit," it is said of Dr. Tenney, "That he was a learned theologian, and a useful preacher —a judicious and faithful pastor, and a man of eminent and steady piety — amiable, just and generous and a true philanthropist."

OTIS CO. BOSTON.

C. J. Tenney -

Rev. Dr. Tyler, late President of East Windsor Theological seminary, in a biographical sketch of Dr. Tenney, says of him, that " he was one of the most impressive preachers I ever heard, but excelled more in the composition than in the delivery of his sermons. They were characterized by a richness of matter, lucid arrangement, thorough discussion and a faithful application of the truth."

Among the published sermons of Dr. Tenney, were two on " Baptism :" at the " ordination of Rev. Royal Robbins," 1816 : on the " death of Rev. John Marsh, D. D.," 1821 : " New England Distinguished, — A Thanksgiving Sermon," 1827 : at the " Funeral of Rev. Samuel Austin, D. D.," 1830.—and at the " Funeral of Rev. Alfred Mitchell," 1832.*

REV. DAVID JEWETT,

son of Jacob and Elizabeth (Cummings) Jewett, born August 16, 1773, and graduated at Dartmouth college in 1801. Studied for the ministry with Rev. Dr. Emmons, D. D., of Franklin, Mass., and Rev. Dr. Spring of Newburyport,—ordained as pastor of the Congregational church at Rockport, Mass., Oct. 30, 1805. He continued in the pastorate of that church for thirty-one years, when he resigned on account of impaired health. During his ministry his church is said to have increased from a membership of ten to two hundred and fifty. Allen, in his American Biographies, says of him, " That he was a man of childlike simplicity and Christian tenderness, but of an iron purpose, resolute, fearless and immovable." Died at Waltham, Mass., July 16, 1841, æt. 67.

An interesting event in respect to Mr. Jewett was the burial of his remains at Rockport, July 13, 1856, fifteen years after his death : a sermon being preached on the occasion by his son, Rev. William R. Jewett, then of Plymouth, N. H., who also made an address at the grave, which was responded to on the part of the people by Dr. Benjamin Haskell.

CAPT. JONATHAN B. EASTMAN,

son of Jonathan and Sarah (Fletcher) Eastman, born in Hollis, January 8, 1780, graduated at Dartmouth college in 1803, enlisted in the United States army, and was appointed Ensign the same year, Lieutenant in 1805, and Captain in 1813. Soon after this last

*Sprague's American Pulpit, Vol. 2, pp. 473, 474, 475, and Allen's American Biography pp. 744, 785.

appointment, Capt. Eastman left the army and returned to Hollis, there passed the rest of his life, and died in Hollis April 26, 1827, æt. 47. Capt. Eastman was with the American army in Canada, in 1812, at the time of its surrender by Gen. Hull, and was then United States paymaster.

NEHEMIAH HARDY, JUN., ATTORNEY AT LAW,

son of Nehemiah and Abigail Hardy, born in Hollis, April 10, 1781, and graduated at Dartmouth college in 1803. Read law in Boston, but did not practise his profession. Removed to Wilmington, North Carolina, in 1807, and there engaged in mercantile pursuits; and afterwards, in 1815, removed to Tennessee and died at Wesley in that State, August 26, 1839, æt. 58.

REV. STEPHEN FARLEY, JUN.,

son of Stephen and Mary (Shattuck) Farley, born in Hollis, October 24, 1779, graduated at Dartmouth college in 1804. Ordained as pastor of the Congregational church at Claremont, New Hampshire, December 24, 1806. Dismissed April 21, 1819. Afterwards he was for several years preceptor of the Academy at Atkinson, New Hampshire, in the mean time supplying the pulpit of the Congregational society in that town. He was reputed to be an excellent and accomplished scholar, a ready writer, and was a voluminous contributor to the periodicals of the day. Died at Amesbury, Mass., Sept. 20, 1851, æt. 71.

REV. ELI SMITH, JUN.,

son of Rev. Eli and Catharine (Sheldon) Smith, born in Sunderland, Mass., July 16, 1787, and came to Hollis with his father in 1793. Graduated at Dartmouth college in 1809. Studied for the ministry in Philadelphia, and was first settled as pastor of a Presbyterian church in Frankfort, Ky. He was pastor of the church at Frankfort for about ten years, and was afterwards, in 1829, installed as pastor of a Presbyterian church in Paris, Ky. It is said of him "that his rank as a minister was inferior to that of no one of his cotemporaries in Kentucky." Died at Frankfort, Oct. 23, 1839, æt. 52.

WILLIAM TENNEY, JUN., ATTORNEY AT LAW,

son of Capt. William and Phebe (Jewett) Tenney, born in Hollis, September 12, 1785. Graduated 1808, read law at the law school of Judges Reeves and Gould in Litchfield, Ct. Was admitted to the bar in Boston in 1811, and first settled in his profession in Salem in 1813; removed from Salem to Newmarket, N. H., in 1815, and practised his profession at that place till his decease, September 13, 1838, æt. 53. Mr. Tenney was assistant clerk of the New Hampshire Senate in 1823.

REV. LEONARD JEWETT,

son of Jacob and Elizabeth (Cummings) Jewett, born in Hollis, October 2, 1787. Graduated at Dartmouth college, 1810, and at the Theological seminary at Andover in 1813. Was licensed to preach and employed for several years as a home missionary in the States of New York and New Hampshire. He was afterwards ordained as pastor of the Congregational church at Temple, N. H.. March 6, 1833. Resigned on account of impaired health in 1844, and afterwards resided in Hollis till his decease. February 16. 1862, æt. 74.

REV. GRANT POWERS,

son of Samson and Elizabeth (Nutting) Powers, and grandson of Capt. Peter Powers, the first settler of Hollis, was born in Hollis, March 31. 1784. and graduated at Dartmouth college in 1810. Studied for the ministry with Rev. Dr. Burton. Thetford, Vt. Ordained as pastor of the Congregational church at Haverhill. N. H., January 4. 1815. Dismissed at Haverhill. April 28. 1829. Installed as pastor of the Congregational church at Goshen, Ct., August 27, of the same year, and continued pastor of the church at Goshen till his death. April 10. 1841. æt. 57. In a biographical sketch of Mr. Powers, it is said of him. "That as a preacher he was able, ingenious, faithful and instructive. That he was endued with much practical wisdom. with uncommon frankness and candor, and great generosity, and that he was highly esteemed for his talents and virtues, and his eminent and agreeable social qualities." He was a ready and popular writer. and an earnest and eloquent public speaker. and the productions of his pen display great good taste, versatility. and literary ability. Publications.—among his published writings are the following: Sermons—"At the ordination of Rev. E. J. Boardman," 1822 ; "At the ordination of Rev. J. D. Farnsworth." 1827 : "At the funeral of Rev. William Andrews." 1838 : "Centennial Address at Hollis," 1830 ; "Centennial Address at Goshen, Ct.." 1838 ; "An Essay upon the Influence of the Imagination upon the Nervous System." 1828 : "Historical Sketches of the Coos Country." 1841.*

*Drake's Biographical Dictionary, p. 735. Allen's Biographical Dictionary, p. 675.

NOAH HARDY, M. D.,

son of Phineas and Sibyl (Shattuck) Hardy, was born in Hollis, March 23, 1785. Graduated at Dartmouth college, 1812: studied medicine and settled as a physician in Hollis, about the year 1814, and practised his profession there till his death at Hollis, December 25, 1850, æt. 65. He was much respected in his profession, and also for his amiable and exemplary character.

LUKE EASTMAN, ATTORNEY AT LAW,

son of Lt. Amos and Ruth (Flagg) Eastman, was born in Hollis, June 22, 1790, and graduated at Dartmouth college, 1812. He read law in Boston and commenced the practice of his profession in that city in 1816. He afterwards in 1820, removed to Sterling, Mass.; thence to Dracut, and subsequently settled in Lowell, as a teacher of music, for which he was distinguished. Died at Lowell, February 3, 1847, æt. 56.

REV. DAVID PAGE SMITH,

son of Rev. David and Hepzibah (Worcester) Smith, born in Hollis, September 20, 1795. Graduated at Dartmouth College, 1823; Studied for the ministry with Rev. Dr. Wood of Boscawen, N. H.; ordained as pastor of the Congregational church at Sandwich, N. H., May 23, 1827; dismissed, June 28, 1832; afterwards installed as pastor of the Congregational church at Parsonsfield, and Newfield, Maine, July 11, 1832; dismissed in 1839, and subsequently, May 8, 1845, was settled in the ministry at Greenfield, N. H. Died at Greenfield, October 11, 1850, æt. 55.

REV. WILLIAM P. EASTMAN,

son of Alpheus and Elizabeth (Ames) Eastman, born in Hollis September 20, 1813. Graduated at Dartmouth college in 1842, and at the Theological seminary at Andover, in 1845. Ordained as pastor of the Presbyterian church at New Comerstown, Ohio, in 1846. Dismissed at New Comerstown, and afterwards installed as a pastor of the Presbyterian church in Union, Ohio, and still (1879) resides in that State.

REV. CHARLES CUMMINGS,

son of Thomas and Mary (Woolson) Cummings, born June 7, 1817. Graduated at Dartmouth college, 1842, and at the Theological seminary at Andover in 1845. Licensed to preach by the

Andover Association in 1846. and after preaching for a short time. gave up his profession. on account of impaired health. For the last twenty years or more he has been principal of the High school in Medford. Mass.. where he still resides (1879).

CHARLES H. MOOAR, ATTORNEY AT LAW,

son of Gardner and Mary (Hardy) Mooar. born in Hollis, June 17. 1822. Graduated at Dartmouth college. 1848. Read law in Covington. Ky.. admitted to the bar in 1850. and settled in his profession at Covington. He was judge of the County Court of Kenton county. Ky.. from 1858 to 1862. Still resides at Covington.

EDWARD F. JOHNSON. ATTORNEY AT LAW.

son of Noah and Letitia (Claggett) Johnson. born in Hollis, October 21. 1842. Graduated at Dartmouth college in 1864. Read law in Nashua, N. H.. settled in and now practises his profession in Marlborough. Mass.. having also an office in Boston.

JOSEPH H. PARKER, ATTORNEY AT LAW.

son of Joseph D. and Lucretia (Smith) Parker, born in Hollis. September 1. 1840. Graduated at Dartmouth college, 1869. For some years after leaving college he was a bookseller and stationer at Hanover, afterwards read law in Nashua. N. H.. and settled in his profession at Nashua. where he now resides (1879).

FRANKLIN WORCESTER. ATTORNEY AT LAW.

son of John N. and Sarah (Holden) Worcester, born in Hollis. October 27. 1845. Graduated at Dartmouth college in 1870. Read law at the law school in Cambridge. practised his profession for a short time at Cambridge. and afterwards engaged in mercantile and manufacturing business with his brothers at Cambridge, and at Hollis. N. H. He was Representative from Hollis to the New Hampshire General Court in 1877 and 1878.

JOHN H. HARDY. ATTORNEY AT LAW.

son of John and Hannah (Farley) Hardy. born in Hollis. February 2, 1847. Graduated at Dartmouth college in 1870. Read law in Boston and settled in the practice of his profession in that city.

CHARLES L. DAY,

son of Rev. Pliny B. and Mary (Chapin) Day, born in Hollis, April 28, 1854. Graduated at Dartmouth college. 1877. Now (1879) reading law in Iowa.

GEORGE W. SAUNDERSON,

son of William P. and Hannah (Marshall) Saunderson, born in
Hollis, April 22, 1854. Graduated at Dartmouth college in 1877.
Now (1879) reading law in Nashua.

GRADUATES OF MIDDLEBURY COLLEGE.

REV. FIFIELD HOLT,

son of Fifield and Anna (Lakin) Holt, born 1784; graduated at
Middlebury college, 1810, and at the Theological seminary at
Andover, in 1813. He was ordained as pastor of the Congregational church and society at Bloomfield, Me., June 14 1815, where
he remained till his decease, at Bloomfield, November 15, 1830,
æt. 45.

REV. SOLOMON HARDY,

son of Solomon and Mary (Bailey) Hardy, born in Hollis, September 27, 1796; graduated at Middlebury college, 1824, and at the
Theological seminary at Andover, in 1827. Mr. Hardy was
ordained as a home missionary, at Andover, November 10, 1827.
He afterwards preached, as " stated supply " or acting pastor, for a
number of years for several churches and societies in Illinois and
Massachusetts, and died while so engaged at Eastham, Mass., September 18, 1842, æt. 45.

GRADUATES OF BROWN UNIVERSITY.

REV. DANIEL KENDRICK,

son of Capt. Daniel and Mary (Pool) Kendrick, born in Hollis.
March 30, 1785; graduated at Brown University in 1810; studied
for the ministry with Rev. Caleb J. Tenney, D. D., at Newport,
R. I. Ordained pastor of the Congregational church and society
at Pittston, Me., November 28, 1812. Died at Wilton, Me., May,
1868, æt. 83.

REV. LUTHER SMITH,

son of Rev. Eli and Ama (Emerson) Smith, born in Hollis, August 11, 1800; graduated at Brown University, 1824; read law
with Hon. B. M. Farley, in Hollis; afterwards studied for the ministry with his brother, Rev. Eli Smith, Jun., at Frankfort, Ky.;
subsequently established, and for many years conducted an academy in Bourbon county, Ky.; June 8, 1874, he was settled in the
ministry as pastor of the Presbyterian church and society, at Zanes-
field, Ohio, where he still resides.

THOMAS ABBOT FARLEY,

son of Dea. Thomas and Susannah (Burge) Farley, born in Hollis, July 8, 1813; graduated at Amherst college in 1838, and at Andover Theological seminary in 1841. Died in Hollis, August 26, 1841, a short time after graduating at Andover, æt. 28.

REV. AMOS F. SHATTUCK,

son of Amos and Margaret (Ball) Shattuck, born in Hollis, July 9, 1832. Graduated at Amherst college, 1859, and at the Union Theological seminary in New York in 1862. Preached for several years in Surry and Charlestown, N. H., and ordained as pastor of a Congregational church at Durham, Me., June 3, 1868. Dismissed at Durham, and afterwards preached in Worcester, Vt., and Hatchville, Mass., till April, 1872, when he ceased to preach on account of ill health. Now resides in Hollis.

GRADUATES OF MARYVILLE COLLEGE, TENN.

REV. PHILLIPS WOOD,

son of Dea. Phillips and Dorothy (Davis) Wood, born in Hollis, July 12, 1801. Graduated at Maryville college in 1831. Studied for the ministry at the Theological seminary at Maryville, and was afterwards ordained as pastor of the Presbyterian church at Blountsville, Tenn. Subsequently removed to Piqua, Ohio, where he died June 11, 1856, æt. 54.

LEONARD WOOD, M. D.,

son of Dea. Phillips and Dorothy (Davis) Wood, born in Hollis, October 22, 1805. Graduated at Maryville college in 1832. Studied medicine, and settled in his profession at Maryville, where he died, August, 1854, æt. 48.

BENJAMIN F. EMERSON,

son of Rev. Daniel and Esther (Frothingham) Emerson, born in Hollis, July 3, 1806. Graduated at Union collge. N. Y., 1830. Read law in Hollis, and settled in his profession, first in Townsend, Mass., and afterwards removed to Nashua, N. H., where he still resides in the practice of his profession.

REV. ELI N. SAWTELL, D. D.,

son of John and Martha (Wallingford) Sawtell, was born in Milford, N. H., September 8, 1799, and came to Hollis to reside when of the age of ten years, his father being a farmer, in very moderate

circumstances. In his early boyhood, young Eli worked upon the
farm with his father in Hollis, but being then of feeble constitution,
farm work was found to be too hard for him, and when about the
age of sixteen, he was apprenticed to a shoemaker to learn his
trade. In the fall of 1817, Rev. Eli Smith, Jun., then of Frankfort, Ky., made a visit to Hollis, one purpose of which was, to
engage a small company of young men, inclined to study for the
ministry, to go to Tennessee to be educated, with that view. Upon
hearing the public address of Mr. Smith upon the subject, young
Sawtell, then of the age of eighteen, and two other Hollis young
men, of about the same age, made up their minds to go to Tennessee the spring following. But when spring came, the courage
of the other two failed. Under the agreement, made with his
master, one year's service was still due on the contract of apprenticeship. Having made up his mind to go to Tennessee, he bought
of his master this last year's time, by giving him his note for $90,
to be paid when he should return as a minister from Tennessee,
which debt was promptly paid eight years after on his first return
to New England.

On the first of May, 1818, Dr. Sawtell, then in his nineteenth
year, started for Tennessee, a distance of eleven hundred miles (a
large part of the way through the wilderness), on foot and alone,
with his whole wardrobe, and library, consisting of a Bible, hymn-
book and primer, tied up in a cotton handkerchief. In this plight,
and with $14 for his expenses, he made his way to Maryville,
Tenn., prepared for college at the school in that place, graduated
at the college in Greenville, Tenn., in 1823, and at the theological
seminary at Maryville in 1825, and was licensed to preach the same
year. After being employed for about a year in collecting funds
for Maryville college, in the year 1826, he came on to New England and spent two years or more, in various States, as an evangelist. He afterwards returned to the west, and in 1829 was settled
as pastor of a Presbyterian church in Louisville, Ky., where he continued till 1836. In the year last named, he was appointed agent
of the American Seamen's Friend Society, and went to Havre in
France, where, through his efforts, a seamen's chapel was built
and a church established, of which he became pastor till 1843,
when he was appointed agent of the Foreign Evangelical Society,
in the service of which he was employed for several years. This
agency led to his travelling and preaching very extensively, in both

Europe and the United States, in the discharge of his duties, he having crossed the Atlantic, on his various missions, no less than eight times. His connection with that society having been dissolved, he established a flourishing female academy at Cleveland, Ohio, of which he was principal till 1854, when he accepted a second appointment to take charge of the seamen's chapel at Havre, where he continued for the next nine years. In 1863 he again returned to the United States, and for a year or more served in the union army in the care of our sick and wounded soldiers. In March, 1865, he was again settled in the ministry, in charge of the Congregational church and society in Saratoga, N. Y., where he continued for about four years, when, by reason of impaired sight and health, he resigned and removed to Brooklyn, N. Y., and after some years to Newmarket, N. J., where he still resides. While in Europe Dr. Sawtell received the honorary degree of D. D., from the college at Maryville, Tenn.

.

CHAPTER XXIX.

MINISTERS, PHYSICIANS AND LAWYERS NOT GRADUATES OF COLLEGE.

REV. NOAH WORCESTER, D. D.,

son of Noah and Lydia (Taylor) Worcester, was born November 28, 1758. The opportunities of Dr. Worcester for attending school were limited to the short public schools in Hollis, which, such as they were, ended with the winter of 1774-5. In the spring of 1775, at the age of sixteen, he enlisted in the army, and was in the Hollis company at the battle of Bunker Hill. In 1776 he went to Plymouth, N. H., where he taught his first school, having (as he says in a short autobiography) "never studied Geography or Grammar, or even had the benefit of a dictionary." While at Plymouth, he says: "After I became an instructor, I felt the importance of learning, and exerted myself to obtain it by such means as were in my power. I found myself deficient in the art of writing, and being at Plymouth where, in the time of the war, it was difficult to procure paper, I wrote over a quantity of white birch bark, in imitation of some excellent copies I found at Plymouth.".

Again in 1777 he was in the army, and was in the Hollis company at the battle of Bennington, where, in his eighteenth year, he was fife major. In September, 1778, having bought of his father the remaining fourteen months of his minority, he went again to Plymouth with the expectation of spending his life as a farmer, except as he might occasionally teach school. The fall after he was married, on his twenty-first birthday.

In 1782 he removed with his family to Thornton, N. H., where he had a small farm, and, while carrying on his farm there, also worked at the trade of a shoemaker, which he had learned in his boyhood. Obliged to practise the most rigid economy in respect to time, when at work upon his shoe bench, he was in the habit of

N. Worcester —

keeping pen and ink by his side to note down any important thoughts as they occurred. In this way he accustomed himself to a rigorous mental discipline, especially in the writing of dissertations on various theological subjects.

In 1785 he addressed a letter, (which was afterwards published,) to Rev. John Murray, the noted Universalist preacher of that day, "On the Origin of Evil." This was Dr. Worcester's first publication, and soon brought him into public notice, and prepared the way for his introduction into the ministry. Upon the recommendation of the neighboring ministers he was licensed to preach in 1786, and on the 18th of October of that year was ordained as pastor of the Congregational church and society in Thornton. He had lived in Thornton for five years before his ordination, and in the meantime had been schoolmaster, selectman, town clerk, justice of the peace, and representative to the general court. From 1802 to 1804 he was the first missionary of the New Hampshire Missionary Society. In 1810 he removed to Salisbury, N. H., and for three years was the assistant of his brother, Thomas Worcester, as minister of that place. While at Salisbury he published his well-known work entitled "Bible News," which afterwards passed through many editions.

In 1813, the monthly periodical called the "Christian Disciple" was established by a number of the prominent clergymen of Boston, and Dr. Worcester was invited to become its editor. On the acceptance of this invitation he removed to Brighton, Mass., and continued to be the editor of that periodical till 1818. While so engaged his mind became very deeply interested in the cause of universal peace, and in 1814 he published his celebrated pamphlet entitled "A Solemn Review of the Custom of War," an essay that was many times republished in this country and England, and was translated into several foreign languages. The publication of this pamphlet, not very long after, led to the formation of the Massachusetts Peace Society, of which Dr. Worcester was elected Secretary. In 1819 a quarterly periodical was established by this society, entitled the "Friend of Peace," of which Dr. Worcester was the editor and principal contributor till the year 1828, when he resigned on reaching his 70th year.

His mind was afterwards directed, with much earnestness, to the examination of the question of the connection of "the Sufferings of Christ with the salvation of men," and in 1829 he published a

small volume entitled the " Atoning Sacrifice—a Display of Love.
not of Wrath." In 1831 he also published a small work entitled
" Causes and Evils of Contention among Christians," and in 1833,
his last work with the title " Last Thoughts on Important Subjects."
Beside the above works he also published the following: Sermon,
at the " Ordination of Rev. Thomas Worcester," and " Friendly
Letter to Rev. Thomas Baldwin," 1791. " Candid Discussion of
Close Communion," 1794 ; " New Hampshire Election Sermon,"
1800 ; " Reasons for declining to adopt the Baptist Theory and
Practice," 1809 : " Appeal to the Candid or Trinitarian Review ;"
1814 ; " Thoughts on the Personality of the Word of God ;" and
" Review of Atheism," 1816. Received the honorary degree of
A. M., from Dartmouth college, in 1791, and that of D. D. from
Harvard in 1818. Died at Brighton, October 31, 1837, in his 79th
year. His monument at Mt. Auburn bears the following inscription :

" To NOAH WORCESTER, D. D.,
Erected by his Friends
In commemoration of his Zeal and Labors
In the cause of Universal Peace,
And the consistency of his character
As a Christian Philanthropist and Divine."

REV. LEONARD WORCESTER,

son of Noah and Lydia (Taylor) Worcester, born January 1, 1767.
Mr. Worcester went to Worcester, Mass., in his youth, and served
an apprenticeship to the printers' trade in the office of Isaiah
Thomas, Esq., a distinguished printer and publisher of that time.
After reaching the age of majority, he was, for several years, editor, printer, and publisher of the newspaper called the " Massachusetts Spy." In 1795, at the age of twenty-eight, he was chosen
deacon of the first church in Worcester, of which Rev. Dr. Austin
was pastor, and without any regular or systematic course of theological studies he was licensed to preach by the Mendon Association, March 12, 1799, and was ordained as pastor of the Congregational church and society in Peacham, Vt., October 30, 1799. He
discharged the duties of his pastorate with much acceptance for
thirty-eight years, till 1837, when he left Peacham on account of
impaired health. He afterwards resided in Littleton, N. H., and
St. Johnsbury, Vt., until his decease at the place last named, May
28, 1846, æt. 79.

Publications of Mr. Worcester, " Letters to Rev. Dr. Bancroft,
on the doctrine of Election," 1794 ; Oration on the " Death of

Washington." 1800; "Fast Day Sermon," 1802; also Sermons on the following subjects—" The Highway and Way"; "On the Atonement;" "On Prayer;" "On the Determination of God;" "On the Trinity;" "Men their worst Enemies;" "The Christian desirous to be with Christ;" "A Defence of the Confession of Faith of the church at Peacham;" at the "Ordination" of Rev. Elnathan Gridley and Rev. Samuel A. Worcester as Missionaries, 1825; "On the Alton Outrage," 1837; "At the close of his Ministry," 1839. Besides the above publications. Mr. Worcester was a frequent contributor to several of the religious periodicals of the time. He received the honorary degree of A. M., from Middlebury college in 1804, and from Dartmouth college in 1827.[*]

REV. THOMAS WORCESTER.

son of Noah and Lydia (Taylor) Worcester, born November 22. 1768. Mr. Worcester studied for the ministry with Rev. Daniel Emerson at Hollis and was ordained as pastor of the Congregational church and society in Salisbury, N. H., November 9, 1791. Objections were made at the time, (by some of the ordaining council) to the ordination of the candidate, mainly, for the reason that he had not had the advantage of a "college education." After considerable delay in consequence of this opposition. Judge Ebenezer Webster, the father of Hon. Daniel Webster, and a member of the society, rose and addressed the council in an earnest and eloquent speech in which he said, "*Mr. Moderator, we have chosen this young man for our minister, and we are satisfied with him; we have invited this council to ordain him, Sir, but if you do not see fit to do it.* (he added with determined emphasis) *we shall call another council that will.*" After this address the candidate was ordained without the call of a second council.

In the year 1807, Hon. Daniel Webster, then a parishioner of Mr. Worcester, united with his church. At the time of so doing, Mr. Webster wrote out his own creed, or confession of faith, which he left with his pastor. The original document in the hand writing of its author, after the decease of Mr. Worcester, was found among his papers, by his executor. Judge George W. Nesmith, and by him deposited in the library of the New Hampshire Historical Society at Concord, where it is still supposed to be.

Some years after his settlement Mr. Worcester embraced the theological doctrines of his brother, Dr. Noah Worcester, as presented in his work, called "Bible News." On this account and also by reason of his failing health, he was dismissed by a mutual council, April 24, 1823. He afterwards remained in Salisbury without charge till his death, December 24, 1831, æt. 63. He received the honorary degree of A. M. from Dartmouth college in 1806. In Dr. Sprague's biographical sketch it is said of Mr. Worcester that he was highly gifted "with the powers of natural eloquence."

Publications : "Oration," July 4, 1798, and "Thanksgiving Sermon" same year, afterwards Sermons as follows, at the "ordination" of Rev. Moses Sawyer. 1802 ; "Little Children in Heaven," 1803 : "On the Education of Children." 1804 ; "On the Glory of Christ :" "On the Testimony by which the Son of God honored the Father." and "on the Sonship of Christ." 1810 ; "Concise view of the Glory of Christ," 1811 : at the "Funeral" of Joseph Wardwell, 1814 : "Letter" to Rev. Dr. Spring. 1811 : "Ecclesiastical Usurpation Exposed." 1815 : "Candid Letters to a Trinitarian." 1817 : "Friendly Letter to a Trinitarian Brother." 1819.*

REV. DAVID BROWN.

son of David and Rebecca Brown, born April 4. 1773. Studied for the ministry in Hollis, and was self-taught. Preached for a time in Hollis and vicinity as an Evangelist, and was afterwards settled as a Baptist minister in western New York.

REV. SAMUEL AMBROSE.

The name of Mr. Ambrose is not found in the Hollis records of births. He was a member of the Hollis Young Men's Religious Association before the Revolution, and of the Hollis militia company in January, 1775, and also a soldier from Hollis in the army at Cambridge in the fall of that year. Married Mary Goodhue, daughter of Dea. Samuel Goodhue, of Hollis, February 20, 1776. Removed to Plymouth, N. H., studied for the ministry, and was settled as pastor of the Baptist church in Sutton, N. H., April, 1782, and dismissed at Sutton in March, 1795, was afterwards employed as a missionary, and in preaching to vacant churches. Died at Sutton. May 30,1830. æt. 77.

REV. JOSEPH WHEAT.

son of Thomas and Mary (Ball) Wheat, born July 18, 1759. He was a soldier from Hollis in the Continental army, and a brother of Thomas Wheat, Jun., who was killed at Bunker Hill. After the war he studied for the ministry, and was settled as pastor of the Baptist church in Grafton, N. H., in August, 1801. Dismissed in 1815. Died at Canaan, N. H., October 28, 1837, æt. 78.

REV. DAVID SMITH.

son of Emerson and Mary (Page) Smith, born September 28, 1769. Mr. Smith learned the trade of a carpenter and joiner, and for several years carried on that business in Hollis, and aided in building the third Hollis meeting-house in 1804. He afterwards studied for the ministry with Rev. Eli Smith in Hollis, and was first ordained as pastor of the Congregational church at Temple, Maine, February 21, 1810. Dismissed January 27, 1819. Afterwards installed as pastor of the Congregational church at Meredith, N. H., March 23, 1819. Died at Meredith, August 18, 1824, æt. 54.

REV. JACOB HARDY.

son of Isaac and Mehitable (Boynton) Hardy, born November 14, 1795, studied for the ministry at the Theological seminary at Bangor, Me., and graduated at Bangor in 1824. Ordained as pastor of the Congregational church at Strong, Me., July 12, 1826. Died at Strong, March 1, 1833, æt. 37.

REV. HENRY H. SAUNDERSON.

son of Jonathan and Lucy (Pool) Saunderson, born September 1, 1810. Entered Yale college in 1828, and left in 1831, without graduating. Studied for the ministry at the Theological seminary at Andover, and graduated at Andover in 1842. Supplied the Congregational church at Ypsilanti, Mich., from October, 1845, to October, 1846. Ordained as pastor of the Congregational church at Ludlow, Vt., April 20, 1848. Dismissed April, 1853. Was pastor of the Congregational church at Wallingford, Vt., from May 1, 1853, to May 1, 1862; at Ludlow, Vt., from 1862 to 1864; at Charlestown, N. H., from 1864 to 1873. Now resides in Swanzey, N. H. Publications of Mr. Saunderson, "Centennial address," at Wallingford, Vt., 1873; "History of Wallingford," also an excellent "History of Charlestown," N. H., 1877.

320 BIOGRAPHICAL SKETCHES.

REV. EDWARD JOHNSON, JUN.,

son of Edward and Sarah (Bruce) Johnson, born October 13. 1813. Received an academical education at Andover. Mass. In 1836 he went as a missionary school teacher to the Sandwich Islands, in the employ of the A. B. C. F. M. While engaged as a teacher there he studied for the ministry, and was ordained as pastor of a native church at Waoli, in the island of Kauai, of which he was for many years the minister. Died in 1868. æt. 55.

PHYSICIANS NOT GRADUATES OF COLLEGE.

ABIJAH WRIGHT,

son of Capt. Joshua and Abigail Wright, born August 15. 1746. Removed from Hollis to Hebron, N. H., before the war of the Revolution, and settled there as a physician. Died at Hebron in 1828. æt. 82.

PETER EMERSON,

son of Rev. Daniel Emerson. (See p. 210, *ante.*)

WILLIAM HALE,

son of Dr. John Hale. (See p. 211, *ante.*)

JOSEPH F. EASTMAN,

son of Jonathan and Sarah (Fletcher) Eastman, born January 14. 1772. Studied medicine in New Boston with Dr. Wm. Gove, and after practising his profession for some years in New Boston, he relinquished it, returned to Hollis, and settled upon his farm near the middle of the town, where he continued to reside till his decease, Sept. 20. 1865. æt. 93. Dr. Eastman was a man of much general intelligence, enterprise and public spirit. He was the Moderator of the annual town meetings in Hollis, in fifteen different years, between 1812 and 1835, and was a Coroner for the county from 1802 to 1849.

JOSEPH BOYNTON,

son of Abraham and Mary (Hartshorn) Boynton, born March 26. 1789, studied medicine in Hollis, and afterwards removed to and settled in the State of New York.

LUKE LAWRENCE,

son of Daniel and Polly (Johnson) Lawrence, born April 14. 1803. Settled in his profession in Lunenburg, Mass. Died in Hollis, January 19. 1832, æt. 28.

CALVIN WHEELER,

son of Zebulon and Mary (Kendrick) Wheeler. born June 7. 1805.
Settled in his profession in Bristol, Ill.

JOHN R. SMITH,

son of Rev. Eli and Ama (Emerson) Smith, born February 12.
1807, studied medicine in Paris, Ky., settled first in his profession
at Paris, and afterwards in Lexington, Ky. He now (1879) resides in the town of Vermont, Missouri.

HENRY W. WILLOUGHBY,

son of Washington and Lucy (Saunderson) Willoughby, born December 21, 1816. Dr. Willoughby entered Amherst college in 1837.
and left college in his junior year, without graduating. He afterwards studied medicine at the medical college in Philadelphia, and
settled in his profession in Hollis, in 1855, where he still resides, in
the practice of it (1879).

JOHN G. WOOD,

son of Moses and Submit (Hardy) Wood. born December 27. 1830.
studied his profession in Philadelphia. and settled as a physician in·
Salem. Mass.. where he died.

JACOB MOOAR,

son of John and Rebecca (Abbot) Mooar, born March 7. 1831,
studied his profession at Hanover and Manchester, N. H.. and
settled as a physician in Manchester.

JOSIAH M. BLOOD,

son of Ebenezer and Elizabeth (Abbot) Blood. born July 3. 1832..
studied his profession in Hollis. and also at the University in New
York, settled as a physician in Temple. N. H.. and afterwards in
Ashby. Mass.

SAMUEL W. FLETCHER,

son of Samuel and Elizabeth (Corey) Fletcher, born September 18.
1831, studied his profession in Cambridge, Mass., New York city.
and also in Paris. France. Settled in his profession in Pepperell.
Mass., where he now resides.

(21)

WILLIAM H. CUTTER,

son of John H. and Susan (Pool) Cutter, born July 17, 1847,
studied his profession at the medical school in Hanover, N. H.,
and settled as a physician in Hollis.

LAWYERS BORN IN HOLLIS NOT GRADUATES OF COLLEGE.

ABEL CONANT,

son of Dea. Abel and Margaret (Jewett) Conant, born June 1, 1784.
Read law with Col. W. Hastings, in Townsend, Mass. Admitted
to the bar at Concord, Mass., in 1813. He practised his profession
in Townsend and New Ipswich, N. H., and in 1834 removed to
Lowell, Mass., and his health having partially failed he relinquished
his profession, and afterwards turned his attention to the study of
Chemistry and Mechanics, and became a useful and successful
inventor. At an early day he is said to have invented the seraphine
or parlor organ, and not long after the hollow auger, so much used
by wheelwrights. While he lived at Lowell, he invented and
patented the mortise door lock, now in common use, and the manufacture of which gives employment to so many persons. He afterwards discovered and patented the process of raising bread with
cream of tartar or other acids, also now in common use, but the difficulty of preventing infringements upon patent rights deprived Mr.
Conant, to a great extent, of personal advantage from his inventions. He is said to have made many other improvements of the
like character, and, to the day of his death, was engaged in per-
fecting several new inventions which he expected soon to make
public. His habits were simple, retiring and exemplary, and his
mind and memory remarkably clear till his last hours. Died at
Lowell, April 12, 1875, æt. 90.

DANIEL MOOAR,

son of Jacob and Dorcas (Hood) Mooar, born May 11, 1815. He
received an academical education at Milford, N. H., and Chester,
Vt. Afterwards he went to Covington, Ky., and read law at that
place and at the law school in Cincinnati, Ohio, and was admitted
to the bar in 1843. "He settled and practised his profession in
Covington for twenty-five years, and established a reputation as a
profound lawyer, a safe counsellor—for business integrity,—and a
high sense of honor, and several times filled the office of District

Judge." His health having become partially impaired by too close application to business, and, having acquired an ample fortune, he afterwards removed to Keokuk, Iowa, where he still resides, and is there engaged in extensive business.

In a biographical sketch of Judge Mooar, published in the Historical Atlas of Lee county, Iowa, in December, 1873, it is said of him " that he is now among the substantial and solid men of Keokuk, and a man of decided ability and varied information. * * Such men are real ornaments to any community and Keokuk has been fortunate in adding such an one to her citizens."

CHAPTER XXX.

PHYSICIANS WHO HAVE PRACTISED THEIR PROFESSION IN HOLLIS, AND MISCELLANEOUS BIOGRAPHICAL SKETCHES.

DR. JOHN HALE.

(See p. 211, *ante*.)

DR. JONATHAN FOX

was from Dracut, Mass. Married Zerviah Jones. Settled in Hollis as a physician in 1778, at the age of 24, and was regarded as a young man of much promise, and soon gained the esteem and confidence of the people. In the years 1779 and 1780, he was several times appointed a member of the Hollis committee for raising men for the army, in which service he was very efficient and successful. He died in Hollis, much lamented, October 26, 1782, at the early age of 28, his death being regarded as a public loss. His only daughter Zerviah, born February 16, 1779, became the wife of Rev. Samuel Worcester, D. D. His youngest son, Ebenezer, a man of great industry and business ability, after being for many years settled in his business in Salem, Mass., afterwards removed to Hollis, and became the owner of the farm now known as the "Fox place," where he died December 6, 1857, æt. 74.

DR. JONATHAN POOL.

(See p. 214, *ante*.)

DR. WILLIAM HALE.

(See p. 211, *ante*.)

DR. BENONI CUTTER

was a son of John and Susannah (Hastings) Cutter, born in New Ipswich, N. H., in 1771. He settled as a physician in Hollis in 1799, and married Phebe Tenney, oldest daughter of Capt. William

Tenney of Hollis, May 20, 1800. He was greatly respected, both as a citizen and as a physician, and in the year 1814 was appointed to the office of deacon of the Hollis church. Died in Hollis, January 17. 1816, æt. 44.

DR. PETER MANNING

was born in Townsend. Mass. He settled in Hollis as a physician in 1814 or 1815, and in 1817 he was a member of the School Committee. He removed from Hollis to Merrimack in 1818, and continued in the practice of his profession in Merrimack till 1838, and afterwards removed to Lunenburg, Mass., where he died.

DR. OLIVER SCRIPTURE,

son of Oliver and Jane Scripture, born in Mason, N. H., June 16, 1783. Married Eliza, the youngest daughter of Hon. Timothy Farrar of New Ipswich. Dr. Scripture settled in his profession in Hollis in the year 1818, as successor to Dr. Manning, and continued his practice as a physician in Hollis till his death, November 7, 1860, æt. 77. The inscription upon his tombstone, in the Hollis central burial ground, " The beloved Physician," is expressive of the affectionate esteem in which he was held by the people of the town. His father-in-law, Judge Farrar, passed the last years of his life in the family of Dr. Scripture, and died in Hollis, February 21, 1849. æt. 101 years, 7 months, 12 days.

DR. ORVILLE M. COOPER

was a native of Croydon, N. H., and graduated at the medical school at Hanover. in 1845. Dr. Cooper settled in his profession in Hollis, in 1846, and died in Hollis, February. 1847.

DR. JOHN L. COLBY,

settled in Hollis as a physician in 1847, soon after the decease of Dr. Cooper, and in 1848 he was a member of the School Committee in Hollis. In 1850 he removed from Hollis to Manchester, Mass., and about two years afterwards to Harlem, N. Y., where he is still supposed to reside.

DR. LOCKHART B. FARRAR

was born in Walpole, N. H., and was a graduate of the medical school in Castleton, Vt. Settled in his profession in Hollis, in 1850, upon the removal of Dr. Colby. In 1852 he also removed from Hollis to Manchester, Mass., and afterwards to the State of Illinois.

DR. WILLIAM A. TRACY,

son of Elisha L. Tracy, was born in Tunbridge, Vt., May 3, 1826. Attended medical lectures at Boston, Woodstock, Vt., and Hanover, N. H. Settled in his profession in Hollis, succeeding Dr. Farrar in September, 1852. Removed from Hollis to Nashua, in August, 1854. Appointed Surgeon of the 6th New Hampshire Infantry, October 25, 1861. Resigned on account of ill health, March 15, 1863, and returned to Nashua. Died at Nashua, March 15, 1864, æt. 37.

DR. HENRY BOYNTON,

son of Isaac Boynton, born in Pepperell, Mass. Studied medicine at the medical school in Woodstock, Vt. Settled in his profession in Hollis in September, 1854, as successor to Dr. Tracy. Practised his profession in Hollis till 1858, when he removed to Woodstock, Vt., and was succeeded by Dr. George P. Greeley. Appointed Assistant Surgeon of the 7th New Hampshire Infantry, October 15, 1861. Resigned January 24, 1864, and returned again to Woodstock.

DR. HENRY W. WILLOUGHBY.

(See page 321, *ante.*)

DR. GEORGE P. GREELEY,

son of Ezekiel Greeley, was born in Nashua, N. H. Attended medical lectures at Woodstock, Vt., Hanover, N. H., and at the College of Physicians and Surgeons in New York city, where he graduated in 1857. Settled as a physician in Hollis in 1858. Appointed Assistant Surgeon of the Second New Hampshire regiment, May, 1861; Surgeon of the Fourth New Hampshire regiment, October 8, 1862; honorably discharged, October 23, 1864. After leaving the army, he settled in his profession, first in Boston, and afterwards, in 1872, removed to Nashua, where he still practises his profession (1879).

DR. ELLERY CHANNING CLARKE.

was a son of Rev. Stillman Clarke, and was born in Winchester, N. H., March 21, 1836; entered Harvard college in 1855, and left in 1857. Studied medicine with Professor Albert Smith of Peterborough, N. H., and graduated at the medical college at Burlington, Vt., in 1860. Settled in Hollis in the spring of 1861, succeeding Dr. Greeley. Appointed Assistant Surgeon of the Eighth New Hampshire United States Infantry, January 18, 1862 ; promoted to Surgeon, June 5, 1863; discharged for disability, August, 1864 ; afterwards settled in Westfield, Mass.

DR. SYLVANUS BUNTON

was born in Allenstown, N. H. Graduated at Dartmouth college in 1840. Studied medicine in Baltimore. Settled in his profession in Manchester, N. H., where he continued till June, 1864, and was then appointed Assistant Surgeon of the 7th New Hampshire U. S. regiment, and in August, 1864, was promoted to Surgeon. Mustered out July 20, 1865, and after leaving the army, settled in his profession in Hollis, where he remained about three years, and then removed to Mont Vernon, N. H.

DR. ADONIJAH W. HOWE,

son of Dr. Luke Howe, was born in Jaffrey, N. H., September, 25, 1825. Graduated at the medical college in Hanover in 1850. Settled as a physician in Dunstable, Mass., in 1851. Came to Hollis in March, 1861. Removed from Hollis in 1865, and now in 1879, resides in Greenville, N. H.

DR. CHARLES G. COREY

was born in Jaffrey, N. H. Graduated at the medical college in Hanover, N. H., in 1857. Settled in his profession in Hollis in 1867, where he remained from three to four years, and then removed to Greenville, N. H., and died at Greenville, October 19, 1878, æt. 54.

NATHAN THAYER,

(Contributed by Miss G. A. Boutwell, a granddaughter.)

son of Elijah and Sarah (Robinson) Thayer, was born in Milford, Mass., July 6, 1781. He was a descendant of Thomas Thayer, who came to this country from England about 1630, and settled in Braintree, which town is supposed to have been named by the Thayer family in honor of their English birth-place. A son of Thomas Thayer settled in that part of Mendon, Mass., which is now known as Milford, about 1665, and for successive generations, and for a period of over one hundred and fifty years, the ancestors of Mr. Thayer were citizens of that ancient town. At the early age of

seventeen, Mr. Thayer came to Hollis " to seek his fortune." He
had for his capital, a common school education, and a good knowledge of the trade of house painting. His name appears first on the
Hollis tax lists in 1803. Mr. Thayer was so good a workman
that he was called frequently to Pepperell, Groton, and even as far
away as Andover to pursue his trade. He took especial pleasure
in the society of those places, and on his return would tell his children pleasant anecdotes of the Prescotts, Lawrences, and the
learned professors of Andover. He was a welcome guest in many
homes in those towns, and one of his daughters, who went to school
in Andover, recalls with pleasure the consideration which she received on her father's account.

For thirty years, Mr. Thayer employed his leisure of the winter
months in teaching school. In the early part of this century,
schools of the higher grades were almost unknown, and all those
inclined to study were dependent upon the district schools, and
many young men, as well as the children, availed themselves of his
instruction. He was an especially good grammarian, and by common consent all knotty questions in grammar were referred to him
by the other teachers.

He was a member of the Hollis examining School Committee in
1817, 1818, 1821, 1822, 1825, and 1827 ; and of the Superintending
School Committee, in 1828, 1829, and 1830. He was also a Justice
of the Peace from 1822 to 1830, and a Representative to the New
Hampshire General Court in 1812, 1819, 1820, and 1821. April 2,
1807, he married Hannah Jewett, daughter of Dea. Stephen Jewett,
Jun. She died March 17, 1824. She was the mother of six daughters and one son, all but one (the fourth daughter) survived her.
Mr. Thayer married March 27, 1825, Mary Jewett, a sister of his
first wife. She was the mother of two children, both of whom died
in infancy. She died October 16, 1833. Mr. Thayer died October
21, 1830, æt. 49.

JAMES BLOOD,

son of Solomon and Priscilla (French) Blood, was born in Hollis,
May 20, 1793, and died in Newburyport, Mass., June 27, 1876, æt.
83 years. For the following obituary tribute to the memory of Mr.
Blood, I am indebted to the Merrimack Family Visitor, published
at Newburyport, of the date of July 1, 1876. "Mr. Blood came
to this city in the year 1825, poor, respectable, industrious and

intelligent. His life was a success, and in all controllable events just what he would have it. We doubt if he would materially change it if he had to live it over again. He enjoyed the most perfect health till old age. He was one of the most industrious persons that ever lived, and his happiness was in his business. He loved to work for the sake of it, and would have continued to do so, though no gains should have come from it. But his business yielded its profits till his estate grew to exceed all his early expectations. His fellow citizens did not fail to appreciate his virtues, his integrity, his independent thought and straightforward action : and they honored him with a seat in the legislature, and many local offices, while, without his own solicitation, he was made Collector of Customs under two national administrations.

"Mr. Blood *enjoyed* life—in his nature he was happy. Under the gravity of his demeanor there was a quiet humor, and in the busiest moments of his most busy days, he was lively and witty—to old age ever seeing the bright side of events and the sunny spots of life.

" He was a man of firm convictions and religious faith which never deserted him. Life and death to him were equally natural and desirable, and he had no wish to stay here when his mission on earth was accomplished, nor any fear that he should not awake from his last sleep to renewed activities and joys. Death was not therefore shaded with fears, nor the grave with gloom. He went not like a cringing slave to punishment, but lay down quietly and hopefully as to pleasant dreams His funeral was from his residence on Friday *morning*, appropriate in time, for he was one of those to say, ' *bury me in the morning, when the sun will be upon my grave.*' "

JAMES PARKER, JUN.,

son of James and Betsey (Wright) Parker, was born in Hollis, April 1, 1815, and died in Springfield, Mass., Jan. 2, 1874, æt. 58. The following appreciative biographical sketch of Mr. Parker is in substance to be found in the October number of the New England Historical and Genealogical Register for 1874, p. 475.

" Mr. Parker was a native of Hollis. In 1833 he ' mounted the stage box' as a stage driver. In 1836 he became agent for Burt and Billings' stage line, between Worcester and Springfield, and continued in that capacity till the Western railroad was opened, when like Ginery Twitchell and others who had shown eminent ability in managing the ' whip and ribbons,' he was taken into the new service of transporting passengers and freight. Mr. Parker had charge of the first train of cars from Boston to Springfield, and his attention to passengers and gentlemanly bearing soon proved that he was ' the right man in the right place.' His pleasant countenance and never-failing urbanity will long be remembered by the thousands who had occasion to pass over that road during many of the earlier years of its existence.

" The first train from Boston to Springfield made the trip in exactly six hours, and Mr. Parker received many compliments, not only for what was regarded as remarkable speed, but also for his accurate observance of that ' old time table.' The train bearing among others, the directors of the road, left Boston at seven o'clock, A. M., and arrived at Springfield at 1 o'clock, P. M., September 27, 1839. The opening of the road was an event of such general rejoicing that it was publicly celebrated in Springfield upon the arrival of the first train under the command of Mr. Parker. So closely did Mr. Parker attend to his new duties, that for nineteen years after he entered upon them, he had been west of the Connecticut river but once, and it was jocosely said of him, that he did not know how the Springfield Armory looked, as he had seen only its back side for fifteen years. When Mr. Parker resigned his position as conductor, he was appointed superintendent of the sleeping cars, between Boston and New York, and in April, 1872, he was made superintendent of all the sleeping, parlor, passenger and baggage cars of all the trains between the two cities. During the twenty-nine years of his service as conductor, he is said to have travelled in that capacity, without serious accident to life or limb of his passengers, more than 1,500,000 miles, a distance equal to sixty times around the globe, and a greater distance, as is believed, than that of any other known railroad conductor.

" Upon Mr. Parker's retirement from office, an elegant gold watch was presented to him by his friends who had often travelled under his assiduous care, and the employees of the road gave him a valuable horse and carriage in token of their high appreciation of his services. In 1871 and 1873, he was elected a member of the Massachusetts House of Representatives. His house was filled with curiosities, old books, rare drawings, and other specimens of handicraft, which show that if he had devoted his life to art or to Archæological pursuits, he would probably have had but few superiors in these departments of knowledge. By reason of his interest in

Henry G. Little

these pursuits, he was admitted to a resident membership in the New England Historical and Genealogical Society, November 24, 1862, and he was also an honorary member of the New Hampshire Historical Society."

HENRY GILMAN LITTLE

was the sixth of the thirteen children of Abner B. and Nancy (Tenney) Little, and was born in Goffstown, N. H., March 31, 1813. During his infancy, his parents removed to Hollis, where he lived till his eighteenth year, enjoying such advantages for education as were then afforded in the Beaver Brook district, viz., two months of school in winter, and three in summer. In 1830, he left his paternal home in Hollis, and spent the next six years in Wethersfield, Ct., partly in study and teaching, and in part in labor. In March, 1836, he married Fidelia M. Stoddard, of Newington, Ct., and removed to the then new State of Illinois, and the next year settled in Henry county, where he passed thirty years of an active and busy life, engaged in agriculture, and filling various important offices of public trust. During the first year of his residence there he took part in organizing the county, and was elected Justice of the Peace, an office he held for twelve years and more. In 1850 he was High Sheriff, and Collector of the whole revenue of the county—at that time a position of great responsibility, there then being neither a safe, bank nor jail in the county. In 1856 he was elected to the Illinois legislature, of which he was for two years a member. He was for five years President of the Henry County Agricultural Society, which he had helped to organize. He was probably at no time free from public trust and duty, either as an officer of State, the county, town, church or school board.

In 1867 he removed to Grinnell, Iowa, on account of the educational advantages afforded by the college at that place. Here for four successive terms he has been elected Mayor of that city, and for most of the time has served as school director, and trustee of the church and society, and at Grinnell, (as in his former home), many substantial and tasteful improvements will long bear witness to his skill and public spirit.

In 1878 he was elected by the Iowa legislature one of the five trustees of the State Agricultural college, a post of high trust and great responsibility, involving the care of the endowment fund of a half million of dollars, together with the direction and management

of the flourishing college of two hundred and fifty students with
its large faculty. and the college farm of eight hundred acres.

At the age of sixty-five Mr. Little remains with unbroken health,
unabated vigor, energy and usefulness. Though afflicted by the
loss of an only son at the age of sixteen. he has reared to woman-
hood a family of five daughters, of whom three have graduated
from college, and all are now married. He has still. as always in
the past, a cheerful, attractive and hospitable home, and as yet has
no thought of retiring from active life.

LUTHER PRESCOTT HUBBARD,

was born in Hollis, June 30, 1808, and was the oldest child of
Luther and Hannah (Russell) Hubbard. Mr. Hubbard, in his
childhood and youth, attended the public schools in the Middle district in Hollis, and was for a short time a pupil in the Pinkerton
academy at Derry. He helped to build the first cotton mill in
Nashua in 1824; afterwards the Bunker hill monument, and also
superintended the fitting of the granite for the Tremont hotel in
Boston.

His views in respect to and against the use of tobacco have been
widely published by the American Tract Society, by the religious
and secular press, and also in the Sailor's Magazine.

Mr. Hubbard has been for twenty years a corresponding member of the Iowa State Historical Society, and is an honorary member of the New Hampshire Antiquarian Society, and is the author
of a Genealogy. entitled "Descendants of George Hubbard from
1600 to 1872," published in the year last named, and tracing his
family line ten generations. The last forty-five years of his life
have been zealously, and usefully devoted, mostly to the interests of
seamen. For many years he has been the financial agent of the
American Seamen's Friend Society, and also Secretary of the New
England Society of the city of New York, both of which offices he
still holds and fills acceptably.

He now resides in Greenwich. Connecticut, the State of his honored progenitor, George Hubbard. one of the first settlers of Wethersfield. Ct., in 1634, but has his office in New York city.

JOSEPH WHEAT, AN OLD-TIME STAGE-DRIVER.

Joseph Wheat, famous eighty years ago as a stage-driver, came
to Hollis in his youth, with his father, soon after the Revolution.

BUFFORD, BOSTON.

L. P. Hubbard

He was by trade a cooper, and built and owned the house on the main road leading from Hollis to Amherst, which, in 1796, he sold to Dea. Enos Hardy, and which was for many years afterwards the well-known homestead of Deacon Hardy. Soon after this sale, Wheat removed to Amherst and became interested in a line of stages, both as owner and driver,—the line running from Concord and beyond to Boston. I am indebted mainly to Rev. Dr. Bouton's History of Concord for the following humorous anecdotes of this primitive stage driver.*

"Of Joseph Wheat, who will be recollected as almost if not quite the first driver of a stage into Concord, and whose *nose* will be remembered *long*, I have two or three anecdotes. At one time being complained of by the people of Amherst, (one of the towns on his stage route,) that he did not give the customary notice of his approach by blowing a tin horn, he replied to this complaint through the Amherst Cabinet, 'that he was too poor to buy a tin horn, but that, in the future, when they should see his nose they might expect the stage in ten minutes.'

"Upon another occasion, stopping for his breakfast one frosty morning, a somewhat dainty passenger, sitting at the table opposite to him, and observing the effects of the cold coming from his nose, rudely requested Wheat to wipe it. 'Wipe it yourself,' coolly answered the driver, ' my nose is nearer to you than to me.'

"Again, when driving his stage from Concord to Hanover, he met Rev. Dr. Wheelock, president of the college, riding in his carriage. As he was about to pass the president, Wheat took hold of his nose and, turning it one side, said, 'I think, Mr. President, you can pass now.' "

It seems that Mr. Wheat, among other gifts and graces pertaining to his calling, had also that of *verse making*. As an illustration of the commendable change in the tastes and habits of the patrons of public stage coaches since the dram-drinking days of eighty years ago, we quote the closing stanza of one of Mr. Wheat's poetic effusions, giving notice to the public of his having established a new line of stages.

"Come, my old Friends, and take a seat
In this new Line with Joseph Wheat,
And when to your journey's end you've come,
Your friend will treat with good old Rum."

*Bouton's History of Concord, p. 577.

Another similar poetic effusion of his was the following advertisement of his business as a cooper.

> " My advice to farmers all
> Is—Pick your apples as they fall,
> And if your cider's pure and sweet,
> Please buy your casks of Joseph Wheat."

THE HOLLIS HERMITS.

DR. JOHN JONES.

There were two persons, formerly living in Hollis, somewhat famous in their day as " Hermits," viz., John Jones, commonly called " Dr. Jones," and Stephen Y. French, better known as " Leather French." Jones, the first named, according to the traditions of him, was the son of a wealthy British military officer of good family, born in England in the early part of the last century, and came to this country while yet a young man. After coming to America he is said to have lived a solitary, wandering life, till he came to Hollis soon after the war of the Revolution.

Upon settling in Hollis, he bought for himself a patch of ground of about four acres in the north part of the town, at a distance from any public road, near Mooar's hill so called, and now a part of the farm of Lot Mooar. Here he built for himself a small humble dwelling, which he called his " Lone Cottage." He set out on his grounds an orchard of choice varieties of grafted apple and other fruit trees, and also many kinds of shrubs, herbs and flowers, which he took great pains to cultivate, and it is said of him that he was the first person to introduce grafted fruit into Hollis.

In his youth Dr. Jones was crossed in love, as a result of which his mind became unsettled and distracted, and his disappointment ended in his eccentricities and wayward mode of life. He is reputed to have been educated for the pulpit, and at the early age of twenty, had had and accepted a call to settle in the ministry, which was broken off by his disappointment and the untimely death of his lady love. He was a person naturally of bright intellect, of much humor and ready wit, reputed somewhat of a poet, and some of his effusions in verse have come down to the present day.

Before coming to Hollis, he had written and published a long ballad, of near forty stanzas, telling the sad story of his life and troubles, entitled the " Major's only son and his True Love." My limits do not allow me to copy but a few extracts from this ballad. In its first stanza, its author says,

> "Come all young people far and near,
> A lamentation you shall hear
> Of a young man and his True-Love
> Whom he adored and prized above
> All riches." *   *   *   *

This ballad was learned by heart and sung sixty years ago by hundreds of the " young people" of Hollis and the neighboring towns, and also was often sung by the doctor himself in loud, sad tones, when alone in his " Lone Cottage." It appears from the recitals in the ballad that both the father and mother of the doctor were persistently and irreconcilably opposed to his marrying the maid of his choice, as he says,

> "Because she was of low degree
> And came of a poor family."

Angry at this opposition of the father and mother of the doctor, one day when Jones was visiting the young lady, *her* father said to him, as the ballad has it,

> "' My daughter is as good as you," and
> Turned this young man without his door
> And told him to come there no more."

After this enforced separation the young lady took to her chamber, sickened, pined away and soon after died. Shortly before her death she sent her brother for the " young man," to whom she told the sad tale of her sickness and sorrow. Taking the engagement rings from her fingers just before her death she gave them to him, saying,

> "Keep them for my sake
> And always when these rings you see,   '
> Remember that I died for thee." *   *
> " Tears down his cheeks as fountains run,
> He cried, alas! 'I am undone.
> No comfort ever shall I have,
> While I go mourning to my grave.'"

The " young man" attended the funeral of his betrothed as chief mourner, as the ballad has it.

> " Dressed in black from top to toe *   *
> And after that distracted run,
> And so forever was undone,
> And wandered up and down, alone."

While living in Hollis Jones supported himself in part by raising and preparing medicinal herbs, and various nostrums from them, which he peddled in Hollis and other towns near, hence his title of

"Doctor." In his wanderings about the country he usually wore a broad brimmed hat with a mourning weed around it, and a long, plaid dressing gown. In his thus going about, he carried with him two baskets, one in each hand, the one of which he named the "Charity," the other the "Pity basket." In these he carried for sale and barter his herbs and nostrums, and also "Liberty tea," so called, and, in their season, juniper berries, and scions for grafting, from his orchard, taking home with him, in the same baskets, the articles he got in exchange. He also kept for sale copies of verses written by him, including the ballad telling the story of his troubles.

Years ago, and within my own remembrance, many anecdotes were told of his impromptu verses and rhymes, and of his humor and wit. His age at his death, as inscribed on his gravestone, was sixty-nine, though he was supposed to have been somewhat older. But on this subject he was very taciturn, and inclined to keep the secret of his age to himself. At one time, an unmarried lady customer of his, to whom he had sold some of his "Liberty tea," of the name of Phebe (herself of uncertain age), took occasion to question him upon this matter, in the hope of solving the mystery. The doctor, in reply, told her that "she might ask him just as many questions as *she* was years old." Nettled at this evasive answer, Phebe reproachfully called him an "old cracked fiddle of one doleful tune," and demanded of him to take back his "Liberty tea" and return her money. In reply to this demand the doctor said to her,

> "Phebe, my dear, my own sweet honey,
> You've got your tea, and I've got my money."

It was his habit, as a spectator, to attend the courts at Amherst, where, as he used to say, the lawyers would try to get a "crumb of sport" out of him. On one occasion, having been bantered by them for one of his impromptu stanzas, he was afterwards invited by the host to eat at a second table, from which the judges and lawyers had just risen from a dinner of roast poultry. Having finished his meal, on rising from the table, in place of his customary after dinner grace, with one eye upon the lawyers, he gave expression to his sentiments in respect to his dinner and the *guests* at the first table in the following terse couplet.

> "Cursed be the owls
> That picked these fowls;
> And left the bones
> For Dr. Jones."

For the following anecdote of Dr. Jones, I am indebted to my
friend, Hon. J. B. Hill, who tells me that it was told him by his
father, Rev. Ebenezer Hill of Mason, who was cotemporary with
Dr. Jones, and for many years a member of the Hollis Association
of ministers. The doctor, as he says of himself in his ballad.
(having been educated for the ministry) at the time he lived in
Hollis, was in the habit of attending the meetings of this Association of ministers, as well as the courts, not as a *member*, but as one
of the persons styled " *company* " in the records of the Association. On such occasions, he sometimes proposed for discussion
questions in theology, which interested him. and at one time the
following, "Was there ever a man that had a tongue which never
told a lie, or a heart which never had an evil thought?" This question was promptly answered by all present with a decided *negative*
and " nailed wi' scripture." The doctor insisted on the *affirma-
tive*—and said to them that he would prove that they were all
wrong, and at once went to the door. and brought in one of his
baskets, and uncovering it showed them the *head* and *heart* of a
sheep. and pointing to them, exclaimed in triumph, " there is a
tongue that never told a lie, and a heart that never had an evil
thought, and they are both mine."

On another occasion, calling at a house where he wished for dinner, he said to the hostess, that if she would provide him one. he
would write for her a suitable epitaph, two lines of which were to
be composed before dinner. and two after. This bargain being
struck. he wrote for her the first two lines."

> "Good old Sarah died of late,
> And just arrived at Heaven's gate."

The good lady concluded that these lines would fit her case, and
provided the dinner. But the entertainment not having been wholly
to the taste of the doctor, on rising from the table. and with one
hand on the door latch, he added to the first two lines,

> "Old Gabriel met her with a club
> And knocked her back to Beelzebub!"

There were at that time, in Hollis, three young men to whom the
doctor was strongly attached, and whom he called his adopted sons,
viz., Thaddeus Wheeler, Jun., Timothy Emerson, and J. Coolidge
Wheat. the last named, by trade, a stone cutter, and maker of gravestones. During the life of Jones, and under his eye and direction.
Wheat had made for him a large, neatly finished gravestone, fully
(22)

completed and lettered, except the date of his death, with the epitaph inscribed upon it, furnished by the doctor, and copied from a
stanza of his ballad.   By his will dated January 1, 1791, the little
estate that the doctor left was given to his three adopted sons, with
the single condition, that Wheat should finish and set up his gravestone. This gravestone is now to be found standing at the grave
of the doctor, near the north end of the central burial ground in
Hollis, with the following inscription :

"DR. JOHN JONES,
Died July 14, 1796, æt. 69.
" In youth he was a scholar bright,
In learning he took great delight,
He was a Major's only son,
It was for love he was undone."

STEPHEN YOUNGMAN FRENCH.

Another somewhat noted hermit, a native of Hollis, was Stephen
Y. French, better known by his acquired name of " Leather
French," a son of Joseph French, a Hollis soldier of the Revolution,
and Mary (Youngman) French, and was born in Hollis, September
23, 1781. Early in life he wandered to Exeter in the State of
Maine, where for many years he lived in his little cabin as a hermit, solitary and alone. Hon. John B. Hill, the author of the
history of Mason, who was settled in his profession as a lawyer
in Exeter for several years, and was well acquainted with this
recluse, says of him, that he was harmless, simple minded, poverty
stricken, and of feeble understanding. That it was manifest that
French and work of all sorts had had a falling out at an early day,
and had parted company forever. Being utterly destitute of family or friends, he took up his abode upon a tract of land in Exeter,
known as the " Hurricane," for the reason that all attempts to settle it had been abandoned, the felled trees having been left on the
ground to rot, over which fires had run, and the land itself left to
an overgrowth of brushwood, brambles and weeds. Upon this
desolate and forsaken spot French built for himself a little hut,
cleared off a small patch of it for corn and vegetables, and there
lived a lonely, weary and poverty-stricken life until, in old age, he
found shelter and a comfortable home in the Exeter alms-house,
where he died, at the age of near eighty years, March 8, 1858.
His entire wardrobe was mainly of tanned sheepskins, hence his

acquired name of " Leather French." His name and fame have
been perpetuated in the following pleasant stanzas to his memory,
copied from a little volume of poems by David Barker, Esq., late
of Bangor, Me., who was a native of Exeter.

"TO LEATHER FRENCH.

"You have haunted the dreams of my sleep, Leather French,
   You have troubled me often and long;
And now to give rest to the waves of my soul,
   Leather French, let me sing you a song.

"I suppose the cold world may sneer, Leather French,
   For it has done so too often before,
When the innermost spirit has snatched up its harp,
   Just to sing o'er the grave of the poor.

"Never mind, let them laugh, let them sneer, Leather French,
   We will not be disturbed by them long,
For we'll step aside from the battle of life,
   While I question and sing you a song.

"You were poor when you lived here below, Leather French,
   And you suffered from hunger and cold,
And it was well you escaped from the storm and the blast
   At the time you grew weary and old.

"Has that old leather garb that you wore, Leather French,
   That you wore, in the days long ago,
Been exchanged for the robe that you named in your prayer,
   For a robe that is whiter than snow?

"And that dreary old hut where you dwelt, Leather French,
   That old hut on the ' Hurricane ' lands,
Was it bartered by you at the portals of death
   For a house not erected with hands?

"When the toys that I love become stale, Leather French,
   And my life's fitful fever is passed,
Shall I safely cross over the Jordan of Death?
   Shall I meet you in Heaven at last?

"Tell me true, tell me all, tell me now, Leather French,
   For the tale you can tell me is worth
More to me than the wisdom, the pleasure, the fame
   And the riches and honors of earth.

"Shall I meet no response to my call, Leather French?
   Tell me quick for I cannot wait long,
For I'm summoned again to the battle of life.—
   Leather French, I have finished my song."

The personal biographical sketches presented in different connec-
tions in this history, it is believed, are more numerous than will be
readily found in any other like town history. Still it is not to be
presumed that these sketches embrace all the natives or permanent
residents of the town whose names deserve honorable mention.

Many others of the descendants of the early settlers, neither "graduates of college," nor known to the public as "ministers," "lawyers," "physicians, officeholders or politicians" are, doubtless, equally worthy. Of these, many emigrated to other States or towns, and by their enterprise, intelligence and personal integrity, became honored citizens in their new homes. More of them, "whose sober wishes never learned to stray," settled in their native town, and, "content to breathe their *native* air on their own ground," have creditably sustained the good name of a worthy and honored ancestry.

CHAPTER XXXI.

NAMES OF SUCH PERSONS AS HAVE DECEASED SINCE THE WAR OF THE REVOLUTION, AT THE AGE OF EIGHTY YEARS OR MORE, WHOSE AGES WITH THE DATE OF THEIR DECEASE HAVE BEEN ASCERTAINED.

1783, May 27, Widow Martha Hardy,	82 yrs.	
" Oct. 14, Rev. Francis Worcester,	85	
1785, July 10, Wid. Hannah Farr,	92	
" Nov. 7, Dea. Samuel Goodhue,	90	
1786, June 2, Wid. Mary Harris,	81	
1787, Dec. 13, Lt. Benjamin Farley, in his 80th y		
1789, Wid. Lydia Ulrich,	104, 4m	
" Wid. Sarah Kemp,	90	
1790, May 25, Mrs. Susanna Jewett,	82	
1791, Oct. 5, Dea. Nathaniel Jewett,	81	
1793, Feb. 2, John Willoughby,	85	
1795, Sept. 23, Wid. Lydia Taylor,	83	
1797, May 20, Wid. Joanna Farley,	80	
1798, Sept. 21, Wid. Anna Powers,	90	
1800, Oct. 2, Wid. Hannah Hunt,	94	
1801, Sept. 30, Rev. Daniel Emerson,	85	
1802, Feb. 7, Ensign Benj. Parker,	82	
1808, Feb. 13, Mrs. Margaret Jewett,	82	
" Mar. 6, James Jewett,	85	
" Mar. 6, Lt. Amos Eastman,	88	
" Apr. 12, Mrs. Abigail Hardy,	82	
" July 27, Wid. Kezia Taylor,	86	
1809, Mar. 20, Zachariah Shattuck,	85	
" Aug. 21, Wid. Catharine Thurston,	90	
1811, Feb. 9, Capt. Reuben Dow,	81	
" Mrs. Esther Scott,	94	
1812, Wid. Abigail Wright,	96	
" Feb. 28, Wid. Hannah Emerson,	90	
" Apr. 26, Wid. Ruth Boynton,	88	
1813, Mar. 7, Phineas Hardy,	86	
" May 24, Samuel Ober,	80	
" Nov. 12, Wid. Mehitable Eastman,	88	
1814, Sept. 24, Nicholas Youngman,	91	
1815, Jan. 10, Nehemiah Woods,	83	
" Nov. 8, Wid. Elizabeth Shattuck,	88	
1816, Nov. 13, Wid. Alice Parker,	83	

1817, Aug. 13, Noah Worcester, Esq.,	81 yrs	
1818, Jan. 2, Abijah Gould,	82	
1819, Apr. 27, Jonas Flagg,	87	
1823, Jan. 31, Wid. Susanna Pierce,	85	
1825, Jan. 3, Wid. Hannah Parker,	95	
" Feb. 13, Miss Alice Powers,	88	
" June 7, Wid. Martha Flagg,	84	
" July 17, Wid. Lydia Dow,	92	
1826, Sept. 25, Benjamin Saunderson,	80	
" Oct. 6, Lt. Ebenezer Jewett,	83	
1827, Jan. 16, Wid. Sarah Hardy,	80	
" Jan. 28, Lt. Ebenezer Farley,	80	
" Mar. 7, Silas Spaulding,	80	
1828, Nov. 7, Thomas Patch,	85	
1829, Jan. 7, Wid. Miriam Dix.	90	
" Jan. 29, Daniel Lovejoy,	83	
1830, April 7, Wid. Sarah Holden,	90	
" Oct. 2, Wid. Elizabeth Hale,	98	
1831, May Wid. Sarah Lovejoy,	83	
" May 24, Wid. Lydia Lovejoy,	84	
" July 2, Wid. Hepzibah Worcester,	85	
1832, Feb. 28, Wid. Hannah Ames,	81	
" May 7, Phineas Hardy, Jun.,	81	
" May 22, Silas Marshall,	86	
" Aug. 2, Amos Eastman, Esq.,	81	
" Oct. 26, Lt. Samuel Willoughby,	86	
1833, Jan. William Ball,	102, 5m	
" April 5, Lt. Caleb Farley,		
1834, Oct. 10, Jonathan Hobart,	81	
" Nov. 6, Wid. Sibbel Spaulding,	88	
" Dec. 12, Abel Brown,	84	
1836, Feb. 19, Wid. Elizabeth Powers,	85	
" April, Wid. Sarah Eastman,	86	
1837, Jan. 13, Stephen Farley,	84	
" Benjamin Abbott,	88	
" Dec. 12, Capt. John Clapp,	80	

1838, Dec. 12, Wid. Abigail Ober, 93 yrs.
1839, Wid. Hannah W. Shattuck, 95
" Nov. 1, Stephen Dow, 82
1841, Jan. 4, Wid. Sarah Brown, 83
" Oct. 10, Wid. Priscilla Blood, 95
" Oct. 29, Wid. Betty Austin, 99
1842, Wid. Susannah Wood, 81
" June 30, Wid. Mary Bailey, 90
" Sept. 3, Mary, wife of Capt. D. Bailey, 84
" Dec. 5, Miss Eunice Marshall, 93
1843, Apr. 11, Silas French, 81
" June 3, Wid. Ruth Farley, 87
" Oct. 19, Wid. Abigail Kittridge, 93
" Dec. 8, Wid. Sibbel Proctor, 90
1844, Sept. 29, Moses Ames, 80
1847, Jan. 1, Capt. William Brown, 80
" Mar. 13, Capt. Daniel Bailey, 91
" April 1, Wid. Sarah Worcester, 85
" May 11, Rev. Eli Smith, 87
" Nov. 25, Jonas Woods, 88
1848, Mar. 9, Wid. Mary Rockwood, 94
" Dec. 30, Wid. Abigail Runnells, 81
1849, Jan. 21, Enoch Jewett, 92
" June 4, David French, 85
" Oct. 5, Wid. Rebecca Ames, 85
1850, May 24, Wid. Mary Jewett, 84
" Aug. 23, Jonathan Saunderson, 84
1851, Mar. 11, Wid. Abigail Colburn, 96
" May 20, Wid. Rebecca Ball, 83
" Aug. 4, Wid. Dorcas Mooar, 81
" Sept. 24, James Jewell, 98
1852, Feb. 13, Wid. Sarah Blood, 85
" May 11, Solomon Hardy, 85
" Sept. 25, Daniel Merrill, 92
1853, Oct. 22, Wid. Azubah Wheeler, 101,11 m
1854, July 31, Daniel Dow, 84
" Oct. 10, Dr. William Hale, 92
1855, Mar. 25, Jonas Lawrence, 81
" Sept. 28, Wid. Abigail Hardy, 84
" Oct. 8, Samuel Smith, 81
1856, May 8, Phineas H. Holden, 84
" Dec. 13, Ruth Hall, 84
" Dec. 15, Wid. Betsey Burge, 82
1857, Jan. 9, Wid. Rebecca Whiting, 88
" May 18, Dea. Enos Hardy, 85
" Nov. 24, Wid. Sybil Holt, 80
" Dec. 22, Capt. Isaac Parker, 85
" Dec. 22, Lt. Edward Johnson, 82
1858, Aug. 19, Wid. Olive Proctor, 80
" Oct. 10, Wid. Esther Hale, 86
1860, Mar. 18, Simon Stone, 83
" Aug. 4, Wid. Ama Smith, 91
" Aug. 4, Wid. Sarah Pool, 90

1860, Nov. 3, Ebenezer Farley, 86 yrs.
1861, Apr. 18, Capt. Thomas Proctor, 81
1862, Jan. 2, Wid. Olive Parker, 89
" Jan. 2, Wid. Fanny Lawrence, 87
" Oct. 18, Wid. Dorothy Wood, 84
1863, Jan. 26, Robert Colburn, 88
1864, " Miss Sarah Farley, 82
1865, Sept. 16, Benjamin M. Farley, Esq., 83
" Sept. 20, Dr. Joseph F. Eastman, 93
" Oct. 30, Nathan Colburn, 80
1867, May 13, Moses Truell, 84
1868, Apr. 25, Daniel Shedd, 83
1869, Mar. 21, Wid. Hannah Willoby, 84
" July 25, Wid. Sally Hardy, 95
" Sept. 26, Jonas Woods, 87
1870, Feb. Wid. Nancy Smith, 86
" Feb. 26, Maj. James Wheeler, 84
" June 21, Jonas Blood, 96
" Wid. Hannah Hubbard, 90
1871, Jan. 9, Thaddeus Wheeler, 97
" Apr. 7, Mary Holden, 85
" Apr. 18, Thaddeus Marshall, 96
" May 6, Wid. Abigail Clough, 82
" Aug. 29, Wid. Esther Wheeler, 84
1872, May 22, Capt. Jonathan T. Wright, 84
" Sept. 18, Simon Saunderson, 81
1873, Feb. 12, Asaph Spaulding, 93
" Feb. 21, Benjamin Ranger, 80
" May 14, John Shedd, 81
" June 12, Wid. Sarah W. Richardson, 84
" Oct. 26, James Farley, 82
" Dec. 3, Dea. William Emerson, 82
1874, Feb. 12, Mrs. Rebecca Baldwin, 87
" Feb. 25, Dea. Isaac Farley, 90
" Feb. 26, Isaac Woods, 82
" May 17, Miss Polly Rockwood, 89
" Nov. 14, Wid. Susan Fox, 84
1875, Jan. 24, Wid. Lydia Colburn, 88
" Mar. 11, Wid. Betsey H. Mooar, 92
" Mar. 11, Wid. Bridget French, 97
" June 25, Wid. Rebecca Blood, 90
" Dec. 9, Wid. Sally Hale, 94
1876, Jan. 31, Joseph Shattuck, 92
" Jan. 31, Wid. Susanna Blood, 94
" Mar. 24, Capt. Jeremiah Dow, 80
1877, Apr. Wid. Nancy Wright, 88
" July 30, Wid. Ruth Farley, 80
" Sept. 12, Wid. Oliver Willoby, 83
1878, Feb. 6, Jesse Hardy, 83
" Mar. 6, Ebenezer Farley, 80
" Apr. 3, Wid. Abigail Smith, 92
1879, Jan. 24, Wid. Elizabeth Woodward, 97
" Feb. 22, Wid. Hannah Russell, 83
" Mar. 8, Wid. Sarah Austin, 93.

CHAPTER XXXII.

MARRIAGES TO BE FOUND RECORDED IN THE RECORDS OF THE DISTRICT OF DUNSTABLE.

1743, Feb. 7, Elias Dickey and Rose McDaniels,both of West Dunstable.
1744, Oct. 9, Samuel Farley and Hannah Brown, " "
"   " John Brown and Kezia Wheeler, " "
" Dec. 11, Benjamin Blanchard and Kezia Hastings, " "
1745, Jan., Thomas Nevins of W. Dunstable and Bridget Snow of Nottingham.
" " 4, Joseph Farley of W. Dunstable and Esther Spalding of Litchfield.
" Feb. 9, Josiah Conant of West Dunstable and Catharine Emerson of Reading.
" Mar. 2, Robert Colburn and Elizabeth Leeman, both of W. Dunstable.
" May 6, John Boynton, Jun. of W. Dunstable and Lydia Jewett of Rowley.
" Nov., Jacob Blanchard and Elizabeth Lawrence, both of W. Dunstable.
" " 26, Wm. Shattuck of W. Dunstable and Experience Curtis of Nottingham.

MARRIAGES RECORDED IN THE FIRST THREE VOLUMES OF THE HOLLIS RECORDS.

1743, May 24, Jonathan Danforth and Anna Blanchard.
1744, " 29, William Adams and Mary Spear.
" Nov. 7, Rev. Daniel Emerson and Hannah Emerson of Malden.
1747, Sept. 12, Joshua Blanchard of Hollis and Sarah Burge, Chelmsford, "publish'd."
" Mar. 21, Robert Colburn of Monson and Elizabeth Smith of Hollis, "
1748, Aug. 12, Nathaniel Clement of Hancock and Wid. Hannah Cummings of H. pub.
1750, Nov. 1, James Wheeler and Mary Butterfield.
" Dec. 4, Jonathan Melvin and Mary Brooks.
1751, Mar. 19, Peter Wheeler and Mehitabel Jewett.
1752, Dec. 27, Oliver Lawrence and Mary Cummings.
1753, Apr. 1, Eleazer Cumings and Martha Brown.
1754, May 1, Timothy Cook of Hollis and Abigail Wheat of Concord.
1754, June 2, Samuel Burge and Joanna Farley.
1755, May 6, Matthew Wallace and Jean Lesley.
" " 20, Whitcomb Powers and Mary Dolliver.
" " 27, Samuel Whittemore and Olive Blanchard.
" June 2, Josiah Fisk and Sarah Colburn.
" Nov. 6, Aaron Colburn of Dracut and Phebe Harris of Hollis.
" " 27, Josiah Blood of Hollis and Sarah Heywood of Chelmsford.
1756, Jan. 1, John Astin and Sarah Hastings, both of Hollis.
" " 29, Moses Smith and Mary Boynton " "
" Mar. 25, Samuel Brown and Mary Glene " "
" Apr. 8, Joseph Bates of New Ipswich, and Phebe Powers of Hollis.
" " 20, Nehemiah Woods of Hollis, and Sarah Lakin of Groton.

1756, Nov. 16,   Edward Taylor and Sarah Sanders, both of Hollis.
1757, Jan.   5,   Stephen Powers of Hollis and Lucy Cumings of Dunstable..
  "   "   5,   John Brooks and Mary Kemp, both of Hollis.
  "   Feb. 22,   Noah Worcester and Lydia Taylor "   "
  "   July 11,   Joshua Smith of Hollis and Hannah Baldwin of Townsend.
  "   Aug. 2,   James Whiting of Hollis and Mary Douglas of Pepperell.
  "   Sept. 13,   Nathaniel Blanchard and Elizabeth Rolfe, both of Hollis.
  "   " 15,   Thomas Colburn of Pepperell and Esther Flagg of Hollis.
1758, Feb. 23,   Ezekiel Jewett and Lucy Townsend, both of Hollis.
  "   Apr. 20,   Zerubbabel Kemp and Hannah Colburn, both of Hollis.
  "   May 30,   Jacob Foster and Lydia Barrett,   "   "
  "   Nov. 16,   Jonathan Russ of Hollis and Lucy Kendall of Litchfield.
1759, Mar. 29,   William Brooks and Abigail Kemp, both of Hollis.
  "   " 21,   Stephen Martin and Patience Worcester, "   "
  "   Dec. 6,   Eleazer Stearns and Elizabeth Pierce,   "   "
1760, Feb. 7,   Caleb Stiles and Elizabeth Townsend,   "   "
  "   Mar. 25,   Richard Warner of Pepperell and Hannah Eastman of Hollis.
  "   Apr. 24,   John Campbell of Townsend and Sarah Barton of Hollis.
  "   July 10,   Jonas Willoughby and Hannah Bates, both of Hollis.
  "   Sept. 1,   James French and Sarah Brooks,   "   "
  "   Nov. 13,   John Atwell and Bridget Cumings,   "   "
  "   " 27,   Josiah French and Sarah Astin,   "   "
1761, Jan. 22,   Samuel Brown and Mary Wheeler,   "   "
  "   Apr. 2,   William Shattuck of Hollis and Zilpha Turner of Lancaster.
  "   Nov. 2,   Francis Blood and Elizabeth Spalding, both of Hollis.
  "   Dec. 24,   David Wright of Pepperell and Prudence Cumings of Hollis.
1762, Jan. 7,   Ephraim Burge and Anna Abbot, both of Hollis.
  "   " 27,   James Hobart and Hannah Cumings "   "
  "   Feb. 23,   Ebenezer Kendall and Lucy Cumings "   "
  "   Mar. 18,   Amos Fisk and Elizabeth Flagg   "   "
  "   June 21,   Zachariah Parker and Elizabeth Brown, both of Hollis.
1762, July 1,   William Waters of Townsend and Mary Lesley of Hollis.
  "   "   7,   Timothy Astin and Elizabeth Ames, both of Hollis.
  "   Sept. 20,   Jonathan Fowler and Lucy Kemp, .   "   "
1763, Feb. 24,   Thomas Boynton and Abigail Elliot,   "   "
  "   "   3,   Eleazer Parker and Dinah Farnsworth. "   "
  "   May 5,   Francis Powers and Elizabeth Cumings, both of Hollis.
  "   June 9,   Joseph Stearns and Mary Shattuck of Monson.
  "   Apr. 27,   Jotham Cumings and Anna Brown, both of Hollis.
  "   Sept. 1,   Isaac Powers and Abigail Sanders,   "   "
1764, Jan. 20,   Nathaniel Blood and Esther Hobart,   "   "
  "   Feb. 14,   Job Harris of Athol and Eleanor Harris of Hollis.
  "   Sept. 27,   Thomas Pratt and Caty Cumings, both of Hollis.
  "   "   8,   Peter Stearns and Abigail Wheat, both of Hollis.
  "   Nov. 28,   Jonathan Powers of Dunstable and Susannah Willoughby of Hollis.
1765, Feb. 28,   Ezekiel Jewett and Anna Williams, both of Hollis.
  "   Apr. 1,   Levi Fletcher of Dunstable and Phebe Stearns of Hollis.
  "   "   2,   Thomas Merrill of Pembroke and Abigail Ambrose of Hollis.
  "   Aug. 27,   James Gould and Mary Lovejoy, both of Hollis.
  "   Oct. 8.   Silas Brown and Lucy Wheeler,   "   "
1766, May 22,   Richard Pierce and Susannah Jewett, both of Hollis
  "   " 29,   Trueworthy Smith and Sarah Taylor,   "   "
  "   June 5,   Elnathan Blood and Deborah Phelps,   "   "
  "   Nov. 6,   Ebenezer Farley and Betty Wheeler,   "   "
  "   " 27,   Swallow Tucker and Lucretia Carter,   "   "
1767, Feb. 26,   Isaac Stearns and Rebekah Jewett,   "   "
  "   Mar. 6,   David Wallingford and Elizabeth Leeman, both of Monson.
  "   June 9,   Christopher Lovejoy and Hannah Kemp, both of Hollis.

1707, Oct. 22, Joshua Davis and Dorothy Wheeler, both of Hollis.
" Nov. 19, Daniel Lovejoy and Sarah Wyman. " "
" " 19, Joseph Pierce and Sarah Phelps, " "
1768, Jan. 28, William Cumings and Mehitable Eastman, both of Hollis.
" Mar. 24, William Nevins and Rebekah Chamberlain. " "
" Apr. 21, James Taylor of Hollis and Lois Butterfield of Dunstable.
" July 7, John Stearns of Hollis and Lucy Shedd of Dunstable.
" Nov. 3, Samuel Cumings, Jun., and Lydia Webster, both of Hollis.
" " 15, Benjamin Shattuck and Mary Proctor, " "
" " 16, Emerson Smith and Mary Page of Hollis.
" " 17, Daniel Emerson, Jun., of Hollis and Ama Fletcher of Dunstable.
" " 24, Benjamin Astin and Betty Farley, both of Hollis.
" " 24, Abel Shipley and Lucy Farley, " "
" Dec. 12, Francis Blood and Abigail Conroy, both of Hollis.
" " 15, James Foster of Temple and Hannah Jewett of Hollis.
1769, Jan. 5, Solomon Blood and Priscilla French, both of Hollis.
" " 9, Josiah Conant of Hollis and Elizabeth Elliot of Mason.
" Feb. 7, Nahum Powers and Mary Wheat, both of Hollis.
" June 22, Ebenezer Nutting and Elizabeth Abbot, both of Hollis.
" Oct. 5, Thomas Kemp and Mehitable Lovejoy, " "
" " 17, Thaddeus Wheeler and Elizabeth Farmer, " "
" " 19, Jonathan Bates of Ashby and Mehitable Willoughby of Hollis.
" Nov. 22, Zachariah Lawrence, Jun., and Rebekah Powers, both of Hollis.
" " 23, Jonas Bancroft of Worcester and Sarah Blood of Hollis.
1770, Jan. 11, Isaac Pierce of Pepperell and Sarah Blood of Hollis.
" Feb. 15, Jeremiah Wheeler of Concord and Kezia Blanchard of Hollis.
" Oct. 18, Ebenezer Ball and Elizabeth Davis, both of Hollis.
" Dec. 6, John Philbrick and Sarah Jewett, " "
1771, Jan. 2, Isaac Stevens and Elizabeth Johnson, both of Hollis.
" " 22, James Fiske and Sarah Leeman, " "
" Feb. 1, Joseph French and Mary Youngman, " "
" Mar. 10, Cyrus Proctor and Sibbel Farnsworth, " "
" " 19, Solomon Pierce and Lucy Parker, " "
" May 3, Timothy French and Anna Willoughby " "
" Aug. 1, James Colburn and Kezia Taylor, " "
" " 20, Solomon Wheat and Sarah Ball, " "
" Sept. 5, Amos Lamson and Mary Stevens, " "
" Nov. 14, Edward Taylor and Mary Worcester, " "
" " 21, Jerahmael Bowers and Martha Tenney, " "
" " 28, Zachariah Shattuck and Elizabeth Farley, " "
" Dec. 19, Jesse Churchill of Plymouth, Mass., and Abigail Worcester.
1772, Jan. 14, Thomas Powell and Elizabeth Stevens, both of Hollis.
" " 22, Simeon Lovejoy and Grace Lovejoy, " "
" Feb. 20, Joseph Nevins and Sarah Powers, " "
" May 12, Ephraim Lund and Alice Wheeler, " "
" Apr. 16, Nathan Blood and Elizabeth Noyes, " "
" Sept. 6, Benjamin Farmer of Hollis and Sarah Emerson of Nottingham West.
" " 30, Noah Worcester and Hepzibah Sherwin, both of Hollis.
" .Nov. 11, Jonathan Ames and Frances Powers, " "
" " 17, Thomas Cumings and Hannah Pool, " "
" Dec. 3, Zachariah Kemp and Sarah Townsend. " "
" " 17, Timothy Wyman and Elizabeth Shattuck, " "
" " 24, John Phelps, Jun., of Hollis and Mary Lakin of Groton.
1773, Feb. 16, Jacob Lovejoy and Elizabeth Baxter, both of Hollis.
" Mar. 1, Lebbeus Wheeler and Elizabeth Carter " "
" Apr. 22, John Kendall of Amherst and Molly Boynton of Hollis.
" " 28, Joseph Brown and Lois Blood, both of Hollis.
" June 29, Ebenezer Stearns and Rachel Ames, " "
(23)

1773, June 29, Jonathan Emerson of Nottingham West and Sibbel Farmer of Hollis.
" Sept. 8, Timothy Wheeler of Plymouth and Mary Nevins of Hollis. .
" Oct. 7, Joshua Stiles of Lyndeborough and Mehitabel Leeman of Hollis.
" Nov. 25, Thomas Wakefield of Amherst and Elizabeth Hardy of Hollis.
" Dec. 23, Levi Fletcher and Esther Bennet, both of Hollis.
" " 30, Christopher Farley and Ruth Jewett " "
1774, Jan. 6, Amos Eastman and Ruth Flagg, " "
" " 13, Jonas Lesley and Elizabeth Dow, " "
" " 20, Jonas Blood and Molly Brown, " "
" Feb. 10, John Goss and Catharine Conant, " "
" " 17, Manasseh Smith and Hannah Emerson, " "
" " 24, John Kneeland of Boston and Ann Hobart of Hollis.
" Feb. 24, Samuel Gerrish of Boscawen and Lucy Noyes of Hollis.
" 8, Obadiah Eastman of Bath and Elizabeth Searle of Hollis.
" June 28, John Willoughby of Hollis, and Elizabeth Sprake of Billerica.
" Aug. 4, Samson Powers and Elizabeth Nutting, both of Hollis.
" Sept. 15, Stephen Hazleton and Esther Hildreth " "
" " 19, Samuel Cunningham and Susannah Carter, " "
" Nov. 22, Samuel Conroy and Alice Blood, " "
" " 24, Nehemiah Hardy and Molly Taylor, " "
" Dec. 15, Benjamin Wright and Esther Taylor, " "
1775, Jan. 3, John Smith of Nottingham W. and Sarah Merrill of Hollis.
" " 4, Emerson Smith of Hollis and Abigail Ayre.
" " 12, Jonathan Lovejoy and Rebekah Ball, both of Hollis.
" Feb. 9, Benjamin Nevins and Annis Moore, both of Hollis.
" " 16, Joshua Blanchard, Jun., and Lucy French, both of Hollis.
" Mar. 16, Timothy Blood and Sarah Dix, both of Hollis.
" " 22, Capt. Jonas Pollard of Westford and Mrs. Elizabeth Abbot of Hollis.
" Apr. 20, Caleb Blood and Rebecca Hopkins, both of Hollis.
" May 18, David Hardy of Wilmington and Hannah Worcester of Hollis.
" Sept. 15, Minot Farmer and Abigail Barron, both of Hollis.
" " 18, Timothy French and Hannah Wright, both of Hollis.
" Nov. 7, Parmenter Honey and Sarah Hale, both of Hollis.
" " 30, Nathaniel Ball and Martha Boynton, both of Hollis.
1776, Jan. 18, Nathaniel Rideout and Susannah Spaulding, both of Hollis.
" Feb. 20, Samuel Ambrose and Mary Goodhue, both of Hollis.
" July 2, Jacob Putnam of Wilton and Wid. Patience Martin of Hollis.
" " 17, Ensign Daniel Merrill of Hollis and Jerusha Williams of Pepperell.
" " 25, William French, Jun., of Hollis and Lucy Fletcher of Chelmsford.
" Aug. 18, Job Bayley and Mehitable French, both of Hollis.
" Sept. 10, Josiah Hobart of Groton and Lucy Kendall of Hollis.
" Nov. 3, Samuel Abbot and Susannah Hobart, both of Hollis.
" Dec. 25, Thomas Jaquith and Rhoda Spaulding, both of Hollis.
1777, Feb. 20, Ebenezer Melvin of Cockermouth and Joanna Bayley of Hollis.
" May 8, James Colburn and Elizabeth Blood, both of Hollis.
" Nov. 12, Daniel Mosher and Lydia Gilson, " "
" " 18, Nehemiah Pierce and Mary Hobart, " "
" Dec. 4, John Ball of Temple and Hannah Farley of Hollis.
" " 18, Moses Thurston and Catharine Conant, both of Hollis.
" " 18, Jonathan Hobart and Alice Wright, " "
" " 18, Joseph Farley and Bridget Powers, " "
1778, Mar. 31, Joseph Stearns and Abigail Wheat, " "
" April 9, Elijah Clark and Martha Runnells, " "
" May 26, Joshua Boynton and Mary Parker, " "
" June 9, William Ayers of Haverhill and Mary Runnells of Hollis.
" Aug. 16, John Warren of New Ipswich and Sarah Eastman of Hollis.
" " 23, William Wood and Susannah Wright, both of Hollis.
" Nov. 5, Samuel Worcester and Lois Boynton, " "

1778, Nov. 5, Benjamin Boynton and Deborah Parker, both of Hollis,
" Nov. 16, Stephen Jewett, Jun., and Elizabeth Pool, " "
" Dec. James Hopkins of Amherst and Mary Taylor of Hollis.
1779. Jan. 28, Stephen Farley and Mary Shattuck, both of Hollis.
" " 28, Nathan Colburn and Abigail Shattuck, " "
" Mar. 17, Jonathan Dix of Raby and Miriam Kneeland of Harvard.
" Apr. 7, Samuel Leeman and Mary Wheeler, both of Hollis.
" " 13, Thomas Pratt and Anna Lawrence, " "
" June 10, Dr. Ebenezer Rockwood and Mary Emerson, both of Hollis.
" Nov. 25, Josiah Fisk and Mary Caldwell, " "
" Dec. 9, John Shattuck of New Ipswich and Mary Farley of Hollis.
1780, Mar. 9, Stephen Wright of Westford and Sarah Carter of Hollis.
" " 29, Nehemiah Hardy of Tewksbury and Wid. Abigail Hardy of Hollis.
" April David Truell of Amherst and Wid. Sarah Fisk of Hollis.
" May 31, Samuel Hill and Jemima Wheeler, both of Hollis.
" June 15, Simeon Blood and Rhoda Youngman, " "
" " 15, Uriah Wright and Eunice Jewett, " "
" June 18, Benjamin Farley, 2d, of Hollis and Lucy Fletcher of Dunstable.
" July 13, Ebenezer Wheeler and Azubah Taylor, both of Hollis.
" Aug. 24, Isaac Boynton and Mary Brooks, " "
" " 24, Jonathan Parker and Naomi Parker, " "
" Oct. 9, Thomas Merrill of Conway and Wid. Elizabeth Cumings of Hollis.
" " 17, William W. Pool and Sarah Farley, both of Hollis.
" Nov. 21, Abraham Boynton of Pepperell and Mary Hartshorn of Hollis.
" Dec. 7, Dr. Jonathan Pool and Elizabeth Hale, both of Hollis.
" " 7, Stephen Runnells and Chloe Thurston, " "
" " 7, Benjamin Cumings and Bridget Pool, " "
1781, Jan. Abijah Hildreth of Townsend and Hannah Smith of Hollis.
" Feb. 9, William Ball and Elizabeth Colburn, both of Hollis.
" Feb. 9, Enoch Noyes, Jun., of Cockermouth and Zillah Fox.
" Mar. 6, Bray Wilkins of Deering and Wid. Lucy Blanchard of Hollis.
" Mar. 13, Lemuel Wright and Widow Mary Johnson, both of Hollis.
" " 15, Aquilla Kimball of Bradford and Anna Tenney of Hollis.
" " 22, David Ames and Anna Wright, both of Hollis.
" Apr. 10, William Elliot of Pepperell and Sarah Honey of Hollis.
" " 12, Caleb Farley, Jun., and Abigail Phelps, both of Hollis.
" " 26, Jonas Woods and Lydia Hobart, " "
" Nov. 19, Jacob Taylor and Betty Boynton, " "
" " 19, Shubael Parker and Betty Brooks, " "
" " 20, Abel Conant and Margaret Jewett, " "
" Dec. 27, Lt. Jeremiah Pritchard of New Ipswich and Elizabeth Smith of Hollis.
1782, Jan. 9, Nathaniel Blood and Martha Spear, both of Hollis.
" " 17, Jonathan Hobart and Elizabeth Lakin, " "
" Feb. 4, Stephen Childs of Upton and Priscilla Wheat of Hollis.
" " 6, Abel Lovejoy and Sarah Fox, both of Hollis.
" " 13, John Connick of Hollis, and Abigail Hartshorn of Dunstable.
" Feb. Daniel Kendrick and Mary Pool, both of Hollis.
" Apr. 24, William Brooks, Jun., and Deborah Parker, both of Hollis.
" " 24, John Ball and Mary Chamberlain, " "
" May 7, Oliver Lawrence, Jun., and Lydia Dow, " "
" " 16, Solomon Hobart and Abigail Brooks, " "
" " 23, Simon Pierce, Jun., and Sarah Boynton, " "
" " 27, John Fox and Sarah Worcester, " "
" " 28, Burpee Ames and Grace Whiting, " "
" June Jesse Worcester and Sarah Parker, " "
" " 13, Eliphalet Brown and Sarah Wright, " "
" " 13, Timothy Jones of Amherst and Elizabeth Kenrick of Hollis.
" Oct. 10, William Spear, Jun., of New Ipswich and Sarah Emerson of Hollis.

1782, Nov. 28, Stephen Bent of Dublin and Elizabeth Darby of Hollis.
1783, Apr. 20, Josiah Woodbury of Hollis and Wid. Abigail Whipple of Mason.
" May 7. Lt. Samuel Farley of Hollis and Elizabeth Powers of Mason.
"   " 22, Thomas Carter and Polly Foot, both of Hollis.
" Oct. 10, Joseph Wheat and Wid. Bridget Farley, "   "
" Dec. 11, Joel Proctor and Caty Blood,   "   "
"   " 25. Phineas Fletcher of Dunstable and Anna Burge of Hollis.
1784, Jan. 1. Thomas Hardy of Dublin and Lucy Colburn of Hollis.
"   " 15, Jacob Mooar and Hannah Shattuck, both of Hollis.
" Feb. 12. Elisha Wright and Anna Sanders,   "   "
" Mar. 4. Daniel Bayley and Elizabeth French, "   "
"   " 18, John Brooks and Elizabeth Woods,   "   "
" Apr. 4. Burpee Ames and Wid. Hannah Cumings, both of Hollis.
"   " 8, Rev. Isaac Bailey of Sterling and Elizabeth Emerson of Hollis.
"   " 15. Benjamin Stearns and Elizabeth Holt, both of Hollis.
"   " 27, Stephen Parker and Rachel Boynton,   "   "
" May 2. Henry Butterfield of Dunstable and Mary How of Hollis.
"   " 13, Ralph Emerson and Alice Ames, both of Hollis.
"   " 20, Nathaniel Patten and Mehitable Blood, "   "
" June 12, Ensign John Senter and Wid. Esther Farnsworth, both of Hollis.
"   " 17, Stephen Dow and Abigail Jewett, both of Hollis.
" Sept. 16, Elijah Noyes of Cockermouth and Mary Lewis of Hollis.
" Dec. 2, Moses Proctor and Ruth Austin, both of Hollis.
"   " 28, David Sanderson and Larana Shattuck, both of Hollis.
"   " 20, George Abbot of Hollis and Naomi Tuttle of Littleton.
1785, Feb. 10, Francis Worcester of Plymouth and Hannah Parker of Hollis.
"   " 14. James Colburn and Susannah Hardy, both of Hollis.

FROM THE HOLLIS RECORDS OF MARRIAGES.

1785, May 12. Asa Baldwin and Rosanna Wheeler, both of Hollis.
"   "   " Phineas Ames of Hancock and Mehitable Jewett of Hollis.
"   " 17. Aaron Bailey and Elizabeth Wallingford, both of Hollis.
"   " 24, Jonas Willoughby and Prudence Saunders,   "   "
" June 12. Levi Parker of Westford and Abigail Pool of Hollis.
"   " 30. Capt. Samuel Douglas of Raby and Wid. Tabitha Fletcher of Hollis.
" July 28, Joseph Frost of Tewksbury and Abigail Leeman, of Hollis.
" Sept. 21, David Wright and Polly Lowell, both of Hollis.
" Oct. 25, Life Baldwin and Polly Holt,   "   "
" Nov. 24, Reuben Blood of Westminster and Lucy Ball of Hollis.
" Dec. 26, James Rideout, Jun., and Sarah Spalding, both of Hollis.
1786, Jan. 16, Peter Cumings of Hancock and Sarah Pierce of Hollis.
" Feb. 16, Silas Hardy and Mary Flagg, both of Hollis.
"   "   " John Edwards and Elizabeth Holden, both of Hollis.
" Mar. 8, Oliver Bacon of Jaffrey and Rebecca Jewett of Hollis.
"   " 21, John Goddard, Jun., and Lucy Stiles, both of Hollis.
" June 16, Silas Swallow of Dunstable and Lucy Emerson of Hollis.
"   "   " Stephen Youngman and Abigail Brown, both of Hollis.
" Oct. 26, John Bonner and Sarah Brooks,   "   "
" Dec. 7, William Ball and Rebecca Kinney,   "   "
1787, Jan. 31, Oliver Willoughby and Sarah Bailey,   "   "
" Feb. 15, Benjamin Farley, 3d, of Hollis and Mary Blodgett of Dunstable.
"   " 25, James Crossman and Rebecca Proctor of Hollis.
1787, Apr. 26, John Goodhue and Rebecca Perham, both of Hollis.
" June 3, David Hale and Elizabeth Holden,   "   "
" Sept. 20, Capt. William Brooks and Hepzibah Powers, both of Hollis.
" Nov. 13. Joel Boynton of Hopkinton and Betty Wallace of Hollis.

1788, Jan.   3. Jesse Hardy and Rebecca Bailey, both of Hollis.
"   Feb.   7, Reuben Hobart of Cockermouth and Isabel Colburn of Hollis.
"   "   17, Caleb Stiles, Jun., and Betty Pierce, both of Hollis.
"   Apr. 17, Josiah Wheat and Sarah Keyes,   "   "
"   Nov.   9, Benjamin Woods Parker and Olive Pratt.   "   "
"   "   13, Isaac Hardy and Submit Wheat,
"   "   27, Jonas Flagg of Gilmanton and Lucy Jewett of Hollis.
"   Dec.   2, Thomas Kemp of Hollis and Wid. Hannah Shattuck of Raby.
"   "   16, Dea. Josiah Conant and Zerviah Fox, both of Hollis.
"   "   29, Asahel Twiss and Wid. Isabel Pierce,
1789. Jan.   1, David Holden, Jun., and Bridget Atwell,   "   "
"   "   6, Solomon Manning of Billerica and Olive French of Hollis.
"   "   16, James Jewett and Lucy Farley, both of Hollis.
"   "   20, William Reed, Jun., and Betsey Burge, both of Hollis.
"   Oct. 19, Daniel Merrill and Phebe Dow,   "   "
"   Dec. 24, Michael Carter and Rebecca Shattuck,   "   "
1790, Feb.   9, Jonathan Hale and Catharine Mosher,   "   "
"   Mar.   7, Jacob Wheeler of Deering and Betsey Dix of Hollis.
"   May   6, Daniel Lawrence and Polly Johnson, both of Hollis.
"   July 28, Shubael Hobart of Hollis and Wid. Prudence Parker of Groton.
"   Nov.   9, Moses Hardy and Abigail Wheat, both of Hollis.
"   "   24, Isaac Baldwin of Amherst and Bethiah Pool of Hollis.
"   "   25, Francis Blood and Wid. Abigail Farmer, both of Hollis.
"   "   30, Henry Wright of Ashby and Hannah Boynton of Hollis.
1791, Jan.   6, Jacob Spaulding of Hillsborough and Mary Barker of Hollis.
"   Feb. 10, Jerathmael Bowers and Hannah Danforth, both of Hollis.
"   "   15, Benjamin Jewett of Gilmanton and Rebecca Boynton of Hollis.
"   "   22, Oliver Prescott, Jun., of Groton and Nancy Whiting of Hollis.
"   Apr. 28, Nathaniel Shattuck, Jun., and Hannah Keyes, both of Hollis.
"   May   5, Samuel Shattuck and Lois Wheat,   "   "
"   Aug.   1, Thomas Hay, Jun., of Merrimack and Rebecca Pool of Hollis.
"   "   25, Solomon Wheeler and Hannah Farley, both of Hollis.
"   Sept. 20, Jotham Robbins of Dunstable and Hannah Fisk of Hollis.
"   "   20, Samuel Runnells and Abigail Smith, both of Hollis.
"   Oct. 18, Jonathan Saunderson and Lucy Pool,   "   "
"   "   24, Zebulon Wheeler and Wid. Mary Kendrick, both of Hollis.
1792, Jan. 31, Oliver Blodgett of Dunstable and Anna Shipley of Hollis.
"   Mar. 15, Ebenezer Jewett and Polly Rideout, both of Hollis.
"   July 12, Abraham Leeman of Hollis and Wid. Olive Jaquith of Dunstable.
"   Oct. 23, Joseph Whipple and Esther Pierce, both of Hollis.
"   Nov. 15, Abijah Shed and Joanna Farley,   "   "
"   Dec. 13, Jonas Smith and Sally Pool,   "   "
1793, Jan. 24, Samuel Barron and Sally Lund,   "   "
"   "   28, Ephraim Burge and Patty Baldwin,   "   "
"   "   28, Leonard Whiting, Jun., and Betsey Conant, both of Hollis.
"   Nov. 21, James Bell and Elizabeth Shattuck,   "   "
"   "   28, John Powers and Hannah Brooks,   "   "
"   Dec. 24, Joel Barker and Sally Foster,   "   "
1794, Feb. 11, Solomon Wheat, Jun., and Hannah Cumings,   "   "
"   "   27, William Merrill of Hollis and Dolly Smith of Raby.
"   Mar.   7, Moses Ames and Rebecca Hale, both of Hollis.
"   Apr.   9, Solomon Wheelock of Leominster and Betsey Ball of Hollis.
"   May   7, Rev. Eli Smith and Ama Emerson, both of Hollis.
"   "   20, Jacob Mooar and Dorcas Hood,   "   "
"   June   9, Solomon Blood, Jun., and Hannah Kinney,   "   "
"   July   3, Isaac Hardy and Mehitable Boynton,   "   "
"   "   13, Benjamin Pool and Sally Fletcher,   "   "
"   "   20, Dr. William Hale and Esther Pool,   "   "

1794, Aug. 20, Daniel Dow and Sally Lovejoy, both of Hollis.
"   "   27, Samuel Lovejoy and Elizabeth Willoughby, both of Hollis.
"   Nov. 13, Nathaniel Shattuck of Hancock and Susannah Jewett of Hollis..
"   Dec. 16, Thomas Farley of Hollis and Polly Jewell of Dunstable.
1795, Jan.   1, David Smith and Hepzibah Worcester, both of Hollis.
"   Feb. 12, Aaron Hardy of Lempster and Sally Shattuck of Hollis.
"   Apr. 16, Abel Shattuck and Sally Blood, both of Hollis.
"   "   24, John Butterfield of Dunstable and Sally Blood of Hollis.
"   May   4, Stephen Lovejoy and Betsey Hood, both of Hollis.
"   "   30, James Bradbury and Catharine Conant, "   "
"   Nov. 29, John Jewett and Jane Ames,   "   "
1796, Jan.   5, Aaron Smith and Ruth Farley,   "   "
"   "   14, Jonathan Eads and Anna Holt,   "   "
"   Feb. 10, David Burge and Betsey McIntosh,   "   "
"   Mar.   4, Silas French and Sally Reed,   "   "
"   "   10, William Willoughby of Hollis and Rebecca Adams of Dunstable.:
"   "   17, David Willoughby and Polly Wood, both of Hollis.
"   Apr. 19, Daniel Blood, Jun., and Esther Rideout, "   "
"   June 2, William Read of Hollis and Wid. Elizabeth Shed of Chelmsford.
"   "   9, Benjamin Barron and Sally Wood, both of Hollis.
"   Aug. 17, Timothy French of Dunstable and Bridget Farley of Hollis.
"   Sept, 4, Nathaniel Jewett and Sally Blood, both of Hollis.
"   "   15, Ebenezer Farley, Jun., and Abigail Farmer, both of Hollis.
"   Nov. 17, David Powers of Dunstable and Polly Blanchard of Hollis.
"   Dec. 22, William Kemp and Sally Shattuck, both of Hollis.
"   "   29, Edmund Williams of Pepperell and Abigail Lee of Hollis.
1797, Jan.   1, Josiah Conant and Lucy Jewett, both of Hollis.
"   "   18, Jacob Mosher and Mary Pierce,   "   "
"   Apr. 19, Josiah Hayden and Polly Patch,   "   "
"   "   19, John Sawtell of Milford, and Martha Wallingford of Hollis.
"   "   24, Jesse Danforth of Amherst, and Sally Wheat of Hollis.
"   Sept. 19, Kendall Kittridge and Sally Whiting of Hollis.
"   "   21, Abel Spaulding and Susannah Marshall, both of Hollis.
"   Oct. 20, Rev. Samuel Worcester of Fitchburg and Zerviah Fox of Hollis.
"   Nov.   5, John Shed and Wid. Lucy Jewett, both of Hollis.
"   "   10, Enos Hardy and Mary Lund,   "   "
"   "   10, Ebenezer Baldwin and Lucy Wheat,   "   "
"   "   26, Levi Nutting of Pepperell, and Persis Eastman of Hollis.
"   Dec. 31, Amos Eastman and Wid. Deborah Woods, both of Hollis.
1798, Feb.   9, Luther Wright of Westford and Priscilla Reed of Hollis.
"   "   15, Daniel Robbins of Dunstable and Betsy Hazelton of Hollis.
"   Mar.   4, James Atwell and Sarah Lawrence, both of Hollis.
"   "   29, Jonas Blood and Priscilla Blood,   "   "
"   June 15, David Woods and Patty Brooks,   "   "
"   Nov. 28, Uriah Reed and Betsey Shed,   "   "
1799, Jan.   1, Eleazer Pierce and Sally Austin,   "   "
"   "   2, David French and Betsey Wheeler,   "   "
"   "   31, Phineas H. Holden of Littleton and Betsey Jewett of Hollis.
"   Mar. 17, Nehemiah Barker and Elizabeth Wallingford, both of Hollis.
. "   Apr. 16, Thomas Farley and Susannah Burge,   "   "
"   "   25, Samuel Smith and Margaret Smith,   "   "
"   May 13, Solomon Pierce and Rebecca Austin,   "   "
"   "   16, Nathan Holt and Sibbel Phelps,   "   "
"   "   23, Dea. Thomas Walker of Sudbury and Mary Hayden of Hollis..
"   June   4, Eleazer Parker and Susannah Flagg, both of Hollis.
"   "   11, Robert Colburn and Kezia Wright,   "   "
"   Oct.   1, Samuel Conroy and Betsey Dix,   "   "
"   "   11, Abel Spalding and Rebecca Ober,   "   "

1799, Oct. 20, William Tenney and Judith Reed, both of Hollis.
" Nov. 28, Moses S. Boynton of Hancock and Hannah Woodbury of Hollis.
" " 28, Hezekiah Kendall of Hollis and Lucy Kidder of Amherst.
1800, Jan. 23, Peter Colburn and Rachel Patch, both of Hollis.
" Feb. 24, Zachariah Alexander of Dunstable and Wid. Mary Messer of Hollis.
" Mar. 13, Leonard Whiting, Jun., and Wid. Rebecca Gilson, both of Hollis.
" " 13, Andrew Bunton of Pembroke and Lavinia Holden of Hollis.
" " 19, Benjamin Austin and Sally Jewett, both of Hollis.
" " 26, Nathaniel Proctor and Olive Goddard, " "
" Apr. 28, Minot Wheeler and Sally Farley, " "
" May 20, Dr. Benoni Cutter and Phebe Tenney, " "
" July 23, Isaac Jewett and Polly Proctor, " "
" Oct. 2, Jacob Cobbett and Phebe Kinney, " "
" Nov. 13, Thaddeus Wheeler and Sibbel Spaulding, " "
" " 13, Reuben Killicutt of Hillsborough and Sally Shipley of Hollis.
1801, Jan. 2, Samuel Parker of Greenfield and Hannah Rideout of Hollis.
" " 12, Josiah Blood and Sally Spaulding, both of Hollis.
" Feb. 3, Phillips Wood and Dorothy Davis, " "
" May 31, James Jewell of Dunstable and Sally Hobart of Hollis.
" July 5, Ebenezer Perkins and Henrietta Goddard, both of Hollis.
" Aug. 13, James Mosher and Hannah Pierce, " "
" Nov. 26, David Rideout and Kezia Wood, " "
" " 27, George Whitefield of Plymouth and Lydia Ranger of Hollis.
" Dec. 7, Ebenezer Perkins and Betsey Austin, both of Hollis.
" " 24, Aaron Kinney and Sally Phelps, " "
1802, Jan. 20, Abner B. Little of Salem, N. H., and Nancy Tenney of Hollis.
" Feb. 17, Ambrose Gould of Greenfield and Susan Farley of Hollis.
" Apr. 4, Joseph Evans of Marlow and Patty Boynton of Hollis.
" " 6, John Ober of Hollis and Sally Peacock of Amherst.
" " 10, Carshina Wood of Littleton and Betsey L. Lawrence of Hollis.
" June 10, Zachariah Ober and Abigail Hardy, both of Hollis.
" Sept. 5, Nicholas How and Anna French, both of Hollis.
" " 7, Ebenezer Parkhurst of Dunstable, Mass., and Hannah Jewett of Hollis
" Nov. 25, Nathan Shattuck and Susanna Wood, both of Hollis.
1803, Jan. 19, Jacob Pierce of Huntington, Vt., and Sarah Jewett of Hollis.
" Feb. 15, William Marshall of Hudson and Polly Smith of Hollis.
" " 22, Emerson Parker and Rebecca Blood, both of Hollis.
" Aug. 15, Jonathan Parker of Lexington and Anna Hobart of Hollis.
" Oct. 17, Jesse Farley and Mary Phelps, both of Hollis.
1804, Jan. 18, William Farley and Elizabeth Robbins, both of Hollis.
" " 26, Daniel Merrill, 3d, and Abigail Colburn, " "
" Sept. 22, Phineas Lovejoy and Abigail Ober, " "
" " 22, Aaron Brooks and Polly Austin, " "
" Apr. 8, Charles Eastman and Rebecca Spaulding, " "
" May 16, Benjamin Fletcher and Abigail Kittridge, " "
" Aug. 30, Gould Robbins of Dunstable and Sarah Johnson of Hollis.
" Oct. 10, Abijah Gould, Jun., and Mary Shattuck, both of Hollis.
" " 11, David Hardy and Anna Colburn, " "
" " 29, David Roby of Dunstable and Ann Johnson of Hollis.
" Nov. 15, Timothy Colburn of Milford and Mary Lovejoy of Hollis.
1805, Jan. 9, Thomas Richardson of Packersfield and Polly Holt of Hollis.
" " 26, Abijah Shed of Pepperell and Catharine Goss of Hollis.
" Sept. Nathaniel Rideout and Sarah Abbott, both of Hollis.
" " 16, Nicholas Youngman and Wid. Lydia Hobart, both of Hollis.
" Sept. 16, Eleazer Hale of Dunstable and Sally Jewell of Hollis.
" Oct. 30, Theodore Wheeler of Hollis and Susannah Hamlet of Dunstable.
" Nov. 28, Benjamin W. Wright and Sarah Hardy, both of Hollis.
" Dec. 26, Eli Hunt of Peterborough and Lydia Rideout of Hollis.

1806, Jan. 1, William F. Phelps and Sukey Farley, both of Hollis.
  "   " 22, Stephen Lund and Rachel Shed,   "   "
  "   " 30, Daniel French of Hardwick, Vt., and Lucy Goss of Hollis.
  "   Feb. 12, Artemas Thayer of Milford, Mass., and Elizabeth Jewett of Hollis.
  "   Sept. 24, Isaac Mooar and Mary Blood, both of Hollis.
  "   Oct. 30, Paul Davis of Mason and Lucy Pike of Hollis.
  "   Nov. 2, Lt. Caleb Farley and Wid. Lucy Shipley, both of Hollis.
  "   Dec. 18, Luther Hubbard of Hollis and Hannah Russell of Carlisle, Mass.
  "   " 18, Isaac Senter of Brookline and Sally Ball of Hollis.
1807, Apr. 2, Nathan Thayer and Hannah Jewett, both of Hollis.
  "   May 4, Foster Emerson and Ruth Proctor,   "   "
  "   Sept. 17, Isaac Shattuck of Washington and Hannah Mooar of Hollis.
  "   " 17, Abijah Gould of Hollis and Mary T. Sargent of Milford.
  "   Oct. 20, Samuel Jones, Jun., of Sudbury and Lucy Phelps of Hollis.
  "   " 20, Ebenezer Youngman and Thankful Phelps, both of Hollis.
  "   Nov. 1, John Grover of Charlestown, Mass., and Rebecca Blood of Hollis.
  "   " 26, Joel How of Milford and Dorcas Colburn of Hollis.
1808, Jan. 14, Nathan Colburn, Jun., and Lydia Jewett, both of Hollis.
  "   " 20, Henry Adams and Sarah Bradley.   "   "
  "   Feb. 25, John W. Kendall and Hannah Colburn,   "   "
  "   Mar. 16, Daniel Mooar of Hollis and Mary Nevins of Amherst.
  "   " 28, Samuel Rideout and Mary Lovejoy, both of Hollis.
  "   Aug. 27, Nehemiah Ranger and Esther Symonds, "   "
  "   Dec. 15, Isaac Farley and Charlotte Woods,   "   "
  "   " 28, William Lovejoy and Susannah Rideout, "   "
1809, Jan. 4, Timothy Colburn of Milford and Rebecca Ball of Hollis.
  "   "   4, Joshua Wright and Rebecca Willoughby, both of Hollis.
  "   " 18, Solomon Hobart of Hebron and Hannah Farley of Hollis.
  "   Feb. 5, Daniel French of Hardwick, Vt., and Sarah Worcester of Hollis.
  "   " 11, Lester Holt of Lyme and Lydia French of Hollis.
  "   " 21, James Rideout, 3d, and Edah Kinney, both of Hollis.
  "   " 28, Jonas Blood of Buckstown, Me., and Eliza Rideout of Hollis.
  "   Apr. 26, Samuel Runnells of Bradford and Elizabeth Lovejoy of Hollis.
  "   June 7, Jonathan T. Wheeler and Esther Spaulding, both of Hollis.
  "   " 23, Isaac French, Jun., and Abigail Farley.   "   "
  "   July 10, Abraham Boynton of Pepperell and Mary Adams of Hollis.
  "   Sept. 28, Jonas French, Jun., of Dunstable and Martha Jewett of Hollis.
  "   Nov. 26, Jeremiah Sanderson of Salem and Lucy French of Hollis.
  "   Dec. 7, Lemuel Wright, Jun., and Mary Farley, both of Hollis.
  "   " 17, Ralph Nutting of Westford and Hannah Wright of Hollis.
  "   " 19, Josiah Kidder of Amherst and Hannah Nevins of Hollis.
  "   " 21, Rev. Stephen Chapin of Mt. Vernon and Sally Mosher of Hollis.
1810, Jan. 18, Samuel French and Naomi Abbot, both of Hollis.
  "   Feb. 1, Benjamin Austin and Wid. Sarah Rideout, both of Hollis.
  "   " 20, Samuel Chapin of Pepperell and Elizabeth Farley of Hollis.
  "   " 20, Jonathan W. French of Hardwick, Vt., and Catharine Conant of Hollis
  "   Mar. 14, John French and Ama Nevins, both of Hollis.
  "   May 8, Alfred Hutchinson of Milford and Lydia Foster of Hollis.
  "   " 14, William Colburn and Rebecca Hardy, both of Hollis.
  "   Aug. 12, Charles W. Knowlton of New York and Sally Wood of Hollis.
  "   Sept. 12, Stephen Lund of Merrimack and Elizabeth Ober of Hollis.
  "   Nov. 22, James Davis and Bridget Wheeler, both of Hollis.
  "   Dec. 18, Benjamin Messer and Abigail Holt,   "   "
1811, Jan. 10, Andrew Willoughby and Hannah Davis "   "
  "   Jan. 22, Richard Clough of Merrimack and Abigail Proctor of Hollis.
  "   Feb. 4, Zachariah Kemp of Groton, N. H., and Elizabeth Powers of Hollis.
  "   " 16, Amos Blood and Susannah Phelps, both of Hollis.
  "   June 20, Oliver Willoughby, Jun., and Martha Hardy, both of Hollis.

1811, Oct. 24, Jesse Hardy and Wid. Mary Smith, both of Hollis.
" Nov. 21, Ralph Lovejoy and Abigail Phelps, " "
1812, May 10, Jabez Chapin of Dorchester, Mass., and Mary Wood of Hollis.
" June 28, Caleb Brown, Jun., of Milford and Sarah Willoughby of Hollis.
" Aug. 18, Simeon Stearns and Lydia Bailey, both of Hollis.
" Sept. 24, William E. Rockwood of Wilton and Abigail Conant of Hollis.
" Oct. 6, Timothy Colburn of Milford and Betsey Ball of Hollis.
" Nov. 1, David Mooar, Jun., of Hollis and Patty Merrill of Dunstable.
" " 12, Ralph E. Tenney and Olive Brown, both of Hollis.
" Dec. 24, Isaac Kimball of Mason and Lucinda Tenney of Hollis.
1813, Jan. 20, Samuel Hamlet and Rebecca Conroy, both of Hollis.
" Mar. 7, Rev. Walter Chapin of Woodstock, Vt., and Hannah Mosher of Hollis.
" " 11, Ebenezer Butterfield of Dunstable and Lucy Hobart of Hollis.
" " 18, Christopher P. Farley and Mary Sherwin, both of Hollis.
" Apr. 1, James Worcester and Mary Lawrence,
" " 22, Ebenezer Duncklee of Amherst and Salome Wright of Hollis.
" June 2, Stephen Lund, Jun., of Merrimack and Mary Hadley of Hollis.
" July 18, Barnabas Sanders and Sophia Bush, both of Hollis.
" Oct. 17, William Youngman and Martha Mooar, " "
" Nov. 1, Amos Wheeler and Mary Rideout, " "
" " 17, Thomas Hamlet and Anna Rideout, " "
" " 23, Amos Foster of Tewksbury and Rhoda Foster of Hollis.
" Dec. 28, Timothy Wyman of Hillsborough and Abigail Dow of Hollis.
" " 28, James Parker and Betsey Wright, both of Hollis.
1814, Mar. 2, Daniel Campbell of Townsend and Susan Colburn of Hollis.
" Apr. 4, Jonathan Stevens and Abigail Foster, both of Hollis.
" Apr. 18, William Emerson and Sarah Jewett, both of Hollis.
" May 1, Jacob McGilvrey of Medford and Betsey Brown of Hollis.
" June 2, Jonathan McIntire of Wilton and Sibbel Reed of Hollis.
" " 6, Jacob Blanchard of Dunstable and Mary Hazelton of Hollis.
" " 12, Jonathan Hale and Lydia Lawrence, both of Hollis.
" " 28, Kendall Cheney of Dunstable and Martha Blood of Hollis.
" July 31, Benjamin Smith and Nancy Jewett, both of Hollis.
" Sept. 6, Thomas W. Stearns and Sally Nevins, " "
" " 22, Daniel Mooar, Jun., and Mary K. Wheat, " "
" Oct. 10, John Shipley and Wid. Susannah Lovejoy, " "
" Nov. 10, Benjamin Farley, 5th, and Rachel Foster, " "
" " 24, Nathaniel Paul and Elizabeth Lamson, " "
" " 28, Levi Kemp and Lydia Hobart, " "
" Dec. 1, Thomas Mooar of Dunstable and Lydia Patch of Hollis.
" " 27, Crista Duncan of Hancock and Lois Dow of Hollis.
" " 27, Samuel Smith of Brookline and Sally Dow of Hollis.
1815, Apr. 13, William Brown, Jun., and Hannah Farley, both of Hollis.
" " 13, Abijah Shed and Sophia Blood, " "
" June 8, Daniel Blood and Wid. Rebecca Chamberlain, " "
" Dec. 28, Levi Pierce and Esther Adams, " "
1816, Feb. 22, William Willoughby and Mary A. Powers, " "
" Mar. 18, Washington Willoughby and Lucy Saunderson, both of Hollis.
" Apr. 15, Lemuel Snow of Worcester, Mass., and Abigail Worcester of Hollis.
" " 15, John Gutterson, Jun., of Milford and Martha Sawtell of Hollis.
" " 18, James Hardy and Mary Smith, both of Hollis.
" " 18, Jeremiah K. Needham of Milford and Olive Parker of Hollis.
" " 18, Jeremiah Preston of Mason and Anna Proctor of Hollis.
" June 6, Eleazer Pierce and Betsey Proctor, both of Hollis.
" July 14, Mather Withington and Nancy Gilson, " "
" Sept. 7, Thomas Davis and Deborah Hobart, " "
" Oct. 17, Jonathan Foster and Leefy French, " "
" Nov. 12, Jonathan T. Wright and Elizabeth Colburn, both of Hollis.

(24)

1816, Nov. 14,   Oliver Stearns of Milford and Mary Willoughby of Hollis.
"   "   14,   Christopher Farley and Constantina Cumings, both of Hollis.
1817, Mar. 13,   Nathaniel Dow and Mary Ames,   "   "
"   "   13,   John Armstrong and Rebecca Hobart,   "   "
"   Apr. 10,   Andrew Shattuck of Dunstable and Phebe Jewett of Hollis.
"   "   23,   James Wheeler and Dorcas Mooar, both of Hollis.
"   May   6,   Loammi Spaulding of Temple and Esther Wright of Hollis.
"   July 10,   Amos Shattuck and Mary Ball, both of Hollis.
"   Aug. 4,   Paul Davis of Mason and Martha Shed of Hollis.
"   "   5,   Ebenezer Shed and Elizabeth Duncklee, both of Hollis.
"   Sept. 16,   Ebenezer Farley, 3d, and Leafy Duncklee,   "   "
"   Nov. 9,   Dr. Noah Hardy and Betsey Farley,   "   "
"   Nov. 18,   Isaac Butterfield of Brookline and Abigail Pierce of Hollis.
"   "   20,   Jonathan Lovejoy of Milford and Sarah Willoby of Hollis.
"   "   23,   Amos Hardy and Mary Cumings, both of Hollis.
"   Dec. 23,   Ebenezer Blood and Betsey Abbott,   "   "
"   "   25,   Daniel Walker of Marlborough, Mass., and Mary Hayden of Hollis.
1818, Jan. 1,   Daniel Dow and Charlotte Farley, both of Hollis.
"   Feb. 5,   Asa Jaquith and Esther Phelps,   "   "
"   "   26,   Jeremiah Dow and Sarah Eastman,   "   "
"   Mar. 6,   John P. Gilson of Dunstable and Rebecca Spaulding of Hollis.
"   Apr. 2,   Capt. Daniel Bailey and Wid. Mary Lawrence, both of Hollis.
"   "   24,   William Brown, 3d, and Hannah Boynton,   "   "
"   Aug. 14,   Ralph E. Tenney and Phebe C. Smith,   "   "
"   Oct. 1,   Benjamin Farley, 4th, and Mehitable Blood, "   "
"   "   29,   Benjamin Wright and Wid. Emma Bradley.   "   "
"   Nov. 22,   Benjamin Carter of Wilmington and Mary Farley of Hollis.
"   Dec. 29,   Moses Kendall of Tyngsborough and Mindwell Reed of Hollis.
"   "   31,   Joseph Patch and Sally Johnson, both of Hollis.
1819, Apr. 1,   Moses Boynton, Jun., and Emma Lawrence, both of Hollis.
"   Sept. 30,   Francis E. Fuller of Hardwick, Vt., and Martha Worcester of Hollis.
"   Nov. 19,   Jesse Hardy and Eliza Mooar, both of Hollis.
"   "   25,   Amos B. Minot of Westminster, Mass., and Mary Hardy of Hollis.
"   Dec. 2,   Isaac French, Jun., and Rebecca Bush, both of Hollis.
1820, June 8,   Leonard Bailey and Mary French,   "   "
"   "   8,   Gardner Mooar and Mary Hardy,   "   "
"   Nov. 5,   Jonas Lawrence and Fanny Lawrence,   "   "
"   "   6,   Minot Farley and Zeraiah Phelps,   "   "
1821, Jan. 4,   Freedom French and Sarah Mooar,   "   "
"   "   25,   Thomas W. Hardy and Mehitable Blood,   "   "
"   "   30,   Benjamin Farley, Esq., and Wid. Susannah Smith, both of Hollis.
"   Feb. 22,   Joseph Rideout, Jun., and Sukey Ranger,   "   "
"   Mar. 15,   Dea. Stephen Thurston of Bedford and Sarah Burge of Hollis
"   June 26,   Asa Beverly of Amherst and Roxana Lovejoy of Hollis.
"   July 4,   Amos Eastman and Wid. Lydia Mooar, both of Hollis.
"   Aug. 12,   Jeremiah Bullard of Rindge and Priscilla Reed of Hollis.
"   "   19,   Samuel L. Hardy and Roxana Duncklee, both of Hollis.
"   Oct. 18,   Jonathan P. Woods and Lucinda Baker,   "   "
"   "   21,   Royal Woods and Catharine Lovejoy,   "   "
"   Nov. 27,   Joel Barker of Milford and Wid. Catharine Lovejoy of Hollis.
1822, Jan. 2,   Daniel Greenwood of Dublin and Rebecca Hardy of Hollis.
"   "   22,   Daniel Holt of Milford and Olive Proctor of Hollis.
"   Feb. 24,   Phineas Cumings and Lucinda Lovejoy, both of Hollis.
1823, Apr. 21,   Luther Wright and Hannah Lillis,   "   "
"   May   1,   Calvin Willoughby and Lucinda Wheeler,   "   "
"   "   17,   Louis Cochran of Andover and Mary Abbott of Hollis.
"   May 22,   Stephen Lovejoy, Jun., and Lucy Hobart, both of Hollis.
"   June 8,   Ebenezer Beard of Boston and Anna Patch of Hollis.

1823, Oct. 30, Joel Hardy and Eliza Johnson, both of Hollis.
1824, Feb. 4, Benjamin Wheeler and Rhoda Rideout, both of Hollis.
" Mar. 23, Abel Ball and Sally French, " "
" Apr. 29, Noah Farley and Ruth Lawrence, " "
" " 29, William Kittredge of Harvard and Lucy Saunderson of Hollis.
" May 13, Samuel Colburn of Groton and Sarah Woods of Hollis.
" " 30, Benjamin Austin, Jun., and Hannah Pierce, both of Hollis.
" July 11, Jefferson Rockwood and Sarah Lovejoy, " "
" Oct. 18, William S. Bradbury and Elizabeth Emerson, " "
" " 23, Leonard Blood of Hollis and Hannah Hale of Dunstable, N. H.
" Dec. 8, Timothy Patch and Hannah Burns, both of Hollis.
" " 28, Ebenezer White of Boston and Susan Hale of Hollis.
1825, Jan. 5, John Minot of Westminster, Mass., and Wid. Mary Minot of Hollis.
" Mar. 27, Nathan Thayer, Esq., and Mary Jewett, both of Hollis.
" Apr. 5, Benoni G. Cutter and Lucy Pool, " "
" May 1, Joel Parker and Eliza Crawford, " "
" " 26, Daniel Lawrence of Hollis and Sarah Fletcher of Pepperell.
" Oct. 11, Francis E. Fuller of Hardwick, Vt., and Hannah Worcester of Hollis.
" " 18, Andrew Dean of Dunstable and Sarah Hale of Hollis.
" Nov. 17, Abel Farley and Elizabeth Farley, both of Hollis.
" " 24, Samuel Quaid and Sarah Boynton, " "
" " 25, Jonathan Cragin of Claremont and Mary Wright, 2d, of Hollis.
" Dec. 14, Ralph W. Jewett and Betsey Farley, both of Hollis.
" " 16, Willard Blood of Dunstable and Sally Blood of Hollis.
" " 27, Alvin Shed of New Ipswich and Laurinda Smith of Hollis.
1826, Jan. 19, Dea. Stephen Thurston of Bedford and Hannah Worcester of Hollis.
" Feb. 14, Washington Willoughby and Elizabeth Wheeler, both of Hollis.
" June 28, Gilbert Brooks of Medford and Martha Burge of Hollis.
" " 29, Silas Hardy of Westminster, Vt., and Abigail Hardy of Hollis.
" Sept. 26, Ebenezer Sargent of Henrietta, N. Y., and Mary Wright of Hollis.
" Nov. 12, George Sherburne and Susannah Runnells, both of Hollis.
" " 15, Ichabod W. Saunderson and Hannah Ball, " "
" Dec. 26, John N. Worcester and Sarah Holden, " "
1827, Feb. 13, Timothy Hodgman and Charlotte Willoughby, " "
" Mar. 8, Oliver Conroy of Hollis and Miranda Fisk of Dunstable.
" " 16, Eleazer T. Merrill and Susan Brown, both of Hollis.
" July 13, James Parker and Susan Woods, " "
" " " Leonard Chafin of Groton, Mass., and Mary Wright of Hollis.
" Nov. 16, William Conant and Sarah Hale, both of Hollis.
" " 19, Calvin Wright of Hollis and Eunice Shattuck of Dunstable.
" Dec. 4, William Gilbert of Francestown and Mary Ranger of Hollis.
1828, Apr. 8, Henry Woods of Groton, Mass., and Hannah M. Thayer of Hollis.
" " 17, John Parker and Mary Ann Gould, both of Hollis.
" May 11, John L. Rix of Haverhill, N. H., and Elizabeth Hale of Hollis.
" " 26, Alpheus Eastman of Hollis and Sally Williams of Warwick, Mass.
" June 5, David Hoyt of Charlestown, Mass., and Sarah N. Pool of Hollis.
" Oct. 9, Rev. Darwin Adams of Camden, Me., and Catharine N. Smith of Hollis.
" " 28, Hiram Wood and Annis S. Jewett, both of Hollis.
" Dec. 30, Ebenezer Runnells and Wid. Lydia Hale, "
1829, Jan. 19, Charles Gilson of Pepperell and Mary Colburn of Hollis.
" Apr. 7, Asahel Reed of Merrimack and Priscilla R. French of Hollis.
" " 9, Obadiah T. Eaton of New Ipswich and Clarissa Farley of Hollis.
" " 9, Leonard Shipley of Dunstable and Sibbel Spalding of Hollis.
" Aug. 10, John B. Hill of Exeter, Me., and Achsah Parker of Hollis.
" " 13, Alpheus Rideout and Lydia S. Powers, both of Hollis.
" " 13, Mark Webster of Lowell, Mass., and Eunice Wright of Hollis.
" Nov. 24, Capt. Leonard Blood and Lucy Dow, both of Hollis.
1830, Feb. 2, Leonard Rideout and Wid. Mary Davis, " "

1830, Feb. 10, Rev. Noah Emerson of Baldwin, Me., and Ama Smith of Hollis.
"   "   22, Luther Hardy and Hannah W. Sawtell, both of Hollis.
"   Apr. 13, Elias Colburn and Thankful Rideout,   "   "
"   "   13, Mark Dow and Charlotte Blood,   "   "
"   Dec. 21, Daniel Wyman of Hillsborough and Louisa Mooar of Hollis.
1831, Mar. 16, Abijah Fletcher of Westford and Louisa Lawrence of Hollis.
"   "   31, Ebenezer Baldwin and Rebecca Bailey, both of Hollis.
"   "   " Winslow Reed and Mary Pierce,   "   "
"   Apr. 5, Timothy U. Patch and Mary Proctor,   "   "
"   May 17, Ira Beaman of Westminster, Mass., and Kezia Colburn of Hollis.
"   "   31, Franklin Abbott of Milford and Indiana Proctor of Hollis.
"   June 9, Sullivan Howard of Mason and Elizabeth B. Little of Hollis.
"   Aug. 4, Douglas R. Patterson of Amherst and Dolly Ann Wood of Hollis.
"   Sept. 22, Asa Farley and Sibbel C. Holt, both of Hollis.
"   Oct. 3, Francis Jewett and Louisa Rideout,   "   "
"   Nov. 17, Silas Spalding and Lucinda Wood,   "   "
"   "   24, David W. Sawtell and Sarah P. Farley,   "   "
"   Dec. 22, David Woods of Hancock and Esther Wheeler of Hollis.
"   "   22, William Bowers of Dunstable and Mary Ann Hubbard of Hollis.
1832, Jan. 19, Daniel Shattuck and Mary Ann Shattuck, both of Hollis.
"   Feb. 27, Bradley Colburn and Naomi Boynton,   "   "
"   Mar. 19, Jesse Templeton and Sarah Foster,   "   "
"   Apr. 5, Nathaniel Hobart and Hannah Colburn,   "   "
"   May 17, Daniel Abbott of Dracut, Mass., and Elsie Marshall of Hollis.
"   Nov. 28, Nathaniel Hardy and Hannah E. Parker, both of Hollis.
1833, Mar. 3, John H. Cutter and Susah F. Pool,   "   "
"   "   21, Daniel Farley and Polly Farley,   "   "
"   Apr. 2, Jacob D. Austin and Lucy S. Wright,   "   "
"   "   9, William Wheeler of Milford and Nancy C. M. Little of Hollis.
"   "   25, Moses Proctor and Indiana Dow, both of Hollis.
"   May 22, Joseph Ober and Rhoda C. Colburn,   "   "
"   June 26, Nathaniel F. How and Almira Rideout,   "   "
"   Aug. 27, Ambrose H. Wood and Mary Ann Colburn, both of Hollis.
"   Oct. 24, Jonathan W. Lovejoy and Elizabeth Colburn, "   "
1834, Feb. 20, John L. Pool and Mary Boynton,   "   "
"   Apr. 8, Ezekiel M. Bradley and Lydia Dow.   "   "
"   May 11, George W. Hubbard of Pepperell and Emma Burge of Hollis.
"   "   20, Mark W. Merrill of Dunstable and Catharine Hale of Hollis.
"   June 1, Daniel Edgerly of Sanbornton, and Mary H. Stevens of Hollis.
"   Aug. 25, Mark Farley and Mary S. Crosby, both of Hollis.
"   Oct. 5, Isaac Jewett of Nashville, Tenn., and Lydia C. Colburn of Hollis.
"   "   30, Luke Hale and Mary Morrison, both of Hollis.
"   Nov. 6, Benjamin G. Searles of Rowley, Mass., and Phebe C. Cutter of Hollis.
"   "   16, Joel Blood and Rachel Lund, both of Hollis.
"   "   27, Charles F. Hall and Martha Willoby, "   "
1835, Jan. 4, George Worcester of Hudson and Wid. Rachel Colburn of Hollis.
"   Feb. 26, Luke Putnam of Dunstable, N. H., and Rebecca J. Hale of Hollis.
"   Mar. 5, Eri Spalding of Chelmsford, Mass., and Ahara Spalding of Hollis.
"   Apr. 12, William Adams and Sarah Ann Adams, both of Hollis.
"   "   19, Ebenezer Ranger and Maria Tozer,   "   "
"   "   29, Charles Walker of New Ipswich and Hannah Walker of Hollis.
"   May 7, Alfred Knight of Lancaster and Mary Butterfield of Hollis.
"   "   21, Mark Mooar and Charlotte Wright, both of Hollis.
"   June 23, Silas French and Esther Saunderson, "   "   •
"   Nov. 24, James Burgess of Dunstable, N. H., and Caroline Holden of Hollis.
"   "   24, Stillman Spaulding and Ann Holden, both of Hollis.
"   Dec. 3, Daniel Livingston of Lowell and Sophronia Lund of Hollis.
1836, Jan. 18, Artemas Hale and Mary Ann Wheat, both of Hollis.

1836, Mar. 31, Joseph D. Parker and Lucretia Smith, both of Hollis.
" June 2, Varnum Wheeler and Mary Wood, " "
" July 1, Gaius Wright, Jun., and Naomi Parker. " "
" Oct. 13, Elbridge Livingston of Lowell and Irene Lund of Hollis.
" " 13, Christopher F. Smith and Rachel R. Farley, both of Hollis.
" Nov. 10, Joseph Brown of Chester and Wid. Patty Patch of Hollis.
" Dec. 12. Charles G. Clapp of Northampton, Mass., and Sarah Lawrence of Hollis.
" " 28, George W. Parker and Mary Woods, both of Hollis.
1837. Apr. 6. Thomas Lund of Hollis and Bridget French of Nashua.
" " 6. Warner Read and Louisa Wright, both of Hollis.
" June 7, John Farley and Hannah Blood, " "
" Aug. 31, Alfred Farley and Lydia Farley. " "
" Sept. 21, William Parker of Pepperell and Martha Patch of Hollis.
" Oct. 4, William Flagg of West Boylston and Louisa Hardy of Hollis.
" " 12, Rev. Dudley Phelps of Groton and Lucretia G. Farley of Hollis.
" " 26, Enoch Jewett and Wid. Sarah Willoby, both of Hollis.
" Nov. 7, Jonas W. Jaquith and Mary J. Austin, " "
" " 21, Freeman Wallace of Bethel, Vt., and Jane Farley of Hollis.
1838, Mar. 19, Eri McDaniells of Brookline and Ann Farley of Hollis.
" Apr. 5, Isaac R. Lawrence and Marinda Wheeler, both of Hollis.
" " 17, James Farley, Jun., and Martha T. Mooar,' " "
" " 26, Capt. Josiah Blood and Wid. Dorcas Spaulding, both of Hollis.
" June 20, Rev. Joseph Warren and Lydia Dale, " "
" July 7, Ethan Willoughby of Hollis and Julia Marshall of Hudson.
" " 8, Amos Wheeler of Nashua and Rebecca Wheeler of Hollis.
" " 19, Samuel Bancroft of Pepperell and Hannah E. Hardy of Hollis.
" Nov. 4, Abial Steele of Milledgeville, Ga., and Betsey Hardy " "
" " 22, Moses Proctor of Boston and Elizabeth Conant of Hollis.
1839. Mar. 7. Harvey A. Powers of Pepperell and Sarah Colburn of Hollis.
" Apr. 2, Charles L. Colburn and Emeline Wright, both of Hollis.
" Aug. 1, Cyrus Whitcomb of Fitchburg and Esther Ann Nichols of Hollis.
" Oct. 7. Eli Spalding of Pepperell and Harriet Eastman of Hollis.
" " 30, David J. Wright and Sarah J. Colburn, both of Hollis.
1840, Jan. 14, Theodore Wheeler, Jun., and Charlotte Wetherbee, both of Hollis
" May 12, Jacob Spalding and Jane Ranger, " "
" Sept. 16. Charles A. Wood of Hollis and Hannah A. Washer of Nashua.
" Oct. 8, Josiah Hayden and Submit Swallow, both of Hollis.
" " 8, Leonard Swan of Nashua and Sabrina Hale of Hollis.
" " 18. Phineas Hardy and Wid. Rebecca C. Hardy, both of Hollis.
" Nov. 19. Reuben Hardy of Hollis and Abigail Stearns of Merrimack.
1841, Mar. 18, Benjamin N. Stearns and Susan E. Colburn, both of Hollis.
1842, Aug. 18, Ezra Shed and Lydia Reed. " "
" Sept. 15, William A. Colburn of Hollis and Mary Hardy of Hudson.
" " 15, Jefferson Farley and Charlotte M. Farley, both of Hollis.
1843, Jan. 31, Charles B. Fletcher of Lyndon, Vt., and Lucy F. Farley of Hollis.
" Mar. 13, Daniel D. F. Johnson and Fidelia Kemp, both of Hollis.
" Apr. 4, William Hardy of Salem, Mass., and Ann M. Richardson of Hollis.
" May 9, Daniel M. Smith of Hollis and Hannah Newton of Nashua.
" " 10, Nathan Willoughby and Elizabeth A. Marshall, both of Hollis.
" June 29, Charles O. Wood and Luella P. Hardy, " "
" Nov. 1, Leonard Lyon of Cambridge, Mass., and Mary D. Farley of Hollis.
" " 9, Reuben F. Foster of Concord, N. H., and Sarah E. Ames " "
" Dec. 7, Horace Field and Sarah E. Farley, both of Hollis.
" " 12, Silas S. Wheeler and Irene Wyman, " "
1844, Feb. 6, Andrew J. Spalding and Mary Ann Wheeler, both of Hollis.
" " 22, John Coburn and Wid. Naomi Colburn, " "
" June 13, John C. Bell and Sarah A. Dow, both of Hollis.

1844, Nov. 13, Edward Emerson of Hollis and Hannah Cumings Pierce of Boston..
  "   "   19, Benjamin G. Searles and Almira Butterfield, both of Hollis.
1845, Jan. 1, John Hardy and Hannah Farley,   "   "
  "   "   29, Rufus N. Wallingford of Milford and Susan Farley of Hollis.
  "   "   29, Nathaniel G. Fernald of Lowell and Harriet Farley of Hollis.
  "   Mar. 6, Luther Proctor of Hollis and Frances P. Wallace of Pepperell.
  "   Apr. 8, George Bancroft of Boston and Sarah G. Farley of Hollis.
  "   "   16, Adolphus Stevens of Pepperell and Nancy J. Wallace of Hollis.
  "   Aug. 5, William S. Young of Fitchburg and Sarah A. Wright of Hollis.
  "   Oct. 16, Caleb Brown of Nashua and Mary Ann Reed of Hollis.
  "   "   10, James S. Rideout and Harriet M. Hartshorn, both of Hollis.
  "   "   21, James Little and Emeline Colburn,   "   "
  "   Dec. 4, Charles Hale and Nancy Ranger,   "   "
  "   "   9, Benjamin Whiting and Esther S. Wright,   "   "
1846, Jan. 1, Mansfield Senter of Nashua and Mary Ann Willoby of Hollis.
  "   Mar. 26, Jonas Blood and Wid. Susannah Wheeler, both of Hollis.
  "   May 12, Frederick Blood and Mehitabel Rideout,   "   "
  "   Sept. 24, Charles P. Wood and Harriet Mooar,   "   "
  "   Nov. 5, Ebenezer T. Wheeler and Mary Ann Blood,   "   "
  "   Nov. 16, Benjamin F. Steele of Wilton and Rachel Colburn of Hollis.
1847, Apr. 25, Nehemiah Woods and Mary Ann Woods, both of Hollis.
  "   May 5, William P. Saunderson and Hannah C. Marshall, both of Hollis.
  "   "   6, Ralph J. Holden and Eliza Ann Hardy,   "   "
  "   Nov. 18, James Blood and Emeline Wheeler,   "   "
  "   Dec. 21, Simeon A. Spalding of Hollis and Catharine P. Sawtell of Brookline.
  "   "   23, David W. Sawtell and Sarah J. Rideout, both of Hollis.
1848, Feb. 1, Minot Wheeler of Hollis and Sarah Ann Hardy of Hudson.
  "   "   15, John C. Foster of Milford and Sophia P. Farley of Hollis.
  "   Mar. 2, Joseph Gates and Susan E. Lovejoy, both of Hollis.
  "   Apr. 4, Jacob R. Bagley and Dorcas C. Woods, both of Hollis.
  "   "   5, Oliver L. Dow of Hancock and Mary Ann Eastman of Hollis.
  "   "   11, Thomas S. Patch and Lucy A. Newton, both of Hollis.
  "   June 4, James W. Wheeler and Kezia A. Wheeler,   "   "
  "   "   20, Nathan M. Ames and Asenath Hardy,   "   "
  "   Nov. 30, Dexter Greenwood and Mary Holden,   "   "
  "   Dec. 14, John B. Perkins and Sophia A. Little,   "   "
1850, Jan. 1, Samuel W. Fox and Abigail A. Lovejoy, both of Hollis.
  "   July 4, Benjamin L. Farley and Elizabeth R. Howe,   "   "
1851, Apr. 2, George Moore and Susan M. Butters,   "   "
  "   "   10, James Willoughby of Milford and Lucretia L. Wood of Hollis.
  "   July 15, Rev. Daniel P. Deming and Abby A. Hardy, both of Hollis.
  "   Oct. 29, Asa Jaquith and Lucy French,   "   "
  "   Nov. 25, Charles Marsh of Bethel, Vt., and Susan E. Farley of Hollis.
  "   Dec. 17, Joseph E. Smith of Hollis and Charlotte Richardson of Pembroke.
1852, May 13, Enoch J. Colburn of Hollis and Elmira Steele of Wilton.
  "   June 3, Oliver Willoby of Hollis and Fanny Nichols of Amherst.
  "   July 27, Thomas Proctor, Jun., and Susan R. Pool, both of Hollis.
  "   Oct. 20, Stephen T. Ellis of Walden, Vt. and Elizabeth N. B. Colburn of Holli.
  "   "   26, Luke M. Blood and Josephine E. Woods, both of Hollis.
  "   Ebenezer Ranger and Sarah Ball,   "   "
1853, Feb. 15, Grant P. Saunderson and Harriet Blood, both of Hollis.
  "   "   24, Augustus R. Lovejoy of Hollis and Jane M. Boutwell of Antrim.
  "   Mar. 14, Rodney J. Hardy of Boston and Sarah E. Tenney of Hollis.
  "   June 2, Alfred M. Hardy of Hollis and Elizabeth J. Sweet of Lowell.
  "   Aug. 7, Addison E. Winch of Westminster and Rosette Rideout of Hollis.
1854, Feb. 2, James Farley, 3d, of Hollis and Mrs. Abby Taylor of Nashua.
  "   "   9, Benjamin W. Rideout and Susan Ranger, both of Hollis.
  "   Mar. 12, Ichabod F. Lund of Hollis and Emily A. Corliss of Nashua.

1855. Apr. 11, Truman Hurd of Nashua and Emeline Rideout of Hollis.
"   " 11, Noah Dow and Mary J. Patch, both of Hollis.
"   Sept. 5, Thomas Lund and Betsey Blood, " "
"   Oct. 3, Luther Cheney of Nashua and Lydia C. Winn of Hollis.
1855. Mar. 31, John R. Parker of Hollis and Cornelia M. Sawyer of Merrimack.
"   Apr. 5, Perry M. Farley and Sarah Farley, both of Hollis.
"   June 28,' Samuel K. Rich of Boston and Frances A. Spaulding of Hollis.
"   Sept. 13, Jabez A. Sawyer of Roxbury and Sarah C. Worcester of Hollis.
"   Dec. 13, Hiram G. Felton of Amherst and Mrs. Jane Austin of Hollis.
1856, Jan. 1, Harvey N. Willoby of Hollis and Mary M. Pease of Weston.
"   " 1, Abel Spencer of Nashua and Melissa Willoby of Hollis.
"   " 3, Albert S. Powers of Milford and Sophia A. Spalding of Hollis.
"   " 25, Isaac Fletcher of Hollis and Phebe J. Draper of Lyndeborough.
"   Mar. 27, David M. Farley and Elvira Wheeler, both of Hollis.
"   Apr. 13, Samuel B. Blood and Sarah Wheeler, "   "
"   May 8, Caleb Farley and Sarah M. Patch, "   "
"   Dec. 30, Josiah Colburn of Hollis and Rebecca Wood of Litchfield.
1857, Jan. 1, Warren K. Lovejoy and Mary A. Wright, both of Hollis.
"   Feb. 5, Asa Noyes of Danvers and Mrs. Rebecca C. Hardy of Hollis.
"   " 25, Levi Abbot and Matilda Abbot, both of Hollis.
1858, Jan. 14, Francis Lovejoy and Ellen M. Hardy, both of Hollis.
"   Feb. 1, Charles Moses of New York and Susan Fox of Hollis.
"   Mar. 11, Nathaniel Pierce and Hannah M. Wheeler, both of Hollis.
"   Apr. 8, James T. Willoby of Hollis and Cornelia L. Pierce of Brookline.
"   " 29, Charles F. Chase of Nashua and Susan A. Blood of Hollis.
"   Nov. 24, Josiah Hayden of Hollis and Mahala Millard.
"   Sept. 9, Mark L. Willoby of Hollis and Maria A. Wentworth of Chelmsford.
"   Dec. 2, Jeremiah K. Needham of Hollis and Elizabeth H. Carlton of Merrimack
"   Dec. 9, Daniel F. Runnels and Sarah E. Farley, both of Hollis.
"   " 9, Oliver P. Eastman and Lucy A. Hardy, "   "
"   " 27, Charles H. Wright and Hattie E. Stratton, "   "
1859, Apr. 5, Milton J. Hardy of Decatur, Ill., and Susan E. Cutter of Hollis.
"   June 2, William Hale, Jun., and Mehitable G. Blood, both of Hollis.
"   July 9, Asa B. Eaton of Manchester, and Roanna S. Farley of Hollis.
"   Nov. 24, Stephen W. Moore of Nashua and Julia Rideout of Hollis.
1860, Mar. 1, Timothy E. Flagg and Susan A. Proctor, both of Hollis.
"   May 14, Charles Richardson of Marlborough and Rebecca F. Hardy of Hollis.
"   " 25, John F. Smith and Mrs. Sarah Smith, both of Hollis.
"   June 28, Francis Tubbs and Mrs. Mary F. Lund, "   "
"   Nov, 29, Albert Shedd and Mary A. Farley, "   "
"   " 29, William H. Gerrish of Boston and Eliza R. Willoby of Hollis.
1861, Nov. 19, Alpheus Rideout of Hollis and Hannah Russell of Lawrence.
"   Dec. 5, John R. Parker and Susan H. Farley, both of Hollis.
1862, Apr. 7, Henry Smithwick of Hollis and Mary A. Smithwick of Nashua.
"   May 6, Silas M. Spalding and Louisa D. Bradley, both of Hollis.
"   Oct. 9, William F. Spaulding and Mary E. Farley, "   "
"   Dec. 11, Dexter L. Blood of Hollis and Cornelia A. Lovejoy of Amherst.
1863, Feb. 28, Albert H. Brooks of Townsend and Mary J. Hardy of Hollis.
"   May 19, Charles P. Ober and Louisa W. Hart, both of Hollis.
"   June 30, Charles S. Spaulding of Hollis and Mercian Barton of Lowell.
"   Nov. 4, Alfred Boynton of Pepperell and Lucy A. Colburn of Hollis.
"   Nov. 14, John H. Pool of Boston and Ellen L. Runnells of Hollis.
1864, June 2, Hale Gage and Jane E. Patch, both of Hollis.
"   Oct. 11, E. C. Frost of Nashua and M. Elizabeth Hills of Hollis.
1865, Feb. 5, Waldo E. Hill and Elvira A. Wood, both of Hollis.
"   June 10, Benjamin L. Farley of Hollis and Persis D. Plummer of Goffstown.
"   Sept 20, Curtis H. Bill of Albany, Vt., and Mary J. Worcester of Hollis.
"   Oct. 19, Alfred Farley of Hollis and Mary W. Eastman of Milford.

1865, Dec. 7, Russell S. Putnam of Malden, Mass., and Sarah T. Colburn of Hollis.
1866, Jan. 7, Charles O. Whittemore of Merrimack and Emma H. Hardy of Hollis.
" Apr. 24, George W. Pierce of Brookline and Emma A. Wood of Hollis.
" Oct. 15, Gustavus S. Moore and Harriet Wright.
" " 30. Frank Dennis and Christene E. Davis.
" " 25, Lyman W. Willoughby and Harriet F. Willoughby.
" " 25, William H. Parsons and Susan M. Leach.
" Nov. 31, Horace Goodwin of Marblehead and Mary S. Wilkins of Hollis.
1867, Feb. 6, Charles S. Runnells and Fidelia A. Wheeler, both of Hollis.
" " 9, Francis M. Lund and Eliza J. Wheeler,   "   "
" Mar. 31, Perley L. Pierce of Brookline and Mary Ann Wood of Hollis.
" April 2, James C. Hildreth and Mary S. Colburn, both of Hollis.
" July 2. J. H. Bond of Waltham and Ella J. Proctor of Hollis.
" Oct. 2, Augustus B. Wheeler and Ellen Wheeler, both of Hollis.
" Nov. 28, Henry Moore of ———— and Letitia A. Hardy of Hollis.
" " 28, Francis A. Wood and Abbie J. Coburn, both of Hollis.
" Dec. 3, George H. Messer and Sarah E. Whiting,   "   "
1868, Feb. 10, John A. Coburn of Hollis and Mary E. Bills of Townsend.
" Mar. 30, Edward H. Wood and Esther Benson, both of Hollis.
" Oct. 27, William P. Cutter and Clara E. Wright,   "   "
" Nov. 25, Henry G. Hildreth of Newton, Mass., and Elizabeth J. Spalding of H.
" Dec. 1, Samuel W. Fletcher of Pepperell and Martha Worcester of Hollis.
1869, Jan. 24, William E. Fox and Eunice T. Ranger, both of Hollis.
" Mar. 11, Clinton Scoville of Conesville, N. Y., and Lydia Fields of Hollis.
" " 19, Josiah N. Hayden and Clara E. Farley, both of Hollis.
" Apr. 30, Alonzo R. Wilson and Eva Shedd,   "   "
" May 19, William E. Howe of Hollis and Hattie G. Lund of Milford.
" " 27, Abel Colburn and Anna L. Heywood, both of Hollis.
" June 24, David McKean of Amherst and Sarah M. Hodgeman of Hollis.
" July 16, Eugene A. Flagg of Worcester, Mass., and Katie F. Spaulding.
" Sept. 14, Nathaniel Whitefield of Francestown, and Mrs. Laurinda Fowler of Hollis.
" Nov. 18, William Worcester and Nellie R. Read, both of Hollis.
" Dec. 3, Charles A. Lovejoy and Ellen H. Day, both of Hollis.
" " Isaac W. Pierce of Pepperell and Lucy A. Blood of Hollis.
1870, Jan. 6, William H. Jordan of Gloucester, Mass., and Harriet E. Worcester of Hollis.
" " 30, Samuel A. Worcester and Lizzie B. Day, both of Hollis.
" Apr. 14, Albert Wheeler of Hollis and Adelia S. Hubbard of Nashua.
" May 28, James E. Hills and Sarah F. Fletcher, both of Hollis.
" Nov. 15, George M. Bradley of Hollis and Maria L. Colburn of Hudson.
" " 24, Amos Fletcher of Hollis and Maria R. Lee of Nashua.
" Dec. 8. Abert J. Farley and Etta F. Wheeler, both of Hollis.
" " 8, Henry S. Spaulding and Eva J. Wheeler, "   "
1871, May 7, Levi B. Crane of New Bedford and Julia Willoughby of Hollis.
" June 14, Norman F. Blood of Groton and Helen A. Smith of Hollis.
" " 15, Isaac F. Fletcher of Lyndon, Vt., and Elizabeth Merrill of Hollis.
" Aug. 13, John H. Hardy of Hollis and Jennie A. Conant of Littleton, Mass.
" Nov. 30, Albert P. Shipley of Nashua and Miriam B. Truell of Hollis.
1872, Feb. 5, David S. Draper of Lyndeborough and Cornelia H. Hall of Hollis.
" " 28, Charles A. Hale of Hollis and Emogene Thomas of Hudson.
" " 28, George Dow of Hollis and Levey V. Draper of Nashua.
" Apr. 29, Albert Lovejoy of Hollis and Charlotte S. Barrett of Nashua.
" Aug. 7, Horace Rideout and Ellen N. Rideout, both of Hollis.
" " 21, Edward S. Colburn, 2d, of Hollis and Abby J. Barnaby.
" Sept. 4, Robert Morse and Grace Burnham, both of Hollis.
" " 18, Albert C. Meady of Boston and Carrie S. Pearse of Hollis.
" Nov. 20. Ramsay C. Boutwell of Hollis and Lucy A. Clark of Lyndeborough.

1873, Feb. 13, John L. Boynton of Pepperell and Josephine L. Fletcher of Hollis.
" June 26, William D. Trow and Nellie A. Hale, both of Hollis.
" Aug. 5, Nathan F. Abbott of Hartford, Ct., and Caroline A. Hills of Hollis.
" Sept. 22, Alphonso H. Powers of Hollis and Frances H. Tufts of Litchfield.
" Oct. 29, Ralph E. Tenney and Sallie A. Cutter, both of Hollis.
" Nov. 26, Amos N. Truell and Clara M. Twiss, " "
1874, Mar. 18, Samuel R. Merrill and Mary L. Smith, " "
" June 2, Leonard Butterfield and Rebecca Noyes, " "
" July 14, Wellington A. Hardy of New York and Mary C. Cutter of Hollis.
" " 14, William B. Whitney of Columbus, Ind., and Lucy F. Cutter of Hollis.
" " 20, Stephen J. Smith and Mary E. Bradley, both of Hollis.
" Aug. 21, Walker H. Blake of Hollis and Augusta E. Jones of Amherst.
" Sept. 24, Henry T. Stimson of Boston and Nellie M. Woods of Hollis.
" Nov. 15, Willard E. Wright and Nellie B. Gates, both of Hollis.
" Dec. 24, Judson J. Willoughby of Hollis and Annie C. Shattuck of Pepperell.
1875, Jan. 21, B. F. Swan and Frances E. Longley, both of Hollis.
" Feb. 17, Frank E. Nichols and Sarah A. Twiss, " "
" Mar. 8, Charles H. Bills of Hollis and Lizzie Mooar of Haverhill.
" " 11, Theodore Brown of Portland, Me., and Clara A. Spaulding of Hollis..
" April 4, Hiram B. Fletcher of Hollis and Cora E. Vaughan of Providence.
" " 8, George H. Blood and H. Augusta Hills, both of Hollis.
" " 20, Elbridge J. Farley and Georgiana Hall, " "
" June 2, Charles E. Gates of Hollis and Adelia A. Peacock of Amherst.
" Aug. 3, James Moore of Nashua and Henrietta L. Hardy of Hollis.
" " 18, George H. Lovejoy and Ella F. Lovejoy, both of Hollis.
" Sept. 9, Henry L. Smith of Hollis and Fannie E. Frost of Arlington.
" " 29, Charles F. Holmes and Nellie M. Bills, both of Hollis.
" Dec. 14, Ralph J. Holden and Loinda Colburn, " "
1876, Jan. 6, Luman C. Drake of Framingham, Mass., and Annie E. Pierce of H.
" " 18, James W. Woods of Hollis and Sarah E. Parker of Pepperell.
" " 20, Lewis G. Woods of Hollis and Nellie M. Plummer of Goffstown.
" Feb. 2, Edward N. Brown of Merrimack and Lizzie M. Holden of Hollis.
" " 2, George F. Hale of Hollis and Addie L. Ruston of Cambridge.
" June 10, Henry Parker of Hollis and Sarah Butterfield of Pelham.
" Aug. 25, Thomas T. Hobart of Hollis and Fannie Woods of Nashua.
" Nov. 29, Charles F Adams and Sarah M. Pierce, both of Hollis.
" Dec. 8, John N. W. Spaulding and Hattie M. Wheeler, both of Hollis.
1877, Jan. 1, Milton A. Parker and Nellie M. Nichols, " "
" " 23, Nathaniel H. Proctor of Hollis and Lizzie S. Billings of Acton.
" " 25, John B. Calderwood and Abbie J. Cameron, both of Hollis.
" Feb. 8, Frederick M. Hill and Ella L. Colburn, both of Hollis.
" Apr. 28, George H. Stearns of Hollis and Laurinda E. Corliss of Hudson.
" May 30, Geo. A. Burge of Hollis and Anna W. Chickering of Somerville, Mass.
" Sept. 3, Albert Kemp of Groton and Clara M. Truell of Hollis.
" Nov. 14, George A. Newton of Hollis and Mary L. Swett of Brookline.

(25)

CHAPTER XXXIII.

FAMILY REGISTERS FROM 1739 TO 1800, COPIED MAINLY FROM
THE HOLLIS RECORDS.

The following lists of Family Registers have been carefully com-
piled, mainly from the first three volumes of the Hollis records, in
which they were originally entered. (without order or method,) for
the most part on the margin of the pages or fractional blank leaves,
from the beginning to the end of each volume. In some cases a
part only of the births in the family registers here presented were
recorded at all in these three volumes—the rest of them, in the
same family in another book, known as the "Record or Book of
Births." In such cases the names of the other children, not found
in the first three volumes, have been copied from the "Book of
Births." The recorded births of a number of the early Hollis
families have also been copied from the original records of the old
town of Monson, and a few others, have been transcribed from
carefully preserved private family records.

In these family registers, as entered on the Hollis records, only
the first or Christian names of the mothers were recorded, not
their full maiden names. In these lists, such family names of the
mothers as were found in the Hollis records of marriages have
been added to their Christian names. The full maiden names of
many others of these mothers, not found in the records of marriages,
are also embraced in these lists, when obtained from sources believed
to be correct. When not so obtained, the names of the mothers
are left as found in the original records.

It is not to be presumed that the family registers recorded in these
first three volumes of the Hollis records embrace the families of
all the early settlers of the town, or that the lists of births in all
the families so recorded and here presented are *wholly* complete.

It is known that the births in some of these early families were not so recorded, and it is also known that there were errors and omissions in some and probably in many of those that were recorded. Still it is believed that the Hollis records, in respect to the genealogies of its early settlers, are more full and better preserved than the like records of most of our older towns, and the information they furnish upon this subject is invaluable to such of their descendants as are interested in preserving the pedigree of their families. It has been the aim of the compiler to exhibit a faithful and accurate transcript of these family lists in a condensed and methodical form, and in such way as would be most convenient to the enquirer, without the toilsome and often fruitless task of a search through the hundreds of pages of the original documents.

The whole number of family registers embraced in these lists, is 337,—the aggregate number of births in them, 2161,—making an average of nearly six and one half to each family, exclusive of such births as may have been omitted in the records.

In thirteen of these families as here presented there was but one birth each; in twenty-four of them but two each; in thirty-six of them but three each; in thirty-four but four each; in thirty-four others, five each; in forty-two of them, six each; in thirty-six of them, seven each; in twenty-seven, eight each; in thirty-four, nine each; in twenty, ten each; in fifteen, eleven each; in six, twelve each; in five, thirteen each; in eight, fourteen each; in two, fifteen each; and in one, sixteen.

BIRTHS, MARRIAGES AND DEATHS.

ABBOT, Capt. BENJAMIN* and ELIZABETH.	
Benjamin,	born April 13, 1749.
Elizabeth,	" Feb. 22, 1751.
Samuel,	" Apr. 15, 1753.
Mary, born Dec. 31, 1754, died Jan. 2, 1755.	
George,	born Dec. 29, 1755.
Joel,	" Dec. 4, 1757.
Jacob,	" Apr. 12, 1760.
*Died Jan. 5, 1776, æt. 46.	

ADAMS, WILLIAM, Jun., and ESTHER.	
Esther,	born Apr. 10, 1784.
Mary,	" Aug. 1, 1786.
William,	" June 3, 1787.
Levi,	" Jan. 22, 1789.
Sarah,	" Jan. 8, 1791.
Samuel,	" Jan. 5, 1793.
John,	" Jan. 9, 1795.
Lucy,	" Aug. 14, 1797.

ABBOT, BENJAMIN, Jun., and SARAH WRIGHT.

Benjamin,	born Dec. 1, 1778, d.
Daniel,	" Aug. 28, 1780.
Jacob,	" Oct. 4, 1782.
Sarah,	" July 3, 1785.
Timothy W.,	" May 4, 1788.
Stephen,	" Dec. 15, 1790.
Betsey,	" June 23, 1793.
Abigail,	" Jan. 9, 1796.
Benjamin,	" Oct. 22, 1800.
John,	" July 2, 1803.
Abial,	" Dec. 29, 1807.

ABBOT, GEORGE and NAOMI TUTTLE.

Married Dec. 29, 1784.

George,	born Oct. 17, 1788.
Naomi,	" Feb. 1, 1790.
Betsey,	" Jan. 11, 1792.
Polly,	" Mar. 11, 1796.
William,	" June 14, 1798.
Harriet,	" July 21, 1802.

ADAMS, WILLIAM* and MARY SPEAR.

Married May 29, 1744.

Mary,	born Oct. 31, 1745.
Lydia,	" Oct. 14, 1747.
Martha,	" June 25, 1749.
Lucy,	" Aug. 17, 1751.
Sarah,	" Feb. 19, 1754.
William,	" Apr. 15, 1756.

*Died Aug. 3, 1757, æt. 39.

AMES, ENSIGN STEPHEN and JANE ROBBINS.

Married Apr. 14, 1731.

Jane,	born Dec. 6, 1733.
Hannah,	" Apr. 28, 1737.
Stephen,	" Mar. 4, 1739.
Elizabeth,	" Feb. 10, 1742.
Rachel,	" Dec. 12, 1744.
Jonathan,	" Apr. 11, 1747.
David,	" May 30, 1749.

AMES, JONATHAN and FRANCES POWERS.

Married Nov. 11, 1772.

Frances,	born Sept. 5, 1773.
Jonathan,	" July 23, 1775.
Anna,	" Dec. 1, 1776.

AMES, Ensign JEREMIAH and JANE.

Jane,	born Sept. 28, 1770.

AMES, BURPEE* and GRACE WHITING.

Married May 28, 1782.

Burpee, Jun.,	born Nov. 14, 1782.

AMES, BURPEE and HANNAH CUMINGS.

Married April 4, 1784.

Jeremiah,	born Oct. 25, 1784.
William,	" Mar. 3, 1786.
Betsey,	" June 9, 1787.
Nathan,	" Oct. 29, 1788.
Poole,	" Feb. 12, 1791, d.
Joseph,	" Feb. 29, 1793, d.
Mary,	" April 13, 1795.
Joseph,	" April 10, 1797.

*Died Nov. 18, 1836, æt. 78.

ASTIN, THOMAS and BEULAH.

Ruth,	born Sept. 27, 1752.
Phineas,	" Jan. 25, 1755.
Thomas,	" July 11, 1758.
Ebenezer,	" Aug. 16, 1760.
Beulah,	" Nov. 16, 1762.
Rebecca,	" April 16, 1765.
Mary,	" Aug. 18, 1767.
Jacob,	" April 6, 1770.
Abner,	" Aug. 26, 1772.
Sarah,	" Jan. 26, 1775.

ASTIN, JOHN and SARAH HASTINGS.

Married Jan. 1, 1756.

Sarah,	born April 3, 1757.
John,	" July 29, 1758.
Andrew,	" Dec. 10, 1759, d.
Mary,	" June 12, 1761.
Martha,	" Mar. 1, 1763.
Benjamin,	" Jan. 25, 1765.
Aaron,	" July 19, 1766.
Eldad,	" April 29, 1768.
Andrew,	" April 12, 1770.

ASTIN, BENJAMIN and BETTY FARLEY.

Married Nov. 24, 1768.

Betty,	born Mar. 22, 1770.
Benjamin,	" July 22, 1773.
Stephen,	" Sept. 2, 1775.

ATWELL, JOHN and BRIDGETT CUMINGS.

Married, Nov. 13, 1760.

John, Jun.,	born June 6, 1761.
William C.,	" May 7, 1763.
Nathan,	" June 15, 1766.
Jonathan,	" Feb. 21, 1768.

Bridget,	born May 24, 1770.
Ebenezer,	" Nov. 22, 1772.
Josiah R.,	" Mar. 27, 1775.
James,	" Feb. 3, 1777.
Becca,	" Jan. 28, 1787.

BALL, EBENEZER and SARAH.

Ebenezer,	born Feb. 26, 1749.
Nathaniel,	" Jan. 24, 1751.
Sarah,	" May 26, 1753.
William,	" April 13, 1755.
Mehitable,	" Aug. 3, 1757.
John,	" Jan. 7, 1759.
Lucy,	" July 4, 1763.

BALL, EBENEZER, Jun., and ELIZABETH DAVIS.

Married Oct. 18, 1770.

Ebenezer,	born Oct. 14, 1771.
Elizabeth,	" Nov. 7, 1773.
Abigail,	" Nov. 12, 1775.
Daniel,	" Mar. 12, 1777.
Sarah,	" Dec. 12, 1779.
David,	" Sept. 14, 1782.
Lucy,	" July 22, 1785.
Phineas, } twins,	" July 24, 1788.
Prudence,	

BALL, ELEAZER and MARY.

Eleazer,	born Jan. 12, 1770.
Mary,	" Dec. 3, 1771.
Submit, born Mar. 27, 1777, d. Oct. 30, 1781.
Samuel,	" Sept. 28, 1779.
Levissa,	" June 26, 1781.

BALL, JOHN and MOLLY CHAMBERLAIN.

Married April 24, 1782.

Molly,	born Jan. 21, 1783.
Sarah,	" March 3, 1785.
John,	" April 21, 1788.
Lucy,	" Jan. 24, 1790.
Submit,	" May 23, 1792, d.
Jesse,	" Nov. 16, 1794.
Ebenezer,	" May 11, 1796.
Submit,	" April 10, 1798.
Samuel,	" Aug. 10, 1800.
Calvin,	" July, 1802.
Lucretia,	" April 7, 1804.

BALL, WILLIAM and ELIZABETH COLBURN.

Married Feb. 9, 1781.

William,	born Nov. 23, 1781, d.
William,	" Dec. 23, 1782.

BALL, WILLIAM* and REBECCA KINNEY.

Married Dec. 7, 1786.

Abel,	born Sept. 8, 1787, d.
Amos,	" Nov. 15, 1789.
Rebecca,	" April 1, 1791.
Abel,	" March 2, 1794.
Margaret,	" July 9, 1796.
James,	" July 4, 1799.
Hannah,	" Nov. 15, 1804.

*Died Jan. 25, 1832, æt. 76.

BARRON, SAMUEL and SALLY LUND.

Married Jan. 24, 1793.

Sally,	born Nov. 29, 1793.
Alice,	" June 8, 1796.
Samuel,	" Sept. 4, 1799.

BARTON, HENRY* and SARAH.

Sarah,	born Oct. 3, 1734.
Mary,	" Jan. 6, 1736.

*Died April 20, 1760, æt. 54.

BAYLEY, DANIEL* and REBEKAH.

Joel,	born Dec. 11, 1751.
Andrew,	" Jan. 4, 1754.
Daniel,	" Dec. 8, 1755.
Joanna,	" Jan. 30, 1758.
Rebecca,	" July 24, 1760.
Sarah,	" May 21, 1763.
Aaron,	" June 28, 1765.
Mary,	" Nov. 16, 1768.

*Died Jan. 15, 1798, æt. 69.

BAYLEY, RICHARD and HANNAH SHATTUCK.

Hannah,	born May 27, 1778.
Eleazer,	" Feb. 20, 1779.
Daniel,	" July 1, 1781.
Job,	" Aug. 5, 1782.

BAYLEY, JOSEPH and ABIGAIL.

Spencer,	born Feb. 2, 1775.
Samuel,	" Sept. 7, 1776.
Abigail,	" Oct. 14, 1779.
Joseph,	" Dec. 8, 1781.
Elizabeth,	" Aug. 26, 1784.
Nathaniel,	" Dec. 24, 1786.
Dolly,	" Feb. 21, 1789.

BAYLEY, TIMOTHY and HANNAH.

Hannah,	born Feb. 22, 1776.
Isaac,	" July 5, 1777.

Timothy,	born Jan. 13, 1780.
Susannah,	" Feb. 6, 1782.
John,	" July 7, 1784.
Leonard,	" June 19, 1787.

Abel,	born Feb. 17, 1761.
Reuben,	" Feb. 1, 1763.
Betty,	" Jan. 21, 1765.
Simon,	" April 10, 1766.

BAYLEY, DANIEL,* Jun., and ELIZABETH FRENCH.

Married Mar. 4, 1784.

Elizabeth,	born Sept. 25, 1784.
Rebecca,	" July 12, 1786.
Lydia,	" April 21, 1789.
Daniel,	" Dec. 31, 1793.
Mary,	" Aug. 28, 1797.

*Died Mar. 13, 1847, æt. 91.

BLANCHARD, JACOB and REBEKAH LAWRENCE.

Jacob,	born Aug. 9, 1750, d.
Jacob,	" Feb. 16, 1753.

BLANCHARD, JOSHUA Jun., and LUCY FRENCH.

Married Feb. 16, 1775.

Joshua M.,	born July 26, 1775.

BENNET, PHINEAS and MARY.

Elijah,	born Mar. 24, 1753.
Tabitha,	" Aug. 2, 1756.
Elizabeth, twin,	" May 3, 1758.
Ephraim, "	" May 3, 1758, d.
Ithamar,	" Aug. 31, 1759.
Mary,	" Feb. 10, 1762.
Ephraim,	" April 12, 1765.

BLOOD, JOSIAH and SARAH.

Josiah,	born July 18, 1743.
Ebenezer,	" May 26, 1745.
Solomon,	" April 17, 1747.
Sarah,	" May 19, 1750. ˙
Caleb,	" May 21, 1752.
Jacob,	" July 24, 1762.
Elizabeth,	" Mar. 27, 1766.

BENNETT, PHINEAS, Jun., and ELIZABETH.

Ede,	born Sept. 7, 1780.
Elizabeth,	" Nov. 3, 1782.
Ezra,	" Nov. 21, 1784.

BLOOD, NATHANIEL* and SARAH.

Nathaniel,	born Mar. 23, 1741.
Daniel,	" Mar. 4, 1743.
Sarah,	" Mar. 18, 1745.
Nathan,	" April 4, 1747.
Francis,	" June 16, 1749.
William,	" Nov. 12, 1751.
Timothy,	" Oct. 15, 1754.

*Died Nov. 11, 1782.

BLANCHARD, JOSHUA and SARAH BURGE.

Married Sept., 1747.

Sarah,	born Nov. 8, 1748.
Joshua,	" Oct. 21, 1750.
David,	" Nov. 10, 1752.
Molly,	" Aug. 30, 1754.
John,	" Sept. 10, 1757.
Lucy,	" June 4, 1760.

BLOOD, ELNATHAN and ELIZABETH BOYNTON

Married Nov. 26, 1741.

Elizabeth,	born Oct. 20, 1742. d.
Elnathan,	" Dec. 4, 1744.
Elizabeth,	" May 22, 1747.
Daniel,	" July 23, 1749.
Jonas,	" Oct. 25, 1751.
Abel,	" July 13, 1754.
Caty,	" Oct. 20, 1760.
Mehitabel,	" Mar. 1, 1765.

BLANCHARD, BENJ. and KEZIA HASTINGS.

Married Dec. 31, 1744.

Benjamin,	born Nov. 15, 1745.
Kezia,	" Mar. 26, 1747.
Abial,	" Jan. 9, 1749, d
Jonathan,	" June 28, 1750.
Abial,	" Dec. 1, 1751.
Isaac,	" April 14, 1753.
Dorcas,	" Feb. 25, 1755, d.
Peter,	" Aug. 17, 1756.
Dorcas,	" Feb. 25, 1757.
Joel,	" Aug. 27, 1759.

BLOOD, DANIEL and PRISCILLA.

Molly,	born May 9, 1767.
Sarah,	" July 24, 1769.
Daniel,	" Feb. 26, 1771.

BLOOD, EPHRAIM and MARY.

Reuben,	born Aug. 10, 1761.
Amos,	" Mar. 10, 1763.
Ephraim,	" April 28, 1764.
David,	" Dec. 15, 1765.
Enoch,	" 1769.
Mary,	" Sept. 11, 1771.

BLOOD, FRANCIS and ABIGAIL CONROY.

Married Dec. 12, 1768.

Abigail,	born Aug. 25, 1769.
Hannah,	" Nov. 12, 1771.
Francis.	" Feb. 15, 1774. d.
Sarah,	" May 10, 1776.
Polly,	" Feb. 21, 1778.
Francis,	" Jan. 30, 1780.
Elizabeth,	" Jan. 8, 1782.
Nathan,	" Jan. 26, 1784.
Daniel,	" Mar. 27, 1787.

BLOOD, SOLOMON* and PRISCILLA FRENCH.

Married Jan. 5, 1769.

Solomon,	born Oct. 7, 1769.
Sarah,	" Dec. 22, 1771.
Joseph,	} twins.
Mary,	

*Died Dec. 6, 1802, æt. 55.

BLOOD, JOSIAH* and ABIGAIL PIERCE.

Married May 24, 1770.

Joel,	born March 7, 1771.
Mary,	" July 10, 1773.
Ebenezer,	" Mar. 15, 1775.
Josiah,	" Apr. 23, 1777.
Sarah,	" April 1, 1779.
Anna,	" April 23, 1783.

BLOOD, JOSIAH and SARAH FRENCH.

Benjamin,	born Mar. 16, 1789.
Abigail,	" April 5, 1791.
Luther,	" Mar. 25, 1793.
Ama,	" Apr. 14, 1797.

*Died Jan. 15, 1816, æt. 73.

BLOOD, NATHAN* and ELIZABETH NOYES.

Married April 16, 1772.

| Nathan, | born April 11, 1773. |
| Elizabeth, | " Feb. 13, 1775. |

*Killed June 17, 1775.

BLOOD, DANIEL, 2d, and SARAH.

Sarah,	born Jan. 4, 1775. d.
Daniel,	" Feb. 5, 1776.
Mighill,	" Dec. 13, 1777.
Sarah,	" Sept. 18, 1779.

BLOOD, ELNATHAN, Jun., and DEBORAH PHELPS.

Married June 5, 1766.

Nathan,	born Feb. 9, 1778.
Rebekah,	" May 14, 1780.
Elizabeth,	" June 6, 1783.
Hannah,	" Aug. 8, 1785.
Martha,	" April 6, 1789.

BLOOD, JACOB* and RACHEL.

Elizabeth,	born Aug. 14, 1785.
Susannah,	" Aug. 28, 1786.
Rachel,	} twins, " April 14, 1788.
Rhoda,	
Nancy,	" Aug. 27, 1790.
Sarah,	" Dec. 11, 1791.

*Died Sept. 11, 1800, æt. 38.

BLOOD, ABEL and SARAH.

| Mehitable, | born Dec. 11, 1788. |
| Abel, | " May 5, 1791. |

BLOOD, SOLOMON, Jun., and HANNAH KINNEY.

Married June 9, 1794.

| Hannah, | born Nov. 28, 1795. |
| Sukey, | " Sept. 3, 1798. |

BOYNTON, JOSHUA* and MARTHA.

Joshua,	born Nov. 26, 1743.
Martha,	" Aug. 39, 1745.
Benjamin,	" Feb. 21, 1747.
Mary,	" June 10, 1749.
Amos,	" June 11, 1751.
Sarah,	" July 12, 1753.
Elias,	" Feb. 24, 1755.
Elizabeth,	" April 4, 1757.

*Died Feb. 4, 1763.

BOYNTON, JOHN, Jun., and LYDIA JEWETT.

Married May 17, 1745.

Margaret,	born Dec. 6, 1745.
Jemima,	" Nov. 10, 1747.
Samuel,	" Mar. 30, 1750.

Lydia,	born Sept. 12, 1751.
John,	" Oct. 18, 1753.
Isaac,	" April 3, 1755.
Balo,	" Sept. 26, 1756.
Sarah,	" Dec. 26, 1757.
Joel,	" Mar. 22, 1759.

BOYNTON, Dea. JOHN* and RUTH JEWETT.

Jeremiah,	born April 29, 1753.
John,	" Aug. 11, 1754.
Jacob,	" Dec. 12, 1756.
Ruth,	" Sept. 10, 1758.
Mehitable,	" Jan. 21, 1761.
Moses,	" Sept. 25, 1763.
Rebekah,	" Nov. 20, 1765.

*Died Oct. 29, 1787, æt. 67.

BOYNTON, BENJAMIN and DEBORAH PARKER.

Married Nov. 5, 1778.

Sarah,	born May 29, 1779.
Deborah,	" July 23, 1781.
Benjamin,	" Dec. 21, 1783, d.
Benjamin,	" Aug. 4, 1786.
Martha,	" Oct. 12, 1788.

BOYNTON, JOSHUA, Jun., and MARY PARKER.

Married May 26, 1778.

Mary,	born May 14, 1784.
Joshua,	" Mar. 19, 1786.
Josiah,	" Dec. 23, 1787.
Samuel,	" Aug. 9, 1789.

BOYNTON, MOSES and HANNAH LUND.

Hannah,	born Feb. 2, 1795.
Moses,	" Mar. 2, 1798.
Rebekah,	" April 3, 1801.
Sarah,	" May 20, 1803.
Naomi,	" July 14, 1805.
Mary, '	" July 15, 1807.
Lucy,	" April 6, 1810.
John,	" Sept. 9, 1812.
Eliza,	" June 21, 1815.
Jacob,	" Dec. 17, 1818.

BRADBURY, JAMES and CATHARINE CONANT.

Married May 30, 1795.

James,	born Jan. 4, 1796.
Catharine,	" Mar. 25, 1798.
William S.,	" Feb. 14, 1800.
Charles,	" July 4, 1802.
Elizabeth,	" Sept. 18, 1804.
Samuel F ,	" Dec. 25, 1806.
Josiah C.,	" Feb. 21, 1809.
Mary Ann,	" May 17, 1811.

BRADLEY, ITHAMAR and MEHITABLE.

Nehemiah,	born May 17, 1779.
Ezekiel,	" April 27, 1781.
Mehitable,	" Sept. 8, 1784.
Ithamar,	" June 22, 1790.

BROOKS, JOHN and MARY KEMP.

Married Jan. 5, 1757.

Mary,	born Dec. 3, 1757.
John,	" Feb. 24, 1760.
Nathan,	" Aug. 26, 1767.
Abigail,	" Dec. 6, 1770.
Hannah,	" Aug. 20, 1772.
Ruth,	" Jan. 15, 1775.

BROOKS, Capt. WILLIAM and ABIGAIL KEMP.

Married March 29, 1759.

William,	born May 1, 1760.
Abigail,	" July 19, 1762.
Betsey,	" July 23, 1764.
Sarah,	" July 6, 1766.
Isaac,	" Oct. 28, 1768.
Marah,	" Feb. 15, 1771.
Samuel,	" Mar. 3, 1774.
Martha,	" Aug. 23, 1776.
Leonard,	" Jan. 29, 1779.
John,	" Nov. 11, 1781.
Susannah,	" Feb. 12, 1783.

BROWN, JOSIAH and ANNA.

Elizabeth,	born Oct. 14, 1742.
Anna,	" Oct. 23, 1744.
Josiah,	" Sept. 24, 1746, d.
Molly,	" Sept. 4, 1748.
Joseph,	" Nov. 8, 1750.
Olive,	" Nov. 1, 1752.
Susannah,	" Aug. 20, 1754.
Sarah,	" Jan. 3, 1757.
Josiah,	" Jan. 31, 1759.

BROWN, SAMUEL AND MARY GLENE.

Married March 26, 1756.

Mary,	born Jan. 1, 1757.
William,	" Nov. 13, 1758, d.
Hannah,	" Nov. 13, 1760.

BROWN, SAMUEL AND MARY WHEELER.

Married January 23, 1761.

Bridget,	born Dec. 31, 1761.
Samuel,	" Jan. 11, 1764.
William,	" Jan. 4, 1766.

BROWN, JOHN* and KEZIA WHEELER.

Married Oct. 9, 1744.

Silas,	born Aug. 11, 1745.
John,	" Jan. 27, 1747.
Kezia,	" Dec. 23, 1749.
Abigail,	" June 10, 1754.
Phineas,	" Nov. 14, 1756.
Rebekah,	" Sept. 21, 1758.
Elizabeth,	" Sept. 10, 1760.
Martha,	" April 8, 1762.
Sarah,	" Mar. 24, 1764.

*Died May 6, 1770, æt. 43.

BROWN, DAVID and REBEKAH.

Rebekah,	born Dec. 13, 1769.
David,	" April 4, 1773.

BROWN, WILLIAM and ELIZABETH NEVINS.

William,	born Mar. 11, 1790.
Betsey,	" Oct. 8, 1791.
Sukey,	" Nov. 5, 1795.
Nathan,	" Aug. 22, 1798.
Lucinda,	" Sept. 11, 1801.

BURGE, EPHRAIM* and ANNA ABBOT

Married Jan. 7, 1762.

Anna,	born Nov. 20, 1762.
Ephraim,	" June 7, 1764.
Josiah,	" April 15, 1766.
Jacob,	" Jan. 7, 1768.
Susannah,	" Dec. 5, 1769, d.
Susannah,	" July 21, 1773.
Abial,	" May 27, 1775.
Sarah,	" May 2, 1777.
Samuel,	" Mar. 28, 1779.
Benjamin,	" Aug. 5, 1782.

*Died July 31, 1784, æt. 46.

BURGE, Dea. EPHRAIM* and PATTY BALDWIN.

Married Jan. 28, 1793.

Ephraim,	born Nov. 8, 1794.
Patty,	" May 9, 1796.
Anna,	" July 13, 1798.
Clarissa,	
Cyrus,	" Sept. 7, 1804.
Emma,	" Nov. 5, 1807.

*Died March 3, 1843, æt. 78.

BURPEE, NATHANIEL and RUTH.

Nabby,	born June 5, 1780.
Sally,	" Jan. 21, 1783.
Nathaniel,	" Nov. 8, 1785.
Benjamin D.,	" Dec. 30, 1788.

(28)

CARTER, EDWARD and MARY.

Mary,	born Nov. 19, 1751.
Elizabeth,	" Mar. 12, 1754.
Susannah,	" June 6, 1756.
Thomas,	" Sept. 5, 1758.
Sarah,	" June 15, 1762.

CARTER, EDWARD, Jun., and ESTHER.

Esther,	born Nov. 8, 1766.
Caty,	" July 8, 1768.
Isaac P.,	" April 27, 1770.
Mary,	" May 27, 1772.
Betsey,	" Sept. 30, 1773.
Edward,	" Aug. 8, 1775.
Thomas,	" July 13, 1777.
Susannah,	" Oct. 12, 1779.
Jonathan,	" Mar. 24, 1782.
Loammi,	" Dec. 21, 1784.

CLARK, ELIJAH and MARTHA RUNNELLS.

Married April 9, 1778.

Hannah,	born Mar. 6, 1779.
Elijah,	" Mar. 18, 1781.
Martha,	" Feb. 19, 1786.
John R.,	" Dec. 14, 1789.

COLBURN, Lieut. ROBERT* and ELIZABETH SMITH.

Married 1747.

Robert,	born April 9, 1748.
Elizabeth,	" Oct. 22, 1749, d.
Benjamin,	" May 11, 1751, d.
Nathan,	" Nov. 6, 1752.
Benjamin,	" May 5, 1755.
Peter,	" Nov. 14, 1756.
Elizabeth,	" April 27, 1759.
Lucy,	" Jan. 12, 1761.
Anna,	" Nov. 27, 1763.

*Died July 9, 1783, æt. 66.

COLBURN, WILLIAM* and ABIGAIL.

Isabel,	born Aug. 16, 1758.
Paul,	" Oct. 4, 1761.
William.	" June 8, 1764.

*Died April 3, 1760, æt. 79.

COLBURN, THOMAS and ESTHER FLAGG.

Married Sept. 15, 1757.

James,	born 1759.
Ruth,	" June 12, 1763.
John,	" Sept. 14, 1765.
Thomas.	" Nov. 1, 1767.

COLBURN, ROBERT, Jun., and DORCAS.

Dorcas,	born Oct. 13, 1773.
Robert,	" April 4, 1775.
Peter,	" Oct. 31, 1776.
Timothy,	" Aug. 10, 1778.
Hannah,	" April 10, 1780.
Anna,	" Aug. 31, 1781.
Elizabeth,	" Jan. 16, 1783.
Washington,	" April 20, 1786.
William,	" March 2, 1789.

COLBURN, PAUL and MEHITABLE.

Mehitable,	born Aug. 16, 1782.
Elizabeth,	" Jan. 13, 1784.

COLBURN, BENJAMIN and ESTHER.

Esther,	born May 29, 1779.
Mary,	" May 5, 1782.
Lucy,	" Feb. 10, 1785.
Elizabeth,	" June 23, 1787.
Mehitable,	" May 16, 1789.
Hannah,	" Mar. 21, 1791.
Joseph,	" May 20, 1793.
John,	" Jan. 24, 1795.
Elias,	" Feb. 15, 1797, d.
Elias,	" Oct. 15, 1800.

COLBURN, NATHAN* and ABIGAIL SHATTUCK.

Married Jan. 28, 1779.

Abigail,	born Nov. 1, 1782.
Nathan,	" Mar. 31, 1785.
Rachel,	" Dec. 11, 1787.
Susannah,	" Feb. 19, 1790.
Elizabeth,	" Nov. 19, 1791.
Nathaniel W.,	" July 17, 1794.
Daniel,	" Oct. 8, 1796.

*Died Feb. 17, 1831, æt. 78.

COLBURN, JAMES* and SUSANNAH HARDY.

Married Feb. 14, 1785.

James,	born Mar. 13, 1786.
Susannah,	" Dec. 30, 1787.
Sally,	" Oct. 7, 1789, d.
Hannah,	" Dec. 27, 1791.
Esther,	" Feb. 26, 1794.
Ruth,	" April 24, 1796.
Sally,	" May 2, 1798.
John,	" Aug. 22, 1799.
Bradlee,	" July 28, 1801.
Amos,	" Jan. 12, 1804.
Mary,	" Nov. 20, 1805.
Almira,	" Oct. 28, 1807.
Louisa,	" Feb. 6, 1811.

*Died Feb. 14, 1830, æt. 70.

CONANT,* JOSIAH and CATHARINE EMERSON.

Married Feb. 9, 1745.

Josiah,	born Oct. 17, 1746.
Catharine,	" Dec. 23, 1748, d.
Catharine,	" Nov. 13, 1753.
Abel,	" Oct. 3, 1855.

*Died Dec. 14, 1756, æt. 44.

CONANT, Dea. JOSIAH* and ELIZABETH ELLIOT.

Married Jan. 9, 1769.

Josiah,	born Feb. 5, 1770.
Elizabeth,	" Nov. 10, 1771.
Catharine,	" Nov. 28, 1773.
William,	" Jan. 16, 1776.
Mary,	" Jan. 7, 1778.
Abigail,	" Aug. 30, 1780.
Ruth,	" Dec. 31, 1782.
Elias,	" Sept. 1785, d

CONANT, Dea. JOSIAH and ZERVIAH FOX.

Married Dec. 16, 1788.

Sarah,	born Sept. 24, 1789.
Joseph,	" July 4, 1791.
Elias,	" Sept. 11, 1792.
Hannah,	" Feb. 29, 1794.
Sophia,	" Feb. 16, 1796.
Elizabeth,	" July 4, 1800.

*Died August 21, 1807, æt. 61.

CONANT, Dea. ABEL* and MARGARET JEWETT

Married Nov. 20, 1781.

Margaret,	born Aug. 30, 1782.
Abel,	" June 1, 1784.
James,	" April 7, 1786.
Catharine,	" Dec. 29, 1787.

CONANT, Dea. ABEL and LYDIA THURSTON.

Susannah,	born May 26, 1791.
Joseph,	" Nov. 24, 1792.
Daniel,	" Dec. 11, 1794.
Lydia,	" April 26, 1796.
Rebekah,	" Nov. 28, 1798.
Moses T.,	" Feb. 3, 1801.
John C.,	" Jan. 30, 1803.

*Died May 2, 1844, æt. 88.

CONROY JOHN and LYDIA.

John,	born Dec. 28, 1761.
Sarah,	" Sept. 13, 1764.
Lydia,	" Jan. 29, 1766.
Thomas,	" April 3, 1769.

William,	born Aug. 3, 1771, d.
William,	" Sept. 26, 1775.
Mary,	" Nov. 6, 1777.

CONROY SAMUEL and ALICE BLOOD.

Married Nov. 22, 1774.

Samuel,	born July 9, 1779.
Alice,	" May 27, 1781.
Jonas,	" Nov. 7, 1783.
Martha,	" Dec. 7, 1785.
Sarah,	" Aug. 23, 1788.
David,	" May 23, 1791.

CONROY STEPHEN and REBECCA BLODGETT.

Married Dec. 13, 1781.

Betsey,	born Feb. 25, 1782.
Eunice,	" Feb. 13, 1784.
John,	" June 13, 1787.
Rebekah,	" April 26, 1789.
Isaac,	" Feb. 9, 1795.
Oliver B.,	" Aug. 28, 1802.

CUMINGS, SAMUEL* Esq., and PRUDENCE LAWRENCE.

Married July 18, 1732.

Mary,	born April 22, 1734.
Sibbell,	" Nov. 1, 1736.
Prudence,	" Nov. 26, 1740.
Samuel,	" Dec. 10, 1742.
Thomas,	" Aug. 21, 1748.
Benjamin,	" Nov. 25, 1757.

*Died Jan. 18, 1772, æt. 62.

CUMINGS, JERAHMAEL* and HANNAH FARWELL.

Hannah,	born July 13, 1737.
Henry,	" Sept. 16, 1739.
Jotham,	" Dec. 29, 1741.
Caty,	" Feb. 28, 1744.
Betty,	" July 17, 1746.

*Died Oct. 21, 1747, æt. 36.

CUMINGS, EBENEZER* and ELIZABETH ABBOTT.

Elizabeth,	born Nov. 23, 1759.
Ebenezer,	" Sept. 15, 1761.
Abigail,	" July 9, 1763.
Bridget,	" June 16, 1765.
Lucy,	" July 9, 1767.
Mary,	" Oct. 23, 1769.
Jacob A.,	" Nov. 2, 1772.
Sarah,	" Feb. 28, 1775.

*Died 1778.

CUMINGS, Lieut. JOHN and REBECCA.

Peter,	born Nov. 12, 1761.
Rebecca,	" Mar. 2, 1764, d.
Sarah,	" Oct. 5, 1766.
John,	" Mar. 8, 1769.
Rebecca,	" Aug. 28, 1771.
Abigail,	" Feb. 11, 1774.
Asahel,	" Jan. 13, 1777.
Henry,	" Nov. 1, 1779.
Benaiah,	" Mar. 21, 1782.

CUMINGS, SAMUEL Jun. and LYDIA WEBSTER

Married Nov. 3, 1768.

Lydia,	born Aug. 21, 1769.
Sibbel,	" May 17, 1771.
Samuel,	" May 30, 1773.
Prudence,	" Jan. 24, 1775.

CUMINGS, PHILIP and MARY.

Philip,	born Sept. 1, 1770.
Thomas,	" Aug. 7, 1772.
Edward,	" Nov. 17, 1774.

CUMINGS, WILLIAM* and MEHITABLE EASTMAN.

Married Jan. 28, 1768.

William,	born Jan. 17, 1769.
Jonathan,	" Aug. 2, 1770.
Daniel,	" July 6, 1772.
Leonard,	" April 19, 1774.
Caleb E.,	" Jan. 9, 1776.
Sarah,	" Dec. 18, 1777.
Elizabeth,	" April 15, 1780.
Molly,	" May 18, 1782.
Bradley,	" April 12, 1784.
Hannah,	" July 17, 1786.
Luther,	" May 6, 1789.

*Died Oct. 2, 1831, æt. 90.

CUMINGS, Lieut. BENJAMIN and BRIDGET POOL.

Married Dec. 7, 1780.

Benjamin,	born Aug. 24, 1782.
Bridget,	" Feb. 3, 1784.

CUMINGS, Lieut. BENJAMIN and SARAH HOLDEN.

Sarah,	born June 7. 1787.
Samuel,	" Nov. 9, 1788.
Thomas,	" Sept. 18, 1790.
David,	" Oct. 13, 1792.
Phineas,	" Mar. 15, 1795.
Betsey,	" April 10, 1797.
William,	" April 25, 1799.

CUMINGS, THOMAS and HANNAH POOL.

Married Nov. 17, 1772.

Hannah,	born April	1, 1773.
Sarah,	"	1774.
Thomas,	" Nov.	1, 1776.

DANFORTH, JONA.* and ANNA BLANCHARD.

Married May 24, 1743.

Anna,	born Feb.	7, 1744.
Jonathan,	" July	20, 1745.
David,	" Jan.	24, 1747.

*Died March 3, 1747, æt. 32.

DANFORTH, JONATHAN, Jun., and HANNAH

Hannah,	born May	5, 1770.
Jonathan,	" July	27, 1772.
Elizabeth,	" May	10, 1774.
Leonard,	" April	9, 1777.
David,	" May	15, 1779.
Luther,	" Oct.	23, 1781.
Anna,	" July	19, 1783.
Asa,	" Oct.	14, 1785.
Rebecca,	" Mar.	23, 1788.

DANFORTH, JACOB and ANNA.

Jacob,	born Mar.	20, 1769.
Timothy,	" June	2, 1771.
Anna,	" Mar.	9, 1773.

DAVIS, JOSHUA and DOROTHY WHEELER.

Married Oct. 22, 1767.

Simeon,	born Mar.	4, 1784.
Hannah,	" May	23, 1786.

DINSMORE, ABRAHAM and LYDIA.

Abraham,	born Jan.	17, 1753.
Zebadiah,	" Jan.	17, 1755.
Lydia,	" Jan.	24, 1757.
Hannah,	" Mar.	2, 1759.
Phebe,	" May	17, 1761.
Thomas,	" Aug.	14, 1763.

DOW, Capt. REUBEN* and LYDIA JONES.

Evan,	born Feb.	4, 1754.
Stephen,	" Dec.	30, 1757.
Lydia,	" May	18, 1762.
Phebe,	" June	22, 1765.
Daniel,	" Dec.	10, 1769.
Lois,	" June	24, 1773.

*Died Feb. 9, 1811, æt. 81.

DOW, STEPHEN* and ABIGAIL JEWETT.

Married June 17, 1784.

Lois,	born Feb.	2, 1786.
Stephen,	" July	14, 1787.
Hannah,	" April	28, 1790.
Nathaniel,	" Aug.	21, 1792.
Jeremiah,	" Jan.	5, 1795.
Abigail,	" April	22, 1797.
Elizabeth,	" Dec.	24, 1800.

*Died Nov. 1, 1839, æt. 82.

DRURY, Lieut. ZEDEKIAH and HANNAH.

Gershom,	born Dec.	31, 1739.
Zedekiah,	" Mar.	1, 1742.
Jonathan, } twins,		
Ebenezer, } twins,	" Aug.	4, 1743.
Thomas,	" April	26, 1747.
Nathan,	" Nov.	23, 1748.
Hannah,	" Aug.	29, 1750.
Elizabeth,	" Aug.	27, 1752.
Mary,	" Feb.	8, 1757.
David,	" May	15, 1759.
John,	" Feb.	28, 1761.
Samuel,	" July	10, 1763.

EASTMAN, Lieut. AMOS* and MEHITABLE
BRADLEY.

Mehitable,	born June	25, 1746.
Jonathan,	" July	19, 1748.
Amos,	" April	28, 1751.
Caleb,	" Oct.	3, 1753.
Sarah,	" Mar.	5, 1756.
Hannah,	" Jan.	6, 1759.

*Died March 6, 1808, æt. 88.

EASTMAN, JONATHAN* and SARAH FLETCHER.

Married Sept. 13, 1770.

Joseph F.,	born Jan.	14, 1772.
Jonathan B., ,	" Jan.	8, 1780.

*Died Dec. 29, 1790, æt. 42.

EASTMAN, AMOS* and RUTH FLAGG.

Married Jan. 6, 1774.

Ruth,	born Oct.	24, 1774.
Persis,	" Dec.	1, 1775, d.
Persis,	" Oct.	27, 1776.
Amos,	" Aug.	4, 1778.
Caleb,	" May	4, 1780.
Charles,	" Feb.	4, 1782.
Hannah,	" June	25, 1783.
Alpheus,	" Oct.	9, 1787.
Luke,	" June	22, 1790.

*Died August 2, 1832, æt. 81.

EMERSON, Rev. DANIEL* and HANNAH
EMERSON.

Married Nov. 7, 1744.

Hannah,	born Sept. 30, 1745.
Daniel,	" Dec. 15, 1746.
Mary,	" Sept. 19, 1748, d.
Peter,	" Nov. 7, 1749.
Lucy,	" Oct. 29, 1751.
Mary,	" Nov. 14, 1753.
Elizabeth,	" May 5, 1755.
Ebenezer,	" Aug. 14, 1757.
Joseph,	" Sept. 28, 1759.
Ralph,	" Mar. 4, 1761.
Rebecca,	" July 5, 1762.
Samuel,	" Sept. 6, 1764.
William,	" Dec. 11, 1765.

*Died Sept. 30, 1801, æt. 85.

EMERSON, Dea. DANIEL* and AMA FLETCHER

Married Nov. 17, 1768.

Ama,		born Aug. 20, 1769.
Daniel,		" July 15, 1771.
Hannah,		" Dec. 7, 1773.
Joseph,		" Oct. 13, 1777.
Ralph,		" Aug. 18, 1787.
Samuel,	twins,	" Nov. 9, 1791.
William,		

*Died Oct. 4. 1820, æt. 74.

EMERSON, THOMAS and JUDITH.

James,	born Aug. 7, 1770.
Thomas,	" Nov. 27, 1774.
William,	" Mar. 28, 1777.
Daniel,	" June 12, 1780.
John S.,	" Aug. 12, 1783.
Asa,	" Sept. 20, 1785.

EMERSON, TIMOTHY and HULDAH.

Timothy,	born Dec. 11, 1776.
Aaron,	" June 11, 1779.
Stephen,	" Mar. 29, 1781.
Huldah,	" April 1, 1783.
Jesse,	" May 15, 1785.

EMERSON, Dr. PETER* and MOLLY.

Susannah,	born Dec. 10, 1781.
Rebecca,	" May 29, 1784.
Mary,	" June 7, 1786.
Daniel,	" Sept. 16, 1788.
Hannah.	" June 25, 1791.
John,	" April 7, 1798.

*Died 1827, æt. 78.

EMERSON, RALPH* and ALICE AMES.

Married May 13, 1784.

Elizabeth,	born Jan. 27, 1785.
Alice,	" Oct. 4, 1790.

*Died Oct. 4, 1790, æt. 29.

EASTERBROOK, JOSEPH and LYDIA.

Mary,	born April 20, 1751.
Elizabeth.	" Nov. 2, 1753.
Lydia,	" Jan. 24, 1761.
Joseph,	" Mar. 28, 1764.

FARLEY, Lieut. SAMUEL and HANNAH
BROWN.

Married Oct. 9, 1744.

Ebenezer,	born Oct. 9, 1745.
Samuel,	" Mar. 14, 1747.
Hannah,	" Jan. 27, 1749.
Benjamin.	" Mar. 11, 1756.
Anna,	" Feb. 19, 1768.

FARLEY, Lieut. BENJAMIN* and JOANNA
PAGE.

Joanna,	born April 21, 1733.
Rebecca,	" April 29, 1735.
Benjamin,	" June 21, 1737.
Molly,	" Nov. 25, 1739.
Betty,	" June 23, 1742.
Lucy,	" Feb. 13, 1744.
Ebenezer,	" Sept. 19, 1747.
Hannah,	" Feb. 8, 1750, d.
Christopher,	" April 1, 1751.
Stephen,	" Jan. 28, 1754.
Hannah,	" Jan. 31, 1757.
Sarah,	" Sept. 28, 1761.

*Died Dec. 23, 1789, æt. 79.

FARLEY, Capt. CALEB* and ELIZABETH
FARLEY.

Elizabeth,	born Aug. 24, 1755.
Joseph,	" May 1, 1757.
Caleb,	" April 3, 1759.
James,	" April 12, 1761.
Benjamin,	" June 27, 1763.
John,	" May 1765.
Thomas,	" Dec. 28, 1769.
Abel,	" July 17, 1773.

*Died April 5, 1833, æt. 102 years, 5 mo.

FARLEY, EBENEZER* and BETTY WHEELER.

Married Nov. 6, 1766.

Benjamin,	born Feb. 1, 1767.
Lucy,	" Sept. 3, 1768.
Joanna,	" Mar. 22, 1770.
Betty,	" Mar. 18, 1772.
Ebenezer,	" Mar. 4, 1774.
Hannah,	" Dec. 1, 1775.
John,	" Dec. 13, 1777.
Daniel,	" Oct. 28, 1779.
Jesse,	" June 26, 1781.
Sarah,	" April 23, 1783.
Rebecca,	" Dec. 13, 1784.
Susannah,	" Feb. 4, 1787.
James,	" May 21, 1791.

*Died Jan. 28, 1827, æt. 80.

FARLEY, CHRISTOPHER* and RUTH JEWETT.

Married Dec. 30, 1773.

Ruth,	born Sept. 19, 1774.
Amos,	" June 6, 1776.
Christopher P.,	" Jan. 30, 1778.
Susannah,	" Jun. 9, 1780.
James J.,	" May 4, 1782, d.
James J.,	" Jan. 12, 1784.
Elizabeth,	" July 28, 1786.
Christopher,	" Oct. 8, 1788.

*Died June 21, 1788, æt. 37.

FARLEY, JOSEPH and BRIDGET POWERS.

Married Dec. 18, 1777.

Bridget,	born Mar. 4, 1778.
Joseph,	" Feb. 7, 1780.

FARLEY, STEPHEN* and MARY SHATTUCK.

Married Jan. 28, 1779.

Stephen,	born Oct. 24, 1779.
Mary,	" Aug. 12, 1781.
Isaac,	" Aug. 21, 1783.
Elizabeth, twin,	" Sept. 18, 1785.
Joanna, " d.,	
Hannah,	" 1787.
Christopher,	" Oct. 19, 1789.
Joanna,	" Aug. 10, 1791.

*Died Jan. 13, 1837, æt. 84.

FARLEY, CALEB, Jun., and ABIGAIL PHELPS.

Married April 12, 1781.

Caleb,	born April 15, 1782.
James,	" Sept. 27, 1783.
John,	" Feb. 15, 1785.

Abigail,	born July 22, 1786.
William,	" Oct. 21, 1787.
Nathan,	" Mar. 16, 1789.
Henry,	" July 9, 1790.
Elizabeth,	" Sept. 14, 1791, d.
Isaac,	" Feb. 15, 1793.
Lucy,	" April 16, 1794.
Hannah,	" July 17, 1795.
Sukey,	" Dec. 2, 1796.
Elizabeth.	" Oct. 10, 1799.
Gilman,	" Jan. 12, 1802.

FARLEY, Lieut. BENJAMIN and MARY BLODGETT.

Married Feb. 15, 1787.

Mary,	born July 27, 1788.
Benjamin,	" May 3, 1790.
Sarah,	" May 5, 1792, d.
Noah,	" Apr. 13, 1794, d.
Leonard,	" Sept. 23, 1796, d.
Charlotte,	" Oct. 22, 1797.
Noah,	" Feb. 10, 1800.
Abel,	" Sept. 19, 1802.
Leonard W.,	" Aug. 9, 1805.
Sarah,	" Aug. 11, 1807.
Caleb, .	" July 16, 1811.

FARLEY, BENJAMIN and LUCY FLETCHER.

Married June 18, 1780.

Sarah, } twins,	born June 3, 1781.*
Betsey, }	
Benjamin Mark,	" Aug. 8, 1783
Lucy,	" Dec. 26, 1784.
Luther.	" Dec. 25, 1786.
Charles,	" Oct. 13, 1788.
Benjamin,	" Feb. 20, 1791, d.
George Frederic,	" Apr. 5, 1793.
Percy,	" Sept. 12, 1798.
Clarissa,	" Nov. 12, 1801.

FARLEY, BENJ., Jun., and ANNA MERRILL.

Benjamin,	born Oct. 3, 1789.
Anna,	" June 30, 1791.
Polly,	" Feb. 18, 1794.
Rebekah,	" Aug. 17, 1796.
Enoch,	" July 22, 1798.
Lucy.	" Oct. 18, 1803.
Merrill,	" May 6, 1806.
Edward P.,	" Dec. 26, 1808.

FARMER, MINOT* and ABIGAIL BARRON.

Married Sept. 15, 1775.

Abigail,	born Dec. 1, 1775.

*Died May 19, 1776, æt. 26.

FISK, Lieut. AMOS and ELIZABETH FLAGG.

Married March 18, 1762.

Betty,	born Jan. 17, 1763.
Hannah,	" Jan. 21, 1765.
Sarah,	" Apr. 7, 1767.

FISK, JOSIAH and MARY CALDWELL.

Married Nov. 25, 1779.

Josiah,	born Nov. 14, 1781.

FLETCHER, OLIVER and TABITHA.

Thankful,	born July 18, 1766.
Sibbel,	" Jan. 15, 1768.
Tabitha,	" Feb. 5, 1770.
Betty,	" Feb. 3, 1772.
Stephen,	" Dec. 1, 1773.
Rebecca,	" Oct. 19, 1775.

FLAGG, ELEAZER* and HANNAH.

Abigail,	born Apr. 16, 1735.
Esther,	" Jan. 30, 1737.
John,	" May 1, 1739.
Mary,	" June 16, 1741.
Jerusha,	" Feb. 1, 1744.
Elizabeth,	" May 11, 1745.
Ruth,	" Oct. 1746.
Joseph,	" June 3, 1750.

*Died August 14, 1757, æt. 53.

FLAGG, Capt. JONAS and MARTHA KNIGHT.

Martha,	born Feb. 3, 1760.
Jonas,	" Mar. 10, 1762.
Jerusha,	" April 27, 1764.
Mary,	" Feb. 23, 1766.
Reuben,	" Aug. 10, 1768.
Joseph,	" Sept. 10, 1772.

FLAGG, JOSEPH and HANNAH BOYNTON.

Hannah,	born Dec. 3, 1795.

FOSTER, EDWARD and PHEBE.

Susannah,	born Feb. 2, 1777.
Elizabeth,	" April 25, 1779.
Patty,	" May 19, 1781.
Bridget,	" April 26, 1783.
Noah,	" Dec. 13, 1784.
William,	" Dec. 5, 1786.
Benjamin,	" Dec. 4, 1788.

FOX, Dr. JONATHAN* and ZERVIAH JONES.

Zerviah,	born Feb. 16, 1779.
Jonathan,	" May 17, 1781.
Ebenezer,	" April 6, 1783.

*Died Oct. 26, 1782, æt. 28.

FRENCH, NICHOLAS and PRISCILLA.

Timothy,	born July 6, 1745.
Priscilla,	" Oct. 2, 1747.
Nicholas,	" June 30, 1750.
Isaac,	" Sept. 1, 1752.
Lucy,	" April 31, 1755.
Sarah,	" Aug. 3, 1758, d.
Jonathan,	" Aug. 21, 1759.
Sarah,	" April 22, 1762.
David,	" Oct. 28, 1765.

FRENCH, JOHN and MARY.

Mary,	born July 12, 1750.
Hepzibah,	" Jan. 31, 1752.
William,	" May 19, 1754, d.
John,	" April 8, 1757.
Elizabeth,	" Aug. 22, 1759.
Jonathan,	" Jan. 9, 1762.
Abigail,	" Mar. 26, 1764.
Whitcomb,	" Oct. 26, 1766.
Rebekah,	" Nov. 3, 1768.
Ebenezer,	" May 7, 1771.
Joseph,	" July 23, 1773.

FRENCH, JOSIAH and SARAH ASTIN.

Married Nov. 27, 1760.

Sarah,	born Aug. 27, 1761.
Rebekah,	" July 31, 1763, d.
Josiah,	" June 27, 1765.
Lucy,	" Aug. 9, 1767.
Daniel,	" Feb. 28, 1771.
William,	" May 25, 1773.
Nathan,	" Feb. 9, 1778.
Rebekah,	" May 14, 1780.

FRENCH, JAMES and SARAH BROOKS.

Married Sept. 1, 1760.

James,	born June 6, 1762.
Sarah,	" Nov. 21, 1766.
Elizabeth,	" Mar. 8, 1769.
Mary,	" May 19, 1771.

FRENCH, TIMOTHY and ANNA WILLOUGHBY.

Married May 3, 1771.

Timothy,	born May 8, 1772.
Anna,	" May 8, 1774.

FRENCH, NEHEMIAH and SUBMIT.

Submit,	born Sept. 22, 1771.
Nehemiah,	" Dec. 11, 1774.
Abraham,	" Jan. 21, 1777.

FRENCH, ISAAC and LUCY WILKINS.

Lucy,		born Sept. 30, 1779.
Priscilla,	} twins,	
Sarah,		" Mar. 6, 1781.
Isaac,		" Oct. 30, 1782.
Susannah,		" Feb. 10, 1785.
Mark,		" July 15, 1791. d.
Mehitable,		" Aug. 7, 1793.
David,		" Mar. 31, 1794.
Polly,		" July 18, 1795.
Lefa,		" May 26, 1797.
Mark,		" Dec. 12, 1798.

FRENCH, JOSEPH and MARY YOUNGMAN.

Married Feb. 1, 1771.

Joseph,	born June 8, 1772.
Mary,	" Mar. 14, 1774.
Ebenezer,	" Oct. 14, 1776.
Tabitha,	" Mar. 20, 1779.
Stephen Y.,	" Sept. 23, 1781.
Mitte,	" June 20, 1784.
Martha,	" Oct. 14, 1786.

GILSON, EBEN'R and ELIZABETH LAWRENCE.

Married August 24, 1769.

Betty,	born Aug. 16, 1775.
Sarah,	" May 19, 1779.

GOODHUE, JOHN and OLIVE.

John,	born April 4, 1763.
Samuel,	" Apr. 30, 1765.
Jonathan,	" Oct. 1, 1767.
Ephraim,	" July 11, 1770.
Joseph,	" Jan. 9, 1774.
Mary,	" Dec. 3, 1776.

GOSS, Capt. JOHN* and CATHARINE CONANT

Married Feb. 10, 1774.

John,	born Jan. 7, 1775.
Samuel,	" Nov. 29, 1776.
Abel,	" Oct. 23, 1780.
Catharine.	" Oct. 11, 1782.
Lucy,	" Dec. 30, 1784.
Anna,	" Aug. 15, 1787.
Mark,	" Oct. 10, 1789.
Luke,	" June 13, 1792.
Elizabeth,	" Nov. 19, 1795.

*Died Sept. 26, 1821, æt. 82.

GOODHUE, JOHN, Jun., and REBECCA PERHAM.

Married April 26, 1787.

Sarah,	born Apr. 13, 1788.
Joseph A.,	" Sept. 5, 1789.
Josiah,	" Mar. 19, 1792.

GOULD, JAMES and MARY LOVEJOY.

Married May 27, 1765.

James,	born Dec. 18, 1765.
Phineas,	" July 18, 1767.
Ralph W.,	" June 19, 1769.

HALE, Col. JOHN* and ELIZABETH HALL.

John,	born Sept. 8, 1756.
David,	" June 8, 1758.
Elizabeth,	" Sept. 28, 1760.
William,	" July 27, 1762.
Rebekah,	" Mar. 26, 1765.

*Died Oct. 22, 1791, æt. 60.

HARDY, PHINEAS* and ABIGAIL.

Elizabeth, born at Bradford July 22, 1750	
Martha,	born June 24, 1752.
Phineas,	" June 25, 1754.
Thomas,	" June 11, 1756.
Noah,	" Sept. 17, 1758.
Jesse,	" Dec. 19, 1760.
Isaac,	" July 9, 1763.
Moses,	" May 17, 1765.
Solomon,	" Aug. 1, 1767.

*Died March 7, 1813, æt. 86.

HARDY, LEMUEL and HANNAH JEWETT.

Silas,	born Mar. 13, 1763.
Hannah,	" May 11, 1765.
Susannah,	" July 17, 1767.
Rebekah,	" Sept. 10, 1769.
Mary,	" Feb. 10, 1772.
David,	" June 19, 1775.
Sarah,	" Mar. 24, 1777.

HARDY, AARON and ABIGAIL DUTTON.

Aaron,	born Oct. 24, 1771.
Reuben,	" Aug. 28, 1773.
Abigail,	" Oct. 12, 1775.

*Died Dec. 26, 1775, æt. 33.

HARDY, NEHEMIAH and ABIGAIL.

Married March 29, 1780.

Nehemiah,	born Apr. 10, 1781.
Kendall,	" Apr. 30, 1785.
John,	" Sept. 27, 1787.
Mary,	" May 9, 1792.

HARDY, ISAAC and SUBMIT WHEAT.

Married Nov. 13, 1788.

Isaac,	born Sept. 9, 1789.
Abraham T.,	" May 7, 1794.

HARDY, ISAAC and MEHITABLE BOYNTON.

Married July 3, 1794.

Jacob,	born Nov. 14, 1795.
John B.,	" Nov. 6, 1797.

HARDY, PHINEAS* and SIBBEL SHATTUCK.

Isaac,	born Nov. 17, 1782.
Noah,	" Mar. 23, 1785.
Sibbel,	" Aug. 5, 1787.
Hannah,	" Sept. 29, 1789.
James,	" Sept. 7, 1792.
Submit,	" May 13, 1795.
Samuel L.,	" May 18, 1798.
Elizabeth,	" April 13, 1803.
John G.,	" April 7, 1805.

*Died May 7, 1835, æt. 81.

HARDY, ENOS* and MARY LUND.

Married Nov. 10, 1797.

Mary,	" Dec. 3, 1798.
Ephraim L.,	" Oct. 14, 1801.
Alvah,	" Sept. 16, 1803.
Levi,	" Sept. 16, 1807.
Louisa,	" Feb. 10, 1811.
Sarah Ann,	" Mar. 21, 1816.

*Died May 18, 1857, æt. 85.

HARDY, MOSES and ABIGAIL WHEAT.

Married Nov. 9, 1790.

Moses,	born April 1, 1791, d.
Thomas W.,	" Jan. 6, 1794.
Moses,	" Sept. 4, 1795.
John,	" Sept. 24, 1797.
Reuben,	" Sept. 12, 1799.
Abigail,	" Oct. 3, 1801.
Phineas,	" May 1, 1803.
Leonard,	" Jan. 20, 1806.
Nathaniel,	" June 27, 1808.
Joseph W.,	" June 21, 1813.

HARDY, JESSE and REBEKAH BAYLEY.

Married Jan. 3, 1788.

Rebekah,	born Feb. 6, 1789.
Martha,	" Aug. 16, 1790.

(27)

HARDY, JESSE and RHODA WOOD.

Jesse,	born July 20, 1794.
Joel,	" Feb. 16, 1796.
Amos,	" Aug. 12, 1797.
Eli,	" Sept. 16, 1799.
Luther,	" Dec. 20, 1802.
Phineas,	" April 29, 1805.
Daniel,	" Sept. 8, 1808.

HARRIS, JOB and ELEANOR HARRIS.

Married Feb. 14, 1764.

Joseph,	born May 16, 1764.
Mary,	" May 2, 1767.
Simon,	" Mar. 26, 1770.

HASKELL, JOSEPH and ANNA.

Betsey,	born Sept. 20, 1778.
Joseph,	" Feb. 6, 1780.
Jane,	" Sept. 27, 1781.
Jeremiah,	" Aug. 31, 1784.
David,	" Mar. 31, 1786.

HAZELTON, STEPHEN and MARY.

Stephen,	born May 25, 1749.
Mary,	" Dec. 31, 1754.
John,	" June 8, 1757.

HAZELTON, SAMUEL and MOLLY.

Benjamin,	born Feb. 25, 1762.
Mary,	" Feb. 23, 1764.
Rebecca,	" Nov. 27, 1765.

HAZELTON, STEPHEN, Jun., and ESTHER HILDRETH,

Married Sept. 15, 1774.

Esther,	born Feb. 7, 1775.
Stephen,	" Aug. 20, 1777.
Elizabeth,	" Oct. 24, 1779.
Rebekah,	" Oct. 8, 1783.
Anna,	" April 30, 1785.

HOBART, Col. DAVID and SARAH.

Sarah,	born Jan. 15, 1745.
Peter,	" Dec. 22, 1747.
Eunice,	" Feb. 5, 1749.

HOBART, GERSHOM and ALEPHIA.

Mary,	born Oct. 16, 1754.
Alephia,	" Dec. 29, 1755.

HOBART, JONATHAN and LYDIA.

Jonathan,	born May 24, 1753.
Joshua,	" Dec. 6, 1754.
Joseph,	" May 7, 1757.
Lydia,	" Feb. 24, 1760.
Jacob,	" May 24, 1762.
Isaac,	" June 13, 1764.
Ruth,	" April 1, 1767.
Asa,	" Aug. 10, 1769.
Sarah,	" Sept. 27, 1771.

HOBART, JONATHAN, Jun., and ELIZABETH LAKIN.

Married Jan. 17, 1782.

Elizabeth,	born Nov. 24, 1782.
Sarah,	" Oct. 18, 1784.
Susannah,	" Sept. 3, 1786.
Polly,	" Oct. 23, 1788.
Jonathan,	" Sept. 27, 1793.
Joshua,	" July 13, 1796.

HOLDEN, DAVID, Jun., and BRIDGET ATWELL.

Married Jan. 1, 1789.

David,	born July 31, 1789.
Cumings,	" Aug. 16, 1790.
Phineas H.,	" May 6, 1792.

HOPKINS, RICHARD and MARY.

Mary,	born Oct. 8, 1763.
Richard,	" June 12, 1765.
Hannah,	" April 4, 1769.
Elizabeth,	" Aug. 7, 1773.
Achsah,	" June 20, 1775.

HOW, EPHRAIM and MARY.

Nicholas,	born May 12, 1781.
Ephraim,	" April 19, 1783.
Mary,	" June 26, 1785.
Betsey,	" May 30, 1787.
John,	" Oct. 11, 1789.
Joseph,	" Feb. 16, 1792.
Sarah,	" June 16, 1794.
Isaac,	" Dec. 28, 1797.
Samuel,	" Aug. 25, 1799.

JAQUITH, THOMAS and RHODA SPAULDING.

Married Dec. 25, 1776.

Rhoda,	born Nov. 28, 1777.
Thomas,	" Sept. 5, 1779.
Enoch,	" April 9, 1781.
Daniel,	" Mar. 9, 1783.
Rebekah,	" April 12, 1786.
Asa,	" Dec. 31, 1788.
Isaac,	" Apr. 25, 1791.

JAQUITH, EBENEZER and RUTH.

| Ebenezer, | born Feb. 6, 1777. |

JEWETT, SAMUEL* and SARAH.

Sarah,	born Mar. 7, 1749.
Mary,	" April 22, 1751.
Ruth,	" May 10, 1753.
Samuel,	" Jan. 1, 1756.
Esther,	" June 29, 1758.
Jacob,	" Oct. 30, 1760.
John,	" April 4, 1763.
Lucy,	" April 28, 1766.

*Died Dec. 29, 1791, æt. 65.

JEWETT, Dea. STEPHEN* and HANNAH (FARWELL) CUMINGS.

Stephen,	born Oct. 14, 1753.
Rebekah,	" Jan. 14, 1756.
Noah,	" Feb. 11, 1758.
Jonathan,	" July 25, 1760.
Lois,	" May 21, 1763.

*Died May 23, 1803, æt. 75.

JEWETT, EZEKIEL and LUCY TOWNSEND.

Married Feb. 23, 1758.

Susannah,	born Dec. 11, 1758.
Nathaniel,	" April 27, 1760.
Isaac,	" July 5, 1763.

JEWETT, EZEKIEL and ANNA WILLIAMS.

Married Feb. 28, 1765.

| Ezekiel, | born May 1, 1766. |
| William, | " Sept. 1, 1768. |

JEWETT, JAMES* and MARGARET.

Ruth,	born Sept. 3, 1755.
Margaret,	" Oct. 18, 1758.
Eunice,	" Sept. 24, 1761.

*Died April 9, 1808, æt. 85.

JEWETT, Lieut. EBENEZER* and MARY RIDEOUT.

Married March 15, 1792.

Ebenezer,	born Feb. 13, 1793.
Polly,	" Sept. 1, 1794.
Nathaniel,	" July 21, 1796.
James,	" Mar. 29, 1799.
Francis,	" May 26, 1801.
Susannah,	" Dec. 16, 1803.
Lydia,	" April 26, 1806.

*Died Oct. 6, 1826, æt. 83.

JEWETT, JACOB* and MEHITABLE MITCHELL.

Abigail,	born June 14, 1763.
Mehitable,	" Mar. 9, 1765.
Susannah,	" Feb. 14, 1767.
Hannah,	" July 20, 1770.
Daniel,	" July 20, 1772.
Ruth,	" Sept. 27, 1774.
Nathaniel,	" Jan. 1, 1777.
Sarah,	" Mar. 27, 1779.
Elizabeth,	" June 28, 1781.
Jacob,	" Mar. 7, 1784.

*Died April 23, 1813, æt. 76.

JEWETT, JACOB, Jun., and ELIZABETH CUMINGS.

James,	born Aug 22, 1767.
John,	" July 2, 1769.
Jacob,	" June 14, 1770.
David,	" Aug. 16, 1773.
Elizabeth,	" Oct. 15, 1775.
Lucy,	" Aug. 9, 1777.
Ralph W.,	" Dec. 8, 1779.
Leonard,	" Oct. 2, 1787.

JEWETT, JAMES, Jun., and LUCY FARLEY.

Married June 16, 1789.

James,	born Sept. 13, 1789.
Cumings,	" Mar. 1, 1793.

JEWETT, Dea. STEPHEN, Jun., and ELIZABETH POOL.

Married Nov. 16, 1778.

Elizabeth,	born June 18, 1779.
Stephen,	" July 7, 1781.
Nancy,	" May 11, 1783.
Hannah,	" Feb. 17, 1785.
William P.,	" Feb. 26, 1787, d.
William P.,	" Feb. 4, 1789.
Sarah,	" Feb. 24, 1790.
Polly,	" July 8, 1792.
Noah,	" Dec. 17, 1794.
Samuel G.,	" Oct. 29, 1798.

*Died Feb. 22, 1829, æt. 75.

JEWETT, JOHN and JANE AMES.

Married Nov. 29, 1795.

John,	born Sept. 13, 1796.
Jeremiah A.,	" May 2, 1798.

JOHNSON, JONATHAN and SARAH.

Elizabeth,	born Aug. 4, 1754.
Sarah,	" May 30, 1756.
Mary,	" April 29, 1758.
Jonathan,	" June 14, 1760.
Hannah,	" June 4, 1762.
David,	" July 4, 1764.

KEMP, ZERUBBABEL and ABIGAIL LAWRENCE.

Married Nov. 23, 1737.

Zerubbabel,	born Feb. 24, 1748.
Zechariah,	" July 26, 1750.

KEMP, ZERUBBABEL and HANNAH COLBURN.

Married April 20, 1758.

Sarah,	born Jan. 30, 1759.
John,	" May 26, 1761.

KEMP, THOMAS and MEHITABLE LOVEJOY.

Married Oct. 5, 1769.

Mehitable,	born Jan. 28, 1771.
Thomas,	" May 21, 1775.
Asa,	" April 18, 1777.
William,	" July 26, 1779.
Zerubbabel, John, } twins,	" Jan. 20, 1781.
Aaron,	" April 13, 1785.
Mindwell,	" July 10, 1787.

KEMP, THOMAS and HANNAH HOBART.

Levi,	born Sept. 6, 1793.
Ralph,	" Mar. 28, 1796.

KENDALL, EBENEZER and MARTHA.

Ebenezer,	born May 11, 1765.
Martha,	" June 26, 1767.
John W.,	" Dec. 16, 1769.
Hacy,	" June 2, 1772.

KENDALL, HEZEKIAH and ABIGAIL.

Abigail,	born Aug. 26, 1793.
Luther,	" May 15, 1802.
Lucy,	" Mar. 15, 1804.
Willard,	" Jan. 7, 1806.
Walter,	" July 11, 1808.

KENDRICK, Capt. DANIEL and MARY POOL.

Married Feb 15, 1782.

Daniel,	born Mar. 30, 1785.
William P.,	" June 20, 1794.

KEYES, ABNER and MARY.

Sarah,	born Sept. 3, 1764.
Mary,	" Aug. 14, 1766.
Hannah,	" July 14, 1768.
Abigail,	" July 2, 1770.
Esther,	" Aug. 24, 1772.
Anna,	" Sept. 15, 1774.
William,	" Oct. 12, 1776.
Rebekah,	" July 31, 1778.
Abner,	" Aug. 2, 1780.
Elizabeth,	" Dec. 9, 1782.
Ruth,	" Feb. 21, 1785.

KINNEY, ISRAEL and HANNAH.

Rebekah,	born Sept. 19, 1766.
Israel,	" Sept. 14, 1768.
Hannah,	" May 3, 1771.
Phebe,	" Feb. 14, 1773.
Moses,	" Oct. 1S, 1775.
Aaron,	" Jan. 10, 1778.
Polly,	" Jan. 22, 1781.
Susannah,	" Jan. 5, 1783.
Edah,	" Nov. 1, 1785.

LAWRENCE, ZACH. and SARAH LAWRENCE.

Married Dec. 5, 1734.

Peter,	born Aug. 20, 1745, d.
Zachariah,	" July 12, 1747.
Jonas,	" Oct. 19, 1751.
Peter,	" Oct. S, 1753.
Josiah,	" Nov. 2, 1756.

LAWRENCE, OLIVER* and MARY CUMINGS.

Married Dec. 27, 1752.

Mary,	born Nov. 4, 1753.
Oliver,	" Oct. 7, 1755.
Peleg,	" Aug. 17, 1757.
Noah,	" Nov. 30, 1760.
Daniel,	" April 26, 1762.
Silas,	" June 19, 1764.
Molly,	" May 25, 1767.
Amos,	" Aug. 6, 1769.
Eben,	" Oct. 25, 1771.
Aaron,	" May 5, 1774.
Sarah,	" Oct. 4, 1777.

*Died April 2, 1797, æt. 68.

LAWRENCE, ZACHARIAH, Jun., and REBECCA POWERS.

Married Nov. 22, 1769.

Daniel,	born Oct. 13, 1772.
Zachariah,	" July 1S, 1777.
Sarah,	" Oct. 10, 1779.
Rebecca,	" June 13, 1784.

LAWRENCE, DANIEL and POLLY JOHNSON.

Married May 6, 1790.

Polly,	born June 16, 1791.
Betsey,	" Oct. 20, 1792.
Charlotte,	" Sept. 5, 1794.
Ruth,	" Nov. 21, 1796.
Daniel,	" April 7, 1798.
Abigail,	" June 10, 1800.
Mark,	" Aug. 20, 1801.
Luke,	" April 14, 1803.
Louisa,	" June 14, 1807.
Caroline,	" Mar. 23, 1810.

LEEMAN, ABRAHAM and ELIZABETH HASTINGS.

Married Jan. 30, 1745.

Elizabeth,	born Feb. 24, 1746.
Mary,	" June 3, 1748.
Hannah,	" July 26, 1750, d.
Hannah,	" Oct. 1, 1751.
Submit,	" June 4, 1753.
Abraham,	" Sept. S, 1754.
Esther,	" Aug. S, 1756.
Abigail,	" May S, 1758.
Dorcas,	" July 13, 1760.

LEEMAN, SAMUEL and LOVE WHEELER.

Married Nov. 7, 1746.

Mehitable,	born Sept. 26, 1747.
Samuel,	" Aug. 7, 1749.
Love,	" Nov. 1, 1752.
Mary,	" Nov. 9, 1754.
Hannah,	" July 2, 1757.
Nathaniel,	" Aug. 6, 1759.
Lydia,	" Dec. 9, 1761.
Sarah,	" Aug. 31, 1764.
Abraham,	" May 13, 1769.

LESLEY, JONAS and ELIZABETH DOW.

Married Jan. 13, 1774.

Elizabeth,	born Nov. 5, 1774.
Jonas,	" Mar. 1, 1776.
Samuel,	" Feb. 23, 1778.
Sarah,	" Feb. 25, 1780.
Joseph,	" April 7, 1782.
George,	" Feb. 2, 1785.

LOVEJOY, CHRISTOPHER and ANNA.

Anna,	born May 26, 1743.
Christopher,	" Oct. 22, 1745.
Abial,	" April 2S, 1749.
Mehitable,	" Mar. 10, 1751.
Benjamin,	" Dec. 25, 1753.
Obadiah,	" June 13, 1756.
John,	" May 2, 175S.

LOVEJOY, JONATHAN and MARY.

Jonathan,	born May 23, 1742, d.
Phineas,	" Nov. 23, 1744.
Daniel,	" Feb. 23, 1746.
Mary,	" Sept. 27, 1747.
Simeon,	" June 6, 1750.
Jacob,	" Feb. 17, 1752.
Jonathan,	" July 3, 1754.
Abial,	" Aug. 3, 1756.
Asa,	" Jan. 28, 1758.
Abel,	" May 6, 1760.
Elizabeth,	" Mar. 24, 1762.

LOVEJOY, DANIEL and SARAH WYMAN.
Married Nov. 19, 1767.

Daniel,	born Aug. 2, 1768.
Samuel,	" July 4, 1770.
Stephen,	" May 22, 1773.
Sarah,	" June 26, 1775.
Phineas,	" Nov. 11, 1778.
Polly,	" Oct. 16, 1784.
Ralph,	" Jan. 3, 1788.

LOVEJOY, ASA and LYDIA NEVINS.

Lydia,	born Nov. 18, 1783.
William Nevins,	" Aug. 17, 1785.
Elizabeth,	" July 28, 1787.
Polly,	" Nov. 8, 1789.
Rebecca,	" Sept. 13, 1793.

LUND, EPHRAIM and ALICE WHEELER.
Married May 12, 1772.

Hannah,	born Sept. 7, 1772.
Sarah,	" Mar. 8, 1774.
Alice,	" April 19, 1776.
Mary,	" May 21, 1778.
Ephraim,	" Aug. 14, 1780.
Stephen,	" Oct. 29, 1783.
Ebenezer,	" July 10, 1786.

McDONALD, JAMES* and SUSANNAH.

Roxanna,	born July 19, 1752.
Randall,	" April 14, 1754.
Susannah,	" Jan. 18, 1756.
Lucy,	" Feb. 8, 1758.
Mary,	" April 5, 1760.
Elizabeth,	" Nov. 10, 1761.
James,	" Jan. 19, 1764.
John,	" June 5, 1766.

*Died April 11, 1801, æt. 83.

MARTIN, STEPHEN and ANNA.

| Stephen, | born Sept. 12, 1749. |
| Jesse, | " Aug. 1, 1754. |

MARTIN, STEPH'N and PATIENCE WORCESTER
Married May 21, 1759.

Anna,	born Mar. 3, 1760.
Jirah,	" June 11, 1762.
Elisha,	" Sept. 22, 1764.
Peter,	" May 27, 1768.

MELVIN, JONATHAN and MARY BROOKS.
Married Dec. 4, 1750.

| Jonathan, | born Jan. 14, 1752. |

MELVIN, EBENEZER and SUSANNAH.

Ebenezer,	born Dec. 28, 1752.
Nathan,	" Nov. 20, 1755.
Eunice,	" Feb. 9, 1759.
Daniel,	" Sept. 8, 1761.
Susannah,	" Oct. 23, 1764.
Seth,	" April 28, 1767.
Enoch,	" Aug. 20, 1769.

MESSER, BENJAMIN and MARY.

| Benjamin, | born Mar. 27, 1784. |

MERRILL, DANIEL and MARY SMITH.

Margaret,		born Nov. 15, 1756. d.
Samuel,		" Jan. 1, 1759.
Daniel,		" Mar. 31, 1761.
Henry,		" July 17, 1763.
Mary,	} twins,	" Dec. 7, 1765.
Ruth,		
Betty,		" April 17, 1768.
William,		" Feb. 15, 1770.
Abigail,		" May 13, 1772.
Margaret,		" Feb. 1, 1776.

MERRILL, SAMUEL and MARY.

Daniel,	born July 1, 1780.
Samuel,	" Aug. 16, 1782.
Isaac,	" June 15, 1784.
Mary,	" Mar. 14, 1787.
Elizabeth,	" June 11, 1791.

MERRILL, DANIEL* and PHEBE DOW.
Married Oct. 19, 1789.

Daniel,	born Sept. 1, 1790.
William,	" June 10, 1792.
Lydia,	" Nov. 9, 1794.
Mary,	" Sept. 13, 1798.
Evan,	" Sept. 24, 1802.
Mark,	" Sept. 20, 1806.

*Died Sept. 25, 1852, æt. 91.

MERRILL, Lieut. WILLIAM and DOLLY
SMITH.

Married Feb. 27, 1794.

Hannah,	born Feb. 9, 1795.
William S.,	" Sept. 24, 1797.
Miranda,	" Mar. 11, 1800.

MOOAR, DANIEL and ANNA.

Anna,	born Dec. 28, 1751.
Martha,	" Nov. 2, 1753.
Daniel,	" July 23, 1757.
Jacob,	" April 8, 1761.
Sarah,	" Mar. 11, 1764.

MOOAR, DANIEL, Jun., and LYDIA NEVINS.

Daniel,	born Mar. 23, 1781.
Isaac,	" Feb. 14, 1783.
David,	" Oct. 6, 1785.
Patty,	" June 12, 1788.
Nathan,	" Feb. 19, 1791.
Ephraim,	" April 26, 1794.
Sally,	" July 15, 1797.

MOOAR, JACOB* and HANNAH SHATTUCK.

Married Jan. 15, 1784.

Jacob,	born July 29, 1784.
Abel,	" Jan. 25, 1786.
Hannah,	" Oct. 21, 1787.
Nathan,	" Aug. 12, 1789.

MOOAR, JACOB and DORCAS HOOD.

Married May 20, 1794.

Gardner,	born Jan. 4, 1795.
John,	" Aug. 11, 1796.
Dorcas,	" Aug. 21, 1798.
Betsey,	" Sept. 7, 1800.
David,	" April 15, 1802.
Jason,	" Jan. 1, 1804.
Louisa,	" July 28, 1806.
Luke,	" July 18, 1808.
Sally,	" July 8, 1810.
Mark,	" Feb. 23, 1813.
Daniel,	" May 11, 1815.

*Died Feb. 2, 1828, æt. 66.

MOSHER, JAMES and EUNICE BLOOD.

Married May 7, 1770.

Catharine,	born Mar. 9, 1772.
Jacob,	" June 3, 1774.
Sarah,	" April 2, 1777.
John,	" May 31, 1779.
Mary,	" Jan. 23, 1783.
Betty, } twins,	
Eunice, }	" Sept. 25, 1786.

MOSHER, ABIJAH and HANNAH.

George,	born Feb. 19, 1777.
Hannah,	" Oct. 6, 1781, d.
Sally,	" Sept. 12, 1783.
Hannah,	" Mar. 12, 1785.

NEVINS, THOMAS and BRIDGET SNOW.

Married 1745.

Bridget,	born Dec. 21, 1746.
Thomas,	" May 25, 1748.

NEVINS, WILLIAM* and MARY.

William,	born July 26, 1746.
Joseph,	" July 20, 1748.
Benjamin,	" Aug. 15, 1750.
Mary,	" Aug. 2, 1752.
John,	" Feb. 26, 1755.
Phineas,	" Feb. 23, 1758.
Lydia,	" July 16, 1760.
Elizabeth,	" Oct. 1762.

*Died Feb. 15, 1785, æt. 66.

NEVINS, DAVID and LOIS PATCH.

John,	born Oct. 12, 1748, d.
Margaret,	" Feb. 3, 1752.
Lois,	" Sept. 16, 1753.
John,	" April 18, 1755.
David,	" July 7, 1758.

NEVINS, Ensign WILLIAM* and REBECCA
CHAMBERLAIN.

Married March 24, 1768.

Susannah,	born Dec. 2, 1776.

*Died 1776, æt. 30.

NEVINS, JOSEPH and SARAH POWERS.

Married Feb. 20, 1772.

Sarah,	born Dec. 3, 1772, d.
Joseph,	" June 10, 1774, d.
Phineas,	" May 5, 1776.
Sarah,	" Dec. 17, 1777.
Hannah,	" June 13, 1779.
Hepzibah,	" June 6, 1781.

NEVINS, JOSEPH and LUCY SAWTELL.

Lucy,	born Dec. 30, 1783.
Polly,	" July 4, 1786.
Anna,	" Mar. 23, 1789.
Gardner,	" Feb. 18, 1792, d
Mitte,	" Mar. 16, 1794.
Gardner,	" Feb. 6, 1797.
Sukey,	" April 12, 1799.
Joseph,	" April 8, 1801.

FAMILY REGISTERS.

NEVINS, BENJAMIN and ANNIS MOORE.

Married Feb. 9, 1775.

Patty,	born Dec. 7, 1775.
Benjamin,	" Oct. 5, 1777.
Lydia,	" April 7, 1780.
Sarah,	" May 25, 1782.
William,	" Mar. 5, 1786.

NOYES, Dea. ENOCH* and ELIZABETH.

Elizabeth,	born Jan. 20, 1749.
Lucy,	" Feb. 16, 1752.
Enoch,	" Aug. 31, 1754.
Hannah,	" Oct. 24, 1756.
Elijah,	" Oct. 2, 1758.
Benjamin,	" Dec. 12, 1760, d.
Jane,	" Aug. 1, 1762.
Rebecca,	" April 23, 1765.
Benjamin,	" Oct. 6, 1767.

*Died Sept., 1796, æt. 80.

PARKER, SAMUEL and MARY.

Samuel,	born April 7, 1740.
Eleazer,	" Mar. 30, 1744.
Lemuel,	" Mar. 4, 1747.
Lucy,	" Mar. 29, 1750.
Mary,	" Mar. 27, 1753.
Esther,	" May 21, 1755.

PARKER, BENJAMIN* and ALICE WOODS.

Sarah,	born Dec. 3, 1763.
Benjamin Woods,	" Sept. 27, 1765.
Patience,	" Feb. 5, 1769.
Ebenezer,	" July 5, 1772.

*Died Feb. 7, 1802, æt. 82.

PARKER, STEPHEN and RACHEL.

| Jane, | born Nov. 8, 1781. |
| John B., | " Aug. 4, 1786. |

PARKER, BENJAMIN WOODS* and ALICE
PRATT.
Married Nov. 9, 1788.

Benjamin W.,	born Mar. 8, 1789.
Olive,	" Nov. 4, 1790.
Calvin,	" July 20, 1792.
John Manly,	" Mar. 31, 1794.
Luther,	" Mar. 19, 1796.
Lucinda,	" July 16, 1797.
Hiram,	" April 6, 1799.
George W.,	" Feb. 27, 1801.

*Died Jan. 2, 1830, æt. 64.

PARKER, BENJAMIN WOODS and DEBORAH
GETCHELL.

| Mary B., | born July 7, 1811. |
| Joseph D., | " April 17, 1814. |

PARKER, Capt. ISAAC* and OLIVE ABBOTT

Olive,	born June 27, 1795.
Hannah,	" May 29, 1797.
Achsah,	" June 24, 1799.
Isaac,	" April 12, 1801.
John,	" July 30, 1803.

*Died Dec. 22, 1857, æt. 88.

PATCH, Dea. THOMAS* and ANNA GILSON.
Married March 25, 1742.

Anna,	born Nov. 20, 1742.
Thomas,	" Jan. 17, 1745.
Sarah,	" Mar. 9, 1746.
Joseph,	" Aug. 24, 1749.
David,	" Aug. 2, 1751.
Daniel,	" Oct. 9, 1753.

*Died May 1, 1754, æt. 40.

PATCH, THOMAS,* Jun., and MOLLY.

Thomas,	born Oct. 10, 1771.
Molly,	" Mar. 1, 1773.
Lydia,	" Sept 21, 1774.
Richard,	" May 26, 1776.
David,	" Oct. 6, 1778.
Rachel,	" May 27, 1780.
Sarah,	" Aug. 21, 1782.
Daniel,	" Sept. 7, 1784.
Joseph,	" Mar. 4, 1791.

*Died Nov. 7, 1828, æt. 85.

PHELPS, FRANCIS and PHEBE.

Francis,	born Aug. 15, 1743.
Timothy,	" Sept. 10, 1745.
Joseph,	" June 19, 1748.
Phebe,	" May 6, 1750.

PHELPS, JOHN and DEBORAH.

John,	born April 20, 1744.
Sarah,	" July 21, 1746.
Nathan,	" Sept. 1, 1749.
Henry,	" April 18, 1751.

PHELPS, JOHN and MARY LAKIN.

Simeon Lakin,	born Mar. 4, 1783.
Sally,	" June 5, 1785.
Luther,	" June 17, 1787.
Betsey,	" Sept. 7, 1789.

PHELPS, NATHAN and MARY FLETCHER.

Nathan,	born Feb. 1, 1780.
William Fletcher,	" Sept. 16, 1781.
Mary,	" Sept. 14, 1783.
Lucy,	" Jan. 12, 1786.
Thankful,	" Sept. 27, 1788.
Susannah,	" July 24, 1792.
Leonard,	" Oct. 12, 1795.
Zeruiah,	" May 10, 1800.

PHILBRICK, JONATHAN and BEULAH.

Jonathan,	born July 3, 1763.
Thomas,	" Dec. 1, 1765.
Mary,	" Feb. 16, 1768.
Beulah,	" Mar. 22, 1770.
Isaac,	" Sept. 3, 1773.
James,	" May 7, 1778.

PHILBRICK, JOHN and SARAH JEWETT.

Married Dec. 6, 1770.

John,	born Sept. 3, 1771.
Sarah,	" Sept. 16, 1773.
Mary,	" Aug. 10, 1777.
Samuel,	" Aug. 22, 1779.
Joel,	" April 24, 1781.

PIERCE, EBENEZER and ELIZABETH.

Daniel,	born April 3, 1755.
Mary,	" June 5, 1757.

PIERCE, EPHRAIM and ESTHER STONE.

Married March 11, 1766.

Betty,	born Sept. 26, 1766.
Mary,	" Jan. 26, 1768.
Esther,	" May 19, 1770.
Susannah,	" April 23, 1772.
Sarah,	" Aug. 11, 1774.
Deborah,	" April 11, 1776.
Ephraim,	" April 12, 1778.
Rebekah,	" July 26, 1781.
John,	" May 8, 1784.

PIERCE, RICHARD and SUSANNAH JEWETT.

Married May 22, 1766.

Warner,	born June 22, 1767.
Nathaniel,	" Jan. 12, 1769.
Ebenezer,	" Feb. 18, 1771.
Jacob,	" Sept. 16, 1772.
Susannah,	" July 23, 1774.
Isaac,	" June 15, 1776.
Eunice,	" Sept. 25, 1778.
Abraham,	" Nov. 14, 1780.
Abigail,	" July 24, 1783.
Daniel,	" Dec. 28, 1788.

PIERCE, SOLOMON and LUCY PARKER.

Married March 19, 1771.

Solomon,	born Sept. 2, 1771.
Lemuel,	" June 13, 1773.
Eleazar,	" April 4, 1775.
Lucy,	" Jan. 11, 1777.
Mary,	" Jan. 1, 1779.
Hannah,	" Mar. 11, 1781.
Samuel,	" May 30, 1783.
Simon,	" Nov. 16, 1785.
Levi,	" July 8, 1789.
Ephraim,	" Mar. 29, 1792.

PIERCE, NEHEMIAH and MARY.

Nehemiah,	born Feb. 5, 1778.
Isaac,	" Mar. 19, 1780.
William, Mary, } twins,	" Mar. 28, 1782.
James,	" May 9, 1784.

POOL, WILLIAM* and HANNAH NICHOLS.

Married June 19, 1751.

Hannah,	born Dec. 20, 1751.
Elizabeth,	" July 18, 1753.
Mehitable,	" Feb. 12, 1755.
William Welsted,	" May 6, 1756.
James,	" Dec. 2, 1757.
Abigail,	" July 31, 1759.
Sarah,	" Dec. 15, 1760, d.
Bridget,	" Aug. 5, 1762.
Mary,	" Feb. 4, 1764.
Rebekah,	" Mar. 29, 1766.
Lucy,	" Sept. 6, 1768.
Benjamin,	" Jan. 17, 1771.
Bethiah,	" Aug. 3, 1772.
Sarah,	" Sept. 20, 1774.

*Died Oct. 27, 1795, æt. 70.

POWERS, Capt. PETER* and ANNA KEYES.

Peter,	born Nov. 29, 1728.
Stephen,	" Oct. 28, 1729,
Anna,	" Mar. 9, 1732.
Whitcomb,	" Oct. 10, 1733.
Phebe,	" Feb. 5, 1785.
Alice,	" Dec. 30, 1736.
Levi,	" June 3, 1739.
Nahum,	" April 11, 1741.
Francis,	" July 15, 1742.
Fanna,	" April 19, 1744, d.
Philip,	" May 20, 1746.
Samson,	" Mar. 12, 1748.
Fanna,	" Mar. 22, 1750.

*Died August 27, 1757, æt. 56.

FAMILY REGISTERS.

385

POWERS, STEPHEN and LUCY CUMINGS.

Married Jan. 5, 1757.

Lucy,	born Oct. 20, 1758.
Stephen,	" April 13, 1761.
Rebecca,	" April 30, 1763.
Peter,	" April 29, 1765.
Bridget,	" Sept. 5, 1767.
Caleb,	" Sept. 15, 1769.
William,	" Dec. 28, 1771.
Catharine,	" May 1, 1775.

POWERS, WHITCOMB and MARY DOLLIVER.

Married May 20, 1755.

Whitcomb,	born April 17, 1756.

POWERS, FRANCIS and ELIZABETH CUMINGS.

Married May 5, 1763.

Francis Grant,	born Jan. 8, 1764.
Elizabeth,	" March 5, 1766.
Anna,	" Feb. 3, 1768, d.
Philip,	" Aug. 17, 1769.
Anna,	" April 13, 1771.
Frances,	" April 4, 1773.
Lucy,	" June 1, 1776, d.
Lucy,	" Mar. 13, 1779.
James,	" Sept. 15, 1781.
Phebe,	" Jan. 1, 1784.
Francis,	" April 3, 1787.
Levi,	" Mar. 19, 1791.

POWERS, SAMSON* and ELIZABETH NUTTING.

Married August 4, 1774.

Mary A.,	born Oct. 16, 1774.
Samson,	" Jan. 17, 1777
Peter,	" Feb. 24, 1779.
Joel,	" Aug. 8, 1781.
Grant,	" Mar. 31, 1784.
Levi,	" Mar. 20, 1786.
Anna,	" Sept. 11, 1789.
Ursula,	" Oct. 3, 1791.

*Died Jan. 2, 1822, æt. 73.

PRATT, THOMAS and CATY CUMINGS.

Married Sept. 27, 1764.

David,	born June 2, 1765.
Caty,	" May 9, 1767.
Hannah,	" July 29, 1769.
Jerahmael C.,	" April 12, 1772.
Betty,	" Jan. 13, 1774.
Molly,	" June 19, 1776.

(28)

PRATT, THOMAS and ANNA LAWRENCE.

Married April 13, 1779.

Anna,	born Sept. 25, 1779.
Stephen,	
Susannah, } twins,	" Oct. 24, 1784.
John,	" Feb. 18, 1791.

PROCTOR, MOSES* and MARY BYAM.

Mary,	born Dec. 31, 1741.
Rebekah,	" April 15, 1744.
Cyrus,	" Sept. 13, 1745.
Moses,	" Nov. 25, 1747.
Philip,	" Mar. 16, 1750.

*Died Aug. 21, 1780, æt. 73.

PROCTOR, EZEKIEL and ELIZABETH.

Abijah,	born Aug. 13, 1772.
Hannah,	" Dec. 16, 1774, d.
Ezra,	" May 15, 1776.
Hannah,	" Oct. 5, 1777.
Esther,	" Jan. 7, 1781.

PROCTOR, CYRUS and SIBBEL FARNSWORTH.

Married March 10, 1771.

Cyrus,	born Jan. 16, 1772.
Timothy,	" Mar. 11, 1774.
Sibbel,	" May 13, 1776.
Nathaniel,	" Feb. 16, 1778.
Thomas,	" Jan. 31, 1780.
Mary,	" Jan. 10, 1782, d.
Elizabeth,	" Oct. 25, 1783.
Hannah,	" June 18, 1785.
John,	" Jan. 25, 1787.
Abigail,	" Dec. 8, 1788.
Amos,	" June 12, 1791.
Anna,	" Sept. 7, 1793.
Mary,	" Feb. 8, 1796.
Susannah,	" June 18, 1799.

PROCTOR, MOSES, Jun., and RUTH AUSTIN.

Moses,	born Sept. 15, 1786.
Ruth,	" Mar. 18, 1788.
Aaron,	" May 7, 1791.

PROCTOR, JOEL and KATY.

Joel,	born June 28, 1784.
Jonas,	" May 24, 1786.

RANGER, NEHEMIAH and LYDIA.

Samuel,	born Oct. 24, 1773.
Lydia,	" Oct. 20, 1779.
Asahel,	" Aug. 11, 1781.
Nehemiah,	" Nov. 8, 1784.
Reuben,	" June 19, 1791.
Benjamin,	" Mar. 22, 1794.

REED, Capt. WILLIAM* and PRISCILLA EMERY.

Samuel,	born Feb. 8, 1763, d.
Polly,	" Dec. 2, 1764.
William,	" July 23, 1767.
Abel,	" Mar. 23, 1769.
Silas,	" Jan. 27, 1771.
Priscilla,	" June 5, 1773.
Asa,	" Nov. 27, 1775.
Sarah,	" Nov. 26, 1777.
Uriah,	" Nov. 13, 1779.
Samuel,	" Dec. 19, 1783.
Abigail,	" Feb. 1, 1786.

*Died July 12, 1817, æt. 77.

REED, JOSHUA and ELIZABETH.

Elizabeth,	born Mar. 9, 1768.
Joshua,	" Mar. 23, 1770.
Hannah,	" June 21, 1772.
Anna,	" Feb. 3, 1774.
Judith,	" Oct. 28, 1776.
John,	" Sept. 13, 1778.
Thomas,	" Jan. 7, 1781.

RIDEOUT, JAMES and MARY.

James,	born April 20, 1765.
Polly,	" Nov. 12, 1767.
Joseph,	" Jan. 7, 1771, d.
Esther,	" Mar. 6, 1772.
Joseph,	" Mar. 27, 1774.
Hannah,	" Nov. 1, 1776.
David,	" May 23, 1779.
Betsey,	" July 1, 1783.
Lydia,	" July 1, 1787.

RIDEOUT, NATHANIEL and SUSANNAH SPAULDING.

Married Jan. 18, 1776.

Nathaniel,	born May 2, 1778, d.
Asa,	" Sept. 8, 1779.
Samuel,	" Oct. 14, 1780.
Jonathan,	" Sept. 17, 1782.
Susannah,	" Oct. 18, 1784.
Diadema,	" Sept. 20, 1786.
Nathaniel,	" Mar. 8, 1788.
Gardner, } twins,	" June 3, 1790.
Huldah, }	
John,	" Jan. 9, 1793.

RUNNELLS, STEPHEN and CHLOE THURSTON.

Married Dec. 7, 1780.

Mary,	born Aug. 4, 1781.
Stephen,	" Sept. 1, 1785.
Hannah, } twins,	" Dec. 10, 1787.
Chloe, }	

RUNNELLS, SAMUEL and ABIGAIL SMITH.

Married Sept. 20, 1791.

Frederick,	born June 28, 1792.
Ebenezer,	" July 5, 1794.
Hannah,	" July 27, 1796.
Persis,	" Aug. 29, 1798.
Josiah,	" Dec. 1, 1800.
Susannah,	" Jan. 28, 1803.
Samuel,	" June 22, 1805.

RUSS, JONATHAN and LUCY KENDALL.

Married Nov. 16, 1758.

Lucy,	born May 9, 1760.
Jonathan,	" Mar. 17, 1762.
Rachel,	" May 20, 1764.
Sarah,	" Dec. 25, 1766.
Nathan,	" May 24, 1769.
Hannah,	" Jan. 20, 1772.

SANDERSON, BENJAMIN* and ESTHER.

David,	born Jan. 23, 1773.
Benjamin,	" Mar. 24, 1777.
Jeremiah,	" Aug. 31, 1779.
Ichabod,	" July 21, 1782, d.
Submit,	" June 7, 1784.
Richard W.,	" Aug. 28, 1788.
Simon,	" Mar. 20, 1790.
Esther,	" June 22, 1795.
John,	" Jan. 23, 1798
Ichabod W.,	" Dec. 8, 1802.

*Died Sept. 25, 1826, æt. 80.

SAUNDERSON, JONATHAN* and LUCY POOL.

Married Oct. 18, 1791.

Lucy,	born Nov. 28, 1792.
Almira,	" Mar. 29, 1796, d.
Marinda,	" Mar. 1, 1798.
Jonathan,	" Dec. 21, 1800, d.
Jonathan,	" Dec. 30, 1802.
Almira,	" Dec. 25, 1804.
William P.,	" Feb. 11, 1807.
Henry H.,	" Sept. 12, 1810.

*Died August 23, 1850, æt. 84.

SANDERSON, DAVID and LAURANA SHATTUCK.

Married Dec. 28, 1784.

| Peter, | born July 18, 1787. |

SARLL, WILLIAM and HANNAH DINSMORE.

Married August 6, 1747.

Elizabeth,	born July 16, 1748.
William,	" Mar. 22, 1750.
Hannah,	" April 19, 1752, d.
Joseph,	" May 13, 1755.
Sarah,	" Jan. 7, 1758.
Mary,	" Mar. 18, 1760.
John,	" Aug. 6, 1762.
Jonathan,	" May 29, 1765.
Hannah,	" June 11, 1767.
Lucy,	" Aug. 26, 1769.

SHANNON, RICHARD CUTTS and ELIZABETH.

James N.,	born Aug. 16, 1774.
Elizabeth,	" June 12, 1776.
Mary Ann,	" Aug. 12, 1778.
Abigail,	" Oct. 21, 1780.
John Langdon,	" July 4, 1783.
Sophia,	" June 4, 1786.

SHATTUCK, ZECHARIAH* and ELIZABETH FISK.

Married March 3, 1747.

Zechariah,	born Nov. 24, 1747.
Elizabeth,	" May 15, 1750.
Mary,	1753.
Abigail,	" June 10, 1755.
Isaac died in the army, 1776.	
Samuel,	
Sibbel,	" March, 1760.
Daniel,	" Feb. 24, 1767.
Abel,	" June 3, 1769.
Nathan,	" June 9, 1774.

*Died March 20, 1809, æt. 85.

SHATTUCK, WILLIAM* and RUTH.

Ruth,	born Nov. 1, 1739.
William,	" Feb. 26, 1741.
Mary,	" Mar. 1, 1743.

SHATTUCK WILLIAM and EXPERIENCE CURTIS.

Married Nov. 26, 1745.

Nathaniel,
Experience,

*Died March 13, 1761, æt 47..

SHATTUCK, WILLIAM and ZILPHA TURNER.

Married April 2, 1761.

Laurana,	born May 12, 1762.
Rebekah,	" May 6, 1764.
Priscilla,	" Oct. 7, 1766.
Sarah,	" May 28, 1770.
William,	" Aug. 20, 1772.
Lemuel,	" Feb. 12, 1776.

SHATTUCK, ZECHARIAH and ELIZABETH FARLEY.

Married Nov. 28, 1771.

Elizabeth,	born 1772.
Sarah,	" May 4, 1774.
Mary,	" Mar. 9, 1776.
Isaac,	" April 9, 1778.
Zechariah,	" July 23, 1781.
Abel,	" Sept. 21, 1782.
Joseph,	" Jan. 20, 1785.
Amos,	" Jan. 11, 1793.

SHATTUCK, SAMUEL and LOIS WHEAT.

Married May 5, 1791.

Samuel,	born Mar. 25, 1792.
Lois,	" Oct. 20, 1793.
Nathaniel,	" June 11, 1795.
Isaac,	" Jan. 25, 1799.
William,	" Feb. 2, 1802.

SHED, JOHN and RACHEL.

John,	born June 17, 1791.
Julia,	" Mar. 15, 1793.
Ebenezer,	" Jan. 24, 1796.

SHED, JOHN and LUCY JEWETT.

Married Nov. 5, 1797.

| Gardner, | born Oct. 9, 1798. |
| Luther, | " April 1, 1800. |

SHIPLEY, ABEL and LUCY FARLEY.

Married Nov. 24, 1768.

Abel,	born Oct. 28, 1769.
Lucy,	" Mar. 15, 1772.
Anna,	" Sept. 26, 1774.
John,	" June 4, 1776.
Sarah,	" June 3, 1778.
Amos,	" Mar. 5, 1780.
Benjamin,	" Sept. 9, 1782.
Betty,	" Sept. 26, 1784.
Page,	" Mar. 20, 1787.

SMITH, MOSES,* and MARY BOYNTON.

Married Jan. 29, 1756.

Mary,	born July	2, 1757.
Elizabeth,	" April	15, 1759.
Moses,	" June	22, 1761.

*Died August 25, 1761, æt. 31.

SMITH, JOHN and SARAH MERRILL.

Margaret,	born April	22, 1778.
Sarah,	" April	25, 1778.
Benjamin,	" April	27, 1780.
Jerusha,	" Oct.	4, 1782.
Daniel,	" Aug.	13, 1786.

*Died Nov. 8, 1807, æt. 59.

SMITH, MANASSEH and HANNAH EMERSON.

Married Feb. 17, 1774.

Hannah,	born Oct.	17, 1774.
Mary,	" Feb.	1, 1776.
Lydia,	" Dec.	15, 1777.
Manasseh,	" Aug.	16, 1779.
Joseph E.,	" Mar.	6, 1782.
Lucy,	" Sept.	22, 1783.
Samuel E.,	" Mar.	12, 1788.

SMITH, Rev. DAVID* and HEPZIBAH
WORCESTER.

Married Jan. 1, 1795.

David Page,	born Sept.	20, 1795.
Noah,	" Sept.	7, 1798.
Hepzibah L.,	" Sept.	7, 1801.
Emmons,	" Dec.	7, 1802.
Martha,	" July	14, 1804.
Mary,	" Sep.	19, 1805.
Hannah,	" Sept.	10, 1806.
Lydia,	" Aug.	1, 1808.

*Died Aug. 18, 1824, æt. 54.

SMITH, Rev. ELI* and CATHARINE SHELDON.

Eli,	born July 16, 1787.

SMITH, Rev. ELI and AMA EMERSON.

Married May 7, 1794.

Daniel E.,	born April	1, 1796.
Ama,	" Mar.	29, 1798.
Luther,	" Aug.	11, 1800.
Catharine H.,	" Aug.	13, 1802.
Joseph E.,	" Dec.	24, 1804.
John R.,	" Feb.	12, 1807.

*Died May 11, 1847, æt. 87.

SMITH, EMERSON and MARY PAGE.

Married Nov. 16, 1768.

David,	born Sept.	28, 1769.
Samuel,	" Mar.	13, 1772.

SMITH, EMERSON and ABIGAIL AYRE.

Married Jan. 4, 1775.

Jesse,	born Dec.	16, 1775.
John,	" April	12, 1777.
Mary,	" Oct.	15, 1779.
Betty,	" Aug.	20, 1782.
Abigail,	" Dec.	12, 1785.
Hannah,	" April	6, 1787.
Ralph,	" Aug.	13, 1791.
Rebekah,	" Jan.	28, 1795.
Joel,	" June	13, 1798.

SPALDING, JACOB and ESTHER SHED.

Married 1782.

Esther,	born Sept.	3, 1782, d.
Abigail,	" May	12, 1784.
Esther,	" July	8, 1786.
Abraham,	" July	17, 1788.
Rachel,	" Aug.	28, 1789.
Isaac,	" Oct.	13, 1791.
Rebekah,	" Jan.	18, 1794.
Sally,	" April	17, 1797.
Betsey,	" April	17, 1799.
Jacob,	" Mar.	8, 1803.
Sybel,	" July	14, 1805.

STEARNS, ISAAC and REBECCA JEWETT.

Married Feb. 26, 1767.

Rebekah,	born Dec.	16, 1767.
Sarah,	" Nov.	9, 1769
Anna,	" Mar.	10, 1772.
Isaac,	" Feb.	17, 1773.

STEARNS, JOSEPH and ABIGAIL WHEAT.

Married Mar. 31, 1778.

Joseph,	born Mar.	21, 1779.
Thomas W.,	" Nov.	15, 1782.
Daniel,	" Mar.	22, 1785.
Abigail,	" Sept.	12, 1789.

STEVENS, ISAAC, Jun., and ELIZABETH
JOHNSON.

Married Jan. 2, 1771.

Elizabeth,	born Mar.	7, 1773.
Isaac,	" July	1, 1774.
Hannah,	" April	19, 1776.
Sarah B.,	" Dec.	2, 1777.

STEWART, JAMES and MARY.

James,	born Oct. 15, 1742.
Thomas,	" Sept. 29, 1744.
Peter,	" June 13, 1746.
Jerathmacl,	" Mar. 14, 1748.

STILES, CALEB and MARY TOWNSEND.
Married Feb. 7, 1760.

Lucy,	born Dec. 21, 1762.
Caleb,	" Feb. 17, 1765.
George,	" Jan. 20, 1767.
Samuel,	" July 17, 1769.
Nathaniel,	" Dec. 14, 1770.
Jonathan,	" May 30, 1773.
Benjamin,	" Oct. 12, 1775.

STILES, ELI and SARAH.

Sarah, •	born Oct. 6, 1768.
Eavry W.,	" Aug. 27, 1770.
William,	" Oct. 12, 1773.
Rachel,	" April 11, 1775.
David,	" Oct. 27, 1777.

TAYLOR, ABRAHAM* and LYDIA.

Olive,	born Jan. 8, 1732, d.
Lydia,	" Oct. 11, 1733.
Leonard,	" Oct. 20, 1735.
Olive,	" Aug. 20, 1737.
Abraham,	" Aug. 11, 1739.
Sarah,	" Oct. 24, 1741.
Submit,	" June 13, 1743.

*Died June 3, 1743, æt. 36.

TAYLOR, EDWARD and Mary.

Daniel,	born Mar. 24, 1749.
Joel,	" Aug. 23, 1752.
Mary,	" June 19, 1754.
Jacob,	" Aug. 21, 1756.
Anna,	" Aug. 28, 1757.

TAYLOR, JONATHAN* and KEZIA.

Kezia,	born June 29, 1749.
Azubah,	" Nov. 12, 1751.
Esther,	" Feb. 19, 1754.

*Died April 7, 1789, æt. 69.

TAYLOR, JAMES and LOIS BUTTERFIELD.
Married April 21, 1768.

James,	born April 16, 1769.
Lois,	" June 4, 1770.
Molly,	" Jan. 31, 1772.

TENNEY, WILLIAM* and ANNA JEWETT.

Benjamin,	born Oct. 28, 1746.
Martha,	" April 13, 1749.
William,	" Mar. 17, 1755.
Anna,	" Jan. 17, 1759.

*Died March 22, 1783, æt. 61.

TENNEY, BENJAMIN and RUTH.

Ruth,	born Dec. 2, 1772.
Benjamin,	" July 7, 1774.

TENNEY, Capt. WILLIAM* and PHEBE JEWETT.

Phebe Jewett,	born Oct. 12, 1777.
Anna,	" Feb. 21, 1779, d.
Caleb Jewett,	" May 3, 1780.
Nancy,	" Jan. 29, 1782.
William,	" Mar. 20, 1784, d.
William,	" Sept. 12, 1785.
Sally,	"• Oct. 22, 1786.
Benjamin G.,	" Dec. 8, 1788.
Ralph E.,	" Oct. 5, 1790.
Lucinda,	" July 16, 1793.

*Died June 16, 1806, æt. 51.

THURSTON, MOSES* and HANNAH.

Hannah,	born Sept. 10, 1744.
Moses,	" July 11, 1746.
Chloe,	" July 15, 1748.
Gilman,	" July 19, 1750.
Mary,	" July 29, 1753.
Lydia,	" July 6, 1756.

*Died April 6, 1800, æt. 79.

WALLINGFORD, Lt. DAVID* and ELIZABETH LEEMAN.
Married March 6, 1767.

Jonathan,	born Sept. 10, 1770.
Sarah,	" July 5, 1772.
Martha,	" Mar. 26, 1774.
David,	" Nov. 26, 1776, d.
David,	" Oct. 12, 1778.
Ebenezer,	" Oct. 5, 1780.
Benjamin,	" Jan. 24, 1782.
Joel,	" Jan. 22, 1784.
Hannah,	" June 29, 1785.
Abigail,	" Jan. 4, 1790.

*Died March 12, 1791, æt. 45.

WARDWELL, SOLOMON and BETHIAH.

Amos,	born July 25, 1779.
Bethiah,	" Feb. 2, 1782.
Daniel,	" Jan. 11, 1784.

WEBSTER, ABEL and HANNAH.

Hannah,	born April 26, 1750.
Nathaniel,	" Nov. 23, 1753.
Abel,	" Dec. 7, 1755.
Mehitable,	" Aug. 31, 1757.
Moses, } twins,	" Aug. 2S, 1759.
Elias,	
Sarah,	" Mar. S, 1762.
Lydia,	" Mar. 30, 1764.

WHEAT, THOMAS and MARY.

Mary,	born Oct. 29, 1746, d.
Abigail,	" Aug. 15, 1748.
Thomas,	" July 7, 1750.
Sarah,	" April 23, 1752.
Priscilla,	" July 3, 1754.
Nathaniel,	" Jan. 20, 1756.
Joseph,	" July 1S, 1759.
Josiah,	" Dec. 1S, 1761.
Lois,	" June 22, 1765.
Hannah,	" Feb. 16, 1767.

WHEAT THOMAS and SARAH.

Submit,	born July 27, 1769.
Abigail Temple,	" June 29, 1771.
Sarah,	" July S, 1773.
Mary,	" May 7, 1775.

WHEAT, THOMAS,* Jun., and ABIGAIL.

Benjamin,	born Jan. 1, 1771, d.
Benjamin,	" Jan. 1, 1772.
Lucy,	" Jan. 17, 1774.

*Killed at Bunker Hill June 17, 1775, æt. 24.

WHEAT, SOLOMON and SARAH BALL.

Married August 29, 1771.

Solomon,	born July 7, 1773.
Josiah Coolidge,	" Jan. 1S, 1775.
Sarah,	" June 11, 1777.

WHEAT, SOLOMON and DEBORAH KIMBALL.

Polly Kimball,	born May 10, 17S7.
Samuel,	" Feb. S, 1790.

WHEAT, SOLOMON and ELIZABETH ROGERS.

Jonathan,	born Oct. 1S, 1795.
Timothy,	" Mar. 25, 1797.
Benjamin,	" Aug. 10, 179S.
Elizabeth,	" July 5, 1S00.
Joel,	" Oct. 2, 1S02.
Daniel,	" April 7, 1S04.

WHEAT, JOSEPH and BRIDGET (POWERS) FARLEY.

Married Oct. 10, 1783.

Nathaniel,	born April 11, 1784.

WHEAT, JOSIAH and SARAH KEYES.

Married April 17, 17SS.

Sarah,	born Mar. 14, 1789.
Ruth,	" April 24, 1791.
Mary,	" Dec. 29, 1792.

WHEAT, SOLOMON, Jun., and HANNAH CUMINGS.

Married Feb. 11, 1794.

William,	born June 13, 1794.
James,	" Oct. 10, 1796.
Hannah,	" Feb. 13, 1S00.
Elizabeth,	" Nov. 19, 1S02.
Mary Ann,	" Aug. 29, 1S06.
Caroline,	" Oct. 27, 1S09.

WHEELER, PETER* and HANNAH.

Lucy,	born June 1, 1744.
Alice,	" Dec. 1, 1745.
Ebenezer,	. " July 15, 174S.
Lebbeus,	" Oct. 15, 1750.
Jemima,	" Aug. 15, 1756.

*Died Mar. 2S, 1772, æt. 67.

WHEELER PETER and MEHITABLE JEWETT.

Married March 19, 1751.

Mehitable,	born Feb. 29, 1752.
Peter,	" Aug. 31, 1753.
Samuel,	" July 1S, 1755.
Esther,	" Jan. 7, 175S.
Hannah,	" Oct. 12, 1760.
Benjamin,	" July 29, 1763.
Joseph,	" Nov. 15, 1766.
Jonathan,	" July 2, 176S.
Nathan,	" Mar. 19, 1774.

WHEELER, JAMES and MARY BUTTERFIELD.

Married Nov. 1, 1750.

James,	born Jan. 29, 1753.
Reuben,	" Jan. 30, 1755.
Mary,	" Nov. 2S, 1756.
John,	" July 2, 175S.
Levincey,	" Aug. 20, 1760.
Abiezer,	" Feb. 2, 1765.
Zebulon,	" Jan. 20, 176S.

WHEELER, TIMOTHY and MARY NEVINS.

Married Sept. 8, 1773.

Timothy,	born Jan. 12, 1774.
Mary,	" Oct. 2, 1775.
Simon,	" July 23, 1777.

WHEELER, LEBBEUS* and ELIZABETH CARTER.

Married Mar 1, 1773.

Lucretia,	born April 3, 1774.

*Died July 10, 1778, æt. 27.

WHEELER, THADDEUS and ELIZABETH FARMER.

Married Oct. 17, 1769.

Elizabeth,	born July 22, 1770.
Thaddeus,	" Oct. 10, 1773.
Minot,	" May 16, 1777.
Theodore,	" Jan. 7, 1780.
Amos,	" July 12, 1783.
James,	" Aug. 6, 1785.
Benjamin,	" Oct. 16, 1790.

WHEELER, EBENEZER* and AZUBAH TAYLOR.

Married July 13, 1780.

Kezia,	born Sept. 17, 1783.
Jonathan Taylor,	" Sept. 6, 1787.

*Died March 15, 1817, æt. 68.

WHITING, JAMES and HEPZIBAH.

Hepzibah,	born July 8, 1741.

WHITING, JAMES and MARY DOUGLAS.

Married Aug. 2, 1757.

James,	born May 17, 1758.
David,	" Mar. 18, 1760.

WHITING, BENJAMIN and GRACE.

Frances Wentworth,	born April 19, 1771.
Martha,	" Sept. 10, 1772.
Grace,	" April 16, 1775.
Sarah,	" Nov. 23, 1776.

WHITING, Capt. LEONARD and ANN.

Ann,	born Aug. 12, 1763.
Leonard,	" Aug. 25, 1765.
Mary,	" Aug. 25, 1767.
Grace,	" Sept. 12, 1769.
Abigail,	" Mar. 25, 1772.
Stephen,	" Feb. 20, 1774.

WILLOUGHBY, JOHN* and ANNA CHAMBERLAIN.

Samuel,	born Feb. 13, 1745.

*Died Feb. 2, 1793, æt. 85.

WILLOUGHBY, JONAS and HANNAH BATES.

Married July 10, 1760.

Jonas,	born May 19, 1761.
Oliver,	" June 2, 1764.
David,	" April 4, 1770.
William,	" June 17, 1774.

WILLOUGHBY, SAMUEL* and ELIZABETH.

Elizabeth,	born Aug. 27, 1774.
Samuel,	" Mar. 1, 1776.

WILLOUGHBY, SAMUEL and MARY GOULD.

Mary,	born Aug. 3, 1777.
Ethan,	" Feb. 26, 1779.
Sarah,	" Mar. 21, 1781.
Beriah,	" Feb. 20, 1783.
Rebekah,	" May 11, 1785.
Anna,	" May 18, 1787.
Luther,	" April 14, 1789.
Calvin,	" Mar. 14, 1791.
Washington,	" April 13, 1793.
John,	" Dec. 23, 1795.
Joseph,	" Nov. 19, 1797.

*Died Oct. 26, 1832, æt. 86.

WILLOUGHBY, JONAS, Jun., and PRUDENCE SAUNDERS.

Married May 24, 1785.

Prudence,	born Oct. 29, 1787.
Jonas,	" Mar. 15, 1790.
Hannah,	" May 7, 1792.
Anna,	" Mar. 22, 1795.

WILLOUGHBY, OLIVER and SARAH BAYLEY.

Married Jan. 31, 1787.

Andrew,	born Aug. 3, 1787.
Oliver,	" July 17, 1789.

WILLOUGHBY, WILLIAM and REBECCA ADAMS.

Married March 10, 1796.

Rebecca,	born Dec. 12, 1797.
Samuel,	" Oct. 28, 1798.
William,	" April 12, 1801.

WHIPPLE, JOSEPH and ESTHER PIERCE.
Married Oct. 23, 1792.

Joseph,	born May	6, 1793.
John,	" Feb.	19, 1795.
Betsey,	" Nov.	1, 1796.
Amos,	" Sept.	12, 1798.
Charles,	" Mar.	7, 1800.
Rowena,	" Feb.	26, 1803.
Irena,	" Aug.	1, 1806.

WOODS, JONAS and LYDIA HOBART.
Married April 26, 1781.

Jonas,	born Feb.	22, 1782.
Lydia,	" Aug.	31, 1784.
Sally,	" Feb.	8, 1787.
Isaac,	" Feb.	16, 1792.
David,	" July	21, 1794.
Asa,	" Aug.	20, 1796.
Betsey,	" June	8, 1801.

WOOD, Ensign WILLIAM* and SUSANNAH
WRIGHT.
Married Aug. 23, 1778.

Susannah,	born Dec.	28, 1779.
William,	" Sept.	24, 1781.
Kezia,	" Feb.	16, 1783.
Ebenezer,	" Sept.	22, 1784.
Henry,	" June	9, 1786.
Abigail,	" Oct.	4, 1787.
Sally,	" April	11, 1789.
Betsey,	" Oct.	1, 1790.
Hannah,	" Jan.	19, 1792.
Polly,	" Oct.	12, 1793.
Mark,	" Jan.	22, 1795, d.
Grace,	" Oct.	21, 1796.
Mark,	" Feb.	11, 1799.
Harriet,	" Oct.	12, 1805.

*Died 1826, æt. 73.

WORCESTER, Dea. FRANCIS* and HANNAH
BOYNTON.
Married Oct. 28, 1741.

Abigail,	born Nov.	5, 1742.
Francis,	" June	16, 1744, d.
Jemima,	" Jan.	22, 1746.
Hannah,	" Jan.	3, 1748, d.
Sarah,	" June	18, 1749.
Beulah,	" Oct.	29, 1750.
Mary,	" Dec.	13, 1751.
Lydia,	" April	26, 1753.
John,	" Dec.	31, 1755.
Hannah,	" Jan.	3, 1757.
Francis,	" Oct.	27, 1758.
Bathsheba,	" April	21, 1763.

•*Died Oct. 19, 1800, æt. 79.

WORCESTER, Rev. FRANCIS* and ABIGAIL
CARLTON.
Married April 18, 1720.

Francis,	born Mar.	30, 1721.
Jesse,	" Sept.	5, 1722.
Hannah,	" Oct.	7, 1724.
Samuel,	" May	7, 1731.
Noah,	" Oct.	4, 1735.

*Died Oct. 14, 1783, æt. 85.

WORCESTER, Capt. NOAH* and LYDIA
TAYLOR.
Married Feb. 22, 1757.

Noah,	born Nov.	26, 1758.
Jesse,	" April 30,	1761.
Lydia,	" Nov.	8, 1762.
Sarah,	" Mar.	24, 1765.
Leonard,	" Jan.	1, 1767.
Thomas,	" Nov.	22, 1768.
Samuel,	" Nov.	1, 1770.

WORCESTER, Capt. NOAH and HEPZIBAH
SHERWIN.
Married Sept. 30, 1772.

Hepzibah,	born June	12, 1773.
William,	" Dec.	11, 1774, d.
William,	" Nov.	29, 1775.
Abigail,	" June	29, 1777.
David,	" April 30,	1779, d.
Ebenezer,	" April 30,	1781.
Hannah,	" Mar.	17, 1783.
David,	" Mar.	25, 1785.
James,	" Feb.	23, 1788.

*Died Aug. 13, 1817, æt. 81.

WORCESTER, JESSE* and SARAH PARKER.
Married June, 1782.

Jesse,	born Nov.	30, 1782.
Joseph Emerson,	" Aug.	24, 1784.
Sarah,	" Mar.	12, 1786.
Lydia,	" Feb.	22, 1789.
Abigail,	" Dec.	15, 1790.
Hannah,	" June	22, 1792.
Leonard,	" Mar.	22, 1794.
Deborah,	" May	22, 1796.
Martha,	" Oct.	24, 1797.
Taylor Gilman,	" April	6, 1799.
John Newton,	" Feb.	7, 1801.
Henry Aiken,	" Sept.	25, 1802.
Samuel Thomas,	" Aug.	30, 1804.
Frederick Augustus,	" Jan.	28, 1807.
David,	" April	13, 1808.

*Died Jan. 20, 1834, æt. 72.

WORCESTER, SAMUEL and LOIS BOYNTON.

Married Nov. 5, 1778.

Lois,	born Dec. 11, 1779.
Mary,	" Sept. 18, 1781.
Samuel,	

WRIGHT, Capt. JOSHUA* and ABIGAIL.

Joshua,	born Jan. 9, 1741.
Esther,	" Nov. 6, 1742.
Abigail,	" Nov. 10, 1744.
Abijah,	" Aug. 15, 1746.
Lemuel,	" Oct. 2, 1748, d.
Ruth,	" Feb. 13, 1751.
Lemuel,	" Dec. 30, 1752.
Uriah,	" Dec. 8, 1754.
Timothy,	" Sept. 8, 1756.
Sibbel,	" Feb. 13, 1759.
Susannah,	" Nov. 25, 1761.
Sarah,	" May 6, 1763.

*Died Aug. 5, 1776, æt. 60.

WRIGHT, BENJAMIN and MARY.

Benjamin,	born Mar. 28, 1752.
Abel,	" Sept. 3, 1754.
Ebenezer W.,	" Sept. 8, 1756.
Mary,	" Feb. 11, 1760.
Noah,	" Dec. 13, 1763.
Joseph, } twins,	
Mary, }	" Feb. 9, 1766.
Hannah,	" Sept. 19, 1769.
Sibbel,	" May 9, 1772.

WRIGHT, BENJAMIN, Jun., and ESTHER TAYLOR.

Married Dec. 13, 1774.

Kezia Taylor,	born Feb. 20, 1776.
Benjamin Winckol,	" July 14, 1778.
Esther,	" April 15, 1781.
Jonathan,	" July 24, 1783, d.
Salome,	" Nov. 28, 1784, d.
Jonathan Taylor,	" Aug. 19, 1787.
Salome,	" Mar. 28, 1790.
Mary,	" Aug. 31, 1792, d.
Mary,	" April 29, 1794.

WRIGHT, LEMUEL and MARY JOHNSON.

Married March 13, 1781.

Lemuel,	born Mar. 18, 1782.
Joshua,	" Feb. 29, 1784.
Noah,	" Jan. 13, 1787.
Miles Johnson,	" Mar. 13, 1790.
Benjamin,	" May 14, 1792.

WRIGHT, URIAH and EUNICE JEWETT.

Married June 15, 1780.

Uriah,	born June 3, 1781.
Eunice,	" Mar. 19, 1783.
Joshua,	" Mar. 9, 1785, d.
James Jewett,	" Mar. 25, 1787.
Margaret,	" July 5, 1789.
Timothy,	" April 13, 1791.
Joshua,	" April 21, 1793.
Jean,	" May 26, 1795.

WRIGHT, SAMUEL and MOLLY.

Samuel,	born Sept. 24, 1778.
Alice,	" Mar. 5, 1781.
Stephen,	" Sept. 19, 1783.
Page,	" April 30, 1785.
Jane,	" Mar. 24, 1788.
Betsey,	" Sept. 19, 1789.
Luther,	" Jan. 7, 1792.
Calvin,	" Oct. 18, 1794.

WRIGHT, ELISHA and ANNA SAUNDERS.

Married Feb. 12, 1784.

Anna,	born Feb. 26, 1785.
Hannah,	" May 5, 1787.
Rachel,	" May 20, 1791.
Elijah B.,	" Mar. 1, 1794.
Mary,	" July 13, 1796, d.
Mary,	" Feb. 14, 1799.
Elisha Winckol,	" Jan. 22, 1802.
William W.,	" Oct. 1805.
Leonard H.,	" Dec. 31, 1807.
Ralph S.,	" Aug. 30, 1810.

YOUNGMAN, JABEZ and SUSANNAH POWERS.

Married March 24, 1785.

Jabez,	born June 26, 1786.
Noah,	" Sept. 14, 1788.
David,	" Dec. 19, 1790.
Susannah,	" Mar. 18, 1793.
Hannah,	" April 4, 1795.

YOUNGMAN, STEPHEN and ABIGAIL BROWN.

Married June 16, 1786.

Ebenezer,	born April 4, 1787.
William,	" Oct. 20, 1788.

ERRATA AND CORRECTIONS.

The reader will please note and correct the following errors :

Page 134, line 11, for "He" read Hon. "Benjamin Pool."

151, line 3, for "Capt. Moor" read "Capt. Moors "

216, bottom line, for "1773" read "1778."

241, line 13 from bottom, for "May 25, 1870" read "Aug. 20, 1874."

242, line 5 from top, for "1858" read "1758."

261, line 18, add "George Moore, representative, 1879."

314, line 4, for "November 28" read "November 25."

354, 11th line from bottom, for "Baker" read "Parker."

360, 16th line from bottom, for "Abert" read "Albert."

361, 18th line from top, for "Charles" read "George."

361, 20th line from bottom, for "Henry L." read "Henry N."

www.ingramcontent.com/pod-product-compliance
Lightning Source LLC
Chambersburg PA
CBHW032258280326
41932CB00009B/618